Village London was first published in 1883 under the title 'Greater London'. Written by Edward Walford, a noted Victorian historian and antiquarian who was concerned to record the history and appearance of the hamlets, villages and market towns that made up the metropolitan area before they were overtaken by the urban sprawl that was then beginning to take place.

There was then a great deal of interest in London's history, but now, when there is little or nothing to differentiate between one district and another except the names on the railway stations, it has become even stronger.

Each village has its own history, in some cases stretching back to Roman or Saxon times and beyond. This is the story of these one-time villages and towns which grew up around coaching inns or river fords, or even Royal palaces – now long since demolished and ancient manors that are now tree lined suburban avenues. Every part of London has its own history and historical characters, ranging from Hampton Court's Cardinal Wolsey and Tooting's Daniel Defoe, to Enfield's Mother Wells. This book tells the fascinating story of Greater London's past, as distinct from its inner city; the battlefields – Epping, Barnet, and Brentford and many more; its palaces – Nonsuch, Croydon, Enfield and Hampton Court. But more importantly it recreates the atmosphere of the old villages, the inns and churches, the pastimes and pleasures of ordinary people as well as the rich and famous.

Edward Walford had the gift of writing history so that it would be of interest to the casual reader as well as the serious student and he brings the long lost days of rural London vividly to life.

VILLAGE LONDON

THE STORY OF GREATER LONDON

by

EDWARD WALFORD, M.A.

PART 2 – North and East

THE ALDERMAN PRESS

First published 1883/4 by Cassell & Co. Ltd.
under the title *Greater London*

Published in hardback by The Alderman Press
under the title *Village London Vol. 1* 1983

British Library Cataloguing in Publication Data.
Walford, Edward
    [Greater London]. Village London: The Story
    of Greater London.
    1. London (England) — History
    I. [Greater London] II. Title
    942.1   DA677

    ISBN 0-946619-11-5 (Pt.1)
    ISBN 0-946619-12-3 (Pt.2)
    ISBN 0-946619-13-1 (Pt.3)
    ISBN 0-946619-14-X (Pt.4)

This edition published 1985
The Alderman Press 1/7, Church Street,
Edmonton, London, N9 9DR.

Printed in Great Britain by
BAS Printers Limited, Over Wallop, Hampshire

CONTENTS.

———◦———

CHAPTER XXIX.

GREAT STANMORE AND ELSTREE.

PAGE

Great Stanmore—Brockley Hill, the supposed Site of Sulloniacæ—Discovery of Roman Antiquities—The Great Forest of Middlesex—The Domesday Notice of Stanmore—Descent of the Manor—The Village—Population—The Bernays Memorial Institute—The Church—Stanmore Park—Bentley Priory—The Property purchased by Lord Abercorn—Queen Adelaide—Sir John Kelk—Elstree—Situation and General Appearance of the Village—The Manor—Parish Church—Burial Places of Martha Ray and William Weare—Female Orphans' Home—Elstree Hill House—Elstree Reservoir—Watercourses—Pudding-stones 297

CHAPTER XXX.

BUSHEY, ALDENHAM, AND RADLETT.

Bushey Heath—The Scenery described—Bushey Manor—The Parish Church—St. Peter's Church—Bushey Hall—Hartsbourne Manor House —Census Returns—Oxhey—Watford—Almshouses of the Salters' Company—Aldenham—Acreage and Population—Descent of the Manor—Kemp Row—Tibhurst Manor—Kendall Manor—Pickets, or Newberry—Aldenham House—Penn's Place—The Parish Church—The Grammar School—Discovery of Roman Remains—Radlett—Christ Church—Gill's Hill—The Murder of William Weare—Medburn —Village Schools and Improved Dwellings 305

CHAPTER XXXI.

SHENLEY, COLNEY, RIDGE, AND SOUTH MIMMS.

Extent and Population of Shenley—Descent of the Manor—Shenley Hall, or Salisbury—Newberries—Old Organ Hall—Porters—Holmes, otherwise High Canons—The Village of Shenley—The Chapel-of-Ease—The Parish Church—Colney House—London Colney— Tittenhanger—Colney Heath—Ridge—The Parish Church—South Mimms—Census Returns—General Appearance of the Village—The Old North Road—The Manor of South Mimms—The Church—Almshouses—Potter's Bar—Dyrham Park—Wrotham Park—Destruction of the Mansion by Fire—Hadley Common—Christ Church 312

CHAPTER XXXII.

HIGH BARNET. ·

Situation and Extent of Barnet—Its Etymology—The Manor—General Appearance of the Town—Census Returns—Markets and Fairs— The Parish Church—The Grammar School—The old "Crown Inn"—Jesus Hospital—Almshouses and Charitable Institutions—The Town Hall—Barracks—Chapels and Meeting-houses—Ravenscroft Park—The "Physic Well"—Historical Associations—Inns and Taverns—The Battle of Barnet—The Obelisk 319

CONTENTS.

CHAPTER XXXIII.

HADLEY, EAST BARNET, AND TOTTERIDGE.

PAGE

Etymology of Monken Hadley—Descent of the Manor—Hadley Green—The Village and Common—Hadley Wood—Gladsmore Heath, or Monken Mead—Dead Man's Bottom—Hadley Church—Two Historic Trees—Almshouses—Noted Residents—Population—East Barnet—Lyonsdown—Census Returns—The Parish Church—The Boys' Farm Home—The Clock House—Cat's Hill—Oak Hill Park—Belmont—Totteridge—Its Etymology—Descent of the Manor—Census Returns—Condition of the Roads—The Church—Yew-trees in Churchyard—The Priory—Pointer's Grove—Copped Hall—Totteridge Park—Wykeham Rise   327

CHAPTER XXXIV.

WHETSTONE, FRIERN BARNET, AND FINCHLEY.

Situation of Whetstone—The Parish Church—Census Returns—Oakleigh Park—George Morland and the Chimney-sweep—General Appearance of the Village—The Manor of Friern Barnet—The Church—Almshouses—Finchley—Situation and Extent—Descent of the Manor—The Old Manor-house—Noted Residents—Church End—Census Returns—Races—The Parish Church—Christ's College—National Schools—East End—The Church, &c.—The " Dirt House "—Cemeteries for Marylebone and St. Pancras and Islington Parishes—North End—Christ Church—The Congregational Chapel—Finchley Common—Encampments and Reviews—Highwaymen—Turpin's Oak—The " Green Man " Tavern—Capture of Jack Sheppard—The Life of a Highwayman   335

CHAPTER XXXV.

COLNEY HATCH AND SOUTHGATE.

Rapid Extension of Colney Hatch, or New Southgate—Its Situation and Etymology—Middlesex County Lunatic Asylum—St. Paul's Church—The Pumping Station of the New River Waterworks—Wood Green—The Drinking Fountain—Nightingale Hall—St. Michael's Church—The Printers' Almshouses—Fishmongers' and Poulterers' Asylum—Fullers' Almshouses—Royal Masonic Institution for Boys—Clock and Watchmakers' Asylum--The Great Northern Cemetery—Southgate—The Village Green and "Cherry-tree" Inn—The Church—Arnold's Court, now Arno's Grove—Minchenden House—Bromefield Park—Bowes Manor—Bowes Park—St. Michael's Church—Culland's Grove—Grovelands—Palmer's Green—Southgate Village Hall—Winchmore Hill—The Church, &c.—Bush Hill Park—Sir Hugh Myddelton and the New River 342

CHAPTER XXXVI.

ENFIELD.

General Description of the Parish—Situation and Boundaries--Parochial Divisions—The Town and Principal Streets—Enfield Court—The New River—Railway Stations—Census Returns—Historical Reminiscences—The Barony of Enfield—Descent of the Manor—Fairs and Markets—Site of the Old Manor House—Camlet Moat—Oldbury—Edward VI. at Enfield—The Palace—Dr. Uvedale—The Market-place—The Parish Church—The Free Grammar School—Schools of Industry—John Keats's Schooldays—Charitable Institutions—Old Park—Chase Park—Chase Side House—Enfield Green—Little Park—Beycullah Park—Enfield Races—Churches and Chapels—The Cemetery—Forty Hall—Elsynge Hall—Sir Walter Raleigh and Queen Elizabeth—Anne Countess of Pembroke—Myddelton House—Gough Park—Distinguished Residents—Beautiful Women of Enfield   347

CHAPTER XXXVII.

ENFIELD CHASE.

General Description of a Chase—Form and Extent of Enfield Chase—Its Early History—The Last of the Staffords, Dukes of Buckingham—Drayton's Description of Enfield Chase—Its Present Condition—The Princess Elizabeth as a Hunter—James I. at Enfield Chase—A Portion of the Chase added to Theobalds—Seizure of the Chase by the Commonwealth—Sale of Different Portions of it—Macaulay's Account of Enfield Chase—Evelyn pays it a Visit—The Chase Re-stocked with Deer by Charles II.—The Chase used as a Sheep-walk—Punishment for Cutting Down and Destroying Trees in the Chase—Its Final Enclosure—Officers belonging to the Chase—Camlet Moat, the supposed Site of the Chief Forester's Lodge—Trent Park—Beech Hill Park—East Lodge—Chase Lodge—Hill Lodge, Claysmore—The Roman Road—Cock Fosters—Dangers of the Roads in Former Times—White Webbs House—The Gunpowder Plot—"The King and the Tinkler"   363

CHAPTER XXXVIII.

ENFIELD HIGHWAY, PONDER'S END, AND THE RIVER LEA.

Position and Extent of Enfield Highway--Population, &c.—The Lower North Road—Mr. Spencer and his Bride—Matthew Prior and John Morley—St. James's Church—Ponder's End—St. Matthew's Church—Lincoln House—Durants—The Manor of Suffolks—Enfield Wash—The Story of Elizabeth Canning, " Mother Wells," and the Gipsy Squires—Roselands--The Manor of Elsynge—The River Lea—Bull's Cross—Capels 371

CHAPTER XXXIX.

THEOBALDS.

PAGE

Situation of Theobalds, and History of the Manor—The Estate Purchased by Sir William Cecil, afterwards Lord Burleigh—James I. at Theobalds—Entertainment to Christopher IV., King of Denmark—Narrow Escape of King James—His Death—Description of the Palace and Gardens—Demolition of the Palace—Present Condition of the Estate 376

CHAPTER XL.

CHESHUNT.

Situation and General Appearance of the Parish—Its Etymology—Supposed Site of a Roman Station or Camp –Discovery of Roman Coins, &c.—The Mound at Bury Green—A Curious Manorial Custom—Census Returns—The River Lea—A Disputed Landmark—Early History and Descent of the Manor of Cheshunt—The Manor of Moteland, or St. Andrew's le Mote—The Great House——The Parish Church—The Cemetery, &c.—Cheshunt College—Pengelly House—Cheshunt Park—The Cromwell Family—Other Notable Residents and Seats—Waltham Cross—"The Four Swans" Inn—The Spital Houses—Holy Trinity Church—The Benedictine Convent—Goff's Oak—St. James's Church 384

CHAPTER XLI.

NORTHAW

Etymology of Northaw—Condition of the District at the Time of the Conquest—Disputed Ownership—Nynn House, and Manor—The Hook—Northaw Place—Acreage and Population—The Village and Parish Church—A Chalybeate Spring 394

CHAPTER XLII.

ENFIELD SMALL-ARMS FACTORY AND WALTHAM POWDER-MILLS.

The History of the Rifle—Situation of the Royal Small-arms Factory—Particulars of its Establishment—Extent of the Buildings, &c.—Perfection of the Machinery and Plant—The Government Powder Mills—Situation of the Buildings—Description of the Works—The Composition of Gunpowder—Quantities produced 395

CHAPTER XLIII.

WALTHAM ABBEY.

Situation of the Town—Its Etymology—Foundation of the Abbey by Jovi—Its Re-foundation by Harold—The Legend of the Holy Cross—Gifts bestowed on the Abbey—Harold's Tomb—The Church despoiled by William the Conqueror—Its Recovery under subsequent Sovereigns—Disputes between the Abbot and Townspeople—Henry III. and the Abbot's Dinner—An Incident touching the Reformation—Income of the Abbey at the Dissolution—Fuller, the Historian—The Conventual Estate passes into Secular Hands—Description of the Abbey Church—Sale of the Church Bells—Present Condition of the Remains of the Abbey—Rome-Land—The Abbey Gateway and Bridge 404

CHAPTER XLIV.

WALTHAM (continued) AND EPPING.

Extent of Waltham Abbey Parish—Census Returns—Rural Appearance of the Locality—Principal Seats and Mansions—Warlies—Copped Hall—Ambresbury Banks—The Story of Queen Boadicea's Conflict with the Romans—Obelisks in the Neighbourhood—Highwaymen and Footpads—The Village of Epping—Epping Church 416

CHAPTER XLV.

EPPING FOREST.

Primeval Condition of the Forest, as the Great Forest of Essex—Gradual Diminution of the Forest—Forest Charters of King John and Henry III.—Laws for the Regulation of the Forest—A Quaint Oath—Lord Warden, Steward, and other Officers of the Forest—The Swainmote Court and Court of Justice Seat—Extent of the Forest in the Middle Ages—Present Form of the Forest—Disposal of the Crown Rights in the Forest—Encroachments by Lords of Manors—The Battle of the Commoners with the Lords of Manors—Parliamentary Scheme for the Preservation of the Forest—The Matter taken up by the Corporation of London—The Case Settled by Arbitration—Dedication of Epping Forest to the "Free Use" of the People—The Science of Forestry—The Deer of the Forest—The Present Condition and General Appearance of the Forest 423

CONTENTS.

CHAPTER XLVI.

EPPING FOREST (*continued*)--SEWARDSTONE, HIGH BEECH, AND CHINGFORD.

PAGE

Preliminary Remarks—Situation and Boundaries of Sewardstone—Seats and Mansions—High Beech Green—St. Paul's Church—Fairmead Lodge—Sotheby and Tennyson—Residents at High Beech—Fairmead House—John Clare—High Beech Hill—The "Robin-Hood" and "King's Oak"—"Harold's Oak"—Queen Victoria's Wood—Lappitt's Hill—Bury Wood and Hawk Wood—Situation and Etymology of Chingford—Its Extent and Boundaries—The Manor of Chingford St. Paul—The Manor of Chingford Earls—Friday Hill—Buckrills—A Singular Tenure—Census Returns—Chingford Old Church—The Ordnance Survey Obelisk—Queen Elizabeth's Lodge—The Royal Forest Hotel—Connaught Water 435

CHAPTER XLVII.

EPPING FOREST (*continued*)—BUCKHURST HILL, LOUGHTON, AND THEYDON BOIS.

Recent Improvements in Epping Forest—Connaught Water and other Lakes—Buckhurst Hill—Its Etymology—Census Returns—The Railway Station—St. John's Church—Congregational Church—Langford Place—The Essex Naturalists' and Field Club—The Epping Hunt—The "Bald-faced Stag"—The "Roebuck"—Situation of Loughton—Census Returns—Descent of the Manor—The Hall—The Old Parish Church—A Memorial Church—St. John's Church—General Appearance of the Village—Staple Hill—The "Lopping" Process—Loughton Camp—Debden Hall—Theydon Bois. 441

CHAPTER XLVIII.

CHIGWELL.

General Appearance of the Village of Chigwell—Its Etymology—Census Returns—Descent of the Manor—Rolls Park—Woolstons—Lexborough—The Warren—Belmont—The Parish Church—Archbishop Harsnett—Local Charities—Club-room—The Grammar School—The "King's Head" Tavern—Charles Dickens's "Maypole" Inn—Chigwell Row—Woodlands—Bowls—Gainsborough's Picture of "The Woodman"—The Mineral Waters 449

CHAPTER XLIX.

WOODFORD AND WALTHAMSTOW.

Boundaries of Woodford—Its Etymology—Its Subdivision—Descent of the Manor—The Manorial Custom of "Borough English"—Woodford Hall—Census Returns—Woodford Bridge—The Church—Claybury Hall—Ray House—Church End, Woodford—The Parish Church—Woodford Hall—Mrs. Gladstone's Convalescent Home—A Pauper's Legacy—Woodford Green—Congregational Church—The Union Church—Art and Industrial Society, and Social Institutions—Harts—Monkhams—The Firs—Prospect Hall—Woodford Wells—"The Horse and Well"—Knighton House—The Manor House—Noted Residents—Walthamstow—Its Area and General Appearance—Walthamstow Slip—Census Returns—Etymology of Walthamstow—Descent of the Manor—Highams—Salisbury Hall—Chapel End—Bellevue House—The Parish Church—Almshouses—Walthamstow House—Benjamin Disraeli's School-days—Noted Residents of Walthamstow—The Town Hall, and other Public Institutions—Hoe Street—Hale End—Marsh Street—St. James's—The Reservoirs of the East London Waterworks Company—Geological Discoveries—An Old Bridge—St. Stephen's Church—Whip's Cross—St. Peter's Church, Forest Side—Forest Grammar School 458

CHAPTER L.

SNARESBROOK AND WANSTEAD.

General Appearance of the Locality—Snaresbrook—The "Rights" of Commoners—The "Eagle" at Snaresbrook and the Eagle Pond—The Infant Orphan Asylum—Merchant Seamen's Orphan Asylum—Christ Church—Almshouses of the Weavers' Company—Area and Population of Wanstead—Its Boundaries, &c.—Etymology—Traces of Roman Occupation—Descent of the Manor—The Earl of Leicester and Queen Elizabeth—A "Spa" at Wanstead—Pepys' Opinion of Wanstead House—Visit of John Evelyn—Wanstead House Rebuilt by Sir Richard Child, afterwards Earl Tylney—Description of the House and Grounds—The Great Telescope—The Maypole from the Strand—Death of Lord Tylney—Subsequent History of Wanstead House—Its Demolition—Wanstead Park secured for the People by the Corporation of London—The Park, Gardens, and Grotto—Lake House, the Residence of Thomas Hood—Cann Hall—The Parish Church—The Village of Wanstead—The George Inn—An Expensive Pie—Park Gate—Wanstead Flats—The Princess Louise Home and National Society for the Protection of Young Girls—Dr. James Pound—The Maypole from the Strand—James Bradley the Astronomer—Admiral Sir William Penn—William Penn, the Founder of Pennsylvania 472

CHAPTER LI.

LEYTON AND LEYTONSTONE.

Extent and Boundaries of Leyton Parish—Walthamstow Slip—Census Returns—Discovery of Roman Remains and other Antiquities—Ancient Earthworks—General Appearance of the Village of Leyton—Railway Stations—Park House—Ruckholt House—The Manor House—Leyton House—Etloe House—The Parish Church—John Strype—The Vicarage—All Saints' Church—Schools and Charitable

PAGE

Institutions—Lea Bridge, and the East London Waterworks—Temple Mills—Eminent Residents of Leyton—Leytonstone—Census
Returns—The Church of St. John the Baptist—Holy Trinity Church—Congregational Church—Union Workhouse—Children's Home . 483

CHAPTER LII.

HAINAULT FOREST AND ALDBOROUGH HATCH.

Situation, Boundaries, and Extent of Hainault Forest—Its Etymology—Its Ownership by the Abbey of Barking—It passes to the Crown—
Subsequent Disposal—Is Disafforested—The Hamlet of Barking Side—Census Returns—The Church—Dr. Barnardo's Homes for
Friendless Children—The " Maypole " Public-house—Fairlop Oak and Fairlop Fair—Aldborough Hatch   489

CHAPTER LIII.

ILFORD.

Chadwell Heath—Chadwell Street—The Old Coach Road—Will Kemp's Dance from London to Norwich—Great Ilford—Census Returns
—Etymology—The River Roding—Ilford Church—Public Reading-Room and Library, &c.—Ilford Hospital—Cranbrook House—
Valentines—Discovery of an Ancient Stone Coffin—Elephants in Essex   495

CHAPTER LIV.

LITTLE ILFORD, WEST HAM, ETC.

Boundaries and Extent of Little Ilford—Census Returns—The Parish Church — Mr. Lethieullier's House at Aldersbrook—Ilford Gaol—
The "Three Rabbits"—West Ham—Its Division into Wards—Population—Market and Fairs—Chemical Works and Factories—The
Parish Church—A Curious Fresco—Upton Park—Forest Gate—Taverns and "Tea-Gardens"—Emmanuel Church—St. James's Church
—Extent and Population of Forest Gate—Pawnbrokers' Almshouses—Legg's Almshouses—Former Condition of Stratford—The Abbey of
Stratford-Langthorne—Pumping Station of the Metropolitan Drainage Works—St. John's Church—Christ Church—St. Paul's—St. Francis
of Assisi Congregational Church—Town Hall—Stratford New Town—Vegetable Market—Old Ford—Bow Bridge—Roman Roads   . 501

CHAPTER LV.

PLAISTOW AND EAST HAM.

Flat and unattractive Appearance of Plaistow—Its Sedate Aspect in Former Times—Its Sources of Wealth—The Destitute Children's Home—
The Metropolitan Main Drainage Works—Census Returns—Silver Town, Canning Town, and Hall Ville—Plaistow Church—St.
Andrew's Church—Congregational Church—East London Cemetery—Poplar Small-pox and Fever Hospital—Chemical Works and other
Manufactories—The Royal Victoria and Albert Docks—North Woolwich—St. Mark's Church—St. John's Church—North Woolwich
Gardens—Distinguished Residents at Plaistow—Descent of the Manor of East Ham—St. Nicholas's Roman Catholic School—A Curious
Manorial Custom—Situation and Extent of the Parish—The Parish Church—Emmanuel Church—St. John the Baptist—Plashet
House—Greenstreet House—Anne Boleyn's Tower—St. Edward's Reformatory—The High Level Sewer—Beckton Gas and Coke Works 509

CHAPTER LVI.

BARKING.

Situation and Extent of the Parish—Census Returns—Etymology—Early History and Foundation of Barking Abbey—The Abbey Burnt by
the Danes—Rebuilt by King Edgar—William the Conqueror takes up his Abode there—The Importance of the Abbey in Saxon Times
—The Convent Damaged by an Overflow of the Thames—Curious Entries of the Revenues of the Abbey—Dissolution of the Abbey—
The Abbey Gateway—Extent of the Original Buildings—Noted Abbesses—Manorial Estates of the Abbey—The Parish Church—The
Rural Deanery of Barking—The Manor of Barking—The Story of Osborne's Leap—The Manor of Clayhall—Malmains—Bifrons—
Eastbury House—The Road to Tilbury—Barking Town—Barking Creek—The Outfall of the Main Drainage Works—Powder
Magazine, &c.—The Roman Entrenchment at Uphall   516

CHAPTER LVII.

DAGENHAM.

Ripple Side, Barking—Ripple Castle—Extent and Boundaries of Dagenham—Census Returns—The Village—Church—Parslowes—Valence—
Dagenham Breach—Discovery of a " Moorlog "—The River Walls of the Thames—Dagenham Lake—Its Proposed Conversion into a
Dock—Failure of the Scheme—Origin of the Ministerial Fish Dinner   527

CONTENTS.

CHAPTER LVIII.

MILLWALL, LIMEHOUSE, AND POPLAR.

PAGE

Situation and Boundaries of Millwall—Origin of the Name of the Isle of Dogs—The Chapel House—Blackwall—Millwall—Acreage of the Isle of Dogs—Fertility of the Soil—Geology—A Submerged Forest—The Manor of Pomfret—Inundations of the Marsh—How Samuel Pepys attended a Wedding Party—Ferries, and the Ferry House—Condition of the Isle of Dogs in the Last Century—Manufactories and Shipbuilding Yards—Roman Cement and Terra-Cotta—The *Great Eastern* Steam Ship—Cubitt Town—St. Luke's Church—Limehouse—Poplar 533

CHAPTER LIX.

THE EAST AND WEST INDIA AND MILLWALL DOCKS.

The Vastness of Trade and Commerce—Arrival of Coal-ships and other Vessels in the Port of London—Number of Barges and other Craft required for Traffic in 1792—Plunder carried on in the Lighters on the River—Institution of the Thames Police—Proposals for the Establishment of Docks—Foundation of the West India Docks—The Opening Ceremony—Description of the Docks—A Curious Museum New Dry Docks—The Wood Wharf—The Rum Quay—The South West India Dock—The Wool Warehouses—The East India Docks—Millwall Dock—Insecurity of Merchandise before the Establishment of Docks or Institution of the Thames Police 549

CHAPTER LX.

THE RIVER LEA.

Etymology of the River Lea—Its Source—Luton—Brocket Hall—Hertford—Ware—Amwell and its Quaker Poet—Haileybury College—The Rye House—Stanstead Abbots—Hoddesdon—Broxbourne—Cook's Ferry—Bleak Hall—The East London Waterworks—Lea Bridge—Fishing on the Lea—Hackney Marshes and Temple Mills—The Navigation of the Lea—Conservancy of the River. 559

CHAPTER LXI.

THE RIVER THAMES.

The Thames as a Political Boundary, and as a Boundary of Counties—Tributary Rivers—Breadth of the River—Its General Aspect and Character of Scenery—The Embankments—Shoals and Floods—Tides—The Thames as the Common Highway of London—Anecdote of Cardinal Wolsey—Sir Walter Raleigh and Queen Elizabeth—Abdication of James II.—Funeral of Lord Nelson—Water Traffic in the Time of Richard II.—The Conservancy of the Thames—Boating on the Thames 568

LIST OF ILLUSTRATIONS.

	PAGE
Bentley Priory	300
Queen Adelaide	301
Bushey Church	306
Aldenham House	307
Shenley Church and Village	312
Tittenhanger	313
Sir T. Pope	313
Wrotham Park	318
High Street, High Barnet	319
Vews in Barnet : the Schools ; the " Red Lion " Inn	324
Hadley Green (Site of the Battle of Barnet)	325
Hadley Church	330
Copped Hall	331
Lord Lytton	331
Alms Houses, Friern Barnet	336
Finchley Manor House and Turpin's Oak	337
Colney Hatch	342
Arno's Grove, Southgate	343
Enfield Church	348
Beach Hill *circ.* 1796	349
Myddelton House *circ.* 1821	349
Queen Elizabeth's Palace, Enfield, 1568	354
The Palace, from the North	354
The Old Market House, Enfield	355
Forty Hall and the Old Gateway	360
Gough Park	361
View in Trent Park	366
In Beech Hill Park	367
Ponder's End	372
Room in Mother Wells' Cottage	373
Old Theobalds Palace	378
The Maze at Theobalds	379
Cheshunt Church	385
Richard Cromwell	389
The Old Manor House, Cheshunt	390
Waltham Cross	391
Enfield Small Arms Factory	396
The Powder Mills, Waltham	397

	PAGE
The Cattle Market, Waltham	402
On the Lea	403
Waltham Abbey—Interior : Nave, Crypt, Lady Chapel	408
Gateway and Bridge, Waltham Abbey	409
Copped Hall, near Epping	414
Ambresbury Banks	415
Map of Epping Forest	421
Views in Epping Forest : Connaught Water, Chingford ; A Glade at Theydon Bois ; On the way to Copped Hall from Loughton ; High Beech	427
Royal Forest Hotel, Chingford	432
Flowers from Epping Forest	433
Chingford Church	438
Queen Elizabeth's Lodge	439
The " Roebuck "	444
The " Bald-Faced Stag "	444
Theydon Bois	445
Chigwell Grammar School	450
William Penn	450
Chigwell Church	451
The " King's Head," Chigwell	456
Churches at Woodford : The Old Parish Church ; All Saints, Woodford Wells	459
Monkhams	462
The " Horse and Well," Woodford Wells	463
Grammar Schools and Almshouses, Walthamstow Churchyard	468
Forest Grammar School	469
The " Eagle," Snaresbrook	474
Wanstead House	475
Monument to Sir J. Child, Wanstead Church	480
Park Gate	481
Monuments in Leyton Church	486
Leyton Vicarage	487
Portrait of Strype	487
Dr. Barnardo's Homes	492
Fairlop Oak, 1800	493
Valentines, near Ilford	498

LIST OF ILLUSTRATIONS.

	PAGE		PAGE
Ilford Hospital	499	Dagenham	535
West Ham Church	504	Millwall Docks	540
West Ham Park	505	Millwall, from the River	541
Royal Albert Docks : Looking East ; Looking West	510	Launch of the *Great Eastern*	546
Anne Boleyn's Castle	511	Limehouse Church	547
Ancient Bell Tower, Barking Abbey	516	West India Docks	553
Barking Creek	517	Vaults at the Docks	555
Eastbury House	522	Entrance to the East India Docks	558
Market House, Barking	523	Cook's Ferry	564
Dagenham Marshes, looking East	528	At Lea Bridge	565
Walls of the Thames	529	The Thames, Barking Reach	570
The Thames from Ratcliffe to Woolwich, in 1588	534	The Thames, Woolwich Reach	571

CHAPTER XXIX.

GREAT STANMORE AND ELSTREE.

Per fines et aprica rura.—HORACE.

Great Stanmore—Brockley Hill, the supposed Site of Sulloniacæ—Discovery of Roman Antiquities—The Great Forest of Middlesex—The Domesday Notice of Stanmore—Descent of the Manor—The Village—Population—The Bernays Memorial Institute—The Church—Stanmore Park—Bentley Priory—The Property purchased by Lord Abercorn—Queen Adelaide—Sir John Kelk—Elstree—Situation and General Appearance of the Village—The Manor—Parish Church—Burial-places of Martha Ray and William Weare—Female Orphans' Home—Elstree Hill House—Elstree Reservoir—Watercourses—Pudding-stones.

GREAT STANMORE, which we have now reached, lies on the border-line of Middlesex and Hertford-shire. The name of the parish, which appears as *Stanmere*, or *Stanmera*, in "Domesday Book," signifies a boundary-mark or stone. In legal documents it is written Stanmore Magna (or Great Stanmore), to distinguish it from the adjoining parish of Stanmore Parva (Little Stanmore), or Whitchurch, which we have just left. Both districts would appear to have formed one parish only at the time of the Norman survey, though the period at which they were divided has not been ascertained.

At the time of the Roman invasion, and probably for a long time afterwards, this locality was thickly wooded, and formed part of that dreary tract which was known in more recent times as the forest of Middlesex. Many interesting evidences of the Roman occupation have been discovered in this neighbourhood, particularly in the north-eastern division of the parish, close by the high ground known as Brockley Hill, about midway between Edgware and Elstree, a spot which Camden, Stukeley, and other writers, have fixed upon as the site of the ancient city of Sulloniacæ. Reynolds, in his edition of the "Itinerary of Antoninus," unhesitatingly ascribes the site of that city to Brockley Hill; and after mentioning the numerous vestiges of Roman habitation which have been discovered there, observes that "no evidence is wanting on the subject, but to show that the distance is agreeable to the numerals." The distance between the presumed site of this city and Verulamium (St. Albans) is estimated, according to Mr. Reynolds, at nine miles and a quarter, which comes very near to the truth.

Roman antiquities, consisting chiefly of coins, urns, rings, fibulæ, and other articles, are said to have been found in large quantities from the site of Bentley Priory, which lies to the north-west of the village of Stanmore, eastward as far as Brockley Hill. These discoveries, says Lysons, gave rise to the following local couplet :—

> "No heart can think, nor tongue can tell,
> What lies 'twixt Brockley Hill and Pennywell."

Pennywell, however, lies at some little distance to the north-east of Brockley Hill, and nearer to Elstree than Stanmore. Norden asserts that Watling Street, which we have mentioned in a previous chapter as having followed the track of the present Edgware Road, crossed over Brockley Hill, passing in its course through a wild and dangerous range of woodland. Matthew Paris, in his "Life of the Twelfth Abbot of St. Albans," describes these woods as "almost of an impenetrable character, and so much infested by outlaws and beasts of prey, that the numerous pilgrims who travelled along the Roman road for the purpose of devotion at the shrine of Albanus were exposed to very imminent danger." Fitz-Stephen, whose "Survey of London" was written between the years 1170 and 1182, says that "beyond the suburbs of the city, which afford corn-fields, pastures, and delightful meadows, an immense forest extends itself, beautiful with woods and groves, and full of the lairs and coverts of beasts and game—stags, bucks, boars, and wild bulls." In this forest the citizens of London enjoyed the right of free chase—a privilege which was confirmed to them by several royal charters. The forest of Middlesex was "disafforested" early in the thirteenth century, but considerable tracts of the ancient wood remained down to much later ages. At the time of the Conquest, although there was probably a preponderance of woodland—from the large and frequent mention of "pannage"—it would appear that much even of this portion of the country was under the plough, and a fair proportion used as meadow-land, or for the purpose of pasturage. The entry in "Domesday Book" respecting this parish is as follows :—"Stanmere is held by the Earl of Moreton. It answered for nine hides and a half. There is land for seven ploughs. In the demesne are six hides and a half, and there are two ploughs therein, and another may be made. The villanes have one plough and a half; and two ploughs and a half might be made. A priest has half a hide there; and there are four villanes of one virgate each, and other two of one virgate ; and three cottagers of ten acres, and other three of one acre. Pasture for the cattle of the village; pannage for twelve hundred hogs, and for herbage twelve pence." *

In the reign of Henry I. the manor was wrested from the Earl of Moreton's successor, and it continued in the hands of the Crown till 1220, when it was given to the monks of St. Albans, under whom it was held till the middle of the fourteenth century by the family of Francis. It next passed, subject to an annual rent to that abbey, to the priory and convent of St. Bartholomew, in Smithfield. After the dissolution of religious houses the manor passed through the possession of various persons, among whom was Sir Peter Gambo, a Spaniard, who was murdered near St. Sepulchre's Church, London, in 1550, by a Fleming named Gavaro. In the reign of James I. the estate was granted to Sir Thomas Lake, of whom we have spoken in our account of Little Stanmore and Canons; and it subsequently underwent various changes, and towards the close of the last century the manor passed, by the marriage of the daughter and sole heiress of James Brydges, third and last Duke of Chandos, to Richard, Duke of Buckingham and Chandos. His Grace, who died in 1839, was the grandfather of the present duke. The ownership of the manor has since passed into the hands of Sir John Kelk, Bart., of Bentley Priory.

The village of Great Stanmore is about a mile in length; it is built on the slope of a hill, and lies on the road to Watford, about two miles north-west from the Edgware Station of the Great Northern Railway. It is quiet and secluded, and the houses generally have a neat and respectable appearance. Both in the village and in the immediate neighbourhood are several good old-fashioned residences, and close by are some large and well-wooded parks and lordly domains.

On Stanmore Hill, a gentle elevation on the north side of the village, the celebrated Dr. Parr opened a school on quitting Harrow,† in 1771; here he received a large number of pupils, many of whom became distinguished in after life. The school was pulled down many years ago, and the site afterwards built upon.

In 1871 the number of houses in the parish was 265, the population at the same time amounting to 1,355. In 1881 it had slightly risen.

A conspicuous building in the village is the Memorial Institute, which was erected by subscription in memory of Mr. Ernest Bernays, a son of the Rev. Leopold John Bernays, many years

rector of this parish, who was accidentally drowned in 1870. The building, which is of Gothic design, is used for concerts, lectures, and similar entertainments.

The church, dedicated to St. John the Evangelist, stands at the western end of the village, and was built, from the designs of Mr. Henry Clutton, in the Decorated style. The foundation-stone was laid by the Earl of Aberdeen (whose son, the Hon. and Rev. Douglas Gordon, was the vicar), in the presence of the Dowager Queen Adelaide, who then appeared for the last time in public. She did not live to see it opened. The building is constructed of stone, and consists of a nave, having north and south aisles, a chancel, with spacious south aisle, and a lofty tower at the north-west corner of the nave, in which is a peal of six bells, removed from Little Stanmore Church in 1720. The east window, by Willement, was erected by subscription as a memorial of Queen Adelaide. There are in the church several other stained glass windows, presented by the rector and others, among them being one presented by the Earl of Wicklow in memory of his two daughters, the Ladies Harriet and Isabella Howard. The font, of Caen stone, was the gift of the Queen-Dowager shortly before her death.

This is the third church in succession that the parish has had within little more than two centuries. The original structure stood at a considerable distance, and its exact site is preserved only by tradition and a single tombstone. The second structure was built about 1632, and was consecrated by Archbishop Laud. It was of brick, in the worst style of ecclesiastical architecture, and was built at the expense of Sir John Wolstenholme, who is said by Newcourt to have been "nursed at this parish." Its consecration by Archbishop Laud constituted one of the accusations afterwards brought against that prelate with fatal success. The extending of the ceremony of consecration to *chapels* was made one of the charges against the archbishop, and this structure was perversely termed a "chapel" by the accuser. In reply, Laud admitted the consecration, but observed that the edifice was "a *parish church*, erected by Sir John *Worstenham*, in the place where he was born, and in the diocese of himself." The remains of this church, roofless, and seemingly held together by the thick clusters of ivy which cover them, are still standing a few yards distant from the western end of the new church. They are built of red brick, square in form, and with an embattled tower at the west end. The porch was designed by Nicholas Stone, who received £30 for work done at this part of the building.* For a monument of Sir John Wolstenholme, the founder of this church, Stone received the sum of £200. This monument, which was on the north side of the communion-table, represents the deceased as lying upon a mattress. There are other monuments and inscriptions to different members of the Wolstenholme family. A large tablet of white marble, with a long inscription, commemorates Catherine, Marchioness of Abercorn, wife of John, first marquis, and daughter of Sir Joseph Copley, Bart., of Sprotborough, Yorkshire. The floor of the old church is carpeted with turf, and in the centre is an elaborate mausoleum, of Gothic design, for the family of the Hollonds, of Stanmore Hall. Lord Henry Beauclerk, who died in 1761, was buried in this church, as also was Mr. John Drummond, M.P., who died in 1774, and other members of the families of Beauclerk and Drummond. Charles Hart, a celebrated tragedian of the seventeenth century, "the Roscius of his age," lies buried in the churchyard. According to Lysons, Hart had a "country house" at Stanmore, where he was enrolled a copyholder in 1679. Close by the entrance to the churchyard is a handsome cottage, erected as a memorial of the late Mr. R. Hollond, M.P., of Stanmore Hall, the aëronaut, who died in 1876.

Almost abutting upon the south-west angle of the churchyard, and stretching away for some distance towards Harrow, is Stanmore Park, the seat of Lord Wolverton. Early in the last century the estate, then known as Belmont, was purchased by Mr. Andrew Drummond, the founder of the great banking-house bearing his name at Charing Cross. Mr. George H. Drummond, who subsequently possessed the property, preserved here a large and valuable collection of original portraits, which were bequeathed to the Hon. Mrs. Drummond by the Duke of St. Albans. The mansion was for a short time occupied by Lord Castlereagh, and later on, early in the present century, it was the residence of the Countess of Aylesford. In 1840 the estate was purchased by the Marquis of Abercorn, and the collection of portraits above mentioned, which comprised among their number several by Kneller and Lely, was shortly after sold by auction. The mansion and estate next passed by sale to Mr. George Carr Glyn, who was in 1869 raised to the peerage, with the title of Lord Wolverton. His lordship died in 1873, and was succeeded by his son, the Hon. George Grenfell Glyn, the present Lord Wolverton.

The mansion is a good modern building, consisting of a centre, with two slightly-projecting wings. The park is extensive and well wooded, and is rendered attractive by fine undulations of surface and a handsome lake. At the southern extremity of the park is a hill, termed Belmont, thrown up by the Duke of Chandos, whence the estate derived its original name. It is approached by a fine avenue, and on its summit is a summerhouse, which is a conspicuous object from several neighbouring points.

Bentley Priory, the seat of Sir John Kelk, Bart., lies to the north-west of the village, and though far nearer to Stanmore than to Harrow-on-the-Hill, actually stands in the latter parish. The estate comprises upwards of 460 acres. The mansion is approached from the high roads, which almost surround the estate, by carriage-drives, with six ornamental entrance-lodges; it is placed on the southern slope of the hill, well sheltered by its own woods from the north, and commanding most charming and panoramic views of its own beautiful terraces, gardens, lawns, and undulating deer-park, adorned with oaks, beeches, and other grand forest trees.

The eastern entrance to the estate is at the top of Stanmore Hill, near the junction of the roads leading on the right to Elstree, and on the left to Bushey Heath and Watford. From the Harrow station of the London and North-Western Railway, a long winding walk, up-hill and "against the collar," through the pretty district of Harrow Weald, leads us past several handsome residences in pretty grounds nearly to Stanmore Common. Turning sharply to the east at Bamford's Corner, and leaving the estates of the Hermitage and Woodlands on the left, and, further off, Lord Wolverton's seat, Stanmore Park, on the right, at the end of about three miles the tall trees which surround Bentley Priory are seen on the left. The house is not visible from the road, as the mansion lies about a mile and a half from the park gates at this point. The Watford road, from Harrow Station, skirts the grounds of the Priory on the north-west. Proceeding to the mansion by this road, the visitor will pass, on his left, the pretty little lodge-house of Harrow Weald Park,* and, as he ascends the hill, obtain a good view of its castellated mansion, the seat of Mr. Alexander Sim. He will find an entrance to the Bentley Priory estate at the top of the hill, near the " Hare " hostelry. The house is called a Priory for as good a reason as that for which the ducal residence of

---

Woburn is called Woburn Abbey; for in the far-off middle ages there stood here a priory, but to what order the monks belonged the local historian makes no mention. The good brethren would seem to have lived the "hidden life" to perfection—

"Far from the madding crowd's ignoble strife."

At all events, very little is known of the history of the house. The Priory did not come to an

The next that we hear of Bentley Manor and Priory Farm is in 1706, when it appears to have belonged to the family of Coghill, who, early in the previous century, had settled in the neighbouring parish of Aldenham. In 1734 it was bequeathed by Thomas Coghill to his nephew, Thomas Whittewronge, who left it in 1761 to a certain Mr. John Bennet. In the following year it passed by sale to Mr. William Waller, who about 1766 alienated it to a Mr. Duberly.

BENTLEY PRIORY. (*From a View taken in* 1849.)

end until the reign of Henry VIII., when it was seized among the lesser monasteries, and suppressed, its revenues being assigned, not to the king, but to the monks of Canterbury. In A.D. 1543 we are told that Cranmer gave to the king, in exchange for other lands, the late Priory of Bentley, with all lands, tenements, &c., thereunto belonging in Harrow and Stanmore, "being parcel of the possessions of St. Gregory's Priory, at Canterbury."

No sooner, however, did the royal tyrant get possession of Bentley than he granted it—doubtless not without good consideration—to Henry Needham and William Sacheverel, who sold the property in the same year to Elizabeth Colte.

It is stated in the additions made to Camden's "Britannia," by Gough, that the house of Bentley Priory was taken down and rebuilt by Mr. Duberly, and it is observed in the same work that a chapel, then appertaining to the structure, but long since demolished, "stood detached on the common."

From Mr. Duberly, Bentley Priory was bought in 1788 by the first Marquis of Abercorn, who made great additions to the original house, converting it into a noble mansion, "in which," says Lysons, in his "Environs of London," "convenience is united with magnificence in a manner rarely to be met with."

Under Lord Abercorn, whose reign here extended over thirty years, Bentley Priory was one of the most celebrated houses in the kingdom for its fashionable and intellectual gatherings. Amongst those who frequented it were Sir William and Lady Hamilton (Nelson's Emma), the "Heaven-born Minister" Pitt, Addington, George Canning, Lord Liverpool, the Duke of Wellington, Sir Walter Scott, and "Athenian" Aberdeen, afterwards our Premier during the Crimean war. Samuel Rogers also was an occasional visitor, in spite of his undisguised preference for Holland House. In fact, during the latter half of the reign of George III., and through a part of the Regency, Bentley Priory was one chief rendezvous of the Tory party, and as such is frequently mentioned in the personal reminiscences of many of our statesmen. Mr. Thorne, in his "Handbook of the Environs of London," tells us that "the Prince Regent (afterwards George IV.) came here with the King of Prussia to meet Louis XVIII. when he left Hartwell to return to France;" this was on the conclusion of the war with the great Napoleon. He also asserts that "in April, 1807, Sir Walter Scott, when on a visit here, corrected the revises of his 'Marmion,' and at the suggestion of Lord Abercorn added the complimentary verses on Fox:

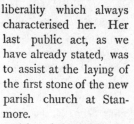

QUEEN ADELAIDE.

> "'For talents mourn, untimely lost,
> When best employ'd and wanted most.'"

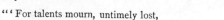

Indeed, Lockhart tells us, in his "Life of Sir Walter Scott," that they "came from the marquis's own pen;" but this may mean only that he had a hand in them.

On the death of the first marquis, in 1818, Bentley Priory came into the ownership of his grandson, the second Marquis (and now Duke) of Abercorn, who, however, did not enter into actual possession of it till he attained his majority. He was sent to school at Harrow, and used to spend his holidays here with his guardian and stepfather, Lord Aberdeen.

The duke resided partly here from 1832 to about 1840; and it was here that Sir Edward Landseer painted one of his most attractive pictures,

in which the younger members of the Abercorn family are introduced.

In April, 1848, Bentley Priory was taken on lease by the Dowager Queen Adelaide, the widow of William IV., who made it her home for the last year and a half of her life. Queen Adelaide, notwithstanding her increasing infirmities, was enabled to take frequent carriage airings in the neighbourhood. She breathed her last here on the 2nd of December, 1849, and by her death the poor of Stanmore and its neighbourhood felt that they had lost a real friend, for her sojourn among them had been distinguished by that active kindness and liberality which always characterised her. Her last public act, as we have already stated, was to assist at the laying of the first stone of the new parish church at Stanmore.

After her death the priory was scarcely used or occupied till 1852, when the estate was bought from the Marquis of Abercorn by Mr. (now Sir) John Kelk, the eminent railway engineer, who represented Harwich in Parliament from 1865 to 1868, and was created a baronet in 1874. He has since purchased the estate of Tedworth, near Andover, in Hampshire, from the Assheton-Smiths, and taken up his residence there, resolving to sell Bentley Priory, which he had largely improved both internally and externally, adding large and well-placed conservatories, several hundred yards in length, which were built at a cost of about £9,000.

The mansion is entered, on the north side, by an ivy-covered *porte-cochère*, with double folding-doors, opening into a spacious entrance-hall, with groined ceiling, supported by fluted classic columns. The grand staircase, on one side of the hall, is of Portland stone, with a carved oak balustrade; the ceiling is enriched, and the walls panelled.

From the inner hall is a corridor, also with groined ceiling, having panelled walls ornamented with medallions, leading to the noble suite of reception-rooms. These are all about twenty feet in height, most artistically decorated. Passing by the boudoir, with its walls of embossed green silk, and the lofty and spacious dining-room, we enter the drawing-room. This is fifty feet by thirty feet; it is highly enriched with painting and gilding, and has two carved statuary marble mantelpieces, surmounted by paintings on panel. The windows of this room open on to a broad portico, from which two flights of stone steps lead to the terraces and Italian gardens. The only other rooms on the ground floor that need be mentioned are the picture-gallery and billiard-room, the library, the smoking-room, the morning-room, or study, and an apartment called "the queen's room," probably from its having been the favourite room of Queen Adelaide. At the western end of the house is the conservatory, whence a corridor leads to a lawn-tennis court or skating-rink. Another important feature of the mansion at this end is a lofty clock-tower.

Immediately in front of the mansion, on the south side, is the Italian garden, intersected by broad terrace walks, and divided into lawns and parterres, adorned with vases on pedestals for flowers. The lawn, studded with oak, beech, plane, and other trees, slopes gently down to the deer-park, which is enclosed by iron fencing, well screened by belts of plantations, and adorned with wide-spreading forest trees. A gravel walk through a shrubbery skirting the deer-park leads to the ornamental "lake," which comprises about four and a quarter acres, a portion of which is covered with water-lilies.

On the margin of the lake is a summer-house, commanding a view of the park and mansion, and it is believed that it was in the quiet seclusion of this charming spot that Scott revised the proof-sheets of his "Marmion." In an adjoining alcove Rogers is said to have written some of his "Pleasures of Memory."

On the north side of the mansion, and approached from the carriage-drive, is a cedar garden and orangery. It is laid out in lawns and flower-beds, and ornamented with cedars, yews, and other evergreen trees. It contains a circular rosary, and in the centre of the garden is the orangery.

Close by is another rosary, and thence a walk leads to a romantic fernery, constructed of rock-work overshadowed by trees. Approached by two shady avenues of lime-trees is a rustic summer-house, containing two rooms; it is situated in the most secluded part of the gardens, and is said to have been the favourite resort of Queen Adelaide.

The plantations and shrubberies adjoining the cedar gardens, and skirting the park, contain many fine specimens of the cedar and fir tribe, cypresses, junipers, &c., with a profusion of laurels and rhododendrons, and other choice flowering shrubs and trees, interspersed with ground covered with brake and ferns, forming a pleasing contrast to the dressed grounds. They are intersected by some miles of winding green walks and drives, which combine a variety of scenery with entire seclusion.

Besides the seats above described, there are a few good residences in the parish, especially in the neighbourhood of the Heath: among them may be mentioned Stanmore Hall, the residence of Mrs. Hollond, an elegant stone-built mansion at the top of the hill; and Broomfield, the seat of the Greigs, a large house of Gothic design, whence, from its lofty situation, extensive views are obtained over the surrounding country. Near the above house, at the edge of the Heath, is The Grove, the residence of Mr. Brightwen. Towards the end of the last century this house was occupied by one Aaron Capadoce, a Jew, who is said to have died here at the age of 105 years. His successor in the occupancy of the Grove House was a German, named Fierville, whose admiration of Rousseau led him to erect a tomb and to form an island on these premises, "in imitation of the tomb and the *Isle des Peupliers* at *Ermenonville*."

A plot of ground between the Grove estate and the high road is known as the Bowling Green. The great Duke of Chandos erected a building close by this spot as a pavilion, or banqueting-house, attached to a bowling-green, which he formed here, in preference to having it near his house at Canons.

We now wend our steps by the cross road running north-east from Stanmore Hill, and, turning northward on regaining the high road at Brockley Hill, soon find ourselves at Elstree. This village, which is pleasantly situated on the brow of a hill, consists mainly of one long street on the St. Albans road. Most of the houses are built of red brick, and have a neat and trim appearance; it is of small extent, for the population does not much exceed 500. It is situated at the intersection of the road from London to St. Albans (the ancient Watling Street) with that from Bushey to Barnet. The latter road separates Middlesex from Herts, and the four parts cut off by these roads are in four different parishes and two dioceses. The north-eastern portion, with the church, is Elstree proper; the north-west is in Aldenham parish, both belonging to Hertfordshire; while the south-east part is in Edgware, and the south-west in Little Stanmore, both in the county of Middlesex. The village is about a mile and a half distant from the Elstree and

Boreham Wood Station, on the Midland Railway. The latter part of the name of Elstree is doubtless "Street," the village being so called from lying on the old Watling Street. In ancient deeds its name figures as Idelstree, Ilstrye, Idelestree, and Eaglestree. The name of Idelstree, or Eaglestree, is still recognised locally.

According to Norden's "Historicall and Chorographicall Description of Hertfordshire," Elstree is "derived from Eaglestree : that is, *Nemus aquilinum*, a place where it may be thought that eagles bred in times past." Lysons, however, contends that the name is rather a corruption of *Eald Street*, or the old road ; in other words, the ancient Watling Street, upon which it is situated.

The manor was granted by Offa to St. Albans Abbey, after the dissolution of which Henry VIII. gave it to Anthony Denny, whose grandson sold part of the estate to the Briscoes, by whom it was possessed down to the middle of the last century, when it passed by sale into other hands; and it has again changed hands on several occasions, finally passing to the Byngs, now represented by the Earl of Strafford.

The manor-house of Elstree Hall, more than three centuries old, was pulled down in 1880–1. It had in it some fine quaint carved chimney-pieces, each of which was adorned with four full-length figures, said by Miss Phillimore, in her "Twelve Churches," to be "exact representations of the fetishes or gods worshipped in Africa and the West Indies." The wood-work was transferred by Mr. H. H. Gibbs to Aldenham House.

The church, dedicated to St. Nicholas, stands on the east side of the street, and its tall spire is conspicuous for miles round. It is a modern Gothic structure, built of brick, and faced with dark flint, with stone dressings, and it consists of nave, aisles, and chancel, with a tower and shingled spire at the south-west corner. Some of the windows are filled with stained glass ; that at the east end of the chancel, a large five-light window, in memory of the Rev. John Morris, D.D., was inserted by his pupils. This edifice was erected about thirty years ago, in the place of the old church, a mean and dilapidated structure, consisting of a nave, chancel, and south aisle, separated by octagonal columns and Pointed arches. The building was one of primitive rudeness and hoary antiquity, and was composed of a number of little patches and compartments, which appeared to have been built at different times. Part of the walls was of rubble-work and of great thickness, and some portion was even composed of timber. The font, which is preserved in the new church, is of antique workmanship, and was perhaps the only interesting feature in the old building. Another feature of the old church which has been retained is the stonework (late Perpendicular) of the doorway known as the "Pilgrims' door."

The monuments are few in number, and of little or no importance. In the church and churchyard are buried two individuals—Martha Ray, and William Weare of Lyons Inn—whose murders may be numbered among the most notorious in the annals of crime; but their graves are without monuments. The former, who was buried on the 14th of April, 1779, was the mistress of the Earl of Sandwich, and mother of Basil Montagu, the editor of Bacon's Works.* She was shot in the piazza of Covent Garden by the Rev. James Hackman, who had conceived a too ardent passion for her, and who fired at her while she was getting into her carriage after leaving the theatre, on the evening of the 7th of the same month. Her frantic murderer, who had made an unsuccessful attempt to destroy himself at the same instant, was tried within a few days at the Old Bailey, and was executed at Tyburn on the 19th of April. Hackman's behaviour after his condemnation, we are told, "evinced most perfect resignation to his fate, united with the settled composure of a man that felt he had survived everything that was dear to him." Hackman's execution became, according to the custom, the subject of some of the most ludicrous verses by the ballad-mongers of the day, of which Mr. Thorne, in his "Handbook," quotes the following as an example :—

" O clergyman ! O wicked one !
　　In Covent Garden shot her;
　No time to cry upon her God,
　　It's hoped He 's not forgot her ! "

Miss Ray was the daughter of a labourer living at Elstree, and hence it was that she was buried here. Weare was a well-known betting-man of his day, and was murdered in 1823 by Thurtell and Probert, two of his associates, near the residence of the latter at Gill's Hill, Radlett, where we shall have again to refer to the subject. The body of Weare was interred at midnight, in the presence of a large number of spectators. The contemporary newspapers rivalled each other in sensational accounts of the ghastly ceremony.

Close by the church was established, about a quarter of a century ago, an institution which in its time has done much good work—namely, the Female Orphans' Home, a charity which has since been transferred to Tangley Park, near Hampton

---

* See "Old and New London," Vol. III., p. 100.

Court. This "Home" had a very humble origin. Towards the close of the year 1855, a private gentleman, not rich in broad acres nor in stores of gold and silver, but pursuing his business as an accountant in the City, resolved to open a "home for destitute orphan girls." He was living with his mother in this pleasant London suburb, when a little girl was left wholly destitute, her father and mother having perished by the cholera. They resolved to adopt the helpless little one, and to make it the "nest-egg" of an orphanage. They were not rich; they had no friends or relatives to "back them up," as the world speaks; they had no funds in hand; but a few pounds were soon subscribed by Christian friends, in coppers, in silver, and in gold, and the newly-adopted stranger was not allowed to be a heavy burden to her foster-parents. Soon another helpless and shipwrecked child was cast at these hospitable doors, borne thither by "the waves of this trouble-some world," and landed happily within reach of friendly aid and succour. Then came another, and then another; and the good work was mentioned privately among friends, and sub-scriptions came in, apparently just as they were needed. A few years ago the founder of the home issued a small pamphlet, or prospectus, in which he tells us that "not only has this particular effort been blessed, but the manager has reason to believe that it has been the means of leading many people to feel, and to act upon, their responsibility in this matter—a responsibility which has been constantly urged upon them from time to time in the reports which have been circulated to some extent. Many similar homes have been opened in London and in the country; and it is hoped that the time will arrive when every *destitute* orphan child will be brought under home influences and sympathies, and thus saved from the cold and withering blight of the union, where, from its very nature, these influences would seem to be im-possible."

Elstree is not very rich in literary memories, but we may mention that here Macready had a country house; it was here that he first met Robert Browning, and introduced the author of "Paracelsus" to John Forster and other friends.

At the entrance to the village from Brockley Hill, on the right-hand side of the road, is a large, old-fashioned red-brick mansion, called Elstree Hill House, which has been converted into a collegiate school; and in the corner of a meadow on the opposite side of the road is a handsome brick-built church, of Gothic design. The meadow is fringed with stately elms, and its farther side shelves down to the Elstree Reservoir, a large sheet of water, which adds considerably to the beauty of the landscape. This reservoir is about three-quarters of a mile in length, and a quarter of a mile across at its widest part. It was formed for the supply of the Grand Junction Canal, and, like the reservoir at Kingsbury,* has become a favourite haunt for wild fowl and "waders." Mr. Harting, in his "Birds of Middlesex," says that when the water has been drawn off for the supply of the canal, or "when it has been much reduced by evaporation and want of rain, the herons are here in all their glory. They are then enabled to wade out to some distance, and regale themselves among the roach and eels with which the reservoir abounds." The reservoir is well known to London ornitho-logists and anglers. It is a beautiful lake, nearly one hundred acres in extent, embosomed in grassy hills, secluded with aquatic trees, and consequently the great attraction of the place.

On our way to Elstree, just before reaching the border of Middlesex and Herts, we cross a water-shed. This watershed runs from Stanmore Heath, on the west, to Brockley Hill and Deacon's Hill on the east, and it divides the botanical district of the Upper Colne, in Hertfordshire, from that of the Upper Brent, in Middlesex. Several small streams originate on the north side of Brockley Hill and on the east of Stanmore Heath, and flow into Elstree Reservoir. The water of this reservoir flows north as a small stream, which is by some writers considered the true Colne, and joins the Colne at Colney Street, in Hertfordshire.

The neighbourhood of Elstree has, indeed, many attractions too for the geologist, the peculiar kind of Hertfordshire stone known as "pudding-stone" being here met with. Mr. Walker, the author of "Rambles round London: Rural and Geological," says:—"The name of pudding-stone is aptly chosen. These blocks are masses of con-glomerate. The matrix is sandstone; it is as thickly studded with pebbles as the popular Christmas pudding is with plums. . . Pudding-stones with flat faces were used as mill-stones in ruder times, the unequal wearing away of the harder pebbles and softer matrix well fitting them for that purpose. Hand-mills of Roman and Saxon times, made of this pudding-stone, are among the antiquities of our museums." In some of the gardens of the villagers at Elstree the pudding-stone may be seen doing duty as clinkers in miniature rockeries, and a "quern," made out of this peculiar stone, is in the Geological Museum, Jermyn Street.

CHAPTER XXX.

BUSHEY, ALDENHAM, AND RADLETT.

"Straight mine eye hath caught new pleasures,
While the landscape round it measures;
Russet lawns, and fallows grey,
Where the nibbling flocks do stray."—MILTON.

Bushey Heath—The Scenery described—Bushey Manor—The Parish Church—St. Peter's Church—Bushey Hall—Hartsbourne Manor House—Census Returns—Oxhey—Watford—Almshouses of the Salters' Company—Aldenham—Acreage and Population—Descent of the Manor—Kemp Row—Tibhurst Manor—Kendall Manor—Pickets, or Newberry—Aldenham House—Penn's Place—The Parish Church—The Grammar School—Discovery of Roman Remains—Radlett—Christ Church—Gill's Hill—The Murder of William Weare—Medburn—Village Schools and Improved Dwellings.

AFTER crossing the Elstree reservoir, and pursuing a westerly course, by Caldecott Hill, a walk of about two miles brings us to Bushey Heath, a breezy spot which, although now greatly curtailed by enclosures, or by the handiwork of the builder, still retains fragments of its former beauty, in the shape of broad open patches of green sward, which in summer time are lighted up with banks of golden gorse and wild flowers. The heath is remarkable for its lofty situation, and the view from it embraces a wide range of scenery on all sides. The towers of Westminster Abbey, Hampton Court, Windsor Castle, and the Surrey hills, are visible on the south side, looking towards Bentley Priory and Stanmore Common; northward, the prospect extends for miles into Hertfordshire, the most prominent object visible in the distance being the lofty tower of St. Albans Abbey. On the northeast, Hill Field Lodge stands out prominently in the middle distance; whilst on the north-west the town of Watford occupies the foreground, the tall clock-tower of the London Orphan Asylum rising conspicuously from amid the surrounding greenery, and further westward the rising smoke marks the situation of the town of Rickmansworth.

Bushey, called *Bissei* in the Domesday survey, was granted by the Conqueror to Geoffrey de Magnaville, or Mandeville, and on the failure of male issue of his family, it reverted to the crown in the reign of King John. Henry III. bestowed it on David de Jarpenvil, who, in the reign of Edward I., obtained, among other privileges, the liberty of free warren and the grant of a weekly market for this manor. Having again reverted to the crown, it was granted by Edward II. to his brother, Edmond of Woodstock, Earl of Kent, who was beheaded through the machinations of Queen Isabella and her paramour, Mortimer, in the fourth year of Edward III. From this period the manor descended through a long line of ill-fated princes. These included Thomas de Holland, Duke of Surrey (grandson of John Plantagenet), who was beheaded at Cirencester, in the rebellion

against Henry IV., and Thomas de Montacute, Earl of Salisbury, who, after obtaining the highest honours in the campaigns in France with Henry V., was killed by the splinter of a window-frame driven into his face by a cannon ball at the siege of Orleans. Richard, the stout Earl of Warwick, another possessor, was killed at the battle of Barnet. George, Duke of Clarence, was murdered in the Tower, and was succeeded in the possession of this manor by Richard Duke of Gloucester (afterwards Richard III.), whose fate at Bosworth Field is well known. The venerable Lady Margaret de la Pole, Countess of Salisbury, another in the long list of unfortunate owners of Bushey, was cruelly beheaded, at the age of seventy-two, in the reign of Henry VIII., seemingly in revenge for a supposed affront by her to her son, Cardinal Pole. Since the above period, the ownership of the manor has passed through various hands, and it is now held jointly by the Earl of Essex and Colonel Walker.

The parish church, dedicated to St. James, is of Early English date, but, having undergone a thorough restoration in 1871 at the hands of Sir Gilbert Scott, it has lost most of the marks of its antiquity. Down to the above date the fabric had remained for many years in a deplorable condition; its walls had been patched and mended at different times, in part covered with plaster and rough-cast, and propped up with large, heavy buttresses. On making some repairs or alterations a few years ago, an inscription of doubtful credit was discovered which stated it to have been "built in the year 1006." The inscription in question was transferred to an iron plate affixed to the wall of the western end of the church. On the restoration of the building at the date above mentioned, the plaster was removed, and a uniform surface given to the walls by facing them with flint and stone, and the church was at the same time enlarged by the addition of aisles to the nave, the interior restored and improved by the substitution of open benches for the high old-fashioned "pews" by which it was formerly encumbered; the open timber roof was repaired, most of the windows were filled with stained glass, and a fresh paving of ornamental tiles laid down. No portion of the present church would now appear to be of the age mentioned in the inscription referred to above. The oldest parts are the chancel and the base of the tower, which are Early English; the present east window, however, a triplet of lancets, was inserted at the restoration in 1871 in place of a gested the inhuman act of disinterring and hanging the bodies of the Protector and certain of the regicides." On a slab in the church, to the memory of two Bakewells, one of whom died in 1643, is the following quaint epigram:—

"Here's two in one, and yet not two but one,
    Two sonnes, one tomb, two heirs, one name alone."

In the churchyard is a tomb, embellished with a carved representation of a palette and brushes, to the memory of Henry Edridge, A.R.A., who

BUSHEY CHURCH.

Perpendicular window of five lights. The chancel is separated from the nave by a carved oak screen. The timber roof of the chancel is decorated with paint and gilding, and on the north side of the altar is an ancient ambry.

The monuments in the church are few and unimportant. In the floor of the chancel is a marble slab inscribed to the memory of Lady Barnard, wife of Gilbert, Lord Barnard; she died in 1728. In 1667 was buried in the chancel Colonel Silas Titus, a Presbyterian Royalist, who has the credit of having planned the escape of Carisbrooke Castle, and with having written the famous tract, entitled "Killing no Murder," with a view to procure the assassination of Cromwell, and who also has the discredit of having "sug- died in 1821, and close by it is an upright slab commemorating Thomas Hearne, a once well-known artist and antiquary, author of the "Antiquities of Great Britain," who died in 1817. "Both these monuments," observes Mr. James Thorne, in his "Environs of London," "were erected by Dr. Munro, the physician, of the Adelphi, a generous friend to young artists, and the early patron of Turner, Girtin, and William Hunt. Dr. Munro had here a country residence, to which he used to invite his young students, that they might sketch in the vicinity. Turner and Girtin have left hundreds of these sketches." There are also in the churchyard some memorials of the Cappers, of Wiggen Hall, in this parish, one of whom purchased the manor of Bushey at the commencement of the last century; also a tomb of Mrs. Elizabeth Fuller, of Watford Place, who founded the Free School in Watford town, and who died in 1709. Mr. William Jerdan, the veteran editor of *The Literary Gazette*, also lies buried here.

St. Peter's Church, which stands in the hamlet of Bushey Heath, is a modern erection of the early English style; its walls are partly concealed in rich clusters of ivy.

From the churchyard, a narrow lane through shops and private houses, with here and there a pleasant shady lane. At the beginning of this century there were about 180 houses in this parish, with a population of about 850. According to the census returns for 1871 the population then reached a total of 4,543, which number in the course of the next ten years had increased to 4,786.

About a mile to the west of Bushey, but rather beyond our beat, lies the hamlet of Oxhey, nestling cosily on the banks of the Colne. The chapel,

ALDENHAM HOUSE. (*See page* 309.)

Little Bushey leads to Bushey Hall, which has been lately fitted up as a hydropathic establishment. The house is built in the Italian style, and has been fitted up in a most elaborate manner, some of the rooms being inlaid with cedar, at a cost of £200,000. There are several other good residences in the neighbourhood, notably Hartsbourne Manor House, the seat of the Sladens, which lies away to the north-west in a pleasant valley watered by the Harts Bourne rivulet, one of the numerous feeders of the river Colne, which it joins after flowing through Carpenders Park.

The main thoroughfare of Bushey stretches for nearly two miles northward on the Berkhampstead road, from Clay Hill, by Stanmore Heath, towards Watford. It is well sprinkled on either side with

which was built in 1612, and which is the only remaining relic of the Jacobean mansion of Oxhey Place, is now used as a chapel-of-ease for Watford.

Bushey has now become a kind of southern suburb of Watford, from which it is separated by the river Colne, which flows through the lower part of the town. As Watford lies just beyond our jurisdiction, we can do no more than express our regret that we are not able to carry our readers with us to Cassiobury, the seat of the Earl of Essex, with its pleasant park and fine family pictures. We must also, for the same reason, leave unvisited the new London Orphan Asylum, which was transferred hither in 1871 from Clapton. The almshouses of the Salters' Company, founded by Beamond and Nicholas, were lately removed hither from London. They are built of red brick with stone dressings, and comprise a centre and detached wings, and an embattled tower. Accommodation is afforded for six men and twelve women.

A walk of about two-and-a-half miles from Bushey Station, on the North-Western Railway, through pleasant rural lanes, by way of Bushey Grove and Berry Wood, brings us to Aldenham, a quiet and retired village, situated midway between the high road to Rickmansworth and that to St. Albans, and about two miles from Radlett Station, on the Midland Railway. The area of the parish is nearly 6,000 acres, and the population, according to the census of 1871, exclusive of the separated district of Radlett, amounted to 1,486. In 1881 they had risen to 1,833.

Long before the Conquest the manor of Aldenham—or Ealdenham, as it was then spelt—belonged to the Abbot of St. Albans, to whom it was given by Wulfsinus, or, as some historians have it, by Offa, King of the Mercians.

Soon after the Conquest the Abbot of Westminster obtained a grant of it for a period of twenty years, for an annual payment of twenty-one hundred shillings and four oxen at Easter, "on condition that he so kept the woods here that persons journeying from St. Albans to London might be safe from the robbers who infested the neighbourhood." The Abbot of Westminster appears to have fulfilled his part of the conditions under which he held the land, but would not give up possession of a wood near Aldenham, which claim the Abbot of St. Albans resisted until long after the expiration of the term.

"There can be little doubt," observes Mr. Cussans in his "History of Hertfordshire," "that the manor of Aldenham really belonged to the Abbey of St. Albans, and that they were unlawfully dispossessed of the greater portion. Constant feuds occurred between the abbots of the two houses of St. Albans and Westminster. At length the Abbot of Westminster brought a suit against his brother of St. Albans, for that the latter had, on Tuesday after Pentecost, in the year 1249, taken fifteen beasts from his manor of Aldenham, and driven them to the manor of Parkbury, in St. Albans; and again, on St. John's Day in the same year, had in like manner taken three other beasts (*haveros*). At the trial St. Albans asserted that the then king had confirmed to their abbey a proportion of the fines coming to the Crown on the circuits of the king's judges within the liberty of St. Albans, a privilege they had held from time immemorial; that certain men belonging to West-

minster, living in that portion of the manor of Aldenham, within the liberty, had been amerced at the last circuit in the sum of five marcs, six shillings and eightpence, whereupon the Abbot of St. Albans seized upon the said cattle. The Abbot of Westminster replied that the same king had granted to his monastery the amercements of all their own men, and the chattels of fugitives and persons condemned. Finally, in Hilary Term, 1256, it was agreed that the abbot and monks of St. Albans should have a View of Franc-pledge in Aldenham once a year, and that on that occasion, whether any fines were levied or not, Westminster should pay St. Albans four shillings, the remainder, if any, to be retained by the metropolitan abbey; that every villein of Aldenham, within the Hundred of Cashio, should render suit at the Hundred Court once in three years, and should attend on juries, &c., when summoned; and if any of the men of Aldenham were amerced (other than at the View of Franc-pledge) before the bailiffs of either the abbeys of Westminster or St. Albans, the said abbeys should equally share such amercement; and, lastly, that the gallows erected in a place called Keneprowe should be common to both abbots, on which to hang persons condemned to death in the Court of Aldenham." Keneprowe—now corrupted into Kemp Row, or Camp Row—is situated between the church and the railway-station at Radlett, and is now a farm. "A man suspended by the neck was supposed to be a wholesome moral lesson, to be taught to so many of his former associates as possible. The abbots, therefore," Mr. Cussans adds, "acted wisely in their selection of Keneprowe, for on its elevated site the result of unlawfully taking a fish from the abbatial waters could be plainly seen both by the men of Aldenham and of St. Albans."

This unsatisfactory state of things between the two abbots came effectually to an end at the dissolution of monasteries, for the manor then "reverted" to the Crown—if the seizure by Henry VIII. of the property of the Church can be called a reversion. It was, however, shortly afterwards granted to the Stepneys, by whom it was sold to Sir Edward Cary, Master of the Jewel Office to Queen Elizabeth and James I., whose son, Sir Henry Cary, was created Viscount Falkland, and subsequently held for some years the office of Lord Lieutenant of Ireland. In the reign of Charles II. the manor was in the hands of Lord Holles. After a few other changes of ownership, it passed, at the end of the last century, to the Thellussons, afterwards Lords Rendlesham, in whose hands it still remains. The advowson of the vicarage, however, was sold by Lord Rendlesham in 1877 to Mr. Henry Hucks Gibbs, of Aldenham House.

There are in the parish one or two manors of minor importance, notably Titeberst, or Tibhurst, and Kendall. The former of these lies on the south-eastern border of the parish, at Theobald's Street, and is owned by the Phillimores, but its history is of little or no importance. The manor of Kendall, the name of which is preserved in Kendall Lodge and Kendall Hall, which lie on either side of the St. Albans Road in the eastern part of the parish, was, in the reign of James I., granted, together with the manor of Tibhurst, to Robert, first Earl of Salisbury. It was afterwards held by the Jephsons, and about the middle of the last century it was bequeathed to Mr. William Phillimore, grandfather of the present owner.

In 1700 Chauncy writes, in his "Antiquities of Hertfordshire":—"Pickets, or Newberry, is another small manor, which William Briscoe, one of the Yeomen of the Guard, held in this vill. Upon his death it came to Edward Briscoe, who was his son and heir, and is the present owner thereof." This manor is now known as Piggots, and is situated near Letchmoor Heath. Although it still retains the name of a manor, the independent rights appertaining to it have long been merged into the manor paramount of Aldenham. As it appears from the above quotation from Chauncy, the manor of Newberry was formerly incorporated with that of Pickets, or Piggots; they are now, however, distinct estates. The manor of Newberry, now called Newberries, is near the railway-station at Radlett, and extends into the adjoining parish of Shenley.

Aldenham House, the seat of Mr. Henry Hucks Gibbs, is a spacious red brick building, standing in a park about 200 acres in extent. The mansion was formerly known as Wigbournes, which, in its turn, appears to have been the successor of a mansion called Penn's Place, or Aldenham Hall, but which, by the way, stood on a small farm now bearing the name, at a short distance from the present house. In dry weather, Mr. Cussans tells us, the foundations of a large building are plainly to be traced. The site, which occupies an acre of ground, is enclosed by an almost rectangular moat, or, rather, the traces of a moat, the eastern side of which, bordering Grub's Lane, has been filled up. The estate derived its name from the family of Penn, to whom it formerly belonged, and it was afterwards owned successively by the Cades, the Coningsbys, and the Coghills. Chauncy, in his "History" above quoted, speaks thus of Penn's Place:—"It is a small manor, situated upon the common where Henry Coghill, Esq., built a fair

house of brick." It is not quite clear from Chauncy whether the "fair house of brick" was the mansion known as Penn's Place and Aldenham Hall, or the house mentioned above as Wigbournes. In the will of Sarah Hucks, dated 1767, Penn's Place is spoken of as a then existing mansion; but in a subsequent deed, executed in 1815, it is described as a farm.

Under its former name of Wigbournes, Aldenham House passed, early in the seventeenth century, to the Coghills; and on the death of Thomas Coghill, in 1734, it passed to his niece, Sarah Hucks, who had already inherited Penn's Place. Her son, Robert Hucks the younger, made sundry additions to the house. After his death, in 1814, the house remained unoccupied for many years, and was allowed to fall into a dilapidated condition. In 1846 Mrs. Gibbs, the mother of the present owner, took up her residence here; but after her death, in 1850, it again remained unoccupied by the family for nearly twenty years, when Mr. Gibbs came again into residence. This gentleman has since thoroughly restored the old building, making many improvements, but in no way altering the character of the building. The family of the present owner was connected by marriage with the families of the Suttons, Hucks, and Coghills, former owners of the estate.

Aldenham is mentioned more than once in the diary of the first Lord Shaftesbury as the seat of Sir Job Harbye, with whom he was an occasional guest.

The parish church, dedicated to St. John the Baptist, stands near the centre of the village, and is an interesting building, chiefly of the Perpendicular period. It consists of a clerestoried nave, with aisles; also a chancel, with aisles, and a lofty embattled tower, surmounted by a shingled spire, at the west end. The nave and aisles are separated by three octagonal columns on each side, from which spring high Pointed arches. The nave-roof is of timber, the principal rafters being painted, and the wall-shafts resting on grotesquely-sculptured stone corbels. The church was restored by Sir Charles Barry in 1840, at which time a timber waggon-headed roof was added to the chancel, and a large five-light window of Decorated character inserted over the altar. This window, and several others in the church, are filled with stained glass. At the east end of the north aisle are faint traces of mural painting.

Among the monuments is one in the chancel, a large altar-tomb, to the memory of John Coghill of Berry, who died in 1714. On the south wall of the chancel, under flat-arched canopies, are the recumbent effigies of two females, whose names are unknown. They form a single monument, and, according to Chauncy's "Antiquities of Hertfordshire," are supposed by tradition " to represent two sisters here entombed, the founders of this church, and co-heirs to this lordship." " The costume of the figures," observes Mr. Cussans, " shows that the monument was erected towards the end of the reign of Edward II.—perhaps as late as the year 1400, but certainly not ten years later. The arrangement of the arms shows that the ladies were not the two wives of one man, nor were they sisters." Near the above is a monument, in the form of a sarcophagus, of coloured marble, embellished with a medallion of white marble, on which are carved in low-relief portraits of Robert Hucks, and Sarah his wife, to whom the monument was erected. In the floor of the chancel are four or five small brasses, but none of any importance.

The south aisles of the chancel and nave were formerly separated by a carved oak screen, which was swept away when the church was restored, in 1840; parts of it, however, remained in the village, and these scattered fragments have lately been collected by Mr. Gibbs, of Aldenham House, and replaced in their original position. A somewhat similar screen on the north side still remains.

In the vestry are preserved two helmets of ancient date. There is also in the church a curious muniment chest, nearly ten feet in length, carved out of a single block of oak, and firmly bound and clamped with iron. The font, in the centre of the nave, between the north and south entrances, has a square bowl of Purbeck marble, resting on a solid circular stem, with detached columns at the corners. It is ascribed to about 1250, the date of the present church, which, by the way, was built on the foundations of an earlier structure.

Aldenham Grammar School, a large red-brick building, of Elizabethan design, is situated on Boydon Hill, in the south-eastern part of the parish. It was founded and endowed, along with six almshouses, in 1599 by Richard Platt, a brewer of London, who entrusted the government of both institutions to the Brewers' Company. In 1875 a new scheme was sanctioned by the Queen in Council, under which the Grammar School was a strictly high-class school, and two lower schools were established out of the endowment, for the use of the parishioners. There are several scholarships, tenable in the school; and there are also three exhibitions a year, tenable at any university.

In 1878, while excavations were being made for the purpose of forming a swimming-bath on the north side of the school, the workmen came upon a large quantity of broken Roman tiles and pottery, at a uniform depth of four or five feet from the surface. It is supposed that there was a pottery factory close by, and that the fragments which were here so plentifully scattered about were broken in the course of manufacture.

Radlett, whither we now direct our steps, is an outlying hamlet of Aldenham, about two miles to the north-east. In 1863 a separate district was assigned to it for ecclesiastical purposes. It lies in a valley, through which runs a stream, called the Leat, or Lete, one of the feeders of the Colne. This stream, before the introduction of the present system of land-drainage, passed through a gravelly soil, and thereby became of a red colour, as it does now in wet weather; and it is from this circumstance that the place is presumed to have derived its name. Rad-lett, or Red-lett, would therefore signify the red mill-stream.

About a quarter of a mile south of Radlett station, on Cobden Hill, stands Christ Church, which was built in 1864 to meet the requirements of the newly-formed ecclesiastical district. It is a cruciform building, constructed of flint and stone, with bands of red brick, and is in the Early Decorated style. The mullions and dressings of the windows are of Bath stone, and the tower is surmounted by an octagonal spire of the same material. Most of the windows are filled with stained glass. The church stands near the site of a small chantry, belonging formerly to the Abbey of St. Albans. In old deeds the name of Cobden Hill is written Copdene Hill, signifying the " Hill at the Head of the Valley." The chantry is stated by Mr. Cussans to have been founded about the year 1510, by Sir Humphrey Coningsby, who endowed it with the following lands lying in the parishes of Aldenham and Elstree :—Paynes, Organ Hall, Tyttescroft, Hilles Stowe, Mole Hill Acre, Chalk Croft, and Woodwards. On the dissolution of religious houses these lands came to the Crown, and were granted by Henry VIII. to Thomas Strete, one of the grooms of his privy chamber. On the accession of Queen Mary, John White, the ejected incumbent of the chantry, was allowed a pension of £5 per annum.

The country round about Radlett is exceedingly rural, much of the land being used for agricultural purposes, the remainder being preserved as parklands. The district is of too recent growth to have a " history;" but early in the present century it acquired some celebrity from the murder of William Weare, of Lyons Inn, whose body, as already stated, lies buried in Elstree churchyard.* The murder took place in October, 1823, close by Gill's Hill cottage, which is reached by a narrow and crooked lane, running westward from Radlett Station towards Batler's Green. Weare was shot by one John Thurtell, his gambling associate, while driving with him in a gig to the house of one William Probert, in the above-mentioned lane. After the murder Weare's body was deposited in a pond behind the cottage, while the murderers divided the spoil, and it was afterwards dragged through a hedge into a field at a short distance from the house. Suspicion having been aroused, a search was made for the body, which was soon discovered. The murderers were forthwith arrested, and Thurtell and Hunt were tried at Hertford, and, being found guilty, the former was condemned and executed, and Hunt was sentenced to transportation for life. Probert, who turned "king's evidence," was discharged, but was afterwards apprehended, tried, and hanged, for horse-stealing.

The details of this old story have been often told; they caused great excitement at the time, and even now read more like fiction than fact. The careful plot, every detail of which fell out quite otherwise than it was planned; the body hidden and sunk, now here, now there; a brother's blood still crying for vengeance; the utter distrust of each other shown by Thurtell's confederates; and the supper on the fatal night, cheered or solaced, as the case might be, by the fitful minstrelsy of Joseph Hunt, an accomplice in the crime; Thurtell's family position, too—for his father was an alderman of Norwich—gave additional interest to the tragedy, which became a fruitful theme for itinerant theatres and peep-shows at country fairs; and "the actual roan horse and yellow gig in which Weare was carried were exhibited on the stage." Poetry came to the aid of the drama—if such doggerel as the following can be called poetry :—

> "They cut his throat from ear to ear,
>   His brains they battered in ;
> His name was Mr. William Weare,
>   He dwelt in Lyons Inn."

Carlyle more than once alludes to the incidents connected with the tragedy; and Sydney Smith pressed the unpromising subject into his service some three years after the event. It happened that in 1826 he was noticing in the *Edinburgh Review* Charles Waterton's "Wanderings in South America." He had to describe a certain Demerara "goatsucker," which, like other birds of its kind, makes night hideous with the most dreadful screeching. This he thought "a stranger would take for Weare being murdered by Thurtell!" Sir Walter Scott not only carefully read the account of the

murder at the time, but more than four years afterwards, when returning from London to the North, did not hesitate to go some two or three miles out of his way in order specially to visit the scene. The author of "Waverley," however, was not happy in his visit to Radlett. He writes in his diary, under date of May 28, 1828 :—

"Our elegant researches carried us out of the high-road and through a labyrinth of intricate lanes, which seem made on purpose to afford strangers the full benefit of a dark night and a drunken driver, in order to visit Gill's Hill, in Hertfordshire, famous for the murder of Mr. Weare. The place has the strongest title to the description of Wordsworth :—

> ' A merry spot, 'tis said, in days of yore,
>   But something ails it now—the place is curst.'

The principal part of the house is destroyed, and only the kitchen remains standing. The garden has been dismantled, though a few laurels and flowering shrubs, run wild, continue to mark the spot. The fatal pond is now only a green swamp, but so near the house that one cannot conceive how it was ever chosen as a place of temporary concealment for the murdered body." Scott's description, however, seems to be somewhat exaggerated. The cottage occupied by Probert, and where Thurtell and Hunt spent the night following the murder, is still standing : it is an ordinary one-storeyed house, with a high-pitched tiled roof. In the rear is the pond which Scott describes as a "green swamp."

Midway between Radlett and Elstree, in the hamlet of Medburn, is a substantial and commodious boys' school, with master's house, garden, and playground. It was built out of the funds of the bequest of Richard Platt, mentioned above, and serves for the boys of both villages. Near Radlett church stands a school for girls and infants, built, in the year 1878, from the designs of Mr. Blomfield, and is in the style commonly named after "Queen Anne." It is of flint, with red-brick dressings, and a tile roof. Since the erection of this latter building, a school at Batler's Green has been converted into cottages.

Mr. William B. Phillimore, of Kendalls Hall, is the chief owner of property at Radlett, and lord of the manor of Elstree and Theobald Street, and his family have been great benefactors to Radlett, by the improvement of the dwellings of the labouring classes. Newberries Park, the seat of Mr. Thomas Bagnall, is a large house in a pleasant park sloping down to the railway. It was purchased from the Phillimores about twenty years ago.

CHAPTER XXXI.

SHENLEY, COLNEY, RIDGE, AND SOUTH MIMMS.

"Per amica silentia campi."—LUCRETIUS.

Extent and Population of Shenley—Descent of the Manor—Shenley Hall, or Salisbury—Newberries—Old Organ Hall—Porters—Holmes, otherwise High Canons—The Village of Shenley—The Chapel-of-Ease—The Parish Church—Colney House—London Colney—Tittenhanger—Colney Heath—Ridge—The Parish Church—South Mimms—Census Returns—General Appearance of the Village—The Old North Road—The Manor of South Mimms—The Church—Almshouses—Potter's Bar—Dyrham Park—Wrotham Park—Destruction of the Mansion by Fire—Hadley Common—Christ Church.

THE village of Shenley lies about two miles east-north-east from Radlett Station on the Midland Railway; the road thither, tortuous, but pleasant,

gave "Scenlea" to the above-mentioned monastery, "in perpetual alms;" "but," as Mr. Cussans infers in his "History of Hertfordshire," "as in a charter

SHENLEY CHURCH AND VILLAGE.

passing for the greater part by the palings of Porters on the one hand, and by those of New Organ Hall on the other.

The parish extends from north to south, a distance of about six miles, from London Colney to Elstree and Chipping Barnet; the parish of Ridge forms its eastern boundary, and a long detached strip, belonging to the same parish, occupies the greater portion of its western side.

The number of houses in Shenley parish in 1871 was 301, the population at the same time amounting to 1,380. Of this number, 382 belonged to the ecclesiastical district of Colney St. Peter. During the next decade the number of the inhabitants had slightly diminished.

From an ancient Chartulary, formerly belonging to the Abbey of St. Albans, but now preserved in the British Museum, it appears that before the time of the Conquest one Thurefleda, a pious lady,

of Edward IV. to the abbey (in which the confirmations of grants by previous kings are all recited at length) there is no mention of Shenley, it is probable that the manor, which in Domesday Book is said to have belonged to St. Albans, was the same manor which was afterwards known as Ridge. This supposition is strengthened by the fact that Ridge is not mentioned in Domesday, and that the abbot's manor of Shenley is there described as being in Albaneston Hundred (the Hundred of Cashio), and the other two within the

Hundred of Danais, or Dacorum." About two hundred years after the Conquest the manor was in the possession of John Fitzacre, who, in 1267-8, granted it, together with the advowson of the church, and the chapel of Colney, to Adam de Stratton, and in the same year obtained from the king a grant to hold an annual fair and a weekly market within this manor. At the close of the thirteenth century the manor was forfeited to the Crown, and shortly afterwards it was granted by Edward III. to Sir John de Pulteney, or Poultney, who was five times Lord Mayor of London. The

of Newberries was formerly known as Old Organ Hall, and appears to have been first called Newberries by its late owner, Mr. Phillimore, from whom it was purchased by Mr. Thomas Bagnall. The building now known as Old Organ Hall, which lies on the east side of the railway, near to Boreham Wood and Elstree Station, is a farmhouse on the estate.

The estate of Porters, mentioned above, covers a large portion of the parish, being no less than 1,300 acres in extent. The mansion, the seat of Mr. Myers, who is lord of the manor, occupies the

TITTENHANGER.

SIR T. POPE.

manor remained vested in the Poultneys for just three centuries, when it was carried, by the marriage of an heiress, to the Crewes, of Crewe Hall, Cheshire. It subsequently passed to the family of Lomax, in whose possession it remained down to 1850, when it was sold to Mr. William J. Myers, of Porters Park, in the parish, and with his descendant it still continues.

The manor of Shenley Hall, otherwise Salisbury, lies in the north-eastern part of the parish, near London Colney. It derived its name from the family of Montacute, Earls of Salisbury, who owned the property in the fourteenth century. The manor subsequently descended in the same way as that of Bushey, and seems to have reverted to the Crown in 1471, on the death of the Earl of Warwick, the "kingmaker," as we shall see presently, at the Battle of Barnet. It now belongs to the Phillimores, late of Newberries. The present mansion

summit of a pleasant hill, commanding an extensive view towards the south-west. Chauncy, in his "Antiquities of Hertfordshire," describes Porters as "an old seat," and Sir Richard Coxe, who died in 1623, is described as "of Porters." From the Coxes, the estate passed by marriage to Sir Edmund Anderson, with whose family it continued for many years. Nicholas Hawksmoor, the architect, a pupil of Sir Christopher Wren, whom he assisted in rebuilding St. Paul's Cathedral, was living here at the time of his death, in 1736; he may, however, have been only a tenant, for in 1750 died Mr. John Mason, who was at that time lord of the manor of Weld, which had become amalgamated with this estate, and who, on his tomb in Shenley churchyard, is described as "of Porters."

The estate of Holmes, otherwise Canons, but

commonly called High Canons, is situated about a mile south-east of the village, on the left of the road towards Barnet. The property derives its name from the fact of its having formerly belonged to the Prior and Canons of St. Bartholomew, in Smithfield, in whose possession it remained till the dissolution of religious houses, when it passed to the Crown. In 1543 High Canons was sold to one Nicholas Bristow, and since that time it has undergone several changes of ownership. Mr. Thomas Fitzherbert, who purchased the estate at the end of the last century, expended a large sum of money in improving the grounds and mansion, which was shortly after again sold. In 1812 the property was purchased by Mr. Enoch Durant, with whose family it now remains.

The village of Shenley fringes the cross-roads at the south-eastern extremity of Porters. It consists of a few straggling cottages and general shops, and, from its lofty situation, possesses some charming views, particularly towards the north-west, where, at a distance of about five miles, the city of St. Albans, with its venerable abbey, is plainly discernible, cresting the opposite range of hills. In 1841, in consequence of the distance of the church from the bulk of the population, a plain brick-built chapel-of-ease was erected in the centre of the village. It consists of a chancel and nave, with a small belfry turret at the south-west angle. Here the afternoon and evening services are performed, the morning service being still continued in the old parish church, to which we will now direct our steps.

This edifice, dedicated to St. Botolph, lies about a mile north-west from the village, at the foot of the hill, and a little to the right of the road to St. Albans. The church originally consisted of chancel, nave, south aisle, and tower; but in 1753, the edifice having become dilapidated, the tower was demolished, the western end built up, the chancel and tower arches and the arcading of the nave pulled down, the open timber roof demolished, and baulks of timber laid from wall to wall, with the result that the structure has been converted into a good-sized rectangular chamber, with a flat plaster ceiling. On the site formerly occupied by the south porch is now a square wooden tower, painted white, with a tiled roof, and containing three bells. The walls of the body of the church are of chalk, faced with squared flints, and the buttresses between the windows have been partially repaired with brick. The windows are of the Perpendicular style throughout. The large four-light east and west windows, and also three or four others, are filled with memorial painted glass. The font is ancient, and stands at the west end of the church under the organ gallery; and in the exterior of the south wall is an old sun-dial. The pulpit and a carved oak reredos and altar-rails were erected by subscription in 1878.

In the churchyard are several fine yew-trees. The tomb of Nicholas Hawksmoor, the architect, mentioned above, is in the churchyard. It is an altar-tomb, the slab of which is broken, and the inscription barely legible. Hawksmoor was the architect of St. George's, Bloomsbury, St. Mary Woolnoth, Lombard Street, and other well-known City churches. Close by the belfry is the memorial of a former parish clerk; it consists of a board supported by two uprights, and bears the following lines :—

"Joseph Rogers, died August 17th, 1828, in the 77th year of his age, having been clerk of this parish a half century.

> "Silent in dust lies mould'ring here
> A Parish Clerk of voice most clear ;
> None Joseph Rogers could excel
> In laying bricks or singing well.
> Though snapp'd his line, laid by his rod,
> We build for him our hopes in God,
> The Saviour God, that He will raise
> Again that voice to sing His praise,
> In Temple blest, which always stands,
> The Church of God not made with hands."

Colney House, in the hamlet of Colney Chapel, about a mile northward from Shenley Church, and the same distance south-west from the village of London Colney, but belonging to the parish of Shenley, is a spacious stone mansion, built about a century ago by Governor Bouchier, at an expense of £53,000, including the charges for laying out the pleasure-grounds and making other improvements in the park, which is about 150 acres in extent. The house is a handsome and regular structure, with slightly projecting wings, and is double-fronted. The principal front, facing the roadway, has a semicircular portico at the entrance, surmounted by a half-dome. The west front, overlooking the park, has a bay-window on either side of the doorway. These bays rise to the level of the second floor, and are surmounted with balustrades. The park contains some fine oak and elm trees, and the pleasure-grounds are extensive. The estate was sold by Governor Bouchier to Margaret of Anspach, who resided here for three years, after which it was disposed of to the Earl of Kingston. Early in the present century it was sold to Mr. George Anderson, with whose family it remained for many years. It was subsequently owned by the Oddies; and in 1871 it was disposed of to Sir Andrew Lusk, Bart., who sold it some years later.

The above estate was formerly part of the extensive manor of the Weald, or Wild, and obtained the name of Colney Chapel, it is supposed, from a religious house which is thought to have stood on a small piece of land in the park, surrounded by a moat, though now planted and laid out in walks.

The river Colne skirts the north side of the park in its course towards Aldenham and Watford. It is crossed by a wooden foot-bridge in the line of the roadway at this point, but is fordable for vehicular traffic. Following the course of this stream in a north-easterly direction we soon find ourselves at London Colney.

London Colney, which is partly in the parishes of Shenley and Ridge, and partly in those of St. Peter and St. Stephen, in St. Albans, is a large village of some 850 inhabitants, and was formed into a separate ecclesiastical district in 1826. It stands on the great high road through Barnet and South Mimms to St. Albans, from which place it is distant about three miles and a half. The principal part of the village slopes upward from the north bank of the River Colne, from which the place derives its name, and which is here crossed by a brick bridge of seven arches. The church, dedicated to St. Peter, was built in 1825, by Philip, third Earl of Hardwicke. It is a plain rectangular brick building, with semicircular-headed windows; that at the east end, of three lights, is filled with stained glass, representing "The Ascension," and was designed by Louisa, Dowager-Marchioness of Waterford; it was erected in 1865 as a memorial to the founder of the church.

The hamlet of Tittenhanger lies to the east of London Colney; it forms part of the parish of Ridge, and consists of two or three humble cottages, nestling pleasantly near the winding Colne, and on the outskirts of Tittenhanger Park, the seat of the Countess of Caledon. The manor of Tittenhanger belonged, at the time of the Conquest, to the Abbots of St. Albans, who frequently resided here, though their manor is stated to have been but a "mean building." About the end of the fourteenth century, however, Abbot John de la Moote commenced the building of a new and stately mansion here, "where," according to Chauncy, "he and his successors might retire for their ease and pleasure, and recreate themselves with their friends and relations, but died before he could finish the same." This was afterwards completed, on a more extensive and elaborate scale, by his successor, Abbot John of Whethamsted, in the reign of Henry VI., and the property continued to belong to the abbots till they were despoiled of their possessions at the dissolution of monasteries. Thorne, in his "Environs of London," observes that "there is a tradition that Wolsey expended a large sum on it, intending to make it one of his residences." In 1528, Henry VIII. and Queen Katherine are stated to have taken up their residence at Tittenhanger during the continuance of the malady known as the "sweating sickness" in London. In 1547, the last year of his reign, Henry VIII. granted the manor and estate to Sir Hugh Paulet, from whose family it was conveyed by marriage to Sir Thomas Pope, the founder of Trinity College, Oxford. Sir Thomas, who had been the fortunate recipient of many grants of the lands of the dissolved monasteries, made Tittenhanger his principal residence, having greatly improved the house; and on his death, without issue, in 1559, it continued in the possession of his widow, Elizabeth, the daughter of Mr. William Blount, of Blount Hall, Staffordshire. This lady was succeeded by her nephew and heir, Mr. (afterwards Sir) Thomas Pope Blount; and from him the estate descended to Philip, third Earl of Hardwicke, in right of his mother, Catherine, first wife of the Hon. Charles Yorke, Lord Chancellor of Great Britain, she being the sole heiress of the ancient Hertfordshire families of Pope, Blount, and Freeman. These Blounts became extinct by the death of Sir Henry Pope Blount about the middle of the last century. On the death of the Countess of Hardwicke, in 1858, the property was inherited by her daughter, Catherine, Countess of Caledon.

The present mansion of Tittenhanger was built about the middle of the seventeenth century by the first Sir Henry Pope Blount, from the designs of Inigo Jones, and it is described by Chauncy as "a fair structure of brick, with fair walks and gardens." The house is of Tudor architecture, large and convenient, oblong in form, and has an inner court. It was originally surrounded by a moat, but this has been filled up; the gardens, too, were long ago destroyed, and much of the park has been broken up and converted into a farm. What there is left of the park is pleasant and well wooded, and is watered on its western side by the river Colne.

Colney Heath, the extreme northern limit of the metropolitan area, and consequently the utmost extent of our wanderings in this direction, abuts upon the north-east side of Tittenhanger Park. The district was formed into an ecclesiastical parish in 1846. The church, dedicated to St. Mark, is a brick building in the Byzantine style, consisting of an apsidal chancel, a nave, and a small bell-tower.

We must now make our way homewards once more, but by way of the high road, through South

Mimms to Barnet. The road for some three or four miles is as "straight as an arrow," and the land on either side pleasantly diversified by cultivation and woods. Ridge Hill, which we ascend about two miles from Colney, takes its name from the quaint little old-world village of Ridge, which lies some little distance away to the right of our road, and is approached through narrow winding lanes. The district is exceedingly rural, and has a population of about 450 souls. Apart from the dozen or more of humble cottages, a general shop, and an inn, forming the village, there are one or two houses of a better class, notably Ridge Hall, Rabley House, and Deeves Hall, with here and there a farm scattered about. The parish, which has really no literary history, probably derives its name from the "ridge" of high ground which runs along its border, and it is wonderfully unchanged among all the changes of time. The green lanes on every side wind between hedgerows of thorns and elders, very much as they must have done two centuries ago ; and the farm-houses have a sleepy and respectable appearance, which seems to indicate that their owners do not care much for " progress."

The parish church, dedicated to St. Margaret, is an ancient building, standing away by itself on the west side of the village. The edifice is small, built of flint and stone, and consists of a chancel in the Early Decorated style, and a Perpendicular nave. The west end is surmounted by a low wooden tower, crowned with a spire. It is as yet "unrestored," so that it still exhibits all the marks of the Georgian interior arrangements. There are high deep pews of deal on either side of the central passage up the nave, with hatchments in abundance, and the royal arms in a conspicuous position. Like Kingsbury, it is quite innocent of aisles, and the distinction between nave and chancel is of the very slightest kind. The structure is chiefly remarkable for the abundant coats of whitewash which have been inflicted on it by successive incumbents and churchwardens. It is also noticeable for the tombs and monuments of the family of the Blounts of Tittenhanger, who lie buried here. Of these, the best known are those of Sir Henry Pope Blount, the author of the "Voyage into the Levant," who died in 1682, and his sons, Sir Thomas Pope Blount, author of "De Re Poetica," &c., who died in 1697, and Charles Blount, the deistical writer, who died by his own hand in 1693, having been driven to frenzy by his unsuccessful endeavours to obtain a license to marry his deceased wife's sister, and her refusal to marry him without it. The event is thus recorded in the Cæsar Manuscripts, under date of August 31, 1693 :—"Mr. Charles Blount, of

Tittenhanger, in Hartfordshire, died in London, *felo de se*, five weeks after he had shot himself into the belly with a pistoll : for love of Mrs. Hobby (his wife's sister), who was a rich widow." Pope, too, commemorated Mr. Blount's death in the following line in his " Epistle to the Satires " :—

"If Blount despatch'd himself, he play'd the man."

Blount's books were reprinted in a collected form by Gildon, in 1695.

The parish of South Mimms is bounded on the west by Ridge, on the north by Northaw and North Mimms ; Monken Hadley and Enfield encompass it on the east, and it stretches away southward to High Barnet. It occupies the northern portion of the Hundred of Edmonton, and is the most extreme point northward of the county of Middlesex. The name of the parish has in times past been variously written as Mims, Mymes, and Mymmes. The additional term of " South " is evidently applied to the village to distinguish it from its neighbour in Hertfordshire, which has become famous as the home of Sir Thomas More, but which, by the way, lies just beyond the limits of our peregrinations. This parish, which includes the hamlet of Potter's Bar, about two miles eastward from the village (where there is a station on the Great Northern Railway), and also the ecclesiastical district of Christ Church, Barnet, has a population of nearly 4,000. In 1871 the number of the inhabitants of South Mimms proper was 775, and the census for 1881 shows very slight change.

The parish contains within its bounds about 5,400 acres of land, of which 1,097 were allotted by an Act of Parliament passed in 1777, on the enclosure of Enfield Chase. The old "Royal Chase" formed the southern boundary of South Mimms, as far as Potter's Bar.

The general outline of the parish is agreeably diversified with hill and dale, and the village itself, with the church in the midst—there is no regular street, in the ordinary sense of the term—is built upon undulating ground along the line of the old road—which is now a picturesque lane, winding up from its lower end to North Mimms, but in ancient times was the great highway northwards. This road is intersected by the present high road, which was formed early in the present century. The course of the old road was somewhat sinuous, but it contrasts pleasantly enough with the dull and monotonous uniformity of the more modern high road to St. Albans. On quitting Barnet, it traversed Hadley Green, and leaving the road by Potter's Bar to Hatfield on the right, was carried thence by Kitt's End under the fence of Wrotham Park to

Dancer's Hill. Here, bending abruptly to the right, along the wall of Dancer's Hill House, it passed over Mimms Wash, and crossing the present high road, reached South Mimms village. After traversing the entire length of this, it followed the present lane, but branched off sharply to the left shortly before reaching the lodge of North Mimms Park. The present high road, continuing in a straight line from Barnet, passes through the village to the east of the church and churchyard, and then almost bisecting the houses of the village, passes on again in an equally straight line to Colney and St. Albans.

The manor of South Mimms is not mentioned in the "Domesday Survey," and it probably then formed part of the royal chase of Enfield, which belonged at the time of the Conquest to Geoffrey de Mandeville, who owned much property in this part of Middlesex. Through several ages, previous to the year 1479, the manorial rights were vested in the Leuknore, or Lewkenor, family, but it afterwards became annexed to the Crown ; and in 1484 it was granted by Richard III. to his zealous adherent, Richard Scrope. It was subsequently owned by the family of Windsor ; and about the middle of the seventeenth century it passed to the family of the Marquis of Salisbury, with whom it still continues.

The church, dedicated to St. Giles, stands almost in the centre of the village, and, from its lofty situation, is visible for many miles round. It consists of a nave and chancel, separated from a north aisle, erected at a later period, by octagonal pillars and six obtuse arches. At the western end is an embattled tower, tall and massive, with a small staircase turret at the south-east angle. The main body of the church is in the Early Perpendicular style, and has the walls faced with flint ; but the north aisle, looking prim and new from recent restoration, is of red brick, and of Tudor architecture, having been built in 1526. There is no chancel arch, but the chancel is slightly narrower than the nave. At the eastern end of the north aisle, and separated from it by a carved oak parclose, or screen, of Gothic design, is the Frowyke chantry, or chapel, now used as a vestry. The chancel was newly paved and decorated at the restoration of the church, by Mr. G. E. Street, in 1868. The font, of Early English character, consists of a plain square block of stone hollowed in the form of a circular basin, resting upon four small circular columns, and a square centre support, with shallow Perpendicular tracery. One or two of the benches are old, and contain some good examples of wood carving. The five windows of the north aisle

contain in their centres some fragments of ancient stained glass, forming a series, thought to have been part of the original decoration of the re-built aisle. In the south wall of the chancel is a trefoil-headed piscina, apparently of the thirteenth century. On the north side of the chancel is an altar-tomb, with an elaborately carved canopy, supported by four Renaissance columns. It is without arms or inscription ; but the initials R. H. are worked into the rose and quatrefoil ornamentation of the tomb. It is very doubtful whom this handsome tomb commemorates. In the Frowyke chapel is an altar-tomb, belonging to the family of Frowyke. It bears the recumbent effigy of a knight in armour, under a rich open canopy. The tomb is without inscription or date. There are in the floor of the church two or three brasses to different members of the Frowkyes.

Close by the churchyard, and facing the street, is a row of almshouses for six widows. They were founded in the year 1687 by James Hickson, between Dancer's Hill and Hadley, but were moved hither in 1856 by the Brewers' Company, who are trustees of the charity.

Potter's Bar, which, as stated above, is an ecclesiastical district of South Mimms, lies about two miles eastward from the latter place. It is a long, straggling village, about a mile in length, with a population of rather more than 1,200 souls. The church, dedicated to St. John, stands towards the north end of the village. It was built in the year 1835, chiefly at the expense of the late Mr. George Byng, M.P., of Wrotham Park. It is constructed of white brick in the Norman style, and several of the windows are filled with memorial stained glass. Here the Byng family were formerly interred; but owing to some differences between them and the incumbent of the parish, Lord Strafford erected in Wrotham Park a mausoleum, which was consecrated by the Bishop of London, as their burial-place.

On the west side of the high road which leads towards Barnet is the estate of Dyrham (or Derham) Park, the seat of the Trotters. The entrance gate, which is approached from the St. Albans road, consists of a tall central arch between Tuscan columns, with entablature and scrolls, and surmounted by a large vase. It is said to have formed originally the triumphal arch which was erected in London by General Monk on the occasion of the public entry of Charles II. in 1660. The old mansion having been burnt down early in the present century, the present house was built by Mr. John Trotter, the then owner of the estate. It is a large and heavy square building in the Classical style, and is situated in the midst of a well-wooded and undulating park of about 170 acres in extent. The estate derived its name from the Derhams, by whom it was possessed in the latter part of the thirteenth century, when it was conveyed in marriage to the Frowykes. This latter family retained possession of the property through many generations, and late in the seventeenth century it became the property of the Austen family. In 1733 it was purchased from Sir John Austen, Bart., M.P. (who lies buried in the churchyard of South Mimms), by Anne, Countess of Albemarle ; and at the end of the last

accidentally destroyed by fire in March, 1883, was a handsome edifice in the Classical Italian style, which was so fashionable in the reigns of the two first Georges. It was erected from the designs of Ware in 1754, its then owner being the unfortunate Admiral Byng, who was executed a few years afterwards, under circumstances well known to every reader of English history. The house bore a strong resemblance to Southill, in Bedfordshire, another seat of the Byngs in the last century. The principal front of the mansion looked to the west,

WROTHAM PARK.

century, having, in the meantime, once more changed hands, it was sold to Mr. John Trotter, the founder of the Soho Bazaar,* and with his family it still continues.

The "Butcher" Duke of Cumberland is said to have turned aside out of the Great North road, on his way back to London, after the victory of Culloden, in order to spend a night or two here before going on to join the king at Kew.

On the opposite side of the road, and occupying some 250 acres of ground in the fork of the two roads, passing northwards to St. Albans and to Hatfield and York, is Wrotham Park, the seat of the Earl of Strafford. The mansion, which was

commanding fine views across the park towards Elstree and Watford. It consisted of a spacious centre, with side colonnades, terminating in octagonal wings ; it had a deeply-recessed tetrastyle portico, and a pediment extending along the second storey ; and the whole was surmounted by a handsome balustrade. The name of the house was derived from Wrotham, near Sevenoaks, Kent, where was the ancient seat of the Byngs, Lords Torrington. The house contained a fine gallery of pictures and an excellent library.

It is somewhat singular that the mansion of Wrotham Park stood a narrow escape from destruction by fire shortly after its erection from the hands of an infuriated mob, during the riots which followed on Admiral Byng's trial and disgrace.

* See "Old and New London," Vol. III., p. 190

Admiral Byng was never married, and at his decease the estate came to his nephew, George Byng, Esq., whose eldest son, also George, was for upwards of half a century M.P. for Middlesex, and who died in 1847. Upon the death of his widow, Wrotham Park reverted to his brother John, a gallant Peninsular officer, who was in 1835 created Baron Strafford, and in 1847 advanced to an earldom; and from him it descended, in 1860, to his son, the present peer, who was well known in his day on the turf, and has held several Court and administrative appointments.

At the southern extremity of the park is Hadley Common, where we meet with the obelisk or pillar set up to commemorate the battle of Barnet; but of this we shall have more to say in the next chapter.

Christ Church, adjacent to the town of Barnet, but in the parish of South Mimms, was built in 1852, at the expense of the late Captain Trotter, of Dyrham Park, but has since been enlarged.

HIGH STREET, HIGH BARNET.

CHAPTER XXXII.

HIGH BARNET.

"I will away towards Barnet presently."—SHAKESPEARE, *Henry VI.*, III., Act V., Sc. 1.

Situation and Extent of Barnet—Its Etymology—The Manor—General Appearance of the Town—Census Returns—Markets and Fairs—The Parish Church—The Grammar School—The old "Crown Inn"—Jesus Hospital—Almshouses and Charitable Institutions—The Town Hall —Barracks—Chapels and Meeting-houses—Ravenscroft Park—The "Physic Well"—Historical Associations—Inns and Taverns—The Battle of Barnet—The Obelisk.

THE small busy town of High Barnet stands at a fork where the road to Elstree and Watford branches off from the Great Northern road, along which Dick Turpin used to ride; and the long High Street still shows marks of having been a street of inns and posting-houses, as being in the old coaching days the first stage out of London on the road both to York and Manchester, for those roads diverge just beyond the northern end of the town.

The town stands high and "wind-swept," extending along a ridge which commands distant views in every direction, and it is from this circumstance that it acquired the prefix of "High." Mr. Thorne, in his "Environs of London," says it is the belief of the older natives that "Barnet stands on the highest ground between London and York." But this, we fancy, can hardly be the case. The town is also called Chipping Barnet, from its market, "which Henry II. granted to the abbots of St. Albans to be kept in this town ; it was famous for cattle, and was held on every Monday."

Barnet is considered to belong to Hertfordshire, but not all the town is in that county, nor does the town lie in a single parish. Middlesex and Hertfordshire interlace here, and so do the parishes of South Mimms, Hadley, and High Barnet, to an extent which makes it difficult to describe the place with accuracy. There is, in fact, great confusion, because there are two Barnets, two miles apart—East Barnet and *Chipping* Barnet, or, as it is commonly called, *High* Barnet ; and to these must be added a third, " New " Barnet, which lies between them both, and is rapidly being covered by modern streets and villas, of the common suburban type. Lying as it does, for the most part, between two lines of railway—the Great Northern main line and the Finchley and High Barnet branch—this central district enjoys the advantage of very frequent communication with London, and therefore is a favourite abode of City men.

As to the origin of the name, Barnet is thought by some antiquaries to be probably at root the same word with Brent, the river which rises in the valley between the town and Totteridge. It is fair to state that it is here called the " Dollis brook "— *i.e.*, boundary, from an old Kentish word, dolestone, a landmark, a word which also occurs in the Homilies.* But according to Chauncy's "Antiquities of Hertfordshire," the name of the town appears in very early deeds as *Bergnet*, " from the high situation thereof ; for the word Bergnet in the Saxon language signifies *monticulus*, a little hill."

In the far-off Saxon times the whole of this district, including East Barnet, formed part of an extensive forest, called Southaw, which belonged to the abbots of St. Albans. The manor continued in the hands of that monastery long after the Conquest ; but after the dissolution it was granted by Queen Mary to Anthony Butler, whose descendants, in 1619, sold it to Sir John Weld. It has since passed through the hands of various families, and is now, according to Kelly's " Directory of Hertfordshire," the property of Mr. William Henry Richardson, of Southampton.

Though High Barnet is now commonly known as " Barnet," without any prefix, yet it must not be supposed that it is the original place of that name. East Barnet, which, as stated above, lies a mile and a half away, nearer to the borders of Essex, is shown, by its Norman church, to be the mother, though the

daughter has risen into greater note, from its situation on the Great North road which led to York and Scotland.

We must, however, mention the daughter first, both because it comes first geographically, and also on account of the extent to which it is mixed up with the adjacent village of Monken Hadley, which really forms its northern suburb.

The main street of the town is about a mile in length, broad and well paved, and bears a strong family likeness to that of Highgate ; the sign-boards of its numerous inns and hostelries indicate the importance of the town before the invasion of the railway, and when upwards of one hundred and fifty stage-coaches passed through it daily. Of late years the town has greatly improved, not only in its general appearance, but also in growth, particularly on its western side, about the Common, or, as it is now called, " Arkley." This suburb of the town is situated on high ground, and commands extensive views towards Bedfordshire and Buckinghamshire on the north, while on the south may be discerned from it the high grounds of Hampstead, Highgate, and Muswell Hill. The neighbourhood is studded with villa residences, a branch railway giving easy access to the City.

According to the census returns for 1871 the number of houses in High Barnet was 601, the inhabitants at the same time numbering 3,375 ; this latter number, in the course of the next ten years, had swelled up to 4,283, or about four times what it was at the beginning of this century.

The market, which was granted to the town by Henry II., is still held, but on Wednesday instead of Monday. The horse and cattle fair held yearly, in September, has made the name of Barnet known not only throughout the kingdom, but even abroad. It is held in the fields surrounding the railwaystation at High Barnet, and many thousand head of cattle from the Highlands change hands here. Even Cossacks from the neighbourhood of the Don, in Russia, have been known to attend the fair, clothed in the costume of their native country. The horse and cattle fair used formerly to be wound up with a pleasure fair and races, which became very popular with London roughs ; but on the formation of a railway, in 1871, the racecourse was broken up, and the races were of necessity abandoned—an event on which the good people of Barnet may well be congratulated.

The parish church, which stands in the middle of the town, at the junction of the north road with that leading to Elstree and Watford, is dedicated to St. John the Baptist, and was originally erected about the middle of the thirteenth century. About

* See Homily for Rogation Week, Fourth Part, " Accursed be he, saith Almighty God by Moses, who removeth his neighbour's doles and marks."

a century later was built the tower, wholly disconnected from the body of the fabric. In 1400, John de la Moote, Abbot of St. Albans, rebuilt the body of the church, which consisted of a chancel, nave, and aisles, separated by Pointed arches rising from clustered columns, with a low embattled tower at the west end. In the chancel was a fine east window, with Perpendicular tracery. A vestry was added to the building in the reign of James I., by a great benefactor of the town, Thomas Ravenscroft, to whose memory there is in the church an altar-tomb, with Pointed arches, supported on Doric pillars, with a recumbent effigy of the deceased in veined marble. He died in 1620; several others of his family are also buried here. In 1839 the church was enlarged, and in 1875 it was thoroughly restored, and further enlarged by the addition of a nave, chancel, and tower, the original nave being converted into a north aisle, while the old north aisle remained beyond it. The old tower, too, was partly taken down, and added to the former nave, and a new tower of flint and stone, in squares, raised at the west end. The church, as it now stands, consists of chancel, south transept, with the mortuary chapel of Thomas Ravenscroft, nave, two north aisles, and tower. The re-building was carried out under the direction of Mr. Butterfield, at a cost of about £16,000, mainly at the cost of the endowments left by Mr. Ravenscroft to the Jesus Hospital, of which we shall speak presently.

The Grammar School is in Wood Street; it flourishes under the shadow of the parish church. It consists of one large and lofty hall, which is as old as the reign of Elizabeth, dating from 1573, and has much of the Tudor style of architecture, with a turret at either end. It is now used as a dining-hall, a new and lofty range of buildings, from the designs of Mr. White, having been erected in the rear. The dormitories above the large hall are almost coeval with the building itself, and the eastern end once contained rooms, in which more than one of the masters lived. These being now removed, the hall now extends to fifty-five feet in length.

The charter for the school (the original of which is extant) was granted "at the humble request of our well-beloved cousin and counsellour, Robert, Earle of Leicester, Knight of the most noble Order of the Garter, Master of our Horse."

Few records of the past history of the school exist; two of its early masters, however, rose to become bishops in Ireland; one of its governors, named Westfield, was Bishop of Bristol in the reign of Charles I.; and another, Sir Robert Berkeley, of East Barnet, suffered imprisonment in the Tower for having, as a judge, pronounced ship-money to be lawful. There is much that is inaccurate in the accounts of the foundation of the school, as given by Lysons, Clutterbuck, and Chauncy; and it seems probable that the fabric owes its erection to a Mr. E. Underne, Rector of Barnet, aided by funds from the Corporation of London, and from one Lonison, or Lannyson, a goldsmith and citizen. Among the earlier governors occur the names of Brockett, Briscoe, Coningsby, Weld, Blount, Berkeley, Lord Coleraine, and other persons of good families connected by ties of property with the neighbourhood.

It appears that from time to time the governors of the school put their hands in their pockets liberally with subventions towards repairs of the buildings and other purposes. By the authority of the Corporation of London collections were made from time to time in the City churches towards the erection and repair of the school buildings here.

The statutes compiled for regulating the school in 1634 ordain that "the master shall be a clergyman, approved by the Bishop of London, and that the scholars be male children, free from infectious disease; that the children of residents in the parish of Barnet shall pay twenty shillings a year, and no more, but that for others a charge may be made, as the parents and the master may agree. The boys are to be catechised on Saturdays, and to attend the parish church on Sundays, and that the daily work of the school be opened and closed with prayers. The employment of the senior boys as Monitors, or 'Præpositi,' is approved; and every scholar shall be taught the 'Qui mihi discipulus' in Lilly's Grammar. There are to be weekly 'Orations' and exercises in prose and verse; the Latin alone shall be spoken in the highest forms, and immoderate correction shall not be used." A further curious statute provides that if the Governors of Merchant Taylors' School, in London, shall choose to send any boy for health's sake to Barnet, he shall be "readily entertained" there; and that if any of the wardens, governors, or masters of Merchant Taylors' School "be pleased to looke into this schoole," the master is to provide a "gratulatorie oration in Latin or English, to be publicly delivered by one of his schollers for their entertainment and welcome."

The school contains over a hundred boys, and the course of studies is modern and practical rather than strictly classical, in the ancient sense of the term. Its pupils some twenty years ago had dwindled down to the most insignificant number; but a "new scheme" was proposed, and warmly seconded by the inhabitants, and in the end the new school was opened in 1875.

According to the new scheme, under the Endowed Schools Act of 1869, the Jesus Hospital was ordered to pay £5,000, and also a yearly sum of £400, towards the advancement of education in the school. The governing body was ordained to consist of twelve persons, mostly of local standing, three of whom were to be nominated by the Visitors of the hospital. These governors manage the financial affairs of the school, but wisely judge it the best course to leave the internal arrangements to the head-master whom they appointed, the Rev. J. R. Lee, of Exeter College, Oxford, formerly second master of the Grammar School at Bedford.

That this school, prior to the above mentioned date, had sunk to a very low ebb, may be inferred from the manner in which, under a thin guise, it was once referred to in a popular periodical.

In *Household Words*, No. 86, November 15, 1851, is given, under the title of "A Free (and easy) School," an account of Queen Elizabeth's " Royal Grammar School at Thistledown," under Dr. Laon Blosse, head-master, who, besides superintending the education of seven foundation or free boys, seeks private pupils of his own, who are to qualify themselves for admission by bringing with them silver forks and spoons. Under scarcely-veiled aliases, the writer describes the approach to " Thistledown " from the railway-station, the general grouping and arrangement of the little town, and the ivy-grown school-room, with its dull, heavy entrance-court, and its flanking round, or rather angular, turrets at either extremity. The writer is, of course, none other than Charles Dickens himself. In no indistinct phrases he informs his readers that the pretence of carrying out the original purposes of the foundation is simply a delusion and a snare, though he confesses to being somewhat affected at the notion of standing in a " school-room built in the old days of Queen Elizabeth, not at all large, but tolerably lofty."

Little is known of its schoolmasters during the sixteenth and seventeenth centuries. " It is to be regretted," writes Mr. Cass, " that that gossiping Samuel Pepys, on that cold August Sunday morning when he visited the Physicke Well, did not look in at the school on his way to or from it ; and that Elias Ashmole never strolled thither by Enfield Chase and Hadley, or across the meadows between Mount Pleasant and the top of Barnet Hill, nor make a halt there when journeying to visit his friends Mr. and Mrs. Hutchinson, at Delrow, near Watford."

The old "Crown" Inn, adjoining the school-house,

was purchased quite recently from the governors of Harrow School, its site and the yard in the rear being added to the school grounds. The inn was a picturesque structure, with overhanging gables. It was at this house, in all probability, that the Lady Arabella Stuart stopped in making her escape from East Barnet to join her husband.*

Almost every town has its local hero or benefactor, and Barnet forms no exception to the rule. James Ravenscroft, a worthy citizen of High Holborn, London, who died in 1680, left a large property in Stepney in order to found a hospital, called Jesus Hospital, for "six poore antient women " in Wood Street, in this town. The recipients of this charity are to be "neither common beggars, common drunkards, backbiters, tale-bearers, common scolds, thieves, or other like persons of infamous life or evil name or repute ; or vehemently suspected of sorcery, witchcraft, or charming ; or guilty of perjury ; nor any idiot or lunatic." The founder lies buried in the church of High Barnet, where, as already stated, a fine Jacobean tomb, with recumbent figures of himself and his wife, commemorates his good deeds. He also left money to support the Grammar School, which dates from just a century earlier, having been established by Queen Elizabeth in 1573. The funds left by Master Ravenscroft for the benefit of the above hospital were augmented by a bequest in 1737, of Miss Mary Barcock, a daughter of a former master of the Grammar School.

The endowments left by James Ravenscroft having largely increased, through the increased value of land at Stepney, have been utilised in various ways at Barnet. Amongst other objects the parish church has come in for a share, having been doubled in size, as stated above, out of the superfluous wealth of Jesus Hospital.

Barnet is tolerably well off for charitable institutions. Besides the above-mentioned almshouses, there are others in Wood Street, founded by John Garrett, in 1729, for six old spinsters or widows, each of whom receives a small dole of money weekly. Palmer's Almshouses (for men and women), beyond the new public gardens, which were part of Barnet Common, all now enclosed, were founded in 1823, from the proceeds of a bequest in 1558 by one Eleanor Palmer, a widow, of Kentish Town, London, for the support of six aged married couples, who receive eight shillings weekly. The Leathersellers' Almshouse, at the junction of Union Street and Wood Street, was erected in the year 1843 by Mr. Richard Thornton, for six poor freemen of the Leathersellers' Company,

---

* See 'Old and New London," Vol. V., p. 404.

and for six freemen's widows. The buildings, of Gothic architecture, are of white brick, and were enlarged in 1865 by the addition of eight new houses.

Barnet is under the control of a Local Government Board, which has been established with a district comprising Chipping Barnet and part of the parishes of Hadley and South Mimms. The Town Hall, which is situate in Union Street, is a brick building, of little or no architectural pretensions; and in the neighbourhood of the town are barracks for a detachment of the King's Rifle Corps.

There are chapels and meeting-houses in the town for the various denominations of dissenters, and there is also a Roman Catholic chapel in Union Street, dedicated to Saints Mary the Immaculate and Gregory the Great.

A large open space of land adjoining the west end of the town was utilised in 1880–81 by being drained, planted, and laid out as a recreation ground. It is surrounded by pleasant villas, and the district has taken the name of Ravenscroft Park, after the local worthy already named.

Beyond the spot which was till lately known as Barnet Common, in a field a mile and a half from the town, on the south of the road to Elstree, is a chalybeate spring of a mild purgative nature, that was discovered about the middle of the seventeenth century, and was formerly in much repute. It is mentioned and extolled in "The Perfect Diurnal" in 1652. In the year 1667 Alderman John Owen, a "citizen and fishmonger" of London left the sum of £1 yearly for keeping the "Physic Well" in repair. It would be surprising to find no mention of it in the diary of the gossiping Samuel Pepys. That worthy paid a visit to the spot in 1667, which is duly recorded under the date of Sunday, August 11, in that year:—

"To the wells at Barnett by seven o'clock, and there found many people a-drinking; but the morning was very cold, so we were very cold all the way in the coach. And so to Hatfield, to the inn next my Lord Salisbury's house, and there rested ourselves and drank, and bespoke dinner; and so to church."

A Dr. Trinder published, in 1812, a small treatise on the medical virtues of this water. But he could not revive or preserve its fame; yet it still exists, for a pound is paid annually for its preservation out of the funds of the Grammar School. It is, however, quite unused, and is a mere survival of past memories. Indeed, the farmer on whose ground it stands, if the truth must be told, does not appreciate the pump, and has painted it green, so as not to attract the notice of passers-by.

The waters of Barnet and Northaw were not very powerful, but they were extremely popular in the reign of Charles II. The Northaw spring was in a bottom, half a mile east of the village. Fuller mentions these waters along with those of Epsom and Tunbridge. Dr. Wittie, in his account of Scarborough Spa in 1669, favours us with these doggrel lines:—

"Let Epsom, Tunbridge, Barnet, Knaresborough, be
  In what request they will, Scarborough for me."

"The old well-house," observes Mr. Thorne, in his "Environs," "was pulled down, and a small farmhouse erected on the foundations in 1840. The well is now covered over, and the water is obtained from it by a small iron pump. To reach it, you go along Wood Street (by Barnet Church) for a quarter of a mile, and down the lane on the left, in front of the Union Workhouse, to where the lane is crossed by a light iron gate. Here turn through a small clap-gate on the left into a field-path, which presently passes through a gap in the hedge, on the right, into a field, in the midst of which the pump will be seen, and above it the well house. The well is quite open to every one, and is still occasionally resorted to by invalids. The visitor who is disposed to test the efficacy of the water will remember Pepys' experience."

Barnet is not without its literary and historic associations. The great conflict between the rival houses of York and Lancaster, commonly known as the "Battle of Barnet," took place really in the parish of Monken Hadley, on the outskirts of the town, as we shall presently see.

At Barnet William Hailes was put to death for heresy, under Queen Mary, in 1555. Here, too, James Thomson lived as tutor to Lord Binning's son, before he became celebrated as the author of "The Seasons;" and here, too—if we may be allowed to pass from fact to fiction—Tom Jones was met by the assumed highwayman on his way from St. Albans to London.*

Though the town of Barnet has no "maltings" and breweries, like Hertford and Ware, yet it is extremely rich in inns, the survivals of old posting-houses of repute in the olden days, when 150 coaches passed through it, either on the up or down journey, and, for the most part, changed horses there. The inns themselves, as is the case still in some other country towns, were patronised exclusively by the "Whig" and the "Tory" magnates; and many persons now living can re-

---

* See "Old and New London," Vol. II., p. 550.

member the day when old and chivalrous ladies refused to change horses when travelling post at any inn that did not bear the colours of their family. The "Green Man," at the junction of the great high road and the new road to St. Albans, formed the head-quarters of the Liberals, "Woolpack," and the "Salisbury"—the latter named, doubtless, after the Cecil family. The interior of it still bears marks of antiquity; and so did its inn-yard till recently. It is now the head-quarters of the neighbouring bicyclists.

There are in Barnet scarcely any side or back

VIEWS IN BARNET.
THE SCHOOLS. THE "RED LION" INN.

while the Tories patronised exclusively the "Red Lion"—possibly as symbolising the British Constitution. Probably the reason why political differences were thus emphasised at Barnet is to be found in the fact that it was half-way to Hatfield, the seat of the Tory Cecils, and that the head of the Whig house of Byng, the lord of Wrotham, lived just outside the town.

Among the chief inns whose sign-boards still hang along the street are the "Red Lion," the streets, and hence the town is remarkably free from "slums." Indeed, it has altogether a thriving and "respectable" appearance—in this respect a pleasing contrast to Staines, Uxbridge, Hounslow, and Brentford.

On the outskirts of the town, in the year 1471, was fought the famous battle between the rival houses of York and Lancaster, which terminated in the death of the Earl of Warwick, and established Edward IV. upon the throne.

The facts of the battle of Barnet, and those which led to it, are to be read in every history of England, and, with some embellishments, in the concluding chapter of Sir Edward Bulwer Lytton's work, the "Last of the Barons." It would be impossible to enter as fully into the latter subject as it deserves without almost writing a fresh history of the Wars of the Roses. It is enough here to refer the reader to other sources of information, and to say that in the early part of the year 1471 (the same year, by the way, in which William Caxton set up his printing-press at Bruges), Edward of York landed from the Continent on the shores of

forming an irregular triangle, of which one side "impinges" on the village of Monken Hadley. Sir John Paston, who fought on that day on the Lancastrian side, fixes the scene of the battle precisely, in a letter written to his mother from London, only a few days after. He states it to have been about half a mile from Barnet; and this agrees with the words of one Edward Halle, judge in the Sheriff's Court, who probably conversed in his lifetime with several who were present :— "This toune (Barnet) standeth on a hill, on whose toppe is a faire plain for two armies to joyne together ;" and on one part of this plain Warwick

HADLEY GREEN (SITE OF THE BATTLE OF BARNET).

Yorkshire, to encounter the deadly opposition of his former ally, Warwick, the "King Maker," who had now thrown in his lot with Henry of Lancaster and Margaret of Anjou. Edward rapidly advanced on London, and entered it in state, having the weak Henry VI. a prisoner in his hands. Warwick and his comrade Montagu hastened from their head-quarters at Coventry towards London to oppose him; but on reaching St. Albans they found that Edward had come out from London to Barnet, about half-way, in order to give them battle. The contest could not be declined; and it is clear that each party knew that on the issue of the battle depended the entire future of the throne and the kingdom.

The heath, to the north of the town, formerly called Gladsmore Common, is the spot which has been fixed upon by most historians as the scene of the encounter. It is still an open space,

"pitched his fielde." Stow, the annalist, also fixes the spot as distant half a mile from Barnet; and the present Hadley Green, with the level ground adjoining it, exactly answers the description.

A very slight glance at the spot will satisfy the most ordinary observer that the spot was well chosen for the purposes of war. "A modern commander similarly circumstanced," writes the Rev. F. C. Cass, in his paper on the "Battle of Barnet," in the "Transactions of the London and Middlesex Archæological Society," "would doubt-less have occupied the town in force, entrenching himself along the high ground sloping towards the south-east, between the top of Barnet Hill and Hadley Church, and have placed his reserves somewhere to the west, on Barnet Common, to secure his right flank from being turned. With his artillery he would have swept the ascent of Barnet Hill, and would have taken care to line the edge of

Hadley Wood with riflemen." And he shows in detail how Warwick, on reaching Hadley Green, or Gladsmore Heath, being first in the field, and having the choice of ground, could hardly have made a different selection, at a time when a tolerably level space was necessary for the movements of heavy-armed horsemen, and horses almost as heavily armed themselves.

On the eve of the battle, which took place on Easter Day, in April, 1471, the king and his troops held the northern suburbs of the town, being quartered along the great northern road; while Warwick came up with his forces along the road from St. Albans. On the common they met face to face, the right wing of Lord Warwick being opposed to the king's left.

"In the profound darkness of the night and the thick fog," writes Bulwer Lytton, in the "Last of the Barons," "Edward had stationed his men at a venture on the heath at Gladsmoor, and hastily environed the camp with palisades and trenches. He had intended to have rested immediately in front of the foe, but in the darkness he mistook the extent of the hostile line, and his men were ranged opposite only to the left side of the earl's forces—towards Hadley—leaving the right unopposed. Most fortunate for Edward was this mistake, for Warwick's artillery, and the new and deadly bombards that he had constructed, were placed on the right of King Edward's army; and the provident earl, naturally supposing Edward's left was there opposed to him, ordered his gunners to cannonade all night. Edward, as the flashes of the guns illumined by fits the gloom of midnight, saw the advantage of his unintentional error; and to prevent Warwick from discovering it, reiterated his orders for the most profound silence. Thus even his very blunders favoured Edward more than the wisest precautions had served his fated foe."

If we may trust the graphic sketch drawn by the novelist's master-hand, the early morning of Easter Day was raw, cold, and dismal; but the signal for battle was given, and the deadly encounter began. On that battle of Barnet, though the numbers engaged in it were small according to modern ideas, depended the ruin or triumph of a dynasty, the fall of a warlike baronage, and the rise of a crafty, plotting, imperious despotism, which ultimately developed into the stern and vigorous rule of the house of Tudor. "The stake was high, the die was cast—the king won, and the Earl of Warwick lost. He proved the last of those power-ful barons who, under the Plantagenets, had held royalty in check. The battle of Barnet secured the crown of England to the House of York, and sent King Henry back a prisoner to the Tower." Lytton describes in detail, doubtless with some little exaggeration, the chief incidents of that hard-fought field, and the doughty deeds of the leaders of either army; but we may accept as true the particulars of the death of Warwick, who, even when he saw that all was lost, refused to fly and save his life. He was hewn down by the battle-axe of one of Edward's officers, and his body, having been placed in a hearse, was carried to London, to be exposed to the gaze of the public in St. Paul's, whence, a few days later, it was carried to its final resting-place in Bisham Abbey, near Marlow.

During the battle, if we may believe Lord Lytton, who follows in this respect the annalists, King Edward was kept in countenance by a sorcerer, one Friar Bungay, who took up his position a little to the east of the battle, near the spot where Monken Hadley Church now stands, the captive King Henry also standing by as a sort of hostage.

As for the "blood-stained" field of Barnet, various estimates are given of the numbers which fell that day; some writers fix them as low as 1,500, whilst others say that 20,000 were slain. Let us hope that the former figures are nearer the truth.

Although the accounts of the numbers engaged in the battle vary very much, and cannot be reconciled, yet as to the details of the engagement there is no doubt. The first shots fired in the early dawn of that Easter Sunday were fired at random, owing to the dense fog which covered the hills, and concealed the foes from each other; but as the morning waxed on to noon, the sun broke forth, and the combatants found themselves face to face. The king and the earl respectively rode along their ranks, each encouraging his followers. One wing of Edward's army was being driven back, when a mistake between the two rival congnizances of the star with five points and the sun with rays threw the hosts of Lord Warwick into confusion, of which Edward was not slow to take advantage, calling into action a reserved force, whilst Warwick's men were too exhausted to answer their leader's call. "The day," writes Mr. Cass, "was visibly lost, and nothing remained but for Warwick to sell his life dearly. By ten o'clock, or at noon according to some writers, victory rested with the Yorkists, and Warwick and Montagu were slain."

The Dukes of Somerset and Exeter and the Earl of Oxford escaped with their lives from the field, but only to die elsewhere. The common soldiers who fell in the engagement were buried on the field, but the exact spot of their interment is not known. The conqueror rode back to London immediately—the captive King Henry following in his train—and presented himself next day at St. Paul's to offer up his standard, and to return thanks to the God of battles.

As a proof that the battle of Barnet was of great practical importance in its results, it is reported that no subsequent Lancastrian rising troubled the reign of King Edward.

There is still on the edge of the common an old moated farm-house, or grange, which some of Lord Warwick's men are said to have occupied on the eve of the battle.

The place where Warwick made his last stand is marked by an obelisk, erected in the last century, and bearing a brief record of the fact and of the date of the battle. The exact spot where he fell is said by tradition to be marked by two trees planted in the place of others which perished from age, about twenty yards north of the obelisk.

The obelisk on the field was erected in 1740 by Sir J. Sambrooke, of Gobions, an estate in North Mimms, more anciently called More Hall, the property of Sir Thomas More.

"Barnet," writes Mr. Cass, "has greatly changed from the little town through which Edward passed on his way to a battle on which his throne depended; but still, behind the plastered or brick-faced fronts of the buildings lining its modern street are perhaps hidden the timbers of dwellings from whose windows men and women and little children looked out upon the victor, as, early on that Easter afternoon, he rode past with Henry in his train." Is it not a satire on Christianity itself that, whilst the service of song and praise was being offered in the church which stood by the battle-field, Christians should have been spending their Sunday in cutting each other's throats and cleaving each other's skulls with battle-axes?

CHAPTER XXXIII.

HADLEY, EAST BARNET, AND TOTTERIDGE.

Etymology of Monken Hadley—Descent of the Manor—Hadley Green—The Village and Common—Hadley Wood—Gladsmore Heath, or Monken Mead—Dead Man's Bottom—Hadley Church—Two Historic Trees—Almshouses—Noted Residents—Population—East Barnet—Lyonsdown—Census Returns—The Parish Church—The Boys' Farm Home—The Clock House—Cat's Hill—Oak Hill Park—Belmont—Totteridge—Its Etymology—Descent of the Manor—Census Returns—Condition of the Roads—The Church— Yew-trees in Churchyard—The Priory—Pointer's Grove—Copped Hall—Totteridge Park—Wykeham Rise.

MONKEN HADLEY—or Hadley, as it is colloquially styled—as stated in the preceding chapter, adjoins on the north the town of High Barnet, of which it forms almost a suburb. The parish, which was formerly a part of Enfield Chase and a hamlet to Edmonton, is bounded on the north-east by the parish of Enfield, and comprises in its area nearly 600 acres, of which about 240 were allotted in lieu of its right of common, on the enclosure of the royal chase above mentioned. According to Lysons and other topographers, the village owes its name to its elevated situation, being "compounded of the Saxon words *Head-leagh*, signifying a high place. The "*ley*" in its designation, however, would seem to imply a meadow, or clear open space in the forest land, as in the case of Cow*ley*, already referred to.* The adjunct *Monken* occurs in many ancient documents, and is adopted in the description of this parish in the Act for enclosing Enfield Chase; and it is probable that it was derived from the former connection of the place with the Abbey of Walden, to which it was given by Geoffrey de Mandeville, Earl of Essex, about the middle of the twelfth century, under the name of the "Hermitage of Hadley."

Hadley is not mentioned in the Domesday survey; but it appears at a very early period to have belonged to the Mandevilles, from whom it was alienated, as above stated, to the monks of Walden, the abbey of which place was founded by Geoffrey de Mandeville. After the dissolution of monasteries, the manor was granted to Thomas Lord Audley, who shortly afterwards surrendered it to the Crown. In 1557 it was granted by Queen Mary to Sir Thomas Pope. A few years later it was alienated to the Kymptons, but was soon after sold to the family of Hayes, in whose hands it remained for about a century. Towards the end of the last century it was purchased by Mr. Peter Moore, who rendered himself unpopular a few years later by asserting a right to enclose Hadley Green, including the whole of the waste, without

See *ante*, p. 226

the consent of the parishioners. This assumed right he defended in a court of law, but failed in his endeavour, as Sir Thomas Wilson failed at Hampstead,* and the immemorial privileges of the parish were fully established on appeal.

The village is situated on the east side of the Great North road, on the margin of Hadley Green, and round about the common—a broad open space which stretches away eastward from the church. The common, with its ponds and trees, much resembles Clapham Common, and is now said to be the only unenclosed portion of the ancient Chase of Enfield. It is a picturesque piece of undulating upland, sloping away rapidly towards the east, where it abuts upon Beech Hill Park. The lower or easternmost part of the common, where it is crossed by the railway, is generally called by the natives Hadley Wood; it is one of the most beautiful pieces of woodland scenery to be found within many miles of the metropolis. This narrow strip of forest scenery runs eastward as far as the hamlet of Cock Fosters.

The high ground towards the west and north-west of the common was sometimes called of old Gladsmore Heath, but more often styled Monkey (or Monken) Mead, and is the spot now generally accepted by antiquarians, as shown in the preceding chapter, as that whereon was decided the great Battle of Barnet. The obelisk which has been set up to commemorate that event stands at the upper end of Hadley Green, in the fork of the two roads leading respectively to Hatfield and St. Albans. It bears the following inscription:— "Here was fought the famous battle between Edward IV. and the Earl of Warwick, April 14th, 1471, in which the Earl was defeated and slain."

The low ground adjoining Monken Mead is named on the early maps "Dead Man's Bottom," either from having been the chief scene of slaughter at the battle of Barnet, or else for being the burial-place of the slain.

Hadley Church, dedicated to St. Mary, stands on the very edge of the battle-field of Barnet. But it is not old enough to have witnessed that engagement, having been built in the year 1494. It stands not very far from the mound on which Lord Lytton, in his "Last of the Barons," represents Friar Bungay as carrying on those solemn incantations which were destined to clear away the fog and mist and to give the victory to the House of York. Close by it there is to the present day a gate across the road, marking the fringe of the Chase, and giving entrance to that royal demesne.

We shall have more to say about it presently. The church is a cruciform building in the Perpendicular style, and consists of chancel, nave, aisles, transepts, and an ivy-covered tower at the west end. This church is finer than most parish churches, and bears a strong resemblance in its general features to those of High Barnet and South Mimms. The church is constructed of black flint and Bath stone disposed in alternate squares. On the top of a turret at the south-west angle of the tower is affixed an iron "cresset" fire-pan or pitch-pot, an almost unique survival of other days. It is supposed to have been placed there as a guide to wayfarers through the neighbouring forest. Mr. Bloxam tells us in his work on "Gothic Architecture," that it was used and fired so late as the year 1745—probably at the time of the alarm caused near London by the Stuart rising in the North. It was also again used more recently at the marriage of the Prince of Wales.

The church was restored, and in part rebuilt, under the rectorship of Dr. Proctor, between the years 1848 and 1850, by Mr. G. E. Street, and the south aisle was added as a memorial of the late rector, Mr. Thackeray. Several new windows were inserted at the time of the above-mentioned restoration. Most of the windows are filled with painted glass; the nave, of four bays, opens into the tower, and it is separated from the aisles by depressed arches resting on octagonal columns. Over the west doorway of the tower is the date 1494, having on one side the device of a wing and on the other that of a rose. Lysons, in his "Environs of London," says that they are probably "the cognizance either of the abbey, or one of the Abbots of Walden." Mr. Brewer, in the "Beauties of England," observes that the same devices occur in Enfield Church, which likewise belonged to the abbey founded by Geoffrey de Mandeville. "It is certain that these emblems," he adds, "had no reference to the arms of Walden Abbey; but they were possibly meant as the cognizance of the abbot at that time, whose name was John Sabysworth, or Sabrisfort." The south porch was erected in memory of Dr. Proctor's son, the Rev. G. H. Proctor, of Balliol College, Oxford, who died before Sebastopol, where he was serving as an army chaplain. Dr. Proctor was a brother-in-law of Mr. John Payne Collier, the learned dramatic author; and he was said to have been the original of the "Dr. Blimber" of Charles Dickens, in "Bleak House."

There are several monuments of the seventeenth century, the most remarkable being that in memory of Sir Roger Wilbraham, solicitor-general of Ireland in the reign of Queen Elizabeth, and his lady,

---

with marble busts of each by Nicholas Stone; and there is a mural brass of the fifteenth century.

Among the fragments of ancient painted glass in the church, is a piece containing the rebus of the family of Goodere, who occupied an important position in this parish and neighbourhood in the fifteenth and sixteenth centuries. It consists of a partridge, with an ear of wheat in its bill, and having on an attached scroll the word "goode" in black letter. On the capital of one of the pillars are two partridges with ears of corn in their beak, an evident reproduction of the above punning device. The Gooderes are thought to have been considerable benefactors towards the rebuilding of the church. Weever, in his "Funeral Monuments," mentions a mutilated inscription to the memory of "John Goodyere, esquyre, and Jone, his wyff," with the date of 1504. This is no longer visible; but a brass still commemorates Anne Walheden, "descended of the Goodere's auncyent race," who was buried in 1575.

In the churchyard, to the east of the chancel, lies under a plain flat slab Mrs. Hester Chapone, the once popular authoress of "Letters on the Improvement of the Mind," addressed to young ladies, and which had a great run in the last century. She died in the year 1801. Her maiden name was Mulso; and among her friends were Mrs. Elizabeth Carter, Mrs. Montagu, and Dr. Johnson, who valued her highly, and condescended even to argue with her. In early life she was a frequent guest at the house of Richardson. Here also are buried Dr. John Monro, who acquired some celebrity as a physician and writer on insanity, at the end of the last century, and Dr. Proctor, the late rector, who died in 1882.

Nearly opposite the church, close by the gate that leads to the common, still stands the weather-beaten trunk of an aged oak, long ago divested of its bark, which is mentioned by Lord Lytton in his "Last of the Barons," when describing the closing events of the battle of Barnet, as the "gaunt and leafless tree" whereon the wizard Friar Bungay, mentioned above, hangs his hated rival, Adam Warner, whilst at its foot lay the life-less form of his daughter Sibyll, "and the shattered fragments of the mechanical 'eureka' on which he had spent the labours of his life." The old trunk was upset a few years ago by some drunken volunteers, but it has been replaced in position, and railed in.

Not far distant is another tree which has become historic, called "Latimer's Elm," from a local tradition that Latimer once preached beneath its branches,

Near the church are the Priory, a modern Gothic edifice, with pleasant grounds and gardens, and also two rows of almshouses: the one was founded by Sir Roger Wilbraham, in 1616, for six "decayed housekeepers," each of whom receive a sum of £18 per annum; the other, founded by Sir Justinian Paget, in the seventeenth century, for three poor men and a like number of women, was rebuilt about fifty years ago.

The mansions facing the east side of Hadley Common have had some celebrated tenants in their day. Mrs. Trollope, the novelist, lived in the house nearest to the Wilbraham Almshouses; and it may be remembered that Anthony Trollope, in his novel, "The Bertrams," alludes to his sister being buried in the adjoining churchyard. The house at the southern end of the same row—called the Grange—was formerly occupied by the grandfather of William Makepeace Thackeray, of the same name, at the beginning of the present century. At The Mount House, on the north-west side of the common, lived for many years Professor Joseph Henry Green, F.R.S., the author of "Spiritual Philosophy, founded on the teachings of the late Samuel Taylor Coleridge." Professor Green died in 1863, about thirty years after the friend whose philosophy he had done so much to interpret and popularise.

In Fuller's "Worthies" it is stated that Sir William Starmford, or Stamford, an eminent lawyer of the sixteenth century, was a native of this place. He was the author of a legal work, entitled "The Pleas of the Crown," and is said by Fuller to have been born in 1509, and to have been buried at Hadley in 1558. Hadley was also the birthplace of Sir Robert Atkyns, the learned author of the "History of Gloucestershire." He was born in the year 1647, being a son of Sir Robert Atkyns, Lord Chief Baron of the Exchequer, who was himself the author of several political pamphlets.

In 1871 the number of houses in the parish of Hadley amounted to 200, the population at the same time numbering 978. In consequence of the increased railway facilities of late years, for communication with the metropolis, the number of the inhabitants has since increased to nearly 1,200.

East Barnet, whither we now direct our steps, lies in a pretty valley about a mile east of the great high road to the north, and some mile and a half south-eastward from Hadley. The parish is bounded on the east by Enfield, on the south by Friern Barnet and Southgate, and on the west by High Barnet and Elstree. The rural aspect of the neighbourhood has been somewhat curtailed since the formation of the Great Northern Railway, and the consequent growth of a town. This, however, is the mother or cradle of the other parishes bearing the name of Barnet, and it is called East Barnet to distinguish it from High (or Chipping) Barnet, and Friern Barnet immediately adjoining. Within the last few years, even, another ecclesiastical district, generally called New Barnet, but legally known as "Lyonsdown," has sprung up, having been formed out of the parishes of Chipping Barnet and East Barnet. A church of Gothic

been erected by an abbot of St. Albans as far back as early in the twelfth century. North Wall, with its small round-headed deep-splayed windows, still remains in its original state. The fabric seems to have remained in its tiny dimensions for centuries; for it was not till the middle of the seventeenth century that the chancel was built, the cost of its erection being defrayed by Sir Robert Bartlet, who was probably a native of the parish. The tower is modern, and poor in the extreme;

HADLEY CHURCH.   (*See page* 328.)

design, in the Decorated style, was built in 1865. It is constructed of coloured bricks, and has an apsidal chancel. In 1871 the number of houses in East Barnet (including the district of Lyonsdown) was 531, the inhabitants being nearly 3,000. According to the census returns for 1881 the population has now reached nearly 4,000.

The manor of East Barnet has been part and parcel of that of Chipping Barnet since the time of the Conquest.

The church, dedicated to St. Mary the Virgin, is the original and mother church of the district, and it is partly Norman. It consists of a nave, chancel, south aisle, with a brick-built tower at the west end. The nave is the oldest part of the building, having

the south aisle, which is constructed of Kentish ragstone, with Bath stone dressings, was added as recently as 1868, at which time the interior of the church was thoroughly restored and refitted.

In the churchyard is the tomb of General Augustus Prevost, a native of Geneva, who died in 1786. He served with distinction in the British army, taking part, in 1779, in the gallant defence of Savannah "against the combined armies of France and America, supported by a powerful fleet." In the corner of the churchyard is a tall Gothic structure, almost like a market cross, erected to the memory of Sir Simon Clarke, who lived at Oak Hill Park, in the parish.

Dr. Richard Bundy, a Prebendary of Westminster, the author of a voluminous Roman history, and of the "Apparatus Biblicus," was rector of this parish in the early part of the last century ; his predecessor was Gilbert Burnet, son of the celebrated Dr. Burnet, Bishop of Salisbury.

At Church Farm, near the church, is the "Boys' Farm Home," a branch of the "Boys' Home" in the Regent's Park Road, near Chalk Farm.* It lodges, boards, and trains for agricultural and industrial pursuits, above eighty poor orphan boys, "not convicted of crime."

the north end of the old village street, and opposite the parish fountain—now a pump—was formerly an inn : it has been said that Lord Macaulay's father lived here ; there is, however, no foundation for the statement.

Cat's Hill is the name given to the steep ascent leading from East Barnet up to Southgate, and is so called from the "Cat" inn which stands by the roadside at its foot. "The Cat," *pur et simple*, is not a very common sign ; though Larwood mentions one at Egremont in Cumberland yet he omits

COPPED HALL.   (*See page* 334.)

LORD LYTTON.   (*See page* 334.)

The grounds cover nearly fifty acres, and the farm is cultivated by the boys, who are admitted between the ages of six and sixteen years. The institution, with its dining-hall, carpenters' shops, &c., which is mainly supported by voluntary contributions, is well worth a visit.

The Clock House, at the foot of Cat's Hill, at

"the Cat" here. The sign is common enough, however, with an adjective, as the "Black Cat" at Lancaster, the "Red Cat" at Birkenhead and at the Hague ; and still more common in connection with some ludicrous appendage, such as the "Cat and Cage," the "Cat and Lion," the "Cat and Parrot," and the "Cat in the Basket." The last named was a favourite sign on the booths when the Thames was frozen over in 1739-40. "The sign," writes Mr. Larwood, "was a living one—a basket hanging outside the booth with a cat in it." In the illustrated "Pennant" in the British Museum is a print representing the Thames at Rotherhithe in the great frost of 1789 : there is a booth with a merry company inside, while the sign over the door, inscribed "The Original Cat in the Cage," represents poor Tabby in a basket. "The sign," writes Mr. Larwood, "doubtless originates from the cruel game, once practised by our ancestors, of shooting at a cat in a basket." It is possible, and even probable, that East Barnet was one of the places where this cruel "sport" was practised by the roughs of North London when out on a holiday.

There are a few good mansions and seats in the neighbourhood. Among them may be mentioned Oak Hill Park, the seat of Mr. Young, and formerly the residence of Sir Simon Clarke. The house occupies an elevated site in the midst of an extensive park, on the east side of the village. Another mansion, near to Oakleigh Park Station, called Belmont, but formerly known as Mount Pleasant, was at one time the home of Elias Ashmole, the founder of the Ashmolean Museum at Oxford.

Totteridge lies to the south-west of East Barnet, on the western side of the Great North road. It is really a "spur" of the long ridge of which Mill Hill forms the central and southern part; and it occupies the extreme south-eastern angle of Hertfordshire, between Highwood Hill and Whetstone, in Middlesex. As to its etymology, it is supposed to have been derived from its situation on the ridge of a hill. The first syllable of the name is derived probably from the Anglo-Saxon word "Tot," or "Toot," a beacon-hill, or from the Welsh word "Twt," a sloping or rising; and it may have been given to it—as in the case of _Tot_-hill, Westminster*—from a beacon placed here, as the highest spot in this district. Taylor, however, in his "Words and Places," thinks such places as Tot Hill and the like "may possibly have been seats of Celtic worship, the names coming from the Celtic deity, _Taith_, the Teutates of Lucan." The antiquary, Mr. Wykeham Archer, too, derives the name from Teut, the chief divinity of the Druids, and the equivalent of Thoth, the Egyptian Mercury, adding that the "Tot," "Teut," "Tut," or "Thoth"—often, by the way, styled "Tuttle" or "Tut-hill" was the spot on which solemn proclamations were made to the people. "Tot" or "Toot," also, in one of its varied forms, is not an uncommon prefix to the names of other places in different parts of England—as _Tot_nes, _Tot_ham, _Toot_ing, _Tot_tenham, _Tut_bury, &c. ; and, it may be added that all these places are considerably elevated, in comparison with the surrounding parts.

The manor of Totteridge in early ages formed part of the possessions of the monks of Ely, and afterwards of the bishops of that see, from one of whom, in the reign of Elizabeth, it was alienated to the Crown, together with Hatfield, in consideration of an annual sum of £1,500, to be paid to

him and his successors in the see of Ely. In 1590 the queen granted this manor to John Cage, from whom it passed in succession to the Peacocks and the Whichcotes. Sir Paul Whichcote, in the year 1720, sold the property to James Brydges, Duke of Chandos ; but it was again disposed of by the second duke to Sir William Lee, Lord Chief Justice of the King's Bench. The manor is now held by the representatives of the late John Lee, LL.D. The advowson of the living is still held, with that of Hatfield, by the Marquis of Salisbury, the annual value of the combined livings being £2,500.

Totteridge is neither a town nor a village, but a group of isolated villas and gentlemen's seats and small parks. The small cluster of houses and shops forming the street fringe the roadway to Mill Hill, at a short distance westward of the church. The village green extends at least a quarter of a mile south from the church, gradually widening out into a leg-of-mutton form, and fringed on either side with rows of elms and other trees of a dark foliage. It is very picturesque and rural.

Totteridge has lately been brought more near to the great metropolis by the opening of a new station in the low ground between it and Whetstone, on the High Barnet branch of the Great Northern Railway.

At the beginning of the present century Totteridge had 48 houses and a population of 280 souls. The census returns for 1871 showed that these had increased respectively to 91 and 474. In 1881 the number of the inhabitants was 656.

The roads about Totteridge are still anything but good in the winter, the soil being hereabouts a stiff clay ; but they are better now than a century or two ago, when the carriage folk would send fagots to be laid in the ruts on the road which they intended to travel, and put four horses to their carriages, not by way of display, but of necessity. We find Lord Montague writing to the Privy Council, in the reign of Charles II., to apologise for his absence from one of its meetings on the plea of the badness of the roads.

The church is generally said to be dedicated to St. Andrew, and Thorne, in his "Environs of London," repeats the blunder. Being attached to Bishop's Hatfield, and thereby connected with the see of Ely, it was dedicated to St. Etheldreda, who was generally known as St. Audrey, and the transition from "St. Audrey" to "St. Andrew" was easy.

The former church, having become rickety and unsafe, was pulled down in 1789, when the present structure superseded it. It was then a plain square preaching room, with large deal pews of the regulation height, and square windows; in fact, as tasteless and common-looking an edifice as could well be conceived. About the year 1870 it was internally re-modelled, the seats being lowered and thrown open, and a small apsidal chancel being added of a more ecclesiastical pattern. An organ and some painted windows have since been added, and the western gallery pulled down. Rising from the roof at the western end of the church is a low, square embattled tower of wood, painted white, and containing two bells. The tower was formerly surmounted by a spire. One monument, now on the wall of the tower, remains to connect the present structure with its predecessor. Among the entries of burials here is one under date of March 2nd, 1802, to "Elizabeth King, widow, for forty-six years clerk of this parish."

In the churchyard is the family tomb of the Pepys family. It contains the bodies of Sir Lucas Pepys, and also of Sir William Weller Pepys, and his brother Lord Chancellor Cottenham who died in 1851. Lady Rothes and Lady Cottenham also lie buried here.

It is quite a popular error to suppose that Lord Mohun, the scampish duellist who fell in Hyde Park,* was buried here. He lies in the vaults under the church of St. Martin's-in-the-Fields.

At the west end of the churchyard is a fine old yew-tree, of great girth, and supposed to be seven centuries old. It does not denote, as would seem at first sight to appear, that a church stood on the spot in the Saxon-Norman times, but is simply the last survival of a yew forest.

It is of classical note, for it is made the subject of communications in the *Gentleman's Magazine*,† and is mentioned by Nichols in his "Literary Anecdotes." Sir John Cullum states that when he measured it, a century ago, it was about twenty-five feet in circumference; and its girth is unaltered now.

Generally, though not always, yews are found in close proximity to the church, where they look like symbols of eternity. But they were also planted for other lasting purposes, as, for example, to mark boundaries of properties, or the courses of primitive roads. It is said that the pilgrims' route from Silchester to Canterbury, across the Surrey hills, can be almost made out by the long line of yew-trees with which it was fringed. The yew, however, served even yet another purpose. In

the will of King Henry VI. is the following item :—"The space between the wall of the church and the wall of the cloyster shall conteyne 38 feyte, which is left for to sett in certaine trees and flowers, behovable and convenient for the service of the same church." Now, it has often been asked, and never satisfactorily answered, "For what purpose were yew-trees anciently planted in churchyards?" In times when it was considered as a matter of importance that the churches should, at certain seasons, be adorned with evergreens, and when to strew branches in the way, and to scatter herbs and flowers into the grave, were practised as religious rites, was it not "behovable and convenient for the service of the church" that every churchyard should contain at least one yew-tree? Several reasons may be assigned for giving this tree a preference to every other evergreen. It is very hardy, long-lived, and though in time it attains a considerable height, produces branches in abundance so low as to be always within reach of the hand, and at last affords a beautiful wood for furniture.

Near the church, at the corner of the Barnet Road, stands an old-fashioned house known as the Priory, and traditionally said to have been occupied by Lady Rachel Russell. But there is no proof of such occupation by Lady Rachel, beyond the statement of Lady Bunsen, on page 284, which may be an error; and it is very doubtful whether Totteridge ever boasted of a prior or prioress. The house, however, dates evidently back to the Tudor times.

Richard Baxter, to whom we have been already introduced at Acton,* lived here for some years in retirement, being probably led to take up his abode here in order to be near Mr. Charlton, whose wife was his sister. His name occurs once as a ratepayer in the village books here.

Totteridge has always been a favourite residence with the wealthier classes in London, and several legal and City knights lived here at one and the same time.

Pointer's Grove (or Poynter's), at the southeastern extremity of the parish, facing the Green, has long been the abode of the Pugets, a family of French refugee extraction. The late Mr. Puget, M.P., built, in 1827, a small chapel and schools on the road to Whetstone. The estate of Pointers belonged, in the middle of the seventeenth century, to Lady Gurney, the widow of Sir Richard Gurney, who died a prisoner in the Tower, in 1647. Later

---

* See "Old and New London," Vol. IV., p. 398.
† See Vol. LXXV., Part II., pp. 1142, 1212.

* See *ante*, p. 11.

on the property was possessed successively by Sir John Aubrey, Sir Thomas Aleyne, Sir Peter Mayer, and Sir John Sheffield, from whom it passed to the Pugets, with whose family it still continues.

Copped Hall, which stands on the Green, facing the Church, was for some years the seat of Sir E. Bulwer Lytton. Whilst staying here he would constantly pay visits to the battle-field of Barnet, to which he has given such interest in his "Last of the Barons."* The estate is about a hundred acres, well timbered, and planted with avenues of limes and other trees. A fine dining-room and conservatory have been added by the present owner, Mr. Bolton.

Half a century ago the property was owned by Mr. William Manning, M.P., and Governor of the Bank of England, the father of Cardinal Manning, who was born here in 1809. The Cardinal was educated at Harrow, and Balliol College, Oxford, and was afterwards a Fellow of Weston College. He resigned his rectory of Graffham, Sussex, and the Archdeaconry of Chichester in 1851, when he became a Roman Catholic. In 1865 he was consecrated Archbishop of Westminster, and he was created a Cardinal in 1875. The Cardinal's elder brother, who died young, lies buried at the east end of the churchyard. Mr. Manning probably came to live at Totteridge on account of its proximity to Highwood, at Mill Hill, where Mr. William Wilberforce was then living, both being "pillars" of the "Evangelical" faith, as taught by Wesley and Simeon.

From the Mannings the estate of Copped Hall passed to the Scarletts, and from them to a building speculator, who sold it to Lord Lytton. His lordship, however, lived here only occasionally, his chief seat being in another part of the county, at Knebworth, near Stevenage. He added largely to this place, however, and re-faced the outside, which he made to resemble an Italian villa, with a terraced front, adorning the upper portion with classical heads, copied from genuine antiques. He hung the library with tapestry, painted the

ceilings of the chief rooms in the Italian fashion, repeating in several compartments his own initials E. B. L., and adding over the mantelpiece the motto so accordant with his taste, "Absque Musis frigent Lares." He stayed here off and on between 1858 and 1875, during which time he wrote "Pelham," "Lucretia," and the "Last of the Barons." The terrace in the rear of the house commands extensive views, extending to Hampstead, Highgate, and Harrow, with peeps of the Surrey Hills beyond. The rivulet which divides the two counties, flows at the bottom of the park-like grounds, and is dammed up into a lake which covers four acres. Mr. Manning planted in the grounds a "spinney," or circular plantation, consisting of a variety of forest trees, to commemorate the jubilee of George III.

The mansion in Totteridge Park, at the western extremity of the village, on the right-hand side of the road leading to Hendon, occupies the site of the old manor house, and its successor, a small hunting-seat, which was purchased from Lord Bateman by Sir William Lee, the Lord Chief Justice mentioned above. He enlarged the mansion, and resided there for many years. The present house, which has been recently converted into a boarding-school for boys, is a large red brick edifice, consisting of a centre and wings, and crowned by an octagonal domed clock-turret. It stands in a finely-wooded park, about 100 acres in extent, and is approached through a broad avenue of elms. In the "Memoirs of Baron Bunsen" it is stated that the Baron lived here in 1848 and the following year, and that during that time he here entertained many distinguished visitors, and greatly enjoyed the grounds, with their "grand trees, those lofty firs, the pride of Totteridge, the fine terrace, the charming garden," and its general surroundings. "Oh, how thankful," he wrote, "I am for this Totteridge! Could I but describe the groups of fine trees, the turf, the terrace walks!"

Among other mansions at Totteridge is one standing in what is now called the Wykeham Rise Estate. It was formerly well known as the residence of the late Dr. Shuttleworth, Bishop of Chichester.

---

* See *ante*, p. 326.

CHAPTER XXXIV.

WHETSTONE, FRIERN BARNET, AND FINCHLEY.

"Ut jugulent homines, surgunt de nocte latrones."—HORACE.

Situation of Whetstone—The Parish Church—Census Returns—Oakleigh Park—George Morland and the Chimney-sweep—General Appearance of the Village—The Manor of Friern Barnet—The Church—Almshouses—Finchley—Situation and Extent—Descent of the Manor—The Old Manor-house—Noted Residents—Church End—Census Returns—Races—The Parish Church—Christ's College—National Schools—East End—The Church, &c.—The "Dirt House"—Cemeteries for Marylebone and St. Pancras and Islington Parishes—North End—Christ Church—The Congregational Chapel—Finchley Common—Encampments and Reviews—Highwaymen—Turpin's Oak—The "Green Man" Tavern—Capture of Jack Sheppard—The Life of a Highwayman.

WHETSTONE lies to the east of Totteridge, from which village it is distant about a mile, the station of Totteridge and Whetstone, on the High Barnet branch of the Great Northern Railway, serving as a means of communication for both places. Till recently it was a portion of the parish of Friern Barnet, which lies to the east of it. It was, however, cut off from the mother parish, and made a separate ecclesiastical district in 1833, a portion of Finchley being at the same time embodied in it. The district round about it still retains some features of its once rural character, in spite of large building operations, and is situated at the north-eastern extremity of the hundred of Ossulston.

Whether the name of Whetstone has anything to do with that vicious locality called Whetstone Park, on the north side of Lincoln's Inn Fields, we know not. Neither Lysons nor the author of the "Beauties of England" offer any suggestion as to the derivation of the name; they simply state that it is the name given to "a manor in Friern Barnet." The local tradition that the place derived its name from a large stone which was there found, and on which the soldiers sharpened their swords and battle-axes preparatory to the Battle of Barnet, is almost too absurd to be mentioned seriously, and may be dismissed with a smile.

The church, dedicated to St. John, stands on the west side of the road at the south end of the village. It is a small brick structure, of the commonplace type of the time, and is shut in from the roadway by a high brick wall, partly overhung with ivy. A chapel is supposed to have been originally built here early in the fifteenth century, in the Perpendicular style. The present building, however, as may be guessed from the date of its erection, is but a poor attempt at Gothic architecture. Till 1879 it was an oblong chapel-like building, with small rectangular turrets or pinnacles at each of its four corners, and a small bell-turret in the centre of the west gable. In the above year, however, a chancel was added to the existing nave, a vaulted roof replaced the old flat ceiling, and Early-English windows were inserted. The window at the east end is of stained glass, and was inserted as a memorial of two members of the Baxendale family, whose residence is in the neighbourhood.

The village contains one or two chapels and schools, and since the opening of the railway the place has rapidly increased in growth and population. In 1871 the number of the inhabitants was over 2,300, and in the course of the next decade this has been considerably increased. A large district, called Oakleigh Park, has lately become in part built over with terraces and modest villas; these, however, have not materially altered the old-fashioned look of the main street, which, as of yore, still contains, for the size of the village, a large number of roadside inns, taverns, and ale-houses.

George Morland, the artist,* whose delight was to pass his time in village taverns, and then perchance to balance his "score" by painting a signboard for the worthy host, met with a slight *contretemps* on one occasion when passing through this village. Allan Cunningham, in his "Life of Morland," tells the following anecdote about him. "He once (we are told) received an invitation to Barnet, and was hastening thither with two friends, when he was stopped at Whetstone turnpike by a lumber or jockey cart, driven by two persons, one of them a chimney-sweep, who were disputing with the toll-gatherer. Morland endeavoured to pass, when one of the wayfarers cried, 'What! Mr. Morland, won't you speak to a body!' The artist endeavoured to elude further greeting, but this was not to be; the other bawled out so lustily that Morland was obliged to recognise at last his companion and crony, Hooper, a tinman and pugilist. After a hearty shake of the hand, the boxer turned to his neighbour the chimney-sweep, and said, 'Why, Dick, don't you know this here gentleman? 'tis my friend, Mr. Morland.' The sooty charioteer, smiling a recognition, forced his unwelcome hand upon his brother of the brush; they then both whipt their horses and departed. This rencontre

---

* See "Old and New London," Vol. V., p. 222.

mortified Morland very sensibly; he declared that he knew nothing of the chimney-sweep, and that he was forced upon him by the impertinence of Hooper; but the artist's habits made the story be generally believed, and 'Sweeps, your honour,' was a joke which he was often obliged to hear."

The long main street, which lies along the high road from Barnet to Finchley, is singularly void of interest, being really little more than a succession of public-houses, small shops, and tasteless villas with tiny gardens in front of them, interspersed

Such being the case, and there being no river or attractive scenery, Whetstone would seem to have had no place among the favourite suburban residences of Londoners, and accordingly it has no literary history, its name being scarcely mentioned, except in connection with the heroes of the "Newgate Calendar."

The principal manor of Friern Barnet, under the name of Whetstone, or *Freren* Barnet, was in ancient times part of the extensive possessions of the Priory of St. John of Jerusalem. The word

ALMSHOUSES, FRIERN BARNET.   (*See page* 322.)

with blacksmiths' forges, or sheds that have done duty as such in the good old days of stage-coaches.

But the good old coaching days, it must be remembered, were also the days of highwaymen and footpads, as we saw when dealing with the locality of Hounslow Heath, next to which the spot of which we now treat enjoyed the highest reputation of any place in Middlesex. Dick Turpin positively loved this highway and its associations, and his "Knights of the Road" followed his taste. So great was the terror which they inspired among the wealthier classes, that many Scotch lords and squires preferred to make the journey from their native hills to the Parliament at Westminster by sea, rather than encounter the terrors of the Great North road within ten or twelve miles of London.

Freren probably means belonging to the friars, *freres*, or brethren of the Order. The name of Barnet, as already remarked, is common to several parishes in England. Lysons says it was anciently written Bernette, or Bergnet, which, as Chauncy remarks in his "Hertfordshire," signifies "a little hill;" the addition of "Friern" or "Friarn" denotes that it was monastic property.

According to Lysons, Sir William Weston, the last of the Priors of St. John of Jerusalem, held a court here in 1539, and Henry VIII., after the dissolution, granted the manor to the Dean and Chapter of St. Paul's, in whose possession it has ever since continued. The manor house, near the church, is described by the above authority as a "very ancient structure." It has undergone many alterations, but a considerable part of the old building, namely, a long passage, or wooden cloister, with a carved ceiling, was remaining far into the present century. "The recluse situation of this manorial house," observes the author of the "Beauties of England," "would seem favourable to tradition and legendary story. Accordingly, it is supposed by some that this was a cell to the the Decorated and Early English types of architecture, and although in the main an ancient building of flint with stone dressings, wears, in consequence of recent restoration and enlargement, a somewhat new and modern appearance. It consists of a chancel, nave, and south aisles, separated by an arcade of four bays, with a square tower and spire at the west end. The south door,

FINCHLEY MANOR HOUSE AND TURPIN'S OAK.

Priory of St. John, and by others that it was an inn or resting-place for the knights in journeys between London and St. Albans. A gateway, which appears to have been formerly the chief place of entrance, is termed the 'Queen's Gate,' an appellation that probably refers to 'a visit of Queen Elizabeth to this house." Norden, writing concerning Friern Barnet in the reign of Elizabeth, says that "Sir John Popham, Knt., Lord Chiefe Justice of England, sometimes maketh this his abode."

The parish church, dedicated to St. James, is of protected by a light porch, is of Norman workmanship, round-headed, and of somewhat rude construction, ornamented only with a moulding of chevron work. On the east wall of the chancel aisle is a mural monument to sundry members of the Cleve family, dated 1726, and in the exterior wall is a small tablet bearing the date February 7th, 1638. The east window of stained glass is new; it was inserted in memory of George and Johanna Homan.

Near the church are schools for boys, girls, and infants, the site of which was given by Mr. John

Miles, of the Manor House. Close by the schools, by the side of the road leading from the church to Whetstone, and shaded by a noble row of elms, stands a row of almshouses, seven in number, and of a somewhat picturesque appearance. They were founded in 1612, by Laurence Campe, for twelve aged persons, and they were repaired and altered in 1843. The parish allows the inmates 2s. 6d. each per week. The long stone front of the houses, with the Tudor arched doorways and square-headed windows, give the buildings a somewhat "collegiate" appearance. On the front are three shields, with the arms of London; of the family of the founder, namely, a chevron between three griffins' heads; and of the Drapers' Company. There are also tablets with such moral and religious inscriptions as these—

> "Every morning before you feed,
> Come to this house, and prayers read;
> Then you about your work may go,
> So God may bless you and yours also."

Another tablet bears the following texts—

"Exhort them that are rich in this world, that they be ready to give, and glad to distribute."—1 Tim. vi. 1.
"He that hath pity upon the poor, lendeth unto the Lord."—Proverbs xv.

A new church, of Early English design, dedicated to All Saints, has lately been completed in this parish. It is of stone, and has at the west end a lofty tower and spire, which is conspicuous for miles round.

Mr. Thorne tells us in his "Environs of London" that "in olden times the Great North Road passed through Friern Barnet by way of Colney Hatch," but that, becoming inconvenient "by reason of the deepness and dirty passage in the winter season," the Bishop of London undertook to make a new and more direct road to Whetstone through his park at Highgate; and that to compensate the inhabitants of Friern Barnet for the loss of traffic on their road, he made them free of the tolls levied at the Bishop's Gate.*

Finchley, although a very large parish, and lying within eight miles of London, on the great high road to the north, is singularly void of historical interest, with the exception perhaps of two or three encampments on the Common. Its name, however, like that of its neighbour, Whetstone, is somewhat largely mixed up with the annals of highwaymen and footpads, who infested these parts in the last century, and gave to them a reputation second only to that of Hounslow Heath. Finchley proper still retains a few vestiges of its once rural character; but it is the same old story over again: its surrounding meadows and pastures are being rapidly covered by untasteful buildings. The parish itself extends about three miles northwards from the district known as East End, to Whetstone, the greater part of which, as stated above, is included in Finchley parish. There are here two stations on the Great Northern branch line to Edgware, and one at Woodside Park, on the High Barnet branch. The river Brent flows along in the valley between the great North Road and Hendon towards the west.

The manor of Finchley, although it does not figure in Domesday Book, belonged from time immemorial to the see of London. In the reign of King John, the bishop and his Finchley tenants obtained from the Crown a grant of freedom from toll, which grant was confirmed by Charles II. In the fifteenth and sixteenth centuries, a manor here, called Finchley Manor, was held by the Marches, Leyndons, and Comptons. In 1577 a license was granted to the Earl of Huntingdon, Anne, Countess of Pembroke, and Henry Lord Compton, to alienate the manor to trustees, for the use of the countess for life, with remainder to Thomas, second son of Lord Compton, and his heirs.

The old Manor House is still in existence, and retains many of its ancient features. It stands between the hamlet of East End and the parish church. The house is a large old-fashioned brick building, but has been much altered to suit modern requirements. It is still surrounded by the moat, which encloses a large oblong area through which passes the public roadway. The mansion is occupied by Mr. George Plucknett, F.S.A., a magistrate for the county, and in its ancient oak-panelled hall justice continues to be meted out to evil-doers, as in days of yore.

Finchley has in times long gone by had some noted residents. Here, for instance, lived Sir Thomas Frowick, the Lord Chief Justice of the Common Pleas under the Tudors. The Frowicks, as we have seen, were influential about South Mimms, Hadley, and the neighbourhood.*

The village locally known as Church End is a rambling and scattered collection of cottages and interspersed houses of a better class. Many of the principal residences are detached; but rows of houses, streets, and terraces, are daily springing up everywhere, and the green lanes are fast disappearing. In 1808 the number of houses in the parish was 250, the population at the same time amounting to 1,500. In 1871 the number of dwellings

---

* See "Old and New London," Vol. V., p. 389.

* See *ante*, p. 317.

had increased to over 1,250, and the inhabitants had reached a total of 7,150, which number, during the next decade, had swelled up to over 11,000.

Races were held here in the years 1869 and 1872, but they have apparently been abandoned as a public nuisance.

The church stands on an eminence in the centre of the village, about a mile from the great north road. It is, like many ancient parish churches, dedicated to St. Mary, and is in the Perpendicular style, from which it would appear to have been erected in the fifteenth century. It was restored in 1872, when the thick coating of plaster with which the stonework was covered up was removed, and the building enlarged by the addition of a north aisle, and an extension of the chancel, and a low embattled tower at the western end, containing a clock and six bells. On the smallest bell, which is dated 1770, is the following inscription :—

> "Good people all that hear us ring,
> Be faithful to your God and king."

The roofs of the chancel and aisles are of open timber; that of the nave is flat, with ornamental panels of plaster set in wooden framework. Most of the windows are new. There are several monuments and brasses of the fifteenth century. On the south wall is a plain marble slab to the memory of William Seward, F.R.S. and F.S.A., who died in the year 1799. He was the author of "Anecdotes of Distinguished Persons," and "Biographiana." Alexander Kinge, who died in 1618, is commemorated by a monument containing two figures kneeling before open books. The oldest brass is that of Richard Pratt, and Johanna, his wife, it is engraved with effigies of the deceased, and is dated 1487. In the chancel is one to Simon Skudemore, gent., and his wife, bearing date 1609, and on the same stone a small plate commemorating Nicholas Luke, gent., and his wife, Elizabeth, daughter of the above-named Simon Skudemore. In the west wall of the church are visible a few traces of rude stonework supposed to be Norman, possibly "suggesting the existence of an earlier fabric." Nothing, however, is known for certainty of the existence of a church here dating as far back as that era. The register dates from the year 1560, and the records of the rectory go no further back than the fourteenth century.

Two of the rectors of Finchley have been elevated to the episcopal bench. Dr. Cotton, who held the living towards the close of the sixteenth century, was promoted to the bishopric of Exeter; and Dr. Bancroft, who was rector in 1608, was raised to the see of Oxford. Dr. John Barkham, Bishop Bancroft's successor in the rectory, was a noted antiquarian in his day, and largely assisted Speed in his "English History."

In the churchyard lies buried Major Cartwright, the once popular political reformer, whose statue now adorns Burton Crescent, St. Pancras, London. His grave is marked by an obelisk bearing the following inscription :—"In this place are deposited the remains of John Cartwright, the son of William and Anne Cartwright, Commander in the Royal Navy, and many years Major in the Nottingham Militia. He was the author of various works on legislation; the earliest, most strenuous, and disinterested Reformer of his time; the intrepid advocate of liberty, whose labours for the public good terminated only with his life, on the 23rd of September, 1824; aged eighty-four. Also the remains of his beloved wife, Anne Catherine Cartwright, who died on the 21st of December, 1834." Thomas Payne, the bookseller of the Mewsgate, "whose little shop," writes Mr. James Thorne, "was the daily haunt of scholars and book collectors," was buried here in February, 1799.

Adjoining the churchyard is Christ's College, which was instituted in 1857 by the late Rev. Thomas Reader White, rector of Finchley, "for the purpose of providing first-class education at a moderate cost." The school is divided between two buildings. The old mansion, which serves the purposes of the lower school, contains also the dining-hall of both schools; the new school is situated on the opposite side of the churchyard. Both buildings are constructed of red brick. The school has acquired a good position among the educational institutions of the country. It is conducted by the principal and resident assistant masters, and several scholarships are awarded annually to boys resident in the college. The average number of pupils in the college is about 200.

The National Schools for St. Mary's, in Ballard's Lane, near the church, were erected in 1852. They are built of brick, with stone dressing, in the Gothic Style, and consist of schools for boys, girls, and infants, with residences for the master and mistresses.

The hamlet of East End lies to the south-east of Finchley proper, and extends to the Barnet Road. It was formed into a separate parish for ecclesiastical purposes in 1846. The church, dedicated to the Holy Trinity, is a stone building, in the Early English style, comprising chancel, nave, and aisles. The Congregational Chapel at East End was built in 1875, in the place of an old chapel which had been burnt down. The building is of brick, in the

Early Decorated style of Gothic architecture, and consists of a nave, aisles, transept, and an apse for the use of the choir. At the north-east angle is a tower, surmounted by a lofty spire. Some of the windows are filled with stained glass.

The "Old White Lion" public-house, at East End, has been for many years locally known as the "Dirt House," a name which was bestowed upon it in consequence of its being the regular "house of call" of the men in charge of the carts and waggons, which, taking hay and other produce to London, usually returned to the country laden with soot, manure, and the like. Near the above inn is a wood, called in old maps "Dirt House Wood," which, it is conjectured, obtained its name from its proximity to the "Dirt House," and to distinguish it from the other small woods in the neighbourhood, all of which are remnants of the great forest of Middlesex.*

The cemetery for the parish of St. Mary, Marylebone, is situated near Church End, and comprises more than thirty acres, with the usual chapel and offices. On the east side of the Barnet Road is the joint cemetery for the parishes of St. Pancras and St. Mary, Islington. It comprises on the whole nearly ninety acres, and contains two mortuary chapels, lodges, and residences for the officers, &c. The grounds are tastefully laid out, and planted with evergreens, shrubs, and trees. Here, in 1855, was buried Sir Henry Bishop, the musical composer: a granite monument, bearing a bronze medallion, marks his grave. This cemetery was taken out of Finchley Common, on another part of which has lately sprung into existence the hamlet of North End, comprising several respectable shops and private residences. The church (Christ Church) was commenced in 1870, but has not yet been completed, the nave only having as yet been built: this is in the Decorated style. North End possesses also a Congregational chapel of the regulation ecclesiastical pattern—Decorated Gothic—with a tower and spire rising nearly one hundred feet in height. It was built in 1865.

Of Finchley Common very little is now left as an open space. At the beginning of the present century it was described as the largest tract of poor land in Middlesex, except Hounslow Heath. It was estimated in 1810, by Messrs. Britton, to contain about 1,500 acres of "somewhat inferior quality, but capable of great improvement under proper cultivation. On this common a large number of sheep and cattle," they add, "is fed in the spring." But this is no longer true.

Dr. Hunter, in his "History of London and its Environs" (1810), writes, "Finchley is chiefly known by being annexed to the extensive Common, a place formidable to travellers from the highway robberies of which it has been the scene." He estimates the common to contain 2,010 acres, and adds, "the waste and uncultivated state of which, so near the metropolis, is disgraceful to the economy of the country." The eastern side of the common, and the northern slopes of Hampstead and Highgate are reckoned by Messrs. Britton, in 1810, as mostly woodland copses.

The few historical events which relate to Finchley are connected with its former common. Here General Monk, in his march to London, previous to the restoration of Charles II., drew up his forces on the 3rd of February, 1660. When the young Chevalier, Charles Edward, was at Derby, during the Scottish rebellion of 1745, there was a great panic in London, and volunteers of all descriptions offered themselves to serve in the ranks. "The whole body of the law," observes the author of the "Comprehensive History of England," "formed themselves into a regiment, under the command of Lord Chief Justice Willes, and were to have done duty at St. James's, to guard the royal family, in case it had been necessary for the king to take the field with the army that lay encamped about Barnet and Finchley Common. Luckily that force was not required, and did little more than scare away the highwaymen from their usual beat. Weavers, and other London artisans, were probably not the best of troops, and it became the fashion to turn the Finchley camp and the march to Finchley into ridicule; but there was, nevertheless, some good regular troops on that point, both horse and foot, with thirty-two pieces of artillery; and the Life-Guards and Horse Grenadiers were ready to march out of London at a moment's notice." Hogarth's famous picture of the "March of the Guards to Finchley," which found a home at the Foundling Hospital,* is well known. Another memorable encampment on Finchley Common was that of the troops, comprising several regiments, hastily brought together here, in 1780, on account of the Gordon riots. This review was the subject of an engraving which was published at the time, and is now very scarce.

Finchley Common continued the favourite "hunting ground" of highwaymen down till near the close of the last century. Sir Gilbert Elliot, afterwards Earl of Minto, in a letter to his wife in 1790, wrote, when within a few stages of London,

---

* See Notes and Queries, June, 1881, pp. 471-2.

* See "Old and New London," Vol. V., p. 362.

that instead of pushing on that night, as he easily could, he should defer his arrival till the morning, for, he adds, "I shall not trust my throat on Finchley Common in the dark."* At the London end of what was once the common, nearly opposite the "Green Man" Inn, at a place called "Brown's Wells," on the Barnet Road, and a little way north of the St. Pancras Cemetery, is an old oak, behind which it is traditionally stated that Dick Turpin used to take up his position. The tree, which is still called "Turpin's Oak," is green and flourishing, though considerably shorn of its upper branches. Pistol-balls, it is stated, which are supposed to have been fired at the trunk to deter highwaymen, have been frequently extracted from the bark. Mr. Larwood, in his "History of Signboards," tells us that the "Green Man" has the following verses under two pipes crossed over a pot of beer:—

> "Call softly, drink moderate;
>   Pay honourably, be good company;
>   Part friendly; Go home quietly;
>   Let these lines be no man's sorrow;
>   Pay to-day and trust to-morrow."

The notorious Jack Sheppard, who kept half London in terror, and who once, at least, effected his escape out of Newgate, was captured on Finchley Common in 1724. He was disguised in a butcher's blue frock and a woollen apron.

As to the life of a highwayman, a writer in the *London Magazine* some years ago remarks:—

"An highwayman is a wild Arab, that lives by robbing of small caravans, and has no *way* o living but the king's *highway*. Aristotle held him to be but a kind of huntsman; but our sages of the law account him rather a beast of prey, and will not allow his game to be legal by the forest law. His chief care is to be well mounted, and, when he is taken, the law takes care he should be still, while he lives. His business is to break the law of the land, for which the hangman breaks his neck, and there's an end of the controversie. He fears nothing, under the gallows, more than his own face, and, therefore, when he does his work, conveys it out of sight, that it may not rise up in judgment, and give evidence against him at the sessions. His trade is to take purses and evil courses, and when he is taken himself, the laws take as evil a course with him. He takes place of all other thieves as the most heroical, and one that comes nearest to the old knights-errant, though he is really one of the basest, that never ventures but upon surprisal, and where he is sure

of the advantage. He lives like a Tartar, always in motion; and the inns upon the road are hordes, where he reposes for awhile, and spends his time and money, when he is out of action. . . . He is more destructive to the grazier than the murrain. When he despatches his business between sun and sun he invades a whole county, and, like the Long Parliament, robs by representative. He calls concealing what he takes from his comrades *sinking*, which they account a great want of integrity. After he has roved up and down too long, he is at last set himself and conveyed to the jail, the only place of his residence, where he is provided of a hole to put his head in, and gathered to his fathers in a faggot cart."

Mr. Harrison Ainsworth, in his "Rookwood," has turned the life and career of a highwayman to good account. We quote from it the following

"CHAPTER OF HIGHWAYMEN.

> "Of every rascal of every kind,
>   The most notorious to my mind
>   Was the royalist captain, gay Jemmy Hind!
>   Which nobody can deny.

> "But the pleasantest coxcomb among them all
>   For lute, coranto, or madrigal,
>   Was the galliard Frenchman Claude Du Val!
>   Which nobody can deny.

> "Yet Tobygloak never a coach could rob,
>   Could lighten a pocket or empty a fob,
>   With a neater hand than Old Mob, Old Mob!
>   Which nobody can deny.

> "Nor did housebreaker ever deal harder knocks
>   On the stubborn lid of a good strong box,
>   Than that prince of good fellows, Tom Cox, Tom Cox!
>   Which nobody can deny.

> "And blither bellow on board highway
>   Did never with oath bid traveller stay,
>   Than devil-may-care Will Holloway!
>   Which nobody can deny.

> "Then in roguery naught could exceed the tricks
>   Of Gettings and Grey, and the five or six
>   Who trod in the steps of bold Neddy Wicks!
>   Which nobody can deny.

> "Nor could any so handily break a lock
>   As Sheppard, who stood in the Newgate dock,
>   And nicknamed the gaolers around him "his flock!"
>   Which nobody can deny.

> "Nor did highwayman ever before possess,
>   For ease, for security, danger, distress,
>   Such a mare as Dick Turpin's Black Bess, Black Bess!
>   Which nobody can deny."

Finchley Common was the scene of the depredations of most of the worthies whose names are introduced in the above piece of verse; but a great change has taken place in it since their time. In fact it is now nearly entirely blotted out of the map, being either enclosed or built over.

---

* "Life and Letters of Gilbert Elliot, first Earl of Minto," Vol. I., P. 372.

CHAPTER XXXV.

COLNEY HATCH AND SOUTHGATE.

" Insanire juvat."—HORACE.

Rapid Extension of Colney Hatch, or New Southgate—Its Situation and Etymology—Middlesex County Lunatic Asylum—St. Paul's Church—The Pumping Station of the New River Waterworks—Wood Green—The Drinking Fountain—Nightingale Hall—St. Michael's Church—The Printers' Almshouses—Fishmongers' and Poulterers' Asylum—Fullers' Almshouses—Royal Masonic Institution for Boys—Clock and Watchmakers' Asylum- -The Great Northern Cemetery—Southgate—The Village Green and "Cherry-tree" Inn—The Church—Arnold's Court, now Arno's Grove—Minchenden House—Bromefield Park—Bowes Manor—Bowes Park—St. Michael's Church—Culland's Grove—Grovelands—Palmer's Green—Southgate Village Hall--Winchmore Hill—The Church, &c.—Bush Hill Park—Sir Hugh Myddelton and the New River.

COLNEY HATCH—or New Southgate, as its inhabitants prefer to style it—comes next in our perambulation. Half a century ago, or less, this

Colney Hatch is in reality a hamlet of Friern Barnet, from which parish it has been cut off for ecclesiastical purposes, the new district having

COLNEY HATCH.

part was rural and retired; but the construction of the Great Northern Railway, with its modern station and the accessories of villas and shops, and that of the still more modern County Asylum for the Lunatics of Middlesex, have largely altered the appearance of the place—it is needless to add, scarcely for the better. As the Asylum is officered by a staff of some three hundred persons, a small village has sprung up, as if by magic, round its gates; and the population of Colney Hatch itself has been doubled in little more than a quarter of a century.

assigned to it the name of New Southgate; and it forms, as it were, a connecting link between Friern Barnet on the west, and Edmonton and the district once known as Enfield Chase on the east. The name of Colney—or Colne—Hatch is mentioned in a Court Roll of the reign of Henry VII.; and in a map published in the last century it is printed Coney Hatch. The term "Hatch" evidently has reference to a side gateway or entrance to the Royal Chase of Enfield. Numerous instances of the term occur in various parts of the country. The " Pilgrims' Hatch," near Brentwood.

is a name well known, as marking the south entrance to the once great forest of Waltham.

The Asylum, which stands close to the west side of the railway station, is a handsome Italian structure, though plain and to a great extent void of ornament. The late Prince Consort laid the first stone of it in 1849, and it was opened for the reception of patients two years later. It has since been considerably enlarged, and now holds a little over two thousand inmates, of whom, as we saw was the case also at Bedlam,* the majority are females.

for which their previous education or trade fits them—as, for instance, in gardening, baking, cooking, &c. In fact, steady kindness and constant employment are the chief machinery used in humanising these waifs and strays of humanity. Such work as painting and decorating the wards, and also the necessary repairs or alterations in the building, are mostly executed by the patients, of course under proper supervision. By this means the Asylum is partly self-supporting, or, at all events, the expenses are largely diminished.

ARNO'S GROVE, SOUTHGATE. (*See page* 346.)

The discipline exercised over them seems to be one of kindness, not of fear or of punishment; and the whips and strait-waistcoats of the days before Dr. Conolly and Dr. Elliotson are not called into requisition, though some cases require to be isolated in rooms with softly-padded walls. The patients enjoy as much liberty as is possible consistent with the maintenance of order; and the monotony of their lives is occasionally varied by dancing. Music they have in plenty, not only in the chapel, but in the larger rooms.

The patients are employed in various industries

It is stated that the cost of erecting the Asylum was a little over half a million, and that about £60,000 a year is devoted to its maintenance out of the rates of the metropolitan county.

The building, which is of brick with stone dressings, was erected from the designs of Mr. S. W. Daukes, and covers about four acres of ground. It occupies an elevated and healthy site, and its ventilating towers and central cupola are conspicuous objects for some distance round. The principal front of the building, nearly 2,000 feet in length, faces the north, and is the only part of the exterior upon which any attempt at architectural embellishment is visible; and even this is not very profuse.

* See "Old and New London," Vol VI., p. 359.

The grounds of the Asylum are enclosed by a brick wall of moderate height, which extends along the roadway from New Southgate westwards towards Finchley. In the centre, facing the principal entrance, are some iron gates and the gatekeeper's lodge. A carriage-drive extends from the gates to the main entrance, in the centre of the north front, having on either side a broad piece of greensward, with gravel-walks, shrubs, and evergreens.

The front part of the central block of building is flanked on either side by a slightly projecting ventilating tower, whilst from the roof rises an octagonal-domed cupola. Across the base of this building runs an open arcade, a doorway in the centre opening into a long corridor, which extends right and left to the wards and offices. In the wall opposite the door is the foundation-stone, bearing an inscription, to the effect that it was laid by the Prince Consort on the 8th of May, 1849. The stone is carved with an ornamental bordering, together with the arms of the county. The chapel, which occupies the centre of the north front, immediately at the back of the corridor mentioned above, is a large square, or rather oblong, room. It is lighted from the roof, and also by windows of tinted glass above the communion-table. It was originally fitted with galleries, the rows of seats rising gradually from one end of the building to the other; but in 1874 the galleries were removed and the seats levelled. The walls of the chapel are painted with a delicate blue tint, and enriched with stencilling and texts of Scripture. The chapel will seat 600, and the services are held twice every week-day and four times on Sundays. The Rev. Henry Hawkins, who has held the chaplaincy since 1867, was for some time chaplain of the Sussex Asylum, at Hayward's Heath. Under his wardenship is an "Association of Friends of the Infirm in Mind." It was instituted in 1871, and has for its object the "after care" of convalescents. The Asylum cemetery was consecrated by Bishop Blomfield in 1851.

The wards and infirmaries are light and airy, and fitted up with every attention to the comfort of the unfortunate inmates. The building includes residences for the principal officers connected with the institution, airing courts, laundry, and workshops, which, with the gardens and airing grounds, cover rather more than one hundred acres. In addition to this, there is a farm adjoining, which comprises another one hundred and fifty acres.

There are separate departments for the several classes of patients, and separate buildings for the two sexes, either wholly unattached, or connected only by the chapel and offices common to both. The accommodation for the female patients is fully one-third greater than that for the males. The ground-plan of the Asylum somewhat resembles the letter **E**, and it is so situated as to afford an uninterrupted view of the country, and to admit the free access of air and sun; whilst the several galleries and wards are so arranged that the medical officers and others may pass through all of them without retracing their steps. On the male side have lately been added two new infirmaries, fitted up after the most approved principles.

As the treatment administered here is in principle the same as that which has long prevailed in Bethlehem Hospital, or "Bedlam," our readers may consider that the remarks on that subject to be found in OLD AND NEW LONDON * may be repeated here—*mutatis mutandis*, of course. As the Colney Hatch Asylum has been in existence for so short a period it has few historical reminiscences, and fewer romantic stories attach to this institution than to its elder sister. This could hardly be otherwise.

A new church, dedicated to St. Paul, was erected in 1873 for this neighbourhood. It is of Gothic design, one of Sir Gilbert Scott's most successful imitations of the Early English period. Not far from it is a pumping-station of the New River Waterworks—a low and unsightly structure, with a lofty campanile in the semi-Italian style.

On the east and south-east sides of the Asylum the land slopes away gradually into a pleasant valley, on the opposite side of which are the rising grounds of Wood Green and Muswell Hill, the latter crowned by the Alexandra Palace and gardens. Twenty years ago, or even less, Wood Green was a retired country spot, hemmed in by green lanes and shady hedgerows, and having here and there a cosy tavern and "tea-garden," whither the ruralising cockney might betake himself—or herself, or both—in the summer-time. The transformation here, however, is almost as great as at Finchley, which we have lately visited. Since the establishment of the Alexandra Palace, and the formation of a railway through its centre, Wood Green has become quite a busy town, built round about the large open space which was once a green and fringing the Southgate road. In the centre of the Green is a drinking-fountain, surmounted by a tall granite obelisk; it is inscribed to the memory of Mrs. Catherine Smithies, of Earlham Grove, Wood Green, the founder of the "Band of Mercy" movement. Not far off is the pleasant seat of Nightingale Hall, standing in its own grounds, and showing by its name that it was once a rural and sequestered spot. St. Michael's Church, on the

---

* See Vol. VI., pp. 353—360.

west side of the Green, is a large and handsome Gothic building, with a lofty spire. What will, perhaps, most attract the attention of visitors to this locality is the architectural beauty of the various asylums and institutions devised by charity and public spirit for the succour of the aged, and the education and protection of the young and help-less. Of these institutions, the Printers' Alms-houses, a handsome Tudor range of buildings near the church, were erected in 1850.* Close by is the Asylum for Aged Fishmongers and Poulterers, a red brick building of Elizabethan architecture, also dating its erection from about 1850. Then there are the Fullers' Almshouses, in Nightingale Lane, and the Royal Masonic Institution for Boys, in Lordship Lane, both of which buildings were erected in 1865.

H. Crabb Robinson, in his "Diary," records a pleasant walk from Hampstead by way of Ken Wood to Finchley Common, and so by "a good turnpike road" to Colney Hatch. "On the heath," he adds, "I was amused by the novel sight of gipsies. The road from Colney Hatch to South-gate very pleasing indeed."

By the side of the pleasant green lane here re-ferred to, and through which we make our way from Colney Hatch in a north-easterly direction towards Southgate, stands the Clock and Watch Makers' Asylum, another picturesque cluster of dwellings, twenty-one in number, that in the centre being occupied by the committee-room, &c. They are of red and black brick, and of Tudor design. This in-stitution was founded in 1853, and is supported by voluntary contributions and by the members of the trades for which it was erected, the funds being largely augmented by the annual subscriptions of the Goldsmiths' and the Clockmakers' Companies.

Leaving on our left the roads to Whetstone and Friern Barnet, and also to the Great Northern Cemetery, which lies stretched out before us like a map on the slope of the opposite hill, we now follow the course of the winding roadway across the valley, and on reaching the summit of the next range of hills find ourselves in the village of South-gate.

Southgate, as its name implies, marks the chief southern entrance into the old Royal Chase of Enfield; and though now possessed of its own church and ecclesiastical district, it is historically but a hamlet of the parish of Edmonton. Though only eight miles from the metropolis, and near stations on two lines of railway, it still retains much of that pleasant rural character which it wore when

it was the suburban seat of the Welds of Lulworth and of His Grace of Chandos.

The shops and villas which compose the village border the high road for some distance, or are tastefully grouped round a green, which once was fringed by tall and shady elms. A few of these monarchs of the forest remain, and the "Cherry Tree" is the name of the village inn, which for a century or more has faced the Green. Mr. Lar-wood, in his "History of Signboards," tells us that the "Cherry Tree" was not uncommon, and that down to the reign of William IV. it was the sign of a famous place of resort in Clerkenwell, with a bowling-green and alley; and doubtless it was not chosen without a like reason at Southgate, as one of the haunts of pleasure-seeking Londoners. The "Cherry Gardens" at Bermondsey* will be remem-bered by readers of Samuel Pepys † as a place of entertainment in the days of the Merry Monarch.

"Southgate," writes H. Crabb Robinson in the "Diary," "is a delightful village. No distant prospect from the Green; but there are fine trees admirably grouped, and neat and happy houses scattered in picturesque corners and lanes. The great houses, the Duchess of Chandos's, &c., have, I suppose, a distant view."

The church, a handsome edifice of the Early English style, built in 1862, from the designs of Sir Gilbert Scott, stands a little to the west of the village, and is said to occupy the site of the chapel attached to the old seat of the Welds, who have always been Roman Catholics. The old chapel was built in 1615 by Sir John Weld, of Arnold's Grove, in this parish. It was a plain brick build-ing, and contained no monument worthy of men-tion, excepting perhaps that of the founder, who died in 1622. The church, which is built of stone, consists of a clerestoried nave, with north and south aisles, a chancel with aisles, and a tower sur-mounted by an octagonal spire. Several of the windows are enriched with painted glass, and the picturesque appearance of the exterior of the build-ing is heightened by the thick cluster of ivy which has overgrown its walls. The churchyard is well kept, and prettily laid out with firs and evergreens.

The seat of the Welds stood in an extensive park on the south side of the church, and was called Arnold's Court, probably after a still earlier possessor; but it was demolished in the reign of George I., when the present mansion was built. Fifty years later it was enlarged by an Irish peer, Lord Newhaven, who had purchased the estate from the Colebrookes. The house, of which an engraving was published by Watts of Chelsea a century ago, and which is also figured in the "Beauties of England," was erected for Sir George Colebrooke. The house is now styled Arno's Grove.

Close by the grounds of Arno's Grove, and adjoining the churchyard, formerly stood Minchenden House, which the Duke of Chandos occupied as a country seat in the last century, after the demolition of Canons.* The house was a large brick-built mansion, shut out from the roadway by a high brick wall and heavy-looking wooden gates. It was built by a Mr. John Nicoll, but was purchased by the Duke of Chandos, and it continued the occasional residence of the Duchess Dowager of Chandos until her death, in 1813, when it passed to the Marquis of Buckingham, in right of his wife, who, as already stated, was the daughter and heiress of the last Duke of Chandos. The old mansion was pulled down many years ago, but its name is kept in remembrance by Minchenden Lodge, a smaller house, which was built some thirty years ago a little further to the north. Mr. Ford tells us, in his "History of Enfield," that a pollard oak still standing in the grounds of old Minchenden House covers a larger extent of ground than any other tree in England. Ten years ago (1873) its spread was no less than 126 feet, and it is still growing.

Bromefield Park, formerly for many generations the seat of a family named Jackson, adjoins Arno's Grove, and is a handsome house of the late Tudor or Early Stuart times, remarkable for its finely preserved staircase of dark oak, richly carved, and for ceilings and walls painted by Sir James Thornhill. The house stands in a park of eighty acres, and has in front an avenue of elms.

Bowes Manor, on the road towards London, lately the seat of Mr. Alderman Sidney, is now destined to be pulled down and obliterated by the all-devouring builder. It is worthy of mention as having been for some years the country seat of Lord Chancellor Truro, who spent here the latter part of his life, and died here in 1855. He lies buried in the family mausoleum in the graveyard at St. Lawrence, near Ramsgate.

Bowes Park is the name given to a small ecclesiastical district, which was formed in 1874, in the neighbourhood of Bowes Manor. The church, dedicated to St. Michael, is in the Palmerston Road, and was built from the designs of Sir Gilbert Scott. It is in the Early English style, and consists of chancel, nave, aisles, transepts, and a bell turret. Bowes Park is a station on the Great Northern Railway.

Another mansion, to the east of the village, is Culland's Grove, which was, early in the present century, the seat of the eccentric Alderman Sir William Curtis, sometime Lord Mayor of and M.P. for London, the same who is said to have first advocated the general teaching of "the three Rs"—reading, 'riting, and 'rithmetic—as a panacea for the evils of society. The house is now called Grovelands. Mr. Harting tells us, in his "Birds of Middlesex," that the sheet of water in these grounds was frequented by some ospreys, which used to catch and eat the fish, and were shot at till they were driven away.

Palmer's Green, a hamlet of Southgate, is a small cluster of houses, with a railway-station, to the south-east of the village, on the road to Winchmore Hill, and is reached by a pleasant footpath to the left of the "Cherry Tree" inn.

Southgate contains a village-hall, a large roomy brick-built structure, of Gothic design, which has been erected by the side of the main street, and is used for concerts and other entertainments.

A walk of about two miles along a pleasant shady roadway skirting the park of Grovelands, and by a footpath through a wood to the left, brings us to Winchmore Hill, a large ecclesiastical district, crowning the eminence from which it takes its name. It contains between 400 and 500 houses, and has a population of some 2,000 souls. Sixty years ago there were only about fifty houses in the district. It is a straggling village; but the houses are mostly built round a large triangular-shaped green, the surface of which is relieved by a circular pond and a few trees. At one end of the green is a railway-station, on the Enfield branch of the Great Northern line, and also a Congregational chapel, built of brick, after the newest style of ecclesiastical Gothic architecture. The village was converted into an ecclesiastical district, out of the civil parish of Edmonton, in 1851. The church, dedicated to St. Paul, stands at the north end of the village, and dates from the close of the reign of George IV. It was consecrated by Bishop Howley in 1828, and partly burnt down in 1844, but subsequently repaired. It is built of white brick, with stone dressings in the Perpendicular style. Crocheted pinnacles rise at each of the four corners, and a bell-turret in the centre of the gable at the western end. The church consists of simply a nave and small recessed chancel. The east window represents, in twelve medallions, the principal scenes and events in the life of St. Paul. Sharon

Turner the historian, and Thomas Hood the poet, resided here for some years. Part of the village, on the east side of the railway, extends over Bush Hill, on the road towards Edmonton.

On Bush Hill was formerly held a fair, called "Beggar's Bush Fair." It was granted by King James I., when he laid out a part of Enfield Chase into Theobalds Park, and is now held at Cathol Gate, on the road leading to Northall.

Of Bush Hill Park, the principal seat in this locality, an account will be found in OLD AND NEW LONDON.* It may, however, be stated here that the property has lately been sold, and is now being laid out for the erection of villa residences. One part of it is called Sambrooke Park. The old Clock-house itself, as the mansion is called, has been sadly spoilt by its new owners, who have destroyed its best features, whitewashing its fine red brick-work, and superseding its iron gates of scroll-work by a paltry wall of modern white brick. The fine summer-house, too, said to have been designed by Inigo Jones, has been pulled down, and the materials sold, and is now (April, 1883), in the course of re-erection in the grounds of Mr. E. Ford, at the Old Park, at Enfield.

At Red Ridge, on the side of Bush Hill nearest to Enfield, Sir Hugh Myddelton resided during the formation of the New River, for the purpose of superintending the works. Some parts of the old building were standing early in the present century, although great alterations and improvements had been effected in the house. The New River was carried across the dell in the grounds by means of a wooden trough or aqueduct, upwards of 650 feet in length. This aqueduct was regarded at the time as a triumph of engineering skill; but it was removed towards the end of the last century, and an embankment thrown up in its place.

Edmonton lies about two miles eastward from Bush Hill. The name of the parish has become famous throughout the length and breadth of the land by Cowper's humorous poem descriptive of "Johnny Gilpin's Ride;" by the residence and grave of Charles Lamb; by the "Merry Devil of Edmonton;" and by the "Witch of Edmonton"— all of which matters will be found fully dealt with in the pages of OLD AND NEW LONDON.* Mr. J. T. Smith, the author of "A Book for a Rainy Day," speaks in high terms of the salubrity of the air of Edmonton, and also of its aristocratic exclusiveness:—"The resident families would not quit their mansions, but kept themselves snugly within their King William iron gates and red brick crested piers, so that there was no longer any opening for new comers, nor would the landowners allow one inch of ground to the builders."

At the Firs, in this village, lived Sir James Winter Lake, Bart., the friend and patron of Mr. J. T. Smith, and to whom he dedicated one of his many works on London. "Sir James," writes Mr. Smith, "was a governor of the Hudson Bay Company—a situation, it is well known, he filled with credit to himself as well as the satisfaction of every one connected with that highly-respected body. Sir James most kindly invited me to take a house near him at Edmonton, where I had the honour, for the space of seven years, of enjoying the steady friendship of himself and family. Lady Lake, who then retained much of her youthful beauty, by her elegance of language and extreme affability charmed every one. Their family mansion was distant about a mile from the 'Angel,' and called the 'Firs.'"

CHAPTER XXXVI.
ENFIELD.

"The Enfield House, that 'longes unto our Queene,
They all behold, and with due reverence
Salute the same."—VALLENS' *Tale of Two Swannes.*

General Description of the Parish—Situation and Boundaries—Parochial Divisions—The Town and Principal Streets—Enfield Court—The New River—Railway Stations—Census Returns—Historical Reminiscences—The Barony of Enfield—Descent of the Manor—Fairs and Markets—Site of the Old Manor House—Camlet Moat—Oldbury—Edward VI. at Enfield—The Palace—Dr. Uvedale—The Market-place—The Parish Church—The Free Grammar School—Schools of Industry—John Keats's Schooldays—Charitable Institutions—Old Park—Chase Park—Chase Side House—Enfield Green—Little Park—Beycullah' Park—Enfield Races—Churches and Chapels—The Cemetery—Forty Hall—Elsynge Hall—Sir Walter Raleigh and Queen Elizabeth—Anne Countess of Pembroke—Myddelton House—Gough Park—Distinguished Residents—Beautiful Women of Enfield.

ENFIELD is one of the many suburban villages whose names are, or have been, associated with royalty, though not to the same extent as Hamp-ton or Richmond. Built upon the fringe of a royal chase, Enfield is just what the old writers would have styled "a right pleasant and joyous place," though somewhat sleepy and quiet in its appearance. Especially in the central square, near the Church Grammar School, High Cross, and Palace, it is decidedly old-fashioned ; and its outlying mansions, for the most part, are such as to keep them company. Once inhabited by princes, and lords and fair ladies, it still wears a courtly look ; and it is not difficult to fancy the youthful princess Elizabeth riding along the pleasant roads which lead in the direction of that Chase which, alas ! is now a chase only in name.

the parishes which we have visited in our perambulations, for it has numbered among its residents, besides two at least of the sovereigns of England, for longer or shorter periods, such celebrities as Sir Walter Raleigh, Isaac Disraeli, Gough the antiquary, Dr. Abernethy, Charles Babbage, Captain Marryatt, and Charles Lamb ; and the annals of the neighbourhood are connected with many other important personages distinguished in the general history of the country.

The parish is nine miles distant from London,

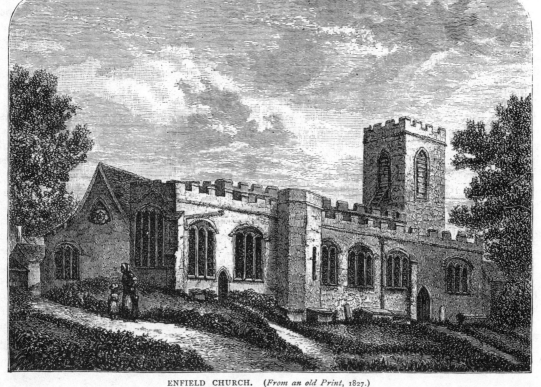

ENFIELD CHURCH. (*From an old Print*, 1827.)

In many, though perhaps scarcely in most places, the "parish" and the "manor" were identical in their limits, but this could hardly be the case in such a widespread locality as Enfield, nearly twenty miles in circumference. On the contrary, it comprised, apparently, no less than eight separate manors, two of which, in old times, were appanages to royalty, viz., Enfield (proper), Durants, or Durants Harbour, Elsynge *alias* Norris or North Farm, Suffolks, Honylands, and Pentriches *alias* Capels, Goldbeaters, Worcesters, and the Rectory Manor. The two royal manors were those of Enfield and Worcesters, each of which had its own palace and park. Enfield is richer in historic and literary associations than many of

almost due north, and it is bounded on the east by a branch of the River Lea, called the Meereditch or Mardyke ; on the west by Hadley and South Mimms ; on the north by Northaw and Theobalds Park, in Hertfordshire ; and on the south by Edmonton and Southgate. From east to west its measurement is between eight and nine miles, and from north to south it is rather more than three miles by the main road, although in some parts it ranges from five to six miles. Norden describes Enfield as "a parish standing on the edge of the Chase, of such extent, that if it were measured by the ring it would be found at least twenty miles in extent, some time parcell of the Duke of Lancaster's lands, now Queene Elizabeth's. The

Chase, called Enfield Chase, taketh its name of this place."

"Few districts in the vicinity of London," writes Mr. Edward Ford in his "History of Enfield," "retain so much of rural and sequestered character, owing no doubt in part to its formerly tedious and circuitous means of access. Since the opening of two new lines of railway, however, this

BEACH HILL CIRC. 1796.

isolation cannot much longer continue. The beauty and variety of the scenery, the upland Chase, still so nobly timbered, the more cultivated lowlands, watered for many a mile by the windings of the New River and the Lea, and the long-sustained character of the parish for health and longevity (rating the second in England), are drawing the attention of the country-loving public to this picturesque and interesting neighbourhood. From the more elevated situations extensive prospects may be obtained in all directions over the adjoining counties—from Camlet Moat and from the Ridgeway Road across the broad expanse of the Chase; far down into Hertfordshire from the wood at Forty Hall; and away into the heart of Buckinghamshire from above Potter's Bar; and the

long range of Epping and Hainault forests from everywhere. The bridle-road across Hadley Common, perhaps the last remains of genuine forest scenery in Middlesex, leads to the highest ground in the parish, whence, looking south, distant gleams of the Thames and the white sails of its shipping may be seen in the far horizon."

The parish is separated into four quarters—namely, the Town Division, which comprises the central part of the parish and the eastern portion of Chase Side; Chase Division, which includes Windmill Hill, the west half of Chase Side, and the whole of Enfield Chase; Bull's Cross Division, embracing Forty Hill, Bull's Cross, and the north-eastern

MYDDELTON HOUSE CIRC. 1821.

section of the parish, stretching away to Enfield Wash; and Green Street Division, which includes Ponder's End, Green Street, and Enfield Highway.

Enfield, on the whole, it is scarcely necessary to state, is a widely-scattered place. It is more than a village, and something less than a town. True, it has its market-place and its square, at one corner of which are painted up in large letters the words "The Town;" but it has nothing that can be styled a High Street, being laid out on the most irregular of plans, if plan it can be called. It is a large cluster of gentlemen's seats and substantial houses of the Dutch and Queen Anne style, with high-browed doorways and heavy-sashed windows, standing for the most part near the road, and screened off from it by lofty red-brick walls and iron gates, some of which afford really handsome specimens of iron scroll-work. Mixed up with these larger houses, in most admired confusion, are small shops and modern villas, for the most part the abodes of industrious City clerks and retired tradesmen.

The central part of the parish, comprising the town, is situated on the cross-road leading from Enfield highway in the east to Barnet and Hadley in the west. The principal feature of the town is the broad central square above mentioned, containing a market-cross and the parish church.

Baker Street and Silver Street are the names of the thoroughfares running northwards from the market-place towards Forty Hill and Cheshunt. In Baker Street is the vicarage, heavy, solid, and sub-stantial, close to the churchyard, and opening into it; Enfield Court, the seat of Colonel Somerset; the old rectory, and Fox Hall, both remarkable for their tall iron gates, surmounted by heraldic bear-ings; and a quaint little square of humble cottages, occupied by the industrious classes, and dating from the seventeenth century, rejoicing in the grand name of Carterhatch Square. One side of it, however, has been cut off to make room for an unsightly Independent chapel.

Enfield Court is the most important mansion in the neighbourhood. The estate, which contains about eighty acres, was formerly part of the manor of Worcesters. The original structure dates from the latter end of the seventeenth century, since which time it has received many successive addi-tions. The southern wing was re-built in 1864, at which time great alterations were made in the gardens and grounds. The garden on the west side of the house still bears traces of having been originally laid out in the time of William III., with its broad terrace walk 400 feet in length, and its clipped yews and hollies of the Dutch style of gardening. At the bottom of this garden stands a quaint and picturesque summer-house, a small building, having an upper chamber and a pointed roof. There is also an oblong fish-pond, crossed by a bridge, the remains of a former " canal."*

The principal thoroughfares, running north and south, extend for about two miles, and are crossed and re-crossed by the New River, which curves and meanders, "at its own sweet will," through the parish, as if loth to leave the woodland Chase through which Sir Hugh Myddelton carried it. Its course within the limits of Enfield cannot be much short of five miles; so that it seems to belong to Enfield more truly than to any other parish in Middlesex.

The New River enters the parish at Bull's Cross in the north, and leaves it at Bush Hill in the south; and it winds about with so many twists and twirls, that it seems to have started on its course with a deliberate intention of visiting every gentleman in Enfield in succession, for really there is scarcely one mansion which has not some part of its grounds washed by its clear waters. One of these seats (Myddelton House), that of Mr. Carring-ton Bowles, stands on the site of a building called Bowling Green House, once the abode of Sir Hugh Myddelton, to whom the New River may be said to owe its existence. Its history from the time when, in the reign of King James I., the above-mentioned worthy knight persuaded the Common Council of London to transfer to him the power granted by certain Acts then recently passed en-abling them to convey a stream of water to London from any part of Middlesex, will be found fully described in OLD AND NEW LONDON.* Sir Hugh Myddelton, who, as we have seen in the preceding chapter, lived at Winchmore Hill whilst super-intending the formation of this river, offered, in four years, at his own risk and charge, to bring the Chadwell and Amwell springs from Hertfordshire up to London, by a route more than thirty-eight miles long; and the work was completed in Sep-tember, 1613. The "Third Report of the His-torical MSS. Commission" gives a melancholy proof, if proof be needed, of the injustice with which this benefactor of London was treated by his fellow-citizens. The patriotic goldsmith, who spent his whole fortune in procuring a priceless boon for the Londoners, never received any recom-pense for his skill and labour; and Lysons tells us that within the memory of his own generation the last male descendant of Sir Hugh was allowed by them to become a pensioner on the bounty of the New River Company. Verily, virtue in this country is too often its own sole reward!

Enfield Highway, the most easterly division of the parish, stretches along the Hertford road from Ponder's End in the south-east, to Enfield Wash and Bullsmoor Lane in the north-east, and will be more fully dealt with in a subsequent chapter. It

---

is connected with the town by numerous lanes and thoroughfares. The River Lea and the Lea and Stort Navigation both flow through the marsh land, a short distance to the east of Enfield Highway. Here, on the banks of the Lea, about a mile distant from the Wash, stands the Royal Small Arms Factory. This, too, we shall presently describe in detail.

Chase Side, as the western division is called, slopes up gradually from the town towards Trent Park (or Cock Fosters) and Beech Hill Park, and so on to Hadley.

Railway communication with the metropolis has of late years been the cause of a great extension of the town in almost all directions, particularly at Chase Side. Here, on Windmill Hill, the Great Northern Railway has the terminus of a short branch line; and close by the "Nag's Head" inn, near the centre of the town, is the terminus of a branch line of the Great Eastern Railway; whilst at Ponder's End, and at the Ordnance Factory, are stations on the main line itself, affording easy communication with Enfield Highway and the eastern parts of the parish.

The parish contains altogether 12,650 acres, inclusive of the Chase, 350 acres of which were enclosed by Act of Parliament in 1801. In 1871 the population was rather over 1,600, to which about 3,000 were added during the next ten years.

The general appearance of the main road running north and south through the town, with its numerous antiquated cottages and mansions, which have been inhabited by generations long since passed away, is quite in keeping with its historical associations, which are by no means small or unimportant.

Almost immediately on the accession of Mary, the jealous Queen sent for her sister Elizabeth, who was at Ashridge on the borders of Hertfordshire and Buckinghamshire, peremptorily ordering her attendance at Court. The Princess, being ill, was obliged to travel in the Queen's own litter, and the rate of progress was so slow that she took four days in making a little less than thirty miles. She was carried, by easy stages, by way of Enfield to Highgate, where she was met by a large number of her friends.

In 1603, when James VI. of Scotland made his triumphal entry into London as James I. of England, his route from Theobalds lay along the road through Forty Hill and the town. "All the road from Enfield to Stamford Hill was lined and thronged with people. I heard many greyheads speak it, that in all the meetings they had seen or heard of, they had never heard or seen the tenth mass of those that were to be seen that day betwixt Enfield and London. Every place in this space was so clogged with company, that His Highness could not pass without pausing, ofttimes willingly enforced, though more willing to have proceeded, if conveniently he could without peril to his beloved people." Such are the fulsome comments of Mr. John Savile on the King's first "progress."

The scenery all round the town is delightfully rural and pleasant, particularly towards the south, in those parts through which we have journeyed hither. H. Crabb Robinson writes in his "Diary": —"I followed a path to Winchmore Hill, and another to Enfield—the last through some of the richest verdure I ever saw. The hills exquisitely undulating, with very fine clumps of oak-trees. . . . Enfield town, the large white church, the serpentine New River, Mr. Mellish's house [Bush Hill Park], with its woody appendages, form a singularly beautiful picture. . . . . Before dinner we lounged round the Green, and saw the cedar of Lebanon which once belonged to Queen Elizabeth's palace, of which only a chimney remains." This last statement, we must add, is not quite accurate.

Enfield conferred the title of Baron on the Nassaus, Earls of Rochfort, the first of whom married a daughter of Sir Henry Wroth, of Durants, and was created Baron of Enfield by William III. in 1695. It now gives the title of Viscount to the Earl of Strafford, whose estates adjoin the Chase.

In Domesday Book the parish is called Enefelde, and the variation in spelling in subsequent records are very trifling—as Endfield, Enfeld, Enefield, Envild, and, lastly, Enfield. As to its etymology, Norden says, "It is called of some Enfen, and so recorded in regarde of the fenny scytuation of some parte thereof, upon the marshes or meerish ground, which, though now brought to be good meadow and profitable pasture, it hath in time past been fenny." "This statement," Mr. Ford observes, in his work above quoted, "is not supported by any authority. The termination 'field' is the past participle of the verb 'fællan,' to fell, and opposed to woodland, as land where the trees have been cleared."

It is stated in the "Domesday Survey" that in the time of Edward the Confessor the manor of 'Enefelde' was held by Asgar, master of the horse to the king, who was likewise lord of the neighbouring manor of Edmonton. At the time of this survey this manorial district was possessed by Geoffrey de Mandeville, from whose family it descended to Humphrey de Bohun, Earl of Hereford. Eleanor, Duchess of Gloucester, was the daughter and co-heiress of the last Earl of Hereford of the Bohun family; and on her death, in 1399, this manor was inherited by her sister Mary, wife of Henry, Duke of Lancaster, afterwards Henry IV. The principal manor of Enfield thus became vested in the Crown, and was shortly after annexed to the Duchy of Lancaster, of which it still continues to be parcel.

Early in the fourteenth century Edward I. granted a license to Humphrey de Bohun and his wife (Elizabeth, Countess of Holland, and the King's daughter), and their heirs, to hold a weekly market here on Mondays; and James I., in 1619, by writ of Privy Council, granted to certain persons therein named license to hold a weekly market here on Saturdays, and at the same time established a "Court of Pie Powder." The market, however, from various causes seems to have been discontinued many years ago; but several ineffectual attempts have been made to revive it, and the very name of "Pie Powder" has been long forgotten.

Two fairs were formerly held in the town annually, in August and November. The first, which, from some unknown cause, had latterly been held in September, and had long ceased to answer any legitimate purposes of trade, but had become a source of lawlessness and disorder, and having grown a nuisance to the inhabitants of the town, was abolished in 1869, on a petition from the leading residents. The other fair, held on St. Andrew's Day, was at one time celebrated as a cheese-fair, but is now chiefly frequented for the sale of horses and cattle.

Richard II. granted to the inhabitants an exemption from certain tolls for their goods and merchandise, and various other privileges, in "all fairs, markets, villages, and other places throughout England, out of the Duchy of Lancaster, in the county of Middlesex." It is stated, however, observes Mr. Ford, that this exemption has been resisted in Covent Garden and Whitechapel markets. The above grant was confirmed and extended by Henry IV. and Henry VI., and other sovereigns, down to George III. An exemption from toll at Ware Bridge was also granted to the inhabitants of Enfield by Queen Elizabeth, and subsequently confirmed by George III.

It is curious, observes Mr. Ford in a supplement to his "History of Enfield," to compare the valuation here given of the mansion and manor of Enfield in the reign of Edward III. with the appraisement, in the same reign, of Holland House and the manor of Kensington, and to note the much higher value of both land and houses in the then much more fashionable and aristocratic suburb of Enfield, the former standing at 32s. 10d., whilst the latter is only 7s. The yearly value of the mansion and dove-house at Kensington is less than that of the Enfield dove-house alone, and the value of woodland per acre is only one-tenth of that of the old park at Enfield.

The site of the original manor house of Enfield has long been a subject of antiquarian research. Camden says that "almost in the middle of the Chase there are the ruins and rubbish of an ancient house, which the common people from tradition affirm to have belonged to the Mandevilles, Earls of Essex." At a short distance from the West Lodge, Trent Park, near the road which leads over the Chase towards Hadley, are still in existence traces of the site above alluded to; it is called Camlet Moat, and is a large quadrangular area, overgrown with briars and bushes. When measured, in 1773, the length of the moat was 150 feet. In describing these remains, Mr. Ford observes that "at the north-east corner is a deep well, paved at the bottom, in which it is pretended lies an iron chest full of treasure, which cannot be drawn up to the top, and that the last owner to whom the Chase belonged being attainted of treason, hid himself in a hollow tree, and falling into this well perished miserably. . . . . The tiles scattered over the area, the well, and the traces of the enclosures and avenues, would seem to be rather the works of the fifteenth or sixteenth centuries than of any earlier period." Here Sir Walter Scott brings some of the characters in "The Fortunes of Nigel," and the place has been, as a matter of course, invested with something of the glamour of his marvellous genius in consequence. It is now almost the only spot where any trace of the original wildness of Enfield Chase can be met with.

In Dugdale's "Baronage" it is stated that Humphrey de Bohun, Earl of Hereford, procured, in 1347, the king's license to fortify his manor house at Enfield. In a meadow to the east of the church, near to "Nag's Head" lane, there are traces of a moat and extensive embankments, with an artificial mount. Lysons and other topographers suppose that these are the remains of Humphrey de Bohun's castle, and that when the manorial residence was removed it acquired the name of "Oldbury," by which it is still known.

Early in the sixteenth century the site of the manor was leased to private individuals; but the lease appears to have reverted to the Crown towards the latter part of the reign of Henry VIII., at which time the house was retained as a royal residence. At that time the original manor house of the Bohuns had fallen into decay, and the royal children, Edward and Elizabeth, were brought up at Elsynge Hall (called also Enfield House), which belonged to the manor of Worcesters.

Here Edward VI. was living when prince, and here he was waited on by many of the Scottish nobility, who had been brought to London as prisoners after the defeat at Solway Firth, and tendered him their homage as destined by the arbitrary king, whose heir he was, to become in due time the husband of the infant Princess Mary of Scotland. But, though a Tudor proposes, God disposes.

At the death of Henry VIII., Prince Edward was living at Hertford, but was shortly after conducted to Enfield, where the Princess Elizabeth was then living, and it was not till then that he was made acquainted with the fact of his father's death, and consequently of his own accession to the throne. On the following Monday Edward was conducted to London. In the State Paper Office is a letter from the Earl of Hertford to the Council : " From Envild this Sunday night att xj. of the clok." He writes, "We intend the King's Matie shal be a horsbak to-morrow by xj. of the clok, so that by iij. we trust His Grace shal be att the Tower."

The following anecdote connected with the garden of the palace at this period is extracted from Tuft's " History of Enfield " :—" There is one very remarkable feature connected with Enfield Palace that has come to light but recently. It was in the garden at Enfield that the Earl of Hertford took the opportunity of communicating to his companion, the master of the horse, *his intention to assume the office of Protector*, in contravention to the late King's will, which had designated eighteen executors, with equal powers.

" We are told that, ' after commoning in discourse of the state,' Sir Anthony 'gave his frank consent to the proposal ;' upon which, as we learn from another letter, Hertford had previously 'devised' with Secretary Paget, who was now left at Court to arrange matters with the other counsellors.

" Edward was not again at Enfield Palace during his reign, but his sister, Elizabeth, continued to reside here ; and there is mention also of the Queen Dowager (Katharine Parr) paying Enfield a visit."

William Wightman writes thus to Secretary Cecil :—" Myne old master, the master of th' orses, albeit, as is commonly known, he did much dissent from the proceedings in matters of religion, yet was I long sins by himself right well assured that he, commoning with my Lordes Grace *in the garden at Endfielde*, at the King's Majesties coom-

ing from Hartforde, gave his franke consent, after communication in discourse of the state, that His Grace should be Protector, thinking it (as indede it was) both the surest kynde of government, and most fyt for this commonwelth." *

And again, another courtier, Paget, writes to the Protector Somerset † :—" Remember what you promised me in the gallery at Westminster, before the breath was out of the body of the King that dead is. Remember what you promised immediately after, *devising with me concerning the place which you now occupy*, I trust in the end to good purpose, however things thwart now."

About the middle of the sixteenth century the manor of Enfield was settled by Edward on the Princess Elizabeth, at which time it is considered probable that he either built, or re-built, on the site of a former structure, the house known as the Palace, some portion of which is still standing on the south side of the High Street, opposite the church and market-place. This house was of red brick, with stone dressings. The principal front of the palace faced the north, and is described by Dr. Robinson, in his " History of Enfield," as consisting of a centre and two wings, with bay windows and high gables. The wings were decorated with the arms of England, crowned and supported by a lion and dragon, with the letters E. R. at the sides. The north-east side of the building, of which an engraving is given in Dr. Robinson's work, was of two storeys, and had a boldly-projecting bay in the centre, terminating in a tall gable, and stone-mullioned square-headed windows.

The greater part of the palace was demolished towards the close of the last century, and the materials were made use of for building purposes. A warrant was issued in 1608 for paying the expenses of taking down what was then called the King's House at Enfield. The materials were by the same order directed to be conveyed to Theobalds, in Cheshunt, there to be used in the intended buildings in course of erection. How any part came to be retained *in situ* is a fact not to be traced in the muniments or records of the period. Considerably later on a further demolition ensued ; and alterations—certainly not improvements—were made, not only in the interior, but in the exterior. What still remains is almost obscured from public view by houses and shops built in front of it, and bears externally nothing to denote any semblance to the residence of royalty, so thorough and complete has been the change effected from the

---

* " Literary Remains of King Edward VI."(printed for the Roxburghe Club, 1558), p. ccxlvii.
† *Ibid,* p. lxxxvi.

mediæval aspect of the ancient dwelling. "Notwithstanding the great alterations which it has undergone, the interior still preserves some vestiges of its ancient magnificence, and a part of one of the large rooms on the ground floor remains nearly in its original state, with its fine fretted panels of oak, and its ornamental ceiling, with pendants of four spreading leaves, and enrichments of the crown, the rose, and the fleur-de-lis. The chimney-piece is of stone, beautifully cut, and supported by Ionic and Corinthian columns, decorated with foliage and birds, and the rose and portcullis, crowned with

the Princess Elizabeth to her brother, Edward VI. It is dated "Enfield, Feb. 14," the year, however, is not recorded. Could it have been sent as a valentine? Other letters by Elizabeth, dated from the same place, are preserved in the Bodleian Library at Oxford. When she became queen at the death of her sister Mary, Elizabeth did not forget her former residence, but frequently went there, holding her court, and enjoying the sport of hunting on the beautiful free and open Chase. That she was well acquainted with the condition of the forest trees growing in her demesne is

QUEEN ELIZABETH'S PALACE, ENFIELD, 1568.

THE PALACE, FROM THE NORTH.

the arms of England and France quarterly in a garter, and the royal supporters, a lion and a dragon. Below is the motto, 'Sola salus servire Deo; sunt cætera fraudes.' The letters E. R. are on this chimney-piece, and were formerly on each side of the wings of the principal building. The monogram is clearly that of Edward VI., as the same room contains part of another chimney-piece, which was removed from one of the upper apartments, with nearly the same ornaments, and the motto, 'Vt ros super herbam est benevolentia Regis,' alluding, no doubt, to the royal grant. Several of the ceilings in the upper rooms are decorated in a similar manner to those below." Among these, the principal are the drawing-room and some sleeping apartments, now used as the boys' bedrooms, for the building has for many years served the purposes of a school.

Among the collection of royal letters in the British Museum there is one * in Latin, written by

evidenced by a letter dated Dec. 30, 1570, wherein she authorises Sir Ralph Sadleir to deliver to Sir William Cecil certain oak timber trees, all to be taken out of the manor of Enfield. Queen Elizabeth was here from the 8th to the 22nd of September, 1561, and again from the 25th to the 30th of July, 1564. The court was here again in July, 1568. Some years later on the queen quitted the Manor House, and fixed her residence at Elsynge Hall.

In 1582 Enfield Palace was leased by Queen Elizabeth to a private gentleman, and did not again revert to the Crown during her reign. From

---

* Harl. MSS., No. 6986, p. 14.

1600 to 1623 it appears to have been held by Lord William Howard; and in 1629 it was granted by Charles I. to Edward Ditchfield and others, as trustees for the City of London, by whom it was afterwards conveyed to Sir Nicholas Raynton, who is commemorated by a handsome monument in the church. About the year 1660 the palace was let to Dr. Robert Uvedale, master of the Grammar School, who acquired great fame in his day for his knowledge of the science of botany, and had some distinguished pupils in his house as boarders.

An account of Dr. Uvedale's garden is given in the "Archæologia," * and in Pulteney's "Anecdotes of Botany" mention is made of a plant called *Uvedalia*, out of compliment to him.

In Robinson's "History of Enfield" the following singular story is told relating to the above-mentioned pedagogue and botanist :—"Dr. Uvedale, in the great plague of 1665, as a preventive against its fatal effects, caused a brick to be put into the fire over night, and the next morning, when red hot, poured a quart of vinegar on it, and placed it in the middle of the hall floor, the steam of which was received by the whole family standing round. They then went to prayers, and afterwards, locking up the house, walked to Winchmore Hill, and on their return went to school. By this precaution not one of the family caught the infection."

A curious knife, found here, is figured and described in the *Gentleman's Magazine*, Vol. IX., page 595. Probably it may have belonged to some of Dr. Uvedale's aristocratic pupils.

In the garden stands a magnificent specimen of the cedar of Lebanon. It cannot claim to be of the time of Queen Elizabeth, having been planted by Dr. Uvedale soon after he took the premises. This worthy, being a scholar and a distinguished botanist, took much pride in his collection of flowers and plants of all kinds. In the year 1793, at three feet from the ground, it is stated to have measured twelve feet in girth, and since then has increased. It was greatly injured by a severe storm in 1794, and lost one of its best branches. It is certainly one of the largest specimens of the cedar known in this country; some say that it is the finest. It may be seen from many points round about Enfield.

The greater part of the palace was pulled down by Dr. Callaway, it having been struck by lightning; he is said to have designed cutting down the cedar also; but he desisted from his intention on account of the remonstrances of the inhabitants.

* See Vol. XII , pp '88-9

The market-place is a large open space in the centre of the town, and in the last century must have been highly picturesque. On the south side stood the palace above described, its gardens bordering the main street, which passes through the town westward at this point. On the east side of the square were in former times the open market and shambles, the south-east corner being occupied by a large hostelry called the "King's Head," with a quaintly-gabled front, and its signboard swinging from an elaborate iron standard. This building is no longer an inn, but is now used as offices by a firm of solicitors, and as the office of the Local Board; it also serves the magistrates as a house

THE OLD MARKET HOUSE, ENFIELD.
(*From Dr. Robinson's "Enfield."*)

for the local petty sessions. A new "King's Head" has sprung up in its place at the south-west corner of the churchyard. The "King's Head" is the most common of all loyal signs, and is most frequently to be met with where the footprints of "bluff King Hal" may be traced. Hence it could hardly fail to be the chief sign in Enfield. In spite of his savage cruelty, still his face and figure, the impersonation of jollity and good cheer, made the royal tyrant popular at all events on the confines of every royal chase.

The old market-house, of which a drawing is given in Dr. Robinson's "Enfield," was a wooden building of an octagonal form, supported by eight columns and a central pillar. There were also a portable pillory and stocks in the market-place, both of which were long ago removed. The stocks, however, found a permanent settlement close by the police-station. The present market-cross—a gingerbread example of the "Strawberry Hill" Gothic, a poor imitation of its neighbours at

Waltham and Tottenham—was built in 1826, at a cost of about £200, which was raised by a subscription among the inhabitants. The structure is built of brick, thickly coated with cement; it stands on an octagonal platform of steps, and is enclosed by iron railings; at the sides are inscriptions recording the date of its erection, and also the date of the several charters granting the market. The cross was restored in 1866, but is again in a somewhat dilapidated condition.

The parish church, dedicated to St. Andrew, stands within a spacious churchyard, on the north side of the market-place. It dates from the thirteenth century, and consists of a chancel, clerestoried nave, aisles, and towers at the west end containing a peal of eight bells. Some of the windows are filled with stained glass. The exterior of the church is somewhat poor and bare, having been "restored" in the very dawn of the Gothic revival, when it was plastered over neatly with cement. There are several engravings of the church in the last century and in the early part of this, showing it with the east window blocked up, and a quaint old parvise, or muniment-room, with a projecting gable, and a sun-dial surmounting the south porch. The fine yew-tree near the south chancel window was at that time cropped into a formal triangle, after the fashion of those which we have seen at Harlington and Bedfont. The embattled tower, built of flint and rubble, with stone quoins in three stages, gradually tapering and without buttresses, has lost much of its ancient appearance by the alteration of its windows in the two lower stages, and by its walls being cased in cement. Inside its proportions are fine, but they are marred by the intrusion of some unsightly galleries. Though the organ has been removed to the east end of the south aisle, yet its "case" still grins down upon the congregation from a gallery across the west end—a tribute to the prejudices of some of the more old-fashioned parishioners. The walls between the arches and the clerestory are coloured with a delicate tint, and stencilled with an effective pattern. These decorations are modern.

The chancel is separated from the nave by a lofty arch, and in the chancel are sedilia and piscina, erected in 1852, in the place of others discovered during some alterations in the building. A lancet-window and hagioscope in the south wall of the chancel were opened during a restoration of the church in 1866, at which time the church was new roofed throughout. Over the arches of the nave are placed alternately the devices of a rose and wing, which are also found on the tower of Hadley Church.* Lysons, in his "Environs of

London," supposes that these emblems had some connection with the Abbey of Walden; but Mr. Ford, in his history of the parish, says "there can be no doubt but that a rose and wing were borne as badges by Sir Thomas Lovell, K.G., who, on the death of Lord Roos, in 1508, without issue, succeeded to the Manor of Worcesters, in right of his wife Isabella, sister to Lord Roos." Pennant mentions in his "Itinerary" that in his time the same emblems, a rose and a wing, were to be seen on a wall which formerly belonged to Holiwell Nunnery, in Shoreditch, to which Sir Thomas Lovell was a great benefactor, and where he was buried in 1524, after his body had been laid in state in Enfield church, on the way from Elsynge Hall to London.

In the year 1777, when the chancel was undergoing alterations, a very curious allegorical picture was discovered, representing the Resurrection, in six compartments, painted on wood; this singular piece of Church antiquity was given to Mr. Gough the antiquarian, who was then residing at Enfield.

The oldest and most interesting monument in the church is that of Joyce, Lady Tiptoft, who died in 1446. She was mother of the learned Earl of Worcester, and wife of Sir John Tiptoft, nephew of Robert, the last Lord Tiptoft. The monument is a large altar-tomb under the easternmost arch on the north side of the chancel, and over it is a stone canopy of later date. The tomb is covered with a slab of grey Purbeck marble, inlaid with a very fine brass, in good preservation, representing the figure of the deceased richly attired in the fashion of the time. She wears an heraldic mantle, and over her head is a triple canopy, on the pillars of which are the arms of Tiptoft, Powes, Holland, and Charlton. Round the edge of the slab is a brass fillet, at the corners of which were the four evangelistic symbols, though only one— that of St. Matthew—now remains. In Dr. Robinson's work, published in 1823, three are represented. The words of the inscription are divided by representations of birds, beasts, fishes, &c. The canopy over the tomb is supposed to have been erected by Thomas, first Earl of Rutland, either as a memorial of Edmund, Lord Roos, or as a memorial of his sister Isabel, Lady Lovell. This monument is enriched with gold and colouring; it was restored a few years ago by the Duke of Rutland, who is a representative of the Roos family.

In the north chancel aisle is a large and richly-

---

* See ante, p. 328.

decorated monument of Sir Nicholas Raynton, of Forty Hall, sometime Lord Mayor of London, who died in 1646, and of his wife Rebecca, who died six years previously. Sir Nicholas is represented in armour, reclining under a canopy, supported by two columns of black marble, in his robes as Lord Mayor; and below him is an effigy of his wife in a similar posture, holding a book in her left hand. Below these again are the figures of his son and his son's wife and their four children. One of the fine Jacobean monuments is "skied" up into the south-west corner of the gallery.

John Abernethy, the eminent surgeon, who died at Enfield in 1831, is commemorated by a mural monument.

On the floor are brasses of William Smith and Jane, his wife, "who served King Henry VIII., Edward VI., Queen Marie, and now Queen Elizabeth." He died in 1592, leaving £4 out of his land "to be given to the godlie poore of Enfield."

There is a beautiful monument on the north chancel pier to the memory of Mrs. Martha Palmer, one of the Palmers of Dorney. It is mentioned by Horace Walpole as the handiwork of Nicholas Stone, sculptor and master-mason to James I., and greatly celebrated for his works. Vertue quotes from his pocket-book an entry of the cost of this monument: "Mrs. Palmer, at Enfield, £16."

Previous to the last restoration of the church, in 1866, there was a brass in the floor of the chancel, inscribed to the memory of Ann, daughter of Richard Gery, Esq., of Bushmead, Bedfordshire, with the following curious epitaph :—

> "Here lies interr'd
> One that scarce err'd ;
> A virgin modest, free from folly ;
> A virgin knowing, patient, holy ;
> A virgin blest with beauty here ;
> A virgin crown'd with glory there :
> Holy virgins, read, and say,
> We shall hither all one day.
>   Live well, ye must
>   Be turn'd to dust."

The vestry, at the north-east corner of the church, is supposed to have formerly constituted a chantry-chapel. Chantries were founded in this church by Baldwyn de Radyngton in 1398, and for the souls of Robert Blossom and Agnes, his wife, in the reign of Edward IV.

At the east end of the churchyard, near the entrance to the vicarage garden, is the tomb of Lord and Lady Napier of Merchistoun. On the grave-stone of John White, Surveyor to the New River Company, is the following quaint epitaph :—

> "Here lies John White, who, day by day,
> On river works did use much clay,
> Is now himself turning that way :
> If not to clay, yet dust will come,
> Which to preserve takes little room,
> Although enclos'd in this great tomb.
> I served the New River Company, as Surveyor, from Lady-
>   day, 1691, to Midsummer, 1723."

The vicarage has numbered among its occupants but few, if any, whose names have become famous in history. We may, however, state that the Rev. Wm. Roberts was ejected from the living of Enfield by the Parliamentary Commissioners in 1642, and that Dr. Maclagan, now Bishop of Lichfield, was for some few years curate-in-charge of the parish, before becoming rector of Newington and vicar of Kensington. He had previously been an officer in the Indian army.

On the west side of the churchyard stands the Free Grammar School, which was founded in the sixteenth century. The school-house was rebuilt in the seventeenth century. It is a large, old-fashioned red-brick building, with dormer windows ; modern sash-windows have superseded the old stone-mullioned frames. The management of the school is in accordance with a scheme drawn up in 1873 by the Endowed Schools' Commissioners, and it is under a board of local gentlemen as governors.

The Established Church and the Dissenters at Enfield have each their "School of Industry," founded in 1806. The former stands in Silver Street, and the latter in Baker Street. A handsome new building for the Church school was opened in 1876, its foundation stone having been laid by Miss Somerset. The school, which had been carried on for seventy years in "The Old Coffee House," now accommodates one hundred children, who are taught washing, cooking, and housework, to fit them for domestic service.

At a school kept here by a Mr. Clarke, John Keats spent the greater part of his childhood and boyhood, from five to fifteen. Here, on half-holidays, when the rest of the boys were at cricket, he would remain indoors, translating his Virgil or his Fénelon. If his master forced him to go out and take exercise, he would walk up and down the garden, book in hand—Shakespeare, or Lemprière's " Dictionary," or Spence's *Polymetis*, or " Robinson Crusoe." He left this school in 1810 to be apprenticed to Mr. Hammond, a surgeon, at Edmonton. The story of the rest of his short life, spent at Hampstead,* in London, and in Italy, is known to most English readers.

This parish is well off for charitable institutions,

---

almshouses, &c. ; and there are also a large number of chapels for Nonconformists of different denominations.

On the south side of the town, near the Great Northern Railway station, is Old Park, so called to distinguish it from the Little Park, or New Park, on the northern side of the parish. The estate, as we learn from Mr. Ford's " Enfield," "was formerly the Home Park of the ancient manorial palace of Enfield, at which the Princess Elizabeth resided." From a survey of 1650, the house appears to have been then a ranger's lodge, and from the remains of massive foundations in every direction, must have been of considerable extent ; but the greater part of the original structure has long since been pulled down, and the remainder transformed into a comparatively modern residence of the early Hanoverian period. In the library still remain the original open chimney and hearth, with fire-dogs, and a "reredos," with figures of the time of James I. There are also several interesting curiosities, autographs of the queen, &c. ; and the original statuette of Oliver Goldsmith, the *chef-d'œuvre* of Foley, graces his library.

The park, about 200 acres in extent, is well wooded, and the lawn in front of the house is surrounded on three sides by a circular entrenchment, from which various interesting relics have at different times been obtained. It is mentioned by Camden as the site of an ancient Roman Oppidum.

A long lease of the Old Park was granted by the merry monarch, on his restoration, to Monk, Duke of Albemarle; but reverting to the Crown on the death of his successor's wife, the second duchess, it was bestowed by William III., in the first year of his reign, upon John, ninth Earl of Rutland. It afterwards passed through the hands of the Clayton and Lewis families; it is now the seat of Mr. Edward Ford, upon whose " History of Enfield" we have drawn so largely in this chapter.

Chase Park, the original house of which stood near the entrance lodge from Chase Green, was formerly part of the Old Park estate. The present mansion, which has been many years in the possession of the Adams family, was built in 1822, about which time the New River Company, under a mutual agreement, formed an ornamental sheet of water in front of the house.

The estate of Chase Side House, the seat of Mrs. Twells, widow of Mr. Philip Twells, M.P., was also originally part of the Old Park, which formerly extended as far as the town, and included the palace, with its gardens, &c. The part of the town in which this property lies was, in the seventeenth century, known as Enfield Green, the pre-sent green being at that time a portion of the unenclosed Chase ; and, as Mr. Ford tells us, down to the present century several trees were still standing, marking the former boundary of the Old Park. In the middle of the seventeenth century Sir Robert Jason was living at Enfield Green, in a house probably occupying the site of the present Chase Side House.

The present green is a broad open space of turf, environed with a few trees, and skirted on the east side by the picturesque windings of the New River, which is here crossed by two or three bridges. It is a pleasant spot, and lies midway between the town and the Great Northern Railway station, on the gentle slope which begins to rise towards Windmill Hill and the Ridgeway. It has long been a favourite lounge. " I sunned myself," writes Henry Crabb Robinson in his " Diary," " on the beautiful Enfield Green."

Thomas Trevor, of Enfield Green, was created a baronet in 1641, and made a Knight of the Bath at the coronation of Charles II. He was the grandson of John Trevor of Trevallin, in Denbighshire, ancestor of the Viscounts Hampden, and son of Sir Thomas Trevor, Chief Baron of the Exchequer.

Little Park, lying between the church and the Chase Side, was built in 1750–60. It is the property of Mr. Cornelius Walford, the eminent authority on insurance matters and other social subjects. The old road from the church to the Chase is said to have passed between some fine dark pine-trees on the estate.

On the west of Enfield, on the hill leading up from the green towards the Ridgeway, and close to the Great Northern Railway station, is Beycullah Park—now being laid out for the erection of villas —where the Enfield races were held. They have, however, been lately given up, much to the satisfaction of the more respectable portion of the community. It is said that this was the first place in the kingdom at which horse-racing was established ; and the statement is probably true, on account of its vicinity to the court held by James I. at Theobalds, near Cheshunt. The races were then called " Bell-courses," because the prize was a silver bell, afterwards altered into a cup. Hence comes the phrase, " to bear the bell."

In this part of Enfield a new church (St. Mary Magdalene) has been erected, at the expense of Mrs. Twells, of Chase Side. It is built of stone, in the Perpendicular style, with a bright red-tiled roof. It consists of a clerestoried nave, aisles, transepts, and chancel, and has a tower with a tall spire, which forms a conspicuous object on all sides. Christchurch Congregational Chapel, at Chase

Side, was built in 1878. It is in the Early English style, and has a tower surmounted by a tall tapering spire. St. Michael's Church, at Chase Side, was consecrated in 1874, as a chapel-of-ease to the parish church. It is built of Kentish rag-stone, with Bath stone dressings, and consists of a chancel and nave, with aisles, and a tower at the western end.

The church of St. John the Baptist, at Clay Hill, is a small building in the Early English style, constructed of brick with stone dressings, and consisting of chancel, nave, and aisles, with a bell-turret at the west end. It was erected in 1857, from the designs of Mr. J. St. Aubyn. All the windows are filled with stained glass.

The cemetery, at Brigadier Hill, is pleasantly situated on a gentle slope, overlooking Clay Hill. It covers about nine acres, and was laid out in 1872, at a cost of about £9,000.

Jesus Church, Forty Hill, at the northern end of the town, on the road towards Cheshunt, was built in 1835, at the expense of Mr. Christian P. Meyer, of Forty Hall. It is a poor imitation of the Early English style. Several of the windows are filled with stained glass; that over the altar is in memory of the founder, and one at the west end is to the memory of Dr. Weir, who held the vicarage from 1863 till his death, in 1874.

On the left hand stands Forty Hall, the seat of Mr. James Meyer. It is the manor-house of the ancient royal manor of "Worcesters."* The house is a heavy but handsome structure, built of brick early in the seventeenth century, and was erected by Inigo Jones for Sir Nicholas Raynton, but was much altered by the Wolstenholmes about the year 1700. It has finely-clustered chimney-stacks, and a lofty tiled roof, reminding the travelled reader of the châteaux of Normandy. The principal rooms are large, and have the ceilings enriched with panelling and tracery. The mansion contains a good collection of pictures by the first masters, including Rubens, Teniers, Canaletti, Annibal Caracci, Raphael, and Bassano; also a portrait of Sir Nicholas Raynton in his civic robes (1643), supposed to be by Dobson, the pupil of Vandyck. The house stands in a park nearly 300 acres in extent, many of the trees of which were full grown in the days when royal Tudors hunted here, and probably formed part of the forest of Middlesex in Plantagenet and even Norman times. The grounds are studded with several fine cedars, limes, and chestnuts, and an ornamental sheet of water in front of the house adds much to its picturesque appearance. The fine old gateway

of the stables, consisting of a semicircular arch, surmounted by a pediment, and a smaller arch on either side, embattled at the top, is still standing. It is said to be the work of Inigo Jones.

The manor of Worcesters belonged, in the reign of Edward II., to the knightly family named de Enefeld, and in 1413 it passed to Sir John Tiptoft, whose descendant was the learned and well-known Earl of Worcester, the Lord High Treasurer, who lost his head in 1471 for his attachment to the house of York. "O good, blessed Lord!" says Caxton of Tiptoft, Earl of Worcester, "what grete losse was it of that noble, vertuous, and well-disposed lord. The axe did then at one blow cut off more learning than was left in the heads of all the surviving nobility."* From this family the manor obtained the name of Worcesters. It was afterwards vested in Thomas, Lord Roos of Hamlake, and in Sir Thomas Lovell, some time Treasurer of the Household. Sir Thomas resided for many years at Enfield, where he was honoured, in 1516, with a visit from Margaret, Dowager Queen of Scotland, and sister of Henry VIII. Sir Thomas died at Enfield, and was buried with great pomp in a chapel which he had founded in the Priory of Holywell. The body lay for eleven days and nights in the chapel adjoining his mansion here. It was removed on the twelfth day to the parish church, and on the following day it was conveyed to the place of interment. On the decease of Sir Thomas Lovell, the manor descended to Thomas, Earl of Rutland, by whom it was given, in 1540, to Henry VIII., together with the manor-house called Elsynge Hall, sometimes also called Enfield House, of which mention has been made above as the residence of Edward VI. and Queen Elizabeth. One of the queen's visits hither is recorded in the memoirs of Carey, Earl of Monmouth, where it is observed that in 1596 "the queen came to dinner to Enfield House, and had toils set up in the park to shoot at bucks after dinner."

Later on the manor of Worcesters was devised by the Crown to Sir Robert Cecil, first Earl of Salisbury, and by the Cecils it was alienated to Sir Nicholas Raynton, Alderman, and sometime Lord Mayor of London. From the Raynton family it passed in marriage to the Wolstenholmes, and at the end of the last century it was purchased by the family of the present owner.

Lysons states that the site of Elsynge Hall is not known for certain, but he is inclined to believe that it stood about a quarter of a mile from Forty Hall, near the stream which runs down to Enfield

---

* See *ante*, p. 348.

* Horace Walpole to Mason, September 19th, 1772.

Wash, where tradition says that Queen Mary had a "palace." He notes some irregularities in the ground, and the outlines, apparently, of some fish-ponds, as still marking the spot. Dr. Robinson, who wrote in 1823, follows suit; but Mr. Ford, in his more recent "History," places the site of this palace further west, "towards the bottom of the avenue at Forty Hall, between the house and the Maidenbridge brook. Here," he writes, "in dry seasons, the outlines of an extensive fabric may be

from the parische-church." Weever ranks it among the princely mansions heritable by the Crown; and Vallens, in his tale of "Two Swannes," as quoted in the motto to this chapter, calls it "Enfield House y^t longs unto our Queene."

The scene of the incident in the life of Sir Walter Raleigh, where he is reported to have gained the favour of Queen Elizabeth by spreading his "new plush coat" on the ground for her Majesty

FORTY HALL AND THE OLD GATEWAY. (See p. 359).

traced on the ground by the withering of the grass; and here the remains of foundations have frequently been dug up."

There can be no doubt that it was at Elsynge Hall that Elizabeth resided, when at Enfield, after her accession to the throne. Norden distinctly states that the mansion was "builded by an Earle of Worcester;" and it is described by him as being a "Howse or Palace of Queen Eli." in his map of Middlesex (1593), where it is represented as surrounded by a park paling, enclosing the "New Park," and about a mile distant from the town; a similar enclosure is placed for the "Old Park," which adjoined the manor-house of Enfield. In the account of Sir Thomas Lovell's funeral, the house is stated to have been "a good myle distant

to step upon, in order not to soil her shoes, has been variously laid at Greenwich and at Kenil-worth. Mr. Ford, however, is inclined to fix upon the grounds of Elsynge Hall as the spot where this little act of gallantry was performed. It is supposed to have taken place shortly after Raleigh left college, and it is distinctly said to have been his *first introduction* to his sovereign. At that time the queen was holding her court at Elsynge Hall, and, as Mr. Ford observes, "every native of Enfield may be excused if, with the evidence before him, he should, with more likelihood, place the scene of action on an autumnal day in 1568, in one of the forest walks of Forty Hall (then Elsynge Hall), leading along the banks of the 'Maiden Bridge Brook.'" Tradition is silent, Mr. Ford adds, as to the origin of this name, but in the earliest survey of the Chase the stream has the less romantic appellation of " Old Pond Gutter." In one of the Forty Hall deeds (temp. James I.), the bridge which crosses it is called " Cole's Bridge, otherwise Maiden's Bridge."

"When the manor of Worcesters was granted to the Cecils," observes Mr. Ford, " Elsynge Hall was reserved to the Crown ; but in 1641 it was sold by Charles I., along with the 'Little Park' and 'The

and the price low. Let them repair to the Coach and Horses, Drury-lane, where they shall have speedy passage every day. The coachman's name is Richard How."*

Myddelton House, mentioned above as occupying the site of the house where Sir Hugh Myddelton lived, stands at a short distance north-east from Forty Hall, and close by Maiden Bridge.

At the upper end of Baker Street, near Forty Hill, stands a good old-fashioned family residence,

GOUGH PARK.

Warren' adjoining (part of the Duchy of Lancaster), to Philip, Earl of Pembroke and Montgomery." It was the widow of this nobleman who wrote the oft-quoted letter to Sir J. Williamson, Secretary of State, who had " presumed " to propose a candidate for her borough of Appleby :— " I have been bullied by an usurper, I have been neglected by a court, but I will not be dictated to by a subject. Your man shan't stand.—ANNE, Dorset, Pembroke, and Montgomery."

The following advertisement, which was published a few years after the death of the Earl of Pembroke, must refer to this house :—" At Enfield House are several wholesome baths erected, wet and dry, cold and moist, for several diseases ; the rates are easy,

once the abode of the celebrated antiquary, Richard Gough. His father, Mr. Harry Gough, sometime M.P. for Bramber, and a director of the East India Company, &c., in 1723, purchased the property, which was much improved by his son. Mr. J. T. Smith, in his " Book for a Rainy Day," mentions having been introduced to the antiquary Gough at Forty Hill. Mr. R. Gough became possessed of this property on the death of his mother, in 1774, and continued to reside here, with the interruption of the various journeys connected with his topographical pursuits, until the time of his decease, in 1809. His extensive library

* " Perfect Passages," Oct. 22, 1632.

of valuable books (with the exception of the department of British topography, which he bequeathed to the Bodleian Library at Oxford) was sold, in pursuance of his own directions, in 1810. Mr. Gough was elected a Fellow of the Society of Antiquaries in 1767, and nominated director in 1771; he was also for some years a Fellow of the Royal Society. He was a great admirer and collector of stained glass, of which a few good specimens, the contributions of friends, were preserved in the windows of his house.

Mr. Gough's residence, still known as Gough Park, is a good two-storeyed building, clearly not built at a more recent date than Queen Anne's reign. The New River winds through the grounds, and at the front and side of the house are two handsome gates of iron scroll work.

The father of John Howard, the philanthropist and prison reformer, was living at Enfield at the beginning of the last century, but he removed to Clapton about the time of the birth of his son, which occurred in 1727.* By some writers it has been doubted whether John Howard was really born here or at Clapton. His father was apparently in good circumstances, as he "paid the fine rather than serve the office of Sheriff of London."

Another distinguished resident at Enfield was Isaac D'Israeli, the father of Lord Beaconsfield. His house, afterwards used as the Eastern Counties railway-station, was a small mansion standing in its own grounds to the east of the town. It was of the Queen Anne period, and was remarkable for the beauty of the details of its brick-work. There is a view of it in Ford's "History of Enfield." The central part of it is now in the South Kensington Museum. "My father," writes the future Lord Beaconsfield, "who came up to town to read the newspapers at the St. James's Coffee House, found their columns filled with extracts from the fortunate effusion of the hour, conjectures as to its writer, and much gossip respecting Walcot and Harley. He returned to Enfield laden with the journals, and presenting them to his parents, broke to them the intelligence that at length he was not only an author, but a successful one."

Benjamin D'Israeli, Lord Beaconsfield's grandfather, appears to have been a man of considerable wealth; he was one of the founders of the "Stock Exchange" of London, and was regarded as a rival of the Rothschilds. Indeed, it is said that on one occasion, early in the present century, the Emperor of Russia, when he required to raise a loan, applied to him for help; and it was only on

his refusal that he placed the negotiation in the hands of the house of Rothschild. He was, as Lord Beaconsfield tells us, "a man of ardent character; sanguine, courageous, speculative, and fortunate; with a temper which no disappointment could disturb, and a brain, amid reverses, full of resource. He made his fortune in the midway of life, and settled at Enfield, where he formed an Italian garden, entertained his friends, played whist with Sir Horace Mann (who was his great acquaintance, and who had known his brother at Venice as a banker), ate maccaroni (which was dressed by the Venetian consul), sang canzonettas, and notwithstanding a wife who never pardoned him for his name, and a son who disappointed all his plans, and who to the last hour of his life was an enigma to him, lived until he was nearly ninety, and then died in 1817, in the full enjoyment of prolonged existence." The date here given, however, is evidently a mistake, for in the *Gentleman's Magazine* for December, 1816, occurs the following notice of Mr. D'Israeli's death: "On the 28th of November, at Stoke Newington, in his eighty-seventh year, Benjamin D'Israeli, Esq." It is remarkable that Lord Beaconsfield never had the curiosity to pay a visit to Enfield, to see his father's house, though he mentions it in the preface to the collected edition of his father's works, quoted above.

At Chase Side Charles Lamb and his sister were living at the close of the life of the former, in 1833. One day in that month (December 19th) he strolled into the "Crown and Horseshoes" inn, as usual, and having taken a drop too much, fell down on the ground on his way home. His face was injured, and a murder having taken place on that day at Enfield, he was for a moment suspected of complicity in it. He was charged, with others, before the magistrates; but the matter was soon explained, and he was set at liberty. He died in the following year.

Major Cartwright, the distinguished politician and writer of the last century, whose burial-place at Finchley we had occasion to notice,* was a native of Enfield. Charles Babbage, the inventor of the calculating machine, passed his early years here, at a school kept by the Rev. Stephen Freeman, in "a large brick house, at the upper end of Baker Street," and where he had as a schoolfellow Captain Marryat, the naval novelist. Frederick Joyce, the inventor of the percussion-cap, was likewise a pupil at this school. Sir William Grey, Lord Bramwell, and his brother Sir Frederick J. Bramwell, the distinguished civil engineer, were educated at the Palace School, under Dr. May. Sir Ralph Abercromby was educated here, by the same master as Isaac D'Israeli. Mrs. André, the mother of the unfortunate Major André, lived at Forty Hill, as also did Dr. Birkbeck.

The unfortunate Lady Cathcart, who was forcibly abducted from Tewin Water by her husband, Colonel Maguire, who imprisoned her in Ireland, was a native of Enfield, being a daughter of one Mr. Malyn, of the Chase, a partner in the brewery in Southwark which afterwards was Thrale's. It is said that Sir Richard Steele, meeting her, when quite young, on horseback in the Chase, was so struck with her beauty that he could never forget it, and that he always regarded her as the pattern of loveliness. She died in 1789. The story of her abduction is told in the "Tales of Great Families" (2nd series). She was met by her Tewin-

bury tenants at Barnet on her return from Ireland; they drew her carriage all the way home; and when upwards of eighty she danced at the Hertford ball.

Lady Cathcart does not appear to have been the only beautiful woman in Enfield, for in the early part of the last century the town was remarkable for the number of handsome women among its inhabitants, a fact which is commemorated by a local poet, a Mr. H. Baker, in 1725, in a dull poem of 140 lines, full of quaint conceits, which is published *in extenso* at the end of Robinson's "History of Enfield," and from which we quote two couplets :—

> "But much superior in each heavenly grace
> Appear the fair ones of the Enfield race ;
> Born to command, supremely bright they shine,
> And with their eyes assert the right divine."

CHAPTER XXXVII.

ENFIELD CHASE.

> " Jove's oak, the warlike ash, veyn'd elm, the softer beech,
> Short hazell, maple plain, light aspe, the bending wych,
> Tough holly, and smooth birch, must altogether burn ;
> What should the builders serve, supplies the forgers' turn,
> When under public good base private gain takes hold,
> And we, poor wofull woods, to ruin lastly sold."   FULLER.

General Description of a Chase—Form and Extent of Enfield Chase—Its Early History—The Last of the Staffords, Dukes of Buckingham—Drayton's Description of Enfield Chase—Its Present Condition—The Princess Elizabeth as a Hunter—James I. at Enfield Chase—A Portion of the Chase added to Theobalds—Seizure of the Chase by the Commonwealth—Sale of Different Portions of it—Macaulay's Account of Enfield Chase—Evelyn pays it a Visit—The Chase Re-stocked with Deer by Charles II.—The Chase used as a Sheep-walk—Punishment for Cutting Down and Destroying Trees in the Chase—Its Final Enclosure—Officers belonging to the Chase—Camlet Moat, the supposed Site of the Chief Forester's Lodge—Trent Park—Beech Hill Park—East Lodge—Chase Lodge—Hill Lodge, Claysmore—The Roman Road—Cock Fosters—Dangers of the Roads in Former Times—White Webbs House—The Gunpowder Plot—" The King and the Tinkler."

BY a Chase is meant a large space of open or forest land, either natural or artificial, and set apart for the purposes of those field sports in which almost all kings and princes, from the days of Xenophon and Cyrus, and those of Herodotus and Xerxes, and even from the ages of Babylonian and Assyrian splendour, have so constantly indulged. The successors of Charlemagne, the French sovereigns of the House of Capet, kept up the tradition, which they handed on in their turn to William the Conqueror and the rest of our Norman kings, under whom the " New " Forest, in Hampshire, was made a royal " Chase," at the cost of sad cruelties, it is to be feared, to the luckless inhabitants. There were other royal chases in Sherwood, Whittlebury, and Needwood Forests, whose broad glades were kept alive during the winter season by the horn of royal hunters in the days of the Plantagenets and Tudors.

Drayton, in the " Polyolbion," describes Enfield Chase thus :—

> " A forrest for her pride, tho' titl'd but a Chace ;
> Her purlieus and her parks, her circuit full as large
> As some, perhaps, whose state requires a greater charge.
> Whose holts* that view the east, do wistly stand and look
> Upon the winding course of Lea's delightful brook."

Enfield Chase is—or was—an extensive tract of land, lying chiefly to the north-west of the town, and stretching into several neighbouring parishes. The name first occurs, it is believed, in a record of the reign of Edward II. " Its form," as we learn from Mr. Ford's " History of Enfield," " was very irregular ; its north and longest side was nearly straight, as was also its west side ; its south and east sides were full of angles. Its greatest length

---

* A term still in use in Hampshire and elsewhere to denote high woods.

was about four miles and a half from east to west—that is, from Parsonage Lane to Ganna Corner; from north to south—from Cattle Gate to South-gate—about four miles; its shortest length from east to west—that is, from Potter's Bar to Hadley Town—two miles and three-quarters. On the north side it abuts on Northaw Common, with which it communicates by Cattle Gate, Stock Gate, Cooper's Lane, and Potter's Bar. On the east it adjoins Enfield parish, its outlets to which are White Webbs, Clay Hill, Cocker or Crook Lane, New Lane, Parsonage Lane, and Enfield Green, or the Town. On this side also it extends into Edmonton parish, communicating with it by Winch-more Hill and Southgate."

In the notice of "Enfelde" in the "Domesday Survey," it is stated that there was "a park" here; but the term park, as used in that record, is of an indefinite character. At that period, and down to the time of its enclosure, the district is supposed by Lord Lyttelton to have formed part of the ancient forest of Middlesex. Previous to the reign of Edward II. it was called "Parcus Extrin-secus," the Outer Park, to distinguish it from the "Parcus Intrinsecus," the Home Park, or Great Park, as it was locally called—though, of course, far smaller than the Chase.

In very early times it formed part of the posses-sions of the Mandevilles, and afterwards of the Bohuns, their successors; but since the marriage of Henry IV. to the daughter and ultimate heiress of Humphrey de Bohun, it has belonged to the Duchy of Lancaster.

In 1483, the Chase, together with the manor of Enfield, is said to have been given by Richard III. to Stafford, Duke of Buckingham, as a reward for his services in raising him to the throne; but if so, it shortly after reverted to the Crown; for, having conspired with the Bishop of Ely to dethrone the king, and been betrayed by his servant, the duke was beheaded in the market-place at Salisbury, without going through the ceremony of a trial. Buckingham, it seems, had claimed the whole or the greater part of the immense inheritance of Humphrey de Bohun in right of descent, which Edward IV. had kept to himself.

The last holder of the dignity and estates of the great family of Bohun, Edward Stafford, Duke of Buckingham, executed on Tower Hill in 1521, was the wealthiest subject in England, the lineal repre-sentative of the Plantagenets, and the mortal enemy of Cardinal Wolsey, whom he had offended. On his way to the Tower from Westminster, he was led to his barge by Sir Thomas Lovel, of Forty Hall, who also treated him with respect, asking the

fallen nobleman to take his seat on the carpet and cushions that he had laid for him. But he de-clined the offer, saying, "When I came here, I was Lord High Constable and Duke of Buckingham, but now poor Edward Bohun, the poorest wretch alive." Holinshed calls him "a most wise and noble prince, and the mirror of all courtesy." With him became extinct the office of Lord High Con-stable of England, which had been hereditary in his family from the days of Magna Charta." On his attainder, his dukedom and earldom and estates were confiscated. His son Henry retained the title of Baron Stafford; but he was so impoverished that he was glad to borrow the loan of a sovereign in the year before his death, in 1588. His son was even more embarrassed; and in 1639 his grandson was deprived by Charles I. of his rank and honour, on account of his poverty and abject condition." Thus ended a noble line, who had flourished for one-fourth of the entire Christian era.

The Chase now consists of a series of farms, of more or less value, and of gentlemen's seats; but in former times—that is, from the period when it became the "happy hunting ground" of royalty down to the time when the district was "dis-chased," in 1779—it was full of trees, and herds of deer roamed in its wild glades.

Whilst residing at Hatfield, under the charge of Sir Thomas Pope, the Princess Elizabeth was gratified by her host with a display of romantic magnificence, which was exactly agreeable to the taste of the times and of herself. "She was in-vited," writes Lucy Aikin, "to repair to Enfield, there to take the amusement of hunting the hart. Twelve ladies in white satin attended her on their ambling palfreys, and twenty yeomen, all clad in green. At the entrance of the forest she was met by fifty archers in scarlet boots and yellow caps, armed with gilded bows, one of whom presented to her a silver-headed arrow winged with peacock's feathers. The splendid show concluded, according to the established laws of the chase, by the offering of the knife to the princess as first lady on the field, and her *taking say** of the buck with her own fair and royal hand."

Whilst staying with Sir Robert Cecil at Theo-balds, on his way from Edinburgh to London, in 1603, King James spent a morning in Enfield Chase, whither he rode, "accompanied by many of the nobility; but his visit was cut short by the showers of rain. He rode," says an eye-witness, "the most part of the way from the Chase between two honourable persons of our land (England), the

---

* Cutting the throat.

Earl of Northumberland upon his Majesty's right hand, and the Earl of Nottingham upon his left hand." Such is the minuteness of the "special correspondents" of three centuries ago.

In 1606 Sir Robert Cecil again entertained King James, and also Frederick III. of Denmark, at Theobalds. About this time the extent of the Chase was considerably reduced, for, according to Clutterbuck's "Hertfordshire," "the king having become enamoured of this place, from its proximity to an extensive tract of open country favourable to the diversion of hunting (his favourite amusement), he prevailed upon his Minister to exchange it with him for his Palace of Hatfield, in the county of Herts. The king, having obtained possession of the manor, enlarged the park by taking in part of the adjoining Chase, and surrounded it with a wall of brick ten miles in circumference."

The Chase remained in the possession of the Crown till after the death of Charles I., when it was seized by the Commonwealth as public property, and, by an order of the House of Commons, was surveyed in 1650, when it was reported to contain 7,900 acres, its value being set down at rather more than £4,700 per annum. Shortly subsequent to that date the district had been divided into parcels and sold to different individuals. A considerable part was consequently enclosed, and several houses built. But the enclosure created great disturbances among those who claimed the right of common, and who were accustomed to obtain their fuel from this waste. In the Bodleian Library at Oxford is preserved an original survey of the Chase, a duplicate of which is in the possession of the vestry clerk of Enfield; it is entitled "A Description of Enfield Chase, situate in the Parish of Enfield, and County of Middlesex, as the same is now divided between the Commonwealth and the Commons, by Edmund Rolfe and Nicholas Gunter, in the year 1658." In this survey the gate of the Chase at Winchmore Hill is called "Highmore, *alias* Winsmore." The Pest House mentioned in Ford's "Enfield" (p. 311) is distinctly marked, standing on the present Green.

In his account of the state of England in 1685, Macaulay observes that Enfield Chase, though hardly out of the sight of the smoke of the capital, was "a region twenty-five miles in circumference, in which the deer wandered by thousands, as free as in the American forests;" still, there is no record of there ever having been more than 3,000 head of deer in Enfield Chase. The last wild boars which had been preserved, here and elsewhere, for the royal diversion, and had been, up to that time, allowed to ravage the cultivated

lands with their tusks, were for the most part slaughtered by the exasperated rustics in the course of the Civil War. It is said that the last grey badger in Enfield Chase was not killed till ten or eleven years after the accession of Queen Victoria.

Evelyn makes the following entry in his "Diary" with reference to a visit which he paid to Enfield. On June 2nd, 1676, he writes :—" I went with my Lord Chamberlaine to see a garden at Enfield towne, thence to Mr. Sec. Coventry's Lodge in the Chase. It is a very pretty place, the house commodious, the gardens handsome, and our entertainment very free, there being none but my lord and myselfe. That which I most wondered at was, that in the compass of twenty-five miles, yet within fourteen of London, there is not a house, barne, church, or building, besides three lodges. To this lodge are three great ponds and some few inclosures, the rest a solitarie desert, yet stor'd with not less than 3,000 deere. There are pretty retreats for gentlemen, especially for those who are studious and lovers of privacy."

In a survey of the manor of Enfield, taken in 1686, it is stated that on a former perambulation the Chase had been found to contain 7,600 acres, of which 500 had been since enclosed in Theobalds Park. This enclosure, as stated above, was made by James I. while he resided at Theobalds. Though at that time the Chase was well stocked with deer, the Parliamentary Army during the Civil War destroyed the game, cut down the trees, and let out the ground into small farms. In this state it remained until the Restoration, when young trees were planted, and the Chase was again stocked with deer.

Another survey was taken in 1698, in order to a fall of timber, by which several new "ridings" were to be formed, and a square lawn of 300 acres laid out for the deer to feed in. The "ridings," marked out when the Chase was to be divided into farms at the time of the Commonwealth, and still distinguished by hedges and ditches, were Cock-Fosters, and the Ridgeway from the gravel-pits by East Lodge to Ganna Corner.

Mr. Ford, in his "History of Enfield," says :— "The Chase was formerly considered to have been a sheep-walk belonging to the family of Coningsby, of Wales, one of whom having a complaint lodged against him for having too many sheep, brought up a parcel of goats, which did great damage. This circumstance, it seems, gave rise to the right of sheep-walk on the Chase annexed to certain farms in this neighbourhood for a certain time of the year. Norden says, 'there ariseth a profit unto

VIEW IN TRENT PARK.

the poore inhabitants there by the use of the Chase, where they have common of pasture for all kinde of cattle, pannage, and wood ;' but the parish, it seems, thought otherwise, finding itself overburthened by numerous and disorderly poor, who availed themselves of the privilege of the Chase to support dissolute lives of idleness and beggary. The deer were stolen and exposed for sale with the greatest audacity ; venison could be purchased cheaper than mutton. The poachers were sometimes transported, but at the expiration of their time returned to their old habits." In 1762 it is recorded in the *Gentleman's Magazine* "that one John Batt, of Potter's Bar, was committed to Bridewell for cutting young beech-trees on the Chase, and carrying them away in a cart. He was sentenced to be publicly whipped in the market-place at Enfield once every month during his imprisonment." The *Public Ledger*, 1764, also records the fact of a woman, "an old offender," being "conveyed in a cart from Bridewell to Enfield, and publicly whipped at the cart's tail by the common hangman, for cutting down and destroying wood in Enfield Chase."

In 1777 an Act of Parliament was passed for the purpose of dividing the Chase, and assigning allotments to such parishes and individuals as claimed right of common ; and in 1801 another Act was passed "for dividing and enclosing the open and common fields, common marshes, and lammas grounds, Chase allotments, and other commonable and waste lands within the parish ;" and the same "have been divided and allotted accordingly, among the tithe owners, lords of manors, and proprietors of freehold and copyhold lands, and others entitled thereto."[*] At the present time nearly the whole of the Chase is enclosed, and but little of its original appearance remains, the wildest parts being at Hadley Common,[†] Trent Park, Winchmore Hill Wood,[‡] and a portion of White Webbs Park. The deer, which, as shown above, were at one time very·numerous, were taken to the estate of the Earl of Bute, at Luton Park, in Bedfordshire. The last red deer killed here was shot by Mr. William Mellish, M.P., of Bush Hill Park, and its horns are now in the possession of Mr. Edward Ford, of Old Park. Still, it is clear that all indications of a Chase have not clean died out, for a woodcock was shot at Old

---

* Ford's "Enfield," p. 52.   † See *ante*, p. 328.   ‡ See *ante*, p. 346.

Park in January, 1874, and a bittern was taken on the banks of the Lea, not far from Ponder's End, in 1847.

The officers belonging to the Chase were—besides the Chancellor, the Receiver General, and the Attorney General of the Duchy of Lancaster—a Master of the Game, a Forester, a Ranger, Keepers, a Woodward, a Steward, a Bailiff, and Verderers, who were annually chosen in the King's Court of the Manor of Enfield, a sort of Supervisor of the Wood. The name of Verderers is still kept up in connection with Epping Forest, as we shall see presently.

There were on the Chase four ancient lodges, called respectively the East, the West, the North, and the South Bailies. These lodges were the official residences of the persons who were connected with the government of the Duchy of Lancaster, some of whom were Chancellors of the Court. These lodges were also used as hunting-seats during the time of Queen Elizabeth, James I., and Charles I.

In the preceding chapter we have spoken of Camlet Moat, now within the bounds of Trent Park, and almost in the centre of the Chase, as having been the subject of much antiquarian speculation. Camden says:—"Almost in the middle of the Chase there are the ruins and rubbish of an ancient house, which the common people from tradition affirm to have belonged to the Mandevilles, Earls of Essex." Lysons, however, considered the tradition to be destitute of any foundation, and suggested that the spot was merely "the site of the principal lodge, and the residence of the chief forester."

Trent Park, the seat of Mr. Bevan, consists of upwards of a thousand acres, and is still covered with such an abundance of timber as to give some idea of what the Chase must have been in early ages. Its charming vistas and forest scenery have been thus graphically described by Sir Walter Scott in the "Fortunes of Nigel:"—"The sun was high upon the glades of Enfield Chase, and the deer with which it abounded were seen sporting in picturesque groups among the ancient oaks of the forest, when a cavalier and a lady sauntered slowly up one of the long alleys which were cut through the park for the convenience of the hunters. . . The place at which he stopped was at that time little more than a mound, partly surrounded by a ditch, from which it derived the name of Camlet Moat. A few hewn stones were there which had escaped the fate of many others that had been used in building different lodges in the forest for the

IN BEECH HILL PARK. (*See page* 368.)

royal keepers. These vestiges marked the ruins of the abode of a once illustrious, but long-forgotten, family—the Mandevilles, Earls of Essex, to whom Enfield Chase and the extensive domains adjacent had belonged in elder days. A wild woodland prospect led the eye at various points through broad and apparently interminable alleys, meeting at this point as from a common centre."

A lease of this property was granted by George III. to his favourite physician, Richard Jebb, on whom he conferred a baronetcy. Dr. Jebb afterwards purchased the freehold; and on his building a residence here, the king gave it the name of Trent Place, "in commemoration of the great skill by which the life of his brother had been preserved in his severe illness at Trent, in the South Tyrol." On the death of Sir Richard Jebb the estate was sold to Lord Cholmondeley, and later on it had among its possessors Sir Henry Lushington. The mansion is a spacious brick structure, stuccoed and whitened, and its situation on gently rising ground, overlooking a broad extent of the park, is very fine.

Beech Hill Park, which lies near the western extremity of the Chase, bordering upon Hadley Common, comprises nearly 700 acres, which was granted to Mr. Francis Russell, a Fellow of the Royal Society, who was some time Secretary of the Duchy Court of Lancaster, and through whose suggestion, it is said, the final enclosure of the Chase was brought about. The house is placed on the brow of a gentle eminence, and, like that of Trent Park, it has the advantage of a fine stream of water flowing through the grounds.

The East Lodge is described in the survey of 1650 as "a brick building, covered with tiles." It was occasionally used by Charles I. as a hunting-seat. Towards the end of the last century the lodge was occupied by Lord Chancellor Loughborough, afterwards created Earl of Rosslyn; later on it was pulled down, and the present house built on its site. West Lodge, which was that occupied by Mr. Secretary Coventry, mentioned above as visited by Evelyn, was rebuilt in 1832, the house having become ruinous, and in danger of falling. South Lodge stands about a mile and a half west of Enfield Town, on the Ridgeway. It was for some years the occasional residence of the Earl of Chatham, to whom it was bequeathed, together with a legacy of £10,000. Mr. Tuff, in his "Historical Notices of Enfield," tells the following amusing story concerning the earl :—" Lord Chatham desired the owner of a windmill, which stood on a post on the top of Windmill-hill, to paint the whole body moving to the face of the wind, on that side next South Lodge, at his expense. The miller did so, but when his lordship looked out of the window and saw the windmill not painted, he sent for the miller, who declared it had been done agreeably to his lordship's direction. The earl pointed to the mill, when the miller informed him that the *wind had changed*, but that he was quite ready to paint that side also on the same terms ! The mill in question was pulled down many years ago, and the present one erected on its site."

Chase Lodge, Hill Lodge, and Claysmore, are smaller estates which have been at different times allotted out of the Chase.

Of Potter's Bar, which formed the extreme north-western limits of the Chase, we have spoken in our account of South Mimms,* to which parish the hamlet belongs ; and Southgate, which, as its name implies, was the southern limit of the royal demesne, has been also dealt with, together with its near neighbour, Winchmore Hill. †

The ancient Roman road, called Ermen, or Ermine, Street, lay through a part of the Chase in its passage to Hertford. From the Cripplegate or Moorgate of London, it passed through Newington, thence through several green lanes to the east of Hornsey, and having entered Enfield Chase, proceeded thence through Hatfield to Hertford. "This was the road (for the present north road was not then in existence) by which the Londoners marched, with King Alfred at their head, against the Danes, in the year 895, to a stronghold or fortification built by them at Hertford." ‡

Cock Fosters is a small village lying to the west of Trent Park, about four miles west from Enfield town, and two miles east from New Barnet railway-station. It was formed into an ecclesiastical parish in 1839. Christ Church, which was built in 1837, at the expense of Mr. Bevan, of Trent Park, is a small plain structure, with a tower and spire, and is profusely overgrown with ivy. The derivation of the name of Cock Fosters—or Forsters, as it is sometimes written—has been the subject of speculation among antiquarians. Mr. Thorne, in his "Environs of London," says, "there can be little doubt that Forsters is a corruption of *foresters* (in either the English or French form). The derivation of Cock is not so palpable. It has been suggested that it comes from *bicoque*, a small house, hut, or collection of huts. Cotgrave renders it *Bicoque*, a little paltry town ; and if the huts of the Chase

* See *ante*, p. 317.   † See *ante*, p. 345.
‡ Tuff's "Historical Notices of Enfield."

foresters and woodmen were collected here, the place may have been called *Bicoque Forestière;* but a more obvious explanation is that here may have been the house of the chief forester, *Coq de Forestières.*"

The roads round about here in times past were not the most inviting to travel in after midnight. Camlet Moat is said to have been the lurking-place of the notorious highwayman and robber, Dick Turpin, whose grandfather, one Nott, kept the "Rose and Crown," by the brook called "Bull Beggar's Hole," at Clay Hill. The moat is distant but a few miles from the scene of Turpin's exploits on Finchley Common, whence he could easily conceal himself in such a place in the then wild state of Enfield Chase.

As lately as December, 1832, in a lane near Enfield Chase, on the road between Enfield and Barnet, was committed a cruel murder on a Mr. B. C. Danby. For this a man named Johnson was executed. The spot where the murder was perpetrated was long marked by an inscription on the bark of a tree by the wayside.

Not only were the roads dangerous in consequence of the highwaymen and footpads who lurked about, but down to early in the present century they were in a very unfit condition for vehicular traffic. Mr. Ford relates that Lady Elizabeth Palk, who resided at Enfield Rectory, was accustomed, when she intended to call on Mrs. Elphinstone at East Lodge, to send out men two or three days in advance to fill the ruts with faggots, to enable her carriage to pass. "Within living memory," Mr. Ford adds, "it was possible to travel from Hadley Church through Enfield Chase, Epping and Hainault Forests, to Wanstead without ever leaving the green turf or losing sight of forest land."

It is singular that there should have been no "haunted house" in the parish of Enfield. "Formerly (says Bourne in his "Antiquities") almost every place had one. If a house was built in a melancholy situation, or in some old romantic manner, or if any particular accident had happened in it—a murder or a sudden death, or such like— to be sure that house had a mark set on it, and it was afterwards esteemed the habitation of a ghost." "The most diligent inquiry," observes Mr. Ford, in his work already quoted, "has been unsuccessful in tracing the vestige of one here, though the Chase was formerly notorious as the residence of witches. The Witch of Edmonton, in the fine drama of Ford and Dekker, was a true story; and the unfortunate old woman, who was condemned and executed for witchcraft in 1622, was a denizen of the Chase."

The estate of White Webbs, as stated above, lies at the north-eastern extremity of the Chase, and is of some historic interest, from its connection with the "Gunpowder Plot." Old White Webbs House stood on a portion of the grounds now belonging to Myddelton House,* which was of old known as Bowling Green House, and originally formed part of the manor of Worcesters and of Goldbeaters. In 1570 Queen Elizabeth granted White Webbs House to Robert Huicke, her physician. The house was, in the middle of the seventeenth century, the property of Dr. Brockenham; it afterwards came into the family of Garnault, and was pulled down about 1790. A tradition, which (says Lysons) is perhaps not much to be depended upon, states that White Webbs House was hired by the conspirators of the Gunpowder Plot for the purpose of watching the signal of their success. The tradition, however, observes Mr. Ford, "is fully substantiated by existing deeds, and by the following extracts from the documents of the State Paper Office, which also identify the locality beyond any doubt. In the confession of 'John Johnsonne (alias Guido Fawkes). he further saith that the Wednesday before his apprencon he went forthe of the towne to a house in Enfielde Chase, on this side of Theobalds, where he stayed till Sunday night following'" (9-10 November, 1665). The report to the Council of the search of White Webbs House says, "The search ended in the discovery of Popish books and relics, but no papers or munitions, and the house was found to be full of trap-doors and passages." In the examination of "James Johnson," it was stated by him that the house "had been taken of *Dr. Hewicke,* by his master, Mr. Meaze, of Berkshire (the Jesuit father Garnet), for his sister, Mrs. Perkins (*alias* Mrs. Ann Vaux); that Mrs. Vaux had spent a month there, and mass had been said by a priest, whose name deponent did not know."

The following paragraph, having reference to the connection of Old White Webbs House with the Gunpowder Plot, occurs in the "Works of that high and mighty Prince James I.," in the discourse on the Gunpowder Treason :—"Meanwhile Mr. Fawkes and myselfe alone (Winter's confession) brought some new powder, as suspecting the first to be *danke,* and conveyed it into the cellar, and set it in order, as we resolved it should stand. Then was the Parliament anew prorogued until the 5th of November, so as we all went down until some ten days before, when Mr. Catesby came up with Mr. Fawkes to an house by Enfield-chase, called

---

White Webbes, whither I came to them, and Mr. Catesby willed me to enquire whether the young Prince came to the Parliament : I tolde him I heard that His Grace thought not to be there. Then must wee have our horses, said Mr. Catesby, beyond the water, and provision of more company to surprise the Prince, and leave the Duke alone."

Mr. Ford mentions the fact that Mr. Bowles, the present owner of Myddelton House, has in his possession a deed, dated 1570, containing a grant of " all the vaultes and all the conduit and pipes of lead laid within the said Chase at the charges and expenses of our servant (Robert Huycke) for the leading and conveying water into the Newe Howse of our said servant, abuttinge in parte uppon the saide Chase, which mansion house is within the parish of Enfield, in our said co. of Midd.," and for supplying water to the mansion house, gardens, ponds, and orchards.

The site of old White Webbs extended across White Webbs Lane (formerly called Rome Road).

White Webbs House was pulled down towards the end of the last century, and the present mansion, bearing the same name, was built on another part of the estate, called White Webbs Farm, which had been purchased by Dr. Wilkinson, the grandfather of Mr. Henry Cox Wilkinson, the present owner. Of late years both the mansion and the park have been augmented ; the latter now comprises about 250 acres, 100 of which are woodland, and covered with old oaks and underwood, the remains of the original Chase, or forest.

In an open glade in the park stands a small brick building enclosing a circular tank, or well of pure water. This is the old " Conduit house," mentioned above as having been granted by Queen Elizabeth to her physician, Dr. Huicke, for the supply of his mansion-house at White Webbs.

An old ale-house, bearing the sign of " The King and the Tinker," in this lane probably retains some of the out-buildings. " With this little beer-shop," writes Mr. Ford, " is popularly identified the ballad of ' The King and the Tinker,' the incident of which is supposed to have occurred during the residence of James I. at Theobalds." Mr. Thorne, in his " Environs," however, says :—" The ballad of ' King James and the Tinkler ' is eminently a border ballad, and is popular throughout the northern counties ; *tinkler* is the northern term for a tinker, but was never used, as far as we know, in the south ; and in the received version of the ballad (though not in that printed by Mr. Ford), the tinkler says—

'The King's on the *border*, a chasing the deer.'

The ballad must, therefore, we fear, be disassoci-ated from Enfield, notwithstanding the beer-house sign." The line above referred to in Mr. Ford's version reads—

" The King is a-hunting the fair fallow deer,"

which, adds Mr. Thorne, " has hardly the old ballad ring." The term *tinkler* is, in Scotland and the border towns and villages, applied not merely to a " mender of pots and kettles," who in England is generally called a " tinker," but it is also used to denote any person who picks up a livelihood by tramping about from place to place, doing odd jobs of any kind, as chance might throw in his way.

Nevertheless, here is the old ale-house called " The King and the Tinker ; " and as local tradition has fixed upon it as being the scene of the incident described in the ballad, we reprint it *in extenso* :—

"KING JAMES AND THE TINKLER.

" And now, to be brief, let's pass over the rest,
  Who seldom or never were given to jest,
  And come to King Jamie, the first of our throne—
  A pleasanter monarch sure never was known.

" As he was a-hunting the swift fallow deer,
  He dropt all his nobles, and when he got clear,
  In hope of some pastime, away he did ride,
  Till he came to an ale-house hard by a wood-side,

" And there with a Tinkler he happened to meet,
  And him in kind sort he so freely did greet :
  ' Now pray thee, good fellow, what hast in thy jug,
  Which under thy arm thou dost lovingly hug ?'

" ' In truth,' said the Tinkler, ''tis nappy brown ale,
  And to drink to thy good health, faith, I will not fail—
  For although thy jacket looks gallant and fine,
  I hope that my two-pence is as good as thine.'

" ' Nay, by my soul, man, the truth shall be spoke ; '
  And straightway the monarch sat down for to joke ;
  He called for his pitcher, the Tinkler another,
  And so they went to it like brother and brother.

" While drinking, the King he was pleased to say,
  ' What news, honest fellow ? come tell me, I pray ; '
  ' There's nothing of news, except that I hear
  The King is a-hunting the fair fallow deer ;

" ' And truly I wish I so happy may be,
  That whilst they are hunting the King I may see ;
  For though I have travelled the land many ways,
  I never saw the King, sir, in all my old days.'

" The King, with a hearty brisk laugh, then replied,
  ' I tell thee, honest fellow, if thou canst but ride,
  Thou shalt get up behind me, and thee I will bring
  To the presence of Jamie, thy sovereign King.'

" ' Perhaps,' said the Tinkler, ' his Lord will be drest
  So fine that I shall not know him from the rest ; '
  ' I tell thee, honest fellow, when thou dost come there,
  The King will be covered, the nobles all bare.'

" Then up got the Tinkler, and likewise his sack,
  His budget of leather and tools at his back ;
  And when they came to the merry green wood,
  The nobles came round him, and bareheaded stood.

"The Tinkler then seeing so many appear,
Immediately whispered the King in the ear,
Saying, ' Since they are all clothed so gallant and gay,
Which is the King? come tell me, I pray.'

"The King to the Tinkler then made this reply—
' By my soul, man, it must be either you or I;
The rest are uncovered you see, all around.'
This said, with the budget he fell to the ground

"Like one that was frightened quite out of his wits,
Then up upon his knees he instantly gets,
Beseeching for mercy—the King to him said,
' Thou art a good fellow, so be not afraid;

"' Come, tell me thy name.'   ' It is John of the Vale,
A mender of kettles, and a lover of good ale.'
' Then rise up, Sir John, I will honour thee here,
And create thee a Knight of five hundred a year.'

"This was a good thing for the Tinkler indeed;
Then unto the Court he was sent with all speed,
Where great store of pleasure and pastime was seen
In the royal presence of both King and Queen."

The sign of " The King and the Tinker " is probably unique; it is not mentioned by Larwood, but sign-boards of a similar character are found in other parts of the country.   "The King and the Miller," for instance, at Mansfield, Notts, celebrates a like adventure of Henry II. and a merry rustic of that town.   Similar stories are told of different sovereigns—such as King John and the miller of Charlton,* after whom Cuckold's Point is said to have been named; of King Edward III. and the tanner of Drayton Basset; of King Henry VIII. and the Abbot of Canterbury; of James V. of Scotland (the " gude mon of Ballangeich "); of Henry IV. of France and the pig-merchant; of Charles V. of Spain and the cobbler of Brussels; of Joseph II.; of Frederick the Great; and even of Haroun-al-Raschid, who used to go about his dominions *incognito*, under the name of Il Bondocani.

There is an old proverb which says that—

" Cobblers and tinkers
Are the best ale-drinkers;"

and possibly this circumstance, be it real or not, may have something also to do with the sign.

CHAPTER XXXVIII.

ENFIELD HIGHWAY, PONDER'S END, AND THE RIVER LEA.

"The old Lea, that brags of Danish blood."—DRAYTON's *Polyolbion*.

Position and Extent of Enfield Highway—Population, &c.—The Lower North Road—Mr. Spencer and his Bride—Matthew Prior and John Morley—St. James's Church—Ponder's End—St. Matthew's Church—Lincoln House—Durants—The Manor of Suffolks—Enfield Wash—The Story of Elizabeth Canning, "Mother Wells," and the Gipsy Squires—Roselands—The Manor of Elsynge—The River Lea—Bull's Cross—Capels.

ENFIELD HIGHWAY—which, as we have stated in a previous chapter,* runs along the eastern division of this parish, from north to south—although of much more recent growth than Enfield Town, is in reality far out-numbering it in population—a state of things which may be accounted for by the fact of its having within its limits several large factories, and more especially the Royal Small Arms Factory, where, on the whole, upwards of 1,500 hands are employed, and of which we shall speak in a subsequent chapter.   According to the census returns for 1881 this division alone contains a population of more than 9,000 inhabitants.   The district comprises the hamlet of Ponder's End, Enfield Highway (proper), the Royal Small Arms Factory, and Frezywater.   Several narrow lanes and thoroughfares radiate from the main road on either side, bearing such names as South Street, Nag's Head Lane, Green Street, Carterhatch Lane, Enfield Wash, Hoe Lane, Welch's Lane (now Ordnance Road, Turkey Street, and Bullsmore Lane. Enfield Highway is the name given to that portion of the Cheshunt and Hertford road which, after passing through Edmonton, enters the parish of Enfield at Ponder's End, and running in almost a direct line due north, parallel with the Great Eastern Railway (Cambridge line), and for a distance of about two miles, leaves it just beyond Bullsmore Lane.   It is made up of the usual admixture of shops and private houses to be met with in villages that are located on main public roads—taverns and ale-houses, as a matter of course, somewhat predominating.

The thoroughfare occupies part of the track of the old Roman road called Ermine Street, described in the preceding chapter.   It is still the modern highway to the north-east, and is now known by the name of the Lower North Road.   It is needless to say that it presents marked differences to what it exhibited a century or so ago, although

* See *ante*, p. 350.

* See " Old and New London," Vol. VI., p. 233.

at that time it was the great northern road, and was the occasional scene of cavalcades and royal "progresses," such as might break the dull monotonous life of the inhabitants. For example, the villagers must have been astonished in December, 1755, at seeing Mr. (afterwards Lord) Spencer and his bride coming up to London from Althorpe, if Lady Hervey's letters are to be trusted, with three coaches-and-six and 200 horsemen. Lady Hervey adds that the country-folk armed

a memorial of his wife. All the windows are filled with stained glass, chiefly in memory of his family.

The hamlet of Ponder's End has lost much of its rural appearance since the formation of the Great Eastern line and the establishment of a railway-station in its vicinity. Besides gas and water works, and two or three large and tall factories, the place can boast of several inns and taverns, and, like most other suburban villages which have been invaded by the "railway king," villas and

PONDER'S END.

themselves with spades and pitchforks, fancying that it was either the Pretender or the King of France who had invaded them!

Along this road must have passed Matthew Prior and his friend John Morley, on their way to dine at the "Bull" Inn at "Hodsdon," *en route* to Down Hall, near Harlow, which had been presented to the poet by Harley, Earl of Oxford.

Enfield Highway was formed into a separate parish for ecclesiastical purposes in 1833. The church, dedicated to St. James, was built in 1831. It is in the Perpendicular style, and comprises a nave, with galleries, an apsidal sanctuary, and a chancel and transepts. The chancel and transepts, which are of Early English architecture, were added in 1864 by the late vicar, the Rev. John Harman, as

"genteel residences" are fast springing up in all directions. The church, dedicated to St. Matthew, erected in 1877, is a chapel-of-ease to St. James's, Enfield. It is built in the Early English style, and consists of a nave and north aisle.

On the southern side of Ponder's End, a little to the west of the high road, stands Lincoln House, which, according to Mr. Ford, is said to take its name from the Earls of Lincoln, of whom Henry and Thomas, the second and third earls, lived here at the beginning of the seventeenth century. In Gough's "Camden," it is stated that the house was the residence of the *Bishops* of Lincoln, "or of that other William of Wickham, bishop of that diocese, who was born here." Mr. Ford, however, says that William of Wickham was born in the manor-house of Honylands, or Pentriches, otherwise Capels, at the northern end of the parish, near Bull's Cross, and of which his father was lessee in the reign of Henry VIII. Lincoln House was a brick building, with heavy buttresses, and bore marks of antiquity. Under one of the windows, between two marble pillars, there was, in 1750, a tablet inscribed "R. L. 1520."

In the "Beauties of England and Wales" it is stated that "there was lately some painted glass remaining in the windows, containing, among other armorial bearings, the arms and quarterings of Howard, with a viscount's coronet, and the inscription 'Henry Howard, 1584.' The whole of this

whose daughter and heiress conveyed it in marriage to John Wrothe; and the manor of Durants, to which that of Gartons was at an early period annexed, descended to their son, William Wrothe, who died in 1408, after which it continued in the hands of the Wrothe family for many generations. Fuller, in his "Worthies," says:—"Sir Thomas Wrothe was of the Bedchamber, and a favourite of King Edward the Sixth, who (as I am informed) at his death passed out of the armes of him, his faithfull servant, into the embraces of Christ, his dearest Saviour. Soon after Sir Thomas found a great change in the English Court, but no alteration, as many did (to their shame), in his own

ROOM IN MOTHER WELLS' COTTAGE.

glass is now (1816) removed, and the building has been newly fronted; but the interior comprises several ancient decorated ceilings." From the above-mentioned arms the house appears to have belonged to Henry Howard, Viscount Bindon, the head of a branch of the ducal house of Norfolk. Other coats of arms in the windows were those of the Lord Keeper, Sir Thomas Coventry (1627), and of George Villiers, first Duke of Buckingham. Some of the rooms were wainscoted, apparently of the date of James I. Part of the house was burnt down a few years ago, but has been rebuilt.

Eastward of the high road, between Ponder's End and Green Street, stood the historic manor-house of Durants, or Durant's Harbour, which was burnt down at the end of the last century. In the reign of Edward I. the manor belonged to Richard de Plessitis; but in default of heirs male, it subsequently devolved upon Thomas Durant,

conscience, in preservation of which he was fain to fly beyond the seas." It was observable, he adds, that the family of this man, who went away for "his own conscience," was the only family in Middlesex, out of all those mentioned by Norden, which was not extinct in his time (1660). A curious letter from his son, Sir Robert Wrothe, who died in 1605, is preserved among the Lansdowne MSS., and printed by Mr. Ford in his "History of Enfield." As this letter vividly depicts the state of the country round about London, and particularly those parts of which we shall have occasion hereafter to speak in these pages, we take the liberty of quoting it:—

"Sir Robert Wrothe to Mr. Michael Hickes.— Intelligence concerning robbers who frequented Layton Heath [? Loughton], in Essex.

(MS. Lansd. 87, Art. 60, *orig.*)

"My very good frende, Mr. Hickes,—I am informed that now, towardes these darke evenings, there are sertaine lewde fellowes—sumtimes horsemen, sumtimes footemen—disguising themselves with beardes that they carry aboute them in their pockets, which doe frequente and use aboute Layton heath and at or about Snaresbrooke, in your brother Colstone's walke.   I have appoynted sum espiciall spyall of them to bewray them and to know them, either by theire horses apparell or otherwise, and I hope in time to have them discifared.   Yet for better surety thereof, I pray you lett me intreate you to speake to your brother Colstone, that with some secresy he woulde take such order with sum of the discreatest keepers he hath, that towardes eaveninges they woulde have an eye upone the heath and about Snaresbrooke for such kinde of persons, and to discry them by their horses or otherwise, if they can.   They come not above one or two in company untill they meete about the heath, and when they have obteyned that they come for, they sever themselves in the like manner; and sumtimes sum of them ride over by Temple Mill, where I pray you take likewise secret order with the miller that he woulde keepe his gate shute up in the nighte; besides sumtimes they ride over by Hackney; and yf they doe discry any of them, that I may have notice thereof, and I doubte not but to have them quickly apprehended, for I have notice of sum of their hauntes.   And so, with my commendations to your good wiffe, I will bid you farewell.   "Your assured frende,

"ROBERT WROTHE.

"Lucton, the 16th of October, 1599.

"One of them usethe to ride on a whit mare.   Let them have a diligent care if they doe see any such man.—To my verie loving friend Mr. Michaell Hickes,* at his house at Duckett, or elsewhere."

The family of Wrothe became extinct in 1673, on the death of Sir Henry Wrothe, the grandson of Sir Thomas, to whose exile, in the reign of Queen Mary, Fuller again refers in his dedication to Sir Henry of part of his "Church History":—"Hence it is that I have seen in your ancient house at Durance the crest of your armes (viz., a lion's head erased), with the extraordinary addition of sable wings, somewhat alluding to those of bats, to denote your ancestour's dark and secret flight for his safety.   However, God brought him home again on the silver wings of the dove, when peaceably restoring him in the dayes of Q. Elizabeth to his large possessions."

On the death of Sir Henry Wrothe, the manor was sold by his executors to Sir Thomas Stringer, whose son William bequeathed the property to his wife Margaret, daughter of the celebrated Judge Jeffreys, who was a frequent visitor here.   It afterwards underwent a few changes of ownership, either by purchase or otherwise; and at the end of the last century it passed into the hands of Newell Connop, Esq, in whose family it still remains.

The entrance to the old moated manor-house was by a bridge of two arches and a large gateway, with a postern, &c.   From the description of the building in Dr. Robinson's "Enfield," the house

seems to have formed a quadrangle, of which part of the north and west sides—standing in 1775—were built of brick; and at the south end stood a chapel, on the south and west sides of which were small Gothic windows with iron bars, and at the north end a square window, with round pillars in the middle and at the sides, and a square tower, with a spiral stone staircase.   "On the east side," wrote Dr. Robinson in 1823, "there was an arch which was stopped up, with some Saxon (i.e., Norman) capitals much defaced; the whole was built of clunch, brick, and masses of pebbles, cemented together with mortar, and plastered over.   Over this building was a room, then used as a pigeon-house.   This chapel appeared to be the most ancient part of the house, the rest probably having been built about the latter end of the fifteenth or the beginning of the sixteenth century, and was pulled down about the year 1776 by Mr. Poe.   At the south-west extremity of the moat, and without it, there was part of another square brick building, with an arched entrance, and a circular room with a fire-place.   Behind the chapel there was a long square canal and the garden, which had been divided into two parts by a brick wall; there are also the remains of two square piers of a gate, on which were two eagles, with wings displayed, holding shields with three eagles' heads on the face.   At right angles with this wall there were parts of others, or rather, two detached walls, near which were steps to the moat.   These two walls were parallel with the north side of the house, which appeared to have formed the south side of the quadrangle, in the centre of which stood a dial on a square block of stone mounted on brick-work.

"On the west side of the moat there was a summer-house, with a balcony and weathercock, surmounted by a flying-horse on a pyramid of ironwork, with Neptune, Bacchus, &c., painted on the west front of the building.   From this summer-house there was an avenue to the road."

The manor of Suffolks, which was also situated near Ponder's End, was, in the fifteenth century, held under the Crown by Sir R. Parr, Comptroller of the Household.   At the end of the last century it passed to Mr. Newell Connop, the then owner of the manor of Durants, with which it became merged.

Enfield Wash is the name now given to that portion of the main road which lies immediately beyond Enfield Highway.   The Wash, observes Mr. Thorne, in his "Environs of London," "owes its name to the little stream which, rising in the Chase, here crossed the road, and spreading out, made the wash, through which horses and carriages had to flounder, but which is now carried under it,

---

* Mr. (afterwards Sir Michael) Hickes, was Burghleys secretary.

and turning to the south-east, falls into the Lea a little below the ordnance factory."

On the east side of the high road at Enfield Wash, at the corner of the lane leading to the ordnance factory railway-station, stands the cottage of "Mother" Wells, a gipsy, once so famous as the scene of Elizabeth Canning's real or fictitious imprisonment, which excited the kingdom for months in 1753–54, divided society into two parties, the "Egyptians" and the "Canningites," and called into existence a whole crop of ephemeral publications: in fact, quite a literature, nearly fifty pamphlets in all, and not far short of twenty portraits, views, etchings, and a plan and elevation of the cottage itself. A ground plan and interior view of the cottage appear in the *Gentleman's Magazine*, vol. xxiii., pp. 306–7, and also in Dr. Robinson's "History of Enfield." The cottage remains substantially the same as it was a century and a half ago. It is a plain wooden-fronted structure, of two storeys, and with a window on each side the door—just such a house as would be naturally the residence of a curate in a country village. The door or window from which Canning effected her escape into the lane is still there, and so is a part of the loft in which she was kept. It is understood that the house will soon be pulled down.

Horace Walpole writes, in a letter to the Countess of Ailesbury, Oct. 10, 1761 :—" I am in such a passion, I cannot tell you what I am angry about—why, about virtue and Mr. Pitt : two arrant cheats, gipsies. I believe he was a comrade of Elizabeth Canning when he lived at Enfield Wash."[*]

The story may be briefly summed up as follows :—Elizabeth Canning, a servant girl about eighteen years of age, went, with the consent of her master, to visit a relation on New Year's Day, 1753. She did not return, nor was anything heard concerning her for nearly a month, at the expiration of which time she went to her mother's house in an emaciated and wretched condition, and accounted for her long disappearance by declaring that she had been "violently assaulted in Moorfields by two men, who had robbed her of her money, and dragged her away into the country along the Hertfordshire road, and that at length they carried her to the house of one Mother Wells, at Enfield Wash, where she said one Mary Squires, a gipsy, and two girls were in the kitchen; and where she had been confined till the day of her return." During the whole time of her confinement, she asserted that she had existed upon a few

crusts of bread and a pitcher of water, and that she had effected her escape by jumping out of a window. In stating the articles of which she had been robbed, she accused Squires of cutting away and taking her stays, and that a young woman named Virtue Hall stood by, and witnessed the act.

In consequence of these charges, Squires, Hall, and Wells, were apprehended, and taken before a magistrate. Hall solemnly denied all knowledge of any such transaction having happened since she had been in Wells' house, and she was discharged; but Squires was committed to prison for the robbery, and Wells for aiding and abetting. They were tried at the Old Bailey, and the former was sentenced to be hanged. Many doubts, however, arose as to the veracity of Canning's depositions, and inquiries took place, which were laid before the king, who referred the case to the consideration of the Attorney and Solicitor General. In the result, the tables were turned : the gipsy received his Majesty's pardon, and Elizabeth Canning was tried and convicted of perjury ; but on quitting prison she returned to England, and inherited a legacy left to her by an old lady of Newington Green, who believed in her innocence. She also still commanded so much sympathy, if not credit, that a subscription was got up to enable her to emigrate to America, where she married a wealthy planter. She died about the year 1773.

Wells came back to Enfield, where she died a pauper, as appears from the register, in 1763. Mary Squires, the gipsy, died in 1762, and was buried at Farnham, Surrey, being followed to the grave by several "Egyptians" as mourners.

Roselands, on the south side of Turkey Street, is an estate some fifty acres in extent, with a goodly mansion, and has been in the possession of the family of the present owner for many years.

The manor of Elsynge, or Norris, according to Mr. Ford's "Enfield," appears to have no connection, beyond its name, with Elsynge Hall. It is said to have been situated in Ordnance Road, and in the middle of the sixteenth century was held under the Crown by a family named Wilforde.

The river Lea, as above stated, forms the eastern boundary of this division of the parish of Enfield. "It begynnethe (says Lambarde) near Whitchurche, and from thence passing by Hertforde, Ware, and Waltham, openethe into the Thames at Ham, in Essex, whence this place is at this day called Lee-mouth. It hath of long tyme borne vessels from London twenty myles towards the head, for in the tyme of King Alfrede the Danes entered Leymouth, whence King Alfrede espied that the channell of the ryver might be in

---

[*] Mr. Pitt lived, however, as stated in the preceding chapter, at Enfield Chase.

such sorte weakened that they should want water to returne. He caused, therefore, the water to be abated by two greate trenches, and setting the Londonners upon them, he made their batteil wherein they lost four of their capitaines. Not long after they were so pressed that they forsoke all, and left their shippes as a prey to the Londonners, which breakyne some and burninge other, conveyed the rest to London."

The old and irregular course of the river is now of little use as a means of transit, having long ago been superseded by the Lea and Stort Navigation.

A curious celt was found some years ago in the Marsh at Enfield, twelve feet below the surface. It is figured in the *Gentleman's Magazine*, 1807.

The hamlet of Bull's Cross, which lies on the northern side of the parish, and in a bend of the New River, about half a mile westward of Enfield Highway, is said to have derived its name from an old cross which formerly stood there. In a deed of conveyance of land in this locality to one John Fforde (*temp.* Edward IV., 1483), it is called "Bedell's Cross." Chapel House, the residence of the Warrens, is situate at Bull's Cross, near the site of the old manor-house of Capels, *alias* Honeylands and Pentriches, which were formerly part of the possessions of Sir Giles Capel, who, in exchange for other lands, conveyed them to the Crown in 1547. The old mansion, together with the estate, was sold by Queen Elizabeth in 1562 to one William Horne, a merchant, and after passing through the hands of various successive purchasers, became, at the end of the last century, the property of the late Mr. Rawson H. Boddam, some time Governor of Bombay. Mr. Boddam pulled down the old manor-house, reserving little more than the stables, and transferred its name of Capel House to his own villa, which is said to occupy the site of the outbuildings of the palace of James I. at Theobalds. The old manor-house stood near a field, now called North Field, where are still the remains of an old garden, with some remarkable trees.

CHAPTER XXXIX.

THEOBALDS.

" You see these lifeless stumps of aspen wood :
Some say that they are beeches, others elms.
These were the Bower, and here a mansion stood,
The finest palace of a hundred realms !
The Arbour does its own condition tell :
You see the stones, the fountain, and the stream,
But as to the great Lodge, you might as well
Hunt half a day for a forgotten dream."—WORDSWORTH'S *Hart Leap Well.*

Situation of Theobalds, and History of the Manor—The Estate Purchased by Sir William Cecil, afterwards Lord Burleigh—James I. at Theobalds—Entertainment to Christopher IV., King of Denmark—Narrow Escape of King James—His Death Description of the Palace and Gardens—Demolition of the Palace—Present Condition of the Estate.

PASSING from Enfieldin to the neighbouring parish of Cheshunt, we cross the border-line which separates the two counties of Middlesex and Herts. Before proceeding with a detailed account of that parish, however, it may be as well to bring before our mind's eye the regal domain of Theobalds, with its magnificent palace—once the favourite residence of the great Lord Burleigh, and afterwards of James I.

The estate—the name of which in ancient documents is variously written Theobals, Tibbolds, or Thebaudes (supposed to be the name of some previous owner)—immediately adjoined, and indeed included, part of Enfield Chase, and the manor of Capels at Bull's Cross, as mentioned at the end of the preceding chapter. The manor was formerly called *Cullynges*, and in the fourteenth century belonged to one William Attemore, of Cheshunt, who, being indebted to William de Tongge in the sum of £101, made over to him this manor, together with an estate named Le Mores, and from him it obtained the name of Tongge. It was afterwards named Thebaudes, and under that appellation was granted, in 1441, by the Crown to John Carpenter, Master of St. Anthony's Hospital, in London, and others, to hold "by the annual rental of a bow valued at 2s., and a barbed arrow, value 3d." The manor subsequently passed through various hands, until it was bought by Sir William Cecil (afterwards Lord Burleigh), from Robert Burbage of Theobalds, in the third year of Elizabeth. Robert Burbage was grandson of a William Burbage, who married Cicely, daughter and heiress of Sir Robert Green of Theobalds, whose mother was a daughter and co-heir of Sir John Cley, also of Theobalds, which would appear, as far back as 1450, to have had a character for feasting and revelry.

Sir William Cecil had been twice member of Parliament, Master of Requests, and Secretary of State to Edward IV. and Queen Elizabeth. In 1570 he increased the estate by the purchase of Cheshunt Park from Mr. Harrington, a fact which is duly entered in Sir William's Diary for the above year.

The original house at this time is supposed to have been placed on a small piece of rising ground, still visible. But in the summer of 1564, Queen Elizabeth having honoured him with a visit, and probably having expressed her intention of repeating it, he conceived the plan of enlarging the house, so as to entertain his royal mistress on subsequent occasions with becoming magnificence. He therefore erected a more spacious mansion, adorning it with beautiful gardens, and surrounding it with a moat filled with water, and wide enough for a pleasure-boat to ply between the "tall flag-flowers" and the turreted walls. The palace and grounds were completed by September, 1571, when the queen visited him again, and was presented with "a copy of verses" and a "portrait of the house." Elizabeth appears to have taken a particular fancy for Theobalds—probably from its proximity to the Chase at Enfield and to Waltham Forest, where she could enjoy the pleasures of hunting—for her visits were pretty frequent. Nor did her Majesty come alone. In 1583 she was attended by a large retinue, and stayed four days; the Earls of Leicester and Warwick, the Lord Admiral (Lord Howard), Lord Hunsdon, Sir Christopher Hatton, and Sir Francis Walsingham, were there with her. In the "Life of Lord Burleigh," "The Compleat Statesman," commonly known as "The Diary of a Domestic," it is written, "Her Majestie sometimes had strangers and ambassadors come to see her at Theobalds: where she hath byn sene in as great royalty, and served as bountifully and magnificently as at any other time or place, all at his lordship's chardg: with rich shows, pleasant devices, and all manner of sports could be devised, to the great delight of her Majestie and her whole traine."

Early in the summer of 1592, during one of her "progresses," the queen paid a visit to this place. It is thus mentioned in a letter from one of his friends to Sir Robert Sidney:—"I suppose you have heard of her Majesty's great entertainment at Theobalds; of her knighting Mr. Robert Cecil, and of the expectation of his being advanced to the Secretaryship. But so it is, as we say in Court, that the knighthood must serve for both." ("Sidney Papers.")

As time went on wealth and honour multiplied upon Cecil. The queen created him Baron Burleigh, and she honoured him with her presence at Theobalds no less than a dozen times. Lord Burleigh entertained her Majesty most sumptuously, each visit, it is said, putting him to the expense of some £2,000 or £3,000. Some idea may be formed of his lordship's style of living from the fact that he had in his train twenty gentlemen, each with £1,000 a year. Indeed, it might truly be said of Theobalds in his day—

"Here he lives in state and bounty,
    Lord of Burleigh, fair and free;
Not a lord in all the county
    Is so great a lord as he."

Lord Burleigh was not a man who thought that greatness consisted in living in a great house; and although his business was much at Court, still he felt he had duties at Cheshunt, and he fulfilled them heartily: relieving the poor, and maintaining, at a cost of £4,000 a year, a style of living which £40,000 a year certainly could not match at the present time. The usual expense of his house-keeping at Theobalds was £80 per week; his stables cost him a thousand marks (£666 13s. 4d.) per annum. The sum of £10 per week was allotted to setting the poor to work in his garden; and 20s. a week was distributed by the vicar of Cheshunt as his almoner.

In the "Diary of a Domestic" it is said in respect of Theobalds that the gardens, fountains, and walks were perfected most costly, beautifully, and pleasantly, where one might walk two miles in the walks before coming to the end. "The house at first," says the "Domestic," "he meant for a little pile, as I heard him say; but after he came to entertain the queen so often there, he was forced to enlarge it, rather for the queen and her great train, and to give work to the poor, than for pomp and glory, for he ever said it would be too big for the small living he could leave his son." Lord Burleigh's character is summed up by his biographer as follows:—"His nature, though cold, was not mean or sordid, nor his heart narrow or selfish; neither, with all his firmness (which some might call sternness), was his temper unkind, or his manners harsh, but the contrary; in thirty years together he was seldom seen angry. He had his children, grandchildren, and great-grandchildren ordinarily at his table. If he might ride privately in his garden on his little mule, or lie for a day or two in his little lodge at Theobalds, secluded from business or too much company, he thought this his greatest and only happiness." At length a heavy loss befel him, and his second wife, Mildred, with whom he had lived on affectionate terms for forty-three years, passed away. He felt lonely and desolate in the midst of shows and tournaments; and his depression of spirits, coupled with the infirmities of old age, brought him to his end in 1598, and in his seventy-eighth year.

At his death Theobalds and the neighbouring estates passed into the possession of his youngest son, Sir Robert Cecil, who became Earl of Salisbury soon after the accession of James I. He not

The king had dined early in the day with Sir Henry Cocks at Broxbourne, and was accompanied by Sir Edward Denny, High Sheriff of Essex, and many of the Scottish and English nobility. An eye-witness of the reception, John Savile, thus describes the scene :—" As his Highness was espied coming towards Theobalds, the concourse of people was so frequent, every one desiring a sight of him, that it were incredible to tell of. And it was wonderful to see the infinite number of horse-

OLD THEOBALDS PALACE.
(*From an Engraving in the "Gentleman's Magazine," 1836. See page 384.*)

only succeeded to his father's country seat, but, like him, held the highest offices of state. He became Prime Minister to Queen Elizabeth, and was confirmed in that office by King James. Although the talents of Sir Robert were not equal to those of his father, yet he was the ablest statesman of his time. In three successive years he was made Baron of Essenden, Viscount Cranbourne, and Earl of Salisbury. In order to conciliate the favour of the new sovereign, Sir Robert embraced the earliest opportunity of honouring him. Accordingly, when his Majesty came from Scotland to take possession of the throne of England, in May, 1603, Sir Robert Cecil gave him a noble reception and princely entertainment at Theobalds.

men and footmen that went from the city of London that day thitherwards, and likewise from the counties of Kent, Surrey, Essex, and Middlesex, besides other counties. . . . When we were come to Theobalds, we understood his Majesty to be within the compass of three-quarters of a mile from the house. At which tidings we divided ourselves into three parts, each one taking a place of special note, to see what memorable accidents might happen within his compass : one standing at the upper end of the Walk, the second at the upper end of the first court, and the third (myself) at the second court's door ; and we made choice of a gentleman of good sort to stand in the court that leads into the hall, to take notice what was said or done by his Highness to the nobility of our land, or said or done by them to his Majesty, and to let us understand of it. All which accidents, as they happened in their several places, you shall hear in as few words as may be.

"Thus, then, for his Majesty's coming up the Walk. There came before him some of the nobility, some Barons, Knights, Esquires, Gentlemen, and others—amongst whom was the Sheriff of Essex and most of his men, the trumpets sounding next before his Highness, sometimes one,

answer that 'he should be heard, and have justice.'

"At the entrance to that court stood many noblemen, among whom was Sir Robert Cecil, who there meeting his Majesty, conducted him into his house; all which was practised with as great applause of the people as could be—hearty prayers and throwing up of hats.

"His Majesty had not stayed above an hour in his chamber, but hearing the multitude thronging so fast into the uppermost court to see his Highness, as his Grace was informed, he showed himself

THE MAZE AT THEOBALDS. (*See page* 382.)

sometimes another; his Majesty not riding continually betwixt the same two noblemen, but sometimes with one and sometimes with another, as seemed best to his Highness; the whole nobility of our land and Scotland round about him, observing no place of superiority, but all bareheaded; all of whom alighted from their horses at their entrance to the first court, save only his Majesty, who alone rode along still, with four noblemen laying their hands upon his steed, two before and two behind. In this manner he came till he come to the court's door, where I myself stood, where he alighted from his horse, from which he had not gone ten princely paces but there was delivered to him a petition by a young gentleman; his Majesty returning his gracious

openly out of his chamber window by the space of half an hour together. After which time, he went into the labyrinth-like gardens to walk, where he recreated himself in the meanders, compact of bays, rosemary, and the like overshadowing his walk, to defend him from the heat of the sun, till supper time. At which there was such plenty of provision for all sorts of men in their due place as struck me with admiration.

"And first, to begin with, the ragged regiment, and such as were debarred the privilege of any court, these were so sufficiently rewarded with beef, veal, mutton, bread, and beer, that they sang 'Holy day' every day, and kept a continual feast. As for the poor maimed and distressed soldiers, which repaired thither for maintenance, the wine, money, and meat which they had in very bounteous sort, hath been a sufficient spur to cause them to blaze it abroad since their coming to London : whose thankfulness is not altogether unknown to myself, some of whom, hearing that I was about to publish this small 'Remembrance,' made means to me to give me true information of such princely exhibition as they daily received during the time of his Majesty's abode at Theobalds."

The king appears to have won golden opinions during his stay at Theobalds by publishing a proclamation ordering that the price of victuals, such as meat, bread, butter, and cheese, should not be raised to exorbitant prices within the verge of his court.   He arrived on Tuesday, the 3rd of May, and proceeded on to London, by way of Stamford Hill, on Saturday, the 7th ; and it is on record that he spent the intervening Wednesday in a visit to Enfield Chase.

In 1606 the earl gave a second entertainment to his sovereign, and to Christopher IV., King of Denmark, who stayed with him four days.   The king was so delighted with Theobalds, and its convenient situation for his favourite amusement of hunting, that he desired to become possessed of this noble mansion, and make it his principal place of abode.   He therefore gave in exchange for it the more valuable mansion of Hatfield, and shortly after commenced the work of improving and embellishing Theobalds by enlarging the park, apportioning, as we have already seen, a good slice of Enfield Chase,* with parts of Northaw and Cheshunt Common.   The king at that time enclosed Theobalds with a brick wall ten miles in circumference, part of which wall still remains in the grounds of Albury House, and other parts at Bury Green and Cuffley.

The scene which presented itself at Theobalds during the feastings and masks in honour of the visit of Christian IV. has been described by one of the guests in the following terms :—"After dinner the representation of Solomon and his Temple, and the coming of the Queen of Sheba, was made, or (as I may say better) was meant to have been made.   The lady who did play the queen's part did carry most precious gifts to both their Majesties, but forgetting the steps arising to the canopy, overset her caskets into his Danish Majesty's lap, and fell at his feet, though I rather think it was in his face.   Much was the hurry and confusion ; cloths and napkins were at hand to make all clean.   His Majesty then got up, and

would dance with the Queen of Sheba ; but he fell down, and was carried to an inner chamber.   The entertainment and show went forward, and most of the presenters went backward or fell down : wind did so occupy their upper chambers.   Now did appear, in rich dresses, Faith, Hope, and Charity.   Hope did essay to speak, but wine did render her endeavours so feeble that she withdrew.   Faith was then all alone, for I am certain she was not joined with good works, and left the court in a staggering condition.   Charity came to the king's feet ; she then returned to Hope and Faith, who were both sick in the lower hall."

Theobalds was exchanged for Hatfield House, with Robert, first Earl of Salisbury, by James I., in 1607, and in 1614 his Majesty received a second visit from the King of Denmark, and entertained him for fifteen days with an uninterrupted succession of feasting and diversions.   Fond as the king was of hunting—so fond that the people used to say, " God's peace be with you, as King James said to his hounds "—he was a bad rider, and often thrown.   Thus, " when staying at Theobalds in the depth of winter, he rode out one day after dinner, and his horse stumbling, he was cast into the New River.   The ice broke, and in plunged his august Majesty head foremost, while nothing but his boots remained visible.   It would have gone ill with him that day had not Sir Richard Young alighted, and ran to the rescue.   His attendants had to empty him, like an inverted cask, of the river water he had drunk so freely against his will ; and a warm bed at Theobalds soon restored him to his pleasures and follies."*

From Ellis's " Letters " we learn that James did many wicked, cracked-brained things at Theobalds, for he had " fools, fiddlers, and master-fools ; " and Jesse tells us how some called him " Old wife," and his minions addressed him as " Your sowship ; " that the ladies of his court rolled about intoxicated, and he himself was carried off to bed, after having proposed five-and-thirty healths ; how oaths were never off his lips, nor cowardice and hypocrisy ever out of his heart ; and how, as the counterpart of all his vice and foolery, he translated the Psalms, wrote books of piety, and welcomed bishops to his presence as warmly as if they had been buffoons.   One of these was Joseph Hall, Bishop of Norwich.   He had previously been curate of Waltham Abbey, and he preached several times before James and his court at Theobalds.   Laud notes in his " Diary," September 17th, 1609:

---

* Ellis's Letters, "Joseph Meade to Sir Martin Stuteville, January 11th, 1622."

"My first sermon before King James at Theobalds."

James died at Theobalds on the 27th of March, 1625, and the blood was hardly cold in his veins when a knight-marshal was seen issuing from the palace to proclaim his successor. His name was Sir Edward Zouch, and when he reached the court-gate, and silence had been secured by the heralds, he solemnly proclaimed James's son Charles as king, but by an unfortunate and, as many thought, ominous slip of the tongue, instead of styling the new sovereign "the rightful and *indubitable* heir," he used the words "rightful and *dubitable* heir," and was corrected in his error by the secretary.

March 27th, 1625.—Laud tells us in his "Diary" that whilst preaching at Whitehall this day he heard the news of the death of James I. "The king died at Theobalds about three-quarters of an hour after eleven in the forenoon. He breathed forth his soul most religiously, and with great constancy of faith and courage. That day, about five o'clock, Prince Charles was solemnly proclaimed king. God grant to him," adds Laud, "a prosperous and happy reign!" Prayers and pious wishes, it would seem, are not always fulfilled. At Theobalds Laud did homage to Charles I. on being made Bishop of Bath and Wells.

On the day following the death of King James, Charles took coach at Theobalds with Buckingham, and went to London, and was proclaimed at Whitehall and Cheapside. The usual route by which the king went from London to Theobalds may still be traced by the names of streets on the north side of Holborn: namely, Kingsgate Street, King Street, King's Road, and Theobalds Road.

Theobalds continued a royal residence till the commencement of the Civil War, and to this place Charles retired when he found himself no longer safe at Westminster. From here, in July, 1635, he wrote to the Earl of Salisbury to obtain a supply of food for his Majesty's deer in the park from the adjoining parishes, for, owing to great drought, Cheshunt could not furnish a sufficient quantity of hay and oats. Here the king received the petition from both houses of Parliament in 1645, and from hence he, a short time afterwards, set out for the north, and raised aloft his standard at Nottingham. During the contest between the king's forces and the Parliamentarians, the palace was plundered and very much defaced, and the manor appears to have been parcelled out among the officers of the Parliamentary army.

Norden, in his account of Hertfordshire in the reign of Elizabeth, states that he found the palace of "Thibauldes, or Theobalde," so vast a subject that he despaired of being able to do it justice. "To speake," he says, "of the state and beuty thereof at large as it deserveth, for curious buildinges, delightfull walkes, and pleasant conceites, within and without, and other thinges very glorious and ellegant to be seene, would challenge a great portion of this little treatise ; and therefore, leaste I should come shorte of that due commendation that it deserveth, I leave it, as indeed it is, a princely seat."

In a survey of the house, taken in 1650, when it was being pulled down, it was stated to consist of two principal quadrangles, besides the Dial Court, the Buttery Court, and the Dove-house Court, in which the offices were situated. The Fountain Court, so called from a fountain of black and white marble in the centre, was a quadrangle, eighty-six feet square, on the east side of which was a cloister eight feet wide, with seven arches. On the ground-floor of this quadrangle was a spacious hall paved with Purbeck marble, and the roof arched with carved timber of curious workmanship. On the same floor were the Lord Holland's, the Marquis of Hamilton's, and the Lord Salisbury's lodging-rooms (for the last-mentioned nobleman was made keeper of Theobalds House by King James in 1619), the council chamber, and the chamber for the king's waiters. On the second floor was the Presence Chamber, "wainscoted with carved oak, painted of a liver colour, and richly gilded, with antique pictures over the same ; the ceiling full of gilded pendants, setting forth the room with great splendour ; there were large windows, and several coats-of-arms set in the same." These windows opened south on the walks in the great garden leading to the gate going into the park, where was an avenue of trees a mile long. There was also the Privy Chamber, the Withdrawing Room, the King's Bedchamber, and a gallery 123 feet long by twenty-one feet broad, "wainscoted with oak, and paintings over the same of divers cities, rarely painted, and set forth with a frett seelinge, with divers pendants, roses, and fleurs-de-lys, painted and gilded with gold, also divers large stagges' heads sett round the same, and fastened to the sayd roome, which are an excellent ornament to the same." The windows of this gallery looked "north into the park, and so to Cheshunt." On an upper floor were the Lord Chamberlain's lodgings, my lord's withdrawing chamber, and several other apartments.

Near the Chamberlain's lodgings, on the east, was a leaded walk, 62 feet in length and 11 in breadth, with an arch of freestone over it ; "which sayd arch and walk," says the Survey, "looking eastward into the Middle Court, and into the highway leading from London to Ware, standeth high, and may easily be discerned by passengers and travellers, to their delight." On the west of the Lord Chamberlain's lodgings was another walk of the same dimensions, looking westward into the Fountain Court. At the corners of these walks stood "fower high, fair, and large towers, covered with blue slate, with a lyon and vaines on the top of each, and in the walk over the hall, in the midst of the fowre corners, one faire and large turrett, in the fashion of a lanthorne, made with timber of excellent workmanship, curiouslie wrought, standinge a great height, with divers pinacles at each corner, wherein hangeth twelve bells for chiminge, and a clocke with chimes of sundrie worke." The walk from the lower gate up to the middle of the Fountain Court is described as leading "through the severall courtes, so that the figure of Cupid and Venus (which stood between the pillars of the fountain) maye easily be seene from the highway when the gates are open." This walk, continues the Survey, "is so delightful and pleasant, facing the middle of the house, and the severall towers, turretts, windowes, chimneyes, walkes, and balconies, that the like walke, for length, pleasantness, and delight, is rare to be seene in England."

The Middle Court was a quadrangle 110 feet square, having on the south side the Queen's Chapel (with windows of stained glass), her presence chamber, privy chamber, bed chamber, and coffer chamber. The prince's lodgings were on the north side; on the east side was a cloister, over which was a green gallery, over 100 feet in length by 12 in breadth, "excellently well painted round with the severall shires in England, and the armes of the noblemen and gentlemen in the same." Over this gallery was a leaded walk (looking eastward towards the Dial Court and the highway), on which were two "loftie arches of bricke, of no small ornament to the house, and rendering it comely and pleasant to all that passed by." On the west of the quadrangle was another cloister of five arches, over which were the duke's lodgings, and over them the Queen's Gallery, 109 feet by fourteen feet.

On the south side of the house stood "a large open cloister, built upon severall large faire pillars of stone arched over with seven arches, with a faire raill and balisters, well painted with the Kinges and Queenes of England, and the pedigree of the old Lord Burleigh and divers other ancient families, with paintings of many castles and battailes, with divers superscriptions on the walls." This cloister was standing in 1765, and the mutilated remnants

of the "pedigrees," as they then existed, were engraved for Nichols's "Progresses of Queen Elizabeth." The whole house was built, as the Survey states, of excellent brick, with coins, jambs, and cornices of stone. "The basement of the house," observes Mr. John C. Earle, in an account of the palace published in 1869, "was faced with fine ashlared limestone, and the cornice, of which a small portion remains, was of the Doric order. The upper storeys were of fine red brick, divided from one another by stone cornices. From what remains of these cornices, it appears that the upper portion of the edifice was of the Ionic or Corinthian order; and it is highly probable that the three classical orders—Doric, Ionic, and Corinthian—were used one above the other, as in many buildings of the same period—Burleigh House, for example, the schools at Oxford, and the second quadrangle of Merton College."

Paul Hentzner, a German traveller, has left us the following description of the gardens of Theobalds, as they appeared in 1598, just after the death of Lord Burleigh :—"Here are great variety of trees and plants; labyrinths made with a great deal of labour; a *jet d'eau*, with its basin of white marble; and columns and pyramids of wood and other materials up and down the garden. After seeing these, we are led by the gardener into the summer-house, in the lower part of which, built semi-circularly, are the twelve Roman emperors in white marble, and a table of touchstone; the upper part of it is set round with cisterns of lead, into which the water is conveyed through pipes, so that fish may be kept in them, and in summer time they are very convenient for bathing; in another room for entertainment very near this, and joined to it by a little bridge, was an oval table of red marble."

In addition to the great gardens were the priory gardens, with other enclosures for pheasants, aviaries, and menageries, for James was very fond of wild beasts, and had a collection of them worthy of a Zoological Garden. In one of his letters to Buckingham, when the latter was at Madrid, we find him inquiring about the "elephants, camels, wild asses," &c. He had always a large camel-house at Theobalds, whilst the tennis-court, stables, kennels, and falconry, were on a scale of magnitude proportionate to the palace.

In the gardens of Theobalds was one of those curious contrivances called mazes, or labyrinths, such as we have seen at Hampton Court.* "In the reigns of Henry VIII. and Elizabeth," observes a writer in the *Archæological Journal* (Vol. xv.,

---

* See *ante*, p. 171.

p. 228), "mazes were much in vogue, and there must then have been a frequent demand for fabricators of verdant subtilties, a maze formed by neatly-clipped hedges being an usual adjunct to the royal residences, and probably also to those of the nobility." Although these mazes have been for the most part destroyed, their past existence is indicated by the retention of the name of Maze in the vicinity of the spots they had once occupied, such as Maze Lane and Maze Pond,* in Southwark, marking the site of the Princess Mary Tudor's residence, alluded to by Miss Strickland in her "Lives of the Queens of England," and called the Manor of " Le Maze " in the reign of Henry VI. ; also by the name of Maze Hill at Greenwich,† which was once supplied with a similar means of amusing the royal inmates of the adjoining palace.

Of Theobalds itself nothing remains but the park, and a few of the walls of the royal gardens and outhouses. Three or four large mansions have been erected on the site of these gardens and terraces, and the noble cedars, poplars, and evergreens, attest the former splendour of the place. The garden walks still remain as of old, though no longer trodden by the feet of brave cavaliers and fair ladies of the court. In one portion of the walls which remain are a number of small niches, which look as if they had been intended for saints, though they were not built till long after the saints were banished from our churches. Their use is a mystery. In one corner of the garden was an alcove in the wall, where Dr. Watts used to sit whilst a visitor here ; and tradition says that he wrote here some of his hymns and poems, including possibly " The Little Busy Bee."

Though Theobalds was demolished by order of Parliament during the Commonwealth, and the money arising from the sale of the materials was divided among the army, self-interest or shame restrained in some degree the violence of the destroyers. The commissioners who were appointed by Parliament in 1650 to make a survey of the palace reported that "it was an excellent building, in very good repair, by no means fit to be demolished, and that it was worth £2,000 per annum, exclusive of the park ; yet, lest the Parliament should think proper to have it taken down, they had estimated the materials, and found them to be worth £8,275 11s." Notwithstanding this report, the greater part of the palace was taken down, and the materials sold ; the royal park was converted into farms, and several "pleasant residences " have been erected where royalty once delighted to assemble and enjoy the beauties of a rural retreat. An almshouse adjoining the stables, built probably by Lord Burleigh, continued to be a refuge for the aged poor. It is mentioned in a " Life of the Earl of Salisbury," printed in 1612, that it was occupied by " aged and over-worne captaines, gentlemen by birth and calling." This building, which had the arms of Cecil in front, and was furnished with a hall and chapel, was standing till about the year 1812.

The park contained 2,500 acres, and was valued, together with six lodges, at £1,545 15s. 4d. per annum. The deer was valued at £1,000, the rabbits at £15, and the timber at £7,259 13s. 2d., exclusive of 15,608 trees marked for the use of the navy, and others already cut down for that purpose. The materials of the barn and walls were valued at £1,570 16s. 3d.

Among the few parts of the palace that were left standing after the dismantlement, about 1650, was one of the chapels, which continued to be used by the Presbyterians till the year 1689, when the site of the palace and the park were granted by William III. to the Earl of Portland. Charles II. had previously made a grant of the park and manor to the man who had seated him on the throne of his father. This was George Monk, Duke of Albemarle. After the death of Monk, in 1607, his son Christopher enjoyed it ; but on his death without issue it reverted to the Crown, where it remained until granted to the Earl of Portland, as above mentioned. Somehow, however, the manor of Theobalds did not go with the park and house ; but after frequently changing hands, it became, towards the close of the last century, the inheritance of Oliver Cromwell, Esq., the last male descendant of Henry, the Protector's son. From the Earl of Portland the property passed to his son, whom George I. created a duke ; and about the middle of the last century the property was sold to one of the Prescott family, who afterwards became possessed of the manor. The last remains of the palace were eventually destroyed, and on their site were erected the houses which now form Theobalds Square, in the village of Cheshunt. About the same time a new park of 200 acres was enclosed by Sir G. Prescott, who also built a handsome brick mansion, on rising ground, about a mile northwest from the site of the palace, and at a short distance from the New River, which runs through the grounds. The new house is somewhat similar in plan to that of St. James's Palace. A considerable improvement and addition was made to it by the late Sir Henry Meux, who held it under Sir George Prescott some years since.

---

* See "Old and New London," Vol. VI., p. 104.
† *Ibid*, Vol. VI., p. 230.

Mr. S. Beazley, the architect, dramatist, and man of letters, designed a new staircase here for the Meuxes, who affected to drop the " x " in pronouncing their names, and to sound the name as if it were " Muse " or " Mews ; " and when done, he styled it in jest a " Gradus ad Parnassum," the latter being the fabled seal of the Heavenly Nine. Lord William Lennox wrote the following *jeu d'esprit* on the name : —

" There's *Meux* entire—called Mews the swells among,
Though *Mieux* is better in a foreign tongue ;
Tant Mieux, why change the sounds? nay, 'tis no myth,
Tayleur was Taylor once, and Smythe was Smith."

The property, which is now called Theobalds Park, was bought by Sir Henry Meux in 1882. It is one of the most compact estates for its size of any within the same distance of London. There are several roads through it, but no right of carriage-way to any but the owner, although the public have the privilege of passing through it on foot.

Sir Thomas Abney had a house at Theobalds, and here Dr. Watts lived with him for some time before his removal to Stoke Newington.* In a

summer-house in the garden, as stated above, he is said to have composed many of his hymns.

In the *Gentleman's Magazine* for February, 1836, there is an engraving of "the Royal Palace of Theobalds," derived from a drawing in the Fitz-william Museum at Cambridge. It had been pre-viously known only from a vignette in Pickering's edition of Izaak Walton's "Complete Angler." The embattled gatehouse, with its oriel window above the archway, and the clock-tower and other buildings beyond, recalls to mind to a certain extent the appearance of Wolsey's Gateway and the older portions of Hampton Court Palace. The central tower, with its turrets and cupola, was doubtless a conspicuous object from many parts of the surrounding country ; at all events, it would appear to have been visible to Izaak Walton's worthy anglers, Auceps and Piscator, in their walk along the banks of the Lea; for the former remarks, "I shall by your favour bear you company as far as Theobalds," and the latter shortly after says, "I must in manners break off, for I see Theobalds House."

CHAPTER XL.
CHESHUNT.

" There the most daintie paradise on ground,
Itselfe doth offer to the sober eye,
In which all pleasures plenteously abownd,
And none does others happiness envye.
The painted flowers, the trees upshooting hye ;
The dales for shade ; the christall running by,
And that which all fair works doth most aggrace,
The art which all that wrought appeared in no place."—EDMUND SPENSER.

Situation and General Appearance of the Parish—Its Etymology—Supposed Site of a Roman Station or Camp –Discovery of Roman Coins, &c.— The Mound at Bury Green—A Curious Manorial Custom—Census Returns—The River Lee—A Disputed Landmark—Early History and Descent of the Manor of Cheshunt—The Manor of Moteland, or St. Andrew's le Mote—The Great House—The Parish Church— The Cemetery, &c.—Cheshunt College—Pengelly House—Cheshunt Park—The Cromwell Family—Other Notable Residents and Seats—Waltham Cross—"The Four Swans" Inn—The Spital Houses—Holy Trinity Church—The Benedictine Convent—Goff's Oak— St. James's Church.

CHESHUNT, which will now form the subject of our remarks, is both extensive and pleasingly diversified with agricultural and park-like scenery. It is, in fact, undulating, well-wooded, and well-watered, and irregular in plan. The most populous part of the village, called Cheshunt Street, is built on either side of the great North Road, a continua-tion of the road from London through Enfield Highway, by Waltham Cross—which, by the way, is really part of Cheshunt—and so on to Ware ; so that the inhabitants, if they had happened to have been at their windows on that eventful day,

would have witnessed John Gilpin's involuntary ride to that place, and also his return journey, though the fact is not commemorated by Cowper in his inimitable ballad. The older part of the parish, however, is grouped round the church, and is called Church Street, or Church Gate. Here were some old mansions, including Pengelly House, and two or three with projecting upper storeys. The parish is intersected from north to south by water. The Lea bounds it on the east, and the New River cuts it through nearer the western limit ; the Great Eastern Railway has two stations in the parish—one at Waltham Cross and the other at Cheshunt.

The name of the parish is a curious admixture

* See "Old and New London," Vol. V., p. 539.

of the Roman and the Saxon element, if it be true, as generally stated, that it is derived from "Ceastre," "Castrum," and "Hunt," implying that it had been a Roman encampment in a forest, or weald. Salmon, in his "History of Hertfordshire," states that here was a Roman station or fortified camp connected with the military road called Ermine Street, of which we have spoken in a previous chapter,* and which road was intersected by another leading

Salmon to place here the *Durolitum* of Antoninus; and this opinion has been thought to receive support from the fact of Roman coins of the Emperors Hadrian, Claudius Gothicus, and Constantine, having been discovered here. These were exhibited at a meeting of the Society of Antiquaries in 1724. In Gough's "Camden," however, it is questioned whether *Durolitum* should not rather be placed at Durnford, vulgarly called Turn-

CHESHUNT CHURCH.

to the camp, which was situated at Kilsmore, near Cheshunt Street. Be this as it may, however, the subject has been one of dispute among antiquarians, some asserting that the supposed vallum and fosse in Kilsmore field were nothing more than a cut originally intended for the New River, but laid aside as less convenient than the present channel. This fosse, at all events, has been entirely effaced by a large reservoir, formed by the New River Company; but the farm close by still bears the name of Kilsmore.

This supposed fosse and military way induced

ford, a little village at the north end of Cheshunt, by Cheshunt Wash. The notion of Cheshunt having been the site of a Roman settlement may seem to be further strengthened by an urn, said to be Roman, having been found here; it is to be seen embedded in the front of an inn called "The Roman Urn," in Crossbrook Street. The urn was found on the spot many years ago, whilst some excavations were being made; but its date is far from certain.

Salmon also makes mention of an old tumulus, or Druidical mound, near Bury Green, with ascending paths corresponding to the four cardinal points; this is also disputed, some topographers

* See *ante*, p. 368.

supposing it to be a hillock on which, in days long gone by, stood a windmill; whilst Clutterbuck thinks it more likely to be the site of an old manor house.

It is supposed that the boundary of the kingdom of the East Saxons passed through Theobalds and across Goff's Lane, to Beaumont Green, and so on to the ancient city of Verulam (St. Albans). It was marked by a bank, but no trace now remains.

One peculiarity of the manors in Cheshunt is recorded by Mr. Thorne, who writes :—"An irregular line, known as the Bank's line, runs north and south through the parish; east of it, or *below bank*, by far the larger and more valuable portion, the land and tenements are subject to borough-English, *i.e.*, descend to the youngest son, while west of the line, or *above bank*, the eldest son succeeds." This custom, observes Salmon, could not have been introduced except by different laws of different governments.

Cheshunt was originally divided into eight villages, or hamlets, namely : Waltham Cross, Carbuncle Street, Turner's Hill, Cheshunt Street, Hamon (now Hammond) Street, Appleby Street, Wood Green, and Cockerams. The parish is divided into three wards, known as Waltham Cross, Cheshunt Street, and Woodside Cross Wards ; and, inclusive of the ecclesiastical districts of Waltham Cross and Goff's Oak, it contains nearly 8,500 acres, and is estimated at thirty miles in circumference, with a population, in 1881, of 7,700, being an increase of rather more than 1,000 during the preceding ten years.

The parish is separated from that of Waltham Abbey by the River Lea, which, forming two channels at that part, has given rise to much litigation and contention between the inhabitants of the two parishes, each party claiming the piece of valuable marsh-land between the streams, and each asserting that to be the original stream which affords the greatest extent of territory. This undecided dominion has sometimes been attacked and defended by the weapons of the law, and at others by personal prowess. These disputes first began between the Abbot of Waltham Abbey and the townsmen of Waltham about the year 1245. The abbot and his convent having possession of the marsh, which they had enjoyed for many years, the townsmen killed some of their cattle and drove out the rest. Disturbances arose ; the subject was brought before the King's Bench ; but the townsmen acknowledging their error, the quarrel came to an end. A fiercer and greater strife, however, soon after broke out with reference to this piece of land between the Abbot of Waltham and the

Lord of the Manor of Cheshunt, but the question does not appear to have been satisfactorily settled, for in 1601, on the men of Cheshunt "beating the bounds," they are considered to have over-stepped the mark, as the following entry in the parish records of Waltham testify :—"The curate of Cheshunt and some of the churchwardens . . . . did come in their perambulation to our high bridge, and for so doing, and coming out of their own liberty, they were for their pains thrust into a ditch, called Hook's Ditch." The situation of the place where this disaster occurred appears to be not far from the disputed piece of marsh-land. The rich and fertile marshes of which those in dispute form a part were laid under water in the time of King Alfred (897), and were then navigable, so that the Danes sailed up the river to Hertford, where they built two forts for the security of their ships ; but in order to secure them from returning, Alfred, with pioneers, divided the principal stream of the Lea with several rivulets, so that their ships were left on dry land, which so terrified them that they abandoned their forts, and being hotly pursued, were compelled to flee the country. These marshes were formally called the King's Meads, many being drained and capable of bearing grass, and the king gave them for "common" to the several adjacent parishes.

Cheshunt contains several subordinate manors. The principal manor, from which some of the others have branched off since the time of the Domesday Survey, was given by the Conqueror to his nephew, Earl Alan, surnamed the "Red," who commanded the rear of his army at the battle of Hastings, and was rewarded with the earldom of Richmond, in Yorkshire, the manor of Cheshunt being assigned to him in order to support his newly-acquired dignity.

Earl Alan was a son of Eudes, Earl of Brittany, by a sister of William the Conqueror. The following is the entry relating to this parish in "Domesday Book" :—"Earl Alan himself holds Cestrehunt. It was rated at twenty hides. Arable land thirty-three carucates. In demesne are ten hides, and there are four carucates, and two may yet be made. Forty-one villanes, with a priest and twelve bordars, have seventeen carucates there. Ten merchants pay ten shillings for custom there. There are eight cottagers and six bondmen, and one mill worth ten shillings. From a stream sixteen-pence. Meadow, twenty-three carucates, and fodder for the lord's horses. Pasture for cattle. Pannage for one thousand two hundred hogs, and forty pence." On the death of Earl Alan, without issue, in 1089, the manor passed to his half-brother, surnamed

Niger, who also died without issue, and was succeeded by his brother Stephen, and with his descendants it remained till the beginning of the thirteenth century, when it was granted by the Crown to William, Bishop of Carlisle. In 1241 Henry III. gave the manor to Peter de Savoy, uncle of Eleanor, his queen, and in the following year granted him the right of holding an annual fair of two days' duration within this manor. Another fair, to last four days, was subsequently granted to Peter de Savoy, but both have died out. Cheshunt Fair, which had from time immemorial been held in Cheshunt Street on the 24th of August, was abolished by the local magistrates in 1859.

The manor, after the death of Peter de Savoy, saw several successive changes of ownership. In 1525 it was granted by Henry VIII. to his illegitimate son, Henry Fitzroy, who was created Duke of Richmond and Somerset, but on his death, at the age of seventeen, it again reverted to the Crown. Edward VI. granted it to Sir John Gates, on whose attainder for high treason in supporting the claims of Lady Jane Grey to the throne, his estates were forfeited, and once more this manor came to the Crown. Queen Mary granted it to Sir John Huddlestone, who shortly after conveyed it to the family of Cock of Broxbourne. It was afterwards owned by Lord Monson, who in 1782 sold it to the Prescotts, Sir George R. Prescott, Bart., being the present owner.

The old manor house of the chief manor has disappeared, and even its site is uncertain. But on the north of Goff's Lane, a short distance northwest of the church, stands a curious old-fashioned house of red brick, among some trees in a meadow. It seems as if it had been surrounded by a moat, and is called St. Andrew's le Mote, though locally known as the "Great House," or the "Moated House," or the "Haunted House." It must be owned that its appearance would give such an impression. It is now a solid square, but evidently has formed part of a larger structure. It must have been built as far back as the fifteenth century at least, and some arches in the cellars (said to be a portion of a crypt or chapel) are probably older still. The great hall, which reaches to the roof, is certainly of a date anterior to Henry VII.; but the story is that it was built by Cardinal Wolsey. For this, however, there is no proof, nor even that he ever lived here, though the Manor of Moteland here was given to him by the tyrant. The building is said originally to have contained more than thirty rooms, and to have been quadrangular in plan. What at present remains consists of the hall above

mentioned, with apartments towards the north, and a vaulted crypt underneath, which is said to have been the chapel, and to have been paved with embossed tiles. The dimensions of the hall are twenty-seven feet by twenty-one, and it is thirty-six feet high. It has an arched roof supported by timber-worked ribs of chestnut, in the Gothic style; the sides are wainscoted, and the floor is paved with black and white marble, so that altogether it remains in much the same state as when the Tudors and Stuarts occupied the throne, except that the minstrels' gallery and the buttery-hatch at the lower end are gone, and that the daïs has also disappeared. The hall is hung with portraits of very doubtful authenticity, and first on the list is one of Wolsey—probably a copy. There are altogether about a hundred portraits of kings, statesmen, court ladies, judges, &c., mostly of the fifteenth, sixteenth, and seventeenth centuries, though some are even more recent. Near the fireplace hangs the portrait of Wolsey, and above this a family piece of the Shaws, who formerly owned the manor, painted by Sir Peter Lely, in which is depicted Sir John Shaw, his wife, and nine children; among the other portraits are Queen Elizabeth, Charles I., and Charles II., ascribed to Vandyck, William III. and Queen Mary, Sir Hugh Myddelton, James II., Richard Cromwell, Archbishops Laud and Juxon, Lord Falkland, Thomas Lord Fairfax, and several members of the Mayo family. The apartment also contains several suits of chain and other armour, many banners, escutcheons, and weapons of war, besides a curious old-fashioned chair and a few other bits of furniture, which, to keep up the tradition of the place, are said to have belonged to Cardinal Wolsey. Nearly all the pictures are in a sad condition of decay, being left to the care of a labourer's family, who live in the back part of the house, and show the place to visitors. In an upper chamber, called the haunted room, and said to have been the scene of a barbarous murder, are an arm-chair and a mutilated rocking-horse, both said to have belonged to Charles I., who, as a child, must often have been at Theobalds. In the vaults below the house is a chopping-block, which the guardians of the place tell the credulous visitor was used by Cromwell in the execution of his captives. Some years ago two skeletons, with a pitcher and a lantern, were discovered enclosed in a cavity in the wall, in a corner of the crypt.

After the time of Wolsey we find the manor in the hands of the families of Dennis and Dacre, whose monuments are to be seen in the church.

From them it passed to the Shaws, one of whom repaired it in the middle of the last century, modernising it in the most tasteless manner ; and early in the present century a subsequent owner, the Rev. Charles Mayo, completed the task of mutilation, destroying half of it in order to provide materials for the repair of the rest, and at the same time filling up the moat which surrounded it.

The parish church, dedicated to St. Mary the Virgin, stands about a quarter of a mile south of the "Great House," and half a mile west of the high road. It is a fine handsome Early Perpendicular structure, very much of the same type with those of Bishop Stortford, Thaxted, Dunmow, Saffron Walden, and other neighbouring towns. It consists of nave, chancel, and side aisles, and a handsome embattled tower, with good western doorway, adorned with shields; there are niches for saints in the angles of the west window, but their occupants are gone. The tower is built of flint and stone, and has an octagonal cupola containing six bells, dating from 1636 to 1760. Early in the present century the body of the church was thoroughly repaired and galleries were erected, and in 1855 it was "re-pewed" and re-arranged. In 1872 the church was considerably enlarged and restored, not overjudiciously, by Mr. Joseph Clarke. The galleries were taken down, the plaster was removed from the walls, and the pillars, which are of Purbeck marble, were divested of the paint with which they had been covered ; but the south aisle was enlarged at the east end in such a manner as to spoil the symmetry of the building. At the north-east angle of the church was an ancient vestry, with a small room over it. Between the nave and chancel on either side is a curious ornamental recess, like a window, pierced through the solid wall. Its object and design is uncertain. On the south side is an opening, through which access was gained to the rood-loft. The new chancel is handsome and spacious, but painfully new. The font is probably that of the original church, long previous to the fifteenth century. Several of the windows are filled with stained glass, as memorials of local worthies.

As might be supposed from the former presence of the Court at Theobalds, the church contains several fine Jacobean monuments. On the north side of the chancel is a Gothic altar tomb to Sir Robert Dacres, a member of the Privy Council of Henry VIII., on the top of which is placed a Jacobean monument to one of King James's physicians. Others, of various types of merit, are to be seen on the walls.

At the west end of the north aisle there is a fine piece of sculpture, a marble statue and tomb of one David Dodson, who died in 1761, and who seems to have had little scruple in blocking up a fine window with his effigy. The statue, however, is evidently by a master-hand, and has not been properly appreciated.

There is a brass under the communion table to Nicholas Dixon, Vicar of Cheshunt, the builder of the present edifice (on the site of a former church). He died in 1448, having held several offices at Court which sound rather secular to our ears— "Clerk of the Pipe Office, Under Treasurer, and Baron of the Exchequer."[*]

At the north-west corner of the churchyard is a large square heavy tomb, under which rest the bodies of several members of the Cromwell family, and of their successors, the Russells. Richard Cromwell, however, though he died here, lies at Hursley, near Winchester. There are also monuments to various members of the Meux, Prescott, and Daking families, and one to the only son of Lord Chancellor Eldon, with an inscription from the pen of his uncle, Lord Stowell.

Near the vicarage gate is an old stone coffin, without a lid, probably of Anglo-Saxon date. This was discovered, bottom upwards, a few feet from the chancel door, in 1872, on digging the foundations for the extension of the south aisle.

The cemetery, in Bury Green Road, to the southwest of the church, was formed in 1855, on land given by the late General Osborn. It is about five acres in extent, and in the centre is a building, with a square tower and spire, and comprising two mortuary chapels.

Two of the houses at the corner of Church Street, on the opposite side of the way, are said to be the originals of the Great and Small House in Mr. Anthony Trollope's novel of "The Small House at Allington," being sketched from the life by the author during a stay in the village.

Nearly opposite the church is Cheshunt College, which was founded in 1768 by Lady Huntingdon at Trevecca, in South Wales, but transferred here after her death, in 1792. The institution, which has since been affiliated to the University of London, is for the training of young men for the Nonconformist ministry. The college was originally a gentleman's mansion, and is of the Queen Anne type. Of this house a part remains, now used as a lecture-room. Other buildings of a commonplace character were erected in 1863 ; these included a chapel and library. In 1872 a new structure, of Decorated Gothic, with some foreign details, was

* Chauncy's " History of Herts," Vol. I.

opened. It contains lecture-rooms and dwelling-rooms for about forty students. Its tall campanile, or spire, is visible for miles round on every side. The library is octagonal. The hall contains some fine portraits and engravings of John and Charles Wesley, Lady Huntingdon, and other members of the Ferrers family—for she was by birth a Shirley—and also of several of the presidents of the college. The grounds, some fifteen acres in extent, are bounded by the New River, which runs at their foot.

On the bank of the water is a summer-house, of the square type so common along the course of the New River. It is called "Dr. Watts' Wig," from some tradition—possibly baseless—that it was haunted by that worthy in his lifetime. Near the college is a narrow thoroughfare, called Dr. Watts' Lane, "from a questionable tradition," writes Mr. Thorne, in his "Environs of London," "that it was the favourite stroll of the great Non-conformist divine during his visits to Richard Cromwell."

Besides the above institution Cheshunt is well supplied with schools, the oldest in point of foundation being Dewhurst's, at Church Gate, which dates from the middle of the seventeenth century. This school was enlarged and considerably improved in 1847.

Pengelly House, near the church, occupies the site of the residence of Richard Cromwell, the deposed Protector, who, after his return from the Continent about the year 1680, assumed the name of Clarke, in order to secure himself from the intrusions of his father's friends, and lived here in retirement as a private gentleman during the remainder of his life. Here also he died, in July, 1712, in the arms of the gardener of Baron Pengelly. To all except his nearest friends Richard Cromwell always avoided speaking of his former greatness. Dr. Watts, who was one of his most frequent visitors, used to say that he never heard Richard allude to his former station except now and then in a very distant manner. In Noble's

RICHARD CROMWELL.

"Memoirs of the Cromwell Family" appears the following singular anecdote concerning Richard, which was related to the Rev. George North, Vicar of Codicote, near Welwyn, by two persons who conversed with him in the last years of his life at Cheshunt:—"When Richard left Whitehall he was very careful to preserve the *Addresses* which had been sent to him from every part of the kingdom, expressing 'that the salvation of the nation depended upon his safety, and his acceptance of the sovereignty,' and many of them proffering him the lives and fortunes of the addressers. In his retirement at Cheshunt no one was admitted to visit him without strong recommendations of being of agreeable conversation and strict honour. One of the two persons above alluded to, named Windus who lived at Ware, was introduced to him as such, with an admonition to conform to his peculiarities, without asking any questions or seeming to make any observations. After an hour or two spent in 'conversation and drinking, Richard started up, took the candle, and the rest of the company, who all knew, except the last admitted man, what was going forward, took up the bottle and the glasses, and followed the quondam Protector up to a dirty garret, in which was nothing but a little round hair trunk. Mr. Cromwell pulled it out to the middle of the room, and calling for a bumper of wine, drank "Prosperity to Old England." All the company did the same. When the new man, Mr. Windus, was called to do so, sitting astride, as they had done, upon the trunk, Cromwell desired him to take care, and sit light, for he had no less than the lives and fortunes of all the good people of England under him. The trunk was then opened, and the original addresses showed him, with great mirth and laughter. This was his method of initiating a new acquaintance.' "

Richard Cromwell was buried at Hursley, in Hampshire, the manor of Hursley having descended to him in right of his wife, though he was obliged to contest the possession of it with his daughters in a court of law. Serjeant Pengelly, who was retained by him on this occasion as counsel, and was afterwards Chief Baron of the Exchequer, is supposed to have been a natural son of his employer, a supposition which Mr. Noble, in his work above quoted, admits to be rendered probable by Richard's gallantry. Richard Cromwell appeared personally in the court at Westminster to contest the action against his daughters, and when he appeared in Westminster Hall, the judge, Sir John Holt, Lord Chief Justice of England, struck with the sad reverse of fortune and the unfeeling behaviour of his daughters, and on account of his old age, conducted him into a private apartment; refreshments were provided for him, and it was ordered that he should be accommodated with a seat in court. The old man gained the cause, and had the painful satisfaction of hearing his daughters severely censured; Queen Anne had the good feeling to applaud the judge for

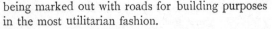

the attention he had shown to one who had once held sovereign power. As Richard was leaving Westminster Hall his curiosity led him to the House of Lords. He was asked when he was there last. "Never," he said, pointing, with a smile, to the throne, "since I sat in that chair."

Pengelly House, during the last ten or twelve years, has been completely transformed and much spoilt in its appearance; but the summer-house in the garden, in which Richard Cromwell used to smoke his pipe, still remains. The house was for some time the residence of Hugh Stracey Osborne, an East India civilian, and more recently of Mr. Benjamin Attwood, a millionaire, but is now (May, 1883) in the market to be sold, the estate

THE OLD MANOR HOUSE, CHESHUNT.

being marked out with roads for building purposes in the most utilitarian fashion.

About a mile north of the church is another property which has for generations been connected with the Cromwells, and their heirs, the Russells: namely, Cheshunt Park. The estate was originally a subordinate manor of Cheshunt, and known as Crossbrook, and also as Cullings. It is not a little singular that, having at one time formed part of the royal manor of Theobalds, which was granted by Charles II. to George Monk, Duke of Albemarle, for restoring the monarchy, it should eventually have come into the possession of the last male descendant of Oliver Cromwell. On the death of Christopher, the second Duke of Albemarle, without issue, the property reverted to the Crown. It appears, however, to have been granted anew to Ralph, Duke of Montagu, who had married the widow of the Duke of Albemarle, as his descendant, John, Duke of Montagu, sold it in 1736 to a Mrs. Letitia Thornhill, from whom it passed to the Cromwells, through the marriage of Richard Cromwell, grandson of Henry Cromwell, Lord Lieutenant of Ireland, with Sarah, daughter of Ebenezer Gatton, and niece and one of the co-heiresses of Sir Robert Thornhill, the father of the above-mentioned Letitia. The estate subsequently became vested in Oliver Cromwell, the great-grandson of Henry Cromwell, son of the Protector. This gentleman practised as a solicitor in London, and became the biographer of his illustrious namesake. He built on his estate here a seat, to which he gave the name of Brantingfay, but which has now become changed to Cheshunt Park. The house contained several ancient and curious pictures and portraits, which ranged from the Protector's parents down to the above-mentioned Oliver. After his death in 1821, at the age of seventy-one, the property descended to his only surviving child, Oliveria, who had married Mr. Thomas A. Russell. Sir Robert Heron, in his "Notes," relates that the last Oliver Cromwell was very desirous of leaving his name to his son-in-law, and "applied several times for the royal license that Mr. Russell should assume it; but the old king, George III., positively refused, always saying, 'No, no; no more Oliver

his unambitious son, Richard. Many other relics of the Protector are in the Rev. J. D. Williams's Cromwellian Museum at Paragon Road, Hackney.

In College Road is a building called St. Mary's Hall, erected in 1868, and used for the purposes of lectures and other entertainments. Here the Petty Sessions and Sessions under the Criminal Justice Act are held. The magisterial business for this division of the county was formerly conducted at the "Green Dragon" inn, at Church Gate.

WALTHAM CROSS.

Cromwells!'" George IV., when Prince Regent, appears also to have thought that the country had had enough of the Cromwells, for he, too, is said to have refused his royal leave and license to a repetition of the request. Mrs. Russell was the last person who bore at birth the name of Cromwell through direct male descent. She died in 1858, and her husband followed her to the grave a few years later. Their eldest son, Cromwell Russell, married the daughter of the Rev. W. A. Armstrong, of Pengelly House, and they left an only child, a daughter, who married the Rev. Paul Bush, Rector of Duloe, Cornwall, and who still owns a variety of Cromwellian relics, including several of the great Protector's autograph letters, and the great seal of

Cheshunt and its immediate neighbourhood abounds in beautiful walks, and in many parts extensive views of the surrounding country are obtained. Many parts of the land are cultivated as market gardens. The soil is particularly suited to the growth of roses, and the old-established nurseries of Messrs. Paul, in Cheshunt Street, form quite a show in the summer months.

Salmon, writing in 1728, observes of Cheshunt that "it changes its inhabitants so often that there are not two gentlemen in the parish who were born in it;" and nearly the same may be said of it at the present day. There are, nevertheless, some good seats and residences in the parish, besides those already mentioned, notably the Cedars; Theobalds, long the residence of Lady Prescott; Wood Green Park, where lived the Hon. John Scott, son of the first Lord Eldon, and who was so pleased with the neighbourhood that, as we have seen above, he desired to be buried in Cheshunt churchyard; Claremont, a good house in a pleasant park a little to the north-east of Church Gate; and Aldbury House, half a mile to the south. Some remarkable men, too, have held property in this parish, among whom may be mentioned Charles, Lord Howard of Effingham, Lord High Admiral of England in 1588, the hero of the Spanish Armada. He was the owner of a farm house in Cheshunt Street, now called Effingham Place, which he gave to one of his captains, named Bellamy, with whose descendants it has since continued. General Whitelock, whose name became notorious at the beginning of the present century for his conduct while in command of the forces in South America, and whose action at Buenos Ayres led to his trial by court-martial and dismissal from the service, afterwards lived here for some time, and was often compelled to hear that

> " Grey hairs are honourable,
> But Whitelocks are abominable."

Here, too, also lived in retirement, after dismissal from the public service, another individual whose name figures in English history, namely, Lord Somers; and Lord Grey de Wilton, who was a Knight of the Garter in the time of Queen Elizabeth, died here in 1562. William Herbert, the editor of "Ames's Typographical Antiquities," died here in 1795; and James Ward, R.A., who gained some celebrity as an animal painter, lived for the last thirty years of his life at Round Croft's Cottage, and died there in 1859.

The hamlet of Waltham Cross, near the entrance to this parish on the London road, derives its name from one of those elegant stone crosses which the pious affection of Edward I. caused to be erected to the memory of his wife, Eleanor of Castile, in the places where her body was rested for the night on its journey from Hareby, in Lincolnshire, to the place of its interment in Westminster Abbey. Of the several crosses which were in this manner erected—namely, at Lincoln, Grantham, Stamford, Geddington, Northampton, Stony-Stratford, Dunstable, St. Albans, Waltham, and Charing—only three remain, namely, those at Geddington, Northampton, and Waltham. Like those at Geddington and Northampton, that at Waltham was originally surrounded by a flight of steps, but these have long been removed, and its base covered in with brickwork. The upper parts of the cross are also greatly mutilated, much of the

foliage being defaced, and the pinnacles and other ornamentation broken. The form of the cross is hexagonal, and it is divided into three storeys, of which the centre one is open, and contains statues of the queen in whose honour it was erected. Each side of the lower storey is divided into two compartments beneath an angular coping, charged with shields pendent from different kinds of foliage, and exhibiting the arms of England, of Castile, Leon, and Ponthieu. The cornice over this storey consists of foliage and lions' heads, surmounted by battlements pierced with quatrefoils. The second storey consists of twelve open tabernacles in pairs, but so divided that the pillar intersects the middle of the statue behind it. These terminate in ornamental pediments, with a bouquet on the top, and with a cornice and battlement, and support the third storey, which is of solid masonry, ornamented with single compartments in relief resembling those below, and supporting the broken shaft of a plain cross. The statues of the queen are crowned; she holds a cordon in her left hand and a sceptre in her right. This cross stands close to the "Falcon" Inn, which has been built up against it, in the angle formed by the high road and another road which branches off eastward towards Waltham Abbey.

The following lines, "suggested by a sight of this cross," appear in the *Mirror* for 1831:—

> "Time-mouldering crosses, gemm'd with imagery
> Of costliest work and Gothic tracery,
> Point still the spots, to hallow'd memory dear,
> Where rested on its solemn way the bier
> That bore the bones of Edward's Elinor,
> To mix with royal dust at Westminster.
> Far different rites did thee to dust consign,
> Brunswick's fair daughter, Princess Caroline !
> A hurrying funeral and a banished grave,
> High-minded wife ! were all that thou couldst have.
> Grieve not, great ghost ! nor count in death thy losses,
> Thou in thy lifetime hadst thy share of crosses."

The cross was completed in 1294, the work having been executed by Alexander of Abingdon, Domenic de Leger of Rheims, and Roger de Crundale. The stone was brought from Caen, in Normandy, and the total cost is stated to have been £95.

In a volume entitled "Memorials of Queen Eleanor," it is remarked that "the Waltham Cross has suffered grievously from neglect and wilful injury, and not a little, we are compelled to say, from modern restoration." The members of the Society of Antiquaries have twice interested themselves in preserving it from decay: once in 1721, and again in 1757, when Lord Monson, the then Lord of the Manor of Cheshunt, at the request of the Society, surrounded the base with brickwork, as the whole of the steps, ten in number, had been taken away. At that time it was discovered that the roof of a neighbouring house, which still disfigures the view of the cross, leaned against one of the statues of the queen. In 1796 the cross was again found in a very neglected condition. Mr. Gough, in the "Velusta Monumenta," observes that the cross probably stood isolated from the town, like that near Nottingham, or at least that the only building near it was "Ye Olde Foure Swannes Hostelrie." At one time there was attached to the cross a board, pointing the direction of the adjacent roads. At the beginning of the present century an attempt was made to remove the entire structure into Theobalds Park; but fortunately the materials were found to be so decayed that the idea was abandoned, and it became an almost shapeless mass of stone, and a few years more would have left nothing remaining of Waltham Cross. About 1830 the attention of the neighbouring gentry and others, however, was called to it, while there was yet time to save something of its pristine form, and while it afforded indications by which much that was deficient might be restored, and a subscription was at once set on foot for the purpose of raising the necessary funds for repairing the monument. In 1833 the work was commenced, under the direction of Mr. W. B. Clarke. The result was the restoration of the cross as it now appears. Her Majesty the Queen and the Prince Consort stopped to inspect this relic of antiquity on their way from Cambridge to London in October, 1843.

The "Four Swans" inn, mentioned above, and which stands on the opposite side of the road, is undoubtedly an old building; but it is questionable whether it can properly lay claim to the antiquity that is locally assigned to it, for in it, according to tradition, "the body of Queen Eleanor remained for the night preceding its solemn entry into London." Salmon considers this inn to have been the original manor-house of the honour of Richmond; and Gough, in the work above referred to, says that "it bears marks of great antiquity in the forms of its chimneys, and the quantity of chestnut timber employed about it." A large signboard, supported on tall posts placed on the opposite sides of the way, swings across the road, having on the inscription, "Ye Olde Foure Swannes Hostelrie, 1260."

In the parish register of Waltham Holy Cross (or Waltham Abbey) there is the following entry:— "Julii, 1612, Margaret, the daughter of Edward Skarlett, of Cestrehunt, was buried 26 daye, dwel-

ling at the signe of Ye Old Swanne in Waltham Cross." In days gone by this inn was a well-known posting-house, and more recently it numbered Charles Lamb among its patrons.

This village being the resort of travellers, and a general halting-place for the stage-coaches on the Great North Road to or from London, rendered another inn upon the spot necessary, and accordingly one was erected at the corner of the road to Waltham Abbey. The cross itself, as shown above, is almost taken into the end of it, whereby much of its beauty is concealed, and many of its ornaments disfigured. It has been suggested that a roadside chapel at one time stood on the site of this inn, which was formerly called "The Falcon," but which is now known as the "Great Eastern."

The hamlet of Waltham Cross was made into a separate parish for ecclesiastical purposes in 1855. The church, dedicated to the Holy Trinity, is a plain brick building, of Gothic architecture. It was built in 1832, and altered and improved in 1872. In 1870 this district was endowed as a vicarage.

There are almshouses for four poor persons at Waltham Cross, called the Spital Houses, the income of which, together with others for ten widows at Turner's Hill, amounts, in the gross, to £550 yearly. The Spital Houses are stated by the Parliamentary Commission survey in 1650 to have been used "time out of mind" for the "entertainment of lame, impotent, and decayed persons." They were rebuilt in 1830.

Here was, before the Dissolution, a small convent of Benedictine nuns, whose name is still kept in memory by the Nunnery Farm, towards the north-east of the village, not far from the banks of the River Lea. But little is known of the history of this convent. It appears to have been founded in the reign of Stephen, by Peter de Belingey, in honour of the Blessed Virgin, for nuns of the Sempringham order. It was afterwards possessed by the canons of that order, but Henry III. placed in it nuns of the order of St. Benedict, and made them independent. After the Dissolution the convent was granted to Sir Anthony Denny, and it has since passed through the hands of several different owners. At the beginning of the present century the remains of the convent formed the domestic parts of a large mansion.

About a mile to the north-west of Cheshunt Church is a small hamlet, called Goff's Oak, from an old survivor of the forest, an oak, now on its last legs, which stands on the south side of the common, in front of a small roadside inn. The traditional history of this celebrated tree is inscribed as follows under a rude drawing of the tree, which is to be seen at the above-mentioned house :—" It was planted in the year 1066 by Sir Theodore Godfrey, or Goffe, who came over with William the Conqueror, and it is not at all improbable but that some neighbouring land, called Cuffley, belonged to this person at that time. The dimensions of the tree are very large, as it is twenty feet in girth three feet from the ground. The trunk is hollow, and several persons can stand in the cavity which time has made. This cavity is now boarded in, but a door admits visitors into the interior; and few persons will regret the time spent in examining it. A respectable inn is within a few yards of the tree, and bears the name of the tree for its sign; its predecessor was burnt down in 1814, and was called the Green Man."

The hamlet of Goff's Oak was formed into an ecclesiastical parish in 1871. The church, dedicated to St. James, had been built some years previously, having been consecrated as far back as 1862. It is a small brick edifice, in the Gothic style, but deserves no especial mention in these pages.

CHAPTER XLI.

NORTHAW.

Etymology of Northaw—Condition of the District at the time of the Conquest—Disputed Ownership—Nynn House, and Manor—The Hook—Northaw Place—Acreage and Population—The Village and Parish Church—A Chalybeate Spring.

This parish, the name of which in old documents is sometimes written Northall and Northolt, lies on a hill to the east of the Great North Road some three miles north-east from Potter's Bar Station on the Great Northern Railway. Its etymology is, doubtless, the same as that of Northolt,* in Middlesex, the north *haw*, or *holt*, which signifies a wood.

At the time of the Conquest all this district probably formed a continuation of the extensive woodland afterwards known as Enfield Chase, or it may have been merely waste ground, producing no revenue to the Crown, as it is not mentioned in the " Domesday Survey." Towards the end of the eleventh century, however, it appears to have belonged to St. Albans abbey, for it was at that time held under a lease from the Abbot Paul by Peter de Valoines, or Valence, and his son Roger. After the death of the abbot, Valoines continued to retain possession by consent of the monastery; but on the latter making a request, at some later date, for possession to be given up, Robert de Valoines, who then held it, refused, and appealed to the king, Henry II., who was then in France. The decision of the king was in favour of Valoines, or, in other words, he commanded the abbot to "give up the wood."

Armed with the king's authority, de Valoines returned to England, and "having obtained the possession, during the short time he enjoyed it (as one who unjustly possess it) often wasted the same, causing it to be cut beyond measure. When the abbot heard these things, he sent officers to view the waste, who found that the damage committed there could not be repaired. Then he hastened to Robert, Earl of Leicester, then Chief Justice of England, and obtained his letters that he would restrain the injurious acts of Robert de Valoines; but he, slighting the commands of the earl, did *twice the damage* he did before, which the abbot hearing, did address himself to Queen Eleanor. . . whose admonitions Robert obeyed for a time, but soon after committed *double damage again*. Then the abbot complained of these wrongs to the Pope, who sent his letters to Theobald, Archbishop of Canterbury, and Hillary, Bishop of Chichester, that they cause the said Robert within thirty days to restore the possession of the wood to the abbot, and upon his contempt to declare sentence of excommunication against him."

The abbot's right to the wood, however, was eventually confirmed by Henry II., and Northaw continued in the possession of the priory of St. Albans until the dissolution of religious houses, when it came to the Crown. In 1539 it was granted by Henry VIII., under the title of the manor of " Northawe, Nynne, and Cufley," to Sir William Cavendish, Gentleman Usher to Cardinal Wolsey, and the author of his " Life ; "* but it was alienated early in the reign of Elizabeth to the Earl of Warwick, in exchange for other property. The earl built here a mansion, called "Nyn House," on the site of the present manor-house. It was a spacious structure of brick, occupying three sides of a quadrangle, with a courtyard in the centre, and graced with "delightful gardens and walks, and sundry other pleasant and necessary devices.* Sir Samuel Pennant, who was Sheriff of London in 1745, died at Nynn House in 1750, during the year of his mayoralty. In 1774 a Mr. John Granger, who assumed the name of Leman on coming into possession of the manor, pulled down the old house, and destroyed the gardens. The materials of the building were used in the erection of the present Northaw House, which stands about half a mile distant from the site of the old mansion.

The manor, on the death of the Countess of Warwick, in 1603—4, passed by deed of settlement to her brother, Lord William Russell, and it was a few years later sold to the Lemans, with whose family it remained for several generations, down to the middle of the last century, when it was bequeathed to the above-mentioned John Granger. About 1822 the property passed into the hands of the Rev. Dr. Trenchard, on whose death it was inherited by his son, Mr. Ashfordby-Trenchard. This family held the manor till 1876, when it was sold to Mr. John P. Kidston, the present owner. This gentleman has greatly improved and enlarged the house. The grounds are extensive, beautifully laid out, and contain an ornamental lake about five acres in extent.

There are a few other good houses in the parish, notably "The Hook," a substantial mansion of the old-fashioned type, on the south side of the village; and Northaw Place, which stands a little to the west of the church, built towards the end of the seventeenth century.

The parish itself, although of considerable extent, embracing no less than 3,000 acres, contains only about 600 inhabitants, showing but a slight increase since the census of 1871. The parish is wholly agricultural.

The village green occupies a central position in the parish. It stands on a hill some three miles north-east from Potter's Bar Station on the Great Northern Railway. On one side of the green stands the parish church, a new building, of Early English architecture. It is built of stone, and consists of chancel, nave, south aisle, transepts, and a square tower at the south-west corner. The church, dedicated to St. Thomas à Becket, was erected in 1882, in the place of one destroyed by fire in the previous year. The predecessor of the present building—a pseudo-Perpendicular structure —was a comparatively modern edifice, dating from the beginning of the present century. It was built in the place of an older church, probably Late Norman or Early English. It was a commonplace cruciform building, covered with a coating of cement.

At Lower Cuffley, a valley lying about midway between the villages of Northaw and Cheshunt, is a chalybeate spring, which, at the time when the royal court was held at the neighbouring Palace of Theobalds, was much resorted to; but it shared the fate of the spring at Barnet * and other similar places, and its medicinal qualities seem to have lost their virtue as soon as the spring ceased to be fashionable. Mr. Cussans, in his "History of Hertfordshire," says that "the water contained a large quantity of iron, and a favourite diversion of the inhabitants was to induce strangers to make tea with it. Though perfectly colourless, as soon as the boiling water was poured on the tea, the iron combined with the tannin, and formed ink— as much to the astonishment of the tea-makers as to the delight of the practical jokers."

CHAPTER XLII.

ENFIELD SMALL-ARMS FACTORY AND WALTHAM POWDER-MILLS.

"Fire answers fire."—SHAKESPEARE: King Henry V, Act IV.

The History of the Rifle—Situation of the Royal Small-arms Factory—Particulars of its Establishment—Extent of the Buildings, &c.—Perfection of the Machinery and Plant—The Government Powder Mills—Situation of the Buildings—Description of the Works—The Composition of Gunpowder—Quantities produced.

BEFORE we leave Hertfordshire and Middlesex for the towers of Waltham Abbey and the green glades of Enfield Forest, we must pause, and devote a chapter to two public manufactories lying close together on the banks of the Lea, the one known as the Enfield Small-arms Factory, and the other as the Royal Gunpowder Factory, Waltham. Practically they belong to no parish or county, but are national to the fullest extent of the term, so we make them a connecting link between the district that we have visited and the county of Essex, on which we are about to enter.

The Royal Small-arms Factory is the establishment through which all the small-arms of every

---

description have been supplied—at all events, since the Crimean War—to the regular army, the militia, yeomanry, and volunteers. Its long ranges of buildings and tall chimneys are conspicuous objects from whatever side they are viewed.

With reference to the special manufacture carried on here, a short account of the rifle itself may not be judged out of place.

"As early as 1498," observes a writer in *Chambers's Cyclopædia*, " the citizens of Leipzig possessed the germ of the future rifle, for their arms had a grooved bore, but the grooves were

vidual skill of the marksman. The spiral groove gives to the bullet, if it fits into the grooves, a rotation rapid in proportion to the force of the explosion and the sharpness of the twist in the spiral. This revolution of the bullet on its own

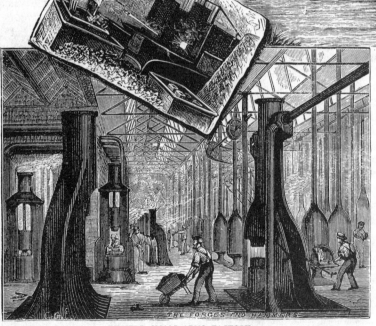

ENFIELD SMALL-ARMS FACTORY.

axis keeps that axis, gravity excepted, in the line in which it leaves the piece. In 1628 Arnold Rotsiphen patented a new way of 'makeing gounes,' which, from a subsequent patent granted him in 1635, appears to have consisted, among other improvements, in rifling the barrels. It would be tedious to enumerate the various principles of rifling which were tried during the two centuries following Rotsiphen; suffice it to say, that scarcely a form of rifling now prevails but had its prototype among the old inventions. The difficulty of mechanical appliances making the rifling true deferred, however, their general introduction, and the cost of rifled arms limited their use to the purposes of the chase. The revolutionary government of France had rifles issued to portions of their troops, but they met with so indifferent a success that Napoleon recalled them soon after he came to power. In the Peninsula, however, picked companies of sharpshooters practised with rifles with deadly effect on both the English and

straight. Not many years after, in 1520, Augustin Kutter (or Koster), of Nürnberg, was celebrated for his rose or star-grooved barrels, in which the grooves had a spiral form. It took its name from the rose-like shape of the bore at the muzzle; and, setting aside superiority of workmanship subsequently developed, Kutter's arm was the veritable rifle, and to him, therefore, so far as history shows, is due the invention of this terrible weapon, which reduces the flight of the projectile to a question of the indi-

French sides. During the American War—1812–14 —the Americans demonstrated incontestably the value of rifles in warfare, but many years were yet to elapse before they were definitively placed in the hands of soldiers, many of those of every nation in the Crimea having fought with the ineffective and almost ridiculous 'Brown Bess.' Soon after the French invaded Algeria they had armed the Chasseurs d'Orleans with rifles, to counteract the superior range of the Arab guns. The inutility of the old musket was shown in a

right, however, to state that this contrivance is claimed for Mr. Greener as early as 1836.) Notwithstanding the many advantages of the Minié system, it was found defective in practice. Experiments were set on foot in all directions, and resulted in 1853 in the production of the 'Enfield rifle,' which had three grooves, taking one complete turn in seventy-eight inches, and fired a bullet resembling the Minié, except that a wooden cup was substituted for one of iron. From 1853 to 1865 this was the weapon of the British army.

THE POWDER MILLS, WALTHAM.

battle during the Kaffir War, where our men discharged 80,000 cartridges, and the damage to the enemy was twenty-five men struck. After experiments with the old musket, it was found that its aim had no certainty whatever beyond 100 yards. It was soon discovered that a spherical ball was not the best missile, one in which the longer axis coincided with the axis of the gun flying truer—the relative length of the axis and the shape of the head being matters of dispute. In England no improvement took place until 1851, when 28,000 rifled muskets to fire the Minié bullet were ordered to be issued. The Minié bullet, being made smaller than the bore of the piece, could be almost dropped into the barrel. (It is

In 1865 the adoption of breech-loading arms caused the Enfield to be converted into a breechloader by fitting the 'Snider' breech mechanism to the Enfield barrel. This arrangement was, however, only temporary; and after a most exhaustive series of trials before a special committee on breech-loading rifles, the Henry barrel was in 1871 adopted, in conjunction with the Martini breech, for the new small-bore rifle for the British army, now known as the Martini-Henry rifle. No fewer than 104 different kinds of breech-loading small-arms were submitted to this committee, who decided that the Henry ·45-inch bore barrel 'was the best adapted for the requirements of the service,' on account of its 'superiority in point of accuracy, trajectory, allowance for wind, and pene-tration,' and also on account of its great durability. The Henry system of rifling is the invention of Mr. Alexander Henry, gunmaker, Edinburgh, and its essential peculiarity consists in the form of the rifled bore. . . . The length of the Henry barrel is $32\frac{1}{2}$ inches. The mean diameter of the bore is ·450 of an inch, and the rifling takes one complete turn in 22 inches. Its bullet is solid, with a slight cavity in the rear, and weighs 480 grains, the charge of powder being 85 grains."

The Royal Small-arms Factory, at Enfield Lock, on the narrow strip of land between the River Lea and the water-way known as the "Lea and Stort Navigation," about a mile and a quarter from Enfield Wash, dates its erection from 1855–6. It is true that a small ordnance factory was established here by the Government early in the present century, where a few thousand muskets were laboriously forged by hand each year; but when the sudden introduction of the rifle and the de-mands of the Russian War called for a supply of arms, which the trade, not only of Birmingham, but of all Europe and America, was unable to meet, the Government determined to erect machi-nery for the fabrication of arms on its own account. For this purpose the factory at Enfield was entirely re-modelled, but the successive adoption of the Snider and Martini-Henry rifles, as above shown, has been the means of producing a great change in the plant.

The manufactory on its present footing originated in the dissatisfaction for some time felt by the Board of Ordnance at being almost wholly de-pendent on private manufacturers for so important a part of the *matériel* of war, and in the recommen-dation, based on that feeling, of a Committee of the House of Commons on small arms, which sat in the session of 1854. The following interesting particulars of the establishment of this factory we quote from Tuff's "Enfield":—"Before 1804, when the manufactory in its original form was established at Enfield, the Government depended on the private trade for their small arms, and when that failed to provide a sufficient supply, recourse was had to the foreign market. At one time, indeed, the art of making muskets became extinct in this country. This occurred in 1802; and Lord Chatham, then Master General of the Ordnance, stated the circumstance publicly. Mr. John Colgate, who held an appointment in the Ordnance Department, was sent to Liège in 1779 to super-intend the setting up of 40,000 stand of arms for the service of the British Government. Major General Miller was despatched to Liège on a similar service in 1794, to Hamburg in 1795, and again to Hamburg in 1800, the store of arms in the Tower being at that time entirely expended. Again, in 1823, the names of not less than twenty English artificers had been ascertained who were in full employment in the national armoury estab-lishments of Russia and the United States, and no doubt many more might have been discovered. This was attributable to the encouragement and inducements to emigrate held out to our skilled artificers in that branch of trade by foreign nations, backed by the want of employment in their vocation at home; and it was apprehended at that time by men conversant with the subject that, unless the fostering care of the Government was continued in support of its armoury institution, the art must again be lost, or so far reduced that the country would a second time be left to depend on the casual supplies furnished by individual manufacturers. It has always been contended by men who have advocated the formation of Govern-ment armouries that the views of tradesmen were confined to individual profit. When they entered upon a contract, their only object was to bring their workmanship to such a state as to pass the official examination; they had no motive, it was said, to improve, or inducement to perpetuate, the art. When the call for arms by the Government ceased with a war, they turned their industry to other occupations, and their workmen were driven to seek employment in foreign countries, or left to neglect the art at home. It was also alleged that a national establishment offered the most perfect means of making experiments for the improvement of the service, and caused the saving of money in time of war as well as of peace, by operating as a check upon the prices of private manufacturers. But its principal object was to keep up among us the art of making military guns.

"It was considerations such as these and others that induced the Government, upon the recom-mendation of the committee of 1854—the year of the Crimean War—to establish a manufactory of small arms to a limited extent, under the direction of the Board of Ordnance."

While the Parliamentary committee was sitting, a deputation of practical men, previously sent out by the Board of Ordnance to make inquiries in the United States of America as to the mode of manufacturing small-arms there, and having ex-tensive powers to purchase machinery to be applied to their fabrication in this country, was pursuing its mission; and on the report of the committee, the House of Commons voted a sum not exceeding £150,000 towards the experiment. It should be mentioned here that down to this date most of the small-arms used by our soldiers were manufactured at Birmingham and in other parts of the kingdom, and purchased by the Government.

Since the above period extensive ranges of buildings have been constructed here. They occupy three sides of a square, are built of brick, in a good substantial manner, but quite devoid of ornamentation. About forty acres of ground describes the extent of the factory premises, including the land used as butts for testing each piece that is turned out. Machinery for the manufacture of rifles was imported from America, and was placed under the supervision of Mr. Perkins, as manager. The factory was subsequently taken in hand entirely by the Government, the first superintendent being Colonel Manley Dixon, R.A., who had charge of the works till 1872, when he was succeeded by Colonel Fraser. The factory at the present time is carried on under the superintendence of Colonel H. T. Arbuthnot, R A., with a staff of military and civil officers, the whole being under the direction of the War Department. The machinery here is probably the most perfect of any gun-making establishment, whether private or Government, at home or abroad; and as the manufacture proceeds it produces the various parts which are ultimately brought together to produce the gun with such accuracy of finish, that if a number of such guns were taken to pieces, and each part thrown together in a heap, the parts could be taken up indiscriminately, and be fitted together to make up guns without the slightest alteration or re-adjustment of either. This great nicety of finish is of immense importance, with regard to both convenience and economy, for if any part of a rifle becomes damaged or rendered unserviceable, the regimental armourer has merely to remove the injured portion, take the corresponding piece from his repository, and at once fit it into its place, without trouble or loss of time.

The mechanism of the "Martini-Henry" is much more simple than either of its predecessors above mentioned, for whilst the old "Enfield rifle" was composed of no less than fifty pieces, and the "Snider" of thirty-nine, the "Martini-Henry" consists of only twenty-seven pieces. Taking the average for the last four years, the number of weapons turned out at the factory in the course of a year is as follows:—Rifles (various), say 40,000; pistols, 5,000; and swords for rifles, 8,000. The plant and general facilities of the factory are in such condition that under great pressure 150,000 arms could be manufactured annually. The motive power is mainly steam, but one water-wheel is still used in certain work. The number of hands employed here is generally about 1,500.

The interior of the factory consists of a series of large work-rooms. The first usually entered by visitors is called the "action shop," from the fact that here everything relating to the action (or breech-loading and lock apparatus) being finished in it. The room is 200 feet in length, and contains nearly a thousand different machines. The turning-lathes, or machines for forming the butt or stock, are of the most ingenious character, and finish the work in such a delicate manner that the "action" can be instantly fitted to it without the slightest trouble or difficulty. The fitting the lock into the stock was a work involving much time and labour when performed by hand. By this machine a lock can be completely let into the stock in three minutes; indeed, the whole process of making and perfecting the stock does not occupy more than half an hour, and the only hand labour employed upon it is that which causes the friction of a little sand-paper along its surface after its removal from the last machine. Besides the work-rooms, several buildings are occupied as stores of stocks, barrels, &c., which are kept constantly in readiness for use as may be required.

The factory is open to visitors, even without previous application, on Mondays and Thursdays; but the proof-house, immediately to the south of the factory, is not usually shown. Every "piece" manufactured here is *tested* in the meadows close by.

The Powder-mills stand on the left hand as you enter Waltham Abbey, between two branches of the River Lea, which, as already stated, here is divided into several channels. They are screened from sight by groves of poplars and willows, mostly planted in long rows diagonally, after the fashion described by Virgil, in his "Georgics," under the name of a "quincunx."* This shelter is useful to keep away all grit and dust, and also, as already noticed, in order to counteract the violence of an explosion. These are the only powder-mills belonging to the Government, those at Faversham, Dartford, and Hounslow, being in private hands. They employ about 250 hands, and they cover a long strip of land about 200 acres in extent, which runs along the banks of the river from south to north.

It is almost needless to add that these powder-mills are very closely guarded, and are shown only to such strangers as have a genuine object in view in inspecting them. There is no special day set apart for their inspection.

---

* Virgil, Georg. II., 277, &c.

The appointment of superintendent of the powder-mills is made by the War Office, and is always held by an officer of the Royal Artillery. It is held generally for five years. The present superintendent is Colonel C. B. Brackenbury.

The visitor who wishes to inspect the works on entering the grounds passes along a very beautiful avenue of poplars, and finds himself at the gates of the superintendent's office. He is here warned that he must not carry lucifer-matches or other explosive articles about him, and that whenever he is required to put on leather-soled boots he will do so, as a single particle of grit from the high road, if it were to be driven into some parts of the mills, would cause an explosion.

The wood used for making charcoal is to a great extent grown on the estate. It is either alder, willow, or dog-wood; the latter comes chiefly from Germany, and each kind of wood is used in the composition of different sorts of powder, and is treated differently.

The wood is stacked about the grounds in every available corner, awaiting the time when it will be wanted, in order to be manufactured into that deadly combustible which renders the hearths and homes of soldiers desolate, and the necessity for which is a scandal to the Christian name. However, we must accept the actual state of things.

All the "hands" employed are bound to be steady and sober; no smoking is allowed on the premises; and each man on coming to work puts on a suit of greyish-black. Many of the "hands" are the sons of parents who were employed here before them; and the fact that they carry their lives constantly in their hands, and work with death ever before their eyes, has a sobering effect on them, and even (so I was informed) on their families at home.

The authorised visitor to the works, having been duly challenged at the gates by the police, and passed to the office of the superintendent, is placed in the care of an experienced guide, and thence conducted to the various "houses" where the several operations of gunpowder-making are carried on. These houses are separated by considerable spaces thickly planted with willow and alder wood. Thus if an explosion were to take place in one house the force would be broken by a screen of trees, and the other houses would not be likely to be affected by it.

The three ingredients of which gunpowder is composed are saltpetre, sulphur, and charcoal. For ordinary English gunpowder the proportions by weight are—saltpetre 75, sulphur 10, and charcoal 15 per cent. The processes required for the manufacture of one of the newest kinds of powder, called prismatic, are as follows:—1, refining the saltpetre; 2, refining the sulphur; 3, burning wood to produce charcoal; 4, mixing the ingredients for the "green" charge; 5, incorporating the "green" charge; 6, breaking down the mill-cake; 7, pressing the powder; 8, granulating; 9, dusting and glazing; 10, prismatic pressing; 11, stowing, to dry the powder; 12, blending prismatic powder.

1. The saltpetre arrives in bags from India, and is refined by boiling in a large quantity of water, and filtering the solution, which then runs into shallow receptacles, where it cools down, being kept in a state of agitation by wooden rakes. The saltpetre crystallises out in a form which closely resembles snow. It is then shovelled into vats, where it receives several washings.

2. The sulphur is next refined by being placed in a retort, and heated until it first melts and then commences to sublime, that is, to pass into a state of vapour. The vapour is led through a pipe kept cool by water outside it, and condenses into a treacle-like fluid, which passes into a receiver, and is then ladled out into tubs, where it sets into the beautiful yellow material which is known as refined sulphur. The impurities are, at the same time, left behind in the retort. Before being used for gunpowder, the sulphur has to be ground into a fine powder.

3. The woods used for gunpowder charcoal are three, as mentioned above. The larger descriptions of powder are made of willow and alder, the willow giving a rather stronger powder than the alder; while the fine-grained powders for use in small-arms are made of dog-wood, which is more expensive, and has not hitherto been grown largely on English soil. The woods are packed in iron cylinders, called slips, and introduced into furnaces also lined with iron. The flame from the fuel plays round the outside of the iron furnace-lining, heating it and the slip within. The various juices of the wood begin to distil, and the gases so produced pass through two holes in the far end of the slip and corresponding holes in the back of the furnace, whence they are carried down into the fire and contribute to the fuel, so that after the process has once been established the wood helps to burn itself. When the work of burning is completed, the slip, with its heated charcoal within, is taken out of the furnace, and placed in an iron cooler for twenty-four hours, after which it is emptied out, but not used for several days, in order to avoid the possibility of any heat existing in it. The charcoal is then ground in an apparatus like a coffee-mill.

4. The next process is that of mixing the ingredients. Hitherto the visitor has entered the houses without any other precaution than the leaving behind of any dangerous material ; but henceforth a new danger has to be provided against. The dust from powder flies about the houses, blackening the floor, and filling every cranny with explosive material, in spite of constant sweeping and washing. It is therefore most important that not a single particle of sand or grit should be introduced, lest the motion of a foot on the floor or any friction in the processes themselves should create heat enough to ignite the smallest atom of powder. All persons who enter the powder-houses are therefore obliged to have their feet encased in special leather boots, which never touch the ground outside. A small threshold board, about a foot high, marks the division between the black powder-house, which is called " clean " in the parlance of the factory, and the beautiful outside world, with its waving trees and glittering streams, which are all classed under the one word " foul." If by inadvertence a visitor plants his outside feet within the charmed precincts, he is instantly obliged to withdraw them, and the spot which he touched is carefully purified with wet mops.

In the mixing-houses the air is full of dust, and we literally breathe powder. Fifty pounds of the thin ingredients are placed in a drum, which revolves with great rapidity in one direction, while an orb armed with forks revolves within it in an opposite direction. In about five minutes the process of mixing is complete, and from that moment the three ingredients begin to be highly dangerous.

5. Though the "green" charge is explosive, it is not yet enough intimately mixed to make good gunpowder. It is accordingly next carried in bags to the incorporating mills, which are heavy iron or stone rollers, travelling round in pairs, each roller following its fellow in monotonous round upon its powder-bed, fenced from the rest of the incorporating house by the inclined sides of a sort of basin. The crushing and grinding motion thus produced brings each particle of the three ingredients into mutual contact, and produces, after a certain number of hours (which differ according to the powder to be produced), a soft cake, which is called the mill-cake. Before the runners are set in motion, the green charge placed upon the bed is sprinkled with distilled water, the quantity of which varies, according to the nature of powder sought and the condition of the atmosphere.

6. The mill-cake is then taken to the breaking-down house, where it is made to pass, carried on a canvas band, between a series of grooved rollers, which crush it into dust much more powerfully explosive than the " green " charge of the mixing-house.

7. The " meal," as it is now called, is next carried to the press-house. The press is a very strong box, containing a number of copper or gun-metal plates, so arranged that the meal can be filled in vertically between them, while they are kept separate by means of grooved plates. When the box is full, the grooved plates are withdrawn, and the spaces left by them filled up with meal, so that nothing now prevents the copper plates from coming together except the meal between them. The side of the box which has hitherto been open is now closed, and the box itself turned over, so that the copper-plates become horizontal. What is now the top of the box is then opened, and the whole placed on an hydraulic press. A ram rising from beneath thrusts the layers of copper plates and powder against a square block of wood above, which just fits into the box. The pressure is continued until the meal has become " press-cake " of the density required for the particular powder which is being made. The time is notified by the release of a spring when the box has risen high enough ; this spring rings a bell in a smaller room, where the powder-men are now ensconced ; for there are always some 800 pounds of powder in the press-box, and any atom of grit might possibly cause an explosion. A huge traverse of masonry stands between the press-house and the room where the men remain during the process. In addition to the lower growth of the willow and groves of alders, walnut and ash trees surround these terrible press-houses, which are thus mysteriously hidden, not only from the outer world, but even from the rest of the works. The dusky shade and the dark reflection of the green trees in the water, and the black powder-houses themselves, lend an air of mystery to these temples of the art of destruction.

8. The press-cake is carried by water, in black roofed boats, not unlike gondolas, to the granulating-house, where it enters a machine not unlike the breaking-down machine already described, but larger, and with toothed instead of grooved rollers. The cake is here cut by the rollers into " grain " of various sizes, and sorted by sieves kept in perpetual agitation under the stream of grain.

9. The dusting and glazing operations are carried on in long cylindrical reels and wooden barrels, of which different sorts are used, according to the work required. For some powders a little black-lead is introduced, to give them a glossy facing.

10. We now come to the prismatic press-house. The grain suitable for making prismatic powder is carried also in boats to the prismatic press-house, where stands an elaborate machine, consisting mainly of a huge iron circular block, which contains thirty holes. In each hole is put a cylindrical plug of phosphor-bronze, the interior of which is cut exactly to the shape of the prism required. A so-called "charger," with thirty funnels corresponding with the thirty holes in the block, moves backwards and forwards on rails. It is filled with the

a considerable amount of moisture; this is now to be expelled by means of heat. For this purpose the powder is placed on trays in drying-chambers, which are gradually raised to a heat differing according to the character of the powder required. For some powder it is as much as 125 degrees Fahrenheit.

12. But in spite of all the care taken, and though a series of scientific experiments follow the powder through all its stages, there always exists a certain amount of difference between quantities of powder,

THE CATTLE MARKET, WALTHAM.

grain outside the machine, then pushed directly over the block; two motions of a handle then cut off exactly the quantity of grain required, and allow it to fall from the funnels into the phosphor-bronze moulds below. The charge is then withdrawn, the top of the machine brought down to seal the tops of the holes, and then, by hydraulic pressure, thirty plungers, one for each hole, rise up and compress the charges of grain, so as to form them into prisms of the size and shape required. The top is then raised, and the pressed prisms are thrust out of their moulds by pressure from below. The skill required in powder-making may be estimated from the fact that the time necessary to press prismatic powder which will produce certain definite effects varies greatly, according to the state of the atmosphere. The variation at Waltham Abbey has been found to be as much as between twenty-five and sixty-five seconds.

11. All powders hitherto made here have in them

which are called "lots," made at different times and under different atmospheric conditions. It is, therefore, very important to bring the material to a certain average, so that the accurate shooting of artillery or of small-arms may be counted upon. For this purpose every "lot" of powder is proved by actually firing a charge of it. The lots which give the higher results are then mixed in strict proportion with lower lots, so that it is impossible, in making up a cartridge, to take an undue quantity of either the higher or the lower lot. This process is called "blending," and after it is gone through, a charge is again taken and fired, to secure the fitness of the powder for its destined use.

All sorts of strange stories are told about the experiences and hairbreadth escapes of employés in these interesting works. Thus, on one occasion a lucifer-match was found to have passed between the rollers of the granulating machine; and on another occasion a key was discovered in the same condition. It seems little less than a miracle that such a thing could have happened without causing an explosion.

The works here can turn out about 30,000 barrels of powder in a year, or about 700 barrels weekly. It may be of interest to add that, in-

allowed to dig in them, these grounds are virgin soil, and accordingly they nourish a profusion of wild flowers which are scarcely known outside. Hence they are a favourite haunt of botanists who can procure admission to them; but the favour is sparingly accorded.

The introduction of gunpowder into England is connected with the honoured name of Evelyn, as that family are said to have brought from Holland the secret of its manufacture. Mr. George Evelyn,

ON THE LEA.

cluding the sidings and canals, there are about ten miles of water on the estate, of which three and three-quarter miles are navigable. In addition to the screens of trees, the more dangerous portions of the works are isolated by solid traverses of earth or brick, to minimise the effects of explosion.

The "works" which I have described can boast of almost a venerable antiquity. In the "Anglorum Speculum, or the Worthies of England" (1684), it it is stated that there were gunpowder mills "on the River Ley, between Waltham and London." In 1735 Farmer speaks of them, in his "History of Waltham," as being the property of a Mr. John Walter; and in the same book there is a delightful description of gunpowder. As nobody is

grandfather of the author of "Sylva," received, about 1590, a licence to set up powder mills at Long Ditton and at Godstone, Surrey.

"The works at Faversham, afterwards for so many years the Government gunpowder factory, date from Elizabeth's reign; but they were then secondary in importance to those at Godstone. There seems reason, however, to suppose that powder-mills existed at Waltham Abbey as far back as 1561, for in that year we find John Thomworth, of Waltham, in treaty, on behalf of Elizabeth, for the purchase of saltpetre, sulphur, and staves for barrels. Fuller also refers, in his "Worthies," to the powder mills of Waltham Abbey, of which he was appointed vicar in 1641. In 1787 these mills were sold to the Crown by John Walton, and reorganised under the superintendence of the famous Sir William Congreve. The old royal factory at Faversham was given up after the Peace of 1815, being let, and afterwards sold, to the well-known firm of John Hall & Co. . . . The Waltham Abbey works have been greatly enlarged in recent years, and no expense has been spared to render them, by the introduction of new and improved machinery, the most complete, as well as the safest, in the world." *

Henceforth our travels will be in Essex.

CHAPTER XLIII.

WALTHAM ABBEY.

Situation of the Town—Its Etymology—Foundation of the Abbey by Jovi—Its Re-foundation by Harold—The Legend of the Holy Cross—Gifts bestowed on the Abbey—Harold's Tomb—The Church despoiled by William the Conqueror—Its Recovery under subsequent Sovereigns—Disputes between the Abbot and Townspeople—Henry III. and the Abbot's Dinner—An Incident touching the Reformation—Income of the Abbey at the Dissolution—Fuller, the Historian—The Conventual Estate passes into Secular Hands—Description of the Abbey Church —Sale of the Church Bells—Present Condition of the Remains of the Abbey—Rome-Land—The Abbey Gateway and Bridge.

WALTHAM ABBEY, or Waltham Holy Cross, as it was once called, must be carefully distinguished from its neighbour in Hertfordshire, which is described in a previous chapter.* It is a large, irregular town, and evidently one of considerable antiquity, as is shown by the variety of projecting gables, and the quaint carved figures which still stand in bold relief at the corner of more than one of its streets, like those with which one meets at Ipswich, Saffron-Walden, and many other towns of the eastern counties. The town is situated on low ground near the river Lea, which here forms a number of small islands, and is skirted by fruitful meadows, that have long been famous for the succulent and nourishing qualities of the grass. The spot was originally part of the Forest of Essex, and it derived the name of Waltham from the Saxon words *weald-ham*, the dwelling or hamlet on the weald, or open forest.

The town is twelve miles north-east from London, and about three-quarters of a mile eastward from Waltham Station on the Cambridge line of the Great Eastern railway. The road thither from the railway station, however, is by no means attractive : it is straight as an arrow, and is little more than a raised causeway between low-lying green meadows, with a deep ditch on either side. The river Lea, which we cross—the Lea of quaint old Izaak Walton—here separates into a variety of streams, and we pass no less than four bridges before we find ourselves at the end of a narrow street, with gabled tenements on either side, and close under the shadow of the tower which has been our beacon.

Waltham appears to have been a place of note long before the Norman Conquest. It is first mentioned in a document dated as far back as the time of Canute the Great, at which period its then owner, Tovi, or Tovius, standard-bearer to that monarch, founded on the outskirts of the forest here a church and a village, placing in the former two priests, and erecting in the latter some tenements for his " villains," and placing in them " threescore-and-six dwellers." After his death, Athelstan, his son and heir, a prodigal young man, squandered his inheritance, and Waltham appears by some means or other to have reverted to the Crown. The religious establishment of Tovi, however, continued, and probably with some augmentation, till the reign of Edward the Confessor, who bestowed certain lands here on his brother-in-law, Earl Harold, son of Godwin, Earl of Kent ; but the grant was made upon the condition that Harold should build a monastery in the place, " where *was a little convent*, subject to the canons and their rules." The " little convent " mentioned in the Confessor's charter, evidently alludes to Tovi's foundation, which might have been augmented by casual donations previous to this mention of it.

In 1062, the year in which the grant was dated, Harold refounded or enlarged the original establishment of Tovi, endowing it as a convent, doubling the number of its canons, settling on them ample estates, and founding hard by a school of religious and useful learning.† Farmer, in his " History of Waltham," says that each of the canons had one manor appropriated for his support, and that the dean had six ; making in all seventeen. From the charter of confirmation granted by Edward the Confessor, it appears that

---

* See *ante*, p. 392.

* Encyclopædia Britannica.
† " Dugdale's Monasticon," Vol. VI., pt. I. p. 56.

Harold endowed his new foundation with the manors of Passefeld, Welda or Walde, Upminster, Wahlfara or Wallifare, Tippedene, Alwartune, Wudeforde, Lambehyth, Nasingam, Brekendune, Melnho, Alrichsey, Wormelei, Nethleswelle or Neteswell, Hicche, Lukintone, and Westwaltham. "All these manors the king granted them with sac, soc, tol, and team, &c., free from all gelds and payments, in the most full and ample manner, as appears by the charter among the records of the tower."

The parish derived its second name of "Holy Cross" from a cross, bearing on it a figure of the Saviour, which was said to have been found. at Montacute, in Somerset, and to have been brought miraculously by oxen, undriven, to this place. The cross itself is said to have shown very miraculous powers; and among the wonders told of it is that Harold was cured of the palsy in consequence of a pilgrimage to it.

The following is a translation of the legend of Waltham Abbey, by the late Mr. W. Burges, from the *De inventione Stæ Crucis*," probably written some time at the end of the twelfth century:— "Once upon a time, when Canute reigned over England, there lived at a place in Somersetshire, named Montacute (but called Lutegaresberi by the common people), a smith who was adorned with all the Christian virtues. Thus he was 'vir magnæ simplicitatis et bonæ indolis, sine malicia timens Deum, &c. Indeed, so much was he respected, that the parish priest committed to his care the water, fire, and lighting of the church. One night, when this worthy man was in a deep sleep, he saw in a vision 'venerandi decoris effigiem,' who told him when he went to his duties at the church next morning, to request the priest to assemble the whole of his parishioners, and after prayer, exhortation, and fasting, to lead them in procession to the top of the hill, and there to dig until he found the treasure hid for ages, viz., the cross, the sign of the passion of our Lord. The smith took no notice of this communication, and accordingly the vision appeared again the night following, but with a severe countenance. The smith, by the advice of his wife, this time also neglected the admonitions of the vision, and thus gave the latter the occasion to make a third visit, thereby completing the usual number. At last the smith did tell the priest, and the latter, with not only his own parishioners, but also with many people from the surrounding country, set off in procession, singing litanies, the smith leading the way: and when they had attained the top of the hill with 'uberrima lacrimarum effusione,' proceeded to dig, and after going to the depth of forty cubits, were rewarded by the discovery of a stone of wonderful size, with a great fissure through the middle. The next thing was to remove part of the stone, which was done 'non minus fletuum ubertate quam manuum impulsione,' and then appeared the wonderful crucifix of black marble (silex), which was destined to work so many miracles, and eventually be the war-cry of the English upon the field of Senlac. Another but smaller crucifix was also found placed under the right arm, and under the left a bell of ancient workmanship, such as are seen round the necks of cattle. The discovery was completed by a book of the gospels.

"Not knowing exactly what to do, a tent was placed over the excavation until the lord of the place could be sent for. The lord was 'Tovi le prude,' a very great man indeed, being described as 'totius Angliæ post regem primus.' He, when he came, 'vidit et gavisus est.' After which it was determined to remove the objects to the atrium of the parish church. The next morning, Tovi and sundry church dignitaries, both episcopal and abbatial, being present, the smaller crucifix was given up to the parish church, but the other objects being placed upon a wagon, 'cum ornamentorum decora varietate,' were to be deposited wherever the twelve red oxen and twelve cows who were attached to the wagon might carry it. Tovi then mentioning the names of his various residences, devoutly prayed that the car and oxen might proceed to one of them, promising, moreover, in that case, that he would endow the servants of the Holy Cross with the revenues of the town where the cross should be deposited; the wagon, however, stood still, nor could all the efforts either of the bystanders or of the oxen get it to move. At last Tovi remembered the poor hunting-lodge he had begun to build at a place called Waltham, when, 'mirabile dictu, fide mirabilius,' the oxen began to move at such a rate that it seemed more as if the wagon impelled the oxen than that the latter drew the wagon. On the day appointed for the exaltation, when the workmen attempted to drive a nail into the right arm, for the purpose of fastening on the jewelled ornaments given by Tovi, immediately, says the chronicler, blood issued from the stone in the same manner as in former time water issued from the rock. The blood was of course preserved, and formed another of the very many relics which enriched the consecrated house at Waltham.

Glitha, the wife of Tovi, presented a splendid golden and jewelled crown, besides the circlet, which she wore in common with all noblewomen, which was fixed round the thigh of the image, while her bracelets and other jewels were fashioned into a subpedaneum, into which was inserted a wondrous stone, whose property was to emit rays during the night, and thus afford light to travellers. Tovi appears to have made a foundation for two priests and other clergy, besides enriching the church with various gifts of gold and silver. . . . After the erection of the new church the crucifix still continued its miracles, the most famous of which took place when Harold was on his way to fight the Normans : he went to Waltham to pay his devotions, and to pray for victory. When he had prostrated himself to the ground in the form of a cross, the image which before looked upwards, now bowed down its head, 'a bad sign indeed, and significant of the future :' and the chronicler adds that he had this fact from Turkil, the sacrist, who was at the altar at the time. . . In 1192 the cross was covered anew with silver, but the ornaments on the figure itself were left untouched, probably in consequence of what had happened a few years before, when the crucifix being under repair, Robert, the goldsmith of St. Alban's, took off the circlet round the thigh (probably that given by the wife of Tovi), and all those present were struck blind for a considerable time."

It was to the "Holy Cross" that Harold dedicated his new foundation, which he enriched with a vast number of relics and costly vessels. We learn from the Harleian Manuscripts that "among other rich gifts bestowed by Harold on his new college were the following:—Seven little caskets or boxes (*scrinia*) for precious things, three of gold, and four of silver gilded, enriched with gems and full of relics. Four great thuribles (*censers*) of gold and silver. Six great candlesticks, two of gold and four of silver. Three large vessels or pitchers of Greek workmanship, silver and richly gilded. Four crosses of gold and silver studded with gems. Another cross of silver of the weight of fifty marks. Five suits for the priests, ornamented with gold and precious gems. Five other vestments ornamented with gold and gems, one extremely rich and weighty. Two copes covered with gold and gems. Five chalices, two of gold and three of silver. Four altars with relics, one of gold, and three of silver gilded. A silver horn, and various other articles. The relics were still more valuable and numerous, and many (if we may credit the legends) were the miracles wrought by them." *

It is the received account that Harold was killed at the battle of Hastings, and that his corpse was carried from the field and buried at Waltham

Abbey. His tomb was shown for many centuries as marking the resting-place of the last of our Saxon kings, though Giraldus Cambrensis among old historians, and Sir Francis Palgrave among modern writers, doubt the fact, and relate a tradition that Harold escaped alive from the field of Hastings, and lived in religious seclusion at Chester, where he ended his days as a monk or lay brother. The latter author considers that the tomb at Waltham was nothing more than a cenotaph, though it bore on it the inscription, " Hic jacet Harold infelix," words which certainly would seem to assert a positive fact ; and Fuller, in his " Church History," gives a circumstantial account of the opening of the monument towards the end of Elizabeth's reign, when a skeleton was discovered inside it. Farmer's history, quoted above, contains a copper-plate engraving of a mask sculptured in grey marble, which, he says, was one of the ornaments of the tomb, and was then in his own possession. The burial of Harold here is accepted as probably true by no less an authority than Dr. Freeman, though disputed by Mr. John H. Parker.

Be this, however, as it may, whether Harold found here his last resting-place or no, it may easily be supposed that William the Conqueror owed little kindness and showed little favour to the religious house which owned his vanquished rival for its founder. He accordingly laid heavy hands upon the church of Holy Cross, robbing it of vestments, plate, and jewels, though, somehow or other, he left the monks in possession of their manors and other estates ; and in subsequent reigns their properties in the neighbourhood appear to have increased, for Matilda, the first wife of Henry I., bestowed on the convent the abbey mill, which still stands close to the gateway shown in our illustration, and was, at that time, a valuable gift ; while the same king's second wife, Adeliza of Lorraine, bestowed on it all the tithes of Waltham, including not only those of her tenants, but of her own demesne land. Stephen appears to have done little more than confirm the charters of his predecessors.

Mr. Freeman, in an article in the "Transactions of the Essex Archæological Society," is inclined to fix the date of the consecration of the new church as 1059 or 1060, and he has at the same time endeavoured to reconcile the various accounts concerning the burial of Harold. He supposes that he was in the first instance interred under a heap of stones upon the sea-coast of Sussex, and afterwards re-buried at Waltham. The new foundation here, as may be easily imagined, suffered greatly under the two first Norman kings ; but as the

---

* Harl. MSS. 3776.

two queens of Henry I. were both connected with the place, it began to recover in his reign, and in that of his successor, Stephen.

Henry II. did not find that the monks of Waltham turned to good account the gifts so generously bestowed on them; and, therefore, as we find recorded in his charter, he dissolved the foundation, and scattered the dean and eleven canons to the wind. The last dean was Guido Rufus, who, having previously been suspended by the Archbishop of Canterbury, resigned his deanery in 1177 to the king. The story is thus told by a local antiquary:—"This preliminary proceeding having taken place, the king visited Waltham on the eve of Pentecost, when Walter, Bishop of Rochester, on the part of the Archbisop of Canterbury, Gilbert Bishop of London, John Bishop of Norwich, and Hugh Bishop of Durham, assembling by precept from the King and mandate of the Pope (Alexander III.), the said archbishop consenting, sixteen regular canons of the Order of St. Augustine, namely, six of Cirencester, six of Oseney, and four of Chich, were inducted into the church, and Walter de Gaunt, a canon of Oseney, was constituted the first abbot of the new foundation. The church was at the same time declared exempt from episcopal jurisdiction; and Pope Lucius III. subsequently by his bull confirmed to this monastery the exemption from all episcopal jurisdiction. The church thus settled was dedicated first to the Holy Cross, and afterwards to St. Lawrence." At the same time, anno 1191, the use of the *pontificals*, namely, the mitre, crosier, ring, &c., was granted to the abbot. The charter of Henry II. thus defines the ancient liberties of Waltham Church:— "Semper fuit regalis capella ex primitiva sui fundatione nulli Archiepiscopo vel Episcopo, sed tantum ecclesiæ Romanæ et Regiæ dispositioni subjecta." It may be remarked that Waltham is still exempt from the Archdeacon's visitation.

Henry not only confirmed to the newly-founded canons the lands which they had held by gift from Harold, but added to them other possessions in the neighbourhood, including the manors of Epping and Siwardston, or Sewardstone; adding to his charter, by way of preamble, the remarkable expression that it was "fit that Christ his spouse should have a new dowry." The convent was further enriched by a charter from Richard I., confirming all former grants, and also bestowing on the canons the entire manner of Waltham, with "the great wood and park called ' Harold's Park,' " the market of Waltham, and most of the village of Nasing—460 acres in all—on the easy terms of the monks paying £60 into his royal exchequer in lieu

of all services. Richard also, by another charter, confirmed all the former grants, and made further gifts to the monastery, among which was the stately mansion called Copped Hall, but appointed the latter to be held in fee, and hereditarily, of the church of Waltham, *Sancte Crucis*, by Robert Fitz-Aucher. Other pious persons, in the course of the same reign, gave broad lands to the monks "*pro salute animarum suarum;*" and Henry III., who frequently took up his residence at the abbey, requited the hospitality of the canons by giving to them the right of holding a fair annually for seven days. He also augmented their revenues with many rich and costly gifts, and from his date the abbey gradually became so distinguished by royal and noble benefactors as to rank with the most wealthy institutions in the kingdom.

Henry's favours to the monastery were not entirely disinterested; for he resided here, it is said, in order to save the expenses of keeping a court; and he occasionally sought and found in the abbot sympathy and help in his distresses.

In 1242, according to Matthew Paris, the church was re-dedicated, though he does not enlighten us as to the occasion on which this ceremony was performed. Most probably it was on the occasion of the addition of new buildings on the south side of the old Norman church, including what now is called "our Lady's Chapel."

"When Simon de Seham was abbot, in the 30th Henry III. (1245), a dispute arose between the abbot and the townsmen of Waltham about the common lands. 'The men of Waltham,' says Farmer, 'came into the marsh, which the abbot and his convent formerly enjoyed as several to themselves, and killed four mares, worth forty shillings sterling at least, and drove away all the rest: the abbot was politicly pleased for the present not to take notice thereof. Next year the same men of Waltham went to the abbot the Tuesday before Easter, in the name of the whole village, and demanded of him to remove his mares and colts out of the marsh. This the abbot refused to do, adding, that if his bailiffs had placed his cattle otherwise than they ought, they might do well to have it amended, and yet so as to defer the matter till the Tuesday after Easter. On that Tuesday, Richard, brother to the king, Duke of Cornwall, came to Waltham, at which time both the men and the women of the town repaired to the gate of the abbey to receive the abbot's final answer.'

"He put them off with the information that he was preparing for a journey into Lincolnshire, to meet the justices itinerant, and said that he would settle the affair at his return. Not satisfied, they, went into the pasture, and in driving out the abbot's mares and colts, drowned three worth twenty shillings, spoiled ten more to the value of ten marks, and beat the keepers, who resisted them, even to the shedding of blood. Fearing, however, that they should be prosecuted, on the return of the abbot, they desired a 'love day,' and

amerced twenty marks, which the abbot remitted; and, on their submission, he *assoyled* them from the excommunication."*

Not long after the above incident the same abbot was engaged with Peter, Duke of Savoy, the king's uncle and lord of the manor of Cheshunt, in a law-suit about boundaries, each asserting his right to some meadow-land lying between two branches of the river Lea, on the west side of the town. Of the altercations that arose in

WALTHAM ABBEY—INTERIOR.

offered to pay damages for the injury committed; but, instead of doing so, they went to London and accused the abbot to the king of having wrongfully taken away their common land, and bringing up new customs, adding that he would 'eat them up to the bone.' The abbot then excommunicated the men of Waltham; and they impleaded him at common law for appropriating their common land to himself. They were unsuccessful, and after a long suit in the King's Bench, were glad to confess that they had done wrong, and they were

consequence of this disagreement we have spoken in a previous chapter.† This dispute about the debatable land was often revived afterwards, and was undecided when the last abbot resigned the convent to Henry VIII.

In 1258, the Parliament having refused money to Henry III., the king prevailed upon the Pope to send a messenger, named Mansuetus, to Eng-

* "History of Waltham," pp. 71--2.   † See *ante*, p. 386.

land, asking a supply from the abbeys and churches. The abbot of Waltham was among the first to be applied to on this occasion; and, partly by threats and partly by entreaties, he was induced to issue a security for 200 marks. A similar application was made at another time to the abbots of Waltham, St. Albans, and Reading, for the sum of 5,000 marks, which the king had promised to the young Earl of Gloucester, as a marriage portion with his niece, the daughter of Guy, Earl of Angoulême.

can hardly digest the breast of a chicken.' The king pledged him in return, and having dined heartily, and thanked him for his good cheer, he departed. A few days after, the abbot was sent for to London, and lodged in the Tower, where he was kept a close prisoner, and, for some time, fed upon bread and water. At length, a sirloin of beef was set before him, on which he fed as heartily as one of his own ploughmen. In the midst of his meal, the king burst into the room from a private

GATEWAY AND BRIDGE, WALTHAM ABBEY.   (*See page* 415).

But this was not successful; the three abbots declaring that they were unable to raise such a sum, nor could they justify such an act, even if they were able.

Farmer relates the following pleasant anecdote of Henry III.; but the abbot who enjoyed the benefit of his prescribed regimen is not named:—"Having disguised himself in the dress of one of his guards, he contrived to visit, about dinner time, the Abbey of Waltham, where he was immediately invited to the abbot's table; a sirloin of beef being set before him, he played so good a part, that the abbot exclaimed, 'Well fare thy heart, and here's a cup of sack to the health of thy master; I would give a hundred pounds could I feed so heartily on beef as thou dost, but my poor queasy stomach

closet, and demanded his hundred pounds, which the abbot gave with no small pleasure, and on being released returned to his monastery with a heart and pocket much lighter than when he left it a few days before."

Such stories have been told also of other English kings, from the early Norman days down to those of Henry VIII.

Stow, in an account of Wat Tyler's rebellion, says that King Richard II. was "now at London, now at Waltham," so that it is clear that more than one king made the abbey a place of residence.

We read but little more of Waltham Abbey until we come to the reign of Henry VIII., when it accidentally became the scene of a conversation, the results of which have ultimately changed the whole course of ecclesiastical affairs in England, by bringing about an event on which the Reformation mainly hinged. It was here that Thomas Cranmer, then a plain Fellow of Jesus College, Cambridge, happened to be resident, on account of the plague, as tutor to the sons of Mr. Cressy, whose wife was the future archbishop's relation, when he was accidentally introduced to Fox and Gardiner, just at the time when the propriety of King Henry's divorce was being canvassed in privileged and "well-informed circles." We allude to the occasion when, in reply to Fox and Gardiner, he said that, instead of waiting month after month and year after year, to learn the Pope's will, it would be better to have the moot-point about a man's marriage with his brother's widow referred to the universities and learned divines of this and other nations. When Fox reported this speech to the king, the latter said, with an oath, that the Cambridge fellow "had the sow by the right ear." And so it proved in the end.

But this service did not save the abbey from the king's greedy commissioners. In 1539, its gross income, according to Speed, was £1,079 12s. 1d., while the clear income is reckoned by Dugdale at £900. And so the fiat went forth. The canons were forced to quit their comfortable nests, and their broad acres and manors were seized by the king and his ministers. The last of a long line of two-and-thirty abbots was Robert Fuller. He was afterwards chosen prior of St. Bartholomew's, in Smithfield, which he held *in commendam*, and which he was also obliged to surrender to the king in 1540. Abbot Fuller may fairly be reckoned among the literati of his monastery; and from his "History," written in a folio volume 460 pages, his namesake Fuller, who was curate of Waltham in the time of the Commonwealth, compiled almost all the particulars of the account of Waltham Abbey, which he appended as a supplement to his "Church History of Britain," published in 1656.

By Edward VI. the conventual estate was granted to Sir Anthony Denny, whose grandson, Sir Edward Denny, the second owner, was raised by Charles I. to the earldom of Norwich. From him it passed, by the marriage of his daughter and heir, to the celebrated James Hay, Earl of Carlisle; and from the Hays it came into the possession of the Wakes, whose head, Sir Herewald Wake, is now lord of the manor. His grandfather, Sir Charles Wake, was an extensive contributor to the funds raised about thirty years ago for beautifying and restoring the noble church, and the east window of painted glass was his donation.

"Originally the abbey church was a very magnificent building, and its curious remains must be regarded as the earliest undoubted specimen of the Norman style of architecture now existing in England. Though erected by Earl Harold, in the Anglo-Saxon period, it cannot be justly referred to any other style than that which the Normans permanently introduced after the Conquest. The great intercourse between the two great countries, which King Edward the Confessor so particularly encouraged previously to that era, and the preference which he gave to Norman customs and Norman artificers, will readily account for this church being constructed from Norman designs. Edward himself caused the abbey church of Westminster to be rebuilt on similar principles; and in respect to the monastery at Waltham, that monarch, as appears from his charter, dated in 1062, may be almost regarded as its coeval founder with Earl Harold."

Sufficient is known of this structure to state that its original form was that of a cross, and that a square tower, which 'contained a ring of five great tuneable bells,' arose from the intersection of the nave and transept; the two great western supporters of which are connected with and partly wrought into the present east end. Some part of the old central tower fell from mere decay; the remainder was purposely destroyed, as we gather from the following entry in the churchwardens' accounts:—" Anno 1556. *Imprimis*. For coles to undermine a piece of the steeple which stood after the first fall, 2s." It was the opinion of the late Sir Gilbert Scott that the central tower of St. Albans abbey was designed to be destroyed in the same way, but that it was saved by an accident.

The interior of the church is certainly striking for its massiveness rather than its beauty. Passing under the western tower we enter the church through a very handsome Pointed arch, adorned with floriated, crocketed, and finialed work, and through a porch or vestibule with a handsome groined roof, both probably of the reign of Henry III.

The first two and most westerly arches of the nave are pointed; but they probably were made to supersede the semicircular Norman originals, six in number, which divide the main body of the church from its side aisles. The columns vary from each other both in diameter and in ornamentation. They are thus described:—"Spiral grooves (deeply cut), proceeding from the base to the capital, diversify two of these columns; and two others are surrounded by indented zig-zags, in successive rows; thus assuming a strict similarity of character with the great columns of the nave in Durham Cathedral. Another tier of large arches, springing from very short columns and pilasters, surmounts the former arches, on each side; except at the west end, where, as before stated, two of the lower ones have been altered into the high-pointed form, and carried up to the string-course of the *triforium*, or clerestory, which contains the principal windows that give light to the nave. These are each fronted by a central and two smaller arches, between which and the windows there is a narrow passage extending along the sides. Most of the mouldings are of the zig-zag form, but there are some distinct variations of character. The length of the church is 106 feet; its breadth, including the aisles, is about 53 feet. A ground plan, a perspective view, and a longitudinal section, of the interior of Waltham church as it was half a century ago, may be seen in Britton's "Architectural Antiquities," Vol. iii.

We have already said that Harold's tomb stood several yards beyond the east end of the present church, and that its site is bare, and that his bones, if they be there, now lie *sub Jove frigido*. But besides the founder Harold, many eminent persons, in the good old palmy days of its glories, found their last resting-place within these monastic walls. "Hugh Nevil, Protho-forester of England, who died 'full of years,' A.D. 1222, according to Matthew Paris, was buried here 'under a noble engraven marble sepulchre;' not the least remnant of which is now known to exist. His son also, John Nevil, the successor to his revenues and offices; and Robert Passelew, archdeacon of Lewes, a despised and discarded minion of Henry III., who died at his house at Waltham, in the year 1252, were also among the number of those interred here. Near the altar rails is a defaced grey slab, which is indented with a mitred figure; this, with two or three brass plates of Queen Elizabeth's time, are the oldest memorials which now remain.

On the south side of the communion rails is the Jacobean tomb of a person of quality, presenting an amusing contrast to another handsome monument on the north to a wealthy and respectable gentlemen of plebeian and commercial antecedents.

As may be easily imagined, the Dennies did not hold the fair abbey lands and monastic buildings of Waltham without leaving their dust behind them in its aisles. Thus, if we search the parish registers, we find that "Edward Denny, first and only Earl of Norwich" (of that creation), was buried in this church in December, 1630. And near the east end of the south aisle is a mural monument in memory of Sir Edward Denny,

Knt.,—"'Sonn of ye Right Honourable Sr Anthony Denny, Counsellor of Estate and Executor to King Henry 8, and of Joane Champernōn, his wife,'—and his Lady who was the daughter of Pierce Edgecombe, Esq., of Mount Edgecombe, and 'svmtime Maide of Honor to Qveene Elizabeth,—and who, 'ovt of meane Fortvnes bvt no meane affection, prodvced this Monvment.' Sir Edward was one of the Counsel of Munster, in Ireland, and governor of Kerry and Desmond. He died on the 12th of February, 1599, aged 52 years, and is represented in plate armour, lying on his side: his head is partly supported by his helmet, and partly by his left hand, the elbow resting upon a cushion; his right hand being brought across the body, rests upon his sword. His Lady has a ruff and close boddice; and kneeling in front are their ten children, *viz.*, four boys and six girls. The inscription states, that 'this worthy Knight, cvt off like a pleasavnt frvite before perfect ripeness,'—was 'religiovs, wise, jvst, right valiant, most active, learnings frinde, prides foe, kindly lovinge, and mvtch beloved;' and that 'he was honored wth ye dignitie of knighthood, by dve deserte, in ye Field.' Over the tomb are the family arms (with quarterings), *viz.*, Gu. a saltire Arg. between Crosses pattée, Or."

About 1864 a partial restoration of the old abbey church was commenced, and the cost of the work done since that time has amounted to upwards of £8,000. The church is now no longer the dreary and dilapidated building that it was less than a quarter of a century ago, although the edifice has not been thoroughly restored, but merely saved from that utter decay and ruin by which it was at one time threatened. The Lady Chapel, on the south side of the chancel, and the most ruinous part of the old structure, has been repaired at a cost of £1,000, defrayed by Sir T. Fowell Buxton, Bart., and has been thrown open into the body of the church; the hideous old deal pens, called "pews," have been replaced by oaken benches all looking eastward, and all the galleries have been removed. The ceiling—the dark colours of which for years only served to add a sense of weight and oppression where all should be light and graceful—has been replaced by one of wood, painted in bright colours, and far more suited to Norman architecture, though perfectly flat and horizontal. Instead of the large square holes in the walls, filled with glass, that had long served as windows, new windows set in a framework of the Norman style have been inserted throughout: and almost all the windows have been filled with painted glass as memorials of departed friends. The chancel was repaired at the expense of the late Sir Charles Wake, Bart., the lord of the manor of Waltham. The new reredos was the gift of Mr. Edenborough, of Thrift Hall, in the neighbourhood of the town ; whilst the remainder of the work has been carried out at the cost of the parishioners and their friends.

The Lady Chapel, which is probably of Henry III.'s time, is supported by graduated buttresses, ornamented with elegantly-formed niches. Beneath it is a crypt, "the fairest," says Fuller, "that ever I saw," the roof of which is sustained by groined arches. The superstructure was modernised, so that scarcely a vestige of its ancient character remained. The crypt was used as a place of worship, and it had its regular priest and other attendants ; the reading-desk was covered with plates of silver. In the Churchwardens' Accounts, mention is made of six annual *Obits*, to defray the expenses of which various lands were bequeathed, and a stock of eighteen cows was let out to farm for 18s. The sum allotted for each *Obit* was thus expended:—To the parish priest, 4d. ; to our Ladye's priest, 3d. ; to the charnel priest, 3d. ; to the two clerks, 4d. ; to the children (choristers), 3d. ; to the sexton, 2d. ; to the bellman, 2d. ; for two tapers, 2d. ; for oblation, 2d. ; &c.

In the burial-ground, close to the south entrance, is a very fine wide-spreading elm, the trunk of which, at several feet above the earth, is nearly twenty feet in circumference. The present tower stands at the west end of what is now the parish church, but was formerly the nave. It is a heavy and uninteresting structure, and is a poor substitute for its predecessor, though good for its time ; it was built by the parishioners in the reign of Queen Mary, out of "their stock in the church box." This "stock" was an aggregate from various sources, as the sale of stone, lead, and timber from the monastic buildings ; but it was chiefly obtained by the sale of the goods of a *brotherhood* belonging to this church, consisting of three priests, three choristers, and two sextons, which was not dissolved until Edward the Sixth's reign. Two hundred and seventy-one ounces of plate, the property of this fraternity (which had been saved from confiscation on account of the avowed intention of the parish to erect the above tower), were sold for £67 14s. 9d. At the same time many rich dresses were disposed of, including a cape of cloth of gold to Sir Edward Denny for £3 6s. 8d., and two altar-cloths of velvet and silk, value £2. It is not improbable but that the brotherhood thus despoiled was that of an *hospital*, which had been originally founded within the precincts of the monastery by

the abbot and convent of Waltham, about the year 1218.

It appears from Fuller that the bells out of the old tower were hung for some years in a temporary frame of timber which stood at the south-east corner of the churchyard, and remained there till the tower was finished, when, the funds falling short, the good people of Waltham resolved to sell their bells to raise money—like some "Vandals" of more recent times at Sandwich—so that Waltham, "which formerly had steeple-less bells, had now a bell-less steeple." It would be unfair to suppress the fact that in the very dark days which mark the beginning of the present century the inhabitants of Waltham did their best to atone for the faults of their forefathers by hanging a new peal of bells in the tower.

Some idea of the former extent of this church may be conceived from stating that the ancient tomb considered to be King Harold's, though situated about forty yards from the present termination of the building, stood in the eastern part of the original choir. This tomb is described as "plain" in form, but of "a rich grey marble"; having sculptured on it "a sort of cross fleury, much descanted on by art." Fuller says that it was supported by "pillarets," one pedestal of which was "in his own possession." In Queen Elizabeth's reign, a gardener in the service of Sir Edward Denny discovered, in digging, a large stone coffin, inclosing a corpse, supposed to be that of King Harold ; but the remains, on touching, mouldered into dust. Near the same spot, about ninety years ago, a second coffin was found, containing an entire skeleton inclosed in lead.

"Waltham Holy Cross," writes the author of "Professional Excursions," in 1843, "as the favourite foundation and the grave of Harold, must not be overlooked, though dilapidated, neglected, and hurrying to decay. Within its cloisters Cranmer, Fox, and Gardiner unintentionally met together, little dreaming of the various positions they were afterwards destined to hold in our ecclesiastical history. The church," he adds, " is a massive deformity, but contains within some curious specimens of Norman architecture, which the dirty lanes and shabby streets must not prevent us from seeking to examine."

With reference to the present aspect of the remains of the monastery, Mr. Burges, in his " Legends of Waltham Abbey, and History of the Church" (1860), quoted above, remarks :—" We know this from the chroniclers, that the church was very magnificent, that it was made of stone, that it had a roof covered with lead, and that in some parts (perhaps in the apse, or in the baldachin over the great altar) there was a great deal of gilding and bronze plates. Now the eastern end of Harold's church has long ago disappeared— most probably it did not last above seventy or eighty years; but the nave and aisles perfectly correspond with the description, of course omitting the gilding and bronze plates, which would naturally be restricted to the east end. Thus the height of the nave walls is fifty-two feet. The aisles have originally been vaulted, the arches are elaborately decorated with chevrons and billet moulds; there are no mouldings to speak of, and every part could be done with an axe—in fact, it is exactly such a building as would be erected without regard to expense in a rude age. . . It was in all probability about the time of Stephen that the apse of Harold's church was taken down, and a new central tower and choir added. This choir was, no doubt, rather a large one . . . sufficiently extensive to afterwards accommodate the new foundation of Henry II., who turned out the seculars, and substituted a much larger number of monks in their place. We know that he did build sundry domestic buildings, which were absolutely necessary for a monastic establishment, and were not so for a body of secular priests, who probably lived in the town; and we are also informed that he did intend to rebuild the church, but upon consideration the monks were inducted into the old building. Most probably the increased accommodation was got by bringing the choir down into the central tower; and perhaps we may assign the northern clerestory of the nave to the first works begun by this monarch, as the style is very advanced and rich Norman, while the building now called the 'potatoe house,' as well as the cloisters (the springing of the groining of which was discovered in the late repairs), must be referred to the end of his reign, or to those of either of his sons, for the mouldings are by no means Romanesque. . . Some time in the reign of Edward II. it was found that the vaulting of the aisles had pushed out the side walls, so the said vaulting was forthwith destroyed. The bays at the west end had also got a lurch towards the west, probably in consequence of want of care in the foundations, or perhaps from the incomplete state of the western towers. The result was that the architect for the time did not make a restoration of the westernmost arches, but boldly got rid of the nave arch, and turned a new-pointed one at the triforium level, thus making a composition of two bays instead of three. It is needless to say that the effect is by no means improved. But the fourteenth century architect was

a man of genius, and when he proceeded to give us a new west front, he really produced a most striking and original composition; and although the great west window has been irrevocably destroyed by the tower in Philip and Mary's time, the beautiful west door and the charming windows and side turrets still remain to call forth our warmest admiration. It is by no means improbable that the same architect erected the 'lady chapel,' but in his later years, for although what remains of the tracery of the western window is very good, yet the mouldings are small, poor, and sub-divided, and utterly unworthy of the architect of the western front. . . A small three-light window is the only trace of Perpendicular work in the building as it at present remains. At the Reformation the east end, as reverting to the Crown, was destroyed, but the nave, belonging to the parishioners, was preserved intact. The tower, which appears to have been a sort of debatable ground, saved all further trouble by falling down in the time of Philip and Mary, and the townsmen, who had bought the bells, then set to work and built up a new tower at the west end of the church out of the old materials of the choir, which they bought or exchanged with Mr. Henry Denny.

" Fuller, who was presented to the curacy in 1648, has given us, in his 'History of Waltham Abbey,' several very interesting extracts from the parish books relative to the sale or purchase of articles required by the church during the various changes in religion which took place in the sixteenth century. An attempt was made to execute repairs in Charles the First's time, but owing to Archbishop Laud not having been consulted, it fell to the ground. Some repairs, however, were undertaken during the reign of Charles II. Among them was the re-facing of the second pillar from the east on the south side, for a coin of that king was found in the foundation. In the eighteenth and the early part of the present century, all sorts of the greatest barbarities were inflicted upon the unfortunate church. The roof was lowered, and a plaster ceiling put underneath; more of the windows of the north side were destroyed; two galleries were erected at the west end, and another in the south aisle, whereby great holes were cut in the pillars, to their no small detriment; and lastly, the whole area filled with very high pews. The roof, being in good repair, although by no means of the original pitch, has been retained, but the plaster ceiling has, of course, been removed, and its place supplied by boarding painted in imitation of the only contemporary ceiling remaining, namely, that at Peterborough. The centres, however, represent the signs of the zodiac, the labours of the year, and the elements."

In 1859 the work of restoring the interior was undertaken by Mr. W. Burges. Nothing, however, was done to the exterior, beyond making necessary repairs. The east end of the church is, except the main walls, entirely new, and in a style much later than the body of the church: namely, that of the first half of the thirteenth century. Within the great arch which spans the eastern wall are three lancet thrown into the church; some ruinous walls; a small bridge and gateway, near the Abbey Mills; and a dark vaulted structure of two divisions connected with the convent garden, and which adjoined the Abbey House, inhabited by the Dennys. Not any remains exist of the Abbey House (which is reported to have been a very extensive building), except, perhaps, the vaulted structure mentioned above; and of a large mansion which was erected upon its site, nothing is left but a plastered wall.

COPPED HALL, NEAR EPPING. (See page 417.)

windows immediately above the altar, and a rose window of early French character. In the process of restoration the greatest care seems to have been taken in the matter of decoration. Thus the altar-piece and the three lancet windows are occupied with subjects representing the human nature of our Saviour, the rose window above illustrating His Divine nature.

Though the buildings of Waltham Abbey were once so extensive as to include a space of many acres, scarcely any part remains but the nave of the abbey church, which, as shown above, is now the parochial church, an attached chapel on the south side, called the Lady Chapel, long used as a school-room and vestry, but now utilised for service, being In the convent garden, which is now tenanted by a market-gardener, is an aged *tulip-tree*, reported to be the largest in England.

To the north of the abbey church is a farm-house, constructed out of the abbot's stables and faced with fine bricks. The gardens are still partly surrounded by the abbey walls, and a small chapel, or oratory, in the grounds, arched with a groined ceiling of fine Early English work, is now used as a room to grow mushrooms. Beyond the farm-house is a quaint old bridge, said to be Norman, and often called after Harold; three out of its five ribs still remain. In a meadow beyond are the abbey fish-ponds, now dry, in which doubtless fine carp and tench were preserved for the brethren on fasting days. They now grow abundance of wild flowers.

Near the Abbey Mill, which is still occupied for grinding corn, is a wide space of ground, surrounded by small dwellings, called the Bramblings, but formerly Rome-land (as at St. Albans and at Norwich), which is conjectured to have been so called from its rents being in former times appropriated to the use of the Holy See. The weekly market is held here on Tuesdays; on one side of

rest on corbels, formed by two demi-angels supporting shields, on which were engraved the royal arms of the time of Edward III.: viz., France and England, quarterly.

The various streams of the Lea in this neighbourhood are said by tradition to flow in the very same channels which were cut by the great Alfred when he turned aside the course of the river, and left the Danish fleet aground.

"Fragments of sculpture, figured tiles, metal

AMBRESBURY BANKS. (See page 418.)

the spot still stands a stack of chimneys, which formed a portion of King Henry's hunting-box. It was probably here that the conversation (related above) was held which affected so deeply the course of the Reformation in this country. If so, this chimney-stack is an historic landmark.

The gateway and bridge shown in the illustration on page 409 stand a little to the north of the abbey, close above the Abbey Mill. The gateway is of stone; but it has been repaired from time to time with bricks of various sizes and hues, which lend it a great variety of colour, and render it a great favourite for the water-colour painter. It consists of two Pointed arches, one larger than the other. The outer mouldings of the larger arch

work, &c.," writes Mr. Thorne, in his "Environs of London," "are occasionally exhumed on the site or in the neighbourhood of the abbey. Considerable quantities of pilgrims' jettons, or groats, have been found in the town. The 'Holy Cross' itself doubtless attracted numerous pilgrims to Waltham. A few years ago a stone mould was dug up in Coleman Street, London, from which metal casts were taken, to be worn by Waltham pilgrims as the badge or insignia of their pilgrimage. The mould was cruciform, with a figure of a cross in the centre, surrounded by the legend, 'Signum Sancte Crucis de Waltham.'"

Among the worthies connected with this place whose names we have not already mentioned was

John of Waltham, Master of the Rolls, Keeper of the Privy Seal, Lord High Treasurer, and Bishop of Salisbury, who was excommunicated by Courtenay Archbishop of Canterbury; he was buried in Westminster Abbey. Another celebrity was Roger de Waltham, Canon of St. Paul's, and the author of several books, under Henry III.

The history of Waltham town is so nearly identified with that of the abbey that the completion of the latter leaves but little to record with respect to the former. Henry III., as we have shown above, was not only a great benefactor to the abbey, but granted to the abbot the right of holding a weekly market and an annual fair of seven days' duration. The demands of the abbot for "stallage" at the fair led to frequent disputes with the citizens of London, and quiet was obtained only after the Londoners had refused to resort to Waltham Fair for some three years or more, when, in 1256, the abbot agreed to refund all distresses, and granted to the Londoners "acquittance of all such stallage for ever." The market is still held weekly on Tuesdays, and the fairs take place in May, June, and September. The old market-house, a building of the Elizabethan era, was pulled down about 1850. In it were preserved for many years a pair of stocks, bearing the date 1598. They are still standing—not, however, in their original place or position, but set up on one end of the roadside, near the church.

William Vallens, in his "Tale of Two Swannes," written in 1590, thus quaintly describes this place as it was under the latter years of Elizabeth :—

" Down all along through Waltham Street they passe,
    And wonder at the ruines of the Abbay
    Late supprest, the walles, the walkes, the monumentes,
    And everything that there is to be seene."

He proceeds to describe at considerable length, and with great minuteness, the "locke" on the river, with its "double doores of wood," and a "cesterne all of planke," both then novelties to the eyes of travellers in the infancy of canal navigation.

The town still in many parts wears an antiquated appearance, and the venerable abbey and gateway give a character of the "olden time" to the scene; but still the place is not behind-hand in the march of progress, for it has its weekly newspaper, its local board of health, its burial and school boards, its literary institute and reading-rooms, two or three cricket-clubs, and a "fishery." The Lea in this locality is much resorted to by the disciples of Izaak Walton—barbel, bream, trout, jack, chub, and roach, abounding in plenty. Free fishing is also afforded on the Lea Navigation. Hofland, in treating of Waltham Abbey in his "Angler's Manual," writes :—"Often have I fished here in May, and, under the gentle influence of the season and the spot, recalled to mind the beautiful lines of the highly-gifted, but unfortunate, Lord Surrey :

' The sovte season that bud and bloome forth bringes,
    With grene hath cladde the hyll and eke the vale;
    The nightingall with fethers new she singes,
    The turtle to her mate hath told her tale ;
    Somer is come, for every spraye now springes,
    The fishes flete with new repayred scale,
    The adder, all her slough away she flynges,
    The busy bee her honey now she mynges.' "

There are in the town and its immediate neighbourhood malt-kilns, a brewery, flour-mills, a manufactory of percussion caps, &c. The cemetery, which was opened in 1857, covers about four acres, and contains two mortuary chapels. The County Court, which was built in 1849, stands on the site of some old silk-printing works. The "Tulip Tree," a celebrated inn here, is, of course, named after the famous tree mentioned above as growing in the abbey precincts.

As was usual in other places, so here the brethren of the abbey supplied the religious wants of the neighbourhood on all sides, and accordingly the region which they served was very large. Hence the parish of Waltham extends over Sewardstone, and High Beech has only recently been cut off, and made into a separate incumbency.

CHAPTER XLIV.

WALTHAM (continued) AND EPPING.

" Sweet sylvan Epping rears its rural head."

Extent of Waltham Abbey Parish—Census Returns—Rural Appearance of the Locality—Principal Seats and Mansions—Warlies—Copped Hall—Ambresbury Banks—The Story of Queen Boadicea's Conflict with the Romans—Obelisks in the Neighbourhood—Highwaymen and Footpads—The Village of Epping—Epping Church.

WALTHAM HOLY CROSS is a very extensive parish, consisting not only of the township of Waltham Abbey, but of a large portion of the country east, north, and south, containing altogether nearly 12,000 acres. Inclusive of Sewardstone and other subordinate districts, it stretches away northward for some three miles to the parish of Nasing, eastward for about three miles to the boundaries of Epping, and southward to the village of Chingford, whilst on the south-east it embraces High Beech, which lies about three miles from the town. Sewardstone and High Beech are situated on the borders of Epping Forest, and will be dealt with in a subsequent chapter. Holyfield in the north and Upshire in the east are two little scattered agricultural hamlets, containing in the aggregate some 7,000 acres. In 1871 the population of Waltham parish, exclusive of the ecclesiastical district of High Beech, amounted to about 4,500, a number which had increased during the next decade to 5,300. According to the census for 1881, the number of inhabitants in Waltham Abbey township alone was close upon 3,000.

The whole of the district comprised within the jurisdiction of the metropolitan police, and lying to the north-east of Waltham town, is exceedingly rural, being mostly meadow-land, used for grazing purposes, intersected by the Cobbin Brook, a tolerable rivulet, which winds and gurgles in a sinuous course by Epping Upland, or Old Epping, and skirting the south-east side of Waltham, unites its waters with that of the river Lea about half a mile south of the town. The country round about is pleasingly diversified with hills and vales, and in parts well wooded, but possesses no history. Warlies Hall and Copped Hall are the chief seats in this district; but there are a few others, with moderate estates attached to them, such as Thrift Hall and Monkham, besides several farms and hamlets, one of which latter bears the name of Harold's Park, and may mark the site of the "great wood and park called Harold's Park," mentioned in the preceding chapter as having been bestowed by Richard I. on the canons of Waltham Abbey.*

A short distance to the west of Harold's Park are Galley Hill and Galley Wood. Thomas Fuller, who lived at Waltham for many years, wrote in 1640:—" On the one side of the town itself are large and fruitful meadows . . . . On the other side a spacious forest spreads itself, where fourteen years since one might have seen whole herds of red and fallow deer." What is left of Epping Forest, originally known as the Forest of Essex, and later on as Waltham Forest, in the immediate neighbourhood of the town, crowns the high ground away to the east and south-east.

Some two or three miles to the east of Waltham Abbey, in a sheltered valley on the road to Copped Hall, lies Warlies, the seat of Sir Thomas Buxton. The property, consisting of about 1,000 acres, was purchased by the late Sir Edmund Buxton, M.P., the son and successor to the honoured name of the first Sir Thomas Fowell Buxton, many years M.P. for Weymouth, and the associate of Wilberforce in his philanthropic efforts to abolish African and West Indian slavery.

Copped Hall—so named from the Saxon "cop," the top of a hill—lies a mile or so eastward, nearer to Epping. It is one of the finest modern seats in the county. It was built about the middle of the last century, near the site of an older structure raised by the monks of Waltham Abbey in the good old days when they had possession of the manor. The park, upwards of 4,000 acres in extent, is situated partly in the parish of Waltham and partly in that of Epping.

Mr. Weldon, in his "Guide to Epping Forest," says :—" In the proceedings of the Privy Council, in the rèign of King Edward VI., there is an account of the Princess Mary, afterwards Queen, living at Copped Hall, and three of her principal servants being summoned before the Privy Council, and commanded to inform their mistress that her chaplains were prohibited from celebrating mass, or using any of the ceremonies of the Roman Catholic religion. On their return she ordered them not to speak to her chaplains, but sent them back with a letter addressed to King Edward, dated from her ' poore howse at Copped Hall, 19th August, 1551,' and, on their refusal to acquaint her with the further charge given by the Council, the Lord Chancellor Riche, Sir Wm. Petre one of the principal secretaries of state, and Sir Anthony Wingfield comptroller of the household, were deputed to wait on her with a letter from the King, and to enforce the orders of the Privy Council. The Princess seems to have received them anything but graciously, saying they ought to ' shewe more favore to me for my fathere's sake, who made the more parte of you almoste of nothing.' She delivered to the Lord Chancellor ' a ringe, for the king, upon her knees; most humbly, with very humble recommendaciones, saienge she would die his true subjecte & sister, & obaye his commandements in all things excepte in theis matters of religeon, towchinge the masse, & the newe service.' Among the same extracts from the proceedings of the Privy Council, three years afterwards, in the first year of the reign of Queen Mary, is a letter, dated March 17, 1554, directed to ' Lord Oxforde, & the above Lord Riche, to be presente at the burninge of such obstinat persones as presently are sent doune to be burned in diverse partes of the county of Essex, & to be aydinge to the Sherife of the said shiere therein.' "

The old hall itself, built in the place of a yet earlier structure, was a large quadrangular red-brick mansion, and it stood to the south of the present hall, on lower ground. It was built in the reign of Elizabeth, from the designs of Thorpe, for Sir Thomas Heneage, the Treasurer of the Royal Chamber and Vice-Chamberlain of the Queen's Household, to whom the estate had been granted by the Crown. The chief feature of the hall in Sir Thomas Heneage's time was the great gallery, fifty-six yards in length.

The author of "Anglorum Speculum, or The Worthies of England," thus writes in 1684 :— "Copt Hall, or Coppice Hall, seated on a hill in the midst of a park, was built by the Abbot of Waltham, and enlarged by Sir Th. Heneage : in which there is the most proportionable gallery in England." He adds :—"An. 1639, a Hericano forced the stones of the great east window, like pellets, quite through this gallery, in length 56 Yards. Dr. Jackson about the same time observed the like wind as Ominous and presaging our Civil Dissentions."

Thorne, in his "Environs of London," says :— "Charles Sackville, the witty Earl of Dorset, and the patron of wits and poets, lived at Copped Hall, and here Shadwell wrote part of his 'Squire of Alsatia.' Charles II. dined with the Earl of Middlesex at Old Copped Hall in June, 1660; and William III., when on his way to Newmarket, dined and stayed the night here, April 4, 1698."

Later on Copped Hall was held successively by the Earls of Winchelsea and the Lords Grey. Between 1753 and 1757 it was rebuilt by its then owner, Mr. John Conyers, who at that time resided at Epping Place, and whose descendants remained seated here for upwards of a century. The family of Conyers appears to have been of very ancient standing in Yorkshire. Tristram Conyers, or Coniers, a gentleman possessed of an ample fortune, settled at Walthamstow early in the seventeenth century, and this branch became naturalised as an Essex family. Several of its members occupied prominent positions in that century. Gerard Conyers was an alderman of London, and received the honour of knighthood ; and Edward, who then represented in Parliament the borough of East Grinstead, became the owner of the manor of Epping and Copped Hall, by purchase from Lord North, about the year 1728. In 1753 Mr. John Conyers found the old hall in such a dilapidated condition, that he determined upon pulling it down, and rebuilding the house on a different site. Time had loosened the foundation of the grand old Elizabethan mansion, and a hurricane had long previously blown down its

great gallery ; and the beautiful painted glass window of its ancient chapel, which is believed to have been originally painted for Henry VIII.'s chapel at New Hall, near Chelmsford, in this county, whence it was obtained, eventually found its way to St. Margaret's Church, Westminster.*

The present mansion of Copped Hall is a spacious building, almost square, consisting of a centre, with pediment and two wings, and, standing on high ground, is visible for miles round. It is constructed of white brick of a superior make, and since its erection it has been much improved and enlarged by James Wyatt. The late Mr. H. J. Conyers was a first-rate sportsman and master of hounds. "Copt Hall," writes the author of "Professional Excursions in 1843," "is remarkable for the smooth and nicely jointed brick-work of the exterior, and the *brusque* manner of its owner ; but he is the spirit of the chase, and Nimrod's hounds apologise for Nimrod's manner." After paying a tribute to Mr. Conyers as a master and landlord, he adds :—"The mansion looks cold and solitary at a distance, perched upon a knoll unbroken by intervening foliage ; but a spirit of improvement prevails over the asperities of Nature, and the neighbouring forest is a theatre of endless amusement and delightful recreation." It now belongs to the family of Mr. Wythes, who was a railway contractor, "raised from the ranks" by his own energy and enterprise.

The traveller, in passing along the narrow roadway which skirts the forest between Waltham and Epping, sees the mansion on a bold eminence away to the left, the land falling from the spot on which he stands to a deep valley, and rising again by easy gradations in groves and plantations, like a succession of wooded terraces, to the park and green lawn on which the hall-door opens. The little river Cobbin steals quietly along on the north side of the park, whilst just on the outskirts of the park, about thirty or forty yards to the south-east, are the remains of an extensive earth-work, probably British, called the Ambresbury Banks, supposed by antiquarians to be a military camp, and the scene of Boadicea's battle and final defeat. The earth-work, which is about half a mile in circuit, is tolerably perfect, and is so largely overgrown with beeches, oaks, hornbeams, and hazels, as to form a favourite spot for picnics in the summer.

With reference to these earth-works, we find in Gough's "Camden" (Vol. II., p. 49) the following remarks, communicated to the author by Mr. Smart Letheuillier :—"This entrenchment is now

---

* See "Old and New London," Vol. III., p. 568.

entirely overgrown with old oaks and hornbeams. It was formerly in the very heart of the forest, and no road near it, till the present turnpike road from London to Epping was made, almost within the memory of man, which now runs within a hundred yards of it, but the entrenchment cannot be thence perceived, by reason of the wood that covers it. Its figure is irregular, rather longest from east to west, and on a gentle declivity to the south-east. It contains nearly twelve acres, and is surrounded by a ditch and high bank, much worn down by time, though where there are angles they are still very bold and high.   There are no regular openings, like gateways or entrances, only in two places, where the bank has been cut through, and the ditch filled up very lately, in order to make a straight road from Debden Green to Epping Market.   The boundaries between the parishes of Waltham and Epping run exactly through the middle of this entrenchment . . . As I can find no reason to attribute this entrenchment either to the Romans, Saxons, or Danes, I cannot help concluding it to have been a British *oppidum*, and perhaps had some relation to other remains of that people which are discoverable in our forest." Mr. W. Winters, in a letter in *Notes and Queries* (4th Series, Vol. X., p. 395), remarks :—" Gough seems to raise a doubt about the exact position of the combatants being Amesbury (or Ambresbury), simply on the ground of what Mr. Letheuillier had stated.   He also affirms that ' the want of barrows is an argument that a great slaughter could hardly have happened here.'   Philip Morant, the Essex historian, not willing to give up the point so easily, states that ' by comparing all accounts and circumstances, he is persuaded that the field of battle was between Waltham and Epping, or thereabouts, not far from London.' "

Another writer in *Notes and Queries* (5th Series, Vol. V., p. 396) suggests that these works are really not a camp, but " part of a series of beacon hills ; " but be that as it may, their form and general appearance bear a strong resemblance to other works of a similar character which are undoubtedly known to have been used for military purposes.   Old soldiers who have served in India and South Africa have been known to have remarked on seeing these earth-works that they must have been a camp, used by Oliver Cromwell or some such officer !

The City arms, on an iron post at the roadside, in front of the works, denote that here is the limit of the jurisdiction of the Lord Mayor of London.

The story of the great conflict between the Britons and Romans, which is said to have taken place here, is graphically told by Coller, in his " History of Essex," as follows :—" The king of the Iceni, the people who inhabited Suffolk and Norfolk, and part of Cambridgeshire, appears to have retained his kingdom under the protection of the conquerors ; and when he died he left half his territory and treasures to the Romans, under the impression that the other half would be secured for his family.   The Romans, however, seized the whole.   Boadicea, the widow, remonstrated.   The extortioners endeavoured to silence her by insult ; she was publicly scourged like a common slave, and her daughters were given over to dishonour by the soldiery.   This outrage aroused all the spirit of the ancient Briton.   The wretched queen, instead of sinking under her miseries, boldly raised the standard of revolt and vengeance, and fearfully were the Romans made to pay for their breach of faith and want of honesty.   Suetonius, the propraetor, was at this period (A.D. 61) engaged in an expedition against the sacred Isle of Mona, or Anglesea, the last home and refuge of the Druids, and this part of the country lay comparatively unprotected.   There was, indeed, a garrison of Roman veterans at Colchester, but they appear to have been paralysed as the storm of war came swelling up from Suffolk.   Conscience—for then, as now, such was the effect of crime—' made cowards of them all ; ' and superstition gave birth to all sorts of hideous portents and omens to unman them.   Tacitus, in his 'Annals,' says that the statue of the goddess of Victory at Camelodunum fell down and turned, as if yielding to the enemy ; howlings were heard in the theatre, and strange noises in the council-house ; a fearful apparition was seen in the estuary of the Thames, towards Mersea Island, which had become a pleasant resort of the Romans ; and enthusiastic women foretold the coming destruction—which, considering the force that was advancing and the panic of the defenders, required no great prophetic powers. When, therefore, the Britons in overwhelming numbers appeared upon the wooded hills around Colchester, and were joined by the men of Essex, who flocked in thousands to the standard of the queen, they met with only a feeble resistance. The ninth legion, which had hastened to the rescue, was defeated, and the whole of its infantry slain ; and the exasperated Britons swept into the capital of the colony, slaughtering all, even the women and children, and mercilessly destroying every object of art and emblem of the Roman sway.   The soldiers threw themselves into the temple of Claudius, which they defended for two days, but at length perished by fire.   Excited by their success, and enriched by plunder, the victors then appear to have turned their backs upon Colchester, leaving it a scene of utter desolation. Boadicea, at the head of her troops, directed her march along the Roman way by Coggeshall, Rayne, and Dunmow, to St. Albans, which also fell a like prey to her fury. Every station that could be reached was devastated; and the number of the Romans and their allies who were thus slain is stated to have been 70,000. The sounds of this calamity at length reached Suetonius, who hurried back with his army. The Britons mustered in arms at least 100,000—some historians state their force at 250,000—far outnumbering the Romans, who had, however, on their side the advantage of experience and skill in the art of war; and Boadicea, retiring at their approach, established herself in an entrenched camp in the forest, where, a short distance from Epping, near Copped Hall, and now known as Ambresbury Banks, the remains of her stronghold may still be traced. Here she decided on awaiting the Roman foe. Some writers have assumed that the last struggle was at Islington, others at Messing; but Morant and others, whose authority is decisive, say—'The famous battle between Suetonius and Boadicea was fought somewhere between Epping and Waltham, near which a fine camp remains.' Here, then, the opposing forces were drawn up. The Britons, like the Russians at the Alma, had brought the ladies to see the fight and witness their triumph. Their wives and children were taken in wagons to the field, and ranged in a line along the rear of the battle—to become its victims, and to swell the slaughter of those they loved. The skilful Romans had chosen ground accessible at only one point, with a forest at the back. Having provoked the enemy to the assault, here they remained till the Britons had exhausted themselves, and expended their darts in the attempt to force the narrow pass; then assuming the form of a wedge, their infantry bore down upon them like an avalanche, while their horsemen with their spears swept the field. The Britons were routed; and hemmed in by the rows of wagons behind, the warriors, their wives and children, fell in one indiscriminate slaughter. The Romans lost only 400, but 80,000 of the Britons were left upon the forest turf; and Boadicea escaped, only to die soon after either of grief or poison. Truly has it been said that 'we dwell amidst the ruins of successive races, and heed them not.' How little does the quiet traveller from Epping to Waltham or Loughton think that a scene of blood like this has passed upon the very spot he is crossing! When, too, the members of the summer pic-nic party gather round the gipsy feast spread upon the table of turf, and within the shade of the brushwood and clumps of hornbeams with which the site of the camp is now overgrown, how little do they reflect that the bones of 80,000 lie beneath the surface, and with them are buried the wreck and remnants of the rule of that people who first possessed power in the land—for this was the last expiring effort of the Britons; and though partial revolts took place, we do not find that they again, as a people, raised the arm against the Romans in battle."

There is an obelisk on some rising ground at Chingford, some five miles to the south-west of Ambresbury Banks, set up some years ago by the Ordnance Survey, and maintained at the instance of the Astronomer-Royal. That obelisk gave rise to a discussion in the pages of *Notes and Queries* in 1882, it having been asserted by one writer that it marked the site of Queen Boadicea's death. Be that as it may, another correspondent writes:—"There still remains the old belief that the great battle between the Romans under Suetonius and the Britons under Boadicea, the widow of Prasutagus, king of the Iceni, was fought a few miles from Chingford; and the story that a stone or obelisk was set up to mark the presumed spot where, after the slaughter of her army, the queen, who had sworn not to survive a defeat, took poison and died, is a popular belief. The description of the field of battle, as given by Tacitus, is very vague. It has, I think, been usually imagined that it was near the old British camp called Ambers' Banks, or Ambresbury Banks. . . . If any memorial stone exists, it might be looked for in that part of the county. In Chapman and André's fine map of Essex, published in 1777, there is an obelisk marked as then standing on Copped Hall Green, and a second obelisk situated about a mile more westward."

The two obelisks here referred to are still standing in the neighbourhood of Warlies Park, which lies about a mile to the north-west of the entrenchment. "If there is any history attached to these obelisks," writes another correspondent of *Notes and Queries*,[*] "it is not to be found in accessible sources. No inscription appears on either; they are of brick, one being stuccoed; and they cannot be older than the eighteenth century. But if any value is to be placed on tradition, it is not dealing unfairly with the tradition that clings to this part of the county of Essex to admit the possibility of the historic site being placed here. The point has not been thoroughly sifted. Morant says, speaking of Ambresbury Banks, 'hereabouts appears to

---

* See 6th Series, Vol. VI., p. 272.

have been fought,' &c., which is only tantamount
to a recital of the ancient tradition. . . . It is
by no means an improbability that the site was
'hereabouts.' Ambresbury Banks was not a
temporary camp; there must have been a British
village or settlement here. It stands on the
highest ground, as British villages would do.
Closely adjacent, a bye-road defiles down the hill
through the forest, itself the site of an ancient
trackway, into the river plain. The higher part of
Copped Hall Green is broken up into irregular
lumps of earth-work, which may be modern or may
be of high antiquity. Obelisk No. 1 stands in a
meadow just northward of this waste spot, and
gives name to the adjoining farm. The narrow
defile through the forest and the open plain below
are fully characteristic of the battle-field familiar to
us in the chronicles. Some such track was occupied by the forces of Suetonius, down which he
issued, cleaving as with a wedge the host of the
British; and it was across such a plain that the
defeated thousands would disperse. Obelisk No. 2
stands in a meadow on the other side of Cobbin's
Brook, and gives name to an adjoining wood.
Here, it may well be believed, the unfortunate
Boadicea retired, in order to crown with her own
death the disasters of the day."

This locality possesses not only the earth-work
known as Ambresbury Banks, but also another
camp some two miles distant, at Loughton, so
that there is really a choice of sites whereon to
fix the scene of Boadicea's famous battle. It is a
commonly received opinion that the Romans had
their camp at Ambresbury Banks, while the British
queen drew up her forces at Loughton. "These
two camps," observes General Pitt-Rivers, in his
report on the excavation of Ambresbury Banks,
"owe their preservation to the fact of this region
having been always forest, and not cultivated
ground; and this is a point worth noting on the
part of those who are inclined to lay stress on the
value of tradition as evidence of time and place.
It is certain that neither Cæsar nor Boadicea, nor
any of the heroes and heroines of olden times, to
whom these things are ascribed, had any special
eye for locating themselves in places which might
not in after years be destroyed by the plough; yet
tradition concerning these people hangs naturally
about such places as remain to us from ancient
times rather than about those innumerable spots
in our long and highly cultivated country in which
ancient monuments have been destroyed by agriculture."

No doubt the existence of the Ambresbury Banks,
as the camp is locally called, has tended to keep

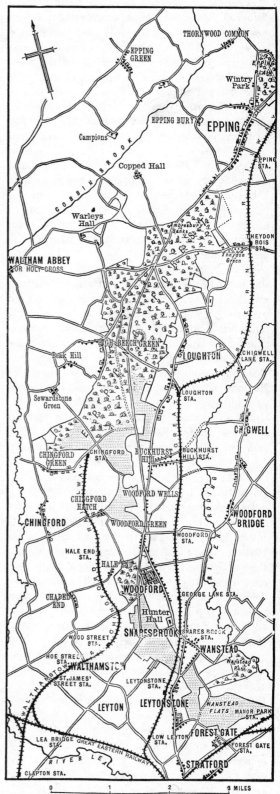

MAP OF EPPING FOREST.

up in these parts the memory, or rather the tradition, of Boadicea's defeat, which without such a *memoria technica* would probably have died out.

"If we are to find a clue to the date of Ambresbury Bank in its name," writes Mr. Frederic Johnson in Weldon's "Guide to Epping Forest," "we cannot make the work more modern than about A.D. 500. The word Ambresbury is commonly said to be much the same as Ambrose-bury, from a patriotic chieftain named Ambrosius Aurelius, who died soon after A.D. 500. This place, like one in Wiltshire, is called Ambresbury and Amesbury, and we must explain the name in each case alike. The story of Ambrosius is connected with the times and legends of King Arthur and the Knights of the Round Table, and it is even said that Ambrose, or Ambrosius, was the true name of the magician Merlin."

In the pages of Morant's "History of Essex" the camp is said to be the fortress of Boadicea, and other writers have followed in his wake. But with the present information it would seem hardly safe to state positively that Ambresbury Camp was actually the work of the Romans. At the same time, it is within the bounds of possibility that Boadicea made here her last stand against the Romans under Suetonius. General Pitt-Rivers, who carefully examined the "Banks" in 1881, wrote upon them a paper which was read at a meeting of the Essex Naturalists' Field Club, and also at the York meeting of the British Association in that year. In it he shows that on the east side a ravine approaches the camp from the valley below, and divides into two forks as it nears the camp, and that the rampart at this place is drawn across the points of these forks, so as to sweep down them. On the south side also advantage is taken of another ravine to strengthen the fortifications on that side. "These are points," adds General Pitt-Rivers, "which, although influencing the principles of defence which have prevailed at all times, are more especially British, as distinct from Roman. The Romans, caring more for their internal discipline and the position of their cohorts than for external defence, arranged their camps on geometrically constructed lines, and often disregarded natural features altogether. It is true that at the northern corner of Ambresbury Camp the rampart turns at an abrupt angle, but this is owing to the fact that at that particular spot there are no natural features to guide campbuilders: the ground is a dead flat, and as the turn had to be made somewhere, it was made abruptly, as so often occurs in British camps."

The camp is an irregular square, and to some slight extent follows the conformation of the ground which surrounds it. This fact would seem to justify a doubt as to its being of Roman origin; and such a negative inference is corroborated by the fact that no Roman pottery or vessels or coins were discovered *in situ* when some explorations were made. There is in the camp a well which feeds a pond of water with a dam across it.

Probably the exposure of these banks to the action of the weather for so many centuries may have rubbed off the angles, and made the square less perfect than once it was. The diagrams appended to General Pitt-Rivers's paper in the "Transactions" of the Essex Field Club show how much the weather has altered the sectional aspect of the camp, lowering the summits, and filling up the trenches to such an extent that it has been uncertain till lately whether the bottom of it was flat or pointed.

The plan given in that paper, drawn by Mr. D'Oyley, the surveyor of the forest, shows six gates or entrances, whereas the Romans, as we know, were usually content with four. Here, however, also, time and exposure may have altered the configuration of the site.

"In choosing their sites, the constructors of both camps seem to have been careful to secure a water supply. The interior of the enclosure is well wooded, and on the south the thicket is so dense as to hide the bank and be almost impenetrable. In modern times the timber has been much diminished, and the diggers for sand and other materials have done much mischief, in some places having destroyed portions of the bank itself. Happily, this is now stopped, and although the camp lies in two parishes, it will be safe from further depredations. It must be borne in mind that the search after antiquities in Epping Forest is a new thing. People have been content to look after butterflies and blackberries, and various other productions of Nature; and they have not gone to look for the work of men's hands. However, a beginning has been made, and already most valuable results have been achieved."[*]

Epping lies about a mile and a half north-eastward from Ambresbury Banks, and is just beyond our limits; as, however, the manor belonged in early times to Harold, and was given by the Conqueror to Waltham Abbey, we may be pardoned for making some little mention of it here. The town, called Epping Street, is situated on the road to Newmarket, on the ridge of hills that run north and south through the forest. In the old "coaching

---

[*] Weldon's "Guide to Epping Forest."

days " the place carried on a flourishing trade in sausages, poultry, and butter, which usually commanded high prices at the London market; and for its size, it also contained a very large number of inns and public-houses, many of which, since the Great Eastern Railway diverted the traffic from the high road, have been converted to other uses. At the time when the neighbourhood was the haunt of highwaymen, some of the forest taverns served as harbours for those "knights of the road," among whom might be reckoned the famous Dick Turpin. As far back as the close of the seventeenth century this locality appears to have been as bad as Hounslow Heath, in respect to its dangers from footpads and highwaymen. Macaulay tells us that on the Peace of 1698, a large number of the discharged soldiers turned footpads and marauders, and that " a fraternity of plunderers— thirty in number, according to the lowest estimate— squatted under the shades of Epping Forest, near Waltham Cross, from which they sallied forth with sword and pistol to bid passengers stand. . . It was necessary that during some time cavalry should patrol every evening on the roads near the boundary between Middlesex and Essex." It sounds almost incredible, but as lately as the year 1775 the guard of the Norwich stage-coach was killed in this forest, after he had himself shot dead three highwaymen out of seven that assailed him.*

The following scrap of information, taken from an old newspaper, shows that the roads hereabouts had their terrors down to even a later date :—"On Tuesday, January 22nd, 1793, a Mr. Alderman Plomer was taking an airing in his carriage in Epping Forest; he was stopped near the eight-mile stone by a single highwayman, who presented a pistol, and robbed him of a watch and about fourteen guineas."

The parish of Epping, which is between thirty and forty miles in circumference, is divided into three parts—the Town, the Upland, and Ryehill Hamlet. Its weekly market is still kept up on Fridays, when the main street of the town wears a somewhat busier appearance than usual. The Town Hall is used occasionally for concerts and lectures.

Near the western end of the street stands the Church of St. John the Baptist, a modern Gothic structure, built a few years ago, in the place of a chapel which the monks of Waltham had set up in days of old to serve as a chapel-of-ease to the mother church. At that time the whole, or nearly the whole, of this parish belonged to the Abbey of Waltham; and the houses of the town or village appear to have been clustered round the church, which lies some two miles away to the north-west, on Epping Upland, the present street being of comparatively modern date. The tall brick tower of the parish church, standing as it does on high ground, is a conspicuous landmark for the country round ; the rest of the building is of little or no interest.

CHAPTER XLV.

EPPING FOREST

" ' 'Midst those trees the wild deer bounded
Ages long ere we were born,
And our great-grandfathers sounded
Many a jovial hunting-horn."—T. CAMPBELL.

Primeval Condition of the Forest, as the Great Forest of Essex—Gradual Diminution of the Forest—Forest Charters of King John and Henry III. —Laws for the Regulation of the Forest—A Quaint Oath—Lord Warden, Steward, and other Officers of the Forest—The Swainmote Court and Court of Justice Seat—Extent of the Forest in the Middle Ages—Present Form of the Forest—Disposal of the Crown Rights in the Forest—Encroachments by Lords of Manors—The Battle of the Commoners with the Lords of Manors—Parliamentary Scheme for the Preservation of the Forest—The Matter taken up by the Corporation of London—The Case Settled by Arbitration—Dedication of Epping Forest to the "Free Use" of the People—The Science of Forestry—The Deer of the Forest—The Present Condition and General Appearance of the Forest.

"THIS is the forest primeval," writes Longfellow of the Forest of Acadie; and he might have applied the epithet to that of Epping, much of which still happily remains in its "primeval" wildness. It was called of old "the forest of Essex," as being the only forest within the county. Afterwards it was known as "Waltham Forest," and it is only within the last two or three centuries that its present name of Epping Forest has prevailed. It covers most of the district lying between the Lea and the Roding. Roughly speaking, the forest is divided into two main portions, lying respectively west and east of the latter river. The west is more properly Waltham Forest, whilst the eastern portion is known as the Forest of Hainault.

Epping and Hainault Forests are comprehended

---

* Annual Register, 1775, pp. 97 and 182.

in the Chase of Waltham; and, according to Evelyn, the first onslaught was made upon them by King Henry VIII., when he suppressed the monasteries, converting the property to his own use, and disposing of the oak timber. Previous to that time but little oak was used in building, the commonest woods sufficing for ordinary habitations, until the general clearance brought about a greater demand for material of a better class.

In its primitive condition, the great "waste" covered the larger part of the county, stretching from the Forest of Middlesex at Waltham, in the west, to Colchester in the east, and hence it was properly called the "Great Forest of Essex." With reference to the forests of Essex and the forest laws, Mr. Coller, in his history of that county, writes:—"The forests were fearful sources of feuds and oppression; and Essex, being covered extensively by one of these royal nuisances, was frequently excited by the occurrences and conflicts to which it gave rise. The wild woodlands which at one period stretched over so large a portion of the county became vested in the Crown, and long after the Conquest these tracts of wilderness were found in the heart of Essex. Here the sovereigns and the gallants of the Courts hawked and hunted during their sojourn at Havering-atte-bower, or the Palace of Chigwell—which appears to have been erected solely for a royal hunting-lodge—or in their visits to the Palaces of New Hall and Writtle. . . In this forest the stag was chased, and the wild boar, an important part of the game of these woods, brought to bay—for the fox appears to have been looked upon with contempt by the Nimrods of those days. Here, in later times, the outlaw, like him of Sherwood, composed of about equal portions of the poacher, the bandit, and the hero, found ready shelter. And here, too, at a period bordering on our own days, the burglar and the highwayman shaped their caves and concealed their plunder. The forest regulations were terrifically severe, though often set at nought. The killing of a stag in these hunting-grounds of the king was regarded as more heinous than murder. The slaughter of a man could be expiated by a pecuniary fine; but one of the game laws of the Conqueror enacted that the killing of a deer, boar, or hare in these forests should be punished with the loss of the offender's eyes. This law was renewed by Richard I., with the addition of further disgusting mutilation. Civilisation, with its multiplying people, increasing the necessity for larger supplies of food, and thus raising the value of the land, has laid so steady a siege to the forest

of Essex that no idea can be formed of its extent from the remnants of it which are left, under the names of Hainault, Waltham, and Epping. It stretched at one period along the whole of the northern boundary, from nearly Bow to Cambridgeshire, filling up the whole of the vast space between Hertfordshire and the line of road from Brentwood and Romford in that direction—even extending beyond it—and running from Bishops Stortford to Colchester. This latter portion was stripped of its forestal character by King John. Stephen had previously disafforested Tendring Hundred, and given it over to the husbandman, who has long since converted it into a fertile and flourishing district. . . Gradually these open woodlands have disappeared. The popular feeling —in no age very strong in favour of game preserving—was aided in this case, when hunting formed so important a part of the pastimes of the nobility, by the barons and the landowners—the predecessors of those who are now the greatest sticklers for upholding the laws of the chase, and the sworn opponents and punishers of poachers of all descriptions. The rights of the Crown, as they were called, trenched seriously upon the privileges of the local lords, land which had long been granted out and grubbed up being still considered as forest. This led continually to the institution of vexatious suits, and the exaction of heavy fines from the king's tenants and the freemen. At length it produced open conflicts with the Crown; and the united barons, by an act of compulsion, wrung from King John the Charter of Forests—'a bar,' says the historian, 'to oppression, and a happy instrument of improving our agriculture.' 'Every article of this charter,' adds Rapin, 'is a clear evidence how the subject was oppressed under the pretence of preserving the royal forest.' The spirit of that charter was jealously guarded. In the conditions exacted from Henry III., an additional charter of forests was included, by which capital punishment for these offences was abolished, and they were made punishable by fine and imprisonment. Further, the proprietors of the land recovered the right of cutting and using their own wood with pleasure. The Commons gave Edward I. the bribe of a fifteenth of all the goods of the kingdom to have its provisions carried out. From this period the Forest of Essex rapidly disappeared, as shown by the perambulations made in the reigns of four succeeding monarchs."

In past ages this vast wilderness, given up to wild beasts and the pleasures of the chase, was governed by certain laws and customs which were unknown outside—a carefully constructed legal organisation, fragments of which have survived until modern times. The laws for the regulation of the forest, and of those who dwelt within its borders, in the olden time were both various and singular. Among them were the following, which we glean from the "People's History of Essex":— "A toll was exacted from a man if he required a passage through the forest, on account of the disquiet it gave to the wild beasts. It was a fine for any one to keep a mastiff there without having three claws of one of its fore-feet struck off; and every inhabitant of the forest, on reaching the mature age of twenty-one, was compelled to take an oath in the following quaint old lines, which certainly were not likely to awe the mind by their dignity, or exorcise evil thoughts by their sweetness; but they were supposed to have a restraining influence in the solitary sylvan ramble when a hare crossed the path, or a stag came within reach of the cross-bow :—

> " 'You shall true liege man be
> Unto the king's majesty;
> Unto the birds of the forest you shall no hurt do,
> Nor to anything that doth belong thereunto;
> The offences of others you shall not conceal,
> But to the utmost of your power you shall them reveal
> Unto the officers of the forest,
> Or to them who may see them redrest.
> All these things you shall see done,
> So help your God at his holy doom.' "

The office of Lord Warden of the forest was formerly a post of great importance and profit. It was for many years held by the late Earl of Mornington, through the marriage of his father, the Hon. Mr. Long-Pole-Wellesley, with Miss Tilney, the great heiress of Wanstead House. The warden had the same duty in the forest as the sheriff had in the county. The right belonged for centuries to the De Veres, Earls of Oxford, the lords of Hedingham Castle. They succeeded the Clares, who were stewards from the reign of Henry III. to that of Edward III. They had considerable rights within its boundaries, and were always keepers of the palace at Havering-atte-Bower. They ranked among the most powerful barons of England, and played a distinguished part in the history of the country from the Conquest to the beginning of the seventeenth century. The office of King's Forester was long held by the Archers of Copped Hall. The steward appointed a lieutenant, a riding forester, and three yeomen foresters; and the perquisites of the warden and steward are thus stated :—"They had all the deer-browsing wood, all wayfs and strays within the limits of the forest; likewise all the amerciaments in the swain-motes and wood comptes, agreeably

to the assize of the forest (the amerciaments for venison and the bodies of oaks only excepted). Upon the sale of every wood they were entitled to the second best oak contained therein; and the buyer and seller thereof were obliged to present them with one bow and one broad arrow, paying at the same time each of them one penny out of every shilling. They likewise received from the sale of every covert or hedge-row, of every shilling one penny." There was also a chief forester, generally a member of some noble family, one of the Fitz-Archers of Copt Hall holding it in the reign of Edward I.; but with the decay and diminution of the forest the office appears to have become extinct. There were also in bygone times four verderers, elected by the freeholders of the county at large. Anciently important duties attached to all these officers. There were three courts in which they exercised their power. The Verderers,' or Forty-day Court, as it was called, from being held every forty days, was the first that took cognisance of offences. The verderers, as judicial officers, appointed to observe and keep the assizes and laws of the forest, were sworn "to view, receive, and enrol the attachments and presentments of all manner of trespasses of vert (that is, anything growing in the forest that would afford cover for the deer) and venison, and to do equal justice as well to the poor as to the rich." They punished trifling offences, but sent other presentments to the Swainmote Court, where the matters were decided upon by a jury, and then returned to the Court of Justice Seat—the highest forest court. This was held by the Lord Chief Justice in Eyre, under the king's commission, and, though limited to forest offences, it seems to have been similar to a Court of Assize. Formerly these courts were held at Chelmsford; but as the forest was driven by the agricultural pioneer to the south-western borders, they were removed to Chigwell.

For the following particulars we are indebted to Weldon's "Guide to Epping Forest."

"Richard Montfitchet, who was reinstated as Forester in 1217, appears to have had his time fully occupied with the duties of his office, the power and privileges connected with which must have been eminently congenial to the sporting tastes of an Anglo-Norman. What these powers were is shown in the close rolls, as well as the care and jealousy with which the ancient forest laws were maintained. It was the duty of the Forester to preserve the boundaries of the forest intact, and to permit no encroachments within them. Should a neighbouring landowner desire to free his woods from the view of the Foresters and Regarders, to cultivate a portion of them, or to enclose a park, and kill the game on his own manors, he had to obtain the royal permission, and an official writ was addressed to the Forester on the subject. Such a writ, on behalf of the Abbey of St. Edmund's-Bury, was despatched from Oxford to Sir Richard de Montfitchet on the 20th of July, 1216. By it he was informed that a charter had been given to the abbot and monks there serving God, granting that their woods at Harlow, Stapleford, and Werketon should be for ever free from regard, waste, and view of the Foresters and Regarders, and that the abbot and monks should have the use of the same woods at their own will, except always driving forth the game. And on the same day, under another writ to de Montfitchet, free warren was granted for ever to the Bishop of London and his successors in his manor of Clackington, and that of Walton-cum-Thorpe, which is the manor of the Chapter of St. Paul's, London. Also that the said bishop and his successors for ever had full liberty to take stags and hinds, and all sorts of wild animals within the limits of the said manors. The Forester was also commanded to make two deer leaps in his great park at Ongar, as he had right and custom to have. And also about the same time Montfitchet received the following mandate :—' We command you to allow the Abbess of Barking her reasonable estovers* in her wood at Hainault for her firing, her cooking, and her brewing, if she has been accustomed so to do, in the time of our Lord King John our father ; also to permit the same abbess to have her dogs to chase hares and foxes within the bailiwick if she was accustomed to have them in the time of our aforesaid father.' The king made numerous gifts of timber and firewood out of the forest, for which writs were issued to the Forester of Essex. For instance, he was ordered to give Rose de Sculiz, a nun of Barking, an oak out of the forest of Essex, to repair her chamber in the said abbey, taken where it would least injure the said forest."

By a charter of King John, dated March 25, in the fifth year of his reign, and confirmed by Edward IV., all that part of the forest which lay to the north of the road from Stortford through Dunmow to Colchester, was ordered to be disafforested. Its extent was further diminished by a perambulation made in 29 Edward I., in pursuance of the Charta de Foresta ; but its boundaries were finally determined by an inquisition and perambulation taken in September, 1640, by a commission under the great seal of England, in pursuance of

an Act of Parliament for settling the bounds of the forests in general. The boundaries as thus fixed include the whole of Wanstead, Leyton, Walthamstow, Woodford, Loughton, Chigwell, Lamborne, Stapleford Abbots, Waltham Holy Cross, Epping, and Nazing, and parts of Chingford, Stratford, East and West Ham, Little and Great Ilford, Barking, Dagenham, Theydon Bois, and Navestock. The extent of the forest was estimated at 60,000 acres, of which 48,000 were enclosed and private property, the remaining 12,000 being unenclosed wastes and woods. What is called Henhault, or Hainault, Forest is a part of this district.

From the earliest times then, as we have seen, this extensive tract of woodland had been a royal forest—one of those districts quaintly described by Manwood as " a certain territory of woody grounds and fruitful pastures, privileged for wild beasts and fowls of forest chase and warren, to rest and abide there in the safe protection of the king, for his delight and pleasure." " Queen Elizabeth, in one of her visits to the lodge bearing her name, is reported to have granted to the poor of several adjoining parishes the privilege of lopping wood. The custom still exists—or did until lately—for the possessors of that privilege to assemble on the eleventh of November in each year, in order to strike an axe into the boughs of the trees at the hour of midnight. This right is also exercised upon parts of the forest which have been for many years enclosed, and extends in full operation till the twenty-third of April in the following year." *

The ancient bounds of the forest have been a matter of controversy from time to time, but from the days of the Long Parliament down to the year 1851, as stated above, it consisted of two parts—the Forest of Hainault and Epping Forest, the former comprising the high ground lying to the east of the Roding, and north of the high road to Romford, and the latter lying between the Roding and the Lea, and stretching northward from Stratford to Epping. Hainault Forest, in which the Crown had a more clearly-defined interest than in Epping, possessing not only rights of forest, but the soil of several large woods acquired at the dissolution of monasteries, was disafforested by Act of Parliament in 1851, and was subsequently enclosed.

The enormous tract of land which was settled under the statute of Charles I., in 1640, as the limits of Waltham Forest, doubtless included very extensive private estates, subject to rights of forest and chase ; the greater part of the residue had been granted or sold by Henry VIII. and succeeding

---

* This word is derived from the French " estoffer," to supply material for any kind of work.

* Weldon's " Guide to Epping Forest."

VIEWS IN EPPING FOREST.

1. Connaught Water, Chingford.   2. A Glade at Theydon Bois.   3. On the way to Copped Hall from Loughton.   4. High Beech.

sovereigns. In its present form the principal portion of Epping Forest commences at Chingford Station, and proceeds northward beyond Theydon Bois to the outskirts of Epping itself. But southward from Chingford Station there is a somewhat broken stretch of forest and waste, reaching down to Wanstead Flats and the City of London Cemetery at Aldersbrook. To that cemetery London is largely indebted for the preservation of Epping Forest as a place of recreation for the people. Extra-mural interment has thus contributed to extra-mural enjoyment; for, if this parcel of land had not been acquired by the Corporation for a burying-place, they could scarcely have maintained the right which served to break down the usurpations of the encroaching " land-grabbers." But on this subject we shall have more to say hereafter.

In Epping Forest an enclosure had never been recommended in the interests of the Crown; but a most complicated system of ownership prevailed. The soil of the open waste belonged to the lords of about seventeen different manors, each owning the part situate within his own bounds. Certain rights of pasturage existed over the whole tract, and certain rights of woodcutting in particular parts; and over all the Crown had the right to preserve deer and to keep the forest *in statu quo* for the sake of the deer, the ancient rights of " vert " and " venison." To these ancient rights the public had, from the time when the forest became of any use for recreation, looked to preserve their playground intact, but their hopes had been somewhat cruelly disappointed. An economic air prevailing at the Treasury and the Office of Woods, it was resolved, soon after the disafforestation of Hainault, to sell the Crown rights in Epping to the lord of the manor, and a pitiful sum of about £18,000 was thus realised for the national exchequer. The consequence of this action was not only to remove the safeguard of the Crown's rights, but to give a false impression that the effect of their acquisition by a lord was to enable him to enclose against all comers.

In 1851, when Hainault Forest was disafforested, the area of the open forest was little short of 6,000 acres, but this in 1871 had dwindled to just under 3,000. In 1882, when Epping Forest was handed over by Her Majesty for " the free use and enjoyment of the people for ever," it extended to about 5,600 acres, nearly the whole of which had been purchased by the Corporation of London, while some 400 acres remained enclosed, partly under such conditions as prevented building, thus tending to enhance the value of the forest as an " open space."

Between the years 1851 and 1863, when the " Open Spaces Committee " was appointed, rapid strides had been made by the encroaching fences in Epping Forest, particularly in the manor of Loughton, where an enclosure of enormous extent had startled the public into a watchful attention from which it never subsequently relapsed. That enclosure comprised in the whole about 1,300 acres—land covered with wood, and situate in the heart of the wildest and most beautiful tract of the forest. It was not carried out without some regard to supposed rights. Having bought the interest of the Crown, the lord of the manor assumed that he had only the commoners in his own manor to deal with. These he compensated by the distribution among them of between 300 and 400 acres of the forest, and, having thus obtained their consent, he put a fence on his own account round the remaining 900 or 1,000 acres. The lord of the manor, however, seems to have forgotten to take into consideration that keen instinct of resistance to enclosure which is seldom wanting among the poor agricultural classes, when their real or presumed " rights " are being entrenched upon. The inhabitants of Loughton, high and low, had been accustomed to get their winter supply of fuel by lopping the trees in the forest. To the poor this practice had been a double benefit, not only furnishing their own hearths, but giving them constant employment during the winter months in lopping for their richer neighbours. They asserted that the right had come down to them from the time of Elizabeth, and was the right of the inhabitants at large, and not to be got rid of by allotments of land to a favoured few.

In the preceding chapter we have spoken of the highwaymen who infested these parts in former times; here we have had to deal with modern thieves and plunderers, in the shape of "land grabbers." Well and wittily wrote Samuel Butler in " Hudibras " :—

> " The fault is great in man or woman
> Who steals a goose from off a common :
> But who shall plead that man's excuse,
> Who steals the common from the goose ? "

It was all very well for the queen to bestow a baronetcy on the Lord Mayor of London, Alderman Ellis, and the honour of knighthood on the two sheriffs, Mr. Reginald Hanson and Mr. William Anderson Ogg; but the real men who fought and won the battle on behalf of the toiling masses were Mr. John T. Bedford, a common councilman, Mr. George Burney, an old member of the Commons Preservation Society, Mr. Frederick Young, the Chairman, and Mr. W. G. S. Smith, the

Honorary Secretary of the "Forest Fund." To these names must be added that of an old forester named Thomas Willingale, whose rude forefathers for generations had lived by the irregular products of that forest. This last-named individual was the "Village Hampden" who organised the bands who pulled down the enclosures—an overt act, which served as a declaration of war. Burney, who was also a commoner in the forest, took down from London three omnibus-loads of navvies, and in the course of a morning's work levelled the fences round the obnoxious enclosures which the commissioners wished to legalise.

It was really, if the full truth must be stated, a sort of triangular duel between the Crown, the lords of the manor, and the people. The Crown sold its rights for mere nominal sums, and then the landowners and the landless multitude were the only combatants, and the former thought that they would be able to drive the latter to surrender their rights on their own terms. But they found, when too late, that they had "reckoned without their host." The lords of several of the manors sold their "waste," as the open lands were called by them, and allowed it in every direction to be enclosed and built upon.

In the end, after long litigation, and after several lawless encounters, the question was brought formally under the notice of the House of Commons, and an Act passed appointing a commission to inquire into the contending rights, and to report to Parliament a scheme for the preservation and management of the forest in the interests of the public.

A few days before this Act received the royal assent, another champion took up the gage on the part of the public. The Corporation of London had an ancient traditionary connection with the forest. It was reputed that certain rights of hunting there had been granted to them by royal charter, and though the existence of the grant could never be established, there were not wanting curious entries in the Corporation records bearing upon the claim. Fortunately, however, a connection of a very different character had recently arisen, which, though it could not furnish the motive for interference, supplied a most powerful weapon of attack. The Commissioners of Sewers had purchased for the purposes of a cemetery the demesne lands of the ancient manor of Aldersbrook. In the time of Charles I. the lord of this manor claimed for himself and his tenants rights of common of pasture for their beasts throughout the length and breadth of the forest waste. Upon this claim (one of many of a similar character) the Corporation, when they had resolved to help the public, founded a Chancery suit, which, commenced on the 14th of August, 1871, was terminated by the memorable judgment of Sir George Jessel, in November, 1874. All the lords of manors were defendants to this suit, and no expense was spared on either side to gain the victory. In the result the case of the Corporation was established at all points, the right they claimed was declared to exist, and all enclosures made within twenty years before the filing of the Bill—that is, since the 14th of August, 1851—were pronounced illegal.

So far, a decisive victory was gained; but still much remained to be done in order to secure its fruits, and to this end the vast resources of the Corporation were devoted. The lords of the manors who had enclosed had sold large tracts of the forest, amounting in all to about 1,000 acres. It was impossible to make all the purchasers parties to the suit, and recourse was of necessity had to the Epping Forest Commission to enforce the judgment against these persons, subject to such modifications as might be found just and expedient. Portions of the land sold had been built over, and it was obviously impossible to pull down streets of villas; but larger portions remained in their natural condition or had been merely broken up for agriculture, and these portions the Corporation and the Commons Preservation Society thought should be restored to the public. Unfortunately, the commissioners took a different view, and thus prolonged the struggle for some years.

On the 23rd February, 1877, the final report of the Epping Forest Commissioners was presented to Parliament. Their recommendations, as summed up briefly by the author of Weldon's "Guide" already quoted, were: "The forest to be disafforested, the Crown rights to cease, the forest to be managed by the Corporation of London as conservators, who are from time to time to appoint a committee, not exceeding twelve in number, to act for the conservators; and Colonel Palmer, Sir Thomas White, and Sir Antonio Brady, the surviving verderers, and one other verderer to be elected, to be members of that committee. In future, two of the verderers to be elected by the parliamentary voters of the northern part of the forest, and two by those of the southern. Rights of common, pasture, lopping, pannage, and so forth, to continue, subject to the scheme. The conservators to keep the forest unenclosed as an open space for the recreation and enjoyment of the public at all times; they shall preserve its natural aspect, protect the timber and other growths, and prevent the digging of gravel or other strata. The conservators to purchase the right of any lord of the manor or other person who owned the soil of any land within the forest at a specified rate; but where such land had been built on before 21st August, 1871, the occupiers were to pay a rent-charge; enclosures on which there was no building to be thrown open within twelve months after the scheme coming into operation. Enclosures made since 1851, the soil of which did not belong to the lord of the manor, should be permitted to be retained by the owners of the soil, and remain enclosed, upon payment of a perpetual annual rent-charge. An exception to those rules was made in the case of churches, chapels, and charitable institutions, as long as they are used for such purposes. The conservators were to cause certain unlawfully enclosed lands to be thrown open; might make bye-laws for the regulation of persons using the forest, both for recreation and under common rights, and generally for preventing its improper use or disfigurement. The Corporation to have power to apply the duty raised by the metage on grain to afford the necessary funds. They were to appoint from time to time, as reeves and assistant reeves, persons who were recommended by the vestries of such parishes, the reeves to be the officers of the conservators, who could reject unqualified persons."

In the end further difficulties arose, and fresh litigation ensued; but towards the close of the Session of 1878 an Act was passed appointing Sir Arthur Hobhouse sole arbitrator, to determine all the nice questions arising between the purchases from the lords and the public, subject to an instruction that nothing was to remain enclosed save what was necessary to render the villas and manors habitable and marketable by their owners. This task—no light one—Sir Arthur Hobhouse completed in July, 1882, to the satisfaction of all concerned. The result was the rescue of some 500 or 600 additional acres, and that without, it is confidently believed, the infliction of any real hardship upon a single individual.

The Act effectually preserves the forest as an open space for the use and enjoyment of the public. It provides for a Ranger of the Forest, appointed by the Crown, and constitutes the Corporation of London conservators, stipulating that in this capacity the Corporation are to keep the forest unenclosed, and to preserve, as far as possible, its natural aspect; especially to protect and preserve the ancient earthworks called Ambresbury Banks, the Purlieu Bank, and other forest marks and boundaries. The conservators are further to protect the timber and other trees, pollard, shrubs, underwood, gorse, turf, and herbage, and to prevent the lopping, cutting, and injuring the same, and the digging of the soil. The ancient house known as Queen Elizabeth's Lodge is vested, by assent of the Queen, in the conservators, for preservation and maintenance as an object of antiquarian interest. The lands held by grantees are to be thrown open, the arbitrator to decide what sum shall be paid in respect of them, and also as to the mode and conditions of quieting in title, of lands not thrown open, with buildings erected thereon. There are to be four verderers elected by the commoners. The verderers are to be members of the Epping Forest Committee, a body consisting of twelve members of the Common Council, in addition to the verderers. Power is given to this body to make bye-laws for various purposes: amongst other things for excluding gipsies, hawkers, beggars, rogues and vagabonds, and for preventing bird-catching, and regulating the killing, taking, injuring, shooting, chasing, or disturbing of deer, game, or other animals, or fishing in the waters.

Two months previously—namely, on the 6th of May—when the queen formally opened this delightful pleasure-ground in its present form, and pronounced it "free to the public for ever," the difficulties which had attended the achievement of the above object became very generally known. His Royal Highness the Duke of Connaught was appointed ranger, and at the above-mentioned date the queen paid a visit to the forest for the purpose of declaring it freely open to the public, her Majesty at the same time planting an oak in commemoration of the event, and signifying her wish that the wood at High Beech, in the neighbourhood of Chingford, hitherto known as Beech Wood, should henceforth be known as "Queen Victoria's Wood."

An article in *The Times*, in July, 1882, on the occasion of the termination of the inquiry into the complicated interests connected with Epping Forest, contained the following interesting remarks:—" The whole science of forestry, with its deep mysteries as to vert and venison, is clean dead and gone. So little remains of the knowledge of the real history of these forests that, by a strange mistake, they are sometimes supposed to have been as beautiful and admirable features of feudal as of modern England. It is the fate of Epping as a forest to pass from the domain of the Crown to that of the people; to the ragged schools and Bands of Hope who picnic under its trees has fallen one of the most important of the *jura regalia*. Only a king might make a forest. No subject, as such, however potent he might be, might have a forest, inasmuch as sovereign prerogatives were incident to it. A subject might own a chase, which possessed no particular laws and where the common law was in force, where there were no verderers, regarders, or agisters, no Court of Attachments, no Swainmote, no Justice Seat. If the king granted a forest to a subject, it fell to the rank of a chase. Precise and important distinctions were drawn between the two. The beasts of the forest were the hart, the hind, the hare, the boar, and the wolf—that is, 'beasts that do haunt the woods more than the plains.' The beasts of the chase were five also—the buck, the doe, the fox, the marten, and the roe. Each forest included also a warren, and the beasts and fowls of warren were the hare, the cony, the pheasant, and the partridge. Venery was then a science with a precise nomenclature, and hunters were as much pedants as feudal lawyers. The hart in its second year must be called a broker, and a boar of the fourth year a sanglier. Good woodmen spoke of a bevy of roes and a rout of wolves, and they referred to the footmarks of the hart as the slot, and to traces of the fallow deer as its 'view.' One cannot study the old forest laws without seeing that our forefathers loved the forests as much as their sons do. Every twig and every cony were sacred in their eyes. It was the duty of the good woodman to preserve with care venison and vert—that is, the beasts of the chase, and the trees and cover which sheltered them. No man might without licence cut down the trees within the forest, even if they grew in his own freehold. Still more heinous was the offence of ploughing up the thickets and covers, or erecting houses, or making inclosures. In every forest a fence month was strictly observed, and for fifteen days before Midsummer, and for as many after, no one was permitted to wander about or drive his flocks in the forest, so that it might be, in the words of one old writer, 'a sanctuary of peace for the wild beasts.' Hawking and hunting within the forest domains, being pastimes for kings and princes, could not, of course, be enjoyed by common people; and to slay a deer, so long as the forest laws were in force, was a crime blacker than murder or arson. The most striking peculiarity of these wastes was the fact that the common law did not extend to them. There, in theory at least, only the judgments and determinations of the king were binding. The word of his vicar, the Lord Chief Justice of the Forest, was supreme. In the Court of Attachments or Woodmote, which sat every forty days, in the Swainmote, which sat thrice a year, and in the Justice Seat, which was held at intervals of three years, were administered laws wholly repugnant in spirit to those which were put in operation at Westminster. All the ordinary rights of property, all the common ideas of law, were set at nought; and history is full of complaints and murmurs respecting the hardships caused by the servile system administered in these 'oases of despotism.'

"Almost all traces of this state of things have long passed away from Epping. The rights of the Crown were in some cases sold, and even before they were extinguished the sharp distinctions of the forest laws had fallen into disuse. The commoners turned their cattle into the forest to feed, subject to the supervision of the reeves and forest courts. From time to time a lord of the manor enclosed a tempting piece of land to round off his property, or a cottager stole a morsel to make a garden. For a long time the forest was almost ungoverned, or was subject only to imperfect usages, indifferently observed and little understood. Thanks to the labours of the Corporation, this is altered. Rights are defined, and a code of management as precise as the old forest laws themselves has been established. One thing we may learn from those old laws the memory of which is disappearing: they were framed by men who prized the greenwood, who regarded every tree as precious, who would not have a bird or a hare disturbed, who viewed with suspicion improvements which affected the forest domains. It was this jealous spirit which preserved them in the past, and its continuance will be the best preservation in the future. Another thing, also, may be gathered from the same sources. The avowed justification of these exceptional domains in the past was that the king's labour 'doth maintain and defend every man's rest and peace;' that 'his diligence doth preserve and defend every man's private pleasure and delight;' and that it was for the advantage of the realm that he should have his fit place of recreation and pastime. All that is the sentiment of a past age, and modern sovereigns need no such means of entertainment. But we shall be keeping up this spirit of zeal for the welfare of the realm by permitting the common people to take their pleasure where sovereigns once found theirs."

Lysons, in his "Magna Britannia," describes the forest as "of large extent, full of game, and well stocked with deer, the fattest and largest in the kingdom." Notwithstanding that the Crown had long ago parted with the ownership of the soil, it still retained the right of "vert" and "venison," that is, the right to keep an unlimited number of deer, with their "herbage, vert, and browse," which is held to include a right over "all the beasts of the forest, the trees, and underwood, and whatever grows within it ; and the power of granting licenses to hunt and shoot within its boundaries."

The result of the purchase of the several manorial rights, and of the supervision of the forest by the Lord Mayor and Corporation, is to be seen in the gradual growth of the trees, and in the number of

bourhood about the "knights of the highway" and other less romantic transgressors.

The forest, it appears, was stocked with both red and fallow deer down to the end of the last century, for in the report of the Commission of 1793, Sir James Tylney Long, at that time warden, although he was "not able to ascertain what number of bucks and does are kept, or abide in the forest in general," stated that "about five brace of bucks and three brace of does have

ROYAL FOREST HOTEL, CHINGFORD.

the deer which browse in its remoter glades. These are supposed to have increased from about eighty to one hundred. They are thought by many naturalists to be of a different breed from those in any park in the kingdom, and to represent with perfect identity the wild denizens of the forest in Anglo-Saxon times. They are but slightly spotted or marked, and when first born they are not spotted at all. Although they are shy and wild, and seldom come near the haunts of men, they fight terribly among themselves, especially at the rutting season, in autumn. The deer, as might naturally be supposed, were terribly thinned by the highwaymen and poachers of the last century, and many strange stories are still told in the neigh-

been, one year with another, killed in the forest, by warrants of authority from his Majesty ; and about fourteen brace of bucks and seven brace of does for individuals who claim a right to have venison in the forest. My claim to red and fallow deer in the said forest is without stint." By 1863 the deer appear to have fallen off in number very considerably. Mr. Howard, in that year, told the committee of the House of Commons that "there are no longer any deer in Epping Forest ; practically they do not exist ;" he added, however, "there may be a dozen, perhaps." But this was probably untrue ; they never were really reduced so low.

Of the Epping Hunt, which was for so many

years associated with the forest, we shall speak more fully in dealing with Buckhurst Hill; and of Queen Elizabeth's fondness of frequenting its sylvan glades for the purposes of the chase, on reaching Chingford.

Fisher, in his "Companion to the History of England," states that "Henry VIII. went out with his hounds, and breakfasted under a great tree in Epping Forest the very day that his once-lov'd wife (Anne Boleyn) was to perish in the Tower."

But the site of this tree is not known, and the story may not be true.

Of the geology of this district there is little at present to be said; and for the best of all reasons: because the Essex Field Club has only just taken the subject seriously in hand. It may be said, however, generally, that the surface of the district is mainly composed of London clay, which overlies the primitive stratum of chalk, and which here and there is capped with patches of gravel and Bagshot sand.

Epping Forest is intersected by railways, with stations at short intervals, so as to furnish points of approach in all directions. It has all the charms of hill and dale, open plain and pleasant avenue, with deep umbrageous recesses here and there, comprising altogether every variety of forest scenery, fringed with far-spreading landscapes, reaching into half-a-dozen counties. As a rule, the oaks and other trees are of somewhat stunted growth, but there are, of course, exceptions. Of the famous Fairlop Oak we shall speak in dealing with Hainault Forest. The neighbourhood of Woodford is particularly rich in its flora, and the "Plantæ Woodfordiensis" of Richard Warner is

still a text-book for botanists. Indeed, nearly every part of the forest is profuse in mosses, wild flowers, grasses, and fresh-water algæ.

In the less frequented parts, and especially in the damp and boggy places, many interesting, and, indeed, uncommon plants occur. Let us hope that the wholesale drainage will not be continued so as to utterly destroy the plants peculiar to naturally damp situations. One of the smallest and most lovely of these Epping Forest plants is the blue Ivy-leaved Bell-flower (*Campanula hederacea*) seen at the bottom of our illustration; another, the rose-coloured Bog Pimpernel (*Anagallis tenella*) seen on the right, and below it the Round-leaved Sun-dew (*Drosera rotundifolia*), an insectivorous plant studied and described by Charles Darwin. Another bog

FLOWERS FROM EPPING FOREST.

plant is illustrated on the top right of our illustration in the lovely drooping Marsh Thistle (*Carduus palustris*). A decidedly uncommon orchid is common not far from High Beech, viz.: the Smaller Butterfly Orchis (*Habenaria bifolia*), illustrated at the top left; many other orchids may be found, notably the Helleborine and Marsh Helleborine *Epipactis latifolia* and *E. palustris*). The Grass of Parnassus (*Parnassia palustris*), also grows in wet places, a most beautiful, interesting, and curious plant. The Butcher's Broom (*Ruscus aculeatus*) may also be found in many damp spots, together with its near ally the Lily of the Valley (*Convallaria majalis*). The Wood Sorrel (*Oxalis acetosella*)— probably the true Shamrock—is very frequent; so are many diverse species of St. John's Wort

(*Hypericum*), together with both the British species of Golden Saxifrage (*Chrysosplenium*). This brief list does not give one-hundredth part of the many beautiful plants of the forest either prized for their beauty, rarity, or, may-be, their botanical interest.

Amongst the ferns of the forest one of the most interesting is the Adder's-tongue (*Ophioglossum vulgatum*), illustrated at the top right, the Hart's-tongue (*Scolopendrium vulgare*), the Scaly Spleen-wort (*Ceterach officinarum*), the Toothed Bladder Fern (*Cystopteris dentata*), the Prickly Shield Fern (*Polystichum aculeatum*), the Male Fern (*Lastrea filix-mas*), Common Polypody (*Polypodium vulgare*), very frequent about old stumps, and illustrated at the foot of our engraving, Wall Rue (*Asplenium ruta-muraria*), upon crumbly old walls, and the Common Brake (*Pteris aquilina*) grows profusely all over the forest.

Many edible species of fungi may be found in the forest, and most of these have been painted by Mr. Worthington G. Smith, the originals being at all times accessible to the public in the New Natural History Museum at South Kensington. The true Mushroom (*Agaricus campestris*) grows in open grassy places, together with the Fairy Ring Champignon (*Marasmus oreades*). The Parasol Mushroom (*Agaricus procerus*) is frequent in partially open places, the Red-fleshed Mushroom (*Agaricus rubescens*) is very common in the woody parts, together with the delicious Edible Boletus (*Boletus edulis*) and the Edible Chantarelle (*Cantharellus cibarius*). The Vegetable Beef-steak—so named by Dr. Bull—is very frequent on the old oaks, and sometimes on old beeches and other trees. The Giant Puff-ball (*Lycoperdon giganteum*) is common in the open grassy places; various truffles have also been found, and many poisonous species, and species of great botanical interest. Many other edible species occur besides the above mentioned, and numerous highly-poisonous plants, as the Scarlet Fly Mushroom (*Agaricus muscarius*) under the birches. Before venturing to eat edible fungi, all beginners should carefully examine Mr. Smith's paintings at the British Museum.

The forest has, however, its insect plagues. A correspondent of the *Times* has remarked that the greatest delinquent among the insects that spoil the foliage of our oak-trees is the larvæ of *Tortrix viridana*, which may be found in abundance during May, rolled in a leaf or between two adjacent leaves connected by a slight silken web. The moth itself appears at the end of June, and is frequently a perfect pest on account of its numbers. "In walking through Epping Forest," he adds, "I noticed that every tap on an oak branch caused a cloud of these insects to fly out. The moth when expanded is something under one inch across the wings, the upper pair of which are of a pure green colour."

Epping Forest is a rare hunting-ground, not only for the botanist and the entomologist, but also for the ornithologist; song-birds of almost all the known species are, at one time or another during each succeeding year, to be met with here. In Mr. Jefferies' book, "Nature near London," many interesting details respecting the feathered visitants of our suburban forests may be found.

The inns and hostelries of the neighbourhood are all reminders of the rural character of the place. Besides the "Royal Forest Hotel," we have the "Foresters," the "Roebuck," the "Warren House," the "Bald-faced Stag," the "Horse and Well," the "Robin Hood," the "King's Oak," and the "Owl." Most of these are still frequented during the summer months by ruralising parties from London, who make the shady bowers and sylvan retreats of the forest in their vicinity resound with their noisy mirth.

The hearthstones of many of the forest cottages were, and some are still, removable; and as they served in Romney Marsh, and in many sea-coast towns, as places for storing kegs of illicit brandy, so about Epping and Loughton and Chingford they supplied the parents and grandparents of many of the present race of cottagers with storehouses for haunches of venison which were not altogether honestly obtained.

The story of the preservation of the forest has been told in pamphlet form by Mr. J. T. Bedford, who, from his position of Chairman of the Epping Forest Committee, was in a position to observe and to recount the various steps which led to the final event—its dedication to the use and enjoyment of the people "for ever." From this pamphlet it appears that the forest now consists of about 6,000 acres, rather more than 5,500 of which have been purchased by the Corporation, and in acquiring which about 1,200 claims had to be considered. The costs incurred in the prolonged struggle to secure this vast tract of land from further encroachment were, no doubt, heavy : the aggregate of the purchase money, compensation for rights of lopping, the price of Wanstead Park, and legal expenses, amounting to some £256,275. But in exchange for this outlay a domain of rare beauty has been secured to ever-growing London, and generations yet unborn are likely to be grateful for the boon that has been conferred upon them; so that the almost romantic story of its rescue ought not readily to be forgotten by those who enjoy its cool shades and sylvan recesses.

CHAPTER XLVI.

EPPING FOREST (*continued*)—SEWARDSTONE, HIGH BEECH, AND CHINGFORD.

" A mound of even-sloping side,
Whereon a hundred stately beeches grew,
And here and there great hollies under them.
But for a mile all round was open space,
And fern and heath."—TENNYSON.

Preliminary Remarks—Situation and Boundaries of Sewardstone—Seats and Mansions—High Beech Green—St. Paul's Church—Fairmead Lodge—Sotheby and Tennyson—Residents at High Beech—Fairmead House—John Clare—High Beech Hill—The " Robin Hood " and " King's Oak "—" Harold's Oak "—Queen Victoria's Wood—Lappitt's Hill—Bury Wood and Hawk Wood—Situation and Etymology of Chingford—Its Extent and Boundaries—The Manor of Chingford St. Paul—The Manor of Chingford Earls—Friday Hill—Buckrills— A Singular Tenure—Census Returns—Chingford Old Church—The Ordnance Survey Obelisk—Queen Elizabeth's Lodge—The Royal Forest Hotel—Connaught Water.

THE topography of the various districts which form integral parts of Epping Forest, and their associations with past history, may perhaps furnish the reader with a few entertaining chapters. Though they lead us far away from literary associations, yet they open up fresh fields for our pilgrim feet. Little importance can, however, be attached to the present celebrity of the once great Forest of Essex, for even the last of historic events connected with it—the Epping Hunt—has become a thing of the past, having lingered among the relics of the ancient sports of London citizens down to a very recent date. The picturesque scenery and historical associations of the forest have, however, more lasting charms, and may tempt the reader hither—not merely in the hurly-burly of the Easter holiday, but on any quiet day when he may enjoy undisturbed the rich beauties of its glades and woody knolls.

The towns, villages, and seats which now stud the district we are about to traverse, and the roads which intersect the sylvan waste, may have been the labours of a few centuries; inns and lodges would be among the earliest adjuncts to a vast district, peopled, as it were, by hundreds of retainers, whose business it was to defend this " royal chase ; " for the privileges of hunting here were confined to the sovereign and his favourites. Again, the thousands who flocked thither with such privilege would well repay the hospitalities of an inn and " hosteller," even were we to leave out of the reckoning the boon companionship of foresters and the debauched habits of marauders who fattened upon the infringement of the royal privilege, as in wholesale deer-stealing for the London markets. Houses of call of this description, to suit the requirements of the wayfarer, from the humble roadside tavern or ale-house to the spacious " hotel," are to be met with in almost every part of the forest.

With these few remarks we will resume our perambulation. Sewardstone, our first halting-place southwards from Waltham Abbey, is a hamlet belonging to that parish. It lies between two and three miles distant, on the lower road leading to Chingford. The district is situate just on the borders of the forest, on its western side, and it stretches away from High Beech and Sewardstone Wood in the east to Sewardstone Mill on the River Lea in the west, and from Waltham Abbey in the north to Low Street, Chingford, in the south. It includes within its boundary Sewardstone Street, Sewardstone Green, Sewardstone Bury, Sewardstone Wood, and Sewardstone Mills, at which last-named place are some extensive dye-works ; with this exception, the locality is almost wholly agricultural. The land is pleasantly broken up into miniature hills and valleys, and in parts is well wooded. Among the better class of residences here may be mentioned Gilwell Park, near the Green ; Sewardstone Lodge, the grounds of which slope down to the Lea ; the Grange, on the north side of the village ; and Yardley House, nearer to Chingford. Mr. Thorne, in his " Environs of London," says:—" Sewardstone has a tradition that it was once a distinct parish, named after one Seward, a great Saxon thane, and used to show a heap of broken ground as the site of the old church."

From Sewardstone, we pass by a narrow winding lane eastward, for about half a mile, to High Beech Green, another hamlet and ecclesiastical district of Waltham Abbey. The cottages and other houses are somewhat scattered and straggling, and close by is a small brick-built church, St. Paul's, which was erected in 1836. Further eastward, by the side of the Epping road, stands another church, which was built in 1872, to serve as a chapel-of-ease to Loughton parish. It is a handsome structure, in the Early English style, erected from the designs of Mr. A. W. Blomfield. The building is cruciform in plan, with a semi-circular apsidal chancel and a tower and tall spire ; the latter is a conspicuous landmark for miles round, and is a pleasing object in the forest scenery at several points. This church, as we learn from

Weldon's " Guide to Epping Forest," was built at the expense of a neighbouring resident, " whose munificence was such that he erected it on ground in which he had not the sole interest."

High Beech Park, Wallsgrove House, and Alder Grove Lodge, are among the seats in this locality. Fairmead Lodge, which lies about half a mile south of the church, and looks out upon Fairmead Plain, was for many years, at the end of the last and beginning of the present century, the home of William Sotheby, who here wrote his " Orestes," and entered the field against Pope by translating the " Iliad" of Homer into English verse. Tennyson also at one time lived in this neighbourhood, at Beech Hill House, a building which has now disappeared ; here he wrote his " Talking Oak" and " Locksley Hall."

To Fairmead House, then a private lunatic asylum, John Clare was taken in 1837, at which time a son of Thomas Campbell, the poet, was also an inmate. The pair soon got upon friendly terms, and became constant companions in their rambles, which, after a time, they were permitted to make into the forest. In one of his poems, written at that time, Clare wrote :—

"I love the forest and its airy bounds,
　Where friendly Campbell takes his daily rounds."

In the summer of 1841 Clare quitted the pleasant shelter which he had found here, and started off, " without a penny in his pocket," to walk to his native town, Northborough, in Northamptonshire, which he reached in three days. He soon found himself, however, in the County Lunatic Asylum, where he continued till his death, in 1864.

High Beech Hill—now known as " Queen Victoria's Wood," since the visit of Her Majesty to the spot in May, 1882—is the highest plateau of the forest. This is, perhaps, the most favourite resort of the many thousands who take holiday in the forest during the summer and autumn. Here the London clay formation reaches its greatest altitude— 759 feet above the sea-level ; and from this elevated spot some beautiful views of the surrounding country are obtained, including a broad sweep of undulating forest. Westward the eye wanders unobstructed over the valley of the Lea, and northward the view extends far into Hertfordshire, whilst to the south-west the vision ranges over a great part of Kent, from Shooter's Hill down to Gravesend.

The scenery here is very beautiful, almost rivalling in effect some parts of the far-famed New Forest, in Hampshire. "Nothing can be more delightful," observes Mr. Weldon in his book above quoted, "than a ramble among the beech woods on a hot summer day. The shadows are so cool and deep ; the belts of golden light that lie across the greensward at every opening among the trees are so bright and sunny ; the far-stretching vistas so mysterious and seductive to the imagination ; and the trunks and branches of the beeches so smooth, round, and well filled, and so covered with heavy masses of beautiful transparent foliage, that you feel as if in an enchanted place. You think longingly of the long-ago times when an English county merited its beautiful poetical name of 'Buckinghamshire'—the home of the beech-trees ; beech being the modern form of the old Teutonic buck, or buch."

Within the immediate neighbourhood of High Beech Hill are two well-known hostelries, the " Robin Hood" and " King's Oak." Near the latter inn is the stump of an old tree, commonly called " Harold's Oak," from which the latter inn takes its name ; and the green close by of late years served as the " meet" for the counterfeit " Epping Hunt," of which we have spoken above, and of which we shall have more to say on reaching Buckhurst Hill. The " meet" of late years had degenerated into a very disorderly gathering of London roughs, and in 1882 the fiat was issued by which this time-honoured custom—certainly "more honoured in the breach than in the observance"—was brought to an end. It is now no more, and we may be sure will not be revived by the Lord Mayor and Aldermen of London.

On the east side of High Beech Hill, in the thick of the forest, is an excavation, almost hidden from sight by the overhanging trees and brushwood, which has become locally known as " Dick Turpin's Cave," from a tradition that it was one of the lurking-places of that notorious highwayman. This part of the forest, as we have seen in a previous chapter,* was anything but safe for wayfarers, unless well armed, down to the end of the last century, deer-stealing being of common occurrence here. In Epping churchyard lies buried a poor fellow whose business it was to convey the venison to the metropolis, but who, in one of his midnight returns, was shot by an unknown hand, the almost headless body being found on the road next morning.

Mr. Thorne, in his " Environs of London," thus paints in glowing colours that portion of the forest lying to the north-east of High Beech Hill, and stretching away to the " Wake Arms" on the

---

* See ante, p. 423.

Epping road, about a mile and a half distant. "Here," as he tells us, "you may explore a charming bit of wild forest, guided by a winding forest road, and keeping the high road well to your right. Rough and broken, in parts open, elsewhere thick with pollard oaks and hornbeams, and an ever-varying undergrowth of hollies, thorns, and sloes, rose-bushes, sweet-briars, and brambles, and not wanting many an unlopped beech, oak, or ash, its sunny glades and gentle undulations reveal as you wander on a thousand peeps of sylvan loveliness. Deep moist dells, rich in fungi, or banks of furze, fern, and heaths, foxgloves, and honeysuckles, tempt your admiration at every turn; song-birds are on every spray; the call of the cuckoo is heard the summer through, and not unfrequently you may catch a glimpse of a nimble woodpecker, blue-tit, or wryneck. A mile beyond 'Wake Arms' is the earth-work known as Ambresbury Banks." Of this interesting relic of early days, however, we have spoken at length in a previous chapter.

On the south side of High Beech Hill, is "Queen Victoria's Wood." It is not often that a crowned head has paid a visit to the county of Essex. Queen Elizabeth reviewed her troops at Tilbury Fort, and George III. once or twice reviewed the regiments of the line and militia at the camps of Warley Common and at Colchester; but beyond that, such records are very scant—if, indeed, any will be found—until we come to the memorable 6th of May, when Queen Victoria here declared the forest to be free and open to the use and enjoyment of the people for ever. It was at this favourite spot, on the high ground close by King's Oak, that the pavilion, with its amphitheatre of seats, was erected on the occasion of her Majesty's visit. The spot, perhaps, could not have been better chosen, for not only is it the most elevated part of the forest, and consequently the best point for obtaining an idea of the extent of the surrounding wilderness, but it is also in itself one of the richest "bits" of forest scenery. The trees of Beech Wood perhaps are not so venerable as the famous Burnham beeches, with their enormous girth of trunk, their gnarled and twisted roots, and rugged limbs; but the beeches here* have the advantage of being all unlopped, well grown, and expansive, and many of them gigantic in stature; they are not the stunted and mutilated giants, as at Burnham, but send out their limbs to the full extent of their natural growth and beauty.

"The trunk of the beech," writes Mr. Walker, in his "Saturday Afternoon Rambles round London," "is itself a beautiful and distinguishing character. Not ribbed and furrowed like the bark of the elm, but with a smooth skin of a beautiful light grey, a noble and soaring pillar carries the eye upwards to clustered columns which spread aloft." The Burnham beeches are pollards, having undergone the treatment which Cowper has described in his picture of

> "Trees that had once a head,
> But now wear crests of oven-wood instead."

"Tradition ascribes the pollarding of the Burnham beeches to Cromwell's soldiers. Probably," adds Mr. Walker, "the only value of the statement is in the testimony it gives to the age of the trees."

It is not, however, merely for the growth of its trees that this part of Epping Forest is famous. Here the naturalist, the entomologist, and the botanist alike, will find full scope for the study of his particular science. Many of the plants here are unmistakably of Northern origin. Ferns in great variety flourish in this neighbourhood, as also do flowering plants and shrubs; whilst birds of almost all kinds seem to abound here more than in any other part of the forest.

Southward from Beech Wood a broad open track winds through the forest towards Queen Elizabeth's Lodge and the new hotel in the neighbourhood of Chingford; whilst a little to the west, by Fairmead Lodge, is another broad green opening, leading on to Lappitt's Hill, whence, near the "Owl" public-house, a good view is obtained across London to the Surrey hills, the "ivy-mantled tower" of Chingford Church being visible away to the left. Other parts of the forest close by, such as Bury Wood and Hawk Wood, are well worth a visit. A large slice of the forest close by Fairmead Plain was some time ago enclosed, and in part built upon; the trees were grubbed up and the forest ways stopped; but where the land had not been utilised for building purposes the greater part has been reclaimed.

Chingford lies on the edge of the forest, and derives its name from the King's Ford,* the ford across the Lea by which the Court crossed to hunt in the royal forests of Epping and Hainault. One of the meadows between the old church and the river Lea still bears the name of the "King's Mead." It is not uncommon to find the aspirate interpolated in words derived from "king." Thus,

---

* The case is far different in other parts of Epping Forest, where the annual lopping process has kept them in the condition of stunted pollards.

* Kelly, in his "Post Office Directory of Essex" says that the name comes "from a ford over the Ching, on the east bank of which rivulet it is situated."

Chigwell, as we shall presently see, is in early records written Cingwell, probably King's Well. The name of the parish, in early records, is written in a variety of ways—Chilgelford, Cingeford, Cingheford, Eehingelsford, Schingelford, Shymgylford; but one and all apparently mean the same— a royal ford over the river, as mentioned above.

The parish of Chingford is seven miles in circumference, and it forms the south-western angle of the half-hundred of Waltham. The Lea divides

In the Domesday Survey the manor of Chingford St. Paul is described as comprising six hides, and containing "50 acres of meadow, pannage for 500 hogs, two fisheries, nine beasts, two sumpter-horses, 27 hogs, and 100 sheep;" and it is also added that there were "always four slaves." The extent of the manorial rights were encroached upon both by Peter de Valoines and Geoffrey de Magnaville; and in a survey of the manor taken in 1245, we find it reduced to five hides. Lysons,

CHINGFORD CHURCH.

it from Edmonton on the west; whilst the land round about, swelling up into eminences, affords fine views across the country into Kent on the one side, and of various places in Hertfordshire on the other. A part of the parish is still open forest and woodland; and most of the habitations of the villagers are somewhat isolated from each other. Several good mansions and residences of the better class, however, dot the landscape.

There are in Chingford two manors: one called Chingford St. Paul, as having belonged to St Paul's Cathedral until the dissolution, and the other called Chingford Earls (originally Chingford Comitis), from having in far distant times belonged to the Bourchiers, Earls of Essex.

in his "Environs of London," mentions some curious customs appertaining to this manor in former times. Among them it is stated that "the tenants were obliged to till the lord's land with a good plough, six horses, and two oxen, and to find a horse for harrowing;" and that "Gilbert de Ecclesia was obliged, by the tenure of his lands, to find a man to gather nuts for the lord of the manor." One of the early records of the manor, about the year 1220, is an agreement between the Abbot of Waltham and the Dean and Chapter of St. Paul's, by which the latter are exempted from several payments and services before due to the hundred of Waltham: among these were "wardpeny" (money paid for watch and ward) and

" borchal-peny." This manor, which enjoyed an exemption from the forest laws, and sundry privileges granted to the Dean and Chapter of St. Paul's, was " surrendered " to Henry VIII. in 1544, and has since been in private hands. Edward VI. granted it to Sir Thomas Darcy, but it was shortly afterwards again surrendered to the Crown, and was given by Queen Mary to one of the ladies of her bedchamber, Susan Tongue, the widow of Thomas Tongue, Clarencieux King-at-Arms. The property

Thomas Boothby, from whose family it descended by marriage to the Heathcotes, by whom it is still owned. The old hall stands near the banks of the Lea, and is now a farm. Friday Hill, a house about a mile to the east of the church, and the seat of the Heathcotes, has long been used as the manor-house of Chingford. A view of Friday Hill House is given in the *European Magazine* for June, 1798.

Lysons identifies the old manor-house of

QUEEN ELIZABETH'S LODGE.

afterwards passed to the Leighs, and later on to the Snells of Brill, in Buckinghamshire. The manor of Chingford St. Paul is now owned by Miss Hodgson.

The manor of Chingford Earls, at the time of the Conquest, was held by " Orgar the Thane, under Robert Gernon." It was at one time in the possession of the Earls of Athol, and subsequently of Lord Roos. In the fifteenth century it was granted to the Bourchiers, Earls of Essex, but was soon after restored to the Roos family, with whom it continued till 1542, when it was given by Thomas, Earl of Rutland, to Henry VIII., in exchange for other lands. In or about 1666 the manor-house, called Chingford Hall, was purchased by a Mr.

Chingford Earls with the building known as Queen Elizabeth's Lodge, of which we are coming to speak.

Another manor here, called Buckrills, is mentioned by Kelly, in his " Directory of Essex," as owned by Mr. James D. Waters; but little or nothing is known about its history.

In this parish is, or was, an estate called Brindwoods, which was formerly held under the rector of the parish by a singular tenure, thus described by Morant, in his " History of Essex:"—" Upon every alienation the owner of the estate, with his wife, man-servant, and maid-servant, each single upon a horse, come to the parsonage, where the owner does his homage and pays his relief in the following manner. He blows three blasts with his horn, and carries a hawk on his fist; his servant has a greyhound in a slip, both for the use of the rector that day. He receives a chicken for his hawk, a peck of oats for his horse, and a loaf of bread for his greyhound. They all dine; after which the master blows three blasts with his horn, and so they depart." According, however, to Lyson's "Environs," by the end of the last century all memory of the custom had clean died out, so far as the rector and the parishioners were concerned. It is strange to find a parish so little conservative of ancient tenures.

Chingford is a very scattered parish, and apparently the chief population has drifted away from its former centre, as the old church stands far away from the abodes of man, except one old farmhouse and the vicarage. Its site is high, for Essex at least. In 1871 the number of the inhabitants was about 1,250, but during the next decade it had increased to nearly 1,400. This increase may be partly accounted for by the fact that since 1874 Chingford has been in direct railway communication with London, the forest branch of the Great Eastern Railway having been in that year opened, with its terminus near the new church at Chingford Green. Here are located the largest number of houses forming the village; others are at Forest Side, about half a mile eastward, and others again form the hamlet of Chingford Hatch, about a mile to the south-east.

The old church, dedicated to All Saints, still stands, though disused for these many years, except for funerals; it is rich in colour, and very picturesque, being almost covered with ivy, the growth of several centuries. It consists of a nave, south aisle, and chancel, with a tower at the west end and a south porch of red brick. The walls are of late Early English or of the Decorated period, but the windows are Perpendicular, inserted at a later date. The south porch has Tudor details. The glass has been taken out from all the windows except those in the chancel, so the wind whistles through the desolate nave, into which the ivy also has crept.

In the chancel are three fine mural monuments of the Jacobean period, and others of a later date on the floor, in memory of Sir J. Sylvester, Recorder of London, and members of the Boothby and Heathcote families. The brasses have been carried off from all. The font was removed into the new church (St. Peter and St. Paul), which stands on Chingford Green, and proclaims as loudly as its style can do that it was built early in the reign of Victoria, before the principles of Gothic architecture were well known. It is, in fact, a nondescript Gothic structure of white bricks, interlaced with squares of dark flints: a poor imitation of Dunstable and Luton churches. It has a stone spire, and looks pretty, but meaningless.

About half a mile to the north-west of this church is an obelisk, built by the directors of the Ordnance Survey, and kept up at the desire of the Astronomer-Royal, as marking the exact meridian of Greenwich. It is occasionally used for the purpose of testing and verifying calculations. In the *Illustrated London News* it is said—but without the least proof—that this obelisk marks the place of the death of Queen Boadicea, and was erected to her memory! Thus, indeed, history is too often written.

The roadway running north-eastward from Chingford Green, by the railway-station, opens directly upon the forest at one of its most frequented points, by the front of Queen Elizabeth's Lodge and the new Royal Forest Hotel, near which is the broad green track to the left that winds away through the forest to High Beech, mentioned above, and also a most charming glade, that of Fairmead, which stretches away towards the north-west.

The old Lodge is a tall, irregular square structure of the Tudor era, consisting of three storeys, with gable ends and high pitched roof. It is built of brick and timber, somewhat rudely plastered, and its exterior is very picturesque, resembling the houses in the West of England. At its door were two fine elms, but both were blown down in 1881–2. The basement is used as a kitchen and parlour, with capacious fire-places and antique fire-dogs. The staircase, which projects into the hall, is wide and large, and composed of strong timbers, which will last till "the crack of doom;" its width is about six feet, and it is divided by six landings, with four stairs between each, and each stair or step consists of a solid oak sill.

The principal room on the first floor has its walls hung with tapestry, in good preservation, and a chimney-piece opening with a flattened arch. The height of the basement and first floor has been sacrificed to the storey above, as they occupy about half of the whole elevation.

The top floor is not cut up into chambers, as usual, but consists of one large room—or hall, if such a term can be applied to an upper room—with an arched timber roof, and not unlike a chapel in its general appearance. Its walls are said to have been hung with tapestry when the manor courts were held in it. It is now used for trade feasts and other gatherings. It is entered from the staircase by a low wide doorway. It is about twenty-five feet in width by about forty feet in length ; it is open to the roof, the tiles being merely hidden by plaster-work, and the sides consist of massive timbers filled in with plaster. It was originally lit by four windows. The roof, it should be added, is supported by timbers springing into two pointed arches, which render it probable that the original roof was of a different form, as well as material, to the present. The timbers of the staircase sides and roof are massive, and spring into arched forms, so as to impress the beholder with their strength and durability ; and it is observable that all the doorways in the building consist of flattened arches. The local tradition reports that Queen Elizabeth was accustomed to ride up the stairs on horseback, and alight at the door of the large room upon a raised place, which was of old called the *horse-block*. Marvellous as the story may seem, the width and solidity and the many landings of the staircase are in its favour ; and in order to test its feasibility, it is stated that early in the present century a wager of ten pounds was won by a sporting celebrity riding an untrained pony up the assigned route of the chivalrous queen. It is well known that Queen Elizabeth was ex-

tremely fond of the pleasures of the chase, and that she hunted at the age of fifty-seven is an established fact, so that her freak of riding up-stairs would be but a trifle to her Majesty.

It is satisfactory to know that by the Act of Parliament of 1878, under which the forest was made over to "the people," the Corporation of London are bound to keep Queen Elizabeth's Lodge in repair, as "an object of antiquarian interest."

The Royal Forest Hotel, which adjoins Queen Elizabeth's Lodge, is the constant resort of London excursionists and holiday-makers. Throughout the summer, and especially at Eastertide, Whitsuntide, and on Bank Holidays, the glassy glades in front of it are crowded with picnic parties.

Near the Lodge, on the road to High Beech, is a large piece of water, still retaining all its rural picturesqueness, frequented by wild fowl, and a great resort for insects, and full of aquatic plants. Hence it is constantly visited by microscopical and naturalist and field clubs. It is now called Connaught Water, after the new royal ranger of the forest. The fine oaks which surround it speak as plainly as in words that "this is the forest primeval."

CHAPTER XLVII.

EPPING FOREST (*continued*)—BUCKHURST HILL, LOUGHTON, AND THEYDON BOIS.

" In this lone open glade I lie,
Screened by deep boughs on either hand,
Where ends the glade—to stay the eye,
Those black-crowned, red-boled pine-trees stand."—MATTHEW ARNOLD.

Recent Improvements in Epping Forest—Connaught Water and other Lakes—Buckhurst Hill—Its Etymology—Census Returns—The Railway Station—St. John's Church—Congregational Church—Langford Place—The Essex Naturalists' and Field Club—The Epping Hunt—The " Bald-faced Stag "—The " Roebuck "—Situation of Loughton—Census Returns—Descent of the Manor—The Hall—The Old Parish Church—A Memorial Church—St. John's Church—General Appearance of the Village—Staple Hill—The " Lopping " Process—Loughton Camp—Debden Hall—Theydon Bois.

IT has been remarked by one of our best writers on landscape that " the forest, like other beautiful scenes, pleases the eye, but its great effect is to arouse the imagination." Mr. William Paul, Fellow of the Linnean Society, in a lecture on "The Future of Epping Forest," delivered in 1880 before the Society of Arts, spoke as follows :— " The scenery of Epping Forest, as a whole, is hardly of a character that can be correctly spoken of as sublime or beautiful, although beautiful spots may occasionally be met with, and it possesses the elements of both picturesqueness and grandeur. But there are no mountains or torrents, no frowning precipices, no furious eddies, no foaming cascades. It would, perhaps, be correctly described

as a tract of woodland and pasture, the surface broken into hill and dale, interspersed with a few fine trees and groves ; the old trees possessing a rare and glorious beauty, but not being numerous or prominent enough to impart dignity to a forest of 6,000 acres. It is picturesque from its natural ruggedness ; it is grand from its extent. These two forms or expressions of beauty—picturesqueness and grandeur, which are inherent—should never be lost sight of, or suffer diminution at the hands of the improver."

Since the forest has been taken in hand by the Corporation of London, alterations have been effected in different parts, which, if they may not be called "improvements" so far as the mere natural appearance of the forest is concerned, may at any rate be put down as works of great utility and convenience, and also as enhancing the enjoyment of visitors in the future.   One of these is the Ranger's Road, a new thoroughfare from Chingford to Loughton, made in 1880, and formally opened by the Duke of Connaught as Ranger of Epping Forest; and another is the large sheet of water mentioned at the end of the preceding chapter, which, from being the dismal swamp that it formerly was, when known as the Forest Pool, has been converted into an ornamental lake, some seven acres in extent, and re-named Connaught Water.   This lake, which contains two islands, and is used for boating, &c., is fed by the little Ching rivulet.   Another lake has also been formed at Staple Hill, near Loughton. As the forest is now well drained, and as many new paths and roadways have been formed through it—one of the latter extending its whole length, from Woodford to Epping—the danger of losing one's way is reduced to a minimum.

A broad roadway, called the Green Ride, skirts the Connaught Lake on the west side, and then passes on through the forest, crossing another roadway called Earl's Path, and so on in a north-easterly direction, by Monk Wood, to Ambresbury Banks and Epping; whilst on the south side of the lake the Ranger's Road leads towards the north-east in the direction of Loughton.

We now pass on eastward from Queen Elizabeth's Lodge across an open part of the forest, keeping in view the tall square tower of the water-works on the top of Buckhurst Hill.

Buckhurst Hill, it has been suggested, may have been so named from Sackville, Lord Buckhurst, the accomplished poet, and favoured flower of Queen Elizabeth's court; but more probably it comes from the Anglo-Saxon *Boc-hyrst*, a beech-forest.   Thorne, in his "Environs of London," says that perhaps the name may be derived from "Book-forest: *i.e.*, a portion of the forest set apart, or severed, by royal charter from the neighbouring open forest."   The vulgar name of the place is, or was, formerly Buckett's Hill: hence John Clare, in one of his sonnets on Epping Forest, writes—

" There's Buckett's Hill, a place of furze and clouds,
    Which evening in a golden blaze enshrouds."

Poor Clare, when he wrote these not very original lines, it must be remembered, was an inmate of Fairmead Asylum, not very far off.

This locality was formed into an ecclesiastical district out of the parish of Chigwell in 1838, since which time the number of its inhabitants has very largely increased.   In 1871 it amounted to 2,500, being nearly three times as many as it was ten years previously, whilst according to the census returns for 1881 it has now reached about 4,000. At the foot of the hill, further eastward, is a railway-station on the Epping and Ongar branch of the Great Eastern Railway, around which are clustered several small cottages and "villa residences." From the top of the hill some beautiful views are obtained over the surrounding country, including the high ground on the opposite side of the valley of the Roding; whilst a pleasant and picturesque piece of the forest ground lies along the old Cambridge road to the left, between Woodford Wells and Loughton.

The church, dedicated to St. John the Baptist, was built in 1837, and occupies a commanding site at the top of the hill.   It is in the Early English style.   It has been enlarged at different periods, and now consists of a chancel, nave, aisles, and a tower with spire.   A Congregational church is a handsome stone building of Gothic architecture, of the Early Decorated style.   The pinnacled tower at its western end is about 100 feet in height, and, like the spire of St. John's Church, is a conspicuous object for miles around.

At the lower end of Palmerston Road, opposite the Congregational church, and on the ground now occupied by a private house called Langford Place, stood the hunting seat or palace of Henry VIII., known as Poteles, or Langford Place.   It remained with the Crown till the reign of Elizabeth, when it passed into private hands. Mr. James Jones, in his "Directory of Woodford," &c., says:—"There is no traceable account when the old building was pulled down.   In the year 1773 a farm-house occupied the spot, known as King's Place Farm; this was, a few years ago, converted into a beautiful villa residence, and retains the royal name of 'Langford Place.'   The Congregational chapel is called King's Place Congregational Church, and the carriage-way commencing near the 'Three Colts' Tavern, Prince's Road, and which crosses the Queen's Road to the entrance of Roebuck Lane, is named King's Place. Some fields to the north-east of the palace site, by the river Roding, are known as the King's Meadow."

The Essex Naturalists' and Field Club has its head-quarters at Buckhurst Hill.   This society has of late years done much towards throwing additional light on the antiquarian objects in the neighbourhood.

Here are two wayside inns of celebrity, both of which, in their turn, have been the scene of the

"Epping Hunt," namely, the "Bald-faced Stag" and the "Roebuck." This assembly took place annually on Easter Monday at the former inn, down to about 1853, when the landlord grew tired, or ashamed, of the company that it brought down from London, and handed over the arrangements to his neighbour, mine host of the "Roebuck." Subsequently, as stated in the preceding chapter, the "hunt" was transferred to High Beech, where a publican kept it going till 1882 ; but as in that year and the previous year it had become a scene of riot and a public nuisance, it was suppressed by the aid of the police, and it is now a thing of the past.

The custom is said to have begun in 1226, when King Henry III. granted the liberty of hunting over this country to the citizens of London. Mr. Rounding, who was the landlord of the "Horse and Well," was the last huntsman, and for some years it was not an uncommon sight to see him with as many as 500 mounted followers. The "meet" formerly took place on the ridge near Buckhurst Hill, overlooking Fairmead. It is asserted that the Lord Mayor and Aldermen of London, as the recognised heads and leaders of the citizens, used to attend the hunt in state ; but this is probably untrue.

From Hone's "Every-day Book," Vol. II. (March, 1827), page 459, we extract the following interesting particulars concerning the Epping Hunt :— "In 1226 King Henry III. confirmed to the citizens of London *free warren*, or liberty to hunt a circuit about their city, in the warren of Staines, &c. ; and in ancient times the lord mayor, aldermen, and corporation, attended by a due number of their constituents, availed themselves of this right of chase 'in solemn guise.' From newspaper reports, it appears that the office of 'common hunt,' attached to the mayoralty, is in danger of disuetude. The Epping Hunt seems to have lost the lord mayor and his brethren in their corporate capacity, and the annual sport to have become a farcical show.

"A description of the Epping Hunt of Easter Monday, 1826, by one 'Simon Youngbuck,' in the *Morning Herald*, is the latest report, if it be not the truest ; but of that the editor of the 'Every-day Book' cannot judge, for he was not there to see : he contents himself with picking out the points ; should any one be dissatisfied with the 'hunting of that day' as it will be here presented, he has only to sit down in good earnest to a plain matter-of-fact detail of all the circumstances from his own knowledge, accompanied by such citations as will show the origin and former state of the usage, and such a detail, so accompanied, will be inserted—

'For want of a better, *this* must do.'

On the authority aforesaid, and that without the introduction of any term not in the *Herald*, be it known, then, that before and at the commencement of the hunt aforesaid, it was a cold, dry, and dusty morning, and that the huntsmen of the east were all abroad by nine o'clock, trotting, fair and softly, down the road, on great nine-hand skyscrapers, nimble daisy-cutting nags, flowing-tailed chargers, and ponies no bigger than the learned one at Astley's ; some were in job-coaches, at two guineas a-day ; some in three-bodied nondescripts, some in gigs, some in cabs, some in drags, some in short stages, and some in long stages ; while some, on no stages at all, footed the road, smothered by dust driven by a black, bleak north-easter full in the teeth. Every gentleman was arrayed after his own peculiar taste, in blue, brown, or black—in dress coats, long coats, short coats, frock coats, great coats, and no coats ; in drab slacks and slippers ; in grey tights and black-spurred Wellingtons ; in nankeen bomb-balloons ; in city-white cotton-cord unmentionables, with jockey toppers, and in Russiandrill down-belows, as a *memento* of the late Czar. The ladies all wore a *goose-skin* under-dress, in compliment to the north-easter.

"At that far-famed spot, the brow above Fairmead Bottom, by twelve o'clock, there were not less than three thousand merry lieges then and there assembled. It was a beautiful set-out. Fair dames, 'in purple and in pall,' reposed in vehicles of all sorts, sizes, and conditions, whilst seven or eight hundred mounted members of the hunt wound in and out 'in restless ecstasy,' chatting and laughing with the fair, sometimes rising in their stirrups to look out for the long-coming cart of the stag, 'whilst with off-heel assiduously aside' they 'provoked the caper which they seemed to hide.' The green-sward was covered with ever-moving crowds on foot, and the pollard oaks which skirt the Bottom on either side were filled with men and boys.

"But where is the stag all this while? One o'clock, and no stag! Two o'clock, and no stag !—a circumstance easily accounted for by those who are in the secret, and the secret is this : there are buttocks of boiled beef and fat hams, and beer and brandy in abundance, at the 'Roebuck' public-house, low down in the forest ; and ditto at the 'Bald-faced Stag,' on the top of the hill ; and ditto at the 'Coach and Horses' at Woodford Wells ; and ditto at the 'Castle,' at

Woodford; and ditto at the 'Eagle,' at Snares-brook; and if the stag had been brought out before the beef, beer, bacon, and brandy were eaten and drank, where would have been the use of providing so many good things? So they carted the stag from public-house to public-house, and showed him at threepence a-head to those ladies and gentlemen who never saw such a thing before; and the showing and carting induced a consumption of eatables and drinkables—an achievement which was helped by a band of music in every house, playing

THE "ROEBUCK."

hungry tunes to help the appetite; and then, when the eatables and drinkables were gone and paid for, they turned out the stag.

"Precisely at half-past two o'clock the stag-cart was seen coming over the hill from the 'Bald-faced Stag,' and hundreds of horsemen and gigmen rushed gallantly forward to meet and escort it to the top of Fairmead Bottom, amidst such whooping and hallooing as made all the forest echo again, and would have done Carl Maria Von Weber's heart good to hear. And then, when the cart stopped and was turned tail about, the horse-men drew up in long lines, forming an avenue wide enough for the stag to run down. For a moment all was deep, silent, breathless anxiety; and the doors of the cart were thrown open, and out popped a strapping four-year-old red buck, fat as a porker, with a chaplet of flowers round his neck, a girth of divers-coloured ribbons, and a long blue and pink streamer depending from the summit of his branching horns. He was received, on his alighting, with a shout that seemed to shake heaven's concave, and took it very graciously,

looking round him with great dignity as he stalked slowly and delicately forward down the avenue prepared for him; and occasionally shrinking from side to side, as some super-valorous cockney made a cut at him with his whip. Presently he caught a glimpse of the hounds and the huntsmen, waiting for him at the bottom, and in an instant off he bounded, sideways, through the rank, knocking down and trampling all who crowded the path he chose to take; and dashing at once into the cover, he was out of sight before a man could say 'Jack Robinson!' Then might be seen gentlemen running about without their horses, and horses galloping about without their gentlemen; and hats out of number brushed off their owners' heads by the rude branches of the trees; and everybody asking which way the stag was gone, and nobody knowing

THE "BALD-FACED STAG."

anything about him; and ladies beseeching gentle-men not to be too venturesome, and gentlemen gasping for breath at the thoughts of what they were determined to venture; and myriads of people on foot running hither and thither in search of little eminences to look from; and yet nothing at all to be seen, though more than enough to be heard; for every man and every woman, too, made as loud a noise as possible. Meanwhile the stag, followed by the keepers and about six couple of hounds, took away through the covers towards Woodford. Find-ing himself too near the haunts of his enemy, man, he there turned back, sweeping down the Bottom for a mile or two, and away up the enclosures towards Chingford, where he was caught nobody knows how, for everybody returned to town, except those who stopped to regale afresh, and recount the glorious perils of the day. Thus ended the *Easter Hunt* of 1826."

The above humorous and clever sketch may be regarded as a fair sample of the Epping "Hunt" as it was known to the parents of the present generation—at all events down to a date long subsequent to the accession of Queen Victoria.

sports; and some surprise existed in the House of Commons when, in 1863, the Epping Forest Prevention Bill being before the Committee, Mr. Alderman Copeland, M.P., in response to an inquiry as to whether the City of London did not claim the privilege of hunting, answered, 'Not that I am aware of.'" The real or supposed connection of the civic authorities with the Epping Hunt has been seized upon by other satirists than D'Urfey. It was made the subject of a poem by Tom Hood, to which George Cruickshank added illustrations. In this poem the author gives the following

THEYDON BOIS.

A correspondent of *Notes and Queries** in 1872, however, states that, being about to publish a guide to Epping Forest, he has made inquiries, but without success, in order to find out whether the Lord Mayor and Aldermen ever attended Epping Hunt in state. He adds:—"I have since come across some lines, printed in Strutt's 'Sports and Pastimes,' which relate—

" ' Once a year into Essex a hunting they go,' &c.

Three stanzas are given, taken from an old ballad, called the 'London Customs,' printed in D'Urfey's collection. From time to time these lines revived the assertion, but it is doubtful with what truth. It is, nevertheless, the fact that the Lord Mayor and Aldermen in times gone by took part in these

ludicrous account of the adventures of a Mr. John Huggins at the Epping Hunt :—

" With Monday's sun John Huggins rose,
    And slapped his leather thigh,
And sang the burden of the song,
    'This day a stag must die.'

" Alas ! there was no warning voice
    To whisper in his ear,
' Thou art a fool for leaving *Chepe*,
    To go and hunt the *deer*.'

" Then slowly on through Leytonstone,
    Past many a Quaker's box—
No friends to hunters after deer,
    Though followers of a *Fox*.

" And many a score behind—before—
    The self-same rout inclined ;
And, minded all to march one way,
    Made one great march of mind.

*   *   *   *

" Now Huggins from his saddle rose,
   And in his stirrups stood ;
And lo ! a little cart that came
   Hard by a little wood,

" In shape like half a hearse—though not
   For corpses in the least ;
For this contained the *deer alive,*
   And not the *dear deceased !*

" Now Huggins, standing far aloof,
   Had never seen the deer,
Till all at once he saw the beast
   Come charging in his rear.

" Away he went, and many a score
   Of riders did the same,
On horse and ass—like High and Low
   And Jack pursuing Game.

" A score were sprawling on the grass,
   And beavers fell in showers ;
There was another *Floorer* there,
   Beside the Queen of Flowers.

*   *   *   *

" Away, away he scudded, like
   A ship before the gale ;
Now flew to ' *h*ills we know not of,"
   Now, nun-like, took the vale.

" ' Hold hard ! hold hard ! you'll lame the dogs,'
   Quoth Huggins. ' So I do ;
I've got the saddle well in hand,
   And hold as hard as you !'

" But soon the horse was well avenged
   For cruel smart of spurs,
For riding through a moor, he pitched
   His master in the furze !

" Now seeing Huggins' nag adrift,
   A farmer, shrewd and sage,
Resolved, by changing horses here,
   To hunt another stage.

" So up on Huggins' horse he got,
   And swiftly rode away ;
While Huggins mounted on a mare,
   Done brown upon a bay.

" And off they set in double chase,
   For such was fortune's whim,
The farmer rode to hunt the stag,
   And Huggins hunted him !

" And lo ! the dim and distant hunt
   Diminished in a trice ;
The steeds, like Cinderella's team,
   Seemed dwindling into mice.

*   *   *   *

" Now many a sign at Woodford town,
   Its Inn—vitation tells :
But Huggins, full of ills, of course
   Betook him to the Wells.

" When thus forlorn a merry horn
   Struck up without the door—
The mounted mob were all returned ;
   The Epping hunt was o'er !

" And many a horse was taken out
   Of saddle and of shaft ;
And men, by dint of drink, became
   The only ' *beasts of draught.*'

" For now begun a harder run
   On wine, and gin, and beer ;
And overtaken men discussed
   The overtaken deer—

" And how the hunters stood aloof,
   Regardful of their lives,
And shunned a beast whose very horns
   They knew could *handle* knives.

" And one how he had found a horse
   Adrift—a goodly gray !
And kindly rode the nag, for fear
   The nag should go astray.

" Now Huggins, when he heard the tale,
   Jumped up with sudden glee ;
' A goodly gray ! why, then, I say,
   That gray belongs to me !'

" And let the chase again take place
   For many a long, long year—
John Huggins will not ride again
   To hunt the Epping deer !

MORAL.

" Thus pleasure oft eludes our grasp
   Just when we think to grip her ;
And hunting after happiness,
   We only hunt a slipper."

The anecdotes of " hair-breadth escapes " of some of the gallant sportsmen, and of other incidents connected with the Epping Hunt, as may be supposed, are "plentiful as blackberries" among the older inhabitants of these parts. Among anecdotes of another kind, the following is perhaps worth recording :—Lord Brougham, when staying in the neighbourhood, went on one occasion to witness the hunt, about which he was " very facetious," and asked many questions. He said to a man, " I suppose you are waiting for the Lord Mayor and Aldermen ? If you will show me them when they arrive, I will give you a crown." The man said, " I do not think I should know them for certain ; but if you will give me half-a-crown, I will show you Lord Brougham alive." This so disconcerted his lordship, that he went home immediately.

The " Bald-faced Stag," which stands by the roadside, at a short distance south of St. John's Church, is one of the oldest houses in the neighbourhood ; it is a large, square, white-washed building, with a high-pitched tiled roof, and is a favourite resort for Londoners during the summer. It contains some curious carving, and a fine portrait of Queen Anne. It was formerly a manor-house. The old coach road, at the beginning of the present century, ran in a straight line northward of the "Roebuck," traversing in its course the ground now covered by St. John's Terrace. At that time the whole locality was covered by forest, but later on the course of the road has been carried in a more direct line.

If it be true that "the finest scenery in the world is improved by a good inn in the fore-ground," the saying is certainly true of the spot which we have now reached. The "Roebuck" is on the main road from London, and between Buckhurst Hill and Loughton ; it stands on high ground, within a few minutes' walk of Buckhurst Hill Station of the Great Eastern line, and close to some of the loveliest parts of the forest. Over-looking as it does one of the finest panoramas in the suburbs of London, no more charming des-tination could be found for excursions, picnic parties, bean-feasts, trade dinners, school outings, and bicycling club runs. The banquet hall, ad-joining the inn, will accommodate from 300 to 500 guests, and is available for balls, meetings, concerts, dramatic performances, &c. The "Hunt" room and the "Elizabeth" room will each seat seventy guests at dinner. The pleasaunce, in the rear of the inn, includes twenty-three acres of meadow land, lawns, and fruit garden.

Loughton, which lies about a mile distant from the "Roebuck," is long and straggling, extending for nearly two miles along the Epping road. It is about twelve miles from London, and six miles south-east from Waltham Abbey. The parish is all within the bounds of Epping Forest, and, according to the census returns of 1881, contains a population of 2,851, being an increase of about 400 during the preceding decade. On the east side of the main road is the Loughton Station of the Great Eastern Railway. The views in and around the village are very picturesque, and the ground of a remarkably undulating character, the views from Golding's Hill and other elevated parts extending to the Thames and the Kentish hills in one direction, to Hampstead and Highgate in another, and eastward across the valley of the Roden to the vicinity of Navestock, some twelve miles distant.

This parish formed a portion of the endowments which were bestowed by Harold on Waltham Abbey, and it continued a part of the abbey lands until the dissolution of that monastery. It was granted by Edward VI. to Sir Thomas Darcy ; but his possession was of short duration, for in the reign of Queen Mary it again reverted to the Crown, by whom it was attached to the Duchy of Lancaster. In the reign of Elizabeth it became the property of the Stonards, from whom it was carried by the marriage of an heiress to Sir Robert Wrothe, of Durants, in Enfield.* The manor continued in the possession of this family for more than a century, when it passed by bequest to the Nassaus, Earls of Rochford. About the middle of the last century it was sold to Mr. William Whitaker, a merchant of London, from whom it descended to the present owner, the Rev. John Whitaker Maitland, the families of Whitaker and Maitland having become united by marriage.

The Hall, which stood about a mile distant eastward of the high road, was burnt down in 1836. It was a large building in the Elizabethan style, and it is said to have received many dis-tinguished visitors. In 1561 Queen Elizabeth honoured the Stonards with a visit here. James I. is reported to have been here on more than one occasion ; and the Princess of Denmark (after-wards Queen Anne) is stated, in the "Beauties of England," to have retired hither from the court of her father, James II., "when she saw him pursuing the arbitrary measures which terminated in his expulsion from the throne." Mr. Thorne, in his "Environs of London," however, considers that it was most likely only for a night or so that the princess was here, "when on her way to Notting-ham, under the escort of Compton, the military Bishop of London."

The present Hall, now a farm-house, was con-structed partly out of the materials of the ancient building. The great gates of the old Hall still remain, and are elaborate specimens of hand-wrought iron-work.

The old parish church of Loughton, dedicated to St. Nicholas, stood near the Hall; but being in a sadly dilapidated condition, and at an inconvenient distance from the village, was pulled down in 1847, with the exception of the chancel, which has been retained for use as a mortuary chapel. In 1877 a new "memorial church" was built on part of the site of the demolished structure. It was erected by Mrs. Whitaker Maitland, in memory of her husband, her sons, and all those members of the family who lie buried in the churchyard. The brasses from the old church have been placed here : among them are three with effigies of John Stonard and his wives, Joan and Catharine, and dated 1541 ; another to William Nodes, gentle-man, and his six sons, dated 1594, has the effigy of a man in the costume of the period, with a ruff round his neck ; and some to the Wrothe family, dating back to 1673.

---

* See *ante*, p. 373.

St. John's Church stands on an eminence at the north-east corner of the village, and is much more conveniently situated for the parishioners than the old parish church. It was erected in 1846, and is a brick-built cruciform structure, in the Norman style, with a low square central tower, containing eight fine-toned bells. Some of the windows are filled with stained glass. The church was enlarged and partly re-seated in 1877.

In the village are six almshouses, founded in 1827 by Mrs. Whitaker, besides which the wants of the necessitous poor are ameliorated by local charities. A pretty drinking-fountain stands at the corner of the roadway leading to the railway-station, and altogether the village wears a "sober, sylvan look."

Nearly opposite the railway-station a road winds to the north-west through the forest by High Beech, and so on to Waltham Abbey. To the right of this road, immediately on entering the forest, is Staple Hill, a spot which has become of historic interest as that where the "lopping" process used to be carried out by the natives of these parts, and of which we have spoken in a previous chapter.* Mr. Coller, in his "People's History of Essex" (1861), writes of Loughton:—"There seems to be a want of energy, and an unwillingness to move from their native place, which greatly characterise the inhabitants, not only of this village, but of this part of the county generally, and which certainly impedes their advancement in the social scale. The proximity of the forest, and the pretext of procuring firewood by means of the loppings of the trees, which the inhabitants claim a right to cut during the winter months, encourage habits of idleness and dislike of settled labour, and in some cases give occasion for poaching, all of which are injurious to the poor."

The forest, indeed, has been so constantly "lopped" that most of its trees are pollards with old and hoary stems, which, having been debarred from their natural growth, have twisted their stems and roots into all sorts of fantastic forms. It is probable that many of these trees, small as they may look, are as old as our Plantagenet kings, if not older still. Among them the beech, the holly, and the hornbeam, are remarkable for their abundance.

The walks in or near the forest at this point are of such a character as to prove a great attraction for visitors; and consequently Loughton is largely patronised by excursionists and others during the summer months. At the top of Staple Hill a "shelter" has been erected for the convenience of visitors, and at the foot of the hill a moderate-sized lake has been formed.

Proceeding for about half a mile along the new grass-covered forest roadway which skirts the base of Staple Hill, and striking off into the wood on the left on reaching the top of the next hill, the rambler, by a little diligent searching, may explore the remains of an ancient earth-work, which was discovered in 1872 by Mr. B. H. Cowper. This camp covers about the same amount of ground as Ambresbury Banks—some twelve acres; but it is more irregular in shape, though, being surrounded by trees on every side, it has stood the ravages of time and the effects of rain and storms far better, though in parts the earth-works and trenches have been partially levelled. It has, however, lain for centuries unnoticed in the shade, and apparently its existence was unknown to Morant, the indefatigable historian of Essex. It follows the configuration of the hill which it crowns, and must have been chosen and fashioned with great military skill, as it commands a spur and ravine by which alone it could have been approached. Mr. Cowper is sanguine enough to believe that he has discovered at the north-west corner the place where Boadicea must have led on her attack, and where, being defeated, her soldiers must have been driven down, the sides of the camp itself being partly demolished and carried down into the valley.

In order to carry out the systematic examination of these two entrenchments—the Loughton Camp and Ambresbury Banks—which had not been cut into before the examination made by the Essex Field Club in 1881, it was resolved to commence upon the Loughton Camp as early as possible in 1882; and permission having been granted by the Epping Forest Committee of the Corporation of London, the work was carried out in the months of May and June of that year. The mode of working was similar to that employed at Ambresbury Banks, and consisted in cutting sections through the rampart and ditch, in order to expose the old surface line. With a view to facilitate the carrying on of the necessarily tedious work of watching the removal of the earth, a sub-committee of the Essex Field Club was appointed to co-operate with those engaged in the work. The first section was twelve feet in width, and its cutting involved the removal of one hundred and fifty cubic yards of earth. But few objects were found in this cutting. On the old surface, nearly under the centre of the rampart, two or three fragments of pottery, several flint "flakes," and pieces of charcoal, were turned up. The pottery is extremely rude, and consists of

* See *ante*, p. 428.

badly-burnt rough clay, containing quartz grains, and showing no traces of lathe turning. The great amount of denudation which this earth-work has experienced, owing to its exposed situation and the light character of the soil, has caused the complete silting up of the ditch in most parts, and it was found in this first section that the silting was so very similar in appearance to the undisturbed earth, that the form of the ditch could not be satisfactorily made out. This last circumstance, combined with the paucity of the evidence obtained, determined the extension of the investigation, and another cutting seven feet wide was therefore commenced. In this second section no pottery was found, but numbers of flint flakes and a partially-finished flint celt, all on the old surface line, and buried well beneath the rampart. Further evidence of human occupation in the way of charcoal and burnt clay, marking the sites of fireplaces, were also found on the original surface. The evidence thus far obtained did not appear to those who had undertaken the work of excavation sufficiently complete to enable them to form any conclusive opinion as to the age of the earth-works, although the relics thus far found, conjoined with the absence of all Roman remains, point to a very early, and most probably pre-Roman, period. Inside the encampment can still be traced the well, and the ditch along which the water used to trickle into a pond, the dam at the bottom of which is almost perfect. The little stream still flows in the winter months.

At a short distance further northward, and a little to the right of the high road, in the midst of some charming scenery, stands Debden Hall, a picturesque and well-built mansion, in a park of some 150 acres, adorned by grand old forest trees, with wooded dells, stream and waterfall, &c.

About half a mile eastward from Debden Hall is Theydon Bois, which lies on the very confines of our survey, at the north-east angle of Epping Forest. It is a pretty village, and with its triangular green fringed with an avenue of oak-trees, has almost a foreign appearance. It is called Bois after a family who in early ages possessed the manor, and who, in their turn, doubtless bore that name from dwelling in the wood, which in Norman and French was "*le Bois.*"

The church here has been transplanted, the original structure, which stood to the south on the high ground, having been pulled down, and its materials worked into the new structure—a tasteful little building, with a tall and tapering spire. One or two monuments and graves, with their contents, were transferred, among them some members of the Hall-Dare family, the squires and patrons of the living.

The old manor-house, called Theydon Hall, long the residence of the Hall-Dares, is situated on rising ground a short distance to the west of the church and the common; it is now a farmhouse.

In the church is a well-preserved painting of the royal arms, and the initials "J. R.," clearly denoting "Jacobus Rex," our first English James. Below the escutcheon is a portrait of the king—an unmistakable Stuart, but more like Charles I. than his father. It was probably owing to the remote position of the church in "the woods" that this royal heraldry escaped the hands of the Parliamentary Roundheads of Cromwell's time. The old churchyard is still enclosed, and its tombs are carefully kept.

Theydon has no literary history; but it has had one celebrated character as a resident within its bounds. John Elwes,* the miser, lived here, and from this place he used to ride up to London with his bacon and eggs.

CHAPTER XLVIII.

CHIGWELL.

" Far as the eye may distant views command,
Here—there—vast oaks in pride of foliage stand."—Lord Leigh's *Walks in the Country.*

General Appearance of the Village of Chigwell—Its Etymology—Census Returns—Descent of the Manor—Rolls Park—Woolstons—Lexborough—The Warren—Belmont—The Parish Church—Archbishop Harsnett—Local Charities—Club-room—The Grammar School—The "King's Head" Tavern—Charles Dickens's "Maypole" Inn—Chigwell Row—Woodlands—Bowls—Gainsborough's Picture of "The Woodman"—The Mineral Waters.

At Chigwell we come once more face to face with Charles Dickens, who has laid in this neighbourhood many of the most striking scenes in his "Barnaby Rudge." It is a very rural and retired village, with a "decent church"—as yet happily unrestored—"topping the neighbouring hill," and with one of the pleasantest and most

* See "Old and New London," Vol IV., p. 242.

attractive of old roadside inns directly opposite. Indeed, Chigwell is generally regarded as one of the prettiest villages in Essex. Although much of the beautiful woodland scenery with which it was formerly surrounded has been given over to the builder, or converted to agricultural purposes, much still remains. Down to within the last quarter of a century or so portions of Epping Forest extended well into the parish on its western and northern sides, whilst eastward and southward lay Hainault Forest; but

ings are afar off, and Chigwell does not partake in their character.

The name of the parish is variously written in ancient documents as Cinghewella, Cingnehella, Chiwellia, Chickwell, and Cykewell. In Anglo-Saxon times it was written Cingwella (*cing* signifying king), *i.e.*, the king's well; the name is supposed to be taken from a well in Chigwell Row.

According to a survey taken in the reign of James I., the number of acres in the parish at that time was 4,027, which included 1,500 acres of

CHIGWELL GRAMMAR SCHOOL.

WILLIAM PENN.

since the latter has been disafforested and the former has been curtailed by enclosures, many characteristics of the Chigwell of former days have been obliterated.

Chigwell is about ten miles from London, on the road to Ongar and the "Rodings," or "Roothings"—a district of Essex remarkable for the stiffness of its clay, the poorness of its soil, and locally for the dulness of its inhabitants. In a word, if Essex be the Bœotia of England, the Rodings are the Bœotia of Essex. But the Rooth-

Epping and Hainault Forests. The present area of the parish, including Buckhurst Hill, is a little over 4,500 acres. The population a quarter of a century ago was 2,600. In 1871 this number had nearly doubled itself; and according to the census returns for 1881 it has now reached 5,400. A fair is held here annually in September. The parish is thickly studded with good mansions, mostly the residences of City merchants; and there are also several fine old halls and manor-houses, where in bygone times dwelt the lords of the soil.

The principal manor-house of Chigwell, called Chigwell Hall, lies a little to the north-west of the church, by the side of the roadway leading to Buckhurst Hill and Loughton. It was once part of the possessions of Earl Harold, but at the time of the Norman Survey it was held by Ralph de

Limeses, Baron of Ulverlie, in Warwickshire, with whose descendants it remained for several generations. The manor was subsequently owned by the Fitzwalters, and in the sixteenth century it was conveyed to Sir Thomas Audley, Lord Chancellor of England, for Brian Tuke, Treasurer of the King's Chamber, and others, for the king's use. Edward VI. granted the manor, together with West Hatch, which lies about a mile south-west from Chigwell Church, to Sir Thomas Roth, with whose family it continued till

tensive hamlet, with a church or chapel of its own. Since the Conquest, however, it has been united to Chigwell. In old records the name of this estate is variously written Ulfelmstun, Wolfamston, Woolvermeston, Walston, and Woolston. In the time of Edward the Confessor, like the rest of the neighbourhood, it belonged to Earl Harold; but after the Conquest it formed part of the royal demesnes, and was farmed by a "sheriff." The estate was given by Henry II. to the De Sandfords, "to be holden by the 'grand sergeantry' of finding a damsel to wait in the queen's chamber on the day of her coronation."

Lexborough—the name of which alone survives in Lexborough Lane—is said to have been a mansion which in the last century was inferior to few in the county. It has long since been pulled down, and is now forgotten.

CHIGWELL CHURCH.

the middle of the seventeenth century, when it was sold to Sir William Hicks of Ruckholts, whose son, Sir Harry, in 1720, built the plain brick residence nearly opposite to West Hatch, called Bowling Green. Chigwell Hall was sold by Sir Harry Hicks to Mr. William Davy, Treasurer of St. Luke's Hospital; but the Hicks family still retained the manor, with which was included more than a thousand acres of the forest.

Rolls Park—or Barringtons, as it was formerly called—about half a mile north-east of the church, by the side of the high road to Abridge and Ongar, comprises a well-built mansion, an estate of some 100 acres, and was for two centuries or more in the possession of the family of the late Admiral Sir Eliab Harvey.

On the opposite side of the road, but nearer to Abridge, is another fine estate, called Woolstons, or Wolverston, which appears at one time to have been a distinct parish, or at all events a very ex-

The Warren, the "great house," the old red brick house that stood in its own grounds within a mile or so of the "Maypole," the seat of the Haredales, is probably in part a creation of Charles Dickens's fertile brain; but it is popularly identified in the neighbourhood with a house between Woodford and Chigwell Row, which has been of late burnt down and rebuilt. The Warren, according to Charles Dickens, was attacked by the rioters because its owners were Catholics, and burnt to the ground. It will be remembered how Mr. Haredale found the mysterious murderer lurking among the ruins, and, with the help of the sexton, conducted his prisoner to Chigwell, and thence to London.

At the west end of the lane, by the church, stood at one time an old moated mansion, but faint traces are visible. Across the meadows to the left of this lane, adjoining the estate of Belmont, is a large modern mansion of red brick, which stands out pleasantly from amidst the surrounding trees.

The church is remarkable for its noble south Norman door, and for a fine brass of very late date (1631) to Archbishop Harsnett of York, who founded the grammar-school in this parish. The church, which is dedicated to St. Mary, is approached on the south side by two avenues of clipped yews, whose interlacing branches have imparted to them a close resemblance to the fantraceried roof of the late Perpendicular period. One of these avenues leads up to the entrance of the chancel, and the other to the wooden south porch. The edifice consists of a nave and chancel, with north aisle, and a tower and spire at the western end. The chancel is modern, and several of the windows are filled with painted glass. The Norman doorway mentioned above is enriched with a plain zig-zag moulding, and the windows are mostly of the Perpendicular style. A gallery extends across the western end of the nave, and in the centre of the aisle is a private gallery, containing the sittings of the lord of one of the neighbouring manors. This gallery is approached by a wooden staircase built on the outside of the north wall, which does not add to the beauty of the building.

Among the monuments in the church is one to Thomas Coleshill, who died in 1595, having been "servant to Edward VI., Queen Mary, and Queen Elizabeth;" it bears the kneeling effigies of himself and his wife. The brass to Archbishop Harsnett is of the highest interest to antiquarians, seeing that it is the latest known example of an ecclesiastic of the Church of England, figured as habited in stole, alb, dalmatic, and cope. The figure of the archbishop is full-length, with mitre and crozier. The inscription on the brass, which is said to have been written by the archbishop himself, is in Latin, of which the following is a translation:—"Here lieth Samuel Harsnett, formerly vicar of this church. First the unworthy Bishop of Chichester, then the more unworthy Bishop of Norwich, at last the very unworthy Archbishop of York, who died on the 25th day of May, in the year of our Lord 1631. Which very epitaph that most reverend prelate, out of his excessive humility, ordered by his will to be inscribed to his memory." This brass was formerly on the east wall, but is now on the floor of the chancel.

"Samuel Harsnett," writes the author of "England's Worthies," "born at Colchester, was Bishop of Chichester, then of Norwich, and at last Archbishop of York, and Privy Councillor to King Charles. He founded and endowed a fair grammar-school at Chigwell. He bequeathed his library to Colchester, provided they (his books) were kept in a decent room, for the use of the clergy of that town. He dyed A.D. 1631."

"Dr. Harsnett," observes Mr. Coller, in his "History of Essex," "was the son of a baker in St. Botolph Street, Colchester; and probably at an early age the eloquent preacher and the future prelate might be seen dealing out from his father's counter the bread which perisheth, his humble parents little imagining he was destined to wield the bishop's crozier instead of the baker's peel. He was born in 1561, and having acquired some learning, was sent to Cambridge, where he made great progress. In 1586 he was elected master of the free school at Colchester, which, after a year, he resigned, and in 1597 became vicar of this parish of Chigwell, for which locality, being perhaps his first ministerial charge, he ever after felt a peculiar interest. Afterwards he became Archdeacon of Essex; and having had charge of various other parishes in the county, in 1609 he was made Bishop of Chichester. On being translated to the see of Norwich, in 1619, he was fiercely assailed by the Puritans, and was accused by the Commons of various misdemeanours. He triumphed over all, however, and in 1628 became Archbishop of York."

Archdeacon Paley was for a short time, about 1770, vicar of Chigwell.

The living of Chigwell is somewhat peculiar, being both a rectory, which is a sinecure, and a vicarage, to which the rector presents. From the year 1329 down to 1408, as we learn from Mr. Jones's local Directory already quoted, the rectory was in the hands of lay patrons, being held by the families of Goldingham, Bourchin, and Doreward. In 1432 John Doreward gave the advowson of this parish church and rectory to the priory and brethren of St. Botolph, Colchester, and they procured a licence to appropriate it to themselves and their successors, by virtue of which they presented twice to the vicarage; but in the reigns of Henry VI. (1451) and Edward IV. (1466) the rectors regained their right, soon after which Thomas Kemp, Bishop of London, founded a chantry in St. Paul's Cathedral, and endowed it with the advowson of Chigwell, and with lands here and at Great Clacton, united it to the office of confessor in that cathedral.

There are several local charities for the relief of the poor, and also three almshouses, called "Coulson's," founded in 1557, and rebuilt by public subscription in 1858; each occupant receives a small sum of money quarterly.

A club-room for working-men was built here in 1876, and is used for reading and recreation.

Near the eastern end of the churchyard is the grammar-school founded by Archbishop Harsnett in 1629. It had long been neglected, and its pupils had dwindled to a very small number. But it is now a spacious brick building, with good playground and class-rooms, and has been very greatly enlarged and improved under the provisions of a new scheme lately given by the Educational Commissioners and the Court of Chancery. Amongst the numerous ordinances made by the founder for the good management of the schools is the following :— "I constitute and appoint that the Latin schoolmaster be a graduate of one of the universities, not under seven-and-twenty years of age, a man skilful in the Greek and Latin tongues, a good poet, of a sound religion, neither papist nor puritan, of a grave behaviour, of a sober and honest conversation, no tippler nor haunter of public-houses, no puffer of tobacco, and above all that he be apt to teach and strict in his government ; and all election or elections otherwise made I declare to be void, *ipso facto*, as if he were dead." The master was also directed to teach Lilly's Latin and Cleonard's Greek grammars ; for phrase and style he was to infuse into his scholars no other than Tully and Terence ; for poets, his pupils were to read the ancient Greek and Latin ; "no novelties nor conceited modern writers." The qualifications required for the other master were :—"That he write fair secretary and Roman hands ; that he be skilful in cyphering and casting of accounts ; and that he teach his scholars the same faculty."

William Penn, the founder of Pennsylvania, was educated at Chigwell, most probably at Archbishop Harsnett's school.

But the chief interest of Chigwell is centred in the "King's Head" tavern, opposite the church : a long plaster-fronted inn, with projecting storeys, fanciful gables, and small diamond-paned lattice windows—a building evidently dating from the Stuart era. "The King's Head" bears on its swinging signboard a portrait of Charles I., painted some years ago by Miss Herring, though the portrait is stupidly supposed by some to represent his father and predecessor, James I.

As we look on the pleasant front of this old inn we fancy that we can recognise most of the features of the old "Maypole" as described by Charles Dickens : through the red curtains of the "common room," by the light of the warm fire glowing within, we can almost see John Willett, the "sturdy" landlord, the "parish clerk and bell-ringer of Chigwell," with his rusty black breeches and coat, and the rest of the convivial company who congregated here in the winter evenings, among whom, of course, were "Tom Cobb, the general chandler," and "Phil Parkes, the ranger." The large room on the first floor is still popularly known as John Chester's Chamber, in allusion, of course, to "Barnaby Rudge." In this room the Verderers' or Forest Courts were held till their abolition in 1855.

Everything about Chigwell is particularised in the most minute manner by Charles Dickens. Even down to "the clock of Chigwell Church, hard by the 'Maypole,' striking two at night," and poor brutish Hugh lazily loitering outside the "Maypole" door : in fact, the village and the whole neighbourhood figures largely in Dickens's historical romance of "Barnaby Rudge," which was originally published in "Master Humphrey's Clock."

Dickens was very fond of the village, and frequently visited it. "Chigwell," he writes to John Forster, "Chigwell, my dear fellow, is the greatest place in the world. Name your day for going. Such a delicious old inn opposite the churchyard, such a lovely ride (drive ?), such beautiful forest scenery, such an out-of-the-way rural place ; such a sexton ! I say again, name your day." The day was named at once, and the whitest of stones marks it in now sorrowful memory. "His promise was exceeded by our enjoyment ; and his delight in the double recognition of himself and of *Barnaby* by the landlord of the nice old inn, far exceeded any pride he would have taken in what the world thinks the highest sort of honour."*

The quaint old kitchen of the "Maypole" is the scene with which the story opens in "Barnaby Rudge ;" but the "Maypole" does not, and did not, really exist at Chigwell, though there is a "Maypole" at Chigwell Row, a mile and a half distant. Under Dickens's description of the "Maypole," the "King's Head" is really sketched in such a masterly style as to render its recognition unmistakable :—

"In the year 1775 there stood upon the borders of Epping Forest, at a distance of about twelve miles from London—measuring from the 'Standard' in Cornhill, or rather, from the spot on or near to which the 'Standard' used to be in days of yore—a house of public entertainment called the 'Maypole ;' which fact was demonstrated to all such travellers as could neither read nor write (and at that time a vast number, both of travellers and stay-at-homes, were in this condition) by the emblem

---

* Forster's "Life of Dickens."

reared on the roadside over against the house, which, if not of those goodly proportions that maypoles were wont to present in olden times, was a fair young ash, thirty feet in height, and straight as any arrow that ever English yeoman drew.

"The 'Maypole'—by which term from henceforth is meant the house, and not its sign—the 'Maypole' was an old building, with more gable ends than a lazy man would care to count on a sunny day; huge zig-zag chimneys, out of which it seemed as though even smoke could not choose but come in more than naturally fantastic shapes, imparted to it in its tortuous progress; and vast stables, gloomy, ruinous, and empty. The place was said to have been built in the days of King Henry VIII.; and there was a legend not only that Queen Elizabeth had slept there one night while upon a hunting excursion, to wit, in a certain oak-panelled room with a deep bay-window, but that next morning, while standing on a mounting-block before the door with one foot in the stirrup, the virgin monarch had then and there boxed and cuffed an unlucky page for some neglect of duty. The matter-of-fact and doubtful folks, of whom there were a few among the 'Maypole' customers— as, unluckily, there always are in every little community—were inclined to look upon this tradition as rather apocryphal; but whenever the landlord of that ancient hostelry appealed to the mounting-block itself as evidence, and triumphantly pointed out that there it stood in the same place to that very day, the doubters never failed to be put down by a large majority, and all true believers exulted as in a victory.

"Whether these, and many other stories of the like nature, were true or untrue, the 'Maypole' was really an old house, a very old house, perhaps as old as it claimed to be, and perhaps older, which will sometimes happen with houses of an uncertain, as with ladies of a certain, age. Its windows were old diamond-pane lattices, its floors were sunken and uneven, its ceilings blackened by the hand of time and heavy with massive beams. Over the doorway was an ancient porch, quaintly and grotesquely carved; and here on summer evenings the more favoured customers smoked and drank—ay, and sang many a good song too, sometimes—reposing on two grim-looking high-backed settles, which, like the twin dragons of some fairy tale, guarded the entrance to the mansion.

"In the chimneys of the disused rooms swallows had built their nests for many a long year, and from earliest spring to latest autumn whole colonies of sparrows chirped and twittered in the eaves. There were more pigeons about the dreary stable-yard and out-buildings than anybody but the landlord could reckon up. The wheeling and circling flights of runts, fantails, tumblers, and pouters, were perhaps not quite consistent with the grave and sober character of the building, but the monotonous cooing, which never ceased to be raised by some among them all day long, suited it exactly, and seemed to lull it to rest. With its overhanging storeys, drowsy little panes of glass, and front bulging out and projecting over the pathway, the old house looked as if it were nodding in its sleep. Indeed, it needed no very great stretch of fancy to detect in it other resemblances to humanity. The bricks of which it was built had originally been a deep dark red, but had grown yellow and discoloured, like an old man's skin; the sturdy timbers had decayed like teeth; and here and there the ivy, like a warm garment to comfort it in its age, wrapped its green leaves closely round the time-worn walls."

The chimney corner at the "Maypole" was, of course, the head-quarter of village gossip—

" And news much older than the ale went round."

That the worthy host, John Willet, considered the "Maypole" the very perfection of what an inn should be may be inferred from the following dialogue which occurred between himself and a traveller whom he encountered as the latter was making his way towards the village :—

" 'Pray,' said the gentleman, 'are there any inns hereabouts?'

"At the word 'inns,' John plucked up his spirit in a surprising manner; his fears rolled off like smoke; all the landlord stirred within him.

" 'There are no inns,' rejoined Mr. Willet, with a strong emphasis on the plural number; ' but there's a Inn—one Inn—the "Maypole" Inn. That's a Inn indeed. You won't see the like of that Inn often.'

" 'You keep it, perhaps?' said the horseman, smiling.

" 'I do, sir,' replied John, greatly wondering how he had found this out.

" 'And how far is the "Maypole" from here?'

" 'About a mile'—John was going to add that it was the easiest mile in all the world, when the third rider, who had hitherto kept a little in the rear, suddenly interposed :

" 'And have you one excellent bed, landlord? Hem! A bed that you can recommend—a bed that you are sure is well aired—a bed that has been slept in by some perfectly respectable and unexceptionable person?'

" 'We don't take in no tagrag and bobtail at our house, sir,' answered John. 'And as to the bed itself——' "

In what follows the reader gets a glimpse of the interior of the "Maypole," painted in Dickens's own masterly style.

" Having, in the absence of any more words, put a sudden climax to what he had faintly intended should be a long explanation of the whole life and character of his man, the oracular John Willet led the gentleman up his wide dismantled staircase into the 'Maypole's' best apartment.

" It was spacious enough, in all conscience, occupying the whole depth of the house, and having at either end a great bay window as large as many modern rooms, in which some few panes of stained glass, emblazoned with fragments of armorial bearings, though cracked and patched and shattered, yet remained, attesting, by their presence, that the former owner had made the very light subservient to his state, and pressed the sun itself into his list of flatterers, bidding it, when it shone into his chamber, reflect the badges of his ancient family, and take new hues and colours from their pride.

" But those were old days, and now every little ray came and went as it would, telling the plain, bare, searching truth. Although the best room of the inn, it had the melancholy aspect of grandeur in decay, and was much too vast for comfort.

" No effort had been made to furnish this chilly waste, but before the broad chimney a colony of chairs and tables had been planted on a square of carpet, flanked by a ghostly screen, enriched with figures grinning and grotesque. After lighting with his own hands the faggots which were heaped upon the hearth, old John withdrew to hold grave counsel with his cook touching the stranger's entertainment ; while the guest himself, seeing small comfort in the yet unkindled wood, opened a lattice in the distant window, and basked in a sickly gleam of cold March sun."

It would seem as if Dickens could never exhaust his pen in describing the comforts of this grand and quaint old inn. "Cheerily," he tells us, "though there were none abroad to see it, shone the 'Maypole' light that evening. Blessings on the red—deep, ruby glowing red—old curtain of the window, blending into one rich stream of brightness fire and candle, meat, drink, and company, and gleaming like a jovial eye upon the bleak waste out of doors ! Within, what carpet like its crunching sand, what music merry as its crackling logs, what perfume like its kitchen's dainty breath, what weather genial as its hearty warmth ! Blessings on the old house, how sturdily it stood ! How did the vexed wind chafe and roar about its stalwart roof ; how did it pant and strive with its wide chimneys, which still poured forth from their hospitable throats great clouds of smoke, and puffed defiance in its face ; how, above all, did it drive and rattle at the casement, emulous to extinguish that cheerful glow, which would not be put down, and seemed the brighter for the conflict.

" The profusion, too, the rich and lavish bounty, of that goodly tavern ! It was not enough that one fire roared and sparkled on its spacious hearth ; in the tiles which paved and compassed it five hundred flickering fires burnt brightly also. It was not enough that one red curtain shut the wild night out, and shed its cheerful influence on the room. In every saucepan-lid and candlestick, and vessel of copper, brass, or tin, that hung upon the walls, were countless ruddy hangings, flashing and gleaming with every motion of the blaze, and offering, let the eye wander where it might, interminable vistas of the same rich colour. The old oak wainscoting, the beams, the chairs, the seats, reflected it in a deep dull glimmer. There were fires and red curtains in the very eyes of the drinkers, in their buttons, in their liquor, in the pipes they smoked."

Lord George Gordon, according to the narrative of the "Gordon Riots," as detailed in "Barnaby Rudge," was one of the visitors of the "Maypole" in March, 1780, a few weeks before he set London in a blaze. The stirring events of that eventful period form, indeed, the chief historical element in the above-mentioned novel. Thus Dickens writes: —"The 'Maypole' cronies, little dreaming of the change so soon to come upon their favourite haunt, struck through the forest path upon their way to London, and avoiding the main road, which was hot and dusty, kept to the bye-paths and the fields. As they drew nearer to their destination they began to make inquiries of the people whom they passed concerning the riots, and the truth or falsehood of the stories they had heard. The answers went far beyond any intelligence that had spread to quiet Chigwell. One man told them that that afternoon the Guards, conveying to Newgate some rioters who had been re-examined, had been set upon by the mob, and compelled to retreat ; another, that the houses of two witnesses near Clare Market were about to be pulled down when he came away ; another, that Sir George Saville's house in Leicester Fields was to be burned that night, and that it would go hard with Sir George if he fell into the people's hands as it was he who had brought in the Catholic Bill."

To the readers of "Barnaby Rudge," the assertion that a century ago highwaymen and footpads were to be met with on the road between Chigwell and Whitechapel will be no news at all. This road too, probably about Stratford, must have been in Dickens's eye when he drew the following picture of the meeting of Barnaby Rudge and Gabriel Varden :—" And now he approached the great city, which lay outstretched before him like bark of dogs, the hum of traffic in the streets; then outlines might be traced—tall steeples looming in the air, and piles of unequal roofs oppressed by chimneys; then the noise swelled into a louder sound, and forms grew more distinct and numerous still, and London—visible in the darkness by its own faint light, and not by that of Heaven—was at hand."

The following lines show us the same road under a different aspect :—" Everything was fresh and gay, as though the world were but that

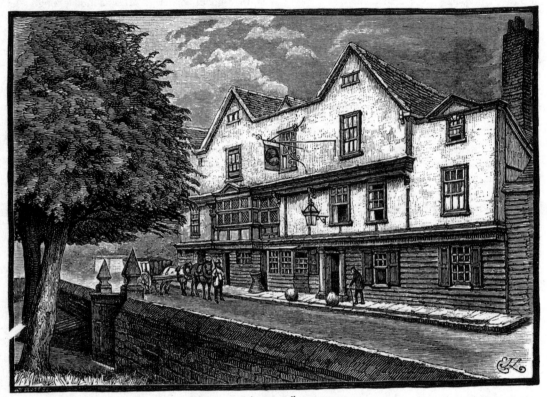

THE "KING'S HEAD," CHIGWELL.

a dark shadow on the ground, reddening the sluggish air with a deep dull light, that told of labyrinths of public ways and shops, and swarms of busy people. Approaching nearer and nearer yet, this halo began to fade, and the causes which produced it slowly to develop themselves. Long lines of poorly-lighted streets might be faintly traced, with here and there a lighter spot, where lamps were clustered round a square or market, or round some great building; after a time these grew more distinct, and the lamps themselves were visible—slight yellow specks, that seemed to be rapidly snuffed out, one by one, as intervening obstacles hid them from the sight. Then sounds arose—the striking of church clocks, the distant morning made, when Mr. Chester rode at a tranquil pace along the forest road. . . . In the course of time, the 'Maypole's' massive chimneys rose upon his view; but he quickened not his pace one jot, and with the same cool gravity rode up to the tavern porch. John Willet, who was toasting his red face before a great fire in the bar, and who, with surpassing foresight and quickness of apprehension, had been thinking, as he looked at the blue sky, that if that state of things lasted much longer it might ultimately become necessary to leave off fires and throw the windows open, issued forth to hold his stirrup; called lustily for Hugh."

*   *   *   *   *

"It was a long time before there was such a country inn as the 'Maypole' in all England: indeed, it is a great question whether there has ever been such another to this hour, or ever will be. It was a long time, too—for Never, as the proverb says, is a long day—before they forgot to have an interest in wounded soldiers at the 'Maypole,' or before Joe omitted to refresh them, for the sake of his old campaign; or before the sergeant left off looking in there now and then; or before they fatigued themselves, or each other, by talking on these occasions of battles and sieges, and hard weather, and hard service, and a thousand things belonging to a soldier's life. As to the great silver snuff-box which the king sent Joe Willet with his own hand, because of his conduct in the Riots, what guest ever went to the 'Maypole' without putting finger and thumb into that box, and taking a great pinch, though he had never taken a pinch of snuff before, and almost sneezed himself into convulsions even then? As to the purple-faced vintner, where is the man who lived in those days and never saw *him* at the 'Maypole,' to all appearance as much at home in the best room as if he lived there? And as to the feastings, and christenings, and revellings at Christmas, and celebrations of birthdays, wedding-days, and all manner of days, both at the 'Maypole' and the 'Golden Key'—if they are not notorious, what facts are?

"Mr. Willet the elder, having been by some extraordinary means possessed with the idea that Joe wanted to be married, and that it would be well for him, his father, to retire into private life, and enable him to live in comfort, took up his abode in a small cottage at Chigwell, where they widened and enlarged the fire-place for him, hung up the boiler, and furthermore planted in the little garden outside the front-door a fictitious maypole; so that he was quite at home directly. To this, his new habitation, Tom Cobb, Phil Parkes, and Solomon Daisy, went regularly every night, and in the chimney-corner, they all four quaffed, and smoked, and prosed, and dozed, as they had done of old. It being accidentally discovered after a short time that Mr. Willet still appeared to consider himself a landlord by profession, Joe provided him with a slate, upon which the old man regularly scored up vast accounts for meat, drink, and tobacco. As he grew older this passion increased upon him; and it became his delight to chalk against the name of each of his cronies a sum of enormous magnitude, and impossible to be paid; and such was his secret ·joy in these entries, that he would be perpetually seen going behind the door to look at them, and coming forth again, suffused with the liveliest satisfaction.

*　　*　　*　　*　　*

"It was remarkable that although he had that dim sense of the past, he sought out Hugh's dog, and took him under his care; and that he never could be tempted into London. When the Riots were many years old, and Edward and his wife came back to England, with a family almost as numerous as Dolly's, and one day appeared at the 'Maypole' porch, he knew them instantly, and wept and leaped for joy. But neither to visit them, nor on any other pretence, no matter how full of promise and enjoyment, could he be persuaded to set foot in the street; nor did he ever conquer his repugnance or look upon the town again."

About a mile and a half to the south-east of the church is Chigwell Row, or, as it really ought to be called, Chigwell Rough,* a hamlet running along the high ridge which extends eastward towards Lamborne and Romford. Half a century ago one would have naturally described it as lying on the borders of Hainault Forest; but, thanks to the lax administration of the Woods and Forests, and the greed of the lords of the surrounding manors and other landowners, those pleasant glades have long since been disafforested and enclosed, and the beauty of the district is gone. It may have come to be called the "Row" because a series of villas and mansions were built along the north side of it, the south side being left open. It commands a fine view of the Thames from London to Gravesend, and over Kent from Shooter's Hill to the Knockholt Beeches near Sevenoaks. At its easternmost end is a "Maypole" Inn, but not the veritable "Maypole" of Charles Dickens's novel. One of the villas on the north side was occupied for some years by Mr. Thomas Faed, R.A., the celebrated Scottish artist; Woodlands, the only large house on the south, was the residence of the late Mr. Joseph Walford, Q.C., a man whose name will be long remembered in these parts, not only as a lawyer, but as a Toxophilite, and the life and soul of the Epping and Harlow Archery Balls.

Chigwell Row has lately been made a separate ecclesiastical district, and a church has been erected for its wants on some waste land, which abutted on the forest.

At the corner of Chigwell Row stands Bowls, the seat of the Stuart family. It probably derived its name from an old inn where bowls were played which once covered its site.

---

* Indeed, it is generally supposed that the word "row" is only a corruption of "rough."

The celebrated picture of "The Woodman," by Gainsborough, from which many prints and drawings have been made, was done from a hale woodcutter who worked for Dr. Webster, of Chigwell Row. Near Chigwell Row was a spring of mineral waters, of a purgative character. It was discovered about the reign of James II. or William III., and written up by Dr. Frewen, a native of Chigwell, but it never attained any great celebrity or popularity.

CHAPTER XLIX.

WOODFORD AND WALTHAMSTOW.

"A noble horde,
A brotherhood of venerable trees."—WORDSWORTH.

Boundaries of Woodford—Its Etymology—Its Subdivision—Descent of the Manor—The Manorial Custom of "Borough English"—Woodford Hall—Census Returns—Woodford Bridge—The Church—Claybury Hall—Ray House—Church End, Woodford—The Parish Church—Woodford Hall—Mrs. Gladstone's Convalescent Home—A Pauper's Legacy—Woodford Green—Congregational Church—The Union Church —Art and Industrial Society, and Social Institutions—Harts—Monkhams—The Firs—Prospect Hall—Woodford Wells—"The Horse and Well"—Knighton House—The Manor House—Noted Residents—Walthamstow—Its Area and General Appearance—Walthamstow Slip—Census Returns—Etymology of Walthamstow—Descent of the Manor—Highams—Salisbury Hall—Chapel End—Bellevue House—The Parish Church—Almshouses—Walthamstow House—Benjamin Disraeli's School-days—Noted Residents of Walthamstow—The Town Hall, and other Public Institutions—Hoe Street—Hale End—Marsh Street—St. James's—The Reservoirs of the East London Waterworks Company —Geological Discoveries—An Old Bridge—St. Stephen's Church—Whip's Cross—St. Peter's Church, Forest Side—Forest Grammar School.

ONCE more, as may be inferred from the lines which we have chosen as a motto for this chapter, we have found ourselves back amidst the dingles and shady groves of Epping Forest, of which there is still a considerable slice remaining within the boundary of the parish of Woodford. This is a very large and scattered parish, extending from Walthamstow in the west to Chigwell in the east, and from Chingford and Buckhurst Hill in the north to Snaresbrook and Wanstead in the south. The parish derives its name from the "ford" over the river Roding, where now is Woodford Bridge, on the road to Chigwell, but which once, doubtless, was in the midst of a "wood" of oaks and hornbeams. The river Roding, it may be added, was at that time of more importance than now, and is said to have been navigable for light barges as high above Woodford as Abridge.

Woodford includes the four districts of Old Woodford (or Church End, as it is popularly called), Woodford Green, Woodford Wells, and Woodford Bridge. Of these, the three first lie, in the order above named, along the high road from London to Epping. They are all remarkable for the broad belts or tracts of open woodland which skirt the road on either side, compelling the houses for the most part to retreat gracefully from the dusty highway.

The parish forms part of the Hundred of Becontree—the last hundred in the county Londonward. This hundred, with the privilege of baronial authority, anciently belonged to the monastery of Barking, but after the dissolution it passed to the Crown. "Woodford," writes Mr. James Jones in his local Directory, "was one of the seventeen lordships given by Earl Harold to the Abbey of Waltham, and was confirmed to that house by the Charter of Edward the Confessor in 1062. The canons of Waltham held it at the time of the survey; and when Henry II. converted the secular canons there into regulars, in 1177, he confirmed to them this manor, as did also Richard I. by his charter of 1198. Among other liberties belonging to this Abbey, they were permitted to assart their lands in Woodford and many other places, and enclose them with a ditch and a low hedge, that they might take of their woods at their pleasure; to have the forfeitures and assarts of their own men, to hunt the fox, hare, and cat, in the forest; that their dogs should not be repudiated." The manor and church of this parish continued in the possession of the abbots and monks of Waltham Holy Cross down to their dissolution, in 1540, when it passed to the Crown. In 1545 John Lyson had the property which, being exchanged with Edward VI., was given by the king to Edward Fynes, Lord Clinton and Tey, from whom it was shortly afterwards conveyed to Robert Whetstone, whose son, Sir Bernard Whetstone, succeeded him in the manor. In 1624 the property was conveyed to the Rowes, by whom it was sold in 1675 to Sir Benjamin Thorowgood, who was Lord Mayor of London in 1685, and whose son conveyed it early in the last century to Richard, Earl Tilney, from whom it descended (through the Tilneys and Longs) to the late Lord Mornington. The manor-house had been in the meantime disposed of, but the manor was devised by Lord Mornington to the present owner, Earl Cowley.

"The custom of the manor here," remarks Mr. Frederic Johnson, in Weldon's "Guide to Epping Forest," "is what is called 'Borough-English,' under which the youngest son inherits. Though the origin of this is not clear, it certainly prevailed greatly in the kingdom of the East Saxons. By its name, it has been observed to have been chiefly used in boroughs, as it is still at Maldon, in this county, and elsewhere; and the term English

which stands near the church, was sold by Lord Tilney to Mr. Christopher Crow, by whom it was disposed of, in 1727, to the Hunts, from whom, again, it was purchased by the Maitlands. A few years ago the estate was bought by the British Land Company, who, after making various roads through it, sold it in plots for building purposes, and it is now known as the Woodford Hall Estate, the Hall itself being purchased by the

CHURCHES AT WOODFORD.

denotes its derivation from our Saxon ancestors. According to Littleton's 'Tenures,' it is very improperly called Borough-English. His words are: 'Some boroughs have a custom that if a man have issue many sons, and dieth, the youngest shall inherit all the tenements which were his father's within the said borough as heir unto his father, by force of the custom which is called Borough-English.' Upon which Sir Edward Coke makes this remark: 'Neither in an uplande towne can there be a custom of Borough-English, or gavelkinde; but these are customs which may in cities or boroughs.'"

The manor-house of Woodford, called the Hall,

trustees of Mrs. Gladstone's Convalescent Home, and most happily utilised in aid of suffering humanity, mostly in the person of Londoners.

The parish of Woodford contains within its bounds some 2,150 acres. In 1821 the population was 2,700, which number had increased in 1871 to 4,600, and this again during the next ten years to upwards of 7,100. Woodford has two stations on the Epping and Ongar branch of the Great Eastern Railway, about a mile apart: one at George Lane, for Church End; and the other further eastward, in Snake's Lane, for Woodford Green and Woodford Bridge.

The hamlet of Woodford Bridge, as stated

above, is so called because it stands near a bridge across the Roding, which here is quite a pretty rural stream, making its way between green meadows and pollard willows, and looking as if it was the haunt of kingfishers and other aquatic birds.

A triangular village green, planted with tall elms, stands on the rising ground by the roadside, near Claybury Hill. Here a new church was erected in 1854. It is built in the Early English style, and forms an ornament. It is sad to record the fact that the beauty of this spot has been sadly spoilt by speculative builders, who have contrived to disfigure the green with most hideous and abnormal structures.

"The road over the bridge, leading to the pretty village of Chigwell," writes a local historian, "is one of the ancient Essex roads into Suffolk and Norfolk. Along this road probably the monks travelled when conveying from London the remains of King Edward the Martyr for re-interment at Bury St. Edmunds in 1013, and which, on their way there, were deposited for one night by the monks in a wooden chapel, or shrine, now the little ancient church of Greenstreet, or Greensted, near Chipping Ongar, Essex."

The following brief notice of this place appeared in the *Ambulator*, published in 1793:—"Woodford Bridge, a village in the parish of Woodford, nine miles from London, on the road to Ongar, situated on a fine eminence, forming a very picturesque appearance. Near the bridge is a neat pump of excellent water, brought hither in 1776 at a great expense by the proprietor of the estate for the accommodation of the poor inhabitants; and not far from this is a manufactory of artificial stone. Near the village is Ray House, the seat of Sir James Wright, Bart. (the proprietor of the artificial stone manufactory), and a pretty villa built by Cæsar Corsellis, Esq., on the site of a house that had been the residence of Mrs. Eleanor Gwynne, mother of Charles first Duke of St. Albans." But the abode of Nell Gwynne in this locality, it is to be feared, is not a very trustworthy tradition.

Claybury Hall stands on high ground southward of Woodford Bridge, near the green, and at one time commanded some extensive views of forest scenery. Towards the end of the last century the estate was enlarged by the then owner, Mr. James Hatch, who had purchased the mansion and grounds of Luxborough House, mentioned in the preceding chapter, the former of which he pulled down, and the latter, with some others, he added to his own demesne.

Ray House is still standing, in Snake's Lane, a little to the west of Woodford Bridge. It was formerly the seat of the Clevelands and Hannots, and was purchased in 1770 by the above-mentioned Sir James Wright, who was some time Governor of Virginia, and afterwards minister at Venice. The manufactory which he established here was for the production of artificial slates, "by a process he had learned at Venice." Lysons, in his "Environs of London" (1796), in speaking of this manufactory, says:—"This slate is used for covering roofs and fronts of houses; for making pendent frames for hay-ricks and stacks of corn, and safe guards to preserve them from vermin; it is also used for water-pipes and gutters. The buildings where the manufacture is carried on are of this slate, and were erected about thirty years ago."

The western end of Snake's Lane opens into the main road through Woodford to Epping. The principal part of Woodford, or Church End, lies a little to the south. It is a village of scattered mansions, nearly all standing in their own grounds. It comprises no regular High Street, and scarcely a row of shops.

The church, dedicated to St. Margaret, is, with the exception of the tower, a commonplace specimen of the Gothic style of architecture which was in vogue at the time of its erection, in 1817, when it was built on the site of a previous structure, ruthlessly demolished in the previous year.

There is a print of the old church as it was before it was pulled down in 1816, but it is very scarce. It was an irregular nondescript edifice, covered over with plaster, so as to conceal any distinctive features. The tower was surmounted by a cupola, and had small pinnacles at the corners, instead of being battlemented, as now. The present church, which is built of brick, coated with stucco, consists of a nave, aisles, chancel, and south porch, with the tower above mentioned, which has been left standing. The nave is separated from the aisles by six pointed arches, carried up to the roof, which is of open wood-work, supported by eight pillars, and surmounted in the centre by an octagonal lantern. The east window is filled with painted glass, containing figures of our Saviour, the four Evangelists, and St. Peter and St. Paul.

A monument in the north-east corner of the church commemorates Elizabeth Lee, Countess of Lichfield; and there is a brass on the south wall to a Mr. Wynche, dated 1590. Near it is a tablet to the memory of Mr. Errington, who died in 1595. On the east wall is a tablet to the memory of a daughter of Sir Josiah Child, brought from Wanstead. A curious monument close by records a lady, Mrs. Anne Thelwall; and on the north wall is the monument to Mrs. Selwyn, grandmother of Bishop Selwyn.

At the south-west corner of the churchyard is a tall Corinthian column of veined yellow marble, surmounted by an urn. On the pedestal is a long inscription, setting forth that it commemorates "the ancient and knightly family of Godfrey, which flourished many years in the county of Kent," one of whom was Sir Edmund Bury Godfrey, whose murder excited much agitation in the reign of Charles II.* This monument, which was raised particularly to the honour and glorification of Mr. Peter Godfrey, sometime M.P. for London, who died in 1742, was designed by Sir Robert Taylor, and was erected at a cost of £1,500. The pillar has lately been restored and re-painted.

In the north-west corner of the churchyard is a mausoleum of the Raikes and Pelby families. Among other tombs and monuments to local worthies is one to Sir Thomas George, Garter King-at-Arms, who died in 1703.

On the south side of the church is a yew-tree of enormous growth; the trunk, at three feet from the ground, is over fourteen feet in girth, whilst its boughs form a circle of nearly two hundred feet. The local tradition is that this tree is as old as the church, but it probably is older even than the fabric which was pulled down in 1816.

On the north side of the churchyard stands Woodford Hall, a large and substantial brick mansion, surrounded by pleasant grounds. The house was formerly the seat of the Hickmans and Maitlands, but, as stated above, is now converted into a convalescent home for the poor of London. The Home was established by Mrs. Gladstone, whose name it bears, in 1866, at Clapton, during the cholera epidemic at the east end of London. In the following year it was incorporated with that of Mrs. Charlesworth at Snaresbrook, and was finally transferred to Woodford Hall in 1869. The institution will accommodate about eighty inmates, from either the hospital or sick-room, who may have been suffering from any form of disease not contagious. They are admitted free of charge. It may be added that this charity depends largely for its support upon voluntary contributions, and that the offices of the Home are at 30, Clarges Street, Piccadilly.

Connected with this parish are several other charities; those in money alone reach to about £80 a year, and some of them had a curious origin.

For instance, a pauper lunatic, one Sarah Ginn—a somewhat suggestive name for a pauper lunatic—having had a legacy bequeathed to her, which realised £59, it was assigned to the parish in consideration of her maintenance, together with an annuity to her husband. The said legacy, which was ultimately to revert to the poor of the parish, was invested in parish trustees, where it remains, and the amount of dividends is included in the distribution of bread to the poor at Christmas. Full details of the various charities in this parish, and also extracts from the old vestry-books, are given in Mr. Jones's "Directory of Woodford," from which we cull the following singular entry:— "Walter Hickman, who died at Woodford Hall in 1540, bequeathed to Clement, his son, four of his best ambling mares, his best gown lined with fitches, and his russit gown lined with fox; to the church of Woodford he left ten pounds to redeem paschal money at Easter, so that everybody in the parish, when they came to God's board, might say a paternoster and an ave for his soul and all Christian souls."

In Weldon's "Guide to Epping Forest" it is stated that in one of the registers is an account of all the collections for charitable purposes (in the nature of briefs) made at Woodford during a great part of the seventeenth century, commencing in 1643. "One of the most remarkable," adds the writer, "is that for the benefit of King Charles's chaplains and domestic servants, collected about twelve months after he was beheaded. Their petition states that they, the late King's Majesty's domestic servants, to the number of forty, being in present distress, by reason that their sole dependence was upon the late King's Majesty, and that their means from the revenue of his late Majesty were still detained, upon some reason known to the committee, and could not be paid, they were therefore so necessitated that they could no wise subsist for the maintenance of themselves, their wives, and families; and they prayed the charity of all good Christians."

Woodford Green, around which are clustered the principal portion of the shops, hotels, and private houses, as well as one or two large and imposing chapels, lies about half a mile northward from the parish church.

The Congregational church, an ecclesiastical-looking edifice in the Gothic style, was built in 1873, and consists of an apsidal nave, aisles, transept, and a lofty tower and spire. The building will seat about 800 persons, and there are schools adjoining. "The history of the Congregational Church in Woodford," writes the author of the local Directory above quoted, "dates back to the latter end of the eighteenth century, when Christian men came from London, and preached the Gospel under a fine old tree which stood on the village green. This led to hiring a room for Divine service in Horn Lane, and in 1798 the first chapel was built, under the direction of two of the trustees of Cheshunt College, in which for a considerable time the students of the college

The village is well supplied with water by the East London Water Company.

Woodford has its Art and Industrial Society, which was formed in 1879, for the purpose of encouraging art and industry, especially amongst the poor. Numerous prizes are competed for each year, and the exhibitions are held annually, in Easter week, in the lecture hall at the rear of the Congregational Church.

MONKHAMS. (*See page 463*).

preached. This chapel is now used as the Mission Room, and is commonly known as the Old British School." In 1837 a new and much larger chapel was erected; but though it was again enlarged in 1862, and otherwise improved, it was taken down in 1873, to give place to the present structure.

The Union Church, so called from its members being composed of "Congregationalists" and "Free Methodists," was erected in 1869, on the site of a former chapel for the Independent Methodists. A conspicuous feature of the building is a tall clock-tower. The Wesleyans have a chapel in Derby Road: it was built in 1876. There are schools in connection with it.

Among other institutions which have been established at Woodford for the social improvement of the working-classes are the Musical and Horticultural Societies, the Becontree Philanthropic and Debating Club, and a "Young Men's Mutual Improvement Society." The "Temperance cause" is well supported here, for besides the Woodford Temperance Society and the George Lane Institute, which have been established for the purpose of affording the working-men of the district the means of social intercourse, mental improvement, pleasant recreation, and non-intoxicating refreshments, there is on the Green, near Higham Hall, a very large and conspicuous Temperance Hotel, or "coffee tavern," named after Sir Wilfrid Lawson, who opened it in May, 1883. It was erected under the auspices of Mr. Andrew Johnston, late M.P. for South-Essex. This latest addition to the public institutions of Woodford has given rise to the following epigram :—

> "All hops abandon ye who enter here:
>   The wicked Wilfrid haunts this watery cavern ;
> No wine, no whiskey, not e'en bitter beer
>   Flows through the channels of the Coffee Tavern.
> The steaming coffee and the fragrant tea
>   Are ready where each eye can plainly see 'em.
> 'Tea-total ' then let each incomer be,
>   And while ' Te Total' let him sing ' *Te Deum.*' "

Several good mansions standing within their

widow of Mr. John Warner, a London banker, who left it to her son, Mr. Richard Warner, the naturalist, who here planted a botanical garden, and very successfully cultivated rare exotics. Mr. Warner was the author of "Planta Woodfordiensis," a work of great value to the botanist, though now a little out of date, as he follows Ray's system of classification and nomenclature ; and as several of the ferns which he describes more or less minutely are now extinct, the work is very much super-

THE "HORSE AND WELL," WOODFORD WELLS. (*See page* 464)

own grounds are still scattered round about in the neighbourhood of Woodford Green. The oldest of these, perhaps, is "Harts," which stands to the north-east. It was built early in the seventeenth century by Sir Richard Handforth, Master of the Wardrobe to James I., who is said to have been frequently entertained here when hunting in Epping Forest. The house was afterwards the seat of the Onslow family, to whom it was conveyed by marriage ; and here Mr. Arthur Onslow, sometime Speaker of the House of Commons in the reign of George II., was born. On the removal of the Onslows into Surrey, this estate was sold to a Mr. Sherman, a draper, of Cheapside. His daughter and heiress disposed of it to Mrs. Warner, the

seded by the "Flora of Essex," by Mr. G. S. Gibson of Saffron Walden. "Warner," writes Mr. Thorne, in his "Environs of London," "was also distinguished as a book-collector, for his critical knowledge of Shakspere, and by translations from Plautus ; and did what he could to advance and perpetuate after his death the tastes he cultivated in life by bequeathing his fine library to Wadham College, Oxford, and a sum of money for founding a botanical lectureship."

Monkhams, the seat of Mr. Henry Ford Barclay, fronts the eastern side of the Green, which extends from his gates northwards as far as the new church of All Saints, the tall spire and fine proportions of which form a charming picture, from whatever side you view them. The church is modern, having been erected by subscription in 1874; it is of stone, and in the Early English and Decorated style. It was built from the designs of Mr. F. E. C. Streatfeild, and consists of a nave, aisles, chancel, north transept (used as a vestry), and tower surmounted by a shingled spire. The north aisle was added in 1876. The reredos, given by one of the churchwardens, is constructed of stone and marble, and is carved with a representation of the Crucifixion of our Lord. The east window, of stained glass, was the gift of Mr. Henry F. Barclay; the organ was presented by Mrs. Barclay, and the font by Mrs. Buxton.

The Firs, on the west side of the Green, opposite Monkhams, is the residence of Mr. Andrew Johnston, who was the colleague of Mr. Wingfield-Baker in the representation of South Essex in Parliament from 1868 to 1874. Mr. Johnston served as High Sheriff of the county in 1881, and in the same year was chosen Chairman of the Essex Quarter Sessions.

Prospect Hall, by the side of the high road at the north end of the Green, is considered one of the finest brick-built mansions in the parish. It dates its erection from the middle of the last century, and was for many years the seat of Mr. Robert Moxon, by whom it was built. It was subsequently occupied as a school, at which time the south wing was added, but was subsequently converted into two private houses.

Woodford Wells, about half a mile farther northward, on the road towards Epping, and lying at the foot of Buckhurst Hill, is connected with Woodford Green by rows of humble roadside cottages, and a few villa residences of a better kind. The hamlet—which has a cheerful rural appearance, situated as it is just on the borders of Epping Forest—received its designation of Woodford Wells from a medicinal spring which appears to have been in repute about the middle of the last century. History is silent as to when or how it was discovered. The "Wells," however, have never reached the popularity attained by those of Hampstead, or Epsom, or Tunbridge, nor, so far as I have been able to learn, is their memory enshrined in any popular novel or comedy. In an "Itinerary of Twenty-five Miles Round London," published towards the end of the last century, the writer thus describes this locality:—"A mineral spring, which rises in the forest at a little distance from the 'Horse and Groom' [now known as the "Horse and Well"], was formerly in good repute, and much company resorted to drink the waters at a house of public entertainment called

'Woodford Wells;' but the waters have long lost their reputation."

The house of public entertainment above referred to had been at that time converted into a private dwelling-house; but the memory of the "wells" is perpetuated by an ornamental drinking-fountain, covered by a tall roof of enamelled slate, which has been erected over a well in front of some wooden cottages opposite the "Horse and Well" Inn.

Among the more important mansions at Woodford Wells are Knighton House, the seat of Mr. Edward North Buxton, one of the Verderers of Epping Forest; and the Manor House, which was formerly used as the parish workhouse, but has been again converted into a private residence. This old house is said to have been once occupied by Robert Devereux, the celebrated Earl of Essex. Mr. James Thorne, in his "Environs of London," states that tradition has fixed upon Grove House, which stood west of Woodford Church, as having been a hunting lodge of the Earl of Essex, and adds, "but there is no authority for the assertion." Mr. Thorne gives the following particulars of Grove House:—"It was spacious, and some of the rooms were large and curiously fitted. One, known as the ball-room, had on the walls twelve paintings in tempera of landscapes and subjects of rural life; the 'water-work' for the walls Falstaff recommends to Mrs. Quickly as a substitute for her tapestry. The house was taken down in 1832, and the site and grounds built over."

A few names of note occur among the residents at Woodford. The pious George Herbert, author of "The Temple," lived here for some time with his brother, Sir Henry Herbert, having removed hither for the benefit of the air when suffering from an attack of ague.

Woodford was the birthplace of Sydney Smith, the witty canon of St. Paul's, of the late eminent ecclesiastical architect, Mr. George Edward Street, and also of Sir Thomas White, who was Lord Mayor of London in 1877.

Sir James Campbell, who in 1649 founded a free school at Great Ilford, was a resident at Woodford, as also was Nicholas Lockyer, some time Provost of Eton, but ejected for nonconformity at the Restoration; he died here in 1685. The Rev. Thomas Maurice, the author of a work on "Indian Antiquities," and an assistant librarian at the British Museum, was for many years curate of Woodford.

Walthamstow, which adjoins Woodford on the west, is a very extensive parish, as may be inferred when it is stated in Kelly's "Post Office Directory of Essex" that it contains over fifty miles of road-way. It is bounded on the north by Chingford, and on the south by Leyton, and has a broad tract of marsh land towards the Lea, by which river it is separated from Middlesex. Altogether, the area of the parish is some 4,500 acres, some considerable portion of which is covered by the delightful wood-land scenery of Epping Forest. Its surface is pleasantly undulated; on the forest side are to be found many spots of sylvan beauty, particularly in the neighbourhood of the "Rising Sun," on the new road made through the forest from Whip's Cross to Woodford, on either side of which are banks and hollows, well overgrown or partially hidden among pollard oak, horn beam, and the luxuriant holly, evergreen in the winter.

Down to about a century ago this district was almost covered by the forest, which extended in parts almost close up to the river Lea; but in 1777 this was disafforested, and has since then been largely cultivated as pasture-land, which is now in turn being rapidly swallowed up for building pur-poses. A considerable portion of the parish, however, on the north side, around Chapel End and Hale End, two outlying hamlets, stretching away to the river Lea, are still broad belts of meadow land, through the centre of which winds the old road to Chingford and Waltham Abbey.

Previous to the embankment of the Thames near the outlet of the river Lea, the marshes here-abouts were frequently overflown, the water extend-ing attimes to a mile in width. Even now, in very wet weather or uncommonly high tides, the marshes in the neighbourhood of Lea Bridge, at the south-western extremity of the parish, are sub-merged.

Running parallel with the entire southern boun-dary of the main portion of the parish, and divid-ing the adjoining parish of Leyton into two parts, is a long strip of land, concerning which there is a tradition that it was acquired by Walthamstow in a very singular manner. In a "History of Waltham-stow," published in 1861, the author observes:—"Tradition says that a dead body was found in the river Lea at this point, and that the parishioners of Leyton would not pay the expenses of burial; that in those days it was customary in such cases for the parish who buried the body to claim as much of the land from the other parish as those persons who carried the body could reach, stretching out their hands in a line, and walking together. They were allowed to walk from the point where the body was found to the greatest extremity of the parish, and claim the land; if so, they certainly availed themselves of the privilege, for they walked through Leyton to the Eagle Point at Snares-brook."

Walthamstow can scarcely be called a town, or even a village, but is rather a collection of distinct hamlets and clusters of houses, called "streets," or "ends," each of which is known by some par-ticular name—as St. James's Street, Hoe Street, Wood Street, Clay Street, Marsh Street, Hale End, Church End, Chapel End, Shernhall Street, Whip's Cross, Higham End, and Woodford Side. The principal part of the parish lies on the roads lead-ing to Waltham Abbey and to Woodford; it is about six miles from the churches of Shoreditch and Whitechapel, and there are four railway-sta-tions on the Chingford branch of the Great Eastern Railway in its transit through the parish, namely, at St. James's Street, Hoe Street, Wood Street, and Hale End. In 1871 the number of the inhabitants was a little more than 11,000, which almost doubled itself within the next ten years.

The more thriving parts of the parish lie on a pleasant slope, well sheltered from the east and north winds; and that its climate is mild may be gathered from the fact that two centuries ago, as we shall see, the vine flourished here sufficiently to produce good wine. It has already been mentioned that the eastern suburbs afford a curious contrast to those of the west and south-west of London, and Walthamstow is an instance in point. It has really next to no literary history; at all events, it figures scarcely at all in the biographical or historical anecdotes of the last two centuries. It has reared few poets, painters, historians, or men whose names have become famous: in fact, its annals are almost a blank; and possibly on that very account it may have been, and may be, all the happier.

The name of Walthamstow does not claim an entry in the Diary of worthy John Evelyn. Horace Walpole lived at its very Antipodes, as far south-west of Charing Cross as Walthamstow lies north-east; and probably, surrounded by his fair Lepels and Waldegraves, he would have disdained the vulgar city whose houses rose on the slopes on the east of the Lea. Besides, though everybody knew the Thames at Teddington and Twickenham, who had ever heard of the Lea, except in connection possibly with Izaak Walton, whom, doubtless, he regarded as having been a sort of myth, and quite out of society? In fact, though he was an occa-sional visitor at Wanstead House, Walpole pro-bably would scarcely have been sure whether Walthamstow was in Essex or in Hertfordshire.

The derivation of the name of the village is simple enough; for Stow, or Stowe, in the Anglo-Saxon, denotes a place, or, according to Halliwell's

Archaic Dictionary, "a place for putting things in," a word which still survives as a verb to "stow-away," and also as a substantive in "stowage." The term is common both as a suffix and a prefix; thus we have Longstow and Bristow (now Bristol), as also Stowmarket and Stow-on-the-Wold.

In the reign of Edward the Confessor the great part of this parish belonged to Waltheof, son of Seward, Earl of Northumberland, other portions being in the possession of Peter de Valoines, Ralph de Toni, and one Halden, "a freeman." Waltheof, it is recorded, defended himself bravely against the Normans; but having submitted to the rule of the Conqueror, was restored to his paternal estates. His bravery and eminent qualities appear to have stood him in good stead with William, for he not only received back his confiscated broad acres, but received in marriage Judith, the king's niece, and had conferred upon him the Earldoms of Northumberland, Northampton, and Huntingdon. Waltheof, however, in the end became drawn into a conspiracy to bring about the king's deposition, the secret of which he unwittingly confided to his wife, who, as the story goes, "having placed her affections upon another, betrayed him, and gladly communicated the intelligence of the plot to her uncle." The result was that Waltheof was condemned and executed. In the Domesday Survey this manor is entered as belonging to Waltheof's widow, the Countess Judith. Waltheof left two daughters, one of whom conveyed this estate by marriage to the above-mentioned Ralph de Toni, who was a son of Toni, standard-bearer to the Conqueror; hence the designation of Walthamstow Toni, which the chief manor bears to this day. It continued with this family till the death of the last heir-male, Robert de Toni, early in the fourteenth century, when it passed, by the marriage of his sister, who had inherited the estate, to Guy de Beauchamp, Earl of Warwick. The manor remained in the Warwick family till the fifteenth century, when it was conveyed by marriage to Thomas, Lord Roos. In the seventeenth century the manor was owned by Sir George Rodney, who sold it to Lord Maynard, with whose descendants it has since continued.

Besides the principal manor of Walthamstow Toni, there are four other manors in the parish, named respectively Low Hall, Higham Bensted, Salisbury Hall, and the Rectory Manor.

The manor of Higham Bensted, or Highams, belonged in the reign of Edward the Confessor to the above mentioned Halden the freeman. It would be not only tedious, but needless, to name its successive owners since that time; suffice it to say that among them have been the knightly families of the Lovels and Herons.

Higham House, a large square brick mansion with wings, occupying a commanding situation on the north side of the parish, on the borders of Woodford, was built in the last century by Anthony Bacon, from whom it was bought by Governor Hornby. It is now the property of the Warner family.

The manor of Walthamstow Sarum, or Salisbury Hall, is situated at Chapel End, on the western side of the parish. It took the name of Salisbury from the unfortunate Margaret Plantagenet, Countess of Salisbury, under whom the manor was held by the Tyrwhit family. In the middle of the sixteenth century it was granted to Sir Thomas White.

Chapel End is so called from having had in former times a chapel there, dedicated to Edward the Confessor. The present church of this district, dedicated to St. John, is a plain, uninteresting structure, of "mixed"—*i.e.*, nondescript—architecture, and was built in 1829.

Bellevue House, a modern erection, is pleasantly situated near the borders of the forest. It is built of brick, with stone dressings, and has a semi-circular portico supported by Ionic columns. The park and pleasure-grounds are extensive; they are beautifully wooded, and contain a fine lake. The house stands on an eminence which commands the vale of Lea, the forest, and a large tract of Essex, with glimpses of the scenery in Herts, Middlesex, Kent, and Surrey.

The parish church, dedicated to St. Mary the Virgin, stands in the district called Church End, about midway between the stations of Hoe Street and Wood Street. The church is built of brick, thickly coated over with cement, and is as devoid of architectural interest as could be wished by the most austere of Puritans. It comprises a nave, aisle, chancel, and an embattled tower at the western end, containing six bells. The building, which stands on the site of an earlier structure, was erected in the early part of the sixteenth century. Sir George Monoux appears to have defrayed the expense of the tower and north aisle, and to have built the chapel at the east end of it, in which he and Lady Monoux are interred; the south aisle was built by Robert Thorne, a merchant of London and Bristol, and the founder of the grammar-school at Bristol. The following inscription was formerly to be seen at the eastern end of the south aisle:—" Christian people, pray for the soul of Robert Thorne, with whose goods this syde of the church was new edyfied and finished in 1535."

In 1817 the church was enlarged, repaired, and "beautified," at a cost of upwards of £3,000; in 1843 £1,000 more were expended in remodelling the nave and in enriching the east window with stained glass; and in 1876 further alterations were made in the interior by reducing the hitherto unsightly galleries to about half their original proportions, converting the old-fashioned pews in the body of the church into open benches, and replacing the ceiling with a roof of stained wood.

The monuments in the church are interesting. Among them is one in the north aisle to Lady Lucy Stanley, daughter and co-heiress of Thomas, Earl of Northumberland, and wife of Sir Edward Stanley; it comprises a life-size kneeling effigy under an arch. On the east wall of the chancel is an elaborate monument to Elizabeth, Lady Merry, wife of Sir Thomas Merry, dated 1632. This monument, which was executed by Nicholas Stone, contains busts of Sir Thomas and Lady Merry, and also of their four children. On the east wall of the north aisle are brasses, with effigies of Sir George Monoux, the founder of this part of the church, and of Ann, Lady Monoux. Sir George, who filled the office of Lord Mayor of London, died in 1543; his wife died in 1500. The brass is also engraved with the arms of the Drapers' Company. At the west end of the south aisle is a large white marble monument, with statues of the deceased, life-size, to Sigismond Trafford, of Dunton Hall, Lincolnshire, who died in 1723, and his wife Susannah, who died in 1689. Dr. William Pierce, Bishop of Bath and Wells, lies buried in the chancel. A small tablet on one of the pillars commemorates Sir James Vallentin, sheriff of London, who died in 1870. There are also monuments to the Bonnells, Maynards, Coles, Lowthers, &c. The churchyard, at the north entrance to which is a fine elm-tree, contains a large number of tombs and monuments, one of which, to Thomas Turner, dated 1714, has a yew-tree growing at each corner.

In the Book of Chantries in Essex, under date of 1547, occurs the following entry:—"Lands and tenements put in feoffment by George Monoux, Gent., to the mayntenance of a priest to sing masse in the church there, and also to teach a few scholars there, during the term of twenty years; and one Sir John Hughson, clerk, of the age of forty years, and of good conversation, literate, and teaches a school there, yˢ now incumbent thereof. The said incumbent celebrateth in the church of Walthamstow; £7 yerely valew of the same doth amount to the sum of £6 13s. 4d.— rent resolute none—goods and chattles none."

In 1650 the commission appointed to inquire into the state of ecclesiastical benefices estimated the annual value of Walthamstow vicarage at £40, including tithes and glebe. The commission reports further that John Wood was their vicar; but that "he is questioned for his abilities, and is disliked by the greater part of the inhabitants, who will not come to church to hear him, whereby there is great distraction in the parish."

In "The Complete English Traveller," published in 1771, the author writes:—"From the architecture of the church at Walthamstow, it appears to have been first built soon after the monastery of the Holy Trinity in 1112, and probably by the same foundress, who was Matilda, the wife of Henry I. However, if it was not built at that time, it was at least soon after; but it has had so many additional repairs since that time, that little remains of the ancient edifice are to be seen." The author speaks of a gallery being at that time at the west end of the church, and adds, "but there are none in the side aisles."

Thomas Cartwright, afterwards Bishop of Chester, was vicar of this parish in the middle of the seventeenth century; and Edward Chishull, a learned antiquary and divine, was instituted to the living in 1708.

In Lyson's "Environs of London" it is stated that among the Cartæ Antiquæ in the muniment-room at St. Paul's cathedral, there is an order for the more solemn observation of processions at Walthamstow, bearing date 1328.

Close by the churchyard stands a picturesque row of red brick almshouses for thirteen pensioners, and also the Grammar School, founded and endowed by Sir George Monoux, whose monument we have seen in the church. Walthamstow is altogether well off for almshouses and charitable institutions, for besides those just mentioned, a Mrs. Mary Squires founded in 1795 almshouses for six poor widows, each of whom receives a certain yearly stipend; and in 1810 Mrs. Jane Collard founded ten almshouses for ten married couples, each couple receiving 4s. weekly. The charities in this parish amount altogether to rather more than £1,150 annually. St. John's Industrial Home, in Shernhall Street, at a short distance eastward from the church, was founded under the auspices of the Roman Catholic body in 1873, and affords a comfortable home and training in various useful pursuits for 150 boys. Shern Hall is a large and ancient brick building, standing in extensive grounds, and was for several years the residence of Cardinal Wiseman.

Walthamstow House, close by, is another large brick mansion, standing within its own grounds. It was built and occupied by Sir Robert Wigram, the second baronet, but has since been occupied as a school, and is now St. Mary's Orphanage.

It may interest many of our readers to know that Benjamin Disraeli, the future Prime Minister of England, was partly educated at a private school kept by a Unitarian minister, Mr. Cogan, at Higham Hill, in this parish.

The writer may be pardoned for quoting from his own "Life of Lord Beaconsfield" the following particulars of his lordship's schoolboy days :— "One of his schoolfellows still living tells me that

"He is said to have had Mr. Milner Gibson among his schoolfellows at the suburban academy at Walthamstow. He never went to either of our great Universities, and the knowledge which he picked up at school was fragmentary and out of the beaten path, though naturally it was subsequently enriched by Continental travel.

"It is remarkable that with both of his early novels he interwove a school-fight, in which an oppressed boy rises against his oppressor, and gains his revenge. Is it possible—or rather, is it not pro-

GRAMMAR SCHOOLS AND ALMSHOUSES, WALTHAMSTOW CHURCHYARD.

as a boy young Disraeli was not remarkable for his attention to his lessons, or for his fondness for classical or mathematical studies ; but that he was a great dandy, and also a devourer of curious and out-of-the-way literature, old romances, plays, and histories ; and that he would often keep the other boys awake at night by telling them all sorts of stories, which he would invent as he went along. 'The child,' in his case, 'was the father of the man.' He was shy and reserved, and would wander by himself in the glades of the forest hard by, his only companions being a book and his master's favourite dog. His holidays were doubtless divided between his father's house in Bloomsbury and his grandfather's villa at Enfield.

bable—that this sketch was so far autobiographical, and that he fought his way among the boys at Walthamstow, having found the finger of scorn pointed at him on account of his Jewish origin ?"

Besides the houses already mentioned, there are still several others to be met with in different parts, which, from their spaciousness, and the fact of their standing apart in their own grounds—to shun, as it were, the obtrusiveness of their humbler neighbours—clearly show that they were in former times the abodes of the flourishing and opulent citizen. Sir Charles Pope, Bart., had a villa here ; as also had Gwillim, the herald, as appears by his account of Queen Elizabeth's funeral, printed in the "Monumenta Vetusta." George Gascoigne, a celebrated poet of the reign of Queen Elizabeth, is, according to Lysons, supposed to have been a native of Walthamstow. Here, at all events, he lived late in life. The dedication of his "Complaynt of Philomeal" is dated from his "pore house at Walthamstow, the sixteenth of April, 1575."

Here lived Sir William Batten and his wife, Elizabeth, Lady Batten, who is frequently mentioned in Pepys' "Diary" as a gossiping friend of his wife, and as occasionally visited by the ill-matched

&c. He read all, and his sermon very simple. Back to dinner at Sir William Batten's; and then, after a walk in the fine gardens, we went to Mrs. Browne's, where Sir William Pen and I were godfathers, and Mrs. Jordan and Shipman godmothers to her boy. And there, both before and after the christening, we were with the woman above in her chamber: but whether we carried ourselves well or ill, I know not, but I was directed by young Mrs. Batten. One passage of a lady that eate

FOREST GRAMMAR SCHOOL.

couple here. Lady Batten married for her second husband a foreigner with a title, possibly a Baron or Count Leyenberg, for as Lady Leyenberg she lies buried here. Her husband was a frequent companion of Pepys in his travels about London and its suburbs. The following entry in the Diary of the latter occurs under date May 29, 1661 :—

"King's birthday: rose early, and put six spoons and a poringer of silver in my pocket, to give away to-day. Sir W. Pen and I took coach, and (the weather and the way being foule) went to Walthamstowe; and being come there, heard Mr. Radcliffe, my former schoolfellow at St. Paul's (who is yet a merry boy), preach upon 'Nay, let him take all, since my lord the king is returned,'

wafers with her dog did a little displease me. I did give the midwife ten shillings, and the nurse five shillings, and the maid of the house two shillings. But forasmuch as I expected to give my name to the childe, but did not, it being called John, I forebore to give them my plate."

It appears from Pepys' "Diary," July, 1667, that good wine was produced from a vineyard adjoining Sir William Batten's house here. "He did give the company that were there a bottle or two of his own last year's wine, grown at Walthamstow, than which the whole company said they never drank better foreign wine in their lives."

Pepys notes in the October following the death of his friend, Sir William Batten, recording also the gratifying fact that his body was carried from London "with a hundred or two of coaches" to its final resting-place at Walthamstow.

The Town Hall, in the Orford Road, a short distance southward of the church, was built in 1876; it is constructed of brick and stone in the "modern French" style, and contains offices for the Vestry and Local and Burial Boards. The building occupies the site of, and is in part incorporated with, an old hall which had been for many years used for meetings and public entertainments. The parish can also boast of its Working Men's Club and Institute, and a Social Club. A cemetery was formed here in 1872. It covers about eleven acres, and contains the usual mortuary chapels.

Besides the mother church of Walthamstow, the parish possesses four or five district churches, besides chapels for Roman Catholics and for the various denominations of Dissenters, among which the Congregationalists largely preponderate.

Hoe Street, or High Street, which crosses the parish from the Lea Bridge Road in the south to Clay Street in the north, was once the chief thoroughfare leading from Walthamstow to Stratford Langthorne Abbey, and thence over Bow Bridge to London. A large number of houses have been of late years erected close by Hoe Street Station, and there are also several good shops.

Hale End, the most northerly hamlet of Walthamstow, bordering upon Chingford Hatch, is for the most part open meadow-land; but a great part of it is laid out in plots for building. This district is said to have been named Hale End from one Thomas Hale, who was the owner of a large house there in the early part of the seventeenth century.

Marsh Street is one of the principal thoroughfares, east and west, through the parish; it runs parallel with the railway on its northern side, by the district known as St. James's Street, and so on towards the Lea and Tottenham. Many of the old-fashioned houses and shops in Marsh Street are giving place to new and more fashionable buildings. The Congregational Church in this street, erected in 1870, is a large stone building of Gothic design, with a tall tower and spire.

The St. James's Street district comprises a large collection of humble cottages, built mostly of wood, and a few houses and shops lining the roadway near the railway-station, a large brewery, &c.

St. James's Church, built in 1840, is a brick building with semi-circular headed windows, &c., but of no interest. St. Saviour's Church, in Markhouse Road, about half a mile to the south from St. James's, was erected in 1874, from the designs of Mr. T. F. Dolman, the cost being defrayed by Mr. Richard Foster and Mr. John Knowles. It is built of Kentish rag, in the Early Decorated style.

To the south-west of St. James's Street, and covering a large space of ground between the railway and river Lea, some 150 acres, are the reservoirs of the East London Waterworks Company, the construction of which was commenced in 1869. These reservoirs, which have the appearance of a miniature lake ornamented with tree-covered islands, are capable of holding 500,000,000 gallons of water. The formation of these reservoirs led to important geological discoveries, the subsoil being found to be very rich in remains of the pre-historical period, extending back to the time when the whole district hereabouts was fen and forest. The area, as we have already shown, formed a portion of the great forest of Essex, which, under the name of Walthamstow Forest, was disafforested in 1777. If history may be relied upon, wolves were met with there so late as the end of the fifteenth century, and early in the twelfth century it abounded in wolves, wild boars, stags, and wild bulls. From an account of the discoveries which were made during the formation of the reservoirs, and which appeared in a monthly magazine in 1869, we quote the following interesting particulars :—

"First underneath the turf is about two feet of clayey loam, a deposit from occasional floods; below this is an irregular bed of peat, usually about three feet thick, abounding in oak and alder timber, and hazel-nuts, now the colour of ebony; next comes a most interesting line of varying thickness, formed of white marly matter, being, in fact, the small shells and calcareous mud of the pools that once dotted the surface. The shell beds may be traced in winding courses, as the bottoms and sides of former shallow pools. The shells are in myriads, with both valves, and in their natural position, as on the banks of the Lea now. Besides the fresh-water shells, there are land shells, blown or drifted into the stream or pools. A pretty collection may readily be made of six kinds of snail-shell, five Limneas, three kinds of Planorbis, two of the Unio, and others : twenty-six species in all.

"But the shells were not the only creatures which resorted to the ponds of the old forest-marsh. In the marl, and a bed of clay and peat below it, there have been and are being found the following :—A few bones of fishes; a few bones of birds; the present ox; the ancient ox (*Primigenius*); the elk, determined by Professor Owen (see *Geological Magazine*, September, 1869; *Times*, September 17th, 1869); reindeer, fallow-deer, abundant; hog, horse, beaver, wolf, dog, goat; and lastly, the traces of man. We may mention two bronze spear-heads, one bronze arrow-head, one bronze knife, one iron sword, late Celtic, part of the bronze sheath of a late Celtic dagger, part of an armlet turned out of Kimmeridge coal, a pierced axe-head of stag's horn, a bone knife, a stag's horn club, various antique pottery, flint scraper, &c. Most of these objects have been sent to the British Museum, and determined by Mr. Franks. Cæsar records the existence both of the elk and the reindeer in the forests of Germany in his time. The remains above mentioned cover the whole historic period, but do not go further back." We shall have more to say with reference to the geological discoveries which have been made in what is called the London Clay when we reach Ilford.

Close by this spot there were formerly some extensive copper mills. These were bought by the Waterworks Company, and a canal made therefrom to convey the water from the former mill-stream to the filter beds. It is stated that in the formation of this canal the remains of anchors and boats were found in the marshes by the workmen. A large number of persons were previously employed at the copper mills. A coin was made there, having on it the figure of a lion, and the inscription, "British Copper Company Rolling Mills, Walthamstow—ONE PENNY."

Many years ago, in consequence of the frequent overflowing of the river Lea, a wooden bridge was constructed from about the foot of Syborne's Hill nearly to Lea Bridge, by which the inhabitants of Walthamstow used to pass on their way towards Hackney and London. In the place of that wooden bridge, which is stated to have been erected by Sir George Monoux, a large bridge of brick and stone, about a quarter of a mile in length, consisting of thirty-four arches, was built about a century ago.

St. Stephen's Church, in the Grove Road, is a large building of yellow brick, of Early English design, and was consecrated in 1878: it consists of chancel, nave, aisles, transepts, baptistery, and a small bell-turret. The "consolidated chapelry" of St. Stephen was formed in 1880 from the parishes of St. Mary, Walthamstow, and St. Mary, Leyton, to meet the requirements of the district lying between the Orford and Beulah Roads on the north and the Lea Bridge on the south; the latter thoroughfare, which communicates with the forest at Whip's Cross, lies almost wholly within the boundary of Leyton. Here within the last few years building has been actively carried on, streets and terraces having sprung into existence with remarkable rapidity; and tramcars ply on the road between Lea Bridge and Whip's Cross.

Whip's Cross is at the extreme southern angle of the parish, and forms the entrance to the forest at the point where the roadway crosses through to the "Eagle" at Snaresbrook. It is supposed that Whip's Cross was so named from having been in former times the starting-point from which persons who were found stealing wood or deer from the forest were whipped at the cart-tail through Wood Street to Stoker's Corner. No doubt this whipping process was of frequent occurrence in former times: that is, if the thieves did not escape with their booty scot free. Among the Remembrancia of the City of London is a letter from Sir E. Phillips, dated in 1614, desiring the arrest of one Harte, as "the greatest destroyer of Deere in Waltham Forest," probably about this neighbourhood.

The church of St. Peter, at Forest Side, is a brick building of no architectural pretensions: one of those, in fact, which may be commended more for their usefulness than their beauty.

The Forest Grammar-school is pleasantly situated in an open part of Epping Forest, near Snaresbrook, but in Walthamstow parish, and forms a large and handsome range of brick buildings, with boarding-houses, spacious school-rooms, &c. This school, which is in connection with King's College, London, was founded in 1834 by a number of the resident gentry of the neighbourhood. There are about 130 pupils, and in each year two scholarships of £35 and £45 respectively are given. The chapel, which is of Gothic design, was built by subscription in 1856, and enlarged in 1874.

CHAPTER L.

SNARESBROOK AND WANSTEAD.

" Everywhere
Nature is lovely : on the mountain height,
Or where the embosom'd mountain glen displays
Secure sublimity, or where around
The undulated surface gently slopes
With mingled hill and valley—everywhere
Nature is lovely ; even in scenes like these,
Where not a hillock breaks the unvaried plain,
The eye may find new charms that seeks delight."

General Appearance of the Locality—Snaresbrook—The " Rights" of Commoners—The " Eagle" at Snaresbrook and the Eagle Pond—The Infant Orphan Asylum—Merchant Seamen's Orphan Asylum—Christ Church—Almshouses of the Weavers' Company—Area and Population of Wanstead—Its Boundaries, &c.—Etymology—Traces of Roman Occupation—Descent of the Manor—The Earl of Leicester and Queen Elizabeth—A " Spa" at Wanstead—Pepys' Opinion of Wanstead House—Visit of John Evelyn—Wanstead House Rebuilt by Sir Richard Child, afterwards Earl Tylney—Description of the House and Grounds—The Great Telescope—The Maypole from the Strand—Death of Lord Tylney—Subsequent History of Wanstead House—Its Demolition—Wanstead Park secured for the People by the Corporation of London—The Park, Gardens, and Grotto—Lake House, the Residence of Thomas Hood—Cann Hall—The Parish Church—The Village of Wanstead—The George Inn—An Expensive Pie—Park Gate—Wanstead Flats—The Princess Louise Home and National Society for the Protection of Young Girls—Dr. James Pound—The Maypole from the Strand—James Bradley, the Astronomer—Admiral Sir William Penn—William Penn, the Founder of Pennsylvania.

NOTWITHSTANDING that the district through which we are about to travel is singularly flat, and that scarcely a "hillock breaks the unvaried plain," lying as it does on the southern margin of Epping Forest, it contains many charming spots of forest woodland, even if the scenery is too tame to be styled beautiful. The Roding meanders through broad green meadows, and in one part in its progress through Wanstead Park opens out into a fine expanse of water, dotted over with little islands. Hence Snaresbrook and Wanstead have long attracted crowds of pleasure-seekers from the metropolis during the summer months, and no doubt in many cases sent them back to the busy world of London with agreeable memories of the charms of country life.

Snaresbrook is really but a hamlet belonging to the parish of Wanstead, but we have taken it first, seeing that it lies nearest to Whip's Cross, the spot with which we concluded the preceding chapter. The forest at this point opens out in the form of a fan, crossed by two good roads, that to the right leading to Leytonstone and Wanstead "Flats," and the other direct on to the "Eagle" at Snaresbrook, on the Woodford Road. If, before the preservation of the forest was taken in hand by the Corporation of London, the "rights" of the commoners extended to gravel and sand-digging, they seem to have exercised those rights to the utmost extent in this part of the forest, causing the destruction of a large number of fine trees, principally oaks, and the formation of numerous cavities, which become ponds in rainy seasons.

The three principal features of Snaresbrook are the "Eagle" Inn, the Infant Orphan Asylum, and the large lake, known as the Eagle Pond, that fronts both of them—a sheet of water some eight acres in extent, which has been secured for public enjoyment, in the shape of angling and boating in summer, and for skating in winter. As late as the beginning of the present century herds of deer roved freely about the forest glades in this locality, whilst the large pond was a favourite haunt for waders and other species of wild fowl. But with the gradual encroachment which has been made on the forest in the way of "enclosures," Snaresbrook has become almost severed from it, whilst rows of "genteel" cottages and smart villas have of late years sprung up, forming a strong contrast to the few old-fashioned houses of the wealthy citizen of which the hamlet at one time mainly consisted.

The "Eagle" Inn, which stands by the side of the roadway at the eastern end of the great lake, has long been a well-known hostelry in this neighbourhood, and, with its large gardens and pleasure-grounds, has become a favourite resort of East End holiday-makers.

As to the "Eagle" itself, let it be noted here that birds have never been plentiful as signs of inns in this country, and of them, the "Cock" and the "Swan" are decidedly the most popular. The "Eagle" is of rarer occurrence, and when it does occur, it is generally in combination, as the "Eagle and Child," the "Eagle and Ball," or the "Eagle and Serpent." It is probably of heraldic origin, though here on the borders of the forest it may have been suggested as a sign from some local occurrence, in which that prince of birds played a prominent part. Mr. Larbord, however, in his "History of Sign-boards," omits all mention of the "Eagle" at Snaresbrook. Tom Coryatt, who travelled over a large part of Europe in the reign of James I., and wrote an amusing account of his travels, gives, in his "Crudities,"* a curious instance of signs representing birds in the neighbourhood of Paris, while in his account of the bridges which span the Seine he mentions one of them as being called the "Bridge of Birdes," instead of the Miller's Bridge, as formerly. He adds that the reason why it is called the Bridge of Birdes is "because all the signes belonging unto shops on each side of the street, are signs of birdes."

On the south side of the lake, with its grounds extending to it, stands the Infant Orphan Asylum, an institution which was founded by Dr. Andrew Reed, for the maintenance and education of the orphans of persons who in former times had "seen better days."

This charity was instituted at Hackney in 1827, and incorporated in 1843, after the completion of the present asylum, of which the foundation-stone was laid by Prince Albert in 1841. It was formally opened by the queen's uncle, Leopold, King of the Belgians, in 1843. The building presents a long front, with projecting wings, in the Elizabethan or late Tudor style. It is built of fine brick, pointed with stone, of which material also are the dressings throughout. The object of this institution is to "board, clothe, nurse, and educate (in accordance with the principles of the Church of England) poor orphan children, or the children of confirmed lunatics." It is designed more especially for such as are "respectably" descended, and many orphans of clergymen, of officers in the Army and Navy, of members of the medical and other professions, and of merchants once in affluent circumstances, have found refuge within its walls; none, however, are excluded whose parents have maintained themselves by their own honest industry, independently of parochial aid. The children are received from their earliest infancy, and can remain in the asylum till they reach the age of fourteen or fifteen years. Elections to fill up vacancies take place in May and November, and the average number admitted annually is about sixty. The number of orphans received into the asylum from its foundation till the year 1880 was 3,000. Nearly the whole of the yearly income is dependent upon voluntary contributions; it may, therefore, not be out of place to state that the head offices of the institution are at No. 100, Fleet Street.

Another very useful charity at Snaresbrook is the Merchant Seamen's Orphan Asylum, situated to the right of the Chigwell Road, a short distance beyond Snaresbrook railway-station. It was established in 1817 at St. George's-in-the-East, in the neighbourhood of Wapping, whence it migrated to the Borough Road. The present building was erected in 1861, from the designs of Mr. G. C. Clarke, and has been twice since enlarged. The buildings are in the Gothic style, of red brick, relieved by bands of black brick, and with white stone dressings. A tall tower and spire forms a conspicuous feature of the building.

The objects of this institution, which is under the patronage of the Queen, and the head offices of which are in Leadenhall Street, London, are the "boarding, education, and maintenance of the children of British Merchant Seamen deceased from all parts of the world." The income of the institution is about £8,000 yearly, and up to 1880 more than 1,400 children had enjoyed its benefits. The number of inmates at the end of 1882 was 270; the premises are available for 300 children. The addition of a chapel to the building in 1882 brought the Prince and Princess of Wales from London to inaugurate it.

By the side of Sprathall Green, which separates the hamlet of Snaresbrook from that of New Wanstead, stands Christ Church, a building of Gothic design, which was erected in 1861, as a chapel-of-ease to Wanstead parish. It has since been enlarged, and a tower and spire added. Some of the windows are filled with stained glass.

A little further to the south are the almshouses of the Weavers' Company, for twelve poor freemen and twelve widows. They were transferred hither about 1860 from the densely-crowded neighbourhood of Potter's Fields and Old Street Road, London, where the charity had existed from the time of its foundation, in 1725.

The parish of Wanstead, including the hamlet of Snaresbrook, covers an area of some 2,000 acres, and contains a population of about 9,500, having doubled itself since 1871. This number, however, includes the inmates of the Infant Orphan Asylum. The village lies to the right of the Chigwell Road, between it and the river Roding. It is about half a mile south-eastward from Snaresbrook station on the Ongar branch of the Great Eastern Railway, and seven miles from Whitechapel or Shoreditch churches. Wanstead Park stretches away on the east: the long level waste known as Wanstead Flats, some 800 acres in extent, lies beyond the village on the south, and Leytonstone bounds it on the west.

The name of Wanstead seems to be derived, according to Lysons, "from the Saxon words *wan* and *stede*, signifying the white place, or mansion."

---

* Coryatt's "Crudities," Vol. I., p. 29.

More recent authorities, however, observes Mr. James Thorne, in his "Environs of London," suppose it to be a corruption of "*Woden's stede, or place,*" implying the existence here of "a mound, or other erection, dedicated to the widespread worship of Woden." Traces of Roman occupation have been found in the southern parts of the parish, in the neighbourhood of Aldersbrook, in the shape of a tesselated pavement, coins, ruined foundations, urns, pateræ, calcined bones, and other relics.

time of the Domesday Survey. After many subsequent changes of ownership, it devolved upon the knightly family of the Herons. Sir Giles Heron, a son-in-law of the great and good Sir Thomas More, held it at the time of the Reformation, and in consequence of his refusal to acknowledge the king's supremacy, he was attainted, and his estates confiscated. The manor of Wanstead remained in the hands of the Crown until Edward VI. granted it to Lord Rich, who made it his "country resi-

THE "EAGLE," SNARESBROOK.

These objects were discovered early in the last century, during the planting of an avenue in Wanstead Park. The piece of Roman pavement which was laid bare measured about twenty feet by sixteen feet, and was formed of small square coloured tesseræ, the centre of which was the figure of a man mounted on a horse, and surrounding it was a scroll pattern border. A small brass coin of the Emperor Valens, and also a silver coin, were among the objects discovered.

The manor of Wanstead was given in Saxon times to the Abbey of St. Peter's, Westminster, and the grant was confirmed to the monks by Edward the Confessor. Soon after, however, it passed— probably by exchange—to the Bishop of London, under whom it was held by Ralph Fitz-Brien at the

dence," and is supposed to have rebuilt the manor-house, then called "Naked Hall Hawe."

Here Queen Mary arrived on August 1st, 1553, on her way from Norwich to London to assume the crown; here she received the congratulations, more or less sincere, of her sister Elizabeth; and from hence she made her formal entrance into London on the 3rd of the same month.

The estate was sold in 1577 to Robert Dudley, Earl of Leicester, who enlarged and greatly improved the mansion, and who, in May, 1578, here feasted his royal mistress, Queen Elizabeth, for several days during the time that he was basking in her favour. For the entertainment of her Majesty on this occasion, Philip Sidney condescended to task a genius worthy of better things with the composition of a masque in celebration of her beauties and royal virtues, entitled "The Queen of May." "In defence of this public act of adulation," writes Miss Aikin, "the young poet had probably the particular request of his uncle and patron to plead, as well as the common practice of the age ; but it must still be mortifying, under any circumstances, to record the abasement of such a spirit to a level with the vulgar herd of Court flatterers."

From Wanstead the virgin queen continued her

not particularised, were valued at £11 13s. 4d. The library, consisting of only an old Bible, the Acts and Monuments, "old and torn," seven Psalters, and a Service Book, was estimated at 13s. 8d. The horses, however, were more numerous, or of good breed, for they were valued at £316 os. 8d.

On the death of the earl, in 1558, Wanstead, with other lands in the adjoining parishes, became the property of the countess, his widow, who afterwards married Sir Christopher Blount ; but by some family arrangement this manor became vested

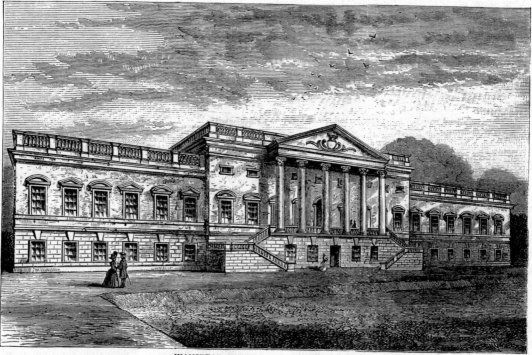

WANSTEAD HOUSE.   (*From an Old View.*)

" progress " through Essex and Suffolk to Norwich, where she was received with great enthusiasm. At Wanstead, in September of the same year, Leicester publicly married Lettice, Lady Essex, a private marriage having previously been performed at Kenilworth.

At the time of his death, in 1588, the earl was much involved in debt, and in consequence an inventory and estimate was taken of all his property, real and personal. From this it would appear that Wanstead House was not very elegantly furnished, for the entire contents of the mansion, including library, pictures, and furniture, and also the horses, &c., were valued at only £1,119 6s. 6d. The pictures, among which were three portraits of Henry VIII., the Queens Mary and Elizabeth, Lady Rich, and thirty-six others

in Charles Blount, Earl of Devonshire, on whose death, in 1606, it appears to have escheated to the Crown. In the autumn of 1607 James I. spent some time here, after his return from a western progress. The manor of Wanstead afterwards became the property of George, Marquis of Buckingham, from whom, in 1619, it was purchased by Sir Henry Mildmay, Master of the Jewel Office. Sir John Chamberlain, a courtier of the reign of James I., under date London, August 23, 1619, writes to Sir Dudley Carleton at the Hague :—
" We have great noise here of a new spa or spring of this nature found lately about Wanstead, in Essex, and much running there is to it daily by both lords and ladies and other great company, so that they have almost drawn it dry already ; and if it should hold on, it would put down the waters

of Tunbridge, which for these three or four years have been much frequented, insomuch that they who have seen both say it is not inferior to the spa for good company, numbers of people, and other appurtenances." The spring, however, would seem to have passed out of fashion, and so out of memory also.

The estate subsequently became forfeited to the Crown, but was granted by Charles II. to his brother James, Duke of York, and he transferred it to Sir Robert Brookes, who was here visited by Samuel Pepys. The genial gossiper writes in his "Diary," under date of May 14, 1665 :—"To church, it being Whit Sunday ; my wife very fine in a new yellow bird's-eye hood, as the fashion is now. I took a coach, and to Wanstead, the house where Sir H. Mildmay died, and now Sir Robert Brookes lives, having bought it of the Duke of York, it being forfeited to him : a fine seat, but an old-fashioned house, and being not full of people, looks flatly."

Sir Robert Brookes, who was for some time M.P. for Aldborough, in Suffolk, held this manor from 1662 to 1667. He afterwards retired to France, and died there in bad circumstances. From a letter among the Pepys MSS., Sir Robert appears to have been drowned in the river at Lyons. As we learn from Pepys' "Diary" (April 17, 1667), there appears to have been some talk of Admiral Sir William Penn, the father of the founder of Pennsylvania, becoming the purchaser of Wanstead House. Under date of May 1, Pepys writes :— "Sir W. Pen did give me an account this afternoon of his design of buying Sir Robert Brookes's fine house at Wanstead : which I so wondered at, and did give him reasons against it, which he allowed of, and told me that he did intend to pull down the house, and build a less, and that he should get £1,500 by the old house, and I know not what fooleries. But I will never believe he ever intended to buy it, for my part, though he troubled Mr. Ganden to go and look upon it, and advise him in it."

From the Mildmays, Wanstead passed by sale to Sir Josiah Child, who spent a large portion of his fortune in improving the grounds, by planting fresh trees and forming canals and a lake. Under date of March 16, 1683, John Evelyn writes in his " Diary ":—"I went to see Sir Josiah Child's prodigious cost in planting walnut-trees about his seate, and making fish-ponds, many miles in circuit in Epping Forest, in a barren spot, as oftentimes these suddenly. monied men for the most part seate themselves. He, from a merchant's apprentice and management of the East India Company's Stock, being ariv'd to an estate ('tis said) of £200,000, and lately married his daughter to the eldest sonn of the Duke of Beaufort, late Marquis of Worcester, with £50,000 portional present and various expectations." And again, under the same date :—"I din'd at Mr. Houblon's, a rich and gentile French merchant, who was building a house in the Forest, neare Sir J. Child's, in a place where the late Earle of Norwich dwelt some time, and which came from his lady, the widow of Mr. Baker. It will be a pretty villa, about 5 miles from White-chapell."

Sir Josiah Child was an alderman and goldsmith of London, and the founder of Child's Bank, at Temple Bar.* He died in 1699, and was buried in the old church at Wanstead. His son and successor, Sir Richard Child, was successively created Baron Newton and Viscount Castlemaine and Earl Tylney. He pulled down the old house, and built a new mansion near its site, called Wanstead House. This building, according to the "Complete English Traveller" (1771), was regarded a century ago as "one of the most elegant houses in England, both for the building and the gardens." In fact, it was a palace nearly equal to Canons in its palmy days, if not superior to it. The writer describes it thus in detail :—"It is constructed according to the best rules in the Corinthian order, and the front entirely of Portland stone. The portico in the centre is supported by pillars of the Corinthian order, and under it is the landing place that leads to the great hall, where there are a vast variety of ornaments and paintings by the best masters in Italy. The dining-room is on the left of the hall, being twenty-four feet square, and adjoining to it is the drawing-room, of the same size. On the right of the hall is another dining-room, twenty-five feet square, and a drawing-room thirty by twenty-five. On the chimney-piece of the drawing-room is the representation of an eagle taking up a snake, elegantly cut in white marble ; and from this room is an entrance to the bed-chamber, from which is a passage into the ball-room, which is seventy-five by twenty-seven feet, and connects the whole front line of apartments.

" The spacious gardens were laid out before the house was begun, and are extremely elegant.

" Mr. Campbell, the author of 'Vitruvius Britannicus,' was the architect employed in contriving this noble house, or rather, palace ; and although in particular parts it has beauties exceeding many of the best houses in the kingdom, yet when all the parts are taken together, it seems to want some of that proportion necessary to set off the whole."

The author adds that the present lord has resided many years in Italy, without any prospect of returning to England, and much regrets the fact that so magnificent a palace should be uninhabited, and left to the care of a handful of servants. As Lord Tylney had no heirs, he augurs that ere long the estate will pass into the hands of some other family, who will prefer English freedom to Italian slavery. He was not far out in his guess; for a few years afterwards Wanstead passed to Sir James Long, who took the name of Tylney.

I have said that Wanstead House was a palace; and in order to justify my words, I add some details of the building. The principal front of the house was 260 feet in length, and in the tympanum of the grand portico in the centre were the arms of the Tylney family, finely sculptured. The building itself consisted of two storeys, the uppermost containing the ball-room, state bed-chambers, and other principal apartments. The great hall was lavishly decorated. The ceiling, by Kent, was gilt, and enriched with paintings of Morning, Noon, Evening, and Night. The walls were ornamented with paintings from Roman history, by Cassali, representing Coriolanus and his mother Porsenna, and Pompey's last interview with his family. Here also were two large statues, brought from the ruins of Herculaneum—one of Domitian, and the other of Livia, the wife of Agrippa. The ball-room was magnificently fitted up, according to the taste of the last century, the furniture being richly embossed and gilt, and the walls hung with tapestry. The latter represented the story of Telemachus and the battles of Alexander. Over the chimney was a fine painting of Portia, the wife of Brutus, by Schalken. In the saloon were several statues, and also a picture of Pandora, by Nollekens, the father of the sculptor of that name. The remaining rooms contained a large number of paintings by the best masters, including Guido, Titian, and Lely.

Lord Tylney, though he lived so much abroad, appears to have been very proud of his new mansion; at all events, Horace Walpole writes thus of him and the place in a letter to Richard Bentley, dated 17th July, 1755 :—" I dined yesterday at Wanstead; many years have passed since I saw it. The disposition of the house and prospect are better than I expected, and very fine. The garden—which, they tell you, cost as much as the house, that is, £100,000—is wretched; the furniture fine, but without taste. The present earl is the most generous creature in the world; in the first chamber I entered he offered me four marble tables that lay in cases about the room. I compounded, after forty refusals of everything I commended, to bring away only a haunch of venison. I believe he has not had so cheap a visit a good while. I commend myself as I ought; for, to be sure, there were twenty ebony chairs, and a couch, and a table, and a glass, that would have tried the virtue of a philosopher of double my size."

On the death of the earl, without issue, in 1784, this manor, with other large estates, devolved upon his nephew, Sir James Tylney-Long, Bart., of Draycot, Wiltshire, whose only son, James, a minor, succeeded to the baronetcy and estates in the year 1794. He died shortly after, when Wanstead became the property of his sister, Miss Tylney-Long, also a minor, who thus became one of the richest heiresses in England. During her minority Wanstead House was taken as the residence of the Prince de Condé. Louis XVIII. and other members of the exiled Bourbon family also occasionally lived here during that time.

There were many suitors for the hand of the young heiress, and the prize was eventually won by the Hon. William Pole-Wellesley, elder son of Lord Maryborough, afterwards Earl of Mornington. They were married amid great ceremony at St. James's Church, Piccadilly, on the 14th of March, 1812, when he assumed the additional names of Tylney and Long. The following details of the dresses worn by the bride and bridegroom, and other particulars of the wedding, culled from the newspapers of the time, may interest some of our readers. The dress of the bride, we are told, consisted of a robe of real Brussels point lace, placed over white satin; the bonnet was made of Brussels lace, ornamented with two ostrich feathers; she likewise wore a deep lace veil and a white satin pelisse trimmed with swansdown. The dress cost 700 guineas, the bonnet 150, and the veil 200. Mr. Pole-Wellesley wore a plain blue coat with yellow buttons, a white waistcoat, buff breeches, and white silk stockings. The lady's jewels consisted principally of a brilliant necklace and earrings; the former cost 25,000 guineas. Every domestic in the family of Lady Catherine Long, the bride's mother, was liberally provided for. The fortune remaining to Mrs. Tylney-Long-Pole-Wellesley, after allowing for considerable sums given as an additional portion to each of the Miss Longs, and an annuity to Lady Catherine, was £80,000 per annum.

At the time of the marriage Mr. Wellesley is said to have been deeply in debt, and matters seemed to have gone from bad to worse afterwards, for in the course of a few years, by reckless expenditure, he contrived to get through the whole of his recently acquired fortune, and had so encumbered the estates, that in June, 1822, the whole of the contents of Wanstead House were swept away under the hammer of the celebrated auctioneer, George Robbins, of King Street, Covent Garden. The sale produced as much excitement as the dispersal of the contents of Strawberry Hill by the same auctioneer, just twenty years later; it lasted thirty-two days, and realised the sum of £41,000. No purchaser could be found for the house as it stood, so it was accordingly taken down, the materials being sold in separate lots. Among the objects of antiquarian interest disposed of were the celebrated ebony chairs and sofa, once the boasted *gems* of Queen Elizabeth, and which are so particularly mentioned by Horace Walpole in one of his letters for their singular beauty and antique character. After experiencing various transfers and vicissitudes of fortune, these articles came into the possession of Lord Tylney. They were purchased at the sale here by Graham, of Waterloo Place, by whom they were afterwards sold to Lord Macdonald.

At the sale of the contents of the mansion the family portraits were reserved; but even these subsequently shared a similar fate, for they, too, were sold in 1851, at the auction-rooms of Messrs. Christie and Manson, " in consequence of the non-payment of expenses for warehousing-room." Their dispersion was the last event in the history of Wanstead House, which once had vied with Canons in its glories, and now came to share the same fate.

On the death of his uncle, in 1842, and the consequent accession of his father to the earldom of Mornington, Mr. Pole-Tylney-Long-Wellesley became Viscount Wellesley; and three years later, on the death of his father, he succeeded to the title of Earl of Mornington, and became head of the noble house of Wellesley. His marriage with the rich heiress of Wanstead turned out to be altogether an ill-assorted union. He not only treated her shamefully, but spent all her princely fortune, and she died, it is said, of a broken heart three years after the sale of her goods and the destruction of her house.

Mr. Wellesley, notwithstanding all his reverses, did not long remain a widower; for, perhaps with the view of retrieving his shattered fortunes, in 1828 he married, as his second wife, a daughter of Colonel Thomas Paterson. The death of this lady in 1869 was thus commented on in the *Athenæum* at the time:—" The Countess of Mornington, widow of the notorious William Pole-Tylney-Long-Wellesley, Earl of Mornington, who died recently, in her seventy-sixth year, adds an incident to the romance of the Peerage. After the ruin into which the reckless earl's affairs fell, some

forty years ago, this lady was for a brief time an inmate of St. George's Workhouse, and more than once had to apply at police-courts for temporary relief. Yet she might have called monarchs her *cousins*. She was descended from the grandest and greatest of all the Plantagenets. Her mother (wife of Colonel Paterson), Ann Porterfield of that ilk, came, through the houses of Boyd, Cunningham, Glencairn, and Hamilton, from Mary Stuart, daughter of King James II. of Scotland, and seventh in descent from Edward I. of England. The earldom of Mornington, extinct in the elder line of the Wellesleys, has lapsed to the Duke of Wellington." The manor of Wanstead, with some adjacent lands, became the property of another Wellesley, Lord Cowley.

" In the latter part of the eighteenth century," writes the author of " Provincial Excursions " in 1843, " Wanstead House still displayed all the splendour which the Childs, the Tylneys, and the Longs, had lavished upon a palace fit for the abode of gentle and royal blood. Little did I dream that in one quarter of a century I should see its proud columns prostrate in the dust, its decorations annihilated, its pictures and sculptures dispersed by the magic of the hammer; at one period simply a deserted mansion, at another a refuge for exiled princes; then for a brief space polluted by riot and profligacy; and ultimately its lawns and gardens swept away, its stately groves and avenues remorselessly destroyed, and myself present at the sad catastrophe. Such, however, were its short and painful annals; and, except the grotto, not one stone now remains upon another. The palace, destined to stand for ages, and on which time had made no inroads, was removed, with the approbation of the Lord Chancellor, when little more than a hundred winters had passed over it: when its features were just mellowed, its woods and plantations in full luxuriance, and all around it smiling in perfection. Wanstead House was the most attractive object (of its kind) near London, and a national ornament." And the writer goes on to lament that the Government did not purchase it for some national institution, scientific or educational, adding his belief that it would not have been allowed to perish if its walls had been covered with ivy, and the fabric been in the last stage of decay. " I was familiar," he adds, " with every little bower and secluded avenue; I knew where its blossoms were fairest and the fruits choicest; could thread the mazes of its delightful foliage and exotic gardens, its limpid waters, and its verdant lawns, all which I have visited at dawn and at sunset, in midday and at night."

Mr. Rush, the American Minister, in his "Diary from 1817 to 1825," writes thus of Wanstead House:—"With our boys we visited Wanstead House, in Essex, the superb dwelling of Wellesley Pole, before it was stripped of its furniture and the whole pulled down; the bare mention of which house makes me remind you of what * * * * told us the rich proprietor once told him: that no wonder he was brought to the hammer, when every one knew that to keep it up with its accustomed hospitality, adding the carriages and servants necessary for the London season, when Parliament was sitting, required at least seventy thousand sterling a year, when all that he had was but sixty thousand."

The park and gardens are thus described by Mr. William Tegg, in his "Sketch of Wanstead Park" (1882):—" In the avenue which led from the grand front of the house to Leytonstone, but which has since had a road cut through it, is a circular piece of water, which seemed equal to the length of the front. On each side of the approach to the house was a marble statue: on the one side Hercules, and on the other side Omphale. To compensate, as it were, for the defect of wings, obelisks and vases extended alternately to the house. The garden front had no portico, but a pediment enriched with a bas-relief, and supported by six three-quarter columns. From this front was an easy descent to the river Roding, which was formed into canals; and beyond it the walks and wildernesses rose up the hill, as they sloped downwards before. A grotto, consisting of shells, pebbles, fossils, and rare stones, looking glasses, and a fine painted window, &c., with domed roof, built at an immense expense by the late Countess of Mornington, is now the only remaining monument of this finely-situated estate."

The outlying portions of what once was the estate of Lord Tylney, after lying waste for years, were purchased from Lord Cowley by the Corporation of London, and conveyed to the Epping Forest Committee, in trust for the public. They have been laid out as a "park" for the people, and were publicly inaugurated as such in August, 1882.

The park includes two or three lakes, with islands, on which the moor-hens and other aquatic birds build their nests, and at the end furthest from the high road a heronry. Near this is the grotto mentioned above: it is much larger than Pope's grotto, which we described at Twickenham.* It is often said that the cost of erecting it was no less than £40,000: but it is to be hoped that this is

an exaggeration. In the "Beauties of England" it is stated that the cost of the construction of this grotto was £2,000, independently of its costly materials.

The main feature of the park is its wild and rustic appearance, the wood being thick and picturesque. Nearly all the ponds are plentifully stocked with fish, and especially perch, and their surface abounds with water-lilies. The Corporation secured this park of 184 acres by an exchange of fifty acres of land scattered about and a payment of £8,000 to Lord Cowley, the latter putting up fences to shut them off from the rest of his estate, and making a road a mile long to give access to them at either end, to Forest Gate Station on one side, and Leytonstone on the other.

At a short distance to the south-west of the site of Wanstead House stood a building called Lake House, which was the last appendage of the mansion, for which it was originally built as a banqueting-hall or summer-house. In it, from 1832 to 1835, Thomas Hood, the author, resided. The house was more generally called the Russian Farm. In a description of the building given by Thomas Hood, junior, in a memoir of his father, the author writes:—"The fact was, it had formerly been a sort of banqueting-hall to Wanstead Park, and the rest of the house was sacrificed to one great room, which extended all along the back. There was a beautiful chimney-piece, carved in fruit and flowers by Grinling Gibbons, and the ceiling bore traces of painting. Several quaint Watteau-like pictures of the Seasons were panelled on the walls. But it was all in a shocking state of repair, and in the twilight the rats used to come and peep out of the holes in the wainscot. There were two or three windows on each side, while a door in the middle opened on a flight of steps leading into a pleasant wilderness of a garden, infested by hundreds of rabbits from the warren close by. From the windows you could catch lovely glimpses of forest scenery, especially one fine aspen avenue. In the midst of the garden lay the little lake from which the house took its name, surrounded by high masses of rhododendrons." Here Hood wrote the novel of "Tylney Hall," much of the descriptive scenery being taken from Wanstead and its neighbourhood; and here he also wrote a little volume containing the poem entitled the "Epping Hunt," from which we have quoted largely in a previous chapter.*

The estate and manor of Canons Hall, now known as Cann Hall, which lies to the south of the

* See *ante*, p. 107.   * See *ante*, p. 445.

site of the Lake House, and is intersected by Cann Hall Lane, connecting Leytonstone Road with Wanstead Flats, was in former times held by the prior and canons of the Holy Trinity in London, from whom it passed successively to the Strelley, Boothby, and Colegrave families.

The parish church of Wanstead, dedicated to the Virgin Mary, stands within the park. It was built in 1790, at the expense of Sir James Tylney-Long,

crowned Ionic turret at the western end. The interior is extremely plain, but well finished: it consists of a chancel, nave, and two aisles, separated by Corinthian columns. The east window is of stained glass. In the chancel is a superb marble monument to Sir Josiah Child, who died in 1699. This monument, which was preserved from the old church, consists of a recumbent life-size effigy of the baronet, with semi-recumbent effigies of his son,

MONUMENT TO SIR J. CHILD, WANSTEAD CHURCH.

in the place of an earlier structure, which had become dilapidated and inconveniently small. The old church is described by the author of the "English Traveller" in 1771 as having been lately "repaired, and fitted up in the neatest manner for Divine service." But only twenty years afterwards the edifice was ruthlessly pulled down, to make room for a bran-new Italian edifice which looks as if it had been put there to match the stables at the other end of the mansion. The new church, built from the designs of Thomas Hardwick, is constructed of brick, cased with Portland stone, and has a Doric portico, and a small cupola-

Sir Richard Child, and his wife.[*] In the churchyard was buried, in 1647, John Saltmarsh, a noted Puritan and divine.

The long, straggling village of Wanstead is pleasantly situated at the southern extremity of Epping Forest, and on the western side of the park. It contains a few picturesque old houses, not the least interesting, perhaps, being the "George" Inn. Let into the side wall of this hostelry is a stone bearing the date 1752, and commemorating a somewhat ludicrous event which then happened.

* Another member of the Child family is buried at Woodford. See *ante*, p. 460.

The inscription, which was restored in 1858, runs as follows :—

> "In memory of yᵉ Cherry Pye
> As cost ½ a Guinea yᵉ 17th of July.
> That day we had good cheer,
> And hope to so do many a year.
> R. C. 1752. Dadᵈ. Terrey."

The story is that during some alterations which were being made in the house at the above date, while the labourers were at work a pie was sent from the Rectory to the baker's shop, next door to

To the south-west of Wanstead Park are several avenues, belts of trees, and broad strips of greensward, which have long been the resort of holiday-makers and school parties in the summer-time. The principal avenue, composed of very fine trees, is nearly a mile long ; and between it and the park is a pretty residence, called Park Gate, the seat of Alderman T. Quested Finnis.

Wanstead Flats—which stretch away southward from the park towards Forest Gate Station on the

PARK GATE.

the "George." The men awaited its return, doubtless in gleeful expectation of a cheap, but delicious, feast. As the pie was being borne home, and as the baker was passing the "George," the men leaned over the scaffold, and took it off the baker's tray. For this little freak they were summoned before the local magistrate, and fined half-a-guinea, which, I presume, was duly paid, for after leaving the court the men decided on placing a stone in the wall to commemorate the joke—if such they considered it—each contributing a small sum towards its expense.

In the village there are chapels for Congregationalists, Wesleyans, and Primitive Methodists, and also a Friends' meeting-house.

Great Eastern Railway, and the Manor Park and the City of London Cemeteries—are about 400 acres in extent, and their area was formerly overgrown with furze, heath, and a few scattered trees ; but of late years its appearance has been considerably changed by the formation of brick-fields, &c. Early in the present century George III. held a review of 10,000 troops on Wanstead Flats, and in 1874 the open portion was secured by the Government for the purposes of military drill and exercise. For very many years this locality was a familiar haunt of the gipsy tribe, and of others who follow the wandering life of that fraternity, their caravans and tents being scarcely ever absent from the borders of the Flats.

At Wood House, on Wanstead Flats, is "The Princess Louise Home and National Society for the Protection of Young Girls." This institution, the objects of which are sufficiently indicated by its title, was founded in the year 1835, since which time it has been the means of rescuing upwards of twelve hundred young girls between the age of eleven and fifteen, who, from various circumstances, had stood in danger of ruin. With such an object and with such results, it need scarcely be added that the institution is one which must recommend itself to the hearty sympathy and support of all.

Dr. James Pound, a distinguished naturalist and astronomer, was rector of this parish from 1707 till his death, in 1724. Pound, who was a friend of Sir Isaac Newton, wrote several papers on astronomy, which were printed in the "Philosophical Transactions." He also taught the science of astronomy to his nephew, James Bradley, who lived with him for some time as a curate, and who later on, succeeded Halley in the post of Astronomer-Royal.

When the maypole which "once o'erlooked the Strand"* was taken down, about the year 1717, it was bought from the parishioners by Sir Isaac Newton, who sent it hither as a present to Dr. Pound, who had obtained leave from his squire, Lord Castlemaine, to erect it in Wanstead Park for the support of what was then the largest telescope in Europe, being 125 feet in length. The maypole, it should be stated, measured 100 feet. It had not long stood in the park, when one morning some amusing verses were found affixed to it, alluding to its change of position and employment. They are given by Pennant as follows :—

> "Once I adorned the Strand,
>   But now have found
>   My way to pound
> On Baron Newton's land,
> Where my aspiring head aloft is reared,
> T' observe the motions of th' ethereal lord.
> Here, sometimes raised, a machine by my side,
> Through which is seen the sparkling milky tide ;
> Here oft I'm scented with a balmy dew,
> A pleasant blessing which the Strand ne'er knew.
> There stood I only to receive abuse,
> But here converted to a nobler use ;
> So that with me all passengers will say,
> 'I'm better far than when the Pole of May.'"

Bradley was born in 1692, and after taking his degree at Oxford, in 1714, resided principally with his uncle at Wanstead. Dr. Pound had fitted up here an observatory, furnished, amongst other in-

struments, with a transit-instrument, some time before its introduction at the Royal Observatory by Halley, and under him Bradley acquired that accuracy and care in observing for which he afterwards became famous. On the death of Dr. Keill, in 1721, Bradley was elected Savilian Professor of Astronomy at Oxford, and in 1727 he commenced a series of observations, which resulted in the discoveries of aberration and nutation. Mr. Bradley had begun his observations at Kew in 1726 with a zenith-sector belonging to Mr. Molyneux, whose telescope was rather more than twenty-four feet in length ; but in 1727 a sector of twelve feet radius was made for him by Graham, and set up at Wanstead. This famous instrument was afterwards transferred to the Royal Observatory at Greenwich, and, on a grant being made in the year 1749 for new instruments, was purchased by the Government.

Another distinguished resident at Wanstead was Admiral Sir William Penn, the father of the founder of Pennsylvania. Born in the year 1664, young Penn spent much of his boyhood at Wanstead, whither his parents had removed soon after his birth ; and here, "playing by the pools or rambling in the leafy shades of the widely-spreading woods of Epping Forest, the lad commenced his active life." Penn's father was one of the greatest sea-captains of his age, and his mother was the daughter of a rich merchant of Rotterdam. "Thus," observes a writer in *Sunday at Home*, "the union of British energy and Dutch shrewdness which surrounded Penn's childhood contributed some appropriate elements towards the formation of that broad statesman-like mind which distinguished the founder of Pennsylvania."

At Chigwell, in the picturesque ivy-covered grammar-school founded by Archbishop Harsnett, as we have already seen,* young Penn's school-days began ; and at the early age of eleven years, we are told, he became the subject of serious religious impressions, which, together with the training which he received there, were the determining causes of his future piety. "His father and mother, though by no means destitute of estimable qualities, were emphatically 'people of the world' —fond of the theatre and dance, the wine and the gaming party." It was well for Penn that his stay at home, after leaving Chigwell, was not long ; but that, at the age of fifteen, he was sent to study at Oxford University. During his stay at Oxford Penn formed the acquaintance of a disciple of Fox,

---

named Thomas Loe, by whose preaching and teaching he became converted to Quakerism. His enthusiasm for his new faith took such a pugnacious form, that he not only absented himself from the services in the college chapel, or refused to wear the surplice of a student, but, along with some companions who had become Quakers, he attacked some of his fellow students, and tore the obnoxious robe off their backs : a proceeding which led to his expulsion from the University. He was soon after sent to pursue his studies on the Continent, and during his residence abroad formed a close friendship with Algernon Sydney. In 1668 Penn found himself an inmate of the Tower, on account of a publication which he had written, entitled "The Sandy Foundation Shaken," and while imprisoned in the Tower he wrote his most famous work, "No Cross no Crown." In 1670 his father died, leaving him an estate worth £1,500 a year, together with claims upon Government for £16,000 ; and in the following year he was again committed to the Tower for preaching, and as he would not take an oath at his trial, he was sent to Newgate for six months. Here, among other works, he wrote a treatise, entitled "The Great Cause of Liberty of Conscience." After regaining his liberty, he visited Holland and Germany in company with Fox and Barclay, for the advancement of the cause of Quakerism. On his return, in 1672, he married a daughter of Sir William Springett, having purchased an estate near Chalfont St. Giles, in Buckinghamshire, at which village also resided for a while John Milton and his secretary, Thomas Ellwood. About ten years later he turned his attention to the New World, obtaining from the Crown, in lieu of his monetary claim upon it, a grant of the territory now forming the State of Pennsylvania. "His great desire," observes the writer of his biography in *Chambers's Encyclopædia*, "was to establish a home for his co-religionists in the far West, where they might preach and practise their convictions in unmolested peace." Penn, with several friends, was well received by the settlers, and shortly afterwards he founded the city of Philadelphia. Towards the end of the reign of Charles II. he returned to England, to exert himself on behalf of his persecuted brethren at home. In 1699 he paid a second visit to the New World, and found Pennsylvania in a flourishing condition. He returned to England two years afterwards, leaving the management of his affairs in the hands of a Quaker agent, named Ford, who for years cheated Penn in every possible way. On Ford's death, his wife and son sent demands on him for £14,000, and these claims were so ruthlessly pressed, that Penn allowed himself to be thrown into the Fleet Prison to avoid extortion. Through the exertions of his friends, however, he was ultimately released, but not until his constitution was fatally shattered, and he lingered on at his residence at Ruscombe, in Berkshire, till July, 1718, when he died. He was buried at Jordans, near Chalfont.

Lord Macaulay wrote thus in praise of William Penn :—"Rival nations and hostile sects have agreed in canonising him. England is proud of his name. A great commonwealth beyond the Atlantic regards him with a reverence similar to that which the Athenians felt for Theseus and the Romans for Quirinus. The respectable society of which he was a member honours him as an apostle. His name has become throughout all civilised countries a synonym for probity and philanthropy."

CHAPTER LI.

LEYTON AND LEYTONSTONE.

Extent and Boundaries of Leyton Parish—Walthamstow Slip—Census Returns—Discovery of Roman Remains and other Antiquities—Ancient Earthworks—General Appearance of the Village of Leyton—Railway Stations—Park House—Ruckholt House—The Manor House—Leyton House—Etloe House—The Parish Church—John Strype—The Vicarage—All Saints' Church—Schools and Charitable Institutions—Lea Bridge, and the East London Waterworks—Temple Mills—Eminent Residents of Leyton—Leytonstone—Census Returns—The Church of St. John the Baptist—Holy Trinity Church—Congregational Church—Union Workhouse—Children's Home.

THE parish of Leyton, which includes the rapidly-increasing hamlet of Leytonstone, extends from Walthamstow on the north side to Stratford on the south ; it is bounded on the east by Snaresbrook and Wanstead, whilst on the west the river Lea separates it from the county of Middlesex, Lea Bridge being its extreme western limit ; and it is from its proximity to the Lea that it is supposed to be derived—Ley, or Lea Town: the Town on the Lea. The village of Leyton, from its situation, is called Low Leyton; whilst the upper part of it by a sort of reduplication, has gradually come to be called Leytonstone, that is, Leyton's Town. The entire parish covers a large area of ground, and the whole district is fast losing its rural character; the sylvan scenery which it once possessed in those parts where it abutted upon the forest, or in the more open parts about Wanstead, being rapidly encroached upon for building purposes.

A portion of land within the bounds of this parish, hardly more than a hundred yards in width, but running from the eastern to the western boundary, or, in other words, from near Wanstead Orphanage to the river Lea, and embracing parts of the Green, Capworth Street, and Beaumont Road, is known as the "Walthamstow Slip." Its singular acquisition by that parish has been already referred to in a previous chapter.* Though lying in the heart of Leyton, this slip of land belongs, for ecclesiastical purposes, to the parish of Walthamstow. For a long time the vicars of the two parishes of Walthamstow and Leyton sought to rid their respective parishes of this anomaly; a scheme was matured, and with a view to the transference of the above-mentioned slip from the parish of Walthamstow to that of Leyton, that portion of the latter parish which lies to the north of Lea Bridge Road, from its junction with Chestnut Walk, near Whip's Cross, to Copeland's Corner, and to the east of Hoe Street from Copeland's Corner to Boundary Road, has been transferred, by an order of her Majesty in Council, to the new parish of St. Stephen, Walthamstow.†

Some idea of the progress made in building here may be formed from the fact that in 1861 the parish, exclusive of the ecclesiastical district of Leytonstone, contained a population of only 4,700, which in 1871 had increased to 10,300, whilst, according to the census returns for 1881, it now numbers nearly 23,000.

It is, or was, generally accepted that Leyton is the same as the ancient Roman station called Durolitum, though some antiquarians fix that at Romford. The discovery of coins, bricks, and pottery of Roman work here would seem to show that it was a place of some importance during the period of the Roman occupation. Indeed, various antiquities have been at different times found in this parish; but the evidence of its having been the site of a Roman station, though supported by Camden and others, does not appear to be sufficiently strong to warrant it being positively asserted. Camden himself speaks with hesitation; and

though willing to suppose it the *Durolitum* of Antoninus, from its name Leyton, or the Town on the Ley, retaining some traces of the former appellation, which "in British signifies *Water of Ley*," acknowledges that, to justify this opinion, the distance of Durolitum from London (fifteen miles) must be regarded as inaccurate. "It is most probable," remarks the author of the "Beauties of England," "that the remains discovered at Leyton and in its neighbourhood belonged only to some Roman villas. That the arguments for the site of Durolitum being in this parish are not incontestable is evidenced by the contrariety of opinions respecting that station: Baxter places it at Waltham, Salmon at Cheshunt, and Stukeley at Romford."

The following particulars of antiquities discovered here are given by Gough, in his "Britannia" (Vol. II., p. 50), from a letter communicated by Mr. Lethieullier:—"In the year 1718, Mr. Gansell (then owner of the manor-house) having occasion to enlarge his gardens, on digging up about two acres of ground, found under the whole very large and strong foundations: in one place all stone, with considerable arches, an arched doorway with steps down to it, but filled up with gravel. In many of the foundations were a great quantity of Roman tiles and bricks, mixed with more modern materials, and several rough and broken pieces of hard stone, some part of which, when polished, proved to be Egyptian granite; two large, deep wells, covered over with stone; and in digging a pond, after the workmen had sunk through a bed of clay about ten feet, they met with a great quantity of oak timber, mortised together like a floor, grown very hard and black, but uncertain how far it reached. Several Roman brass and silver coins, both Consular and Imperial, to the time of Julius Cæsar, were scattered about, as well as some silver coins with Saxon characters. The ground where these discoveries were made adjoins the churchyard, where, some time before, a large urn of coarse red earth was found."

At a place called Ruckholts, about a mile to the south of the church, are the remains of some old entrenchments with a square double embankment, and fortified by what once was a moat. They are about 100 feet across, and are supposed to date from the Roman or Early British times. These remains are situated on a small eminence rising from the banks of the Lea, and trees have been planted over the chief part of the area.

Before the Conquest the monks monopolised the greater part of the lordships and lands of this parish. Part of the lands were given by Harold as

---

an endowment to the Abbey of Waltham; the manor of Leyton belonged to the Abbey of Stratford Langthorne; whilst the Priory of St. Helen's, in Bishopsgate, owned the estate of Marks.

It is less, however, for its antiquarian interest than for its fine old houses, half concealed amid "ancestral" trees, the prim suburban villas scattered about, the views over meadow and marsh land, and the glimpses of forest scenery, that our attention is arrested as we pass the twin villages of Leyton and Leytonstone.

In spite of the efforts of the modern bricklayer and builder, who has lined every roadway with villas of the suburban type, Leyton still retains a few old cottages, with timbered fronts and sides and red-tiled roofs, which tell of the times when the Stuarts sat on the throne. A few also of the limes and chestnuts which once graced these roadways remain in front of the houses to which they served as screens; but these are growing fewer year by year, while

> " Trade's unfeeling train
> Usurp the land and dispossess the swain."

The market-gardens, too, and the farm-houses which gave the village a rural aspect at the accession of her present Majesty, have nearly all been swallowed up in like manner by the building societies, who have parcelled out the land into unsightly plots. The village is between five and six miles from London, and has a station on the Great Eastern Railway. There is also a station at Leytonstone.

Like Chigwell and Walthamstow, and other suburban villages eastward of the metropolis which we have visited, Leyton was in former times the abode of a large number of City merchants and other wealthy personages; these, however, have mostly migrated westward, but many of their fine old houses still remain.

At Knott's Green, a hamlet on the road from Snaresbrook to Low Leyton, is the seat of Mr. G. Gurney Barclay, surrounded by gardens and grounds which have attained a local celebrity, and which has become famous for its observatory.

Park House was another fine mansion; but this has been enlarged, and converted to educational purposes, and is now known as St. Agnes' Roman Catholic Poor School.

Ruckholt House, a good-sized modern building, near the railway-station, occupies the site, or at all events has been built in the place of the old manor-house of that name, which was taken down about the middle of the last century. The old house, which was originally the seat of the Hickes family, seems to have degenerated towards its latter years,

for in 1742 it was taken by one William Barton, who opened it as a place of public amusement for breakfasts and afternoon concerts, after the fashion of Belsize at Hampstead,* and Kendal House at Isleworth.† The concerts were held weekly during the summer, oratorios being occasionally performed. In some of the advertisements announcing the performances here, the old mansion is stated to have been one of Queen Elizabeth's palaces, but there does not appear to have been any foundation for the assertion.

The seats of most pretension now standing are the Manor House, belonging to the Pardoes; Leyton House, a large mansion, standing in its own extensive grounds, some time the residence of Mr. Alderman Sidney; and Etloe House, a large white-fronted building, about a quarter of a mile north-west of the church. This last-named house was erected rather more than a century ago, and was for some years the residence of Cardinal Wiseman.

The parish church of Low Leyton, dedicated to St. Mary, is constructed of brick, in part plastered over, and is altogether poor and ugly. It consists of a nave, chancel, and north aisle, and a tower at the western end.

The church is neatly modernised; not a single trace of antiquity remains. The tower was pulled down and rebuilt in the seventeenth century, the nave and chancel underwent the same process in the eighteenth century; and all that remains to show what once has been is a really fine collection of Jacobean monuments. On the walls are one or two modern specimens of the skill of Flaxman and Chantrey. Near the vestry door, at the south-east corner, is a rather boldly-sculptured mural tablet to Sir Robert Beachcroft, Alderman and Lord Mayor of London, with the date of 1721. Below are the insignia of his office: the Lord Mayor's fur cap, sword, and mace.

At the north-west angle is a mural monument with a Latin inscription to William Bowyer, the printer, and friend of Dr. Johnson, who succeeded Edward Cave as proprietor of the *Gentleman's Magazine*. It was apparently erected by his son-in-law, John Nichols, whose name is added below.

The monuments have nearly all been displaced and replaced in the various beautifying processes which the church has undergone of late. Two large and stately memorials of the Hickes family, which formerly stood on the north and south of the communion table in the chancel, are now

---

* See "Old and New London," Vol. V., p. 495.
† See *ante*, p. 59.

under the tower at the west end, where they are lost to view. These are described by Lysons in his "Environs of London." One of them, formerly on the south side of the chancel, commemorates Sir Michael Hickes, whose effigy in armour, life-size, is represented in alabaster; the monument also comprises the effigy of his wife, in a mourning habit, holding a book. Sir Michael Hickes died in 1612. The other monument commemorates Sir William Hickes, who died in 1680; another Sir William Hickes, his son (1702), and Martha Agnes, Lady

of either, stands erect, but helpless, at the other end. The sculptor, however, has thrown great spirit into his figures, though at the present day they will appear to most people utterly unsuited to a sacred edifice.

On the walls are two or three brasses, of different dates and styles; one of the time of Henry VII. commemorates a maiden lady, Ursula Gasprey, her father's only child, who utters a prayer in Latin verse—

"Ursula Virgineis me pia junge choris;"

MONUMENTS IN LEYTON CHURCH.

Hickes, wife of Sir William Hickes the younger (1723). On the first-mentioned monument the knight and his lady are lying with their feet together and their heads apart, as if they had just had a conjugal "row." This idea, however, is negatived by the language of regret at parting, and of hope to meet in another and better world which are ascribed to them in Latin verses of doubtful correctness and elegance. On the other monument Sir William Hickes is dressed in a court suit, wig, and ruffles, reclining in a semi-defiant attitude, with his bâton as Warden of Waltham Forest in his right hand. At one end of the tomb stands his son, also in a court suit, and in a military attitude; whilst his lady, who for her age might be the wife

another, apparently of the reign of James I. or Charles I., exhibits a London tradesman in the habit of the day, with his wife and a bevy of children, also suitably attired.

The third brass has a quaint English inscription in rhyme—I cannot say in poetry. It records the death of a Lady Mary Kingestone in 1557:—

"If you wyll the truythe have,
　Here lyethe in thys grave,
Dyrectly under thys stone,
　Good Lady Mary Kyngestone;
Who departyd thys world, the truth to say,
　In the month of August, the XV day;
And, as I do well remember,
Was buryed honorably 4 day of September,
　The yere of our Lorde, rekynyd truly,

MVc fourty and eyght varely ;
Whos yerly obyte and anniversary
Ys determined to be kept surely,
At the costs of hyr sone, Sʳ Henry Jernynghame
truely ;
Who was at thys makyng,
Of the Quenes gard cheffe capteyn."

Lady Kingestone—or Kingston—was the wife of Sir William Kingston, and daughter of Richard, Lord Scroope. She had been first married to Edward Jerningham.

Among other monuments in the church may be mentioned those of Charles Goring, Earl of Norwich,

part of the last century. John Strype, the celebrated historian and antiquarian, lies buried in the chancel, but his gravestone has been covered and concealed by the new flooring. He was duly licensed by the Bishop of London, and though never actually inducted, held this vicarage during the long period of sixty-eight years. He died at the residence of his grand-daughter, at Hackney, in December, 1737, at the age of ninety-four.

Strype is said to have been of German descent, but to have been born at Stepney in 1643. He graduated at Cambridge, and on being admitted to

LEYTON VICARAGE.

PORTRAIT OF STRYPE.

who died in 1670, and of Sir Richard Hawkins, dated 1735. Not the least interesting memorial, however, is a tablet to the memory of William Bowyer, the eminent printer, and author of "Critical Conjectures on the Greek Testament," who died in 1777, and whose " Life," as written by Mr. John Nichols, " his apprentice, partner, and successor," and at whose expense the tablet was erected, contains many interesting particulars of the state of literature and of literary characters through a great

holy orders, was presented to the incumbency of Theydon Bois, but resigned a few months afterwards, on being appointed minister of this parish. He was for some years "lecturer" of Hackney, until his resignation of that post in 1724, and he held also with his Essex living the sinecure of Tarring, in Sussex, to which he was presented by Archbishop Tenison. The history of Strype's long life, in so far as it is of any public interest, consists merely of the list of his successive publications, among the more important of which may be mentioned " Memorials of Archbishop Cranmer," " Life of Sir Thomas Smith, Principal Secretary of State to Edward VI. and Elizabeth," " Historical Collections relating to the Life and Acts of Bishop Aylmer," " Annals of the Reformation," Lives of Archbishops Grindal, Parker, and Whitgift, and

"Ecclesiastical Memorials of the Church of England under Henry VIII., Edward VI., and Queen Mary." In 1720 he produced an edition of Stow's "Survey of London." Strype probably spent the first fifty years of his life in collecting the materials of the voluminous works which he gave to the world in the succeeding forty.

The churchyard is full of handsome tombs, showing that the dead who lie here occupied highly "respectable" positions in life. Amongst others who are so recorded are Sir John Strange, Master of the Rolls, and author of some legal reports; and Pope's friend, David Lewis, author of the forgotten tragedy of "Philip of Macedon." A gravestone to the memory of Mrs. Elizabeth Wood bears upon it the following punning inscription:—

" Wail not, my wood, thy trees untymely fall,
    They weare butt leaves that autumn's blast could spoyle;
  The bark bound up, and some fayre fruit withal,
    Transplanted only, she exchanged her soyle.
  She is not dead, she did but fall to rise,
    And leave the woods, to live in Paradise."

The Vicarage, which stands at the fork of two roads in the high street, was built by Strype, and has some nice carvings of the Stuart era on the lintel and posts. The following extract from one of the old parish registers, probably written by Strype himself, may interest our readers:—

" *An Account of ye Building of ye Vicar's House of this Parish.*"—" The Vicarage House of this Parish of Low Leyton, having been of a long time very ruinous, and being at its best state but mean and unfit to receive a Minister with his family, ye present Incumbent, John Strype, M.A., having lived seven years and upwards in ye said Parish, and officiated there as their Minister, thought fit at ye general Vestry at Easter, Anno 1677, to acquaint ye Parishoners with a promise they had made him, at his first coming among ym: wch was, to repair, or rather if need were, to rebuild ye said Vicarage House. Upon wch Motion, ye Vestry appointed Matthias Goodfellow and Robert Harvey, Merchants, to take a view of ye old Vicarage House, and to consider and report ye charge of rebuilding it. Wch was done wthin a short time after by ye former of them, having taken a surveyor and workmen along with him. And a report thereof was accordingly returned at ye next Vestry, wth a Model drawn by Mr. Richard Sadleir, an Inhabitant of this Parish, for ye intended new House, Containing 30 Foot in Front and 26 Foot in Rear. Hereupon a Voluntary Subscription was made by divers of ye wel-affected Parishoners, towards ye charge of ye work . . . . Upon this encouragemt ye said Incumbent undertook ye Building thereof himself,

and entered into articles wth John Mount of Walthamstow, Bricklayer, to build and finish ye House wth al manner of Workmanship and Materials necessary thereunto. And so ye Foundation of this House was begun to be laid in ye Month of August, Anno 1677, And al finished in ye Month of September ye year following. And ye abovenamed John Strype came into it, to dwel and reside there (by ye Favour of God), ye 26th day of September, in ye year 1678."

During the time of the Civil War a captain of a troop of horse, under the Parliament, named Kem, was foisted on the parish as vicar or parson. He preached, as Laud tells us, one Sunday in August, 1641, in the chapel of the Tower of London, before the illustrious prisoner, "in a buff coat and a scarf, but with a gown on. He told the people they were all blessed that died in this (Parliamentary) cause, with much other such stuff."

In consequence of the great increase in the population of Leyton of late years a new church (All Saints') was built in 1864. It is constructed of brick and stone, cruciform in plan, with south and west porches. The architecture is of the Decorated style, and the east window, of five lights, and also two others in the chancel, are filled with stained glass.

The National Schools, built in 1847, are in the Elizabethan style, and were raised by subscription, at a cost of £1,200, on the site of the old free school founded at the end of the seventeenth century by Robert Osler, who endowed it with a rent-charge of £12, for seven boys of Leyton and seven of Walthamstow.

There are several charities in the parish, chiefly gifts in money and bread to the poorest inhabitants. The parochial almshouses, by the churchyard, a low range of eight single-roomed tenements, were founded by one John Smith, a merchant of London, in 1656. In the Lea Bridge Road are the Almshouses of the Master Bakers' Pension Society.

Lea Bridge and the road thence to Woodford were made in 1756–7. The bridge itself is partly in the parish of Hackney. It consists of a single arch, built of iron; the approaches to it being of brick with stone dressings and facings. Close by the bridge are the reservoirs of the East London Water Company, the engine-houses, with their tall brick shafts being conspicuous objects by the roadside. Near the bridge is a station on the Great Eastern Railway. The Lea at this point divides itself into two or three different channels in its course through Hackney Marshes. On one of these branches, about a mile southward from Lea Bridge, were the old Temple Mills, said to have anciently belonged to the Knights Templars, and afterwards to the Knights of St. John of Jerusalem.* In 1720 these mills were used for brass works; but at the beginning of the present century they were appropriated to the manufacture of sheet lead, and subsequently used as flock mills. The building, which was principally of wood, was pulled down many years ago; and the stream which worked the mill is now under the control of the East London Water Company, above mentioned. The mill spanned the stream, and adjoined the "White Hart" public-house, an hostelry well-known to anglers in these parts.

Among the natives of Leyton was Sir Thomas Rowe, or Roe, Ambassador for James I. to the Great Mogul and to the Sultan of Turkey, and author of a narrative of his travels in that capacity. On his return from the East, Sir Thomas was made Chancellor of the Order of the Garter, and also sworn a Privy Councillor. The celebrated Alexandrian Manuscript of the Greek Testament, of which a *fac-simile* was published by Dr. Woide towards the end of the last century, was brought to this country by Sir Thomas. He died in 1644.

Thomas Lodge, the dramatic poet and actor, known also as a translator of the works of Josephus and Seneca, &c., lived at Low Leyton, as he dates from that place one of his plays, "The Wit's Miserie," which was printed in 1596.

The hamlet of Leytonstone lies to the east of Low Leyton, and stretches for about a mile along the Epping Road in its course from Stratford, from which place it is about two miles north as the crow flies. The main street runs parallel with the Epping and Ongar branch of the Great Eastern Railway, the railway-station being close to the church. The district was formed into a separate ecclesiastical parish in 1845. In 1861 the population of Leytonstone was about 2,400. This number had doubled itself in the course of the next ten years, since which time there has been a proportionate increase, streets and rows of "villas" having rapidly sprung up in all directions, particularly eastward, towards the districts once covered by Hainault Forest.

The church of St. John the Baptist was built in 1843; it is constructed of white brick, with stone dressings, and consists of a chancel and nave, with a pinnacled tower at the western end, containing a clock and six bells. The east window, a triple lancet, is filled with stained glass.

In 1879 another ecclesiastical district was formed at Harrow Green, at the north-western extremity of the parish, abutting upon Ruckholts. This new district has been made up of portions of the several parishes of Leytonstone, Leyton, Wanstead, West Ham, and St. Paul's, Stratford New Town. The church, dedicated to the Holy Trinity, was built in 1878.

The Congregational Church, built in 1877–78, is a large edifice of Lombardo-Gothic design. There are also chapels for other denominations of Dissenters. The Union Workhouse for the parish of West Ham, the inmates of which generally number between 700 and 800, is situated at Leytonstone, as also is the Bethnal Green Industrial School, which was erected in 1868, and provides a home for some 400 children. Another useful philanthropic institution here is the Children's Home, in Forest Place, established in 1865.

Much of the land in the parish which has not been already swallowed up by the greedy builder is cultivated either as market-gardens or as nursery-grounds for choice flowers and ornamental trees.

CHAPTER LII.

HAINAULT FOREST AND ALDBOROUGH HATCH.

"To Hainault Forest Queen Anne she did ride,
And beheld the beautiful Oak by her side;
And after viewing it from the bottom to top
She said to her Court, 'It is a Fair-lop!'"– OLD SONG.

Situation, Boundaries, and Extent of Hainault Forest—Its Etymology—Its Ownership by the Abbey of Barking—It passes to the Crown—Subsequent Disposal– Is Disafforested—The Hamlet of Barking Side—Census Returns—The Church—Dr. Barnardo's Homes for Friendless Children—The "Maypole" Public-house—Fairlop Oak and Fairlop Fair—Aldborough Hatch.

HAINAULT FOREST, as we have stated in a previous chapter,† was that portion of the Forest of Waltham which *lay* (alas! I can no longer write "which *lies*") to the south and east of the River Roding. In former times, as already stated, it extended northward as far as Theydon Bois, embracing Chigwell and Woodford Bridge, its southern entrance being at Aldborough Hatch. The word Hatch, as my readers are probably aware, was the old Saxon term for a wicket-gate, and it still survives in the buttery-hatch of our colleges and old manor-houses. From constant enclosures, however, the area of the forest had been so far diminished, that since the commencement of the present century Chigwell Row and Forest Gate may be said to have formed its northern boundary, whilst it extended from Woodford and Leytonstone in the west nearly to Havering-atte-Bower in the east. According to the survey of the Commissioners of Land Revenue, made in 1793, and the estimate of the Commissioners of Woods and Forests, the entire area of Hainault Forest at that time was about 17,000 acres; but by 1851, when it was resolved to "disafforest" and enclose it, these acres had dwindled down to about 4,000, of which nearly 3,000 were comprised in the "King's Woods," or royal forest. Almost the only part which has remained unenclosed since 1853, when the work of reclamation began, is Crabtree Wood, which lies a short distance eastward of Chigwell Row. There are a few other patches adjoining Claybury, and at Hog's Hall, near Barking Side.

Hainault Forest is supposed by some writers to have been named from Hainhault, in Germany, "on account of its having been stocked with deer from that place," and by others that it was so called out of compliment to Philippa of Hainhault, the consort of Edward III. Mr. James Thorne, in his "Environs of London," however, says:—"The name, formerly _Hen holt_, has been derived from the Anglo-Saxon _hean_, poor, of little value (having reference to the character of the land, as in Hendon, Henley, &c.), and _holt_, a wood. Dr. Morris has suggested that it may come from _hayn_, a cleared and enclosed space, and _holt_.* It is not unlikely, however," adds Mr. Thorne, "looking at the character of the district, that it was originally _héan holt_, the high wood."

Down to the present century this district was wild and uncultivated, in a great measure covered over with forest trees—chiefly pollard oak and hornbeam—and underwood, and with here and there broad sweeps of turf dotted with golden furze, and purple with broom and heather, affording safe retreats for the gipsy tribes who located themselves in these quarters.

The portion of Hainault Forest lying within the manors of Barking and Dagenham belonged to the Abbey of Barking, and at the Dissolution it passed to the Crown. From the time of Charles I., however, different portions of the forest have been sold, and the manor of Barking alienated, but what was called the "soil of the King's Woods, together with the timber growing thereon," was reserved, as well as the right of "vert and venison." In 1851 an Act of Parliament was passed empowering the Government, after giving full compensation to the lords of manors, freeholders, and others, in respect to their several rights in the forest, to "destroy or remove the deer, cut down the timber, enclose and appropriate the land, make roads," &c.; and in 1853, as stated above, the work of clearance and reclamation was begun in earnest, Messrs. Charles Gore and Thomas F. Kennedy being then the Commissioners of Woods and Forests. The trees, over 100,000 in number, were laid low by the woodman's axe, and produced nearly £21,000, which went a great way towards paying the preliminary expenses of the proceedings. The Crown had obtained, either by allotment or purchase, some 2,000 acres and the whole of the timber; and the remainder was appropriated to the several parishes and lords of manors. The Crown lands were thoroughly drained and fenced, and now form a compact property, known as the Crown Farm. What was once Hainault Forest has thus become—from a wild and desolate, but beautiful, waste—a broad expanse of productive, fertile land, the property being cut up and divided by roads, and for the most part put under cultivation as farms. But the rights of the British public were ignored, no village Hampden having up here, as at Loughton, come forward to assert and vindicate them.

On the south-west side of this district, which now figures on the map simply as Hainault—or Henhault—is the straggling hamlet of Barking Side. The village consists of a few small houses and labourers' cottages by the roadside, a church, a public-house or two, and a charitable institution. It lies some two miles south from Chigwell Row, and three miles north from Ilford station on the Great Eastern Railway, and it was formed into an ecclesiastical district in 1841, out of Great Ilford and the civil parish of Barking. Its area is some 2,500 acres; whilst its inhabitants, principally employed in agricultural pursuits, number nearly 3,000, or about double of those enumerated in the census of 1871.

The name of Barking Side would seem at first very inappropriate to a place which lies in the opposite direction of Barking from Ilford; but it must be remembered that the name was given with reference, not to that place, though it may have been the Eald Ford, but to the Forest, which was older still.

---

* "Etymology of Local Names," p. 55.

The church, dedicated to the Holy Trinity, is a small building in the Norman style, erected in 1840: it consists of a chancel and nave, with a bell-turret.

Dr. Barnardo's Village Home for Orphan and Destitute Girls is the principal feature in this village. This institution, called the East End Juvenile Mission, and one out of eighteen depôts established in the eastern districts of London, was founded in 1866, for the purpose of "reclaiming, educating, and benefiting, spiritually and physically, adults and children of the poorest classes."

The Homes surround a space of about four acres, which is laid out as a sort of college quadrangle, the houses being grouped around it on all sides. Each of these is fitted for the reception of twenty girls, who are mostly between four and fourteen years of age, though some remain till seventeen, and some are infants only a few weeks old. The total of the houses is at present thirty; but ground has been secured for the erection of ten or twelve more as soon as donors are forthcoming. Many of those already in working order were opened by the Princess Mary of Teck, as recorded on stones let into their fronts; others were given or opened by Lord and Lady Cairns, Lord and Lady Aberdeen, the Duchess Dowager of Manchester, and other titled persons; whilst not a few commemorate a parent or a child. The inscriptions on their fronts are quite touching.

The girls are all brought up for domestic service, and are taught reading, writing, arithmetic, and needlework; and all take their turns at laundry and house work. The steam laundry alone, when in full operation, is a sight worth a visit; and the size of it may be inferred from the fact that often 10,000 articles are washed in it in a single week. The washing, not only of all the thirty "Homes," but that of all the boys at the Home at Stepney Causeway—a kindred institution—is done here. The girls are allowed, in some cases, to remain till seventeen, when they are drafted off into service. Some hundreds of them have been despatched to Canada, for service there; and they cannot be sent too young for the wants of the colonists. Some who are delicate have been sent for a winter sojourn on the north coast of Africa. Two adjoining mansions, with grounds and gardens, have been absorbed into the institution; the one serving as an infirmary, whilst the other is appropriated as school-rooms for the various classes. The whole of the school staff is under Government inspection, and has a resident master and mistress, who have a separate house assigned to them.

The children have their meals and, for the most part, sit and play in their respective Homes, though they meet on equal terms in the common ground. In the centre of the quadrangle is a dovecot or pigeon-house, and little gardens are attached to every cottage. Nothing can be prettier or neater than the general appearance of these Homes; and the bright happy faces of the children tell more plainly than words can do that they are well cared for and well treated. In fact, after a month or two in the Home, the faces of even the dullest and stupidest-looking children show a marked improvement. It is said that the demand for servants from the Homes average a thousand in a year, while the supply can never reach a hundred. The average death-rate of all the children in the several Homes is under one per cent.

The whole of the large sum collected annually by Dr. Barnardo is expended on the children, their clothing, education, and maintenance; and some of the ladies in charge of the Homes give their services gratuitously from love of the work. All the Homes have been erected by private donors, individually or collectively. It is said that the sums collected amount to over £40,000 yearly.

Prizes are distributed annually to a large number of former occupants of these Homes who, by their industry and good conduct, may have retained their situations with credit, after leaving the institution, for a number of years. At a meeting held at Exeter Hall for the above purpose in June, 1883, presided over by Earl Cairns, it was stated that during the preceding year 4,100 boys and girls had enjoyed the advantages of the Homes and institutions connected with them. A new Home, the "Leopold," had been opened during the year, and a Servants' Free Registry added. A scheme had been elaborated for sending 100 boys and 100 girls to the Colonies — emigration being the best possible mode of completing the rescue of many of those who have been trained in the Homes. One of the supporters of the Homes, having purchased 1,000 acres of land in one of the Midland counties, had offered to take 100 boys to train as agriculturists. The income of the year, it was announced, had been £45,136, a considerable increase over the most prosperous of previous years.

The old "Maypole" public-house here has been popular in its time with East London holiday-makers, on account of its proximity to the spot whereon formerly grew the famous Fairlop Oak; but it is open to question whether the worthy host was justified in placing in his bar the following couplet:—

"My liquor's good, my measure's just;
Excuse me, sirs, I cannot trust."

The Fairlop Oak stood about a mile to the east of the "Maypole," on ground which now forms part of the Crown Farm. It has been noticed as not a little singular that the survey of the Board of Agriculture makes no mention of this oak in its list of particular trees in the county.

Mr. Coller, writing of the forest in his "History of Essex" (1861), observes :—"The parts of it about Leyton and Woodford are pleasant airing-grounds for the inhabitants of eastern London on holidays, to whom it is a luxury to breathe the fresh air of a real forest. Doubtless it is a special delight for the fair labourers in the factories of fashion to escape from their prison-houses, and, as a wag has sung—

oak, and of the scenes enacted beneath its spreading branches :—

> " Deep in the forest's dreary tracts,
>   Where ranged at large fierce Waltham blacks ;
>   Where passengers with wild affright,
>   Shrunk from the terrors of the night,

there stood that pride of Hainault Forest, the Fairlop Oak, which for so many years overshadowed with its verdant foliage the thousands who

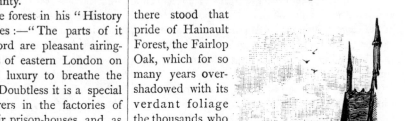

DR. BARNARDO'S HOMES.

> " ' Like Robin Hood, to feel themselves the free,
>   And draw their *beaux* beneath the greenwood tree.'

Even in this respect, however, the popularity of the forest has fallen off since excursion trains have stood at all the outlets of London, ready to whirl the parties further countryward, though the rabble rout that burlesques the grandeur of the old royal hunting party is still to be heard in the forest on Easter Monday. Fair and bright, too, have been the days of forest life under the Fairlop oak, which stood near Great Ilford." Not only, however, as we have already shown,* has the Epping Hunt become a thing of the past, but both the Fairlop Oak and the saturnalia which for a century or so were known as Fairlop Fair have now altogether disappeared.

A writer in the *Literary Chronicle* for 1823 gives us the following particulars of this celebrated

crowded under it, and the antiquity of which the tradition of the country traces half-way up to the Christian era. This vegetable wonder, which was rough and fluted, measured at three feet from the ground about thirty-six feet in girth, and the shade of its branches was proportionally large.

" Under this oak a fair was long annually held on the first Friday in July, which was founded by one Daniel Day, a block and pump maker, of Wapping, commonly called *Good* Day, who died on the 19th of July, 1767, aged 84. Mr. Day was the proprietor of a small estate in Essex, at a short distance from Fairlop Oak. To this venerable tree he used, on the first Friday in July, to repair, having previously invited a party of his neighbours to accompany him, and here, under the shade of its thickest branches and leaves, the party dined on beans and bacon. For many years Mr. Day continued annually to visit this favourite tree ; and attracting public curiosity to the spot, a sort of

* See *ante*, p. 443.

fair was established, which caused a great circula-tion of money, and introduced that kind of civilisa-tion which is the sure concomitant of commerce in a part of the country which had for ages been wild, dangerous, and almost unexplored.   In addition to the entertainment given to his friends, Mr. Day never failed, on the day of the fair, to provide several sacks of beans, with a proportionate quantity of bacon, which he distributed from the trunk of the tree to the persons there assembled.

was applied to the extremities of its decaying branches, to one of which was affixed a board with this inscription :—' All good foresters are requested not to hurt this old tree, a plaster having lately been applied to its wounds.'

"But these precautions were insufficient to protect it from thoughtless visitors, who would make a fire within the cavities to cook their provisions ; and in the month of June, 1805, the tree was thus set on fire, and continued burning until the

FAIRLOP OAK, 1800.

"For several years before the death of the benevolent, though eccentric, founder of this fair and public bean-feast, the pump and block makers of Wapping, to the number of thirty or forty, went annually to the fair in a boat made, like an Indian canoe, of one piece of timber.   The amphibious vehicle was covered with an awning, mounted on a carriage, and drawn by six post-horses, the whole being adorned with ribands, flags, and streamers, and furnished with a band of musicians.

"The oak, so long the great object of attraction, after having endured the fury of the whirlwind and the tempests of ages, at length fell, sub-dued by Time ; for ' what will not Time subdue?' About twenty years ago the tree was fenced round with a close paling, and Mr. Forsyth's composition

following day, by which the trunk was considerably injured, and some of the principal branches wholly destroyed ; but though thus mutilated, ' the stately ruin yet still wonder gained,' and might then have been apostrophised in the language of the poet :—

" ' Thou wert a bauble once, a cup and ball,
    Which babes might play with ; and the thievish jay,
    Seeking her food, with ease might have purloin'd
    The auburn net that held thee, swallowing down
    Thy yet close-folded latitude of boughs.
Time was when, sitting on thy leaf, a fly
Could shake thee to thy roots, and time has been
When tempests could not.
Time made thee what thou wert—king of the woods ;
And time hath made thee what thou art—a cave
For fowls to roost in.'

"The high winds of February, 1820, however,

stretched its massy trunk and limbs on that turf which it had for so many ages overshadowed with its verdant foliage; and thus it exhibited a melancholy memento of the irresistible power of time to bring to an end not only the flower of a season, but the towering growth of many ages.

" But, although the oak is gone, and the only remains of it, we believe, are to be found in the neighbouring church of Wanstead, where the pulpit has been made of a part of it, yet the fair is still held regularly, and is a place of great resort to the inhabitants of London, who flock in crowds, and, forming gipsy parties, spend the day. But the poet Gay must describe the scene :—

" ' Here pedlars' stalls with glitt'ring toys are laid,
     And various fairings of the country maid.
     Long silken laces hang upon the twine,
     And rows of pins and amber bracelets shine.
     Here the tight bass-knives, combs, and scissors spies,
     And looks on thimbles with designing eyes.
     The mountebank now treads the stage, and sells
     His pills, his balsams, and his ague-spells ;
     Now o'er and o'er the nimble tumbler springs,
     And on the rope the vent'rous maiden swings.
     Jack Pudding, in his party-coloured jacket,
     Tosses the glove, and jokes at ev'ry packet ;
     Here raree shows are seen and Punch's feats,
     And pockets pick'd in crowds, and various cheats.' "

The pulpit of St. Pancras Church, in the Euston Road, it may be added, was also made from the wood of this famous oak.*

The author of a *brochure*, entitled " Fairlop and its Founder," printed in 1847, varies the account of the origin of the fair with a few additional details. He writes :—" When entire, the oak is said to have had a girth of thirty-six feet, and to have had seventeen branches, each as large as an ordinary tree of its species. . . . Far back in the last century, there lived an estimable block and pump maker in Wapping, Daniel Day by name, but generally known by the quaint appellative of *Good Day*. Haunting a small rural retreat which he had acquired in Essex, not far from Fairlop, Mr. Day became deeply interested in the grand old tree above described, and began a practice of resorting to it on the first Friday in July, in order to eat a rustic dinner with a few friends under its branches. His dinner was composed of the good old English fare, beans and bacon, which he never changed, and which no guest ever complained of. Indeed, beans and bacon became identified with the festival, and it would have been an interference with many hallowed associations to make any change, or even

addition. By-and-bye, the neighbours caught Mr. Day's spirit, and came in multitudes to join in his festivities. As a necessary consequence, trafficking people came to sell refreshments on the spot: afterwards commerce in hard and soft wares found its way thither; shows and tumbling followed : in short, a regular fair was at last concentrated around Fairlop Oak . . . . . Mr. Day had thus the satisfaction of introducing the appearances of civilisation in a district which had heretofore been chiefly noted as a haunt of banditti.

" Fun of this kind, like fame, naturally gathers force as it goes along. We learn that for some years before the death of Mr. Day, which took place in 1767, the pump and block makers of Wapping, to the amount of thirty or forty, used to come each first Friday in July to the Fairlop beans-and-bacon feast, seated in a boat formed of a single piece of wood, and mounted upon wheels, covered with an awning, and drawn by six horses. As they went, accompanied by a band of musicians, it may be readily supposed how the country-people would flock round, attend, and stare at their anomalous vehicle, as it hurled madly along the way to the forest. A local poet, who had been one of the company, gives us just a faint hint of the feelings connected with this journey :—

" ' O'er land our vessel bent its course,
     Guarded by troops of foot and horse ;
     Our anchors they were all a-peak,
     Our crew were baling from each leak.
     On Stratford Bridge it made me quiver,
     Lest they should spill us in the river.

" The founder of the Fairlop feast was remarkable for benevolence and a few innocent eccentricities. He was never married, but bestowed as much kindness upon the children of a sister as he could have spent upon his own. He had a female servant, a widow, who had been eight-and-twenty years with him. As she had in life loved two things especially, her wedding-ring and her tea, he caused her to be buried with the former on her finger, and a pound of tea in each hand—the latter circumstance being the more remarkable as he himself disliked tea, and made no use of it. He had a number of little aversions, but no resentments. It changed the usual composed and amiable expression of his countenance to hear of any one going to law. He literally every day relieved the poor at his gate. He often lent sums of money to deserving persons without any charge for interest. When he had attained a considerable age, the Fairlop oak lost one of its branches. Accepting the fact as an omen of his own approaching end, he caused the detached limb of the tree to be fashioned

---

* See " Old and New London," Vol. V., p. 353.

into a coffin for himself, and this convenience he took care to *try*, lest it should prove too short. By his request his body was borne in its coffin to Barking Churchyard by water in a boat."

Gilpin, in his "Remarks on Forest Scenery," written in the last century, describes the branches of Fairlop oak as "overspreading an area nearly 300 feet in circumference. About a yard from the ground," he adds, "where its rough fluted stem is thirty-six feet in circumference, it divides into eleven vast arms ; yet not in the horizontal manner of an oak, but rather in that of a beech." In his day it had "suffered greatly from the depredations of time." In 1805, as stated above, it lost some of its greater branches, and was otherwise considerably injured by a gipsy party, who had kindled a fire in too close proximity to its aged trunk ; and although considerable care was afterwards taken to preserve it, the work of decay went on gradually, until, in the month of February, 1820, the "grand old oak" was blown down in a violent gale. The fall of the tree, however, did not put a stop to the "fair," notwithstanding that it was popularly supposed to have been held "by charter, under the shadow of the great oak." Even when the power of holding it was supposed to have been taken away by the Disafforesting Act in 1852, so firm a hold had the idea of celebrating Fairlop Fair taken on the minds of the East Londoners, that they still hovered round its site for their annual "outing" for some three or four years, until the ground was actually enclosed. Mr. Thorne, in his "Environs of London," says that "even now (1876), on the 'first Friday in July,' the block-makers of Wapping visit Barking Side in their ships, drawn by six horses, and after skirting the scenes of their old revels, dine at the 'Maypole,' or one of the neighbouring inns. A sort of

fair continues to be held on the unenclosed waste, but it is a fragmentary, disreputable mockery . . . It may be noticed," he adds, "as illustrating the tenacity with which the memory of Fairlop is held, that the London Foresters named the lifeboat which they presented to the Lifeboat Society in 1865 'The Fairlop.'" Indeed, down to within the last few years Fairlop Fair, on the first Friday in July, was a favourite Cockney holiday-making, and almost as celebrated at the east end of London as the Epping Hunt used to be at Eastertide. The open space of ground whereon the old tree once flourished was on this one particular day in the year crowded by company of every description.

"Lord, what a group the motley scene discloses !
  False wits, false wives, false virgins, and false spouses."

Aldborough (or Aldbury) Hatch is a small hamlet and ecclesiastical district of Barking. It lies about two miles north-east of Ilford, and is a straggling little place, with a population of about 500. The church, a small Gothic structure, was opened about the year 1863. Here, on the verge of the old forest (as implied by the name), is a dreary level district, lately disafforested, and largely built over with straight roads and middle-class dwellings. It is a woodland district simply spoiled.

Morant, in his "History of Essex," says that the place was called Aldbury Hatch, as "denoting an old seat near a hatch, or low gate, belonging to the forest." According to Lysons, a mansion stood here at the beginning of the present century. There are other places in this neighbourhood bearing the same affix to the name, as Pilgrims' Hatch, Howe Hatch, &c., all of which mark the entrances at former times to the once great Forest of Waltham, just as Colney Hatch* has reference to a side entrance to the Royal Chase of Enfield.

CHAPTER LIII.

ILFORD.

"There rolls the deep where grew the tree.
  O Earth! what changes hast thou seen!
  There, where the long street roars hath been
  The stillness of the central sea."—TENNYSON.

Chadwell Heath—Chadwell Street—The Old Coach Road—Will Kemp's Dance from London to Norwich—Great Ilford—Census Returns— Etymology—The River Roding—Ilford Church—Public Reading-Room and Library, &c.—Ilford Hospital—Cranbrook House—Valentines—Discovery of an Ancient Stone Coffin—Elephants in Essex.

MAKING our way southward, by a winding country lane, past Hatch Farm, towards the main road which runs east and west through the heart of the county of Essex from Colchester, Chelmsford, and Romford, through Ilford and Stratford to London,

we leave on our left the uninteresting locality of Chadwell, and the outlying hamlets of Padnall and Great and Little Newberies. Chadwell Heath is intersected by the London road, about two miles west of Romford. In the last century it was perhaps as dangerous for the solitary wayfarer as Hounslow Heath or Finchley Common, being in those days much infested by highwaymen. The road across the heath is now dotted with a few commonplace cottages and a roadside inn, whilst a windmill or two, at a short distance off from the main road, imparts a picturesque variety to what might otherwise be a very dull and monotonous scene. There is also a station here on the Great Eastern Railway. By the side of the high road, at the eastern end of the heath, stands Whalebone House, so called from two large whalebones which grace the entrance to its grounds. These bones have long been objects of curiosity to passers-by, being fixed in a conspicuous position by the road-side. They are said to have belonged to a whale caught in the Thames, and placed here in memory of Oliver Cromwell, it having been taken the same year in which he died. Their original length was twenty-eight feet.

A little to the west of the heath is another cluster of houses, of a similar character to those which we have just left, and known as Chadwell Street. The inhabitants of both these hamlets depend chiefly upon agriculture for their means of livelihood. One row by the roadside has been occupied for generations by a colony of poor Irish. Chadwell Heath is a hamlet of the parish of Dagenham, whilst Chadwell Street forms part of Barking. In the fields round about here, and also in the neighbourhood of Ilford, Stratford, and other suburban parts in this locality, oxen were largely used till lately by the farmers for draught and for ploughing, instead of horses, as in most other counties.

The road from Chadwell Street to Ilford runs almost in a straight line westward, passing between broad stretches of meadow and tillage lands, which have not been obliterated by the "demon of bricks and mortar." The coaches and waggons on this road in the good old days before railways were invented were quite a sight just before Christmas and New Year's Day. A wag writes to Sir Harry Bunbury :—

"Can you, dear sir, a man of taste,
Revive old whimsies gone and past?
And fie! for shame, without reproach,
Stuff as you do the Bury coach.
With strange old kindness send me presents
Of partridges and dainty pheasants?"

Along this road the Earl of Oxford and Lord Robert Dudley conducted the Duke of Finland in state from Colchester to London when he came as a suitor for the hand of Queen Elizabeth, soon after her accession.

Along this road, too, Will Kemp danced his frolic dance for a bet, from London to Norwich, in 1600. He writes :—"Many good fellows being there (at Stratford and Langton) met, and knowing how well I loved the sport, had prepared a bear-baiting ; but so unreasonable were the multitudes of people that I could only hear the bear roar and the dogs howl ; therefore, forward I went with my hey-de-gaies to Ilford, when I again rested, and was by the people of the town and country thereabout very well welcomed, being offered carouses in the great spoon, one whole draught being able at that time to have drawn my little wit dry ; but being afraid of the old proverb, 'He hath need of a long spoon that sups with the devil,' I soberly gave my boon companions the slip."*

The "great spoon" at Ilford would appear, from a marginal note in the original narrative, to have been no spoon at all, but a jug holding above a quart.

Ilford, or rather, Great Ilford—for there is a distinct village known as Little Ilford, some three-quarters of a mile off to the south-west—is situated between six and seven miles from Whitechapel Church, and has a station close to the town, on the Colchester line of the Great Eastern Railway. It forms a "ward" of Barking parish, and is described in the "British Traveller," in 1791, as "a small village, where there are some agreeable houses." Since that time, however, the little village has grown into a town almost equalling in population that of the mother parish, from which, for ecclesiastical purposes, it has become separated, and constituted a district parish. The population of Great Ilford, according to the census of 1871, was close upon 3,700, a number which, during the next decennial period had swelled up to 4,400.

In the Domesday Survey the name of the place is entered as *Ilefort*. As the River Roding here crosses the road close by the western end of the village, there can be little doubt that the name of Ilford was derived from that circumstance ; but it is doubtful whether the ford was of such a dangerous character as to be called an "*ill* ford," as Morant suggests ; it is far more possible, as Lysons supposes, that in the Saxon times it was known as the " eald (old) ford."

The Roding, or Roden, rises near Easton Park, not far from Dunmow, and flows in a southerly direction past Chipping Ongar, Kelvedon Hatch, Navestock, Loughton, and Chigwell, to Woodford Bridge, and so, past Ilford and Barking, into the Thames. After passing Ongar, its banks are low

* See Kemp's "Nine Days' Wonder," performed in a dance from London to Norwich. (Camden Society.)

and rather marshy, and from Ilford and Barking its course is protected by artificial embankments. Under the name of Barking Creek, it is navigable up to Ilford, and doubtless in former days it was in this part of its course a "creek" rather than a river. Its entire course is a little over thirty-five miles.

The district through which this river winds its course north of Ongar is collectively styled "the Rothings," or "Roodings," and its inhabitants are thought by the rest of the county to be very dull. Hence they say of a stupid fellow, all over Essex, that he "comes from the Roothings." The stream takes its rise a little to the south of the village of Great Camfield, whence it passes through the green meadows of several villages, which derive their names from their position on or near the river. These are : High Rothing, Aythorp Rothing, Leaden Rothing, White Rothing (West), Margaret Rothing (East), Abbot's Rothing, and Rothing Beauchamp. Rothing Berners and Rothing Morrell are also named from this river. We have already made the acquaintance of the Roding at Woodford.* There are large corn-mills and wharves by the side of the river at Ilford, and some extensive lime-works and brick-fields not far distant; but the High Street is a dull and unthrifty-looking place, with a mouldering air about it.

The "Red Lion" and "Angel" were great posting-houses in former times, but their "occupation is gone ;" notwithstanding that the town has a quieter appearance than it had in the old coaching-days, before the formation of the railway, much of its prosperity is doubtless derived from the navigation of the Roding up to this point from its junction with the Thames.

In 1830, Great Ilford, Barking Side, Aldborough Hatch, Chadwell Street, and a portion of Hainault Forest, were formed into a separate parish by the Ecclesiastical Commissioners, the combined district being now known as the Vicarage of Great Ilford; but this is for ecclesiastical purposes only. As we have already shown, a sub-division was made in 1841 on the north side of Ilford, the ecclesiastical district of Barking Side being formed, which was followed in 1863 by that of Aldborough Hatch.

The church of Great Ilford, dedicated to St. Mary, was built in 1830, and enlarged in 1866. It is constructed of brick, a poor specimen of the Early English style, and consists of an apsidal chancel, nave, aisles, western porch, and a tower and spire. The last named portion, which contains a clock and six bells, as we learn from Kelly's "Directory of Essex," was erected in 1866,

to the memory of Mr. J. Davis, of Cranbrook Park, and his wife, by their children. The pulpit, of carved stone, also a memorial of Mr. Davis, was erected by subscriptions. The chancel windows are stained, and were inserted in memory of Mr. Davis by the magistrates of the Petty Sessions, of which that gentleman had been chairman for many years. Five other windows are also filled with painted glass, in memory of some members of the family of Thompson, of this parish.

A reading-room and lecture-hall for the benefit of the working-classes, and also a drill-hall for the use of the volunteers, were erected by the late Miss E. Thompson. The reading-room has a library attached to it.

On the south side of the road stands Ilford Hospital, dedicated to St. Mary and St. Thomas the Martyr, an institution founded by Adeliza, Abbess of Barking in the reign of Stephen, for a prior, chaplain, and thirteen poor brethren, or lepers. It was endowed with the tithes of part of Barking parish, and strict statutes for its *régime* were drawn up by Stratford, Bishop of London, in 1346. At the Reformation its revenues were valued at £16 annually. Queen Elizabeth granted these tithes and the site to the Fanshawes, by whom it was converted into an almshouse for six poor men, with a chaplain to perform Divine service in the chapel. Each inmate receives the sum of £2 11s. annually, and the salary of the chaplain was fixed at £14 a year. The estate is now vested in the Marquis of Salisbury, who is the master of this semi-ecclesiastical establishment, and who pays the yearly stipends. The hospital occupies three sides of a small quadrangle ; the apartments of the pensioners are situated on the east and west sides, the chapel being between them, on the south. The chapel appears to date from the fifteenth century ; it is a long and narrow structure, 100 feet by 20 feet, and was the only place of worship for the inhabitants of Great Ilford before the erection of the new church. In the garden court is an ancient well.

About half a mile northward from the village is Cranbrook Park, a large old-fashioned mansion, but in parts modernised and improved, in accordance with the tastes of the present day. It was the seat of Sir Charles Montague, who died in 1625, and whose monument we shall see on reaching Barking Church. It contains a noble suite of rooms overlooking the garden front.

Valentines,* which adjoins the above estate on the north, was built towards the end of the seven-

* See *ante*, p. 458.

teenth or beginning of the eighteenth century by Mr. James Chadwick, son-in-law of Archbishop Tillotson, and is now the seat of Dr. C. M. Ingleby, whose name is so well known as a Shaksperian scholar. In the house is some fine carving by Grinling Gibbons. The mansion was enlarged and the grounds improved by Mr. Robert Surman, who purchased the estate from the family of the Raymonds, baronets. Gilpin, in his "Forest Scenery," speaks of a remarkable grape-vine here, which would seem

and about eight feet high. A walk in the grounds, between two rows of yew-trees that seem to have long seen their best days, and which form an avenue like those in the gardens of Trinity College, Oxford, is known as Bishop's Walk : it was doubtless so called in honour of Tillotson. Having been in early days curate of Cheshunt, and afterwards the occupant of a country house at Edmonton, Tillotson must have been familiar with the forest lands of the north-east of London, and

VALENTINES, NEAR ILFORD.

almost to have rivalled the famous vine at Hampton Court,* of which, indeed, it is often said to be the parent stem. It was of the Hamburg sort, and was planted in a hot-house in the garden in 1758, and produced from three hundredweight to four hundred and a quarter of fruit annually. The profits on the grapes in some years have been supposed to amount to £300. It has, however, been dead for many years past, and looks like a withered gate-post, but it has thrown out from the root a strong rod which still bears fine grapes. Mention is also made of a fine tulip-tree planted here, which was upwards of four feet and a quarter in girth,

doubtless was a frequent visitor at his son-in-law's quiet home, after his warm debates with Papists and Calvinists. This estate has long been celebrated for its trees and gardens, the latter being rich in evergreens. The grounds include a lake about nine acres in extent, formed by damming up a brook that trickles down from what once was the forest.

Lysons states that "in a field behind Valentines a stone coffin, containing a human skeleton, was found in the year 1724;" and that "in the same field was discovered, in 1746, an urn of coarse earth, filled with burnt bones." These remains were, no doubt, Roman, but they do not seem to have been preserved.

The great Roman encampment at Uphall, now a

* See *ante*, p. 170.

farm, is in the Ilford ward ; but as it lies nearer to the town of Barking, we shall deal with it under that heading.

A large quantity of remains of elephants, and of other animals belonging to a Pleistocene epoch, have from time to time been dug up here and in the neighbourhood. The Ilford brick-fields, by the London road, and also at Uphall, have become classic ground with geologists, in consequence of the large number of these remains which have been gether from various parts of the county. "In this collection," observes Mr. Clarke, in his "History of Walthamstow," "there are fossil bones of the hyæna, hippopotamus, and other large animals, and many tusks and teeth of the mammoth—an animal of the size of which we may form some idea when we consider that the head alone has been found to weigh 400 lbs. There have also been found embedded in the London clay, which extends to, and forms part of the soil of, Walthamstow, organic re-

ILFORD HOSPITAL.

found in them. They occur chiefly in the lower brick-earth, underlying what is called the Thames Valley gravels, and comprise not merely elephants, but several other species of mammalia, among them being the rhinoceros, the bear, tiger, wolf, bison, great stag, ox, horse, and beaver. Mr. Phillips, in his "Geology of the Valley of the Thames," says that the place of these deposits in time is probably "somewhere between that of the late pre-glacial and early post-glacial ages, when the levels of the country were different from what they are at present."

Mr. J. Brown, F.G.S., of Stanway, a well-known geologist of Essex, formed a very extensive collection of fossils and organic remains, brought to-

mains of the crocodile and turtle, together with various specimens of vegetable remains, and among them some tropical plants . . . At Ilford, in 1812, while digging for brick-earth, the bones and teeth of huge elephants, differing from those of Asia and Africa, identical with the Siberian mammoth, were found ; and the teeth and tusks of the hippopotamus, and bones of the rhinoceros and of large oxen, have also been found there. The remnants of these giants of ancient days have enriched various geological museums." The magnificent collection of Pleistocene mammalia formed by Sir Antonio Brady, and which found its way into the British Museum, was formed almost exclusively from the Ilford pits.

Mr. Manley Hopkins, in an interesting article on this subject in *Once a Week* (1860, Vol. III., p. 53), writes :—" To 'those who understand their epoch,' it is a result of exceeding interest to have witnessed a great science grow in their own life of forty years, from stammering childhood to adolescence : to have seen almost the first uncertain beams of geology struggling in the morning sky, and then, from hour to hour, pouring in a flood of accumulating facts, and classifying them into a marvellous system. Persons born since the commencement of the present century remember geology in its pre-scientific condition, and will recall with a thoughtful smile the detached fact, the isolated mineral specimen, or remarkable local formation which first drew their attention to the subject.

" The long, grey, old church of West Ham, which stands half a mile river-ward of Stratford, contained in years past some objects likely to attract the wandering eyes of a child during a sermon. The great silken colours of the West Ham Volunteers hung dustily and discoloured below the tall chancel arch. Below them, an elaborate lion and unicorn, the size of cubs, smiled ferociously on the preacher as he passed between them to his elevated pulpit ; and at the east of the church, leaning against an altar-tomb, two immense bones rested— one being a shoulder-blade, three feet in length, and the other a rib—concerning which relics the inquirer was shortly answered that they were *mammoth bones.* The spark of interest thus kindled in our own breast towards osteology might have easily died out again, had it not been followed, some two-and-thirty years ago, by a neighbour presenting to our youthful collection of curiosities a few pieces of fossilated ivory, exhumed at Ilford, in a spot where the ground had been opened for brick-making. Many persons visited the *diggings* daily ; but until lately, when an enlightened curiosity has been established, the discoveries ceased to command attention ; and doubtless great numbers of mammoth relics have been found, and then lost for ever. During the last two years, however, greater care has been taken. The proprietor of the brick-field gave to a gentleman in the neighbourhood, much devoted to geology, full powers over all the animal remains discovered, and—what was of the highest importance—left orders that his workmen should notify to Mr. Brady their having come across any bones. Thus he was enabled to examine them *in situ,* and to prevent in a great measure their injury or destruction. In this one field (and there are two other brick-fields near it) the remains of at least eight elephants have been brought to light. A short account of their discovery was read by Mr.

Brady at a meeting of the British Association at Aberdeen, in September, 1859. The bones of the elephant (*Elephas primigenius*) are found associated with those of the rhinoceros, the Irish elk, the horse, and the ox. An immense tusk was discovered fourteen feet below the level of the soil, to see which, before it was disturbed, Sir Charles Lyell and other eminent geologists were invited. The tusk was deficient of both extremities, but the portion rescued was nine feet long, and of great thickness. Since that time a bone of enormous thickness, belonging to a whale, has been extracted.

" The geological position of these relics is the Pleistocene, or latest tertiary formation. The vein in which they occur varies from five to six feet in thickness, and consists of sandy gravel. It underlies the band of brick-earth already mentioned, into which some of the bones intrude, and thus attract the notice of the brick-makers. Above the brick-earth is the extensive and valuable bed of scarlet gravel for which this part of Essex is celebrated. This bed, with the vegetable mould which covers it in, is from four to six feet in depth at Ilford. In other spots the gravel has been worked as deep as twenty feet. Beneath all is the great deposit of the London clay.

" Though the excavations at Ilford have been singularly productive in the discovery of animal remains, it is not to be understood that they exist in that site only. In other parts of Essex, and also in Middlesex, coming within the basin of the Thames, similar bones have been brought to light. Remains of the elephant have been met with at Grays, at Harwich, at Erith, at Brentford, at Kingsland, and, within a few months past, at Charing Cross. At Erith the lion and hyæna, and at Grays the bear, add the carnivora order to the list of animals given above.

" A view of the circumstances leads to the plausible conjecture that, in its main features, the configuration of land and water was the same when these herds of strangely-associated animals lived as it is now. The estuary of the Thames probably ran up farther inland, and the waters of the river, before they had cut themselves deep channels, and before the hand of man was at work to confine them within useful limits, spread widely in marsh and morass, till they touched the feet of the hills in Kent and Essex . . . It must always be remembered, in the case of the Essex deposits we have described, that they are in the *drift*—a name at once suggestive of the washing together, or other transportation of rocks and organisms, which may previously have been scattered, and distant from each other. Indeed, where carnivora abound, the weaker kinds among the other orders must necessarily disappear. To meet with traces of their association in one place would indicate a disturbance either of the surface on which they dwelt or of their very natures. We can hardly conceive of 'a happy and united family' upon so grand a scale, and without the restraints of a cage or a keeper."

It is remarkable that along with these traces of the elephant and the mammoth there are no vestiges whatever of man or of his works; so that, in all probability these huge beasts lived here in a wide and lonely forest, which in a comparatively recent age was submerged, and became in course of time, first an arm of the sea, and ultimately a riverside plain, as we see it now.

CHAPTER LIV.

LITTLE ILFORD, WEST HAM, ETC.

"Miratur portas strepitumque et strata viarum."—VIRG. *Æn.* I.

Boundaries and Extent of Little Ilford—Census Returns—The Parish Church— Mr. Lethieullier's House at Aldersbrook—Ilford Gaol—The "Three Rabbits"—West Ham—Its Division into Wards—Population—Market and Fairs—Chemical Works and Factories—The Parish Church—A Curious Fresco—Upton Park—Forest Gate—Taverns and "Tea-Gardens"—Emmanuel Church— St. James's Church—Extent and Population of Forest Gate—Pawnbrokers' Almshouses—Legg's Almshouses—Former Condition of Stratford—The Abbey of Stratford-Langthorne—Pumping Station of the Metropolitan Drainage Works—St. John's Church—Christ Church—St. Paul's—St. Francis of Assisi—Congregational Church—Town Hall—Stratford New Town—Vegetable Market—Old Ford—Bow Bridge—Roman Roads.

LITTLE ILFORD, which nearly adjoins its great sister south-west, is a quiet, out-of-the-way village. The River Roding, winding its way through fields and market-gardens, forms its boundary on the east, separating it from the parish of Barking. On the south and west lie East Ham and Stratford, whilst to the north the parish stretches away to Wanstead, and includes within its boundary in that direction the City of London and Manor Park Cemeteries, the former covering upwards of 250 acres, and the latter about 45 acres. They are both neatly laid out, and planted with trees and evergreens of the ordinary type.

In 1871 Little Ilford had a population of 675, which during the next decade had become nearly 1,000.

The church, which hides itself in a grove of elms and chestnuts, and is dedicated to the Virgin Mary, is poor and uninteresting. It is built of brick, and consists of chancel, nave, north chapel, and bell-turret. From the frequent coats of plaster it is impossible to make out the date of its erection, but two of the windows at the west end of the nave are as early as the Norman era, and may, indeed, be Anglo-Saxon. Among the monuments preserved from the old church is one on the north wall of the chancel to William Waldegrave, who died in 1610, and his wife, who died in 1595; it comprises coloured effigies of the deceased, with kneeling figures of their three sons and four daughters. There is a brass to Thomas, son of Sir John Heron, private secretary to Henry VIII. He died at Aldersbrook, in this parish, in 1517. Another brass

records Anne, only daughter of Barnard Hyde, of London, who died in 1630, and her brother William, who died in 1614. One of these brasses represents a lady in a ruff of the Jacobean type, and also includes a baby in swaddling clothes. Two more brasses, long buried under the floor, were discovered in 1883, by the Vicar, the Rev. Arthur Shadwell, a son of the late Vice-Chancellor Sir Lancelot Shadwell. There are also monuments to the Fry family, formerly residents, and well known for their philanthropy; also to the Lethieulliers, a family whose name occupied a high position in Essex in the last century. One of these latter monuments—to be seen in a sort of chapel on the north side of the nave—commemorates the learned antiquarian whose writings we have had occasion to quote in describing this neighbourhood. The inscription runs as follows:—"In memory of Smart Lethieullier, Esq., a gentleman of polite literature and elegant taste, an encourager of art and ingenious artists, a studious promoter of literary inquiries, a companion and a friend of learned men; industriously versed in the science of antiquity, and richly possessed of the curious productions of nature, but who modestly desired no other inscription on his tomb than what he had made the rule of his life—to do justly, to love mercy, and to walk humbly with his God. He was born Nov. 3rd, 1701, and died without issue Aug. 27th, 1760."

This Mr. Lethieullier lived for some years at Aldersbrook, a manor-house in this parish. He is said to have much improved the grounds, in which he built a small "hermitage," as a shrine for many of the antiquities that he had collected in his travels. This structure, however, was pulled down, together with the manor-house, by Sir James Tylney Long, who purchased the property a few years after the death of Mr. Lethieullier, and built a farm-house on the site of the old mansion.

Ilford Gaol, or House of Detention for the county of Essex, a large brick building, was erected on the north side of the London and Romford road, about fifty years ago. It has lately been pulled down, and its site covered with cottages, the only prison in the county being at Springfield Hill, near Chelmsford, and the prisoners from this district being conveyed to the metropolitan prison.

Lysons, in his "Environs of London," says that in the parishes of Ilford, East Ham, West Ham, Leyton, and Wanstead, on the level part of Epping Forest—that is, on Wanstead Flats—"a great mart for cattle brought from Wales, Scotland, and the north of England, is held annually, from the latter end of February till the beginning of May. The business between the dealers," he adds, "is principally transacted at the sign of the 'Rabbits,' on the high road, in Little Ilford parish." This "mart," whatever it may have been towards the end of the last century, when Lysons wrote, has long been done away. The "Three Rabbits," however, is still a favourite "house of call" for graziers and cattle-dealers of Essex on their way to and from London.

West Ham is a very extensive parish, stretching from Wanstead and Leyton in the north to the Thames in the south, and from Little Ilford and East Ham in the east to the river Lea in the west. It is divided into three "wards," namely, Church Street, Stratford, and Plaistow. This division has reference chiefly to secular matters; for ecclesiastical purposes it is divided into several districts. The population of the entire parish in 1871 was 62,900, and that of Church Street, or West Ham proper, 7,900; but such has been the rapid extension of building in the parish since then that these numbers have more than doubled. In the middle of the last century West Ham and the low-lying district surrounding it was largely inhabited by merchants and wealthy citizens of London; but the mansions which they occupied have mostly disappeared, or been so altered to convert them to other purposes that they are scarcely distinguishable. In an official return made in 1762, the number of houses in West Ham parish was stated to be 700, of which by far the larger proportion were entered as "mansions." In Morant's "History of Essex," written about six years later, this place is described as "the residence of several considerable merchants, dealers, and industrious artists." Even at the beginning of the present century the number of the inhabitants of the parish did not amount to 6,500, the number of houses being about 1,100.

West Ham formerly had a market, the charter for which was procured, in the middle of the thirteenth century, by Richard de Montfichet, whose ancestor, William de Montfichet, founded an abbey at Stratford-Langthorne, in this parish, endowing it with the manor of West Ham and other estates. An annual fair of four days' duration was granted at the same time, but both have fallen into desuetude for many years. Much of the prosperity of West Ham and its adjoining townships is due to the formation of the Victoria and Albert Docks at Plaistow, the construction of the railway-works at Stratford, and the establishment within the bounds of the parish of extensive chemical works, flour-mills, smelting and copper works, shipbuilding establishments, and other large works and factories, where employment is given to thousands of hands.

The parish church of West Ham, dedicated to All Saints, occupies a central position in what would formerly have been called the village, and about half-way between the main road at Stratford and Plaistow. It is a large building of brick and stone, partly ancient and partly modern, and principally of Perpendicular architecture. It consists of a chancel, with north and south aisles, nave and aisles, and an embattled tower at the western end. The church contains the monuments of several eminent persons who have been buried here, including Sir Thomas Foote, Bart., Lord Mayor of London in 1650, who died in 1688; Henry Ketelby, who held a law office under the Crown in the reign of Henry VIII., and other members of his family are also commemorated. Robert Rook, who died in 1485, has an altar-tomb in the north chapel, with figures of himself and family. Sir James Smyth, sometime Lord Mayor of London, who died in 1706, has an elaborate monument.

In 1844 a large mural painting was discovered in this church, but after a brief exposure, was again covered with lime-wash. An anonymous pamphlet was published at the time, purporting to give a description of the picture; but, as Mr. H. W. King observed at a meeting of the Archæological Institute in November, 1865, the writer evidently did not understand the subject, and was unacquainted with Christian iconography, therefore his account was inaccurate and of no archæological value. "The renovation of the interior of the church in September, 1865," remarked Mr King, "afforded a favourable opportunity for endeavouring to disclose the picture anew, and under the super-intendence of the Rev. R. N. Clutterbuck, of Plaistow, it was successfully developed, though apparently in a less perfect condition than when exposed in 1844. Its situation was upon the eastern part of the wall of the north clerestory, and it extended as far as the second pendant of the roof, measuring eight feet in width by five in height. It does not appear that more than this was visible when previously exposed; but, from some heads which were found on the south side of the chancel arch, it seems clear that this is only one wing of the subject, which probably extended over the east wall of the nave, and to an equal distance on the north and south sides. The whole subject undoubtedly represented the ' Final Doom of Mankind.' Upon the east wall was doubtless depicted our Lord as Judge. The right wing, which remained, represented the ' Reward of the Righteous,' and the left the ' Condemnation of the Wicked,' but not a trace of the latter could be discovered. Was this a forecast of the theology of to-day?

The picture upon the north wall, representing the ' Resurrection of the Just,' was executed not in distemper, but in oil colours, on very rough plastering, and covered also part of the stones of the arch; in one place, where a beam of the aisle-roof comes through the wall, it was continued upon the surface afforded by its section. It appears to be the work of the latter part of the fifteenth century, and was of inferior, though some-what elaborate, execution. The upper part of the painting, extending as high as the wall-plate, and forming a background to the whole, was richly grouped, though rudely executed, tabernacle work, chiefly white shaded with grey, the windows and crochets strongly outlined in black; and some of the windows were coloured red. From the general treatment, it seems clear that this tabernacle work is a conventional representation of the Heavenly Jerusalem. In the niches were several celestials, each wearing a circlet, with a small cross over the forehead, and among them two of the heavenly choir playing upon gitterns. At the lower part of the painting, below the basement of the canopy, were two angels raising the righteous by the hand. They seem to have issued through the portcullised gates behind them. There are two of these gates at the lower part of the picture, besides that in the upper part of the canopy, into which one of the blessed is entering. From one of them the angels who are assisting the risen seem themselves to have issued, and to be leading the righteous into the other. The risen saints were grouped along the line of the arch in that crowded manner usual, as Mr. Clutterbuck remarks, with mediæval lim-ners. They are singularly irregular in size, the largest being placed just over the crown of the arch, and diminishing as they approached the caps of the columns. All were nude, with their hands either joined in prayer or extended as if in ad-miration. Among the group were two eccle-siastics with red mitres, and a cardinal with a red hat.

The writer of the pamphlet above referred to also noted a figure with a beard, which is supposed to represent a ' monk, friar, or priest,' and a royal personage wearing a crown of gold. The two angels mentioned as raising the blessed were larger than the other figures, and in pretty good preservation : their faces painted with care, and not without dignity. They were vested in white albs, without cincture or apparels. Close to the angle of the wall, where the painting was much mutilated, three demons were visible ; one seemed to be falling headlong, as if to denote the abortive malice of the evil spirits unable to hurt the re-deemed, now placed beyond their power. It appeared to the author of the pamphlet that the lower one had a person in his arms, as if bearing him away, with an expression of malicious pleasure in his countenance. The writer also conceived that he saw in this part of the picture the represen-tation of flames in which others were tormented, which he supposed to be ' the suburbs of Hell.' If such existed, it might possibly have represented Purgatory, but it was not apparent either to Mr. Clutterbuck or myself. ' The Doom of the Lost' was no doubt depicted upon the opposite wall, upon the left hand of the Judge, and there was but the least possible space upon the north side for the introduction of any other portion of the Judgment scene. Since I offered a brief unpre-meditated description of this painting at the meeting of the Institute, the Rev. R. N. Clutter-buck has kindly placed in my hands the memoir which he has prepared for the Journal of the Essex Archæological Society ; and in the present report I have, with his permission, availed myself of his more detailed observations. As the picture was very imperfect, and wholly unintelligible except to those who could read it by a scaffold, Mr. Clutterbuck observes that he could not suggest any sufficient reason for its preservation, all the rest of the plastering having, moreover, to be removed, for the purpose of pointing the inner masonry. There were indications that the whole interior of the church had been freely polychromed in distemper, but only one small portion of diapered pattern of late date could be copied. We are indebted solely to the exertions of Mr. Clutterbuck for the development of this interesting example of mural decoration."*

In the churchyard lies buried a distinguished naturalist, Mr. George Edwards, F.R.S., who was born at Stratford in 1693, and died at Plaistow in 1773. He became celebrated for his knowledge of natural history, more especially with regard to birds; and besides various papers in the "Philosophical Transactions," he published seven large quarto

Richard Jebb, who was some time physician-in-ordinary to George III., who conferred upon him a baronetcy.*

West Ham is well off for charitable institutions. Near the church are almshouses for twenty poor women, each of whom receive a small sum of money weekly. Roger Harris's Almshouses, in Gift Lane, provide homes for six others ; and there are also numerous bequests to the poor of the parish, amounting in the aggregate to about £450 per annum, left from time to time by various

WEST HAM CHURCH.

volumes on subjects in natural history, upwards of 600 of which, it is said, had never before been described. Here, too, is the tomb of James Anderson, LL.D., the editor of "The Bee," and author of several papers on agricultural and industrial subjects.

Dr. George Gregory, author of the "Economy of Nature," a "Dictionary of Arts and Sciences," and a translation of Bishop Lowth's "Lectures on the Sacred Poetry of the Hebrews," was vicar here from 1804 till his death, in 1808.

Dr. Samuel Jebb, a noted physician in his day, author of several professional works, and editor of the works of Aristotle and Bacon, was baptised in West Ham Church, in 1729, and lived in the parish for many years. He was the father of Dr.

benefactors, whose gifts are distributed by a local charity board. In West Ham Lane is the West Ham, Stratford, and South Essex Dispensary, erected in 1878, on a site given by Mrs. Curtis.

The Congregationalists, Unitarians, Wesleyans, and other Nonconformist bodies, have chapels here, and there are several schools.

The hamlet of Upton lies about a mile to the north-east of West Ham Church, its northern extremity bordering on the London road. Here are one or two interesting old houses, notably the "Cedars," formerly known as Upton Lane House. It was for many years the residence of Mrs. Elizabeth Fry, the prison reformer, sister of the late Mr. Samuel Gurney, the equally well-known philanthropist, who lived at Upton Park, close by. His residence, called Ham House, was taken down a few years after his death, which occurred in 1856. The park, comprising about eighty acres, lies between Ham Lane and Upton Lane, and formerly belonged to Dr. Fothergill, by whom the gardens were laid out ; it still contains many trees which he first introduced to this country in the early part of the last century. Shortly after the house was demolished an offer was made to purchase the park for building purposes ; but, fortunately, this proposal was met by another to secure it as a public park and recreation-ground for the poor of this rapidly-increasing locality. Mr. John Gurney, the grandson of Mr. Samuel Gurney, accepted the latter proposition, and offered it for that purpose for the same sum that had been named by the building society, namely, £25,000, the Gurney family at once contributing £10,000 towards that amount. The Corporation of London also voted £10,000, and the remainder having been made up by local subscriptions, the park—under the new name of West Ham Park—was formally opened by the Lord Mayor on the 20th July, 1874, and has since proved an inestimable boon to the neigh. bourhood. The cost of maintaining the park and gardens is entirely defrayed by the Corporation of London.

Forest Gate, a rising and populous hamlet of West Ham, lies to the north of the London road, and stretches away to Wanstead Flats. It has a station on the Colchester line of the Great Eastern Railway, near the entrances to the Manor Park and Ilford Cemeteries. Near the railway-station is the " Eagle and Child " tavern, and not far distant is the " Spotted Dog " ; each has " tea-gardens " and

WEST HAM PARK.

pleasure-grounds attached, and both are well-known resorts for East-end holiday-folk.

A district, embracing parts of Upton and East Ham, was formed into a separate parish for ecclesiastical purposes in 1852. The principal church of the district, dedicated to Emmanuel, stands at the corner of Upton Lane, in the main road. It was built by Sir Gilbert Scott, but has since been enlarged ; it is of Gothic design, and consists of chancel, nave, aisles, and central bell-turret. St. James's Church, built in 1881, is a pseudo-Gothic structure of the most simple kind. The district contains two or three temporary iron churches, besides several chapels for different denominations of Dissenters. The Jews' Cemetery, and also the West Ham Cemetery, are in this district.

The area covered by the district of Forest Gate, although only 8oo acres in extent, comprises a population of more than 20,000, or nearly treble of what it was ten years ago.

In Woodgrange Road are the Pawnbrokers' Almshouses, which were founded in 1849 by the Pawnbrokers' Charitable Institution—they provide homes for seven couples; whilst Legg's Almshouses, in Forest Lane, founded in 1858 by one Jabez Legg, of Stratford, afford homes to six poor women.

West Ham, although third in point of size of the nine parishes comprised in the Hundred of Becontree, is by far the most densely populated. "West Ham," writes Mr. Coller in 1861, in his "History of Essex," "from its traffic, trade, and importance the capital of the Hundred, is the most thickly-peopled parish in Essex, more than doubling the whole population of some of the smaller Hundreds in the county. It has, in fact, become a busy suburb of the metropolis, which has rubbed off its once rural character. Its little hamlets have grown into large towns. Fields over which the plough passed a quarter of a century ago are covered with workshops and teeming factories. On its river bank have risen up the largest ship-building works in the world. Its quiet creek and marsh land have been converted into mighty docks, furnishing a haven and a home for commerce from all countries of the earth. Its pleasant spots, on the edge of business, but just beyond reach of the sound of the hammer and wheel, and the wearying hum of the London hive, are studded over with handsome residences."

We touched so lightly upon Stratford in OLD AND NEW LONDON,* that there is ample opportunity for a further description. This place is described in the "British Traveller," 1771, as "formerly a small village, but now greatly increased by a vast number of additional buildings. It stands," he adds, "in the parish of West Ham, and is only parted from Bow in Middlesex by the river Lea, over which there is a bridge." This is the celebrated Bow Bridge, said to have been the first stone bridge built in England. †

It is amusing to read in the work above quoted:— "Many of the rich citizens of London have fine houses in Stratford and its neighbourhood, it being particularly convenient for such as live eastward of the Royal Exchange. Almost all the lands in the neighbourhood are either let out to gardeners or improved in the culture of potatoes. Vast quantities of all kinds of roots, herbs, and greens, are daily sent hence to the London markets; and upon the whole the place is in a very thriving condition, having many good inns, with other places of public entertainment. If the new buildings from Mile End to Bow, and from thence to Stratford, are continued, both these places will be, as it were, joined to London." What would the writer have said if he could have looked forward a century, to see a population of 30,000 covering the market gardens, and the place "joined to London" literally by railways, tramcars, and omnibuses.

The Abbey of Stratford-Langthorne stood on the marshes, a little to the west of West Ham. The pumping-station of the northern system of the Metropolitan Main Drainage Works at Abbey Mills occupies part of the site, whilst a few fragments of the old monastery may with difficulty be traced in the walls of the "Adam and Eve" public-house, close by. The abbey itself was founded about the year 1135 by William de Montfitchett for brethren of the Cistercian order, and was dedicated to the Virgin Mary and All Saints. It was richly endowed by its founder, who gave it all his lordship here. In the days of its splendour it possessed 1,500 acres of land in this parish, with the manors of West Ham, Wood-Grange, East Ham, and Plaiz (now Plaistow); thirteen manors in other parts of the county, besides lands in other counties. The abbey grounds and gardens covered sixteen acres, and were enclosed by a moat; but at that time no scientific improvements had been made in the way of drainage, and the consequence was that the waters of the Lea occasionally invaded the sacred precincts of the monks. On one occasion they were actually driven away by the floods, and were compelled to seek refuge on their property at Billericay, some miles off.

The story is thus told by Leland :—

" This house, first sett amonge the lowe marshes, was after with sore fludes defacyd, and removed to a celle or graunge longinge to it called Burgestide, in Essex, a mile from Billirica. These monks remained in Burgestide untyll entrete was made that they might have sum helpe otherwyse. Then one of Richards, kings of Englande, tooke the ground and abbey of Strateforde into his protection, and recdifienge it, brought the foresayd monks agayne to Strateforde, where among the marshes they re-inhabytyd."

Thus re-established, the abbey seems to have gone on prosperously, and to have taken a leading position among the religious houses in the kingdom, many high personages resorting to it. In 1307 the abbot was summoned to Parliament; in 1335, John de Bohun, Earl of Hereford and Essex, High Constable of England, was buried within its precincts; and the Countess of Salisbury, whom the remorseless Henry VIII. caused to be beheaded in her old age on a charge of high treason, appears to have resided in the abbey about the time of its dissolution, at which period its revenues were valued at £652 3s. 1¼d. Its possessions were subsequently granted to Sir Peter Mewtis, or Meautis, who had been Ambassador to the Court of France. The building itself, like many of these religious edifices, was allowed to fall into decay when the monks had been expelled. Early in the seventeenth century a descendant of Sir Peter alienated "the site of the abbey, with the abbey mills and 240 acres of land," to Sir John Nulls, and since that period the property has passed through many different hands.

In the "Beauties of England," published in 1803, Mr. Britton writes:—"The chief remains of the monastic buildings now standing are a brick gateway, which was formerly the entrance to the conventual precincts, and an ornamental arch, which appears to have been the entrance to the chapel." Lysons, writing a few years previously, observes:—"The foundations of the convent were dug up and removed by the present proprietor, in doing which, no antiquities worthy of note were found, except a small onyx seal, with the impress of a griffin, set in silver, on which is the following legend: '*Nuncio vobis gaudium et salutem*,' perhaps the priory seal of one of the abbots." The "brick gateway" and the "ornamented arch" have now disappeared from the scene. Indeed, the obliteration of the abbey has been so complete that we cannot even record of it, in the words of the poet, that—

"The sacred tapers' lights are gone,
Grey moss has clad the altar stone,
The holy image is o'erthrown,
    The bell has ceased to toll;

The long-ribbed aisles are burst and shrunk,
The holy shrine to ruin sunk,
Departed is the pious monk:
    God's blessing on his soul."

With the exception of a few that may have been worked into the walls of some of the neighbouring houses, it would be difficult for the most diligent searcher to discover a stone of the once important abbey of Stratford-Langthorne.

The pumping-station in connection with the northern sewer of metropolitan main drainage at Abbey Mills covers about seven acres of the ground once covered by Stratford Abbey. The sewer itself enters the parish at Old Ford, and crosses the West Ham Marshes by a grass-covered embankment. It afterwards traverses Plaistow, and then passes eastward in a straight line through East Ham, on its way to the outlet into the Thames, at the mouth of the Roding at Barking Reach. The works at Abbey Mills are of great capacity, comprising sixteen pumps, worked by steam-engines of immense power, their combined force being capable of lifting some 15,000 cubic feet of sewage per minute from the low-level sewer, and forcing it through large iron cylinders into the outfall sewer. The buildings, which are mostly of brick, are of an ornamental character, two octagonal chimney-shafts, each more than 200 feet high, being conspicuous for miles round.

The ecclesiastical parish of St. John was formed in 1844 from the mother parish of West Ham. The church, a handsome building in the Early English style, had been built about ten years previously. It stands in the middle of the town, at the point where the main road from the east of London diverges towards Romford and Leytonstone.

Christ Church was formed into an ecclesiastical parish in 1852 out of the parish of West Ham. The church, which stands in the High Street, close by the Main Drainage Works, is built of stone in the Decorated style, and is conspicuous by its tall spire.

St. Paul's Church, in the Maryland Road, Stratford New Town, dates its erection from 1865, when the district was carved out of the mother parish, and converted into a separate ecclesiastical parish.

The Roman Catholic Church of St. Francis of Assisi, in Grove Crescent Road, was built in 1868, and is in the Italian style of architecture. Near it is a Congregational Church, also of Italian design, but erected in a much larger and more costly manner.

The Town Hall, in the Broadway, at the corner of West Ham Lane, is a large and handsome building, of Italian design, opened in 1869. The façade towards the Broadway consists of a portico of two stages, formed with columns of polished red granite. To the right of the main front is a tower 100 feet high; the building itself is surmounted with statues of Science, Art, Commerce, Britannia, St. George, &c. Stratford is included in the Local Board district of West Ham.

Stratford New Town may be said to owe its existence to the Great Eastern Railway, the two main branches of which, leading respectively to Cambridge and Colchester, diverge at this point.

Here, about the year 1847, the company established its chief depôt for carriages, engines, and rolling stock, and yards for their repairs. Employment is here given to about 3,000 hands.

A market for the sale of vegetables, fruit, &c., has been established, adjoining Stratford Bridge Station, by the Great Eastern Railway Company, warehouses and sidings being constructed for the development of the trade.

In the olden days, when a pilgrimage to the image of "Our Ladye of Berkynge" was thought conducive to the health of the soul, a procession of courtly equipages was no unfrequent sight on the dull road leading through Whitechapel into Essex and the other eastern counties, though now almost wholly abandoned to farmers, graziers, and butchers. For example, the Princess Maud, after she had become the consort of King Henry I., would often strive to keep alive the flame of that piety which, as a child, she had imbibed in the convent of Romsey, by going on this pilgrimage at Eastertide or Whitsuntide.

At this period the river Lea was crossed by the pilgrims and other travellers at the Old Ford, as the place is still called, but the inconvenience and danger of wading through so considerable a river induced the royal devotee to turn the road to a more convenient part of the stream, where she erected Bow Bridge, which is said to have been the finest example of pontine architecture then in the kingdom, and of which, as well as of its successor, an account will be found in OLD AND NEW LONDON.*

The name of Stratford evidently points to the existence near this spot of a ford, which doubtless connected London with the old Roman street or road (*stratum*) to Camelodunum, whether that was at Maldon or, as is more probable, at Colchester. At Old Ford have been found several sarcophagi of a plain description, with flat covers. They are fully described, and some of them are engraved, in the third volume of the "Transactions of the London and Middlesex Archæological Society;" whilst in a lane at Stratford, called Blind Lane, between Old Ford and Leyton, were dug up about the middle of the last century a large Roman urn and fragments of pottery, confirming the derivation of Stratford from the Latin *stratum*.

The line of communication anterior to the erection of Bow Bridge was, in the opinion of Dr. Stukeley, who wrote very largely—and sometimes very fancifully—upon the Roman remains in this country, by a road extending from Chichester

to Dunwich, in Suffolk, which, having crossed the Watling Street at Tyburn, passed along Old Street, north of the city, continued forward to Colchester, following as nearly as possible the course of the high Essex road of the present day. The same author also informs us that "when the Romans enlarged the city, and enclosed it by a new wall, they also made a branch from St. Giles's, which is now called Holborn, built a gate at Newgate, and continued the road to Cheapside." This line of communication was continued east of the city; and Maitland, in his "History of London," describes it to be the "Roman vicinal way through Aldgate by Bethnal Green, to the trajectus or ferry at Old Ferry," where it, no doubt, joined the *Via Icenaia* described by Dr. Stukeley. From this it would appear that the great Roman road into Essex crossed the river Lea by means of a ferry at Old Ford, in which direction it continued for many centuries after the Romans left this island, or, in fact, until the erection of a bridge at Bow.

Morant, in his "History of Essex," has particularly noticed these roads, as also the circumstances which led to the erection of the bridge. "The ancient road from this county to London was by Old Ford, that is, through the ford there without a bridge; but that passage being difficult and dangerous, and many persons losing their lives or being thoroughly wetted, which happened to be the case of Maud, Queen Consort of King Henry I., she turned the road from Old Ford to the place where it now is, between Stratford, Bow, and West Ham, and caused also the bridges and causeway to be built and made at her own charge."

In the Itinerary of Antoninus, two of the great Roman roads are stated to have passed through Essex. One of these followed very nearly the track of the present highway through Stratford and Ilford, and some remnants of what appear to have been parts of its banks are, or were till recently, visible at West Ham, and again near Ingatestone, this conclusion being strengthened by the fact that this road was made long prior to the fixing of boundaries of the ancient forest on that side.

The native Britons, as readers of ancient history know, suffered severely under their Roman masters, large bodies of them being forced to work in making causeways across marsh lands, cutting down woods, draining morasses, and embanking the Thames with river walls. Campbell writes thus of the Roman roads in England, Vol. II., p. 250 :— "The commodious communication between the several parts of a country by means of roads, causeways where necessary, and bridges over intervening rivers, is of general convenience to the inhabitants, a constant source of opulence, and a signal proof of sound policy. The Romans were distinguished by their attention to the straightness, solidity, and admirable disposition of their larger and their lesser roads, which, though used for other purposes, were chiefly intended for military ways; and this wise economy of theirs was carried through all the provinces of their extensive empire. It is, however, remarkable that scarce in any of the countries they possessed there are still remaining more authentic monuments of these useful and stupendous works than in Great Britain, which, with indefatigable pains and most extensive learning, have been studiously traced, accurately described, and the stations on them, with as much certainty as might be pointed out by our industrious and laborious antiquaries.

"The Roman roads, while yet in a great measure entire, appeared of such amazing grandeur and solidity, manifested such a wonderful sagacity in the design, and such prodigious labour and expense in the execution, that it is no wonder, in the barbarous ages succeeding to the ruin of that empire, we find these noble and stately works confidently ascribed to giants and art magic. The intention of these military ways was worthy of the genius, and expressive of the policy, of that wise and potent people. They were so many links or lines uniting the provinces to the seat of empire.

"They extended, therefore, from Rome to the limits (however remote) of her dominions. To form some idea of them, the shortest and surest method is to consult the Pentingerian Tables. It is evident from hence that they were very numerous, and the certainty of this is confirmed by the remains which are still to be seen in many countries. In our own, as Camden observes, they are most visible, or, in other words, best preserved, and the manner of their construction (by which they have lasted more than twelve centuries) most apparent in wild heaths, over which they were carried, because near towns and villages they were pulled to pieces for the materials. In the 'Itinerary' ascribed to Antoninus there are fifteen roads, with the stations marked upon them, and the distances between them in miles, which, taken all together, make a total of two thousand five hundred and seventy-nine miles, the construction of which must have necessarily consumed much time, required much toil, and demanded immense treasures."

The Saxons, on becoming masters of the south of England, showed their appreciation of the use and value of the roads bequeathed to them by their predecessors, the Romans. The Danes, however, wreaked their vengeance on them as well as on the churches, and after the Norman Conquest, when trade and commerce were at a low ebb, they fell into disrepute, and were allowed to be gradually destroyed, especially in the neighbourhood of towns, where their materials were made of use for building purposes.

CHAPTER LV.

PLAISTOW AND EAST HAM.

"Upon a fertile spot of land
Does Plaistow, thriving Plaistow, stand."

Flat and unattractive Appearance of Plaistow—Its Sedate Aspect in Former Times—Its Sources of Wealth—The Destitute Children's Home—The Metropolitan Main Drainage Works—Census Returns—Silver Town, Canning Town, and Hall Ville—Plaistow Church—St. Andrew's Church —Congregational Church—East London Cemetery—Poplar Small-pox and Fever Hospital—Chemical Works and other Manufactories—The Royal Victoria and Albert Docks—North Woolwich—St. Mark's Church—St. John's Church—North Woolwich Gardens—Distinguished Residents at Plaistow—Descent of the Manor of East Ham—St. Nicholas's Roman Catholic School—A Curious Manorial Custom—Situation and Extent of the Parish—The Parish Church—Emmanuel Church—St. John the Baptist—Plashet House—Greenstreet House—Anne Boleyn's Tower—St. Edward's Reformatory—The High Level Sewer—Beckton Gas and Coke Works.

THOUGH level and dull, this locality has inspired the poets; at all events, there is extant a poem of eight pages, "In Praise of Plaistow"—from which the motto of this chapter is extracted—printed anonymously, without the author's name, place, or date, about the middle of the last century. At that time the land hereabouts was to a great extent unencumbered by houses, and no doubt highly productive, from an agricultural point of view. Potatoes would seem to have been the chief product of the soil, whilst the grass-land in the marshes served for the fattening of sheep.

"Potatoes now are Plaistow's pride,
Whole markets now are hence supplied;
Nor finer mutton can you spend
Than what our fattening marshes send." *

Plaistow, as shown in the preceding chapter, is a "ward" of the parish of West Ham, and the place is passed over in the "British Traveller"

---

* White's "Eastern Counties," Vol. II., p. 299.

(1771) with the curt remark that it "contains several genteel houses." These houses were occupied mostly by wealthy citizens and merchants of London, among whom were the Howards, the Gurneys, and the Sturges. Altogether, the village in those days must have worn a very sedate appearance. There was no church in the hamlet, but there was a Friends' meeting house and a Congregational chapel. The former now serves the purposes of a School Board school, and the latter has been adapted to business purposes.

The huge sewer of the Metropolitan Main Drainage Works passes through the village, and is then carried over the level market-gardens and meadow-land south-east to its outfall at Barking Creek. From a little, straggling, obscure village of "genteel houses," Plaistow has grown to be the larger ward of West Ham parish; and the population, which a century ago amounted to but a few hundreds, may now be reckoned by thousands, the combined districts of Plaistow (proper), Canning Town, and Silver Town, containing rather more

The Victoria Docks, and the large manufactories and centres of industry of Canning Town, Silver Town, and Hall Ville—all of which places lie southward of the village of Plaistow—have absorbed the greater part of the marsh-land and market-gardens between it and the Thames. Since the introduction of these works into the neighbourhood, the whole aspect of the locality has changed. Most of the old mansions have been either pulled down, cut up into tenements, or converted to other uses than those for which they were built. One antiquated building in the Broadway, formerly known as the "great house," or Broadway House, is now a "Destitute Children's Home;" it was established in 1872, is supported by voluntary contributions, and provides a home for sixty outcasts.

than 67,000 inhabitants, or more than double the number when the census was taken in 1871. Silver Town is the name given to the district that has sprung up around Mr. Silver's India-rubber Clothing Works at North Woolwich; and Canning Town and Hall Ville are also named after the principal employers of labour in their respective districts. The most thickly-populated parts are in the neighbourhood of the docks. The London and Tilbury Railway Company have two stations here, and the North Woolwich branch of the Great Eastern line has a station in the Barking Road, Canning Town.

Plaistow was constituted an ecclesiastical parish, formed out of the mother parish of West Ham, in 1844. The church, which was erected a few years previously, is a small brick building of Gothic design, consisting of chancel, nave, and aisles, and containing a monument to the late Sir John Henry Pelly. The first Sir John Pelly, a friend of Sir Robert Peel, who died in 1852, was the owner of the manor of East Ham Burnels. He was also a Governor of the Hudson's Bay Company, and for some time Governor of the Bank of England. Pelly Road, in this parish, is, of course, named after him.

The works and manufactories which have added so largely to the growth of this neighbourhood of late years cover an immense space of marshland, which had been used principally for grazing purposes. These various branches of industry comprise chemical, creosoting, artificial manure, and other works ; but the most important sources of employment in this district are the docks and the various places of business adjoining connected with the shipping.

ANNE BOLEYN'S CASTLE.   (*See page* 515.)

St Andrew's Church, in St. Andrew's Road, was built in 1870, and is a spacious and lofty edifice in the Early English style.

The various bodies of Nonconformists are well supplied with chapels, one of the most imposing being the Congregational Church in Balaam Street. There are several schools in the district; and on the west side of the village, covering between forty and fifty acres of ground, is the East London Cemetery, which was opened in 1871.

The Poplar Small-pox and Fever Hospital, in the Southern Road, is among the most recent additions to the public institutions of Plaistow. It was erected in 1880, and consists of three large blocks of brick buildings, with accommodation for about one hundred patients.

The Victoria Docks, which cover an area of about 200 acres, are situated at a short distance eastward of Bow Creek, or the entrance of the river Lee. These docks were formed in 1855 ; they contain upwards of a mile of wharfage and quay frontage, and are under the management of the London and St. Katharine's Dock Company. They are fitted with all the most recently invented appliances for loading and unloading vessels, whilst its basins are capable of accommodating the largest-sized vessels that come into the port of London. The entrance-lock is 320 feet long and 80 feet wide, and has a depth on the sill of 28 feet at high water. The hydraulic lift dock, which has long been worked here, is an ingenious contrivance for the dry-docking of vessels. It is thus described in the *Globe Encyclopædia*:—" On two parallel sides of a channel, 300 feet long and 60 feet broad, sixteen upright cast-iron columns, in a row, are sunk in the ground. At the base of each column there is a hydraulic press, and the top of each piston or ram carries a cross-head, from the ends of which two iron girders are suspended by iron bars. These girders extend across the excavation to the cross-head of the corresponding column on the opposite side. There are thus thirty-two girders, forming a kind of platform capable of being raised or lowered. On this platform rests a wrought-iron pontoon, open at the top, having sufficient buoyancy to support a vessel. To apply the apparatus, the girders and pontoon, weighted with water, are sunk to the bottom of the lift, and the vessel to be raised is drawn in directly over the centre of the pontoon. The rams are then slowly raised by hydraulic power, the vessel being at the same time secured by wedges and blocks. When out of the water, the pontoon is emptied by valves, which are afterwards closed. The girders being again lowered, the pontoon, with the vessel upon it, remains afloat, and may be towed to a convenient spot. As many vessels as there are pontoons can be docked in a similar manner."

In cutting through a peat bog in the formation of the Victoria Docks there were found a large quantity of hazel, yew, oak, nuts, and other vegetable remains, more or less fossilised. The late Sir Antonio Brady, by whom this discovery was noticed at the meeting of the British Association in 1859, afterwards came into possession of the huge bones of a large whale, which had been dug out of this peat bog at a depth of fourteen feet below the surface of the soil, together with a very perfect millstone, about twenty-two inches in diameter, and a brass dish, " clearly indicating," as Sir Antonio observed, " that the marsh, wherein now dwell thousands of human beings, had been formed in the historic period."

In 1880 an extension of the Victoria Docks eastward was opened, the combined docks being named the Royal Victoria and Albert Docks. By this addition the quays of London have been brought three miles and a half lower down the river than they had hitherto extended, and great ocean steamships have been enabled to avoid the dangerous and expensive towage to Blackwall. The Albert Docks help to separate the heavy goods traffic from the lighter trade of the Thames ; they are not merely a luggage siding, but afford a direct route for reaching the Victoria Docks. A line of railway extends the whole length of the docks. There are three stations : so that from Fenchurch Street and Liverpool Street, as termini, and from several junctions, travellers can be conveyed to the river gates of the docks. The quays are intersected and connected everywhere by railways for moving coal, iron, and other merchandise. The land for the docks was bought in 1864. It was at first intended to form merely a canal, to avoid Woolwich Reach ; but instead of a mere channel, a basin was cut nearly 500 feet wide, more than a mile long, and flanked by large sheds for receiving and warehousing goods. The combined docks are two miles and three-quarters long, with a water area of 175 acres, and about seven miles of quays. The entrance for vessels is at the point where the river, at the mouth of Galleon's Reach, widens into a lake, and affords ample room for the larger ships to manœuvre in.

The entrance lock is 500 feet long, by 80 feet wide, and has four pairs of wrought-iron gates. The depth of water at the sills is thirty feet at Trinity high water. Beyond the lock is a porch, or entrance basin, of about twelve acres, where passenger ships take their living freights on board. A passage 300 feet long and 80 feet wide, spanned by a swing-bridge, leads thence into the main dock, which is about a mile and a quarter long, and has a uniform width of 490 feet. The walls of the dock are about forty feet high, five feet thick at the top, and nineteen feet at the base. The sheds for the reception of goods are respectively 360 feet long by 120 feet broad. The sides and roof are constructed of corrugated iron. On the north side alone these sheds are sixteen in number. The hydraulic cranes, for loading and unloading vessels, travel by wheels along the quays. The great main basin of the Albert Dock is connected with the Victoria Dock by a passage 80 feet wide.

The total cost of construction of the Albert Docks was a little more than £1,000,000. A considerable saving in expense in their formation was effected by the use of large blocks of concrete, made chiefly of material dug on the spot, mixed with Portland cement, instead of using bricks, for the walls of the basins. Each leaf of the dock gates weighs 80 tons, making 160 tons for the gates ; but they are adjusted to such a nicety that four men at the windlass can move them, and when they are closed a penknife could not pass between the gate and the sill.

The Albert Dock, like the Victoria, was sunk through peat soil, enriched with the remains of successive growths of forest trees, marshy with water which everywhere showed traces of iron, and containing a few horns of deer and a few relics of pre-historic man. A canoe twenty-seven feet long, found during the excavations, was deposited in the British Museum.

The effect of the construction of the Albert Dock is that the part of the north shore of the Thames which contains North Woolwich and Silvertown is now completely cut through by a straight line of water. The Victoria Dock previously extended nearly half across the isthmus of this peninsula.

An army of 12,000 labourers ply their calling daily in this and the other docks (the St. Katharine, the London, and the Victoria), under the control of the London and St. Katharine's Dock Company. The Victoria and Albert Dock is lighted throughout by electricity, by which means ships can be loaded or unloaded at night in cases of necessity.

North Woolwich, which lies between the Victoria and Albert Docks and the river, and forms the extreme southern point of the peninsula above referred to, belongs really to the county of Kent, although it is surrounded by, and locally within, the county of Essex. The place was formerly included in the ecclesiastical district of St. Mark, Victoria Docks, but in 1877 it was separated into a distinct parish. The church, dedicated to St. John the Evangelist, was built in 1872. Here is a terminus of a branch of the Great Eastern Railway; and close by, skirting the river-side, are North Woolwich Gardens and Royal Hotel. The gardens form a popular resort for holiday-folks from London during the summer. They extend for some distance along the north bank of the Thames, beyond the steamboat pier and railway-station, and at the entrance to the gardens is the large hotel with which they are connected. One of the chief attractions of this place of amusement is its "monster platform" for open-air dancing, with such occasional extra attractions as "barmaid contests," "baby shows," and the like; the gardens, however, have never acquired the celebrity of those of Vauxhall or Cremorne, which to a certain extent they have been designed to imitate.

Besides the personages already mentioned as living at Plaistow, the parish has numbered among its inhabitants one or two other distinguished residents. Here, for instance, lived Aaron Hill, a dramatic writer of some note in the early part of the last century, and here he wrote several of his poems. Here Edmund Burke, who was fond of the country, resided for a short time before buying Gregories, his favourite seat at Beaconsfield, in 1767. Prior, in his "Life of Burke," writes :— "About this time (1759) he occasionally resided at Plaistow, in Essex. A lady, then about fourteen years old, and residing in the neighbourhood, informs me that she perfectly remembers him there. His brother Richard, who found employment in the City, was with him frequently, and both were much noticed in the neighbourhood for their agreeable and sociable qualities. Among their visitors calculated to attract notice in the country are several known as popular authors, and a few as men of rank." Luke Howard, a distinguished Fellow of the Royal Society, and author of an important work on the "Climate of London," lived for many years in a large house in Balaam Street. The house, however, has been much altered since Howard's time.

It may be added that there is another Plaistow, near Bromley, in Kent, about which we shall have to write in another volume.

East Ham, whither we now direct our steps, is —or was till recently—a dreary, outlandish place, of very little or no interest, except, perhaps, to market-gardeners. At a very early period, before the Conquest, East and West Ham formed one parish, and this part of it, which then belonged to the Crown, was given to the Abbey of Westminster—a grant which was confirmed by Edward the Confessor. In the reign of Henry III. the property belonged to the Montfitchets, and early in the fourteenth century it was divided, the easternmost manor—since known by the name of East Ham—being given by John de Lancaster to the abbot and convent of Stratford, in whose hands it remained till the dissolution of monasteries. The Manor House, near the church, was many years ago converted into a farm-house; it now serves the purposes of St. Nicholas's Roman Catholic School.

The parish comprises several hamlets and manors, as Wall End, Plashet, Manor Park, Green Street, and East Ham Burnels. Mr. Coller, in his "History of Essex," tells us that there used to be a tradition current amongst the "homagers" of the different manors to the effect that "the tenants of the manor of East Ham are obliged to treat and entertain the tenants of the other manors of West Ham, West Ham Burnels, and Plaiz, the origin of which custom is said to be this : that when the lord of these manors was taken prisoner in France, and sent to his tenants for relief, the tenants of all the other manors complied, and those of East Ham refused; so that, to punish them for their disobedience, he laid the burthen upon them."

East Ham was originally a long, straggling village, built for the most part along the sides of the cross-road which runs from Little Ilford, in the north, to the Thames, opposite Woolwich, in the south, and intersected by the road to Barking. It is between five and six miles from Whitechapel Church, with which it has a direct communication by the lower road through Poplar, leading to Barking and Grays. There is a station of the Tilbury and Southend Railway on the north side of the village, and the church stands at the south side, nearly two miles distant. East Ham is described in the " British Traveller," in 1771, as "a small, but pleasant, village, situated on an eminence, from which there is a view of the Kentish coast, the whole being extremely rural." For the "eminence" and " the view of the coast " it is feared the writer must have drawn largely upon a lively imagination. The extent of the parish, according to Kelly's " Directory of Essex," is about 2,500 acres ; whilst the population, which in 1871 was a little over 4,300, now amounts to upwards of 9,300.

The church, dedicated to St. Mary Magdalen, is built of flint and stone, very ancient, and in a dilapidated condition. In the "Transactions of the St. Paul's Ecclesiastical Society" for 1882 will be found a detailed account of this little church, certainly a Norman structure. It stands near to what was once the high road ; but it now seems as if the village had deserted it, leaving it as an outlying bulwark against the marshes, which stretch away southwards towards the Thames at Barking. It consists of nave and chancel, without side aisles, and its eastern end is apsidal. In the chancel is a Norman arcade of intersecting arches, carried round continuously, but sadly spoiled and mutilated by pews of the worst type. On the walls are the remains of some good Early English fresco paintings. It is sarcastically remarked that the condition of the entire fabric is such as would delight the Society for the Preservation of Ancient Buildings with its " extreme simplicity, high pews, modern windows, and obstructive gallery—a typical unrestored church ! " The tower is low and massive, with double buttresses at the angles, the lower part being of Norman workmanship and the upper part modern. Most of the windows are modern and uninteresting, but there are traces of Early English windows, now built up. The apsidal sanctuary is lighted by three narrow lancets. In the south wall is a piscina, with a double drain, divided by a column forming two plain pointed arches, between which is a bracket for a lamp. Behind the communion-table is a sumptuous monument of black and white marble to Edmond Nevill, Lord Latimer, and (reputed) seventh Earl of Westmoreland, of that family. The monument comprises life-size effigies of Lord and Lady Lati-

mer, with their seven children, in devotional attitudes. At the back, over some eulogistic verses, is the following inscription :—" In memory of the Right Honorable Edmond Nevill, Lord Lattimer, Earle of Westmerland, and Dame Jane, his wife, with the Memoralls of their 7 children, which Edmond was lineally descended from the honorable blood of Kings and Princes, and the 7th Earle of Westmerland of the name of Nevills." Close by is the following epitaph to a daughter :—

"Upon the Death of the right Vertuous faire Noble Ladie Katherin Nevell, first daughter of Edmond, Earle of Westmerland, and Jane, his wife, who died a Vergine, the fifth of December, 1618, being of the Age of xx3 years.

> " Surviving Marble, choysly keep
>   This noble Virgine Ladye to sleep.
> A Branch, untimely Fal'n away
>   From Nevelles Royallized Tree ;
> Great Westmerland, too deere a Pray
>   For Death, if she could ransomd bee.
>
> " Hir Name was Katherine, not in faine
>   Hir nature held referance,
> Hir Beutie and hir parts againe,
>   Were all compos'd of Excellence.
>
> " Blud, Beuty, Vertue, did contend—
>   All Thies avanc'd in Eminence—
> Which of them could her most commend,
>   When Death, Enamord, tooke her hence.
>
> " Yet Marble tell the time to come,
>   What Erst she was when I am Dumbe."

Edmond Nevill's claim to the earldom of Westmoreland, which terminated in 1570 with the attainder of Charles Nevill, the sixth earl, was expressly disallowed by the Lords Commissioners in 1605. There are two seventeenth century brasses in this church, and in the churchyard lies buried the celebrated antiquary, Dr. Stukeley ; he was interred here in 1765, " in a spot which he had long before fixed on, when on a visit to the Rev. Mr. Sims, the vicar." His grave is not marked by any monument, and the turf, agreeably to Stukeley's own request, was laid smoothly over it.

In 1863 a new church, called Emmanuel, was built near the Barking Road. It is in the Early Decorated style, and was erected from the designs of Mr. A. W. Blomfield. It is constructed of Kentish rag, and is cruciform in plan, with a central square tower, surmounted by a dwarf spire. The church of St. John the Baptist, built in 1866, is also cruciform.

There have been several charitable bequests to the poor of East Ham ; and there are also in the parish almshouses, founded, with property left for the purpose, by Giles Bream, in 1621.

Plashet, a quiet little hamlet of East Ham, is chiefly noticeable for its manor-house—called Plashet House—which, from the early part of the present century, was for many years the residence of Mrs. Fry, the prison philanthropist, whom we have already mentioned in our account of West Ham.* Here she was visited by the King of Prussia and other distinguished personages.

Green Street, about half a mile southward of Plashet, and lying between Ilford Lane and Plaistow, is another hamlet of East Ham. Greenstreet House—commonly called "Anne Boleyn's Castle"—is a large, old red-brick mansion, supposed to occupy the site of the seat of the Nevills, whose tomb we have seen in the East Ham Church. The most conspicuous feature of the building is a tall tower, locally called Anne Boleyn's Tower, from a tradition that that unhappy lady was confined in it. Indeed, there are many legends connected with Anne Boleyn lingering about this fine old house. One is that "the tower was built for her by her royal lover in the days of his courtship; and that here the beautiful Anne sat listening to the wooing of a king, with the parting sigh of the cast-off Catherine still fresh in his ears. The tale, as told by an old writer, is that—'Anne Boleyn was betrothed to a young nobleman, who died. About ten months after his death the king demanded her hand; she, as was the custom, requested to be allowed to complete the twelvemonth of mourning for her lover, to which Henry agreed, and for her amusement built the tower in question, from which she had a fine view of the Thames from Greenwich to below Gravesend.' Further, it is asserted that when the fickle passion of the king—and as fatal as fickle—had been quelled, and the axe was sharpening for the beautiful neck which he had here embraced, the fair victim was confined for a time in this building, whence she was taken to Greenwich, and so on to the Tower. These traditions have been questioned; and the sceptic has pointed to marks about the building evidently of later date than the eighth Henry. These, however, have been accounted for as modern reparations; and it is not improbable that upon these old window-sills Anne Boleyn rested her fair arm while meditating, first upon the sunrise, and then upon the clouded setting, of her greatness. Certainly some of the apartments were at one period fitted up with royal magnificence."† It is stated that a room in the tower was hung with leather richly embossed with gold, but that an avaricious owner of the property

rent this down and burnt it, in order to collect the precious metal.

From the Nevills this property passed to the Holcrofts, and still later to the Garrards. In 1869 the house, together with fourteen acres of land adjoining, was purchased, and converted into St. Edward's Catholic Reformatory School. The house, which has been enlarged, now affords a home for some 200 boys, who are taught agriculture and various useful trades and occupations.

The Metropolitan Northern High Level Sewer crosses the broad expanse of East Ham Level about midway between the church and Beckton Road. The sewer itself, which is of brick in three channels, each nine feet in diameter, is covered in by a high turf-covered embankment. During the excavations for ballast to form this embankment in 1863, about 900 yards west of the church, the workmen came upon what appears to have been a rather extensive Roman cemetery. The remains discovered consisted of leaden coffins, with a sarcophagus of stone, which were disinterred on the high ground abutting on the marshes. Cinerary urns, with other Roman *fictilia*, were found near the coffins, showing that the spot had been used as a place of sepulture by a Roman colony.

East Ham Level was a portion of the estuary of the Thames until the construction of the river wall. Mr. Ynyr Burges, in describing before the Archæological Institute the Roman vestiges which had been discovered here, remarked that the Anglo-Saxons could scarcely have had the ability to carry out so gigantic an operation as the drainage of the marsh, and added that we may reasonably conclude that the undertaking had been achieved by the Romans, who were, as Mr. Burges observed, skilled alike in the arts of peace as in those of war—the Roman general, as a rule, *Idem pacis erat mediusque belli*. A public roadway crosses East Ham Level from the church to North Woolwich, where there is a steam ferry to Woolwich.

A large portion of East Ham Level, between he entrance to the Albert Dock and the River Roding, is occupied by the Beckton Gas Works. These works, which were established in 1869, and cover some 150 acres, have a river frontage of about 1,000 feet, protected by a substantial wall of brick and stone, from which extends an iron pier. The gas is conveyed from these works to the City and West End of London through several miles of tubes. These works, and the buildings to which they have given rise in their immediate neighbourhood, have converted the once dreary waste of East Ham Level into a thriving, if not altogether picturesque and charming, colony.

---

* See *ante*, p. 504.   † Coller's "History of Essex."

ANCIENT BELL TOWER, BARKING ABBEY.

CHAPTER LVI.

BARKING.

"It hath a very ancient and fish-like smell."—The Tempest, Act II., Sc. 2.

Situation and Extent of the Parish—Census Returns—Etymology—Early History and Foundation of Barking Abbey—The Abbey Burnt by the Danes—Rebuilt by King Edgar—William the Conqueror takes up his Abode there—The Importance of the Abbey in Saxon Times—The Convent Damaged by an Overflow of the Thames—Curious Entries of the Revenues of the Abbey - Dissolution of the Abbey—The Abbey Gateway—Extent of the Original Buildings—Noted Abbesses—Manorial Estates of the Abbey—The Parish Church—The Rural Deanery of Barking—The Manor of Barking—The Story of Osborne's Leap—The Manor of Clayhall—Malmains—Bifrons—Eastbury House—The Road to Tilbury—Barking Town—Barking Creek—The Outfall of the Main Drainage Works—Powder Magazine, &c.—The Roman Entrenchment at Uphall.

LITTLE or no romance now attaches to the parish of Barking, though once it was holy ground. It lies at a short distance eastward of the district which we have just explored, on the opposite side of the Roding, which, below the town, before falling into the Thames, widens out into Barking Creek, a great place for small coasters. But more practical interests have superseded the halo of sanctity which once hung around it. Barking is by no means the little fishing village which it was at one time reputed to be, but a town which has been of late years much improved, with good houses and shops, and a population of 8,000, the number of its inhabitants having nearly doubled in the course of the last quarter of a century.

Its name, possibly, is derived from the Anglo-Saxon *beroc*, or *beorce*, "a birch-tree," and *ing*,

"a meadow," denoting a meadow of birch-trees; but more probably a corruption of *Burgh-ing*, "the meadow fortification." This latter presumption seems to be borne out by the fact that an "encampment" is still to be traced of the most extensive dimensions—being more than forty-eight acres in extent—on the north side of the town, and which we shall visit in due course. It may be remarked that the syllable *—ing*, generally as a termination, is very frequent throughout Essex: as Margarett*ing*, *Ing*rave, Mountness*ing*, &c.

As was usually the case with parishes in which large monastic houses stood, Barking was very extensive, being nearly thirty miles round, reaching up to the borders of Hainault Forest, on the north of the Chelmsford Road, and including the hamlets of Ilford, Chadwell, Aldborough Hatch, and Barking Side.* But most of these have been cut off, and erected into separate ecclesiatical districts. The advowson belongs to All Souls College, Oxford, to which it was given by William Pownsett, of Loxford, who had been steward to the last abbess.

It was proposed as far back as 1650 that the parish should be divided into three. The entire parish contains upwards of 12,300 acres, and, according to the census returns for 1881, the population of the whole amounts to nearly 17,000.

London (the founder also of Chertsey), who died here in A.D. 685, and was buried in St. Paul's, where his shrine was one of the chief attractions.*

The abbey was dedicated to the Blessed Virgin, and was of the Benedictine Order. St. Ethelburgha, sister to Erkenwald, was abbess of the convent, where she led an austere life, and where she died in the odour of sanctity in 676. She was succeeded by her sister, Hildelha, who died in 700. Edilburga, wife of Ina, King of the West Saxons, having lived during her widowhood as a nun here,

BARKING CREEK.

Barking is believed to have formed part of the demesne lands of the East Saxon kings ; but little or nothing is known of its early history until the foundation of the abbey, about the year 670, in the reigns of Sebbi and Sighere, kings of the East Saxons ; the founder was a grandson of Uffa, the first Saxon king of the East Angles, and the first bishop who sat in the see of London after the erection of St. Paul's by Ethelbert. This was one of the earliest, as well as largest, of conventual houses near London, and its site must have been chosen, not for its beauty, but its solitude. It owed its foundation to St. Erkenwald, Bishop of

was canonised after her death, as also were two of her successors.

The history of the abbey is briefly told. It was burnt by the Danes, A.D. 870, and, after having lain desolate for a century, was rebuilt by King Edgar, as an offering in satisfaction for an insult offered by him at Wilton to a holy recluse, the same who became Abbess of Barking, and was canonised as St. Wulphilda. Under its Saxon abbesses Barking became one of the sacred spots of England, and Bede gives us, in his "Ecclesiastical History," a long list of the miracles worked within its walls.†

* See *ante*, pp. 490, 495.

* See "Old and New London," Vol. I., p. 236.
† See Chapters VII.—XI.

At the Conquest it was a place of note, and the Conqueror is said to have visited the place on his way to take up his abode at the Tower of London. Here, under the shadow of the venerable abbey church, and within a few miles of the reputed tomb of his rival Harold, William withdrew after his ill-omened coronation; and here he established a Court, which gradually attracted many, if not most, of the nobility of the south of England, thus making it for a time the head-quarters of "rank and fashion"—a strange contrast to the present appearance of the place.

From the gate of Barking Abbey also William is said by historians to have set out on his first royal progress through his newly-conquered kingdom.

Richard of Barking became Abbot of Westminster, Councillor to Henry III., Chief Baron of the Exchequer, and Lord Treasurer of England. He died A.D. 1246, and was buried in his abbey church.

The convent, under Algifa, Queen Maude, Adeliza, and other great Norman ladies, became one of the chief places of education of the daughters of noble families; here was also a school for youths, and amongst the children here brought up were the two sons of Catharine, widow of Henry V. Eleanor, Duchess of Gloucester, after her husband's murder, found a refuge in the Abbey of Barking, and died here A.D. 1399. "On her brass in Westminster Abbey," observes Mr. Thorne, "she is represented as a nun of Barking." In right of their large temporal estates the Abbesses of Barking held a seat in the great council of the kingdom.

It has often been asked whether women ever sat and voted in the Upper House of Parliament. As a step towards the solution of the question, attention may be drawn to the fact that in the Saxon times four abbesses—those of Barking, Wilton, Shaftesbury, and St. Mary's, Winchester—held seats in the Witenagemot, or great council of the kingdom. But whether they voted is not satisfactorily known. It appears that the Abbess of Barking enjoyed precedence above her other sisters.

It would seem that the first blow to the prosperity of the abbey was caused by a breach of the river banks at Dagenham, which flooded its low-lying lands, and caused a "public appeal" for assistance. The "Harleian Manuscripts" tell us that King Richard III. issued a license to the Prior and Convent of the Holy Trinity, in London, to grant the Abbess of Barking an annuity of twenty pounds—which was a large sum in those days—"probably," suggests Mr. Thorne, "to assist her in her efforts to reclaim the drowned lands."

It may show the importance which was attached to this abbey in former times when it is stated that the Church of All Saints, or Allhallows, in Tower Street, had the distinguishing title appended thereto by the Abbess and Convent of Barking, to whom the vicarage originally belonged. King Richard I. added a chapel to the Church of Allhallows–Barking; and Edward I. presented a statue of "Our Lady of Barking" to the treasures of the church.

The abbess possessed thirteen knights' fees and a half, and she held her lands of the king as a barony; and though her sex prevented her from attending the king in the wars, yet she always furnished her quota of men, and had precedence over the abbesses. In her convent she always lived in great state; her household consisted of "chaplains, an esquire, gentlemen, gentlewomen, yeomen, grooms, a clerk, a yeoman cook, a groom cook, a pudding-wife, &c."

The following curious entries from the records of this house, extracted from the Harleian MS., 433, are worth the notice of the antiquarian readers :—

"Maistr. William Talbot hath the psonage of Alhalowes Berking, of London."

"Elizabeth abbess of Berking hath annuyte of xv li. graunted by Docto. Talbot pson of Berking in London, and the same graunt to hir and hir successors is confirmed by the king."

"A licence given to M. Chaderton dean of Berking, and to the chanons there to graunt to Elizabeth abbesse of Berking an annuyte of xv li. to them graunted by yre."

"The pryor and convent of the Holy Trinitie in London have a licence to graunt for ever unto th' abbess of Berking an annuyte of xx li. of al yre lands in London."

The amount of the rents received from several of the above places, as well as the kind of household anciently kept up in this monastery, appears from the following statement preserved among the Cottonian manuscripts and in the *Monasticon*, and which, for its curiosity, we are induced to give at length.

"This is the charthe longynge to the office of the celeresse of the monasterye of Barkinge as hereafter followethe :—

"First she must luke whanne she commethe into here office, what is owynge to the said office, by diverse fermours and rent gedererers, and see that it be paid as soone as she may."

She was then to receive "yerly of the collectore of Werley" at the two feasts of St. Michael and Easter, each 1. s. And of the collectors of the following places the following sums. Bulfanne yearly v l. Mockinge iiii. l. and of the "fermes ther" lx. s. Of the collector of Hockley at the two feasts of Easter and Michælmass x. l. Tollesbury, * * * Wigberewe x. l. Gynge at Stone, xlviii. s. Slapton viii. l. Of the fermour of Lytlyngton xv. l. Uphall "by yere" vi. l. xiii. s. iv. d. Dunneshall lvi. s. viii. d. Wanynges iv. l. x. s. Of the collector of Barkinge "of the rentis and fermes of Barkinge and Dagenham, to the longing to the sayd office, by the yere, xij. l. xviii. s." "Of the chanons of Seynt Powles," a rent of xxii. s. "Of the prior and convent of Seynt Bartholmewes in London," xvij. s. And of John Goldington for a yearly rent of divers tenements at "Seynt Mary Schorehogge," xxii pence. For a tenement in Friday Street yearly xxiii. s. and iiii. d. "but it is not knowen wher it stonds," and "she shuld receive yerly xxx. s. of the rent of Tybourne, but it is not paid."

Then follow the various particulars the cellaress was to provide for the convent.

The Issues of the Larder.—"And also she must be charged with all the orskeyns that she selleth; and of all the inwardes of the oxen; and with all the tallowe that she selleth, coming of hyr oxen: also of every messe of the beyofe that she selleth: and all these be called the yssues of the larder.

The foryn Receyte.—"And also yf she sell oney hey at ony ferme longynge to her office, she must charge her selfe therwith, and it is called a foryn receyte.

"Some totalis of all the said charthe . . . .

Beyinge of Greynys.—"Wher of what parte of the said some sche must purvey yerly for three quarters malte, for the tounes of St. Alburgh, and Cristmasse, eche of them xij. bushell, and than must sche pay to the brewer of each toune xx. d. And then must sche purvy for a quarter and seven bushells of whete fore pitaunce of William Dune, Dame Mawte Loveland, Dame Alys Merton, Dame Mawte the kynges daughter: and for russeaulx in Lenton and to bake with elys on Schere Thursday. And then must sche pay to the baker for bakinge of every pitaunce vi. d. And also sche must purvey for one bushell of greyne beanes for the covent ayenst missomer.

Beying of Store.—"And sche must purvy for xxii. gud oxen by the yere fore covent.

Providence for Advent and Lentten.—"Also sche must purvy for two cadys of heryngs that be rede for the covent in Advent: and for vii cadys of red heryng for the covent in Lenton: and also for three berell of white heringe for the covent in Lentyn: and also sche must purvey for xii. c. lib. almondes for the covents in Lentyn, and for xviii salt fish for the covent in Lentyn; and for xiv. or ellys xv. salt salmones for the said covent in Lentyn: and for three peces and xxiv. l. fyggis: and one pece reysenez for the covent in Lenton. And also for xxviiil. l. ryse for the covent in Lenton; and for viii galons mustard for the covent.

Ruscheaw Sylver.—"And also sche must pay to every lady of the covent, and also to the priorisse, to two celeresse and kechener, for ther doubls, for ther rushew sylver, by xvi. times payable in the yere to every lady, and doubill at eche time ob. but it is paid nowe but at two times that is to say, at Ester and Michelmes: also sche must paye to every lady

of the covent, and to the said foure doubles, to eche lady and double ij. d. for their cripsis and crumkakes alway payd at Shroftyd.

Anniversaryes.—"And also sche must pay for v anniversaries, that is to say, Sir William Vicar, Dame Alys Merton, Dame Mawte the kynge's daughter, Dame Mawte Loveland, and William Dun: and also to purvey for xii gallon good ale for the pittance of William at the day of anniversary.

Offeringes and Wages, and Gyftes of the Selleris.—"And also sche must pay in offryng to two celleresses by yere xii. d. and then shall sche pay to the steward of howshold, what tyme he brynght home money from the courtis, at eche tyme xx. d. and then schall sche gyve to the steward of howshold at Cristymes xx. d. and to my lady's gentylwoman xx. d. and to every gentilman xvi. d. and to every yoman as it pleaseth her to doo, and gromes in like case: and then must sche bye a suger looffe for my lady at Cristmas: and also sche must pay to hyr clerk for his wages thirteen shillings fourpence; to hyr yoman cooke twenty-six shillings eightpence: and sche shall pay for a gown to her grome coke and her poding wief by the yere ii. s.

Fitance of the Covent.—"And also sche must purvy for iii. casse of multon for the covent, for the pitaunce of Sir William Vicar: also sche must purvey for a pece of whete, and iii. gallons melke for firmete on Seynt *Alburgh's* daye: also she must purvey iiii bacon hojis for the covent, for pitance of Dame Alys Merton, and Dame Mawte the kinge's daughter, at ii times in wynter; and sche must bye vi grecys, vi sowcys for the covent, and also vi inwardys, c. egges to make white podinges: also bred, peper, saferon for the same podinjes: also to purvey iii galons gude ale for besons. And also to purvey marybones to make white wortys for the covent: and then must sche purvey at Seynt *Andrewestyd* a pitance of fysche for my lady and the covent: and then must sche pay at Shroftyde to every lady of the covent, and to iiii doubles, for their cripcis, and for the crumkakes to every lady and doubill ii. d. and thanne must sche purvey for my lady abbess against Shroftyd, viij. chekenes: also bonnes for the covent at Shroftyd. Also iiii galons melke fur the covent the same tyme: and yen must sche purvey for every Sonday in Lenton pituance fysche for the covent: and also to be sure of xii stubbe elles and lx. schafte eles to bake for the covent on Schere Thursday: and also one potel tyre for my ladye abbess the same day, and two galons of rede wyne for the covent the same day: and also to purvey three galons of good ale for the covent every weke in Lenton, and to have one galone red wyne for the covent on Ester evyn: and also to purvey for three casse of multon for the covent, for the pitaunce of William Dune: and also to purvey for every lady of the covent, and v double to every lady, and double di. gose delivered at the fest of the Assumption of our Lady.

Eysylver.—"And also sche must pay to xxxvii ladyes of the covent for their *eysylver* fro Michelmes tyll Allhallowday, to every lady by the weke i. d. ob. and then to every lady by the weke fro Allhallowe-day tyll Advent i. d. ob. q. and then to every lady be the weke fro advent Sonday till Childermas day i. d. q. and then to every lady for the same eysylver be the weke fro Cheldermesday unto Aschwednesday i. d. ob. q. and then fro Ester unto Michelmasse to every lady be the weke i. d. ob. and then must sche paye to eche lady for ye eysylver for eche vigill fallyng within the yere ob. and then must sche pay to the priorie eche weke in the yere, except Lenten xxxii. egges, or elles ii. d. ob. q. in money for them every weke, except iiii weke in Advent, in the wheche sche shall not pay but xvi. egges be the weke : and also sche must pay to the said priorie for every vigill fallynge within the yere viij. egges, or elles ob. dim. q. and iiii. part of q in money for the same.

Beyinge of Butter.—" And then must sche purvey for fest butter of Seynt Alburgh for xxxvii lades and iiij. doubles, that is to say, the prioresse, ij. celleressys, and the kechener, to every lady and double i. cobet, every disch conteynyng iii cobettes : and then must sche pay to the sayd ladys and doubles for the storying butter by v tymes in the yere, that is to wite, in Advent, and three tymes after Cristmas, to eche lady and double at every ob. and also sche must purvey for the said lades and doubles for the fest butter at Ester and Whitsontide, lyk as sche dyd at Seynt Alburgh's tyde : also sche must purvey for the sayd lades of the covent, and the said iiii doubles, and the priory for ther fourtnyght butter fro Trinitie Sonday unto Holy Rounde daye, that is to seyd, to every lady double, and priory, at eche fourtnyght betweene the sayd two festes i cobette butter, iii cobetts makyng a disch : and also sche must purvey to the said ladys with ther doubles to the fest butter of Assumption of our Lady, to every lady and double i. cobett butter.

Hyreing of Pastur.—" And then must sche be sure of pasture for her oxen in tym of yere, as her servants can enforume her.

Mowyng and making of Heye.—" And also to see hyr heye be mowe, and made in time of ye yere, as yeryng requeryth.

Costys of Reparations.—" And thanne must sche see that all manner of howses within her office be sufficiently repayred as well withought at hyr fyrmes, manners, as within the monastery.

This ys the Forme of brening of the Celeresse Beofe ; foist the Clerke shall enter into her Boke as followeth.—" The Satyrday the xx daye of September she answereth of iiii or v messes remaynyng in store of the last weke before, and of lxiii messes of beofe comyng of an oxe slayn that same weke : and also sche must answere of iiii. xx messes of beofe be byr boughte of the covente, of that they lefte behynd of ther lyvere paying for every messe i. d. ob. las in all by i. d. ob. *summa* cxlvii. messe, thereof delyvered to eche lady of the covent for iii dayes in the weke iii messe of beofe, that is sonday, tewesday, and thursday : and thanne schall sche pay to the priory for the seid iii dayes vi messes of beof, for eche day ij messe ; and yff there fall no vigill in the sayd iii dayes, and where ther falleth a vigill in ony of the iii. and the next settyrday sche must loke what beof every houshold will have, and thereafter must sche purvey her beofe in the market ; for she shall stey but every fortnyght, and yff sche be a good huswyff.

The Levery of Red Herynge in Advent.—" First sche schall delyvere ‘to eche lady of the covent every weke in Advent for monday and wednysday, for eche day to every lady iii heryngs : and to the priory every weke in Advent for the sayd ij days viii heryngs.

The Levery of Almonds, Rysse, Fyggs, and Reyssons in Lenton.—" First to my lady abbesse in almondes for Advent and Lenttyn iiii. l. and to every lady of the covent for Advent and Lentten ii. l. almondis, and to the prioresse ii celarisses and kechenere for ther doubill to eche doubell ii. l.

Rysse.—" And eche lady of the covent for all the Lentten D. l. ryse, and eche of the said iiii double to eche double for all the Lentten D. l. rysse.

Fyges and Reysons.—" And eche lady of the covent every weke in Lenton i. l. fyges and reyssons, and eche of the sayd iiii doubles every weke in Lentton i. l. fyges and reysons, and to the priori every weke i. l. fygs and reysons.

Levery of Herynge.—" And to every lady of the covent for every day in the weke in Lentton iiii heryngs red and white, that is, every lady xxviii herynges be the weke, and to the priori be v dayes, that is, monday, tewsday, wedynesday, thursday, and sattyrday ; and the sonday they recevy fische, and for the friday fygs and reysons.

Levery of Fische.—" And to every lady of the covent in Lentton eche oder weke, one messe salt fysch, and to the prioresse ii celleresses and kechener for the doubles eche other weke in Lentten, to eche double i messe salt fysch ; and to the priory eche other weke in Lentton ii messe salt fysch, every salt fysch conteyning vii messe.

Levery of Salt Salmon.—" And to every lady of the covent in Lentton eche other weke i messe of salt salmon ; and like wyse to eche of the sayd iiii doubles i messe of salmon ; and in lykewyse each other weke to the priorye ii. messe of salt salmon yeldyng ix messe.

The Levery of Sowse—" Be it remembered that the celeresse must se that every lady of the covent have hyr levery of sowse fro my lady abbesse kychen at Martynmese tyme ; and every lady to have three thynges ; that is to say, the cheke, the ere, and the fote, is a levery ; the groyne and two fete ys anodyr levery ; soe a hoole hoggs sowsse, shall serve three ladyes. And thanne must sche have for three doubles in lyke wyse, to every double three thyngs ; and the three doubles be the prioresse, the high celeresse and the kychener ; the under celeresse schall not have of double : and then must gyff to every lady and double beforesaid of sowce of hyre owne provisione two thyngs to every lady ; so that a hoole hogg sowse do serve four ladyes.

Pitaunce Pork.—" And sche must remember to aske for the covent at my lady abbesse kychen allwey at Martynmesse pittaunce porke for every lady one messe, and for foure doubles, that is to sey, the priorisse, two celliresses, and the kychener, to every double one messe : and then must sche purvey pittaunce porke for the covent, wheche longeth to hyr owne office, for to doo at two tymes in wynter, and that is, ones for Dame Alys Merton and another for Dame Mawte the king's daughter, at eche tyme to every lady one messe, and eche double one messe ; and every hogge shall yield xx messe.

Pittaunce Mutton.—" And also sche must aske for the covent at my lady abbesse kychen pittaunce mutton three tymes in the yere, betweene the Assumption of our Lady and Michelmasse, at eche tyme to every lady one messe, and to the priorisse the high celleresse, and to the kychener for three doubles, for every double one messe, and every mutton shall yelde xii messe. And then must sche purvey for pittaunce mutton for the covent wheche longeth to hyr owne office to doo at two tymes in the yere, that is, once for Syr William Vicar, and another tyme for William Dune ; to every lady and doubell beforesaid, one messe mutton at eche tym, every mutton yeldynge xii messe.

Soper Eggs.—" And the under celeresse must rememder at eche principal fest, that my lady sytteth in the fraytour ; that is to wyt, five tymes in the yere, at eche tyme shall aske the clerke of the kychen soper eggs for the covent, and that is Estir, Wytsontyd, the Assumption of our Lady, Seynt Alburgh, and Cristynmasse, at eche tyme to every lady two eggs, and eche double two eggs, that is the priorisse, the celeresse, and the kychener.

Rusheaulx in Lenton.—" Also sche must remembir rusheaulx in Lenton, that my lady abbesse have viii of the . . . .

Leveray of Geese and Hennes —" Also to remembir to aske of the kychyn at Seynt Alburgh's tyme, for every lady of the covent halfe a goose, and for six double, for every double *dim.* goose, that is, the priorisse, two celeresse, the kychener, and two chaunteresse. Also to eche at the said fest of Seynt Alburgh of the said clerke, for every lady of the covent one henne, or elles a coke, and for ix doubles, to eche double a henne, or elles a coke, and the be iii priorisses, the chaunteresses, ij cellerysses, the kychener, and the two freytouresses.

Leveray Bacon.—" Also to remember to aske the levery bacon for the covent alwey before Cristmasse, at my lady abbesse kychyner, for every lady of the covent iiii messe, and that is, to the priorisse the cellerysse, the kychener ; and sche shall understond that a flytch of bacon conteynigh x messe.

Levery Ottmeale.—" Also to remember to deliver every lady of the covent every moneth in the yere, at eche tyme iiii dyshes of otemelle, delivered to the covent coke for rushefals, for Palme Sundaye, xxi pounder fyggys. *Item* delyveryd to the seyd coke, on Sherthursday viii pounde ryse. *Item* delyveryd to the said coke for Sherethursday xviii pounde almans *Memorandum* that a barrell off herring should contene a thousand herrings, and a cade off herryng six hundereth, six score to the hundreth."

At the dissolution of monasteries, Barking had, according to Speed, an income of £1,085, and was surrendered to the greedy king by its last abbess, Dorothy Barley, who "retired on a pension." The king leased the abbey and its adjoining lands to one of his courtiers, Sir Thomas Denny. It was granted under Edward VI. to Lord Clinton, who sold it forthwith to Sir Richard Sackville, and it has since changed owners repeatedly, like most of such properties. The Manor of Barking, which once was an appendage to the abbey, was seized by Henry VIII., has passed from royal into private hands, and now belongs to Sir E. Hulse.

Of all the once magnificent buildings of the abbey nothing now is left, except a solitary embattled gateway, once known as the " Chapel of the Holy Rood Loft atte Gate," but now commonly called the "Fire-bell Gate," from a tradition that it contained the bell rung for curfew and for alarm of fires. The gateway is substantially in good condition, though the mullions and tracery of its windows have been sadly mutilated. The gateway still guards the entry into the churchyard and church ; in the room over the entrance is still to be seen a relievo of the Crucifixion, much defaced by " pious " iconoclasts. It is needless to say that the fire-bell is no longer there ; nor are there any traces of its position. Another gateway leading into the precincts of the abbey was needlessly taken down in 1881.

A few yards north of the church stood the abbey itself, but of the conventual buildings scarcely a stone remains, except a few fragments of the walls, which now serve as the walls of a market-garden that covers the sacred spot. Bones and other remains have often been dug up here. Lysons, in his " Environs of London," gives a ground plan of the abbey church, " taken from the ruins of its foundation in 1724." But Mr. Thorne sees reasons for doubting the accuracy of its details. According to this plan, it was a hundred and seventy feet long, and cruciform in shape, the width of the transepts being a hundred and fifty feet. This was erected in the middle of the thirteenth century, in the place of an older and smaller structure.

No print or painting of the church remains, the work of the " Reformers " being complete here ; but it was doubtless a noble building in its time. According to the plan in Lysons it consisted of nave, chancel, and transepts, the two former with side aisles, and the Lady Chapel east of the chancel. Besides the high altar, there were in it altars of Our Lady, of the Resurrection, and of St. Peter and St. Paul, and the shrines of St. Hildelitha and St. Ethelburgha. In the year 1876 the foundations of the Lady Chapel and the skeletons of two ladies, probably abbesses, buried in front of the altar, were discovered in the grounds belonging to the national school, a part of the site which does not appear to have been excavated previously.

"As for Barking Abbey" (writes the author of " Professional Excursions " in 1843), " where canonisation descended as an heirloom, and miracles grew like mushrooms, the owl has forsaken it and the bat disdains it. The curfew has fallen from the belfry, and the *pudding-wife's* occupation is gone."

Mr. Thorne tells us that "the library of Magdalen College, Oxford, possesses a relic of the abbey in the shape of a beautiful French manuscript, containing the Lamentations of St. Bernard, the Meditations of St. Augustine, and a Life of St. Louis, presented to the convent by the Countess of Oxford—the wife of the twelfth earl of the old line of De Vere."

Many charters and privileges, as might be expected, were bestowed on the convent by our Norman kings.

Among the names of the ladies who sat in the abbess's chair are to be noticed those of De la Pole, Montacute, Merton, De Vere, and à Becket—the last named being a sister of the martyred archbishop.

Among the possessions of the abbey long before the Conquest, and possibly from its first foundation, was the manor of Barking ; this was seized by the greedy tyrant, Henry VIII., and remained vested in the Crown until sold by Charles I. to the Fanshawes, from whom it passed, through some intermediate hands, to the Lethuilliers, and from them again to the Hulses, its present owners.

The abbess had not only a host of dependants and retainers, but also a prison in which to detain offenders ; and if any of her servants married his daughter beyond the limits of the manor, he had to pay a fine to the abbey.

There were in Barking several subordinate

traces of Early English and Perpendicular work. It contains some fine monuments : the best and finest is in memory of Sir Charles Montagu, of Cranbrook, Essex (brother of the first Earl of Manchester), who is represented as dying on the field of battle, a page holding his horse at the door of a tent. There are three good brasses on the chancel floor ; and other mural tablets deserve attention, especially one to Sir Orlando Humfreys. One or two curious aumbries still remain in the north side of the chancel.

EASTBURY HOUSE. (*After Lysons.*)

manors, as those of Wangay, Fulks, Loxford, Malmains, Cranbrook, Westbury, Eastbury, &c.

The parish church, dedicated to St. Margaret, is large ; it comprises nave, chancel, and north and south aisles, with a tower at the west end. It must once have been fairly handsome, but it has been terribly " beautified " and modernised, its once open timber roofs having been replaced by ornamental plaster ceilings of the Stuart period. It was built chiefly in the fourteenth century, but its date is not at all clearly shown by its architecture, the tracery of its windows having been superseded by modern insertions. One portion of the church, including the piers between the nave and north aisle, near the western end, is Norman, and there are

In the church were three chantries : one at the altar of the Resurrection, in the north transept, and others at the altar of King Edward and the shrine of St. Ethelburgha.

It appears that the vicars of Barking were considered as part of the household of the lady abbess, and had a seat and a knife and fork (if forks were then invented) at the chaplain's table, their servants sitting " below the salt," with the domestics of the convent ; but this right, being found troublesome, was commuted for a money payment.

Barking is a rural deanery, in the diocese of St. Albans ; and the Bishop of St. Albans Fund, which was established a few years ago, is, in point of fact, a home mission and church extension society for the metropolitan portion of the diocese situated in this deanery. Its sphere includes thirty ecclesiastical parishes, embracing the town districts of Stratford, Canning Town, Victoria Docks, and North Woolwich, and suburban places like Barking, Leyton, Leytonstone, Walthamstow, Wanstead, and Woodford. These districts now contain a population of about 224,000, being nearly double the population of 1871. Many parts of the deanery are inhabited by clerks and workmen who have been forced out of London by the

has been already told by us in OLD AND NEW LONDON.*

The manor of Clayhall, in this parish, was held under the abbess and convent of Barking by the following singular services: namely, that every tenant should come in person to the abbey church on the vigil of St. Ethelburgha the Virgin, and there attend and guard the high altar from the first hours of vespers till nine the next morning; and that he should be ready at all times, with a horse and a man, to attend the abbess and her steward when going upon the business of the con-

MARKET HOUSE, BARKING.

reduction of cheap house accommodation; and the publicans are often almost the only people in the parish who keep a domestic servant. At the commencement of 1883 there were 88 Dissenting and seven Roman Catholic chapels in the deanery, with a total of 32,100 sittings, while the total provision made in churches, with mission-rooms, &c., was 28,600.

After the Dissolution, the manor of Barking, which was paramount over the Hundred of Becontree, remained with the Crown till the time of James I., when it was sold to the Fanshawes. In the reign of Queen Elizabeth the property was in the hands of Sir William Hewitt, Lord Mayor of London. The story, as given by Strype, of the manner in which it passed into the possession of Mr. Osborne, the ancestor of the Dukes of Leeds,

vent anywhere within the four seas. And, lastly, that the abbess should have, by way of heriot, upon the death of every tenant, his best horse and accoutrements; these services, however, did not exempt them from the quit rents. Besides the above tenure, there were other "vexatious contingencies," namely, one Robert Gerard was, among other services, "to gather a full measure of nuts, called a pybot, four of which should make a bushel; to go a long journey on foot once a year to Colchester, Chelmsford, Ely, or the like distances, on the business of the convent, carrying a pack, and other shorter distances, such as Brentford, &c., and maintaining himself upon the road. He was to pay a fine upon the marriage of his daughter, if she married beyond the limits of

* See Vol. I., p. 401

the manor. If his daughter had an illegitimate child, he was to make the best terms he could with the abbess for the fine called Kyldwyte. It appears, also, that he could not even sell his ox, fed by himself, without the abbess's permission."

In former times there were several manor-houses in the parish, but they have mostly disappeared, or been altered to suit other purposes.

Malmains, which stood about a mile and a half north-east from the church, was the residence of Sir William Hewitt, mentioned above. Bifrons, on the road between Barking and Eastbury House, was in the last century the seat of Bamber Gascoigne, M.P., a maternal ancestor of the Marquis of Salisbury. It was so fancifully named because of its double front.

Eastbury House, on the road to Dagenham and Rainham, about a mile from Barking, is a large, dreary, tumble-down mansion, square in plan, of an almost collegiate type, built of red brick, with tall gables, square mullioned windows, and stacks of graceful chimneys, which still retain their original freshness. The rooms inside were panelled, and some of them were painted in fresco; but the interior of the house has been modernised.

A representation of the house, in Lysons' "Environs of London," shows two tall towers, which rise above the top of the house; but now there is only one: the other was destroyed by lightning some years ago. It is said, but erroneously, that Lord Monteagle was staying here when he received the letter which, being submitted to James I., led to the discovery of the Gunpowder Plot.

"Eastbury House," writes the author of "Professional Excursions," "has some pretensions to be immortalised as the reputed residence of Lord Monteagle, who was so singularly instrumental in discovering the Gunpowder Plot, which still annoys us with its barbarous ceremonies on the 5th of November. It is a wretched, neglected building, fit only for 'treason, stratagems, and spoils,' and has only a few whimsical shafts to recompense the trouble of leaving the highway and encountering an ague." The old mansion is called by the natives "Gunpowder House," from a tradition that Guy Fawkes and his fellow conspirators used it as a rendezvous; but there is no historical evidence of this, and even the tradition is confused and contradictory.

It is religiously believed by the natives that preparations had been made by those connected with the "Gunpowder Plot" to witness the catastrophe from the top of the great tower, which commands a view over London. We have, however, shown in a previous chapter that the conspirators hired a house for that purpose at White Webbs, Enfield,* in which they also held their secret meetings. The house belongs to the Sherry family, and entrance to it is most churlishly refused to visitors.

The road by Eastbury House leads on by Grays to Tilbury and Southend. It must have been by this road that Queen Elizabeth rode down to her camp at Tilbury to inspect her troops on that historical occasion just when the panic of the great Spanish Armada had reached our shores, and when she addressed to her gallant soldiers those words which are recorded in every English History :—" My loving people," said the queen, "we have been persuaded by some that are careful of our safety to take heed how we commit ourselves to armed multitudes, for fear of treachery; but I assure you I do not desire to live to distrust my faithful and loving people. Let tyrants fear; I have always so behaved myself that, under God, I have placed my chiefest strength and safeguard in the loyal hearts and good-will of my subjects; and, therefore, I am come amongst you at this time, not as for my recreation and sport, but being resolved in the midst and heat of the battle to live or die amongst you all, to lay down for my God, for my kingdom, and for my people, my honour and my blood even in the dust. I know that I have but the body of a weak and feeble woman; but I have the heart of a king, and of a King of England too, and think foul scorn that Parma, or Spain, or any prince of Europe, should dare to invade the borders of my realms."

The town of Barking is mainly agricultural; it is straggling and irregular in plan, and is joined to London by a double line of railway: the one to Fenchurch Street, and the other by way of Stratford to Bishopsgate. It is on the route to Southend.

In the High Street is an old market-house (said by Lysons to have been built by Queen Elizabeth), around which a market is still held on Saturday. The streets are poor, narrow, squalid, and badly drained. By the wharf at the end of the town is a corn-mill, standing on the site of the old Abbey Mill. From this wharf, Pepys tells us in his "Diary," under date August 18th, 1662, the timber cut down for the navy in the royal forests of Hainault and Epping was shipped for Woolwich. The chief traffic now consists of fish, coals, and corn.

At Uphall, a farm a little to the north of the

---

town, near the Roding, are the remains of a square fortification nearly forty acres in extent. They are certainly Roman, and are supposed to mark a fortification, or else the site of a town or military station, probably the first of a series on the road between Augusta (London) and Camelodunum, Maldon, or Colchester. The banks and trenches minutely described by Lysons have been partially effaced by the plough, but near the north-western angle is still to be seen a "very fine spring of water, which was guarded by an inner work and a high keep, or mound of earth." The mound is still there, and the spring still bubbles up as it did in the days of Julius Cæsar. Probably the stones of the encampment were utilised in building the abbey at Barking which the Danes destroyed.

The men of Barking would seem to have been bold and adventurous. One of them, David Ingram, gives an account of his voyage to North America, along with "Master" Hawkins, and his travels in Mexico and in other parts of that continent in 1582. His curious narrative is to be seen in the first edition of "Hakluyt's Voyages," though omitted from later issues. It was probably thought too wonderful to be true.

From the town wharf down to its junction with the Thames, the banks of Barking Creek are artificially raised by strong walls, along which there is a public path. But the walk is not attractive. Nor, perhaps, are its attractions increased by the fact that just above it, on its western side, is the outfall into the Thames of the main drainage works of London, which were carried out under Lord Palmerston's premiership by Sir Joseph Bazalgette.*

Mr. Thorne, in his "Environs of London," states that here 10,000,000 cubic feet of sewage are brought daily down from London in a concrete sewer which crosses the marshes, and deposited in a reservoir, which is discharged into the Thames at high water.

The reservoir, or main outfall, is constructed on lands in Barking parish. It is built on the marshland on the west side of the mouth of Barking Creek, and covers an area of nearly ten acres. It is divided into four compartments, and will hold 39,000,000 gallons of sewage. The walls are of brick, the floor of stone, and the concrete foundations are carried down to a depth of about twenty feet. At Lodge Farm, Barking, some of the sewage is scientifically applied to agricultural purposes, and with great success; and it seems a very great pity, to say the least, that all the London sewage is not applied in like manner towards reclaiming and fertilising all the waste lands on the Essex borders.

"Primarily the duties of the Metropolitan Board of Works," observes the *St. James's Magazine*, "are constructional in character, and all the other details of its finance and government are merely subordinate to this original object. This fact has endowed the body with more than ordinary importance, for its main functions are spending ones, and resulting in the realisation of great structural works, designed for the benefit of the inhabitants of the metropolis. Instituted almost solely for remedying the defects and dangers of an undrained, or at least imperfectly drained, city, its first task was a solution of the vexed and unsatisfactory problem of 'London drainage.' The polluted character of the river Thames at the period of the Board's inauguration was a notorious fact, and, aided by the designs of many eminent engineers, it set about its work with well-meant and disinterested energy. With almost unlimited funds at its command, no obstacle prevented the carrying out a scheme of efficient drainage, which it was fondly hoped would set at rest for all time the dangers associated with congested sewers, and their intermittent efflux into a tidal river. The final scheme as now carried out was the construction of a series of main drains parallel to the Thames, whose functions were to intercept everything seweral in character from the houses within the superficial boundary of the Board's jurisdiction; in short, collecting, or rather directing, the overflow of London's sewage (so as to prevent its mingling with the river through the City and suburbs) to a more distant point of disemboguement . . . . Let us now, after a few years' interval, examine in all seriousness the *gain* derived from so large an expenditure. There was undoubtedly a fundamental error in deciding to concentrate the daily discharge of seven or eight hundred thousand tons of sewage into the river Thames, at points abutting on the eastern boundaries of the metropolis itself. It was assumed by the engineers of the Board that pumping out this large and fluctuating volume of semi-liquid sewage could be beneficially effected at the top of the tide, resulting in the final dispersion of the corrupt mass by tidal and river influences. In the early days of this great engineering feat, adverse criticism from any quarter met with scant courtesy. Even those experienced chemists and agriculturists who besought the Board to consider the value of that which was thus ruthlessly consigned to what they regarded as annihilation, and beyond the reach of being a danger to the metropolis, at

---

See "Old and New London," Vol. V., pp. 41, 42.

least were snubbed. The loss of £4,000,000 (besides the cost of its dispersion) was as nothing, for was the Thames not purified between the bridges, so much so as to enable steamboat passengers to enjoy a sail in warm weather without the disgusting dangers of noisome smells from a malodorous stream? The first serious challenge of dissent offered to this assumed happy condition of things, and which somewhat disturbed the equanimity of the Board and its engineers, proceeded from the River Thames Conservancy, which, from a carefully prepared river chart and innumerable soundings, showed that mud-banks of an abnormal character were being formed, and that these were attributable to deposits from the Crossness and Barking sewer discharges. Notwithstanding the apparent accuracy of these asseverations, proceeding from an important body, the whole affair was speedily settled by the Board proving, from its own and independent engineering evidence, that the very idea of such a state of things was absolutely preposterous. The River Thames Conservators did not need to be apprehensive of stoppage to navigation, for the millions of tons of sewage matter pumped into the river Thames in the course of the year was sent away, by a happy condition of natural influences, to seaward, where its baneful and dangerous character would be utterly destroyed. The contentions of the Metropolitan Board have been unavoidably persistent as well as consistent, for it is invariably argued, and with much plausible appearance of reason, that all the filth of London, through its agency, is rendered harmless and innocuous, and that neither water, air, land, or sea can be injuriously interfered with, in consequence of its system of drainage. A body of undoubted importance, entrusted with an onerous task, was naturally treated with much forbearance in the past; for during the early years of its existence much allowance had to be made for the novelty of dealing in so comprehensive a manner with a leviathan undertaking such as the disposal of London's sewage. Germs of disease deposited on the river sides and at the bottom of the stream are simply storehouses for future supplies of forces charged with danger and death, the natural result of the collection of London's sewage into vast longitudinal sewers, which at intervals may be dammed back to meet tidal or other exigencies, and which, when so retarded must push back with force the gases produced from the accumulation and churning of such varied qualities of filth. Sewer gas, as it is now called, under such circumstances, readily escapes from the sources of its generation, and with its deadly influences and surroundings permeates the dwellings with which the system of London drainage so effectually entangles the homes of the ratepayers. New types of disease, frequently baffling the skill of the most accomplished physicians, are the result of such baneful contamination from a source which is difficult to control. The main drainage system of London (and by its example and teachings provincial cities and towns as well) has created new professions, in whose ranks special experts have risen up to grapple with dangers and inconveniences before unknown."

The drainage system of London, on the north side of the Thames, comprises the High Level, the Middle Level, the Low Level, and the Western District Sewers, together with the Outfall at Barking Creek. The High Level drains Hampstead, Highgate, Kentish Town, Highbury, Stoke Newington, Hackney, and passes under Victoria Park to Old Ford; its length is about nine miles. The Middle Level runs by way of Kensal Green, Kensington Park, Notting Hill, Bayswater, Oxford Street, and so under a number of minor streets, to Old Ford, being about twelve miles long. The Low Level commences near Pimlico, and will pass along under the Thames Embankment to Blackfriars, and thence through the City and Whitechapel to West Ham. The Western District Sewers drain Acton, Hammersmith, Fulham, Chelsea, &c., on a plan different from that of the main drainage in other localities. The Outfall, an immense work, six miles long, continues the Upper and Middle Level Sewers from Old Ford to West Ham, and all the three sewers thence to Barking Creek, where we now leave it.

At the mouth of the creek, on the east side, are a powder-magazine, a coastguard station, and some large factories.

It is mentioned as a notorious fact by Campbell, in his "Political Survey of Great Britain," that the drainage and reclaiming of the fens and marshes along our rivers was principally the work of the clergy, who in the Saxon times were the most learned and the most wealthy order in the country. And there is no part of England where such qualifications were more in demand than along the banks of the Lea and the Thames, in the neighbourhood of London.

CHAPTER LVII.

DAGENHAM.

"Rivus multâ mole docendus aprico parcere prato."—HORACE.

Ripple Side, Barking—Ripple Castle—Extent and Boundaries of Dagenham—Census Returns—The Village—Church—Parslowes—Valence—Dagenham Breach—Discovery of a "Moorlog"—The River Walls of the Thames—Dagenham Lake—Its Proposed Conversion into a Dock—Failure of the Scheme—Origin of the Ministerial Fish Dinner.

BEYOND Barking Level the land immediately abutting upon the Thames is mostly a dreary marsh, crossed and intersected by straight dykes and sluggish pools, but further inland are broad stretches of pasture-land, serving as an admirable grazing-ground for cattle. The roadway running eastward from Barking towards Rainham, for the first mile or two, till past the high ground whereon stands Eastbury House, is called Ripple Side. A square brick-built house by the roadside, near the commencement of Dagenham parish, erected about a century ago, is somewhat pretentiously named Ripple Castle, doubtless on account of the taste of the builder having led him to ornament its parapet with battlements, and to flank the front of the house with circular towers pierced with narrow loopholes, but it is a poor imitation of a castellated structure, at best.

Dagenham, which is the next parish in succession eastward of Barking, extends from the banks of the Thames far northward, by Chadwell Heath, into what used to be Hainault Forest, a distance of some seven miles inland, the northern border being fully five miles off from the straggling village. The eastern boundary of the parish is the Beam rivulet, which unites with the Rom. The village lies away about a mile northward of the high road from Barking to Rainham, two miles north-west from Rainham Station, on the Tilbury and Southend line of the Great Eastern Railway, and twelve miles from Whitechapel Church. The area of the parish is 6,600 acres, and the population in 1881 was 3,400, being an increase of about 600 during the preceding decade. This number is inclusive of the inhabitants of Becontree Heath, which gives its name to the Hundred, and lies away towards the north, in the vicinity of Chadwell Heath.

Dagenham is not mentioned in "Domesday Book," being included under the general heading of Barking, it having originally formed part of the abbey demesnes. In Hodelerd's grant to the convent it is called Dechenham. There are four manors, or reputed manors, in this parish, namely, the manor of Dagenham proper, and also those of Cockermouth, Parslowes (or Parsloes), and Valence.

The village is surrounded on all sides by corn-fields and market-gardens. It is a long, straggling village, made up of rows of small cottages, and one or two houses of a better class, with the ordinary admixture of general shops, &c. The church, which stands near the eastern end of the street, is dedicated to St. Peter and St. Paul, and consists of chancel, with north aisle, nave, and an embattled tower at the western end, surmounted by a slated spire, and containing a peal of six bells, put up in the early part of the reign of George the Third. The stone-work of the tower is ancient, but has been partly encased with brick and otherwise altered, whilst on an arch above the doorway is carved the inscription: "Wm. Mason, architect, 1800." The chancel and aisle date from the thirteenth century. The nave was rebuilt, and the remainder of the church in part "restored" by a brief in 1800. But the restoration was not satisfactory; at all events, the building was again thoroughly "restored" in 1878, the walls of the chancel being refaced, the floor of the church lowered, open benches substituted for the old-fashioned "pews," the north gallery taken down, and the ceilings throughout fresh plastered, and painted with a flowing leaf pattern. During these repairs and alterations, the original altar-slab, bearing the five marks symbolical of the wounds of Our Saviour, was discovered; it has been replaced on the present table. The remains of an ancient piscina, which had been bricked up and obscured by plastering, was also brought to light, and has been repaired.

In 1878 a stained glass window was inserted in the chancel in memory of Mr. T. L. Fanshawe, of Parslowes, in this parish. Among the memorials in the church is a tomb, with brasses, to Sir Thomas Urswyk, a former Recorder of London, dated 1470: it bears the effigies of himself, his wife, four sons, and nine daughters. A monument of white and grey marble, comprising the effigy of a judge in his robes, and also one of his lady in a mourning attitude, bears the following inscription :—" Here lyes interr'd the body of Sir Richard Alibon, Knt., a person of extraordinary, both natural and acquired, parts, eminent in ye knowledge and practice of the law, of the honourable Society of Gray's Inn, recommended by his merits to the favour of King James the Second, to whom he was a council learned in yᵉ laws, and advanced to be one of the Justices of the Court of King's Bench, being the first of yᵉ Roman faith these 150 years who had bin called to a place of so high a rank." He died August 22nd, 1688, aged fifty-three. This monument was erected by his widow, "Dame Barbara Alibon, who was daughter to John Blakestone, Esq., and granddaughter to Sir Wm. Blakestone, Knt., of Gibside, in the county of Durham." Two helmets and some fragments of gauntlets of ancient date, belonging to the knightly

under the Abbess of Barking. The house is a good old modernised mansion, surrounded by a moat. The lawn and pleasure-grounds slope down to the edge of the moat, and contain some fine cedars.

A turning out of the main road, by the side of the "Chequers" Inn, leads to the river-side at Dagenham Reach, about a mile distant. To the left of the road thither is a large sheet of water, an inlet from the Thames, nearly two miles in length, and covering an area of upwards of forty acres.

DAGENHAM MARSHES, LOOKING EAST.

family of the Fanshawes, or some other former lords of the soil in these parts, are preserved in the church. In the churchyard is a memorial to George Clark, a police constable, who was murdered at Eastbrook End, in this parish, in 1846. It was "erected by the inhabitants and his brother officers of the K division."

Langhorne, the poet, was for some time curate of Dagenham.

Parslowes, the seat of the Fanshawes for the last two centuries, stands on the west side of the parish, a little to the north of the Rainham Road. It is a spacious brick building, with an embattled pediment and turrets, but dating, however, only from the beginning of the present century, when the house was new fronted. The gardens and pleasure-grounds alone surrounding the mansion are about seven acres in extent; the estate altogether, however, extends to about 600 acres.

The estate of Valence, which lies a short distance further to the north, is so named from having been held by the Valences, Earls of Pembroke,

This sheet of water is a lasting mark of the inundation known as Dagenham Breach, which early in the last century laid desolate this part of the parish.

Morant, in his "History of Essex," gives the following detailed account of the breach:—"It happened 17th of December, 1707, at an extraordinary high tide, accompanied with a violent wind, and was occasioned by the blowing up of a sluice, or trunk, made for the drain of the land-waters in the wall and banks of the Thames. If proper and immediate help had been applied, it could have been easily stopped, with a small charge, the ditch, or drain, of the marsh grounds, which led to such sluice, being, at the first blowing up of the sluice, not above fourteen or sixteen feet broad, and might in a day or two have been easily stopped by the bringing on a small dam, in form of a semicircle, to the Thames wall, if many hands had been employed; but, through the neglect thereof, the constant force of the water setting in and out of the levels soon made the gap wider, so that a large channel was torn up, and a passage made for the water, of one hundred yards wide, and twenty feet deep in some places. By which unhappy accident, about 1,000 acres of rich land in the levels of Dagenham and Havering, worth about

of Havering and Dagenham. By which Act, for ten years, from 10th of July, 1714, the master of every ship or vessel coming into the port of London was obliged to pay threepence per ton, coasters three shillings each voyage, and colliers one penny per chalder, except fishing-vessels, ships in ballast only, and coasters, particularly Harwich boats. Colchester packet-boats to be charged with the duty of three shillings a voyage only four times in the year."

The work of repairing the breach was then

THE WALLS OF THE THAMES.

£3 an acre, were overflowed, and a sand-bank was raised in the Thames, at the mouth of the breach, which reached half across the river, and near a mile in length, likely to prove a great obstruction to, and even utterly to destroy, the navigation. The expense of repairing this breach was, at first, laid upon the proprietors of the lands, but after many wearied and unsuccessful attempts of theirs for about seven years, until they had expended more than the value of the land, it was given wholly over as impracticable. However, being deemed a public concern, upon application to Parliament an Act was obtained for the speedy and effectual preserving the navigation of the River Thames by stopping the breach in the levels

undertaken by one William Boswell, who, for the sum of £16,500, agreed to stop up the gap in the river-wall, and remove the shelf that had been thrown out into the Thames, but after the trial of various schemes he found himself unable to complete the undertaking, and the work was abandoned. In 1715 an engagement was entered into with Captain John Perry, who had been employed by the Czar Peter in building the city of Veronitz, upon the River Don. Captain Perry undertook the work for £25,000, and a promise that if that sum was not sufficient he should be recommended to Parliament for a further grant. By the time he commenced his work the breach had been worn into several large branches, like the natural arms of a river, by the force of the reflux water from the marshes on every turn of the tide. The longest of these branches extended upwards of a mile and a half, and was in some places between 400 and 500 feet broad, and from twenty to forty feet deep. By extraordinary exertions, by driving dove-tail pieces in a peculiar manner, and by various other expedients, Captain Perry at length, after about five years' labour, succeeded in stopping the breach, but not before the works had been *three* times nearly destroyed and washed away by the strength and rapidity of the tides. The expense of this important undertaking amounted to £40,472, only £25,000 of which was allowed by the original contract; but £15 000 was afterwards voted by Parliament to Captain Perry, who was, nevertheless, after all, a loser of several thousands of pounds by his successful work.

But this is not the only occasion on which the river has proved wantonly destructive to the low-lying districts on its north side. In 1376, we are told, the tide made a breach at Dagenham, which drowned so many acres of land belonging to the abbey at Barking* as seriously to affect the wealth and prosperity of that institution, and to drive some of the "religieuses" to take refuge on the high ground at Billericay. We do not learn how the misfortune was repaired.

During the progress of the work carried out by Captain Perry, the workmen cut into a "moorlog," or vein of buried wood, which appears to run for miles along the side of the river, and they thought that a buried "forest primeval" lay revealed beneath their feet. It was discovered three or four feet under the surface of the marsh, and was found to be about ten feet in depth. It contained yew-trees from fourteen to sixteen inches in diameter, and perfectly sound; willows more than two feet in girth, but like touchwood; and mingled with it was small brushwood, and even hazel-nuts, which appeared sound to the eye, but crumbled to the touch. Several stags' horns were also met with lying about the moorlog. Coller, in his "History of Essex," says:—"Some have indulged learned surmises that these are the remains of the devastation of the Deluge; others that they are the remnants of the old forest beaten down and buried by storms and inundations at a later age; but the most practical conclusion is that they were purposely laid there by some of the rude engineers of olden times, as foundations for works to shut out the troublesome flow of the Thames on to the neighbouring lands."

Mr. Smiles, in his work on "Engineers," informs us that the Thames is kept in its bed by 300 miles of embankment between London Bridge and the Nore. How the River Thames came to be reduced to reasonable dimensions and confined to its present channel, how it is kept within it, and how the thousands of acres of low land lying between both banks and the higher grounds are kept protected from overflow at every tide, at full and new moon, or during particularly wet seasons, are questions of no common interest, and on which a very general ignorance prevails. The average rise of the tide in the Thames is, at London Bridge, eighteen feet, at Deptford, twenty, at Purfleet, seventeen, at Holy Haven, fifteen, and at the Nore, fourteen.

"From Fulham to the Nore," observes a writer in *Once a Week*,* "every high tide would lay a very large proportion of the neighbouring country under water, and at spring tides would restore the appearance of the basin of the Thames to what it must have presented to Cæsar's eyes if he chanced to sight it first at flood tide, were it not for the system of embankments which line both sides of the river, as well as of its tributaries.

"Conjecture has ever been busy among local and general historians as to the origin of these embankments, and the credit of their construction has been very generally given to the Romans. Indeed, this mighty nation of fighting and paving men share the honour of many of the most stupendous works which are scattered over the face of Europe pretty equally with a certain personage, who, if he have rightly earned the titles of the 'first Whig' and the 'first gentleman,' might seem equally deserving—to judge from the works ascribed to him—of that of the 'first engineer' as well. . . . What public works, however, of enormous dimensions and immense difficulty cannot be clearly traced to the Great Enemy and his gang are generally fathered next upon the Romans—and with far more solid grounds for the conjecture. Old Rome's public works stand to this day the noblest memorial of her greatness, and are still food for wonder to an engineering and scientific age. A very curt enumeration of the baths, sewers, aqueducts, amphitheatres, temples, and other public buildings, which are due to Roman enterprise, would fill a volume; whilst the long lines of hard, durable road which to this day intersect the countries they conquered are solid and striking memorials of their large perception of what are the tangible appliances of a centralised government, as well as of their skill as paviors. Roman soldiers, we know, were 'navvies' as well as fighting-men, and could handle the spade and basket as well as 'the sword and the buckler.'

"No wonder that in the days of our youth, when we were of that inquiring turn of mind which prompts children to ask disagreeable questions of their elders and betters, the sight of Romney

---

Marsh, with its four-and-twenty thousand acres rescued from the tides, should have prompted the question, 'Who did it?' and as little wonder that the prompt reply should have been, 'The Romans, my lad!' As little wonder that, travelling on the long, dreary, monotonous roads that traverse the huge flats of Cambridgeshire and Lincolnshire, we should have asked the same question about the banked-out rivers there, and have met with the same reply; or, again, that, peering over the side of that primitive Ramsgate steamer, the old *City of London*, in her tedious dawdle down the Thames, the miles after miles of river embankment which protected the low ground on each side from inundation should have caught our observant eye, and elicited the same question, with the same result; or that thereupon our young, active imagination should have fallen to work at once to conjure the well-bleached stakes which, in tier above tier, support the bank into the thigh-bones of the old Roman soldiers of whom we had read so much at school—not without much suppressed execration of them and their historians—and should have forthwith much commended this original mode of utilising the remains of ancient heroes. It was not, however, until years and years after those inquiring days, when we had travelled between these Thames embankments scores of times, in all sorts of craft and at all periods of the tides, had taken long walks along their summits, examined their construction, and lost ourselves in the prairie wilderness and among the network of drains that lie in their rear, that we began to be conscious that they constitute a national work, which, if hardly deserving the higher title of 'stupendous,' may fairly lay claim to that of 'enormous,' both in regard to their extent and their utility. . . . The marsh-lands on each side are intersected by tributary streams and creeks, and a moment's consideration will elicit the reflection that every one of these must be banked on each side throughout the whole of its course through the flat country, and until land of a higher elevation than the highest spring tides is attained, or of course the water would, as the tide rose, steal round the back of the principal embankment by the channel of these creeks and tributaries, and render them simply useless. Indeed, nothing will tend more to a due conception of the importance of every yard of these enormous works than the reflection that the failure of the smallest portion of any part of them tends instantly to the destruction of the object of the whole; it is like the springing of a leak in a ship, or the snapping of one imperfectly welded link in a chain-cable. The failure itself may be trifling, but its consequences are

almost illimitable. . . . The uplands on each side of the River Thames below London, and with these the swamps which fringed them, were in large measure bestowed on ecclesiastical bodies in very early times. The Abbey of Stratford, for instance, was founded and endowed in 1135, and that of Lesnes, near Abbey Wood, in Kent, 1178. On the one shore were this Stratford Abbey, the famous nunnery at Barking, the cell at Grays Thurrock, St. Osyth, and others; and on the south shore Lesnes, Dartford, Ingress, &c. The monks and nuns, finding themselves not unfrequently flooded out of their dwellings, and obliged to seek refuge in the higher lands, very early set on foot a process of what was called then, and for many centuries, 'inning' their marsh-lands, that is, enclosing them with embankments; and as early as Henry II.'s time this process began to be deemed a matter of national importance. It is remarkable, by the way, that to the same monarch—as Count of Anjou— the French historians ascribe the consolidation of the great Loire embankment. But that from the time of Edward II. downwards the 'inning' process continued to be considered a national affair is evidenced by the perpetually recurring commissions to view, take order for the repair of the banks, ditches, &c., and for the safeguard of the marshes from the overflowing of the tide, as well as by the continued assessments or taxes on the neighbourhood granted for defraying the expenses of the works. According to the rule of these more advanced days, however, there is also to be detected a constantly recurring difficulty in collecting the taxes. . . . The works remained uncompleted, the low lands were constantly overflowed, and at length private enterprise stepped in to supply public torpor—and not without making a good bargain for itself out of the transaction. Thus, in Queen Elizabeth's days 'one Jacobus Aconcius, an Italian,' undertook to 'in,' or reclaim, about 2,000 acres of drowned land in Plumstead and Erith Marshes, on condition of getting one-half of his recovery in fee-simple for his pains. In 1622, one Jonas Croppenburg, a Dutchman, made a similar bargain about Canvey Island, only, more modest than Jacobus, he restricted his demand to one-third of the land recovered; and about the same time one Cornelius Vermuyden, a German, undertook the recovery of Dagenham and Havering Marshes on similar conditions. The same Vermuyden, some thirty years later, when he is described as a Colonel of Horse under Cromwell, superintended the rescue of something between four and five hundred thousand acres of similar land in the counties of Lincoln, Cambridge, and Hunts, and must have been a genius and a man well ahead of his age.

" By some such process, then, as these, it seems most probable that the Thames embankments gradually crawled into existence during the centuries which intervened between the days of the Henry Second and those of the Protector, comparatively small detached portions of embankment being pushed forward, like military outworks, from the higher lands first of all, and by degrees being extended and united, until the work resolved itself into what at first sight might appear to be one uniform settled plan, acted on at once and from the beginning—an idea consistent only with the exploded theory of Roman construction. That the vestiges of the old approaches have been gradually swept away in order to make the most of the space, and in proportion as their utility was superseded by the more advanced works, has, no doubt, favoured the Roman theory. It is, however, impossible not to regret that so much of them, at any rate, as might provide for accidents was not allowed by common prudence to remain, in spite of the levelling and economising mania. A fracture of even a small portion of the system is a disaster the extent of which there is no foreseeing. This has been already alluded to in the way of illustration. A few facts will help out the theory. A breach of the embankment, in 1324, laid 100 acres of the valuable land between what is now St. Katharine's Docks and Shadwell under water for a year. In 1376 the whole of the lands about Dagenham, and those belonging to the nunnery at Barking, were inundated. Some 1,000 acres at Stepney were flooded in 1448. The whole of Plumstead Marshes were drowned in 1527, and not completely recovered until 1590. The entire country from Purfleet to Grays was laid under water in 1690. And even cockney anglers can tell something about the great inbreak of 1707, which swept away 400 feet of the river wall at Dagenham, overflowed 1,000 acres, and was only repaired after years of labour by Captain Perry, at an expense of £40,472, leaving behind its mark in the shape of that little winding lake in which bream and eels so plenteously swarm."

The " Dagenham Lake Subscription Water"— for such is the name by which this unreclaimed portion of the drowned land has long been known to London anglers—is well stocked with pike, carp, roach, and eels. It is somewhat irregular in shape, particularly on the north side ; on the east side it unites with the Beam, and thence, flowing on southward to the Thames, forms an island nearly a mile square. In the " Memoirs of Eliza-

beth Fry," it is stated that that lady used for some years (1826 onwards) to spend her summers in a cottage by Dagenham Lake, " surrounded by trees, mostly willows, on an open space of lawn, with beds of reeds behind them, and on either side covering the river bank." This, in all probability, was the cottage still standing on the west side of the island : it is a picturesque old building, with a thatched roof, and an external wooden gallery communicating with the upper storey. On the south side of the island, in former times, stood a building known as the Breach House—or, as it was sometimes called, the Beach House ; but this has long ago disappeared, and has given place to a large factory.

About twenty years ago a company was started, and an Act of Parliament obtained for the purpose of purchasing Dagenham Lake, and converting it into a dock. Sir John Rennie and Mr. J. Murray were appointed engineers, and some progress was made with the works ; but at the end of about a twelvemonth they were stopped, owing to the monetary difficulties at that time, and have not since been resumed. According to the original prospectus, this dock was to have been "one of the largest in the Port of London, and be capable of receiving the largest ships afloat." All that is now visible in connection with the undertaking is included in some half-dozen wooden sheds, standing by what was doubtless intended as the entrance to the great tidal basin, and another wooden structure by the side of the lake ; an elevated tramway running from the river-wall, or embankment, some half a mile inland, for the carriage of material ; a large brick building, that was for many years afterwards used as an ice-house ; and, finally, a large board, placed conspicuously by the river-side, bearing the inscription, " Dagenham Docks to be Sold."

It would not be supposed à priori that there would be any more intimate connection between Dagenham Breach and the Ministerial Whitebait Dinner than there was between Tenterden Steeple and the Goodwin Sands. But the contrary is the case. The annual whitebait dinner was originally a private feast, given by Sir Robert Preston to his friends, who went down the river annually to inspect the sea-walls at Dagenham Breach, and it gradually grew to the importance of a State entertainment. The story of the origin of this annual festivity is thus told by Mr. John Timbs, in his "Club Life of London":—"On the banks of Dagenham Lake or Breach, in Essex, many years since, there stood a cottage, occupied by a princely merchant, named Preston, a baronet of Scotland and Nova Scotia, and some time M.P. for Dover.

He called it his 'fishing cottage,' and often in the spring he went thither with a friend or two, as a relief to the toils of his parliamentary and mercantile duties. His most frequent guest was the Right Hon. George Rose, Secretary of the Treasury and an Elder Brother of the Trinity House. Many a day did these two worthies enjoy at Dagenham Reach; and Mr. Rose once intimated to Sir Robert that Mr. Pitt, of whose friendship they were both justly proud, would, no doubt, delight in the comfort of such a retreat. A day was named, and the Premier was invited; and he was so well pleased with his reception at the 'fishing cottage'—they were all two- if not three-bottle men—that, on taking leave, Mr. Pitt readily accepted an invitation for the following year.

"For a few years the Premier continued a visitor to Dagenham, and was always accompanied by Mr. George Rose. But the distance was considerable; the going and coming were somewhat inconvenient for the First Minister of the Crown. Sir Robert Preston, however, had his remedy, and he proposed that they should in future dine nearer London. Greenwich was suggested; we do not hear of whitebait in the Dagenham dinners, and its introduction probably dates from the removal to Greenwich. The party of three was now increased to four, Mr. Pitt being permitted to bring Lord Camden. Soon after a fifth guest was invited— Mr. Charles Long, afterwards Lord Farnborough. All were still the guests of Sir Robert Preston;

and one by one other notables were invited—all Tories; and at last Lord Camden considerately remarked that, as they were all dining at a tavern, it was but fair that Sir Robert Preston should be relieved from the expense. It was then arranged that the dinner should be given as usual by Sir Robert Preston—that is to say, at his invitation— and he insisted on still contributing a buck and champagne; the rest of the charges were thenceforth defrayed by the several guests, and on this plan the meeting continued to take place annually till the death of Mr. Pitt.

"Sir Robert was requested, next year, to summon the several guests, the list of whom, by this time, included most of the Cabinet Ministers. The time for meeting was usually after Trinity Monday —a short period before the end of the session. By degrees the meeting, which was originally purely gastronomic, appears to have assumed, in consequence of the long reign of the Tories, a political or semi-political character. Sir Robert Preston died; but Mr. Long (now Lord Farnborough) undertook to summon the several guests, the list of whom was furnished by Sir Robert Preston's private secretary. Hitherto, the invitations had been sent privately; now they were dispatched in Cabinet boxes, and the party was, certainly for some time, limited to members of the Cabinet. A dinner lubricates ministerial as well as other business; so the 'Ministerial Fish Dinner' may contribute to the grandeur and prosperity of our beloved country."

CHAPTER LVIII.

MILLWALL, LIMEHOUSE, AND POPLAR.

"Where could I wish myself now?
In the Isle of Dogs."—BEAUMONT AND FLETCHER.

Situation and Boundaries of Millwall—Origin of the Name of the Isle of Dogs—The Chapel House—Blackwall—Millwall—Acreage of the Isle of Dogs—Fertility of the Soil—Geology—A Submerged Forest—The Manor of Pomfret—Inundations of the Marsh—How Samuel Pepys attended a Wedding Party—Ferries, and the Ferry House—Condition of the Isle of Dogs in the Last Century—Manufactories and Ship-building Yards—Roman Cement and Terra Cotta—The *Great Eastern* Steam Ship—Cubitt Town—St. Luke's Church—Limehouse—Poplar.

IN the preceding chapter we have reached the utmost limits of our perambulation in an easterly direction, but there still remains a district north of the Thames as yet unexplored by us in our pilgrimage, and to which we will now direct our attention, as it is unrecorded in OLD AND NEW LONDON. Down to the end of the last or beginning of the present century, the region in question was almost uninhabited, but of late years it has become one of the busiest and most thriving

localities in the suburbs of London. Millwall— or, as it is commonly called, the Isle of Dogs— forms part of the parish of All Saints, Poplar. It is in the parliamentary division of the Tower Hamlets, and it belongs to the Hundred of Ossulston, in the county of Middlesex. It was formerly included in the parish of Stepney, and in ancient times it was known by the name of Stepney Marsh. The district is bounded on the north by the London and Blackwall Railway, on the east by Blackwall and the River Thames, on the west by Limehouse and the Thames, and on the south by the Thames opposite Greenwich. Its formation is that of a horseshoe, the curve being described by the River Thames between Limehouse and Blackwall, a distance of about four miles.

There are various conjectures as to the origin of the name of the Isle of Dogs. In Strype's edition of Stow's "Survey," we read :—"The fertile soil of the marsh here is much admired, usually known

Lysons similarly questions the tradition. "On the common tradition of the origin of the name Isle of Dogs," he remarks in a foot-note, "I much doubt the fact, as it would have been much more convenient to have their dog kennels on the other side of the water." In Fearnsides Tombleson's "Thames" appears the following version of the story :—"The name of the Isle of Dogs is traditionally derived from the circumstance of King Edward III., when the court resided at Greenwich,

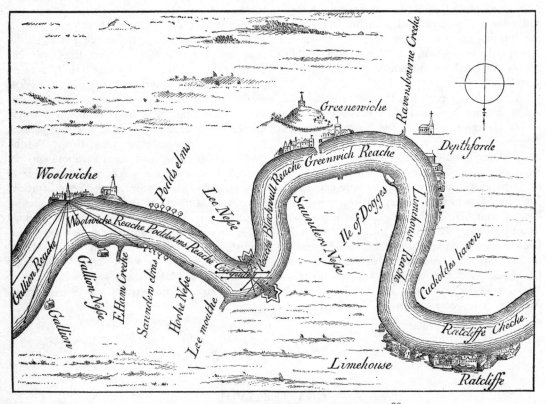

THE THAMES, FROM RATCLIFFE TO WOOLWICH, IN 1588.

by the name of the Isle of Dogs, so called because when our former princes made Greenwich their country seat, if for hunting (they say), the kennels for their dogs were kept on this marsh, which, usually making a great noise, the seamen and others thereupon called the place the Isle of Dogs: though it is not an isle, indeed scarce a peninsula, the neck being about a mile in length." Mr. Brewer, in the "Beauties of England and Wales," implies a doubt as to the above tradition. He writes :—"The origin of this term is not known. A futile tradition says that the place derives its name from the king's hounds having been kept there when the royal family resided formerly at Greenwich Palace, to which it lies opposite."

having kept there his hounds;" whilst in the "Encyclopædia Londinium" the details are slightly varied, thus :—"Although it is now converted to commercial purposes, the Isle of Dogs derived its name from being the depôt of the spaniels and greyhounds of Edward III., and this spot was chosen because it lay contiguous to his sports of woodcock shooting and coursing the red deer in Waltham and the other royal forests in Essex, for the more convenient enjoyment of which he generally resided in the sporting season at Greenwich." Mr. B. H. Cowper, in his "Historical Account of Millwall," questions this derivation, and observes :— "This same tradition has named Henry VIII., Charles II., and other monarchs as having kept their dogs here. But surely if it had been so there would be some historical proof; in this case no one has pretended to adduce it. Therefore, this tradition must be for the present regarded as uncanonical and apocryphal. There is, however," he adds, "another story, which is thus given by Strype and Seymour:—'The next place to be noted on the Thames,' says the latter, 'is the Isle of Dogs, a low marshy ground, so called, as it is reputed, from a waterman's murdering a man in this place who had a dog with him, which would

reign of Elizabeth." Among other instances, he adduces the following:—

"In 1656, on the trial of James Naylor, the celebrated Quaker, for blasphemy, mention is made of the Isle of Dogs. The case of the prisoner was debated by the Parliament. 'The debate turned on the questions of slitting the tongue or boring it; of cutting off his hair; of whipping; of sending him to Bristol, the Isle of Scilly, Jamaica, *the Isle of Dogs*, the Marshalsea.' (See 'Footsteps of our Forefathers,' by J. G. Miall, p. 281, London, 1851.)

DAGENHAM.   (*See page* 527.)

not leave his master till constrained by hunger to swim over to Greenwich, and doing this frequently, it was observed by the watermen plying there, who, following the dog, by that means discovered the body of the murdered man. Soon after the dog, swimming over to Greenwich, snarled at a waterman who sat there, and would not be beaten off, which the other watermen perceiving, and knowing of the murder, they apprehended this strange waterman, who confessed the fact, and was condemned and executed for it.'"

Mr. Cowper, to whom we are mainly indebted for the material for this notice of the Isle of Dogs, writes:—"I have not met with any reference to or use of this name earlier than the close of the

"In Beaumont and Fletcher's *Thierry and Theodoret*, Act II., sc. 2 (Dyce's Edition, Vol. I., p. 154), this passage occurs:—

"*Theodoret:* 'There's something for thy labour.'

"*Bawdber:* 'Where could I wish myself now? In the *Isle of Dogs*, so I might 'scape scratching, for I see by her cat's eyes I shall be clawed wonderfully.'

"Middleton and Dekker, in the *Roaring Girl*, have this passage:—

"*Moll Cutpurse:* 'O, sir, he hath been brought up in the *Isle of Dogs*, and can both fawn like a spaniel and bite like a mastiff, as he finds occasion.'

"I am indebted to Cunningham's 'Murray's

Handbook of London' for the two last references, as well as for the next one.

"'Thomas Nash wrote a play called the *Isle of Dogs,* for which, in 1598, he was imprisoned in the Fleet. Mr. Dyce is of opinion that it was a place where persons took refuge from their creditors and the officers of justice (Middleton's Works, Vol. II., p 535). But this I doubt.'

"Norden, in his Map of Middlesex, 1593, designates this locality 'Isle of Doges Ferme,' and indicates the existence of some building about where Chapel House now stands. The sign used denotes 'Howses of Knightes, Gent., &c.' In this place a stream is represented as running from Limehouse to Blackwall, as well as others which do not exist now. There is no further reference to the Isle of Dogs in this work, but under Blackwall we read: 'neere which is a harbor in the Thamis for shipping. The place taketh name of the blackenes or darkenes of the water bankes or wall at that place.'"

In a map entitled "Thamesis Descriptio," dated 1588, and of which a copy, drawn by Joseph Ames, was published in 1738, two islets are shown between the bed of the river and the embankment which there curves inward, at the point now occupied by the "mast pond." The larger of these islands is termed the "Ile of Dogges."

With reference to the Chapel House mentioned above, which at the commencement of the present century was used as a farm-house, Maitland writes: —"The Chapel House, in the Isle of Dogs, or Poplar Marsh, is the ruins of a stone chapel, but when or by whom built is unknown." In Strype's "Stow" the following particulars are given:— " There is in this marsh, just opposite to Greenwich, a house called the Chapel House, where are the remains of a chapel built of stone. And near this are foundations of houses found, and sometimes hooks of a great size, as though if some great gate taken up, which maketh it probable that hereabouts were inhabitants formerly, perhaps fishermen, or such as had their livelihood from the water. And that, by some inundation, or the unhealthiness of the situation, they left those parts for some more safe and commodious settlement." Mr. Brewer, in his "Beauties of England and Wales" (1816), observes:—"The cold and swampy character of this tract of land would appear repulsive to all thoughts of human habitation ; but piety, which in its obsolete modifications sometimes sought strange recesses, induced an unknown devotee to found a chapel in the midst of the marsh, which is believed to have been dedicated to St. Mary. The site of this small religious structure is now occupied by a disconsolate dwelling, termed Chapel House Farm.

This building exhibits no marks of antiquity, excepting the lower part of the walls, which are composed of small stones and flints, but a Pointed window was destroyed some few years back." Again, the account of this place given by Lysons in 1795 is as follows :—" In the Isle of Dogs stood an ancient chapel, called the Chapel of St. Mary, in Stepney Marsh. It is mentioned by that name in a will of the fifteenth century.* The object of its foundation does not appear. It is not likely that the marsh should ever have had many inhabitants. Perhaps it was a hermitage, founded by some devout person for the purpose of saying masses for the souls of mariners. This chapel has been converted into a neat farm-house, which stands upon the same foundation, and is the only dwelling-place upon the marsh. It exhibits no remains of antiquity, except in the lower part of the walls, which are full of small stones and flints. A Gothic window was removed about three years ago."

For the above string of quotations we are indebted to Mr. Cowper's "History of Millwall," wherein the author observes :—" In all probability Lysons derived his principal fact—that of the designation of the chapel—from Strype. His theory is confessedly a mere supposition. My own view of the original design of this place is that it was a chapel connected with and dependent upon the monastery of St. Mary of Graces, near the Tower of London. This hypothesis is borne out in part by facts, and is, in the whole, more probable than any of the many I have heard. It is matter of regret that our information is so exceedingly scanty, that during its existence this chapel has not been observed to be mentioned more than once. . . . I think it was connected with the monastery in question, which we know held possessions in the marsh ; and we cannot say this of any other. St. Thomas of Acons and St. Katharine's do not appear to have had any possessions here at the dissolution of the monasteries ; in fact, after the estate of St. Mary of Graces fell into the hands of the Bishop of London, he appears to have been sole proprietor for some years. Another fact worthy of consideration is that the chapel was

* "Strype, writing in 1720 (Appendix to Survey, i., p. 120), says, In the Bishop of London's Register of Wills are mentioned these places in this (*i.e.,* Stepney) parish, above 300 years ago.
"*Capella Beatæ Mariæ in Marischo in parochia de Stepney (i.e.,* the Chapel of St Mary in the Marsh, in the parish of Stepney).
" Lymeostes, otherwise Lymehouse, in Stepney. ·
" *Roger Potter de Popiler in parochia de Stebunheath (i.e.,* Roger Potter, of Poplar, in the parish of Stepney). These references must relate to about the year 400.
"I may observe, in passing, that an ancient ferry in the Isle of Dogs is known as Potter's Ferry. The coincidence is noticeable, but no proof of the ferry being named after such an individual."

also dedicated to St. Mary. A third fact worth notice is that the lands in this marsh must have been owned by the monastery prior to any mention made of the chapel. My impression is that its situation and its distance from the monastery on Tower Hill rendered this appropriate as a retreat for spiritual exercises, or as a species of penal colony, to which refractory and erring brethren (for such there were sometimes) were commanded to retire for salutary discipline and penance."

Thirty years ago the condition of Chapel House was much the same as it was when Lysons wrote his description. Two or three additional tenements had been erected on the west side of it, but they were mean and inconvenient, and the trees had been nearly all removed. The ground near Chapel House in every direction showed traces of having been at some remote period occupied with buildings, &c., but more especially to the south-west, from the Chapel House to the river. On the formation of the Millwall Dock, in 1867-8, all traces of the Chapel House were swept away, its site being absorbed in the new docks.

Mr. Cowper, in his work already quoted, inclines to the opinion that the term "Isle of Dogs" was not originally applied to the whole of the district of which we are treating, but to the larger of two islets indicated in Adam's Map of the Thames (1588), above referred to. This map Mr. Cowper regards as "teaching us the important and satisfactory truth that what is now known as such is not the Isle of Dogs proper. The Isle of Dogs," he continues, "is the little spot or island which lies within the curve of the river wall, at the place indicated. Unfortunately for us, this part has been very much altered, and hence we should scarcely expect to find many or any of its original features. However, there is an almost island which answers pretty well to the position of that laid down in the map. This is in the mast pond at the establishment of Messrs. Ferguson. It is a small spot on the south side of the pond, adjoining Tindall's Dock and the mast house (which pond is an indentation of the river bank, and called Drunken Dock), and appears to remain as the last vestige of the primary Isle of Dogs. There is no difficulty in saying how the name became applied to the entire marsh, it being natural to suppose that this was gradually accomplished. Norden's Map is confirmatory to some extent, and explanatory, inasmuch as he calls the portion of the marsh adjacent to Chapel House 'Isle of Dogs Farm.' It seems reasonable, then, to suppose that the term was applied first to the islet in question; secondly,

to the farm nearest to it, and to which it perhaps belonged; and afterwards to the entire marsh. Such is the conclusion to which I have come; and I have called it satisfactory because it shows that there was nothing in the place itself which should make it deserve such a cynical and uninviting name as this. The existence of the original Isle of Dogs has not been noticed by any previous writer on the subject, so far as I am aware.

"The question, however, still remains unanswered—how was the name Isle of Dogs originated? Those who have passed along Millwall (*i.e.*, the western embankment) may have observed, what renders it very probable, that the vast majority of dogs, &c., which find a grave in the river are thrown up and left here by the tide. Indeed, some portions of the embankment, where it slopes toward the river, are a perfect charnel-house of the canine race. Probably it has long been so, and the *original* Isle of Dogs would stand as a net to the stream, by which such substances or objects would be arrested in their course, and left high and dry at low water. Hence, I suspect, the elegant appellation under consideration. I should have been more diffident in reference to this delicate theory, had I not (since it first occurred to my own mind) heard it propounded by others, and stated to actually exist in print."

The Isle of Dogs—or, as it was called, Stepney Marsh—was included in the parish of Stepney probably as far back as the time when England was first divided into parishes; but it now forms part of the parish of Poplar, which, with Limehouse and Blackwall, is of more recent origin than Stepney. Blackwall is the name given to the eastern side of the district under notice. The earliest mention of the locality under that name, observes Mr. Cowper, on the authority of Dugdale, occurs in a deed dated 1377, wherein John Bampton, William Rykhill, Thomas Aspale, and Thomas Mylende, were appointed commissioners for viewing and repairing the banks of the Thames between "Blakewale" and the Hospital of St. Katherine. "In 1480 (20th Edward IV.), Thomas, Bishop of London, Edmund, Abbot of Graces, William Wursley, Dean of Paul's, Sir J. Ebryngton and Sir Thomas Frowyk, Knts., and others, had the like assignation for those embankments, &c., betwixt the town of Lymeostez and the wall called Black Wall." The reference here made to "the wall called Black Wall" justifies the theory propounded in 1592 by Norden, who wrote:—"Black Wall, neere which is a great harbor for shipping in ye Thames, known also by ye name of Black Wall, so called of ye blacke banke or wall of the Thamise." This quotation, remarks Mr. Cowper, is literal as it stands in the MS. ; probably the first Black Wall should be *Bleak* Wall, or Blake Wall. Stow, in his "Survey" (1603), calls it Blake Wall.

The name of Millwall originated from the circumstance of a number of windmills standing along the river wall on the west side of the marsh. These mills were seven in number, and occupied the marsh wall, overlooking Deptford. In a view of London, taken from One Tree Hill, in Greenwich Park, and published in the middle of the last century, these seven mills are represented upon the river bank, opposite Deptford, together with the same number of smaller buildings, one beside each of the mills. Chapel House is also shown in this view. Another view, dated 1754, in the *Gentleman's Magazine*, is similar in all respects.

Mr. Cowper, in his "History of Millwall" (1853), says that the foundations of two or three of the mills may yet be traced, and adds that "one of them without its sails still exists on the premises of Mr. Weston." The premises here referred to, which have long been known as Weston's Roman Cement Works, are now partly occupied as a rosin-oil distillery. The basement of the old mill stands in this part of the premises, now called Barrell's Wharf, and down to very recently it was in use as a flour-mill, but worked by steam power instead of as a windmill. The remains of the mill form an octagonal brick building of three floors, and it still contains some of the internal fittings which were used in the grinding of corn. These works adjoin the old "Windmill" public-house, close by Millwall pier.

The whole aspect of the Isle of Dogs is altogether changed from what it was previous to the end of the last century. By a survey taken in 1740 it was estimated that there were 836 acres of land in marsh. This was reduced to 500 by the formation of the West India Dock at the beginning of the present century, and more recently further reductions have been made in the marsh-land by the construction of Millwall Dock. The island is now traversed from north to south by the North Greenwich and Cubitt Town branch of the Blackwall Railway, whilst the various dock basins and warehouses, &c., have usurped the greater part of the land, which at one time was famous for its fertility, and consequently for its value for grazing purposes. In Strype's edition of "Stow" we read :—"Such is the fertility of this marsh, that it produceth sheep and oxen of the largest size, and very fat. They are brought out of other countries, and fed here. I have been assured by a grazier of good report

(saith the Rev. Dr. Woodward) that he knew eight oxen sold out of this marsh for £34 each. And all our neighbourhood knew that a butcher undertook to furnish the Club at Blackwall with a leg of mutton every Saturday throughout the year that should weigh twenty-eight pounds, the sheep being fed in this marsh, or he would have nothing for them, and he did perform it." Again, in the same strain, Maitland writes :—"The Isle of Dogs, or Poplar Marsh, is a spot of ground of such fertility and excellence of grass, that it not only raises the largest cattle, but it is likewise the great restorative of all distempered beasts." Middleton says :—"It is, perhaps, the richest grass in the country, but if it were the most barren in the kingdom, it might be enriched by the easiest of all possible means : namely, by only opening the sluices to admit the tide, and thereby lay the land under water ; and after the water had remained long enough for the rich substances which are constantly floating in the river, so near the metropolis, to have subsided, permitting the water to drain off by the same sluices into the Thames again. This operation repeated a few times would not fail to improve the land in a very high degree."

"The surface soil of the marsh," observes Mr. Cowper, "is dark, and underlaid in general by a bed of clay or mud, belonging to the *Pleistocene* formation. In some places beneath the soil a bed of pebbles is met with near the surface ; in other places, however, beneath the surface soil and clay, and above the gravel or pebbles which overlie the great clay deposit of the London basin, a stratum, consisting of mud and vegetable matter, is met with." Brewer says :—"Small quantities of peat have been found in this marshy district." In Weale's "Survey of London" we find :—"Subterranean forests exist at Purfleet, Grays, Dagenham Marsh, and Tilbury Fort. In the Isle of Dogs a forest of this description was found at eight feet from the grass, consisting of elm, oak, and fir trees, some of the former of which were three feet four inches in diameter, accompanied by human bones and recent shells, but no metals or traces of civilisation. The trees in this forest were all laid from south-east to north-west, as if the inundation which had overthrown them came from that quarter." "In making the excavations for the Docks," observes a writer in the "Encyclopædia Londinensis," "a wonderful phenomenon of nature was discovered. Eight feet beneath the surface appeared a forest, concealed for unnumbered centuries from every human eye. It presented a mass of decayed twigs, leaves, and branches, encompassing huge trunks rotted through, yet perfect in every fibre; the bark was uninjured, and the whole evidently torn up by the roots. A great deal of this timber was dried and burnt by the inhabitants of Poplar. Some violent convulsion of nature, perhaps an earthquake, must have overturned the forest, and buried it many feet below the present high-water mark; but when or how it happened is beyond the tradition of the most remote ages."

The extent of this deposit appears to have been considerable. When the City Canal was in course of formation, large quantities of submerged wood, with bones, &c., were brought to light; and Lysons tells us that during the construction of the Brunswick Dock (now the export basin of the East India Dock), in 1789, "a great quantity of fossil nuts and wood were found." As far back as the middle of the seventeenth century these discoveries appear to have been going on, as the following entry in Pepys's "Diary" will show. Under date of September 22, 1665, he writes:—"At Blackwall. Here is observable what Johnson* tells us that in digging the late dock, they did, twelve feet under ground, find perfect trees overcovered with earth. Nut-trees, with the branches and the very nuts upon them; some of these nuts he showed us, the shells black with age, and their kernal upon opening decayed, but their shell perfectly hard as ever. And a yew-tree, upon which the very ivy was taken up whole about it, which, upon cutting with an addes (adze), was found to be rather harder than the living tree usually is. The armes, they say, were taken up at first whole about the body, which is very strange." Pepys's description of the nuts, &c., found at Blackwall two hundred years ago would answer exactly for similar discoveries which have been made during excavations which have been carried on within the last twenty or thirty years. "The extent and character of these relics," remarks Mr. Cowper, "justify the opinion that they are found where they grew, and that they were submerged either by the elevation of the bed of the river, or, as I consider the more probable view, by the subsidence of the entire district in which they are found. . . . The subterranean forest which is thus from time to time disturbed is, it would appear, of considerable extent. It is traced from the river-side opposite the dockyard at Deptford, across to the East India Docks, and reappears in Essex. The species of wood which have been

identified appear to be chiefly these:—elm, oak, fir, yew, and hazel; besides which there are ivy, rushes or reeds, land and fresh-water shells, and traces of man, the elephant, and the deer. . . . As it respects the human and elephantine remains, there may be some mistake; it is, however, asserted that such have been found here."

With reference to the early history of the Isle of Dogs, we cannot do better than quote from Mr. Cowper's very interesting work:—"By many it is conjectured that this tract of land was reclaimed under the Romans, who, it is well known, executed many important works in all parts of the kingdom. They possibly commenced this work by raising mounds and banks to define the course of the river, for the guidance and safety of the vessels which navigated it, and they may have actually reclaimed it. There may be said, however, to be nothing certain known. Whether the land was recovered in successive portions or by one effort, history says not. When such enclosures were made by private individuals or the lord of the manor, records could scarcely be expected at so early a period as that to which we must refer part at least of those in the Isle of Dogs. . . . The date of its recovery must have been considerably earlier than the reign of Edward the Confessor.

"In endeavouring to arrive at a fair conclusion respecting the period of our embankments, a careful consideration of data is necessary. It has been stated that our history does not reach back to the period of their construction, and yet we have more than vague conjectures in support of the opinion which would assign them to the time of the Roman occupation of Britain."

It is somewhat singular that the number of "mills" enumerated in "Domesday Book" as belonging to Stibenhede (Stepney) is seven, the precise number which we have seen occupied Millwall at the commencement of the century.

In the "Testa de Nevill," which relates to times of Henry III. and Edward I., William de Vere is described as holding of the Bishop of London a fourth part of his estate in "Stubeneth." Mention is also made of Ricardus de Pontefract, or Pomfret, who held a third part of his estate in Stebeneth. "It is not stated," remarks Mr. Cowper, "in what part of the parish the estate of De Vere lay. It seems to have been parted with in 1396, when the reversion of the manor of Poplar was granted by the celebrated William de Wickham (of Wykeham), Bishop of Winchester, Sir Aubrey de Vere, and others, to the Abbey of St. Mary de Graces." The estate of the Pontefracts, or Pomfrets, was in Stepney Marsh. The manor

---

* Johnson appears to have been the originator of Blackwall Dock during the Commonwealth. He was a friend of Samuel Pepys.

of Pomfret consisted of eighty acres of land, a windmill, &c. Maitland, speaking of the old chapel in this marsh, supposes it may have "belonged to the manor of Pountfret, which anciently lay in this parish, the capital mansion whereof, by the discovery of large foundations and gate hooks, may not only be presumed to have stood here, but likewise diverse other houses, which probably were inhabited till the great inundation toward the close of the fifteenth century, occasioned by a breach in the Blessed Virgin, in the 26th year of Henry VI., a breach made in the said bank of the before specified John Harpour for the length of twenty rods, unto the land of John Fyloll, insomuch as a thousand acres of land lying within the said Marsh were drowned. And that he, the said John, and all those whose estates he then had, were obliged, in respect of their land adjoining to the said bank, to take care of its amendment."

The portion of the embankment thrown down on

MILLWALL DOCKS.

the bank of the River Thames near the great ship-yard at Limehouse Hole."

In the fourteenth and fifteenth centuries considerable repairs seem to have been rendered necessary to the river wall and embankments, in consequence of the damage caused by inundations. Upon an inquisition taken in 1449, the jurors presented, "that by the violence of the tides upon the banks of Stebenhithe Marsh, a great part of the banks adjoining to that Marsh was then ruinous and broken, through the neglect of the landholders there. And that through the default of one John Harpour, gentleman, in not repairing his banks opposite to Deptford Strond, there was, on the Monday, being the Feast of the Annunciation of the above occasion has preserved to modern times the name of the "Breach," in the same manner as Dagenham Breach, already described.* From this breach it has been considered probable that what was called "Poplar Gut" derived its existence. About the middle of the seventeenth century the river again broke in at the same place, which, it would appear, had never been properly repaired. This breach is referred to by Pepys in his "Diary," under date of 23rd March, 1660, which was probably within a few days of the occurrence :—" In our way we saw the great breach which the late high water had made, to the loss of many thousand pounds to the people about Limehouse." In a survey of the parish by Gascoyne, taken in 1703, this part of the river wall is called "Old Breach, the Forland, now a place to lay timber;" and the long strip of water known as Poplar Gut, till its removal on the construction of the West India Docks and City Canal, was designated the Breach. Among the plans and designs published by order of Parliament, in reference to the docks projected in the Isle of Dogs, &c., at the close of the last century, there is one in which this part of the buttons, and gold broad lace round my hands, very rich and fine. By water to the Ferry, where when we come, no coach there; and tide of ebb, so far spent as the horse boat could not get off on the other side the river to bring away the coach. So we were fain to stay there, in the unlucky Isle of Doggs, in a chill place, the morning cool and wind fresh, above two, if not three hours, to our great discontent. Yet, being upon a pleasant errand, and seeing that it could not be helped, we did bear it very patiently; and it was worth my

MILLWALL, FROM THE RIVER.

embankment is named the Breach. Even down to the present day the spot is remembered by this name by the older inhabitants, and also as a place where timber was laid.

There have been ferries across the Thames from Greenwich and Deptford to the Isle of Dogs from a very early period, and two of the principal thoroughfares in the island are the "West Ferry" and "East Ferry" Roads. Our old friend Pepys favours us with one or two amusing entries in his "Diary" respecting these ferries, and the condition of the locality in his time. Under date 31st July, 1665, he writes:—"Up and very betimes by six o'clock at Deptford, and there I find Sir George Carteret and my Lady ready to go; I being in my new coloured silk suit, and coat trimmed with gold observing to see how upon these two scores, Sir George Carteret, the most passionate man in the world, and that was in great haste to be gone, did bear with it, and very pleasant all the while; at least, not troubled much so as to fret and storm at it. Anon the coach comes; in the mean time, there coming a news thither with his horse to go over, that told us he did come from Islington this morning, and that Proctor, the vintner of the Miter, in Wood Street, and his son are dead this morning there of the plague; he having laid out abundance of money there, and was the greatest vintner for some time in London for great entertainments. We, fearing the canonical hour would be past before we got thither, did, with a great deal of unwillingness, send away the licence and wedding ring. So that when we come, though we drove hard with six horses, yet we found them gone from home; and going towards the church, met them coming from church, which troubled us."

The troubles of the genial secretary, however, notwithstanding that he was too late to witness the wedding ceremony, soon wore off, for on the conclusion of the day's festivities, and the retirement of the bridal party for the night, he had the satisfaction of kissing the bride in bed. But it will be best perhaps to record the fact in Pepys's own words:—"I kissed the bride in bed, and so the curtaines drawn with the greatest gravity that could be, and so good night. But the modesty and gravity of this business was so decent, that it was to me indeed ten times more delightful than if it had been twenty times more merry and jovial."

From the above quotation it would appear that there was a communication between the Deptford Ferry and the old ferry opposite Greenwich; it was probably a footway, by what is mentioned by Peter Cunningham in his "Handbook of London" as a "Half-penny Hatch." Norden, writing in 1592, mentions the Ferry House in the Isle of Dogs, and adds that there are "horse ferreyes at Greenwich." Mr. B. H. Cowper considers it probable that the one referred to was "the old Willow Bridge Ferry, or not far from thence." He adds: "no doubt this ferry was the means of communication between Greenwich, Chapel House, and Blackwall." The "news," or postman, alluded to by Mr. Pepys took this route on his way from Islington to Greenwich. Later on, we find Pepys again in the Isle of Dogs. He had evidently been enjoying himself with some friends, probably at Hackney. In his record of the event he writes:— "We set out so late that it grew dark, so as we doubted the losing of our way; and a long time it was, or seemed to be, before we could get to the water side, and that about eleven at night, where, when we came, all merry, we found no ferry boat was there, nor no oares to convey us to Deptford. However, afterwards "oares" was called from the other side at Greenwich; but when it come, a frolick, being mighty merry, took us, and there we would sleep all night in the coach, in the Isle of Dogs. So we did, there being now with us my Lady Scott; and with great pleasure drew up the glasses and slept till daylight; and then, some victuals and wine being brought us, we ate a bit, and so up and took boat, merry as might be, to Sir George Carteret's: there all to bed." Again, he writes under date of 17th December, 1665:—

"Word brought me that Cutler's coach is, by appointment, come to the Isle of Dogs for me, and so I over the water, and in his coach to Hackney; a very fine, clear, cold, frosty day."

Beyond the seven mills on the west side of the island, of which we have already spoken, there appears to have been but few, if any, buildings standing near the river-side down to the beginning of the last century. In "An Actual Survey of the Parish of St. Dunstan, Stepney, *alias* Stebunheath," taken in 1703 by Joel Gascoyne, the circuit of the Isle of Dogs is thus laid down. Starting from north-west corner, we first come to "Fowler's yard," and then to the "Star," a public-house lying a little off from the river-side. The "Old Breach," of which we have already made mention, is next indicated; after which come the "seven mills." Then follows the "Drunken Dock," near the mast house, and further on is a building called "Starch House," which stood close to the ferry. Proceeding along the river-side, the next places marked are—" Roult's Yard," occupying the site of the present Canal Dock; "Cold Harbour," "Globe Stairs," and "Sir H. Johnson's upper dock." "In the body of the map," observes Mr. Cowper, to whom we are indebted for this description, "the 'Chappell' is the only building indicated. The old road is laid down, and its direction very exactly indicated. The other road, which crossed over the east end of the Breach (Poplar Gut), is also given; it appears to have been at this time a field-way, and to have gone south no further than Chapel House, with which, however, it does not appear to have been connected. The ditches seem to be all marked, and the number and form of the fields well defined."

In a survey of the Marsh, taken in 1740 by Dr. Scattiff and T. Willson, the mills are represented as eleven in number, and extend from the Breach to the inlet called the mast-pond. A little to the south of the Canal Dock yard is "the Folly," or "Folly House," which stands upon the river wall: this house is not marked in the survey of 1740, but in 1790 it is mentioned by Pennant, who writes:— "We finished our walk, and dined at a small house, called the Folly, on the water's edge, almost opposite to the splendid hospital at Greenwich, where we sat for some hours, enjoying the delicious view of the river, and the moving picture of a succession of shipping perpetually passing and re-passing."

On the 2nd of February 1791, there was a very high tide; the Thames again overflowed its banks; and the Isle of Dogs was once more inundated.

As we have shown in the preceding chapter, the basin of the Thames, between London and the Nore, consists of a long and very irregularly-shaped flat, lying between high grounds, which sometimes, as at Purfleet, Greenhithe, and Northfleet, come quite down to the river itself, and sometimes recede for miles up into the country, as at Pitsea, where the basin is seven miles in width. The river, as we have seen, is prevented from periodically or occasionally covering the whole of the floor of this basin by a system of embankments, which extend, with occasional interruptions by high lands or houses, from Fulham and Putney above bridge down to the sea, a distance of upwards of fifty miles. A great extent of the river-side streets and houses form, in effect, part of the system of embankment of the river in its course through London—most of Southwark, Lambeth, Deptford, and Greenwich on the one side, and of Shadwell and Limehouse on the other, lying below the level of high water spring tides, and being, in fact, all afloat whenever the tide flows higher than usual. The long straggling street at Millwall presents a good specimen of this sort of embankment; for in walking down it it is impossible not to be aware that it is constructed on artificially raised ground, from which one looks down on the Thames on one side and the flat Isle of Dogs on the other; indeed, the very name of the place, or rather, its termination, is suggestive, the title of "wall" being—both in Kent and Essex—universally applied to the embankments; and the names "Millwall," "Blackwall," "Rotherhithe-wall," "Narrow-wall," "Broadwall," all denote either places built upon the embankment, or streets which owe their existence to its protection.

Since the commencement of the present century there has been a constant growth of factories and establishments of various kinds in the Isle of Dogs, and consequently a corresponding increase in its population and the number of its houses. The East and West India Docks, and the Millwall Docks, which occupy what may be called the central part of the island, we shall describe in the next chapter.

With reference to the progress of factories here, Lysons, in 1811, makes the following remarks in the supplement to his "Environs of London":— "Some very extensive iron-works have been lately established at Millwall, near the Canal and West India Docks, by Jorkes, Coulson, & Co. In their forge and rolling-mills, which are worked by two powerful steam-engines, one of sixty, the other of twenty-horse power, are manufactured from scrap iron bar and bolt iron, for the use of ship-builders and coachmakers, and iron-hoops, sheet and rod iron for home consumption and exportation. Various other articles are made at the manufactory, such as anchors and mooring-chains of any size; and all kinds of heavy forged iron-work for the navy and land service, for various purposes of machinery, &c. Near the same spot Sir Charles Price & Co. have a mill for crushing rapeseed and linseed, a turpentine distillery, and a manufactory of rosin."

At the present time there is almost a complete belt of docks, factories, and engineering establishments extending along the bank of the Thames from Limehouse to Blackwall; these include, besides the above-mentioned works, a large number of others, mostly connected with ship-building and mercantile interests. Among the largest establishments are armour-plate rolling-mills, chemical works, rope manufactories, constructive iron and bridge works, timber wharves, and works for the manufacture of anchors, chains, buoys, &c. Among the oldest establishments on the island are the extensive premises of Messrs. Ferguson, mast and block manufacturers, which have been in existence here upwards of a century.

Messrs. Blashfields' cement and terra-cotta works, which were established here early in the present century, have acquired celebrity for the manufacture of Roman cement, plaster of Paris, Portland cement, and useful and decorative objects in terra-cotta. The following account of these works, communicated by Mr. J. M. Blashfield, appears in Mr. Cowper's "History of Millwall":— "The cement commonly known as Roman cement was first discovered by Parker in 1796, and was then made from nodules of indurated clay, or septaria, found upon the beach of the Isle of Sheppy. Since the expiration of Parker's patent, it has been chiefly made from similar material found off the coast of Harwich. Nearly two-thirds of the brick-work of the Thames Tunnel is united with a cement formed by a combination of the Harwich and Sheppey stones, and was made at these works. Here was also made the cement for the Nelson Pillar, the Royal Exchange, the foundation walls of the new Houses of Parliament, the Lyceum Theatre, the St. James's Theatre, many of the great railway tunnels, and other important works.

"The largest manufactory for plaster of Paris in England is at these works. The raw material is procured partly from Rouen, in Normandy, and partly from Newark, in Nottinghamshire; the latter is most celebrated for its whiteness of colour, but is not so hard as that made from French stones. The cement invented by Mr. Aspdin, of Wakefield, and known as Portland cement, is now made here, and is composed of clay and limestones, washed together in given proportions, then dried, burnt, and ground to powder ready for use.

"Terra-cotta of a light colour is made by combining the clays of Dorset and Devon with silica and other fusible bodies, and mixing them to the consistence of painters' putty or bakers' dough. It is then wrought by an artist into the required shape by hand, somewhat similar to the mode adopted for modelling a statue which is intended to be carved in marble or cast in bronze. The work, when finished, is slowly dried, and when quite dry removed into a reverberatory kiln, and burnt to a white heat in the same mode as burning china. If a number of articles are required of similar design, a plaster mould is made from the clay model, into which the prepared clay is pressed ; and after about an hour's time the mould is removed, and the pressed model worked, finished, and dried. By this latter mode, architectural works which are to be repeated may be made with great economy.

"The red terra-cotta made at these works is from a marble obtained in the township of Bedford, near Bolton, and is, when burnt, equal in hardness and colour to the best ancient specimens of pottery. Etruscan and Greek vases are made of this, and it is of this material the roof of the Alhambra courts of the Crystal Palace at Sydenham is made. The roof of the Pompeian House at Sydenham was also made here, and is, in part, of this red marble.

"Statues of heroic size, and the largest pieces of pottery ever fired, have lately been wrought at this place, in the Dorset and Devon clays. The great statue of Australia, modelled by Mr. Beli for the terrace of the Crystal Palace, was made here in this way. So also was the Venus de Medici and the colossal Triton for the fountains of the same place. Capitals of columns, busts, vases, consoles, balustrades, chimneys, flower-pots, and a variety of other articles, are constantly being fabricated here, and artists of the first eminence are employed upon the models."

On the portion of Millwall immediately opposite Deptford are some extensive iron-works and ship-building yards. The premises known as Millwall Iron-works were filled out in 1836, by Mr. (afterwards Sir) William Fairbairn, the celebrated engineer, of Manchester, and were planned on a very elaborate scale, comprising engineers' fitting and erecting shops, joiners' and pattern-makers' shops, iron and brass foundries, smithies, &c., besides every appurtenance in the yard for constructing vessels of the largest class, both in wood and iron. Here were built several vessels of war for the navy, including the *Grappler, Megæra,* &c. These iron-works were for many years held by the eminent ship-building firm of Messrs. Scott Russell & Co., and were partly destroyed by fire in 1853, when the damage done was estimated at £60,000. Mr. Scott Russell became well known in the engineering and mercantile world for his researches and experiments, which resulted in the practical application of the "wave-line" theory in connection with ship-building, and he also acted as the secretary of the Great Exhibition of 1851, of which he was one of the original promoters.

These premises possess a river frontage of great extent, and are an object of great attraction to the steamboat traveller, from the interest naturally excited in witnessing so many vessels constantly in course of construction.

Here was built the largest vessel that ever floated in the Thames, or, indeed, anywhere else : namely, the *Great Eastern.* This huge steamship, whose subsequent career perhaps has hardly been on a par with the interest which was evinced during her construction, occupied about six years in building, having been commenced in 1853, and equipped ready for sailing by January, 1860. It was built for the Eastern Steam Navigation Company, and was intended for the Indian and Australian route by the Cape of Good Hope. During the construction of the vessel, the proportions of the ship were seen to great advantage as she lay with her broadside to the river, her form being to a great extent free from the forest of poles which usually serve as the stages used in ordinary ship-building.

The hull of the vessel is built entirely of iron, and is 680 feet in length, 80 feet in breadth, and 58 feet in height from keel to deck. The ship is divided transversely into ten separate compartments of 60 feet each, rendered perfectly water-tight by bulkheads, having no openings whatever lower than the second deck, whilst two longitudinal walls of iron, 36 feet apart, traverse 350 feet of the length of the ship.

Some idea of the magnitude of these dimensions may be formed when it is stated that the *Great Eastern* is six times the size of the *Duke of Wellington* line-of-battle ship ; that her length is more than three times that of the height of the Monument on Fish Street Hill, while her breadth is equal to the width of Pall Mall ; and that a promenade round the deck affords a walk of more than a quarter of a mile. She was designed by Mr. Isambard Kingdom Brunel, F.R.S., the "father of Transatlantic steam navigation." The hull of the ship, together with the paddle-engines, were built by Messrs. Scott Russell and Co., whilst the screw-engines were manufactured by Messrs. Watts and Co., of Birmingham. Mr. Scott Russell, to whom the entire merits of the ship as a piece of naval architecture belong, wrote during its construction :—" It is to the company's engineer, Mr. J. K. Brunel, that the original conception is due of building a steamship large enough to carry coals sufficient for full steaming on the longest voyage. He, at the outset, and long before it had assumed a mercantile form, communicated his views to me, and I have participated in the contrivance of the best means to carry them into practical effect. I think, further, that the idea of using two sets of engines and two propellers is original, and was his invention. It was his idea also to introduce a cellular construction, like that at the top and bottom of the Britannia Bridge, into the construction of the great ship. These are the main characteristics which distinguish this from other ships, and these are Mr. Brunel's. Her lines and her structure in other respects are identical with those of any other ships which are constructed like this on a principle of my own, which I have systematically carried out during the last twenty years, and which is commonly called the 'wave' principle. In other respects, also, her materials are put together in the manner usual in any other ships."

The bottom of the ship is almost flat. Up to the water-mark the hull is constructed with an inner and outer skin, nearly three feet apart, and each composed of three-quarter inch plates. Between these, at intervals of six feet, run horizontal webs of iron plates, which materially increase the power of resistance both of the inner and the outer skin. About 10,000 tons of iron plates were used in the construction of the hull. These plates are 30,000 in number, and are each secured by 100 iron rivets.

The distinguishing feature of the *Great Eastern*, in addition to her vast size, is the combined application of steam-power through the paddle-wheel and the screw. The engines are considerably larger than any hitherto made for marine purposes. The vessel has ten boilers and five funnels, and the boilers are placed longitudinally along the centre of the ship, and are entirely independent of each other. Each paddle-boiler has ten furnaces, and each screw-boiler twelve furnaces, thus giving to the whole the large number of one hundred and twelve furnaces. Independent of her steam-power, her means of propulsion is aided by six masts, no

less than 6,500 square yards of canvas being used in the construction of her sails. The paddle-wheels are fifty-eight feet in diameter, and the weight of each wheel is computed at ninety tons, whilst the screw propeller is twenty-four feet in diameter, and the engine shaft 160 feet in length. The ship was designed to accommodate 4,000 passengers—800 first class, 2,000 second class, and 1,200 third class —independently of the ship's complement of about 400 hands. Her registered tonnage is 23,000.

The first attempt to float this monster vessel was made in November, 1857, but unsuccessfully. On Sunday, January 31st, 1858, however, in the presence of a vast concourse of spectators, she yielded to the hydraulic pressure that was brought to bear upon her, and glided slowly, but gracefully, into the Thames, where she lay at rest, while being fitted for sea, till September, 1859, when she was towed down the river to Gravesend. In the following June the *Great Eastern* made her first sea trip. It may be of interest to record that when first floated the vessel registered sixteen and a half feet aft, and fourteen feet eleven inches forward, or within six inches of the amount calculated.

In a work entitled "A Floating City," by Jules Verne, some interesting particulars of the great ship and its subsequent career are given. From it we learn that "after twenty passages from England to America, one of which was marked by very serious disasters, the use of the *Great Eastern* was temporarily abandoned, and this immense ship, arranged to accommodate passengers, seemed no longer good for anything. When the first attempt to lay the Atlantic cable had failed—partly because the number of ships which carried it was insufficient—engineers thought of the *Great Eastern*. She alone could store on board the 2,100 miles of metallic wire, weighing 4,500 tons. She alone, thanks to her perfect indifference to the sea, could unroll and immerse this immense cable. But special arrangements were necessary for storing away the cable in the ship's hold. Two out of six boilers were removed, and one funnel out of three belonging to the screw-engine ; in their places large tanks were placed for the cable, which was immersed in water to preserve it from the effects of variation of the atmosphere ; the wire thus passed from these tanks of water into the sea without suffering the least contact with the air. The laying of the cable having been successfully accomplished, and the object in view attained, the *Great Eastern* was once more left in her costly idleness."

The vessel was afterwards taken in hand by a French company, which was floated with a capital of 2,000,000 francs, with the intention of again conveying passengers across the Atlantic, and the immense ship was accordingly re-arranged for that purpose. The interior of the ship was fitted with every convenience, and even luxury, to suit the requirements of passengers. The ladies' saloon and the grand saloon were ornamented with lustres, swinging lamps, and pictures, and the magnificent rooms lighted by side skylights, supported on

Since the launch of the *Great Eastern* the Millwall Iron Works have been in the hands of Messrs. Mare & Co.; and more recently the premises known as the Northumberland Works have been utilised for the manufacture of the machinery and other necessaries used in the supply of the electric light. The *Northumberland* armour-plated ship was launched from these premises in 1866.

Immediately beyond Potter's Ferry, which lies

LAUNCH OF THE GREAT EASTERN.

gilded pillars, and communicating with the upper deck by wide staircases with metallic steps and mahogany balusters. The laundries and the crew's berth are shut off at the fore part; on deck are arranged four rows of cabins separated by a passage, and at the stern three immense dining-rooms run in the same direction as the cabins; a passage leads from the saloons at the stern to those at the bows round the paddle-engine, between its sheet-iron partition and the ship's offices.

The ill-fated vessel, however, never seems to have prospered; and more than once she was nearly lost in the Atlantic, through failing to answer her helm, or through some other accident. Now it appears that she is likely to be used for conveying coals from Newcastle to the port of London.

directly opposite Greenwich Hospital, is Cubitt Town, so called from the fact of a large portion of the land here having been some years ago taken by Messrs. Cubitt & Co., builders, for the construction of works in the manufacture of all kinds of ceramic ware used in building, &c. Rows of streets and houses were built in the neighbourhood of the works, and in 1853, Mr. William Cubitt, M.P., erected a church here for the use of the inhabitants. This edifice, built of brick, with stone dressings, and in the Early English style, stands at the south-eastern extremity of the island, its tower and spire being a conspicuous object from the river.

St. Luke's Church, in Stratford Street, Millwall, consecrated in 1870, is a stone building of modern Gothic design, with a heavy-looking tower and spire.

Limehouse is situated on the north-western side of the canal which separates the Isle of Dogs from the mainland. It is so called from a lime-kiln, generally known as the lime-house, which stood here. Pepys, under date of October 9th, 1661, writes, in his "Diary" :—"By coach to Captain Marshe's at Limehouse—to a house that hath been their ancestors' for this 250 years, close by the lime-house, which gives the name to the place."

Norden, writing in 1592, adopts the derivation of Limehouse from the lime-kiln, which, according to Mr. Cowper's statement in his work above quoted, exists to this day; but Stow gives the derivation as a corrupt spelling for Lime-host, or Lime-hurst, the latter of which denotes a plantation, or

designs of Nicholas Hawksmoor, a pupil of Sir Christopher Wren, and was consecrated in 1730. The original drawings and plans for the building are preserved in the British Museum. The steeple of the church is conspicuous from the river, but is not remarkable for its beauty; indeed, this church, like others of which Hawksmoor was the architect, exhibits a style remarkable for its solidity of ap-

LIMEHOUSE CHURCH.

a place of lime-trees. It may be remembered that Shakespeare introduces the name in the play of *Henry VIII.* (Act v., sc. 3), where Porter says :—"These are the youths that thunder at a playhouse, and fight for bitten apples : that no audience but the Tribulation of Tower-hill or the limbs of Limehouse, their dear brothers, are able to endure."

The district was originally a hamlet of Stepney, but was made into a distinct parish in the reign of Queen Anne. The church is one of the fifty which were authorised to be erected by an Act of Parliament passed in the ninth year of that reign. It is dedicated to St. Anne, and was built from the

pearance and singularity of design, which may be described as Romanesque. The edifice is constructed of Portland stone, and was built at a cost of about £38,000. The principal entrance, approached by a flight of stone steps, is formed in front of the segmental vestibule, which is finished with square pilasters, with enriched capitals, supporting an entablature and semi-dome roof. The third storey of the tower forms in the plan a curious outline, and in its elevation is equally unsightly with the part rising immediately above it. The walls forming the vestry-room at the north-east angle of the church, and those corresponding on the opposite side, are carried up several feet above the large cornice, and form two curiously ornamented towers. In the interior of the church there is nothing remarkable as to the general arrangement. The Roman style is preserved throughout. Stone columns, of the composite order, standing upon square pedestals, support an enriched cornice, continued only over part of the side aisles. Small Ionic columns of wood are placed as supports under either gallery, the entrances to which are equally crude in design with many other portions of this edifice. The east window, of painted glass, from a design by West, was executed by Mr. Buckler, the painter of the window in the "Barons' Hall" at Arundel Castle. The pulpit is an elaborate specimen of carved work, and is stated to have occupied two years and a half in its execution.

The "fine and beautiful" Commercial Road, as Baron Dupin calls it in his "Commercial Power of Great Britain," constructed under the direction of Mr. Walker, an eminent engineer in his day, runs directly through the parish. It is seventy feet in width, and forms a direct communication between Whitechapel and the West India Docks.

The Lea Cut and the Regent's Canal both enter the Thames at Limehouse. The former was executed in 1772 for the purpose of obtaining a more direct communication between the Pool and the River Lea, which it joins at Bromley. The Regent's Canal is of more recent formation. Its route is traced through nine parishes; it is eight miles in length, and its mean width thirty-seven feet. It rises eighty-four feet by means of twelve locks, is crossed by about forty bridges, passes by means of a tunnel (upwards of half a mile in length) under the New River and part of Islington, and by another tunnel (a quarter of a mile in length) at Paddington, and communicates with the Grand Junction Canal.

Poplar, which adjoins Limehouse on the east, was likewise originally a hamlet of Stepney, from which parish it was separated in 1817. The district embraces the Isle of Dogs. Dr. Woodward, in "Strype" (Circuit Walk, p. 102), writing in 1720, observes :—" Popler, or Poplar, is so called from the multitude of poplar-trees (which love a moist soil) growing there in former times. And there be yet remaining, in that part of the hamlet which bordereth upon Limehouse, many old bodies of large poplars, standing as testimonials of the truth of that etymology."

The parish church, dedicated to All Saints, was consecrated in 1823. It is a large building, with a handsome steeple, which contrasts favourably with that of Limehouse Church. Poplar Chapel, called also the East India Company's Chapel, was built during the Commonwealth, and contains two or three monuments to distinguished men, among them being one to Robert Ainsworth, the Latin lexicographer, who died in 1743, and whose epitaph was his own composition; and another to George Steevens, the Shakesperian critic and editor, who died at Hampstead in 1800, and was buried here. This latter monument was executed by Flaxman.

The old manor-house of Poplar, an ancient wooden building, was situated on the south side of the present East India Dock Road, but was partially pulled down early in the present century. The old house was formerly owned by Sir Gilbert and Sir William Dethick, who held successively the appointment of Garter King-at-Arms in the reign of Queen Elizabeth. The Town Hall and the offices of the Local Board of Works for Poplar are handsome and commodious buildings, the latter being of recent erection.

"To Poplar adjoineth Blackwall"—so wrote Dr. Woodward in "Strype's Appendix"; and added that it is "a notable harbour for ships, so called because it is a wall of the Thames, and distinguished by the additional term Black from the black shrubs which grow on it, as on Blackheath, which is opposite to it, on the other side of the river.'

In the reign of Edward III. Sir John de Pulteney possessed the manor of Poplar. His London house was at Cold Harbour, in Upper Thames Street. Mr. Cowper conjectures that if he ever resided in this neighbourhood, it was at Blackwall, where there is a place called Cold Harbour. "Near the ancient ferry, called Globe Stairs, opposite the 'Artichoke' Tavern," he observes, "there stands an ancient house, which tradition says was successively occupied by Sebastian Cabot and Sir Walter Raleigh. Whatever value may attach to the tradition, the house in question is both curious and interesting. Its framework is of wood, and still likely to last for years. Some grotesque heads and other carvings adorn the outside. The floor of the house is considerably below the present level of the street, and the principal entrance is blocked up. Though now in a narrow and confined situation, originally its windows looked out upon the rising sun, and commanded an extensive view up and down the river, as well as across into Kent. By the gradual encroachments of buildings all around, it has been hemmed in as we now find it."

The Brunswick Wharf, at Blackwall, was opened for the reception of steam-packets in 1840. Lovegrove's Tavern, the "Brunswick," was for many years famous for its fish, and particularly for whitebait dinners.

CHAPTER LIX.

THE EAST AND WEST INDIA AND MILLWALL DOCKS.

" Where has commerce such a mart,
So rich, so thronged, so drained, and so supplied,
As London—opulent, enlarged, and still-
Increasing London?"--COWPER.

The Vastness of Trade and Commerce—Arrival of Coal-ships and other Vessels in the Port of London—Number of Barges and other Craft required for Traffic in 1792—Plunder carried on in the Lighters on the River—Institution of the Thames Police—Proposals for the Establishment of Docks—Foundation of the West India Docks—The Opening Ceremony—Description of the Docks—A Curious Museum—ew Dry Docks—The Wood Wharf—The Rum Quay—The South West India Dock—The Wool Warehouses—The East India Docks—Millwall Dock—Insecurity of Merchandise before the Establishment of Docks or Institution of the Thames Police.

THE docks of London show at once to the most casual observer the great enterprise and prosperity of the metropolis. It will readily be conceived that a population of more than 3,000,000 souls must necessarily, to a great extent, be supported by its trade and commerce, its proceeds in money value far exceeding in amount that of any other community in the world. The merchant is the dealer with the trading universe, the tidal Thames bringing with its flow the treasures of near and distant nations ; and, with the aid of steam, persons of all nations come to us with objects of business and mutual interchange.

Charles Knight, in his " London," says :—" The stranger, especially from an inland county, who takes a passage by one of the steamers which leave London Bridge every half-hour for Greenwich, will be astonished at the apparently interminable forests of masts which extend on both sides of the channel, where a width of three hundred feet *should* be kept for the purposes of safe navigation, but which the crowd of ships from all quarters of the globe, of colliers, coasters, steamboats, and river craft, renders it difficult for the harbour-masters to maintain. If the tide be running upward, laden coal-barges are thronging the channel, proceeding to the wharves in the upper part of the river, and colliers at their moorings are at all times discharging their cargoes into barges alongside. By the regulations of the coal trade, only a certain number of coal-ships are allowed to unload at the same time, the others remaining lower down the river until their turn arrives ; and the coal-meters, who are appointed by the City, are also limited in number. But for these restrictions the river would present a still more crowded appearance, as it has happened that above three hundred colliers have arrived in the lower pool in one day, and even now a very large portion of the river is occupied by this one branch of commerce. Seventy years ago, not only coal-ships, but vessels of every other kind, discharged their cargoes into lighters while at anchor in the stream ; but such a practice would now be impossible, so great has been the increase of commerce. East Indiamen in general came only as far as Blackwall, where they discharged their cargo into decked lighters of from fifty to one hundred tons, and, the hatchways being secured under lock and key, they proceeded to the wharves. West India ships discharged in the river, and the cargoes also, were conveyed in lighters to the legal quays. All other vessels, except they were of small size, were in like manner compelled to use lighters in discharging their cargoes. At the present time the majority of the barges and river craft are solely employed in transporting the cargoes of coal, corn, and timber ships : comparatively speaking, only a small proportion being required for the conveyance of all other commodities, the chief of which are of a bulky kind, and do not offer any great temptation to pilferers."

In 1792 the number of barges and craft required for the traffic between the ships in the river and the quays was 500 for timber and 1,180 for coal, each averaging 33 tons ; 402 lighters of 39 tons ; 338 punts of 20 tons ; 57 lugger boats of 24 tons ; 6 sloops of 27 tons ; 10 cutters of 71 tons ; and 10 hoys of 58 tons : making a total of 3,503 craft. Property of the most costly and valuable description, and every kind of merchandise, was daily exposed to plunder in these open boats, for only the lighters of the East India Company were decked, and it was considered that even they afforded a very insufficient protection. The temptation to pilfering was almost irresistible, those who were honestly disposed taking their share, under the plea that waste and leakage were perquisites. So many persons were engaged in the work of depredation on the river that it was carried on in the most daring and open manner, lightermen, watermen, labourers, the crews of ships, the mates and officers in some instances, and to a great extent the officers of the revenue, being combined in this nefarious system, while on each side of the river there were hosts of receivers, some of them persons of opulence, who carried on an extensive business in stolen property. In 1798, the Thames Police, called then the Marine Police, was instituted for the repression of these offences, but the source of the evil was still untouched, the temptation remaining undiminished so long as the exposure of property was rendered unavoidable by the absence of sufficient accommodation in quays and warehouses.

During the last century scarcely an effort had been made for the accommodation of the vastly increased trade of London, and the mercantile interests experienced, in consequence, impediments and losses, which it is wonderful did not arouse them earlier to provide a remedy. About the year 1793 the complaints of the merchants began to attract more attention than they had hitherto received, and they held meetings, at which various remedies were proposed, but for a time no substantial improvement resulted therefrom. Many plans were brought forward, among them being the following, each of which embraced the Isle of Dogs in their scheme :—

The City plan, of which the chief feature was a dock of 102 acres in the Isle of Dogs, to contain above 400 ships, and another at Rotherhithe, of the same extent, for colliers. Another plan, drawn up by a Mr. Walker, was to excavate fifty-five acres for docks, thirty-five acres additional being intended for quays, wharves, and warehouses. One of the entrances was to be by a canal intersecting the Isle of Dogs, at a point near the southern shore. The cost was estimated at £880,000.

The last of these plans was designed by Mr. Reaveley ; it displayed considerable ingenuity, and its chief features were :— (1) To form a new channel for the river in a straight line from Limehouse to Blackwall, the Long Reach round the Isle of Dogs thus constituting a dock, with flood-gates at each entrance. (2) To continue the new channel below Blackwall towards Woolwich Reach, so as to convert another bend of the old channel into a dock. (3) To make a new channel from Wapping, and to form three docks out of the three bends, to be called Ratcliffe Dock, Blackwall Dock, and Greenwich Dock.

In 1799 an Act of Parliament was passed for rendering more commodious and for better regulating the Port of London ; and in that same year another Bill was also passed for the formation of the West India Docks. These docks, which occupy the whole length of what may be called the " neck " of the Isle of Dogs, from Limehouse to Blackwall, are said to be the largest in the world. They are nearly three times as extensive as the London Docks, and are almost 300 acres in extent.

The West India Docks were the first public wet-docks constructed on the north bank of the Thames in the port of London. There had, however, been for many years a wet-dock at Blackwall, at the ancient ship-yards there ; besides which, a Mr. Perry, in 1789, had constructed the Brunswick Dock, which, as we shall presently see, was afterwards enlarged to form the export basin of the East India Docks.

The Act empowering the formation of these docks includes the City Canal, or South Dock ; and the preliminaries having been duly arranged, the works were commenced in February, 1800, and the " first stone " was laid in July of the same year. Inscriptions setting forth the objects for which the docks were made, written on two rolls of vellum, one in English and the other in Latin, together with several coins of different values, were enclosed in glass bottles, which were deposited in the first stone, at the south-east corner of warehouse No. 8.

The docks were formed from the designs of Mr. Jesson, and were formally opened on the 27th August, 1802, the opening ceremony being performed by Mr. William Pitt, the then Prime Minister, in the presence of a vast concourse of spectators. The first ship to enter the new docks was the *Henry Addington*, a vessel newly built, and one of the finest in the West India trade. For twenty-one years after the opening of the docks all vessels in the West India trade frequenting the port of London were compelled to use them.

The principal, or western, entrance to the docks is near the West India Dock Station of the Blackwall Railway, a little to the east of Limehouse Church. It is surmounted by the model of a sailing-vessel, and over the entrance is inscribed :— " The West India Import Dock—begun 12th July, 1800 ; opened for business 1st September, 1802."

At the principal entrance is a bronze statue, erected to perpetuate the memory of Robert Milligan, " a merchant of London, to whose genius, perseverance, and guardian care, the surrounding great work principally owes its design, accomplishment, and regulation." This statue, which was executed by Sir R. Westmacott, is of life-size, placed on a granite pedestal, and enclosed by an iron railing. Close by are two guard-houses, which were erected for the accommodation of small detachments of troops, detailed by the Government when first the docks were constructed for the more efficient protection of the company's property. These troops supplied a cordon of night sentries round the docks, each sentry having in his sentry-box a bell, which he sounded at regular intervals.

There were originally only two docks, one for imports and the other for exports. The original plan was not filled up by the completion of the docks before 1805. Since that period many additions and alterations have been made.

The whole system of West India Docks now comprises three parallel docks, with warehouses, quay sheds, and sheds for export goods, covering an area of 264 acres, of which 160 acres are land, and 104 acres water. The storage capacity of the warehouses in the West India Dock system is 166,700 tons of goods. The area of the Western and South Dock quays is 1,566,500 square feet, and of the warehouses 1,141,000 square feet. The Dock Company employ on their permanent staff about 2,500 persons. In addition to these a very large number of persons are employed as the exigencies of the work may require. The staff employed at the West India Docks alone is as follows :—

	WEEKLY COST.	ANNUAL COST.
Major or controlling Staff ... ... (184)	£400	£21,000
Minor Staff ... ... (454)	525	27,000
Porter and Labour Staff and extra Labourers } averages (1717)	2,336	120,000

Visitors usually commence their inspection at the northernmost or Import Dock. This dock contains in water space thirty superficial acres ; it is 2,600 feet long, and 500 feet wide, with warehouses half a mile in extent. Ships from all parts of the world discharge here, and their cargoes are housed in the adjoining warehouses, which contain canes, horns, camphor, tea, pepper, pimento, rice, tin, copper, ginger, sugar, molasses, coir, coffee, plumbago, oils, &c.

At No. 11 warehouse, which was partially destroyed by fire on the 28th December, 1873, is a small museum, containing specimens of the various kinds of goods housed at the docks. As a sample of the interest attaching to this museum, it may be mentioned that cochineal, one of the products here exhibited, is the dried carcase of an insect, and produces a brilliant crimson dye. About 70,000 of the insects are required to weigh one pound. They are of two kinds : the black, females which have produced young ; and the grey or white, which have arrived at maturity and have not bred. As the finest dye is in the skin, the black insects are the most profitable, being apparently all skin, and being hollow are known as "shelly cochineal." The insects are suffocated and dried in ovens.

In this warehouse can be seen a machine worked by hydraulic pressure for sampling tin. One ingot of tin in each ten is "sampled" for the market, and, the sample being sent to the brokers in the City,

the sale is effected and the value of the ten ingots is fixed by the evidence of the sample cut from one. The value of the metals, tin and copper, lying at this warehouse is nearly £30,000, and the weight is 350 tons. The weight of an ingot of tin is from ninety to a hundred pounds, and the value about £3 10s.

The vessels from China, which arrive early in July laden with the new season's teas, are generally discharged here ; and when, as is now usual, pressure is put upon the company, it is not uncommon for a ship bringing 50,000 packages of tea to be discharged within twenty working hours.

On the north quay of the Import Dock many cargoes are to be seen. In the warehouses along the quay the article chiefly housed is sugar ; the floors and quay are stained with sugar drainage, and in some parts saturated with molasses from the lower-class sugars. Sugar is imported of many different qualities, and in various kinds of packages, the large hogsheads being the most unwieldy. Mauritius sugar comes in mats formed of leaves, and East India sugar in bags woven from jute. Jaggery is a very low quality sugar from the Madras coast, and the bags in which it is imported become so thoroughly soaked with sugar that after being emptied of their contents they are sold to itinerant dealers, who boil them to extract the sugar, and sell the bags to the paper-makers. All the bags are raised from the hold of the ship by cranes, worked like the majority of cranes in the docks, by hydraulic pressure.

The coffee imports are concentrated at No. 10 warehouse, and about one-sixth of the imports of coffee into London comes to this warehouse. The warehouse is supplied with machinery for the bulking, re-filling, and beating of casks of coffee by hydraulic power, superseding manual labour. All coffee of one mark and of the same quality or description, frequently from fifty or more packages, has to be mixed together on the floor of the warehouse, to ascertain the net weight for Customs duty and for trade purposes, and also to ensure the quality being of one average. In former years this mixing was done by hand, and as the company's housings of coffee are about 20,000 casks in a year, in addition to about 70,000 bags, it follows that much labour was required. It is now the practice, after turning out the contents of the casks, to scoop the berries into iron hoppers, whence they run into the casks on the floor below. In order to make the coffee lie close, so that the actual quantity turned out might be re-filled into the package, it was the practice for a gang of five men to beat the casks with wooden mallets, and even then the whole of the contents could frequently not be returned to the packages, and bags, named by the trade "overtakers," were used to take the surplus; but the mechanical beaters of this patent machinery perform in one minute the work which occupied five men six minutes; moreover, the whole of the coffee can now be easily returned to the original packages. There are eleven of these machines in use.

In passing to the West Wood Wharf, a siding or line of railway will be observed at the south end of No. 10 Warehouse, in which trucks are placed with goods from the steamers, which discharge at Southampton. The trucks are loaded alongside the vessels at Southampton, and run direct to this siding, whence the goods are raised by the crane to the loophole, and manipulated as if coming from vessels discharging alongside the quay in these docks.

The swing bridges carrying the railway over the adjoining locks weigh 300 tons each, and are moved by hydraulic machines, requiring only one man to set them in motion.

Blackwall Basin, which is on the east side of the northern bridge, is the tidal basin for the reception of ships entering the West India Dock; and on the south side of the basin is a dry dock for repairing and painting ships, which was opened on the 6th March, 1878, and was constructed at a cost of from £60,000 to £80,000. Its dimensions are: length 480 feet, breadth of bottom 80 feet, and entrance 64 feet, depth on gill 23 feet.

At the Wood Wharf, large quantities of mahogany, furniture wood, and teak, amounting to about 50,000 tons per annum, are stored, and the heavy logs are carried with comparative ease by travelling machinery. Quantities of lignum vitæ from Jamaica are seen; this is used chiefly for blocks, pulleys, rulers, &c. Satinwood and ebony, in considerable quantity, are also to be seen here, as also logwood, sapan wood, red sanders wood, and other woods used for dyeing purposes.

The largest log of mahogany ever known to have been imported arrived on the 30th of October, 1879, by the *Grizzehaum* from Tabasco. It was more than 60 feet long, and nearly 12 tons in weight.

The Rum Quay is the depôt for all wines and spirits in the Company's charge, and is capable of storing 40,000 puncheons. The average quantity of the rum in the vaults and warehouses is 35,000 puncheons, containing about 3½ million gallons, and of the value of £700,000, the Customs duty, at 10s. 2d. per proof gallon, being in addition about £1,800,000. The vaults are good specimens of groined brickwork, the arches being elliptical, and springing from octagonal stone piers. Notwithstanding the forest of casks (which, however, do not intrude themselves in the prevailing darkness, though the odour of rum does), the visitor might easily suppose he was in the crypt of some immense cathedral. The only light obtained is from side windows, outside which are fixed concave reflectors; and as the vaults are 154 feet wide, the centre, without the aid of the reflectors, would be, in winter time, totally dark.

Each puncheon is marked in white paint with the "rotation" number and year of bonding, and the contents and "ullage," and a reflector formed of a piece of tin, nailed on a stick, is used to throw the borrowed light on these marks by the cooper whose duty it is to sound each cask daily, to ascertain that it remains in good condition. By the sound which the blow of the hammer produces, he is able to tell within half a gallon the vacuity of each cask, and should it appear to increase he marks the cask to watch it, and have it removed for examination should any flaw develop itself.

The plan of using reflectors is adopted on the score of safety from fire, no candle or lamp being allowed to be taken on the Rum Quay. Balmain's luminous paint has been used in the vaults with success.

On the vatting floor of this department are vats varying in capacity from 320 to 15,000 gallons, their aggregate capacity being 59,210 gallons. In these vats merchants are allowed to mix rum intended for exportation.

The centre dock is the Export Dock, covering 24 acres of water, 2,600 feet long by 400 feet in width, in which ships of light draught are accommodated to load.

The South West India Dock, commenced in 1866, and opened on 5th March, 1870, contains upwards of 26 acres of water, is 2,650 feet in length, and 450 feet in width, with a uniform depth of 29 feet. Some of the largest ships carrying colonial and East Indian cargoes which arrive in the Port of London discharge and load in this dock. The Import ships discharge usually on the south side, and the Export ships load chiefly on the north side; two berths, however, at the eastern and western ends of the south side are reserved for loading.

In the basin at the east end of the dock are loaded the fine vessels of the Glen Line, trading between London and China.

The extensive wool warehouses, situated on the south quay of this dock, were erected in 1873, for the storage and showing of wool, and have show room for 15,000 bales at one time. 113,000

WEST INDIA DOCKS.

J R Well

bales were housed and shown here in 1879, and 133,000 in 1880.

Other objects of interest to visitors are the steam fire engines, the cooperage, chain-testing house, and sawmills, together with the various workshops, where at times 400 mechanics and labourers are employed, in connection with the maintenance and repair of the docks, warehouses, and machinery of the company.

The East India Import and Export Docks and basin, at Blackwall, contain a water space of 32 acres ; they were formerly the property of the East India Dock Company, and were constructed chiefly for the accommodation of East India shipping. The then capital or joint stock of the company was £463,876, and with, or out of, this capital were constructed the above-mentioned docks, including necessary warehouses, quays, roads, &c.

As far back as 1592 Blackwall was noted for its "great harbour of shipping," which harbour in all probability gave rise to the idea and subsequent formation of docks. Before the East India Docks existed, there was a wet dock constructed in 1789 by a Mr. Perry, called the "Brunswick Dock," which was afterwards enlarged to form an export dock to the East India Dock. In excavating for this dock a great quantity of fossil nuts and wood were found.

Pepys, in his "Diary," dated September 22nd, 1665, writes :—"At Blackwall, in digging the late docke, they did, twelve feet under ground, find perfect trees over-covered with earth. Nut-trees, with the branches, and the very nuts upon them ; some of these nuts he [Johnson] showed us. Their shells black with age, and their kernel, upon opening, decayed, but their shell perfectly hard as ever."

The following inscription is placed under the clock tower of the principal entrance to the dock in the East India Road :—

"Under auspices of our most Gracious Sovereign George III., the sanction of his Majesty's Government and the patronage of the East India Company, these Wet Docks appropriated to the commerce of India and ships in that employ, were accomplished in those eventful years 1804, 1805, and 1806, the first stone being laid March 14th, 1804. They were opened by the introduction of five ships from 1,200 to 800 tons, with valuable cargoes, on August 4th, 1806. The grand undertaking originated in the laudable endeavours of the managing owners of ships in the Company's service, and the important national objects of increased security to property and revenue, combined with improved accommodation, economy, and dispatch, were thus early realised through the liberal subscriptions of the proprietors, and the unremitting attentions of the Directors of the East India Dock Company.—Joseph Cotton, Chairman ; John Woolmore, Deputy Chairman ; John Rennie, Ralph Walker, Engineers."

In May, 1838, the East India Dock Company was amalgamated with the West India Dock Company, and the name of the Company was changed to the "East and West India Dock Company."

The East India Dock Basin was originally five acres in extent, but in 1874, in consequence of the increase in the size and draught of ships using the port of London, it was deepened and enlarged, and a new river entrance lock was constructed to the eastward of the old entrance. These works, from the peculiar situation of the basin between the rivers Thames and Lea, involved considerable engineering difficulties; but they were all successfully surmounted, and the basin, in its present form, was opened for business by the admission of one of the large steamers of the Orient Steam Navigation Company, in August, 1879.

The basin now has a depth of thirty-three feet of water at ordinary spring tides, with thirty-one feet of water on the sills of the new entrance lock. It thus provides, even at the worst neap tides, sufficient water to admit the largest vessels using the port of London, and is superior in depth and consequent accommodation for deep-draughted vessels to any other dock on the Thames.

On the north and east quays of the basin extensive warehouses have been erected, the ground floors being constructed for the reception of export, and the upper floors for import goods. A novel feature in the construction of these warehouses and quays is the overhead gallery, or crane-road, at the first floor level, on which travelling hydraulics for discharging cargoes into the loopholes of first and upper floors are worked without interference with the lower quay, and the railway lines thereon provided for the accommodation of export business. Numerous loopholes opening into reception and delivery yards at the rear or sides of the warehouses are also provided to enable the extensive land carriage business to be conducted without interference with the quay-side work. Contiguous to the East Quay berth are the extensive premises of Messrs. Donald Currie and Co.

In July, 1879, nearly the whole of the south quay of the Eastern Import Dock subsided suddenly, owing to the disturbance of a treacherous vein of quicksand on which the walls were founded. The accommodation at this quay was formerly insufficient for the rapid discharge of the large vessels using the docks, and advantage was taken of the accident to reconstruct it in the present form, increasing the width of quay space considerably, and providing sufficient quay shed accommodation to enable the Company to at once land any cargoes under cover.

A special feature in this quay is the adoption of the plan of having two-storey quay sheds, which was first introduced in the South West India Dock of this Company.

Owing to the great variation in the length of the ships using these docks, it was found convenient, and for the greater facility of the Company's business, to substitute movable for fixed cranes. The Dock Company, therefore, in reconstructing the quay, converted all the existing fixed hydraulics into travelling cranes, by which means any number

The whole of these extensive works, involving an outlay of nearly £60,000, were completed in the very short period of sixteen months from the date of commencement.

Millwall Dock is situated in the centre of the Isle of Dogs, to the south of the West India Docks, and has entrances in both Limehouse Reach and Blackwall Reach. This dock, and the adjoining land belonging to the Company, cover altogether an area of nearly 200 acres. The dry dock, inside the wet dock, is 430 feet in length, and 65 feet

VAULTS AT THE DOCKS.

required can be concentrated at one ship, and the goods, as discharged, can be placed direct from the ship's holds on to the ground or first floor of the quay sheds.

The new quay was constructed without interfering with the business of the dock, or using any cofferdam, the system adopted being a close timber-piled quay, strongly secured by land ties at the rear of the old wall, the dock bottom behind the timber piling being dredged down to the London clay, and a massive concrete wall built *in situ*. Special means were adopted for mixing and putting the concrete into position, without the large percentage of loss of cement which frequently occurs in the construction of concrete work under water.

wide at the bottom. Millwall Dock, which was opened in 1868, has a trade with all parts of the world, but is especially the dock for grain import. Not only was the last vestige of the old Chapel House swept away on the formation of this dock, as mentioned in the preceding chapter, but the work saw also the removal of the last of the old metropolitan turnpike gates.

Some idea of the immense advantage to merchants and others obtained by the formation of the docks of London may be gained when we state that the number of ships entering the East and West India Docks alone is upwards of 2,000 annually. Even the entries in the port of London during a single week are enormous, as will be seen from the following return for the week ending June 30th, 1883 :—Number of vessels entered in, 238 ; number of steamers entered in, 154. Number of vessels entered out, 133 ; number of steamers entered out, 93. Number of cargo vessels cleared out, 123 ; number of cargo steamers cleared out, 92. Tonnage of vessels entered in, 149,593 ; tonnage of steamers entered in, 109,252. Tonnage of vessels entered out, 81,949 ; tonnage of steamers entered out, 59,568. Tonnage of vessels cleared out, 78,092 ; tonnage of steamers cleared out, 60,523. Total number of British vessels cleared out, 96 ; British tonnage cleared out, 64,372. Number of British steamers cleared out, 75 ; tonnage of British steamers cleared out, 50,304. Number of British sailers cleared out, 21 ; tonnage of British sailers cleared out, 14,068.

To form a proper conception of all the benefits to society, and to the mercantile world in particular, from the establishment of the India Docks, would require a mind of no common powers, and no small share of acuteness. What has been saved by these docks, and by the adoption of a general warehousing system, assisted by the river police, can be appreciated only by a recapitulation of what had been lost, previous to the introduction of the measures connected with these valuable improvements.

Mr. Colquhoun, in his work on "The Commerce and Police of the River Thames," written as long ago as the beginning of the present century, says:— " Let the mind only contemplate the commerce of a single river, unparalleled in point of extent and magnitude in the whole world, where 13,444 ships and vessels discharge and receive in the course of a year above 3,000,000 packages, many of which contain very valuable articles of merchandise, greatly exposed to depredations, not only from the criminal habits of many of the aquatic labourers and others who are employed, but from the temptations to plunder, arising from the confusion unavoidable in a crowded port, and the facilities afforded in the disposal of stolen property. " It will then be easily conceived that the plunder must have been excessive, especially where, from its analogy to smuggling, according to the false conceptions of those who are implicated, and from its gradual increase, the culprits were seldom restrained by a sense of moral turpitude, and this at a time too when, for want of a marine police, no means existed whereby offenders could be detected on the river. The fact is, that the system of river depredations grew and ramified as the commerce of the port of London advanced, until at length it assumed a variety of shapes and forms,

each having as many heads as a hydra. The first of these were *River Pirates*.

" This class was mostly composed of the most desperate and depraved characters ; and their attention was principally directed to ships, vessels, and craft in the night, which seemed to be unprotected. Among many other nefarious exploits performed by these miscreants, the following was not the least remarkable :—" An American vessel lying at East Lane Tier was boarded in the night, while the captain and crew were asleep, by a gang of pirates, who actually weighed the ship's anchor and hoisted it into their boat, with a complete new cable, with which they got clean off. The captain, hearing a noise, came upon deck at the moment the villains had secured their booty, with which they actually rowed away in his presence, impudently telling him they had taken away his anchor and cable, and bidding him good-night."

Much about the same time the bower anchor of a vessel from Guernsey was weighed and carried off with the cable. " Previous to the establishment of the docks, ships being very much lumbered were considered as the harvest of the river pirates, with whom it was a general practice to cut away bags of cotton, cordage, spars, oars, and other articles from the quarter-deck, and to get clear off even in the day-time. And as all classes of labourers, lumpers, &c., were in a manner guilty, they naturally connived at each other's delinquency, so that few or none were detected. It was frequently the practice of river pirates to go armed, and in sufficient force to resist. Their depredations were extensive among craft wherever valuable goods were to be found ; but they diminished in number after the commencement of the war ; and now, since the establishment of the docks and the marine police, a solitary instance of robbery is scarcely ever heard of. . . . . What were called *Night Plunderers* were composed of watermen, associated in gangs of four or five in number, and their practice was likewise to get connected with watchmen employed to guard lighters and other vessels while cargoes were on board, and to convey away in lugboats every portable article of merchandise they could lay their hands upon.

" These corrupt watchmen did not always permit the lighters under their own charge to be pillaged ; but their practice was to point out others which lay near their own, perhaps without a guard, and which on this account might be easily plundered. An hour was fixed upon for effecting this object ; and the receiver, a man generally of some property, was applied to to be in readiness at a certain hour before daylight to warehouse the goods. A lugboat was seized on for the purpose, and the articles removed into it out of the lighter, conveyed to a landing place nearest the warehouse of deposit. The watchmen in the streets leading to the scene of villainy were generally bribed to connive at it, under the pretence that it was a smuggling transaction, and thus the object was effected. Several cargoes of hemp obtained in this manner were conveyed up the river, and afterwards carted in the day-time, till, by the vigilance of the police-boats, a detection took place, and the whole scene of mischief was laid open. In many instances where goods could not be plundered through the connivance of the watchmen, it was no uncommon thing to cut lighters adrift, and to follow them to a situation calculated to elude discovery. In this way, whole lighter loads, even of coals, have been discharged at obscure landing-places on the river, and carted away during the night. Even the article of tallow, from Russia, which, from the unwieldiness of the packages, appears little liable to be an object of plunder, has not escaped the fangs of these offenders. The class called *Light-Horsemen*, or nightly plunderers of West India ships, are said to have originated in a connection between some mates of West India ships, and some criminal receivers residing near the river, who used to apply to them to purchase what is called *sweepings*, or rather, the spillings or drainings of sugar remaining in the hold, and between decks, after the cargo was discharged, and which were generally claimed as perquisites. In getting these articles on shore, it was necessary the revenue officers should connive, which they did, and the quantity of spillings was, of course, gradually increased year after year. In fact, to such a pitch of infamy was the business carried that, an agreement being entered into with those concerned on board, and a gang of plunderers on shore, composed of receivers, coopers, watermen, and labourers, they were permitted, on payment of from thirty to fifty guineas, to come on board in the night; to open as many hogsheads of sugar as were accessible, and to plunder without control. For this purpose, a certain number of bags, dyed *black*, and which went under the appellation of *Black Strap*, were provided. The receivers, coopers, watermen, and lumpers, all went on board at the appointed time. The hogsheads of sugar, packages of *coffee*, &c., were opened, the *black bags* filled with the utmost expedition, carried to the receivers, and again returned to be re-filled, till daylight, or the approach of it, checked the pillage for a few hours. On the succeeding night the depredations were renewed, and thus, on many occasions, from fifteen to twenty

hogsheads of sugar, a large quantity of coffee, and in many instances rum (which was removed by a small pump called a jigger, and filled into bladders with nozzles), was plundered in a single ship, in addition to the excessive pillage committed in the same ship by the lumpers, or labourers employed during the day in the discharge of the cargo. And, previous to the establishment of the docks, it has been estimated, upon credible authority, that above one-fifth of the vessels on the Thames suffered by nightly plunder. The ships subject to this species of robbery, generally known from the character of the mates or revenue officers on board, were denominated *Game Ships*. On board some of these, the labourers, called lumpers, would frequently solicit to work without wages, trusting to the liberty of plundering. Another class called *Heavy Horsemen*, made up of lumpers, &c., were exceedingly depraved. They generally went on board ships furnished with habiliments made on purpose to conceal sugar, coffee, cocoa, pimento, ginger, and other articles, which they generally conveyed on shore by means of an under-waistcoat, containing pockets all round, and denominated a *Jemmie*; and also by providing long bags, pouches, and socks, which were tied to their waists under their trowsers. These miscreants have been known to divide from three to four guineas apiece every night, from the produce of their plunder, during the discharge of what they called a Game Ship, besides the hush-money paid to officers and others for conniving at their nefarious practices; *Game Watermen* were so denominated from their having been known to hang upon ships under discharge for the whole of the day, in readiness to seize and instantly convey on shore bags of sugar, coffee, and other articles, pillaged by the lumpers. By such connections as these, mates, boatswains, carpenters, seamen, and shipboys have been seduced, and even taught to become plunderers and thieves, who would otherwise have remained honest and faithful to the trust reposed in them. Many of these watermen lived in ease and affluence.

" *Game Lightermen* were those who used to be in the habit of concealing in the lockers of their lighters sugar, coffee, pimento, ginger, &c., which they received from mates and others on board of West Indiamen. The lockers in these lighters were generally secured by a padlock, and these were seldom taken out till after the lighter had been supposed to have been completely unloaded. It was then the practice to remove to the road where empty craft used to be abreast of the Custom House quay, and then carry away the stolen or smuggled articles. And it has not seldom happened that many of these *Game Lightermen* have, under pretence of watching their own lighters, actually plundered the goods under their charge to a very considerable amount, without detection. The artful and insidious conduct of these lighter-men was also exhibited in a very glaring point of view in the case of a Canada merchant, who had been accustomed to ship quantities of oil annually to the London market. Finding a constant and uniform deficiency in the quantity landed greatly exceeding what could arise from common leakage,

the effect of design, he began now to discover one of the causes at least of his great losses. He therefore attended the discharge of the lighter until the whole of the casks were removed, when he per-ceived a great quantity of oil leaked out, which the lightermen had the effrontery to insist was their perquisite. The proprietor then ordered casks to be brought, and filled no less than nine of them with the oil that had thus leaked out. He next ordered the ceiling of the lighter to be pulled up, and found between her timbers as much as filled five casks

ENTRANCE TO THE EAST INDIA DOCKS.

which his correspondents were unable to explain, and having occasion to visit London, he was re-solved to see his cargo landed with his own eyes, so as, if possible, to develop a mystery heretofore in-explicable, and by which he had regularly lost a considerable sum for several years. Determined, therefore, to look sharp after his property, he was in attendance at the wharf in anxious expectation of a lighter which had been laden with his oil on a preceding day, and which, for reasons that he could not comprehend, did not get up for many hours after the usual time. On her arrival at the wharf, the proprietor was confounded to find the whole of his casks stowed in the lighter with the bungs downwards; and convinced that this was

more. And thus, but for his own attendance fourteen casks of oil would have been appropriated to the use of the lightermen who, after attempting to rob him of so much property, complained bitterly of his ill-usage in taking it from them.

"*Mud-Larks* were those who played a smaller game, being accustomed to prowl about at low water under the quarters of West India ships, with pretence of grubbing in the mud for old ropes, iron, coals, &c., but whose object in reality was to receive and conceal small bags of sugar, coffee, pimento, and sometimes bladders containing rum. These auxiliaries were considered as the lowest cast of thieves. As for the revenue officers, many of them found means not only to promote pillage in West India ships, but also in ships from the East Indies, and in every ship and vessel arriving and departing from the River Thames. This class of officers generally made a point of being punctual upon duty, and, never being found absent by their superiors, they obtained preference to those particular ships which afforded the best harvest, either from being under the care of mates or others with whom they were connected; or from the cargo being of a nature calculated to afford a resource for plunder. They were also generally acquainted with the *copemen*, or receivers; and at those seasons of the year when the crowded state of the port rendered it necessary to have *extra* and *glut* officers, the general distress of this class of men rendered them very easy to seduce, and to become the willing instruments of plunder.

"*Scuffle-Hunters* were so called from their resorting in numbers to the quays and wharves where goods were discharging under pretence of finding employment as labourers, &c., and then taking advantage of the circumstance of disputes and scuffles arising about who should secure most plunder from broken packages, &c. These men were reckoned the very scum of society. But with the establishment of the docks, these and every other pest of the community already mentioned have sunk into that obscurity and nothingness best befitting the present improved state of commerce and morals." Still, as a memento of the dangerous depravity to which we are no longer subjected, a few more instances, as quoted by Mr. Colquhoun, may not be without their effect :—" The receivers, or *copemen*, he observed, who formed the junto of wholesale dealers, and were accustomed to visit ships on their arrival, carried on their negotiations in a language whose terms were peculiar to themselves. They also procured bladders with wooden nozzles for the purpose of containing rum, brandy, and other liquors, and furnished boats to convey the plunder from the ships during the night. Some of these receivers, to tempt and seduce those who would permit them to plunder the cargo, would advance them considerable sums, which, however, rarely amounted to a moiety of the value of the goods obtained, and frequently not one-fourth part. Other classes of receivers being generally engaged in business as small grocers, or chandlers, and old iron and junk sellers, they were accustomed to protect the plunder in its transit from one criminal dealer to another by means of small bills of parcels."

CHAPTER LX.

THE RIVER LEA.

"This Prince in many a fight their forces still defyd,
The goodly River Lee he likewise did divide;
By which the Danes had then their full fraught naivès tew'd,
The greatnesse of whose streame besiegèd Harford rew'd."—DRAYTON's *Polyolbion*.

Etymology of the River Lea—Its Source—Luton—Brocket Hall—Hertford—Ware –Amwell and its Quaker Poet– Haileybury College—The Rye House—Stanstead Abbots—Hoddesdon—Broxbourne—Cook's Ferry—Bleak Hall—The East London Waterworks—Lea Bridge—Fishing on the Lea—-Hackney Marshes and Temple Mills—The Navigation of the Lea—Conservancy of the River.

DURING our perambulations, since we first reached the banks of the Lea, in the neighbourhood of Enfield Highway and Waltham Abbey,* we have occasionally touched slightly upon this very "fishful" stream. The Lea, however, is so essentially the Londoner's favourite river, next to, if not equally with, the Thames, that we may well be excused if we dwell a little longer upon its charms before we take our leave of the north suburban district once and for all.

The name of the river, which is of Saxon origin, has been variously written, but the most common spelling in the present day is *Lea*. The Conservancy, however, still adhere to the old form *Lee*. By some of the older historians it was spelled *Luy*. In Shakespeare's *Henry VI.* it is written *Ley*. Drayton, in his "Polyolbion," spells it both *Lea* and *Lee;* and Sir John Hawkins, in his "Life of Walton," spells it *Lea*.

The Lea, however, belongs really more to Hertfordshire than to Essex or Middlesex, as it bounds the latter counties on the west and east for only the last ten or twelve miles nearest London. It meets the Essex border at the point where it receives the Stort,* at Roydon, and flows nearly

---

* See *ante*, pp. 375 and 404.

* The Stort, which gives its name to (Bishop) Stortford, rises in Hertfordshire, but soon enters Essex, along the western border of which it flows till it meets the Lea at Roydon. Its whole course is not above twenty-four miles, the last ten of which are navigable. The Stort and Lea, in spite of modern railways, are still largely used to convey corn malt, wood, and agricultural produce to London.

due south near Broxbourne, Hoddesdon, and Cheshunt in Herts, and Waltham Abbey, Chingford, Leyton, and Stratford in Essex, in its course to the Thames, a distance of about twenty miles. Its banks are low and marshy, and greatly overspread by floods in the winter. The marshes are from half a mile to a mile in width. The stream is frequently divided into several channels, so that it is difficult of navigation. In some places also cuts have been made to shorten or improve its course. Some of the Acts of Parliament relating to this navigation are 400 years old.

The source of the river, according to Drayton, is to be found in some springs at Lea Grave, about a mile north of Luton, of which he sings as—

"The head,
Whence Lee doth spring, not farre from Kempton* towne."

A quaint account of the course of this river, wonderfully exact and accurate upon the whole, may be seen in Vallen's "Tale of Two Swannes" (1590), from which I have taken some few of the mottoes for my chapters, and which is reprinted in extenso at the beginning of Mr. J. E. Cussans' "History of Hertfordshire."

Lambarde, however, describes its course in a more prosaic manner. He writes:—"It begynnethe near Whitchurche, and from thence passinge by Hertforde, Ware, and Waltham, openethe into the Thames at Ham, in Essex, whence this place is at this day called Lea-mouth. It hath of long tyme borne vessels from London twenty myles towards the head, for in the tyme of King Alfrede the Danes entered Ley-mouth, whence King Alfrede espied that the channell of the ryver might be in such sorte weakened that they should want water to returne. He caused, therefore, the water to be abated by two greate trenches, and setting the Londonners upon them, he made their batteil, wherein they lost four of their capitaines. Not long after they were so pressed that they forsoke all, and left their shippes as a prey to the Londonners, which breakyne some and burninge other, conveyed the rest to London."

The actual source of the Lea, however, is in a field at Houghton Regis, about a mile from Dunstable, and, like that of most other rivers, it soon spreads out in the form of a pond. Although there may be nothing particularly attractive in the spring or its immediate surroundings, the village of Houghton Regis, with its clusters of thatched-roofed cottages and its fine old church, is one which may be admired for its picturesque rural scenery. For

some distance from its source the Lea is little more than a ditch in appearance, and it is not until it reaches Luton—a place of note for its straw-hat factories—that it becomes anything like a respectable stream. Luton Church, a large building of Perpendicular architecture, contains many interesting features, but has suffered much from the hands of would-be restorers. The river next passes through Luton Park, the seat of Mrs. Gerard Leigh, in its course supplying two large lakes in the grounds, said to contain, the one fourteen, and the other forty acres. The mansion, called Luton Hoo, was visited by Dr. Johnson and his friend Boswell when it was the seat of Lord Bute. It was almost wholly burnt down in 1843, but has since been rebuilt. Having passed the little town of Whethamsted, the river flows on for about two miles to Brocket Hall, once the seat of Lord Melbourne and of Lord Palmerston. The house is a large brick structure, and the Lea spreads out before it in the form of a spacious lake. After leaving Brocket Hall, the Lea flows on through a fertile country—somewhat level, perhaps, but pleasant withal—and, leaving the town of Hatfield on the right, winds its way through a corner of Hatfield Park, the seat of Lord Salisbury. The mansion, called Hatfield House, is a large and stately building of brick with stone dressings, in the Tudor style, and it contains the finest collection of ancient manuscripts of any mansion in the kingdom. Elizabeth was for some time a prisoner here before her accession to the throne, and an old oak at a corner of an avenue on the northern side of the park is called the "Queen's Oak," from a tradition that it formed the boundary of her daily walk.

On reaching Hertford the Lea is joined by another stream, and is visibly increased in volume. Although the town of Hertford is one of great historic interest, a portion of the castle is almost the only antiquarian object existing; this consists of two or three brick towers with a few chambers attached, and some portions of the outer walls. The first lock on the River Lea is about midway between Hertford and Ware. This latter place is supposed to have derived both its origin and its name from a "weare" or dam constructed by the Danes in the reign of King Alfred (A.D. 896), for the purpose of protecting a large fort which they had erected at the spot whereon the town of Ware now stands. By the concurrent testimony of old writers, the Lea was once navigable for ships as far as Hertford, up to which the Danes came by water. Alfred blocked them up in the fortress which they had built, and deprived them of their

---

ships. The injury done to the river was not repaired till the seventeenth century, and the navigation restored. On the banks of the Lea, a short distance from Ware Church, and just beyond Ware lock, are slight remains of a Benedictine priory, which was founded here in the reign of Henry III.

A little to the south of Ware, nearly opposite Ware Park, and at a point where the Lea trends southward towards Essex and Middlesex, lie Chadwell Springs, which form the source of the New River, by means of which so large a portion of London is supplied with water. The site of the principal spring is marked by a stone erected by the New River Company, and bearing an inscription which sets forth that it was opened in 1608, and that the water is conveyed forty miles.

As we leave Ware a vision of Alfred rises up as we think of his memorable exploit of diverting the channel of the Lea, leaving the Danish ships high and dry behind their *weir*. Following the course of our river, we soon reach Amwell—the Emme-well of the Domesday Book—perhaps the prettiest village on the banks of the Lea. This spot, which is well wooded, is invested with an interest of its own, as having been the residence of the Quaker poet, John Scott, on whom a pleasant and chatty paper from the pen of Charles Knight appears in the first volume of *Once a Week*. The house which Scott formerly occupied still stands. It is an old-fashioned, comfortable, red-brick building of no great pretensions. Its gardens and grounds, which once covered upwards of twenty acres, were sold in 1864 for building purposes; but his curious grotto, inlaid with spar, shells, and fossils—once regarded as a rival to that of Pope at Twickenham, and visited by "the quality" from London, and by such learned philosophers as Dr. Samuel Johnson—forms now the central attraction in some tea-gardens, and visitors are admitted to it on payment of 6d. a head. The grotto is curiously cut out in the chalky soil on which the village stands, and comprises six or seven chambers.

Amwell can boast of having numbered among its residents one other poet at least in the person of William Warner, an "attorney of the Common Pleas," who held fair rank as a poet in the reign of Queen Elizabeth, and was the author of "Albion's England" and other poems. Warner is said to have been a Warwickshire man, and to have been educated at Magdalen Hall, Oxford. He died here in 1608–9.

On Amwell Hill are traces of ancient fortifications or earthworks, and others are visible between Ware and Hertford. These are supposed to be the remains of those thrown up by the Danes and King Alfred.

On a stone upon an eyot, or ait, at the source of the New River at Amwell, are the following lines, from the pen of Archdeacon Nares :—

> "Amwell! perpetual be thy spring,
>   Nor e'er thy source be less,
> Which thousands drink who little dream
>   Whence flows the boon they bless.
>
> "Too often thus ungrateful man
>   Blind and unconscious lives ;
> Enjoys kind Heaven's indulgent plan,
>   Nor thinks of Him who gives."

Nowhere in its entire course does the Lea run clearer or purer than about Amwell, where the soil is chalky. It must have been about here that was caught "that great trout, near an ell in length, which had his picture drawne, and now to be seen at mine hoste Rickabie's at the 'George,' in Ware," as honest Izaak Walton writes in chapter iv. of his delightful "Angler." Amwell was one of the favourite meets of Walton and his friend "Venator," as all readers of his "Complete Angler" are aware ; and it was probably about here that "Piscator" conducted his friend to "an honest alehouse," where is to be found "a cleanly room, lavender in the windows, and twenty ballads stuck about the wall."

Scott has paid his tribute to Izaak Walton, who, he writes :—

> "Oft our fair haunts explored ; upon Lea's shore
> Beneath some green turf oft his angle laid,
> His sport suspending to admire their charms."

On a woody knoll, just above the New River, and in the midst of the village, stands Amwell Church, an exceedingly picturesque old edifice. Its situation has been beautifully described by John Scott in the following lines :—

> "The pleased eye, which o'er the prospect wide
> Has wandered round, and various objects marked
> On Amwell rests at last, its favourite scene.
> How picturesque the view ! where up the side
> Of that steep bank her roofs of russet thatch
> Rise, mixed with trees, above whose swelling tops
> Ascends the tall church tower, and loftier still
> The hill's extended ridge."

Scott's style throughout is strictly pastoral, as his description of the view from Amwell Hill will show :—

>   "How beautiful,
> How various is yon view ! Delicious hills
> Bounding smooth vales, smooth vales by winding streams
> Divided, that here glide through grassy banks
> In open sun, there wander under shade

Of aspen tall, or ancient elm, whose boughs
O'erhang grey castles, and romantic farms,
And humble cots of happy shepherd swains.

*   *   *   *   *

Far towards the west, close under shelt'ring hills,
In verdant meads by Lea's cerulean stream,
Hertford's grey towers ascend ; the rude remains
Of high antiquity, from waste escaped
Of envious time and violence of war."

Amwell Church displays the architecture of the fourteenth century ; its very perfect apse peeps from behind the richest foliage ; and, altogether, the place would be interesting without its associations. Besides William Warner, mentioned above, and whom John Scott calls "the gentle bard, by fame forgotten," here lie at rest among the "rude forefathers of the hamlet" Robert Mylne, the engineer of old Blackfriars Bridge, and the Rev. Richard Jones, some time Professor of History and Political Economy at Haileybury College. Scott himself lies buried in the Quakers' burial place at Ware.

Within the limits of the parish of Amwell, though nearly two miles from that village and church, stands Haileybury College, once the chief place of training for cadets destined to enter the old East India Company's Civil Service, as Addiscombe was for its Military Service. The buildings are very extensive, and surround a quadrangle larger than that of Christ Church, Oxford, and equal to Trinity College, Cambridge. They are in the classical style, and heavy and dull to the last degree ; they were designed by W. Wilkins, R.A. In this college Sir James Mackintosh, Malthus, Empson, and other well-known men, were professors ; and Lord Brougham and other leaders of the old Whig party were frequent visitors within its walls. In 1862, the buildings having been closed since the abolition of the great Company whose nursery it was, a public school was founded here by a proprietary connected with Hertfordshire. Fresh buildings, and a handsome new chapel, from the designs of Mr. Blomfield, have been added. The result is a public school of 500 boys, mostly destined for a university career, and holding its own in the competition for Oxford and Cambridge scholarships, and in the cricket-field and at football, with the rest of our public schools. Its first master under the new *régime* was the Rev. Arthur Butler, who was succeeded by Dr. E. H. Bradby.

But we must leave Amwell and follow as closely as we may the windings of the Lea as it meanders in "silver thread" through the green pastures of Hertfordshire to the old Rye House—that favourite retreat of the thoroughbred cockney, where he may find "art, science, history, romance, boating, fishing, horticulture, a lovely English landscape, and jolly English cheer, all in one short holiday." We can scarcely wander through the valley of the Lea as honest Izaak wandered ; for the river has been made navigable by long formal cuts, and the old stream is in most places strictly preserved ; so we are compelled to pursue our way in part along by the less picturesque New River.

The celebrated Rye House, so well known as a place of entertainment to Londoners, especially those from the northern and eastern parts, is situated in the parish of Stanstead Abbots. It is so called from being within the manor of Rye, formerly belonging to the Abbey of Waltham. It was alienated about 1440 to Sir Andrew Ogard, who erected on it a small castle, which is described by William of Worcester in the minutest detail, with the exact measurement of each court, the moat, the granary, &c. The purchase-money, he tells us, was £1,130, a large sum in those days.

The Rye House was noted for the "plot" laid there in 1683 against the lives of Charles II. and his brother James. The place, which lay on the then road to Newmarket, was in the occupation of a maltster named Rumbold, one of the conspirators, and the place was hit upon as the most convenient to intercept the royal party on their return from the races ; but the scheme failed, owing to the king's return taking place some days sooner than was anticipated.

The story of the "Rye House Plot," for alleged complicity in which the noble Sidney and Lord William Russell were brought to the scaffold, is told in every History of England, but nowhere better than in Mr. A. C. Ewald's "Life and Times of Algernon Sidney." Russell, Sidney, and Hampden, with three other Whig statesmen, had formed themselves into a "Council of Six," and were concerting measures to exclude James, Duke of York, from the throne. "Whilst the Council of Six were meditating their plans, whatever they might be, an inferior order of conspirators were holding meetings and organising an insurrection perfectly unknown to the Council. The chief of these conspirators were West, an active man, who was supposed to be an Atheist ; Colonel Rumsey, an officer who had served under Cromwell, and afterwards in Portugal ; Ferguson, an active agent of the late Lord Shaftesbury ; Goodenough, who had been Under-Sheriff of London ; Lieutenant-Colonel Walcot, a Republican officer ; and several lawyers and tradesmen. The aim of these men seems to have been desperate and criminal in the extreme. They talked openly about murdering the King and his brother, and even went so far as to organise a scheme for that purpose. Among this band was one Rumbold, a maltster, who owned a farm called the Rye House, situated on the road to Newmarket, which sporting town Charles was accustomed to visit annually for the races. Rumbold laid before the conspirators a plan of this farm, and showed how easy it would be to intercept the King and his brother on their way home, fire upon them through the hedges, and then, when the deed of assassination was committed, escape by the bylanes and across the fields. The murderous scheme of the maltster was, however, frustrated by Charles having been obliged to leave Newmarket eight days earlier than he had intended, owing to his house having taken fire. Treachery now put a stop to any further proceedings of the conspirators."

False witnesses, however, were found to connect the honoured names of Russell and Sidney with this villainous scheme, and the result was that orders were given for the arrest of the members of the Council of Six. The sequel is but too well known.*

"The Rye House," writes Mr. Cussans in his noble "History of Hertfordshire," "has become celebrated in history for its having been tenanted by Rumbold, a maltster, one of the persons engaged in the alleged conspiracy to assassinate Charles II. and his brother the Duke of York, on their journey from Newmarket to London; but the scheme failed, in consequence of the royal party returning sooner than was anticipated. Lord William Russell and Algernon Sidney were said to have been inculpated in the plot; and after a trial in which their connection with this scheme was by no means satisfactorily proved, however much they may have been concerned in other treasonable designs, they were publicly executed."

Mr. Cussans adds that for many years, till the passing of the new Poor Law Act, the Rye House was used as a workhouse for the parish of Stanstead. "Little of the old building," he writes, "remains. A tavern has been built in the ancient forecourt, upon the banks of the Lee, and is much frequented by the lower classes from London. The moat, at one time an important part of the fortification of the castle, is now used as a bed for water-cresses. Mr. Teale, the present tenant, purchased the property in 1867."

The remains of an embattled gate-house of brick, with a stone doorway and vaulted chambers, are shown to visitors as part of the original structure built in the reign of Henry VI. The place now forms one of the attractions of a modern hostelry, and the grounds are pleasantly laid out, with the extra advantages of a maze, bowling-green, &c. Among the curiosities preserved here is the "great bed of Ware." Little if anything is satisfactorily known of the origin of this curious piece of furniture, which is said to be sufficiently capacious to accommodate six couples. At the head is carved the date, 1435, and it is referred to in Shakespeare's "Twelfth Night":—

Sir Anthony Aguecheek:—"Will either of you bear me a challenge to him?"

Sir Toby Belch:—"Go write it in a martial hand; be curt and brief; it is no matter how witty, so it be eloquent and full of invention. Taunt him with the licence of ink; if thou *thou'st* him some thrice, it shall not be amiss; and so many lies as will lie in thy sheet of paper, although the sheet were big enough for the bed of Ware in England."

Charles Knight, in the article in *Once a Week* above referred to, thus sums up the attractions of the Rye House:—"Hither come for their annual festivals clubs of Odd Fellows and of Jolly Fellows —the skilled artisans of great London establishments, such as printers and pianoforte makers. They dine in a vast saloon, formed out of an extension of the old offices of Rumbold the maltster, who dwelt in the Rye House. Up the old turret they climb, and look out upon the green fields through which the Lea flows amidst osiered banks. They crowd into punts, and aspire to angle where Walton angled. They speed over the meadows, and try their unaccustomed hands at trap-ball and quoits. The provident host of the Rye House is justly proud of the patronage of these great associations of ingenious workmen, who dine economically, and care more for ale than champagne. His dining-room is radiant with bright gilt frames, holding pleasant certificates of their excellent fare from the representatives of the merry and contented hundreds who have thus forgot their accustomed lot for the summer holiday long to be remembered. The form of enjoyment is changed: the conveniences for enjoyment have multiplied since Walton described his holidays— 'stretching our legs up Tottenham Hill;' 'taking our morning draught at the Thatched House at Hodsden;' 'leading our mates to an honest alehouse, where we shall find a cleanly room, lavender in the windows, and twenty ballads stuck about the wall;' listening to the song of 'a handsome milkmaid, that had not yet attained so much age and wisdom as to load her mind with any fears of many things that will never be.' We have no time in our days for such lingering delights; we have no taste

---

for such simple luxuries. We ourselves rejoice to find as good a dinner at the Rye House as at the Bedford, instead of bringing out of our fish bags 'a piece of powdered beef and a radish or two.' We sit contentedly sipping our sherry and water and puffing our cigar under alcoves festooned with roses, instead of indulging in such rare gratification as that with which happy Isaak finished his three days' sport—'a bottle of sack, milk, oranges, and sugar, which all put together make a drink like nectar—indeed, too good for anybody but anglers.'

No milkmaid's mother sings 'an answer to it, which was made by Sir Walter Raleigh in his younger days.' The forms of our pleasures and their accompaniments in other respects incessantly change, but their natural backgrounds are eternally fresh and perennially welcome."

Stanstead Abbots is so called because it formerly belonged to the Abbey of Waltham. Of the church there is little to say, except that it contains some fine monuments, and dates from the latter half of the 14th century. In this parish is an old

COOK'S FERRY. (*See page* 566.)

The habitual economy of those times enabled the industrious tradesman to be occasionally expensive in his tastes. The cheapness and rapidity of modern conveyance permits the London artisan to have a full day's relaxation with that best of economies, the economy of his time. Our holiday enjoyments are perhaps not quite so poetical as when the cheerful old Piscator went out with a determined purpose to be happy. On the banks of the Lea no milkmaid now charms us with 'that smooth song which was made by Kit Marlow,' of

> ' Come live with me and be my love,
> And we will all the pleasures prove
> That valleys, groves, or hills, or field,
> Or woods and steepy mountains yield.'

endowed school and almshouses, founded in 1636 by Sir Edward Baish, a gallant Royalist, who spent nearly all his fortune in the cause of the King. Close by is Easney, more properly Isenye, a seat of the Buxton family, erected by Waterhouse in 1868--70. At Stanstead Bury are the remains of a Roman fortress, in which was a small chapel.

Once more resuming our pilgrimage along the banks of the Lea, we soon pass under the railway-bridge of the Cambridge branch of the Great Eastern Railway, and shortly after arrive at the junction of the Stort with the Lea, at which point Essex begins. Close by is a fishing cottage, which stands on the most northerly detached portion of Epping Forest, whence a footpath across a couple of fields leads to Nether Hall; little is left of the old moated building, however, beyond the ruined gateway, which is of brick, consisting of two floors, with a half hexagon tower on each side of the entrance.

Our river now flows on a little to the east of Hoddesdon, or, as it was formerly written, Hodsdon. The village possesses no interesting features to detain us on our way; but it is worthy of note from its association with the River Lea through the pens of Izaak Walton and Matthew Prior. The "Rambles by Rivers," says that a cottage at the northern extremity of the village has been pointed out as the original "Thatcht House" where Venator proposed to "drink his morning's draught;" but, he adds, it is very doubtful if it be so. The river about this part has long been a favourite resort of the London angler; trout, chub, pike, perch, barbel, gudgeon, dace, and roach, are enumerated in almost every chapter of Walton's "Angler" as found about Amwell, Hodsdon, and Waltham Abbey; indeed, the first-named fish

AT LEA BRIDGE.

latter, in his ballad of "Down Hall," makes mention of the "Bull" Inn here as the place where he stopped on his way to take possession of his residence of that name :—

"Into an old inn did their equipage roll
  At a town they call Hodsdon, the sign of the Bull,
  Near a nymph with an urn that divides the highway,
  And into a puddle throws mother of tea ;
        *   *   *   *   *
  She roasted red veal, and she powdered red beef ;
  Full well she knew how to cook up a fine dish,
  For tough were her pullets and tender her fish,
        Down, down, derry down."

The "nymph with an urn," it may be added, has long ago disappeared, and the "Bull" has been rebuilt since Prior's time. Mr. Thorne, in his gave its name to Trout Hall, which is so constantly mentioned by Walton, though its exact site is disputed, and near which the pretty milk-maid sang to the "brethren of the angle" Kit Marlow's well-known lines, above quoted. The scene must be laid somewhere near Hodsdon, for Peter says, "My friend Coridon and I will go up the river towards Ware;" to which Piscator replies, "And my scholar and I will go down towards Waltham." The "fresh sheets" at the inn "smell of fresh lavender," and the discourse on the way to the river-side and back is on the nature of the trout. The spreading birches and sycamore trees, of which honest Izaak Walton talks so much, should surely help to identify the spot.

"Coridon and I," observes Piscator later on, "have not had an unpleasant day, and yet I have caught but five trouts; for, indeed, we went to a good, honest alehouse, and there we plaid at shovel-board half the day. All the time that it rain'd we were there, and as merry as they that fished."

Sir John Hawkins, in his notes on the "Complete Angler," relates the following story:—"A lover of angling told me he was fishing in the river Lea, at the ferry called Jeremy's, and had hooked a large fish at the time when some Londoners, with their horses, were passing: they congratulated him on his success, and got out of the ferry-boat; but, finding the fish not likely to yield, mounted their horses, and rode off. The fact was, that angling for small fish, his bait had been taken by a barbel, too large for the fisher to manage. Not caring to risk his tackle by attempting to raise him, he hoped to tire him; and, for that purpose, suffered himself to be led (to use his own expression) as a blind man is by a dog, several yards up and as many down, the bank of the river; in short, for so many hours that the horsemen above-mentioned, who had been at Walthamstow, and dined, were returned, who, seeing him thus occupied, cried out—'What, master, another large fish!'—'No' (says the Piscator), 'the very same.'—'Nay' (says one of them), 'that can never be; for it is five hours since we crossed the river!' and, not believing him, they rode on their way. At length our angler determined to do that which a less patient one would have done long before: he made one vigorous effort to land the fish, broke his tackle, and lost him."

After passing Dobbs' Weir and the lock, the Lea forms a decided curve westward to Broxbourne, the next place of interest at which we arrive. The church and parsonage, standing on rising ground above an old water-mill, look highly picturesque, as seen from the river. The church dates from the time of Henry II.; it is of considerable size, and the tower is surmounted by a plain spire and beacon turret. On the north side of the chancel is a chapel, built by Sir William Say, and containing an altar-tomb in memory of the founder, who died in 1559. This church contains many other monuments and brasses, which will be regarded with interest, as illustrating the costumes of the Tudor period.

The parish of Nazing borders the Lea for some distance on the opposite, or Essex, side of the stream. Nazing Church is visible away on a distant hill, whilst Holyfield Hall,* with its contiguous farm-buildings, surrounded by venerable elms, occupies the rising ground nearer the river, which now flows onward in almost a direct line due south.

Wormley Church, a little farther on—on the Hertfordshire side of the river—is a small building, partly of Norman workmanship, and containing several ancient brasses. The remains of Cheshunt Nunnery lie near the river-side, just beyond Wormley; and, farther on, we pass Cheshunt Mill Lock and Waltham Common Lock, above which a private canal runs across the Gunpowder Wharves. Our river about here is divided into several different channels, narrow and tortuous; the Navigation Cut, however, affords an almost direct route for the next half-dozen miles. Enfield and Waltham Abbey, with the Small Arms Factory and Powder Mills, which we now pass, have each and all been fully described in these pages.*

At Cook's Ferry, which is now occupied by a bridge, and forms the communication between Edmonton and Chingford, stands or stood a small building called "Bleak Hall," the house to which, by tradition, Piscator is said to have taken his "scholar," and which was then, according to Izaak Walton, "an honest alehouse, where might be found a cleanly room, lavender in the windows, and twenty ballads stuck about the walls; with a hostess both cleanly, and handsome, and civil." This house is generally called Bleak Hall, and is pointed out and engraved in Sir H. Nicolas's Notes to the "Complete Angler" and elsewhere as the original Bleak Hall of Izaak; but, unless he made a slip of the pen, it cannot be so, for in the conversation on the night spent there (Chap. v.), as quoted above, Piscator speaks of going with his scholar "down *towards* Waltham," whereas this is some miles *below* Waltham.

Stonebridge and Tottenham locks come next in order as we follow the course of the Lea, and then we arrive at the reservoirs belonging to the East London Waterworks Company, at the point where the old copper-mills of Walthamstow formerly stood.† A canal as straight as an arrow, formed by raised embankments, connects the Walthamstow reservoirs with those by Lea Bridge, of which we have already spoken. The East London Waterworks Company draws largely on the Lea for its supply. This company is the largest purveyor of any of the metropolitan water companies; the quantity of water sold by it in the course of a year amounts to upwards of 11,000 million gallons, against 10,000 million gallons supplied by the New

---

River Company, the next largest; but while the working expenses of the latter during the same period absorbed nearly £146,600, those of the former amount only to about £89,800.

"In the year 1828," writes Mr. F. Johnson, in "Weldon's Guide to the Lea," "objections were made to the source from whence the East London Company obtained their water, it having been asserted that, as the tide of the Thames affected the water of the Lea in that part where the Company raised their water, the water 'partook of the nature of Thames water.' To remove all doubt on the point, the Company obtained Parliamentary powers, in the year 1849, to change the source of supply; they constructed the reservoirs and canal at Lea Bridge, for the purpose of bringing water from a part of the river which was far above tidal influence. They had already purchased out the Hackney Common, which had been established here about 1750, whose water-wheels drove machinery to grind corn and raise water for the supply of the neighbourhood."

Lea Bridge was built in 1821, at a cost of £4,500. Close by it, and extending some distance along the banks of the river, are places for the hire of boats for rowing on the Lea; here are also the head-quarters of several rowing-clubs. Both fishing and boating are carried on in the neighbourhood of Lea Bridge to a very great extent; indeed, the incipient cockney fisherman and aquatic sportsman generally seem to regard the several streams and channels into which the Lea is divided in its course between Walthamstow and Bow as the chosen and highly-favoured scene of their diversions. Bathing also is here largely indulged in during the summer months, notwithstanding the very dangerous condition of the stream for that purpose, being full of weeds and deep holes. The result is that, with the reckless boating exploits of inexperienced young men and women from the eastern quarters of London, and the frequent fatalities resulting therefrom, as well as from bathing, the deaths by drowning in the River Lea add considerably to the death-roll of the metropolitan area. During each of the five years ending December 31, 1881, the number of bodies found in the Lea were respectively 47, 49, 55, 39, and 46; making a total of 236.

One of the most noted houses resorted to by anglers in the neighbourhood of Lea Bridge was the "Horse and Groom," but it was swept away on the extension of the waterworks. The fishery along the Lea is carefully preserved, with the exception of two or three intervening spots from Ware to Temple Mills, and let out for the most part to the persons who rent the several public-houses on its banks. From these the angler obtains permission to ply his cunning on payment of a yearly subscription, or the occasional angler may pay by the day.

At the old "White House," on the banks of the river, about the middle of Hackney Marshes, are the head-quarters of a fishery extending to Temple Mills. This house is traditionally said to have been the residence of the noted highwayman, Dick Turpin, before he took up his abode in the recess in Epping Forest now called Turpin's Cave.

The "Navigation Cut" crosses the marshes between high embankments a little to the west of the old river, which forms picturesque bends and meanderings, through the level meadows of which Hackney Marshes are composed. At Hackney Wick Bridge the old turnpike-road—following the course of the Roman road spoken of in a previous chapter[*]—after passing through Homerton, enters Essex. It crosses the Navigation Cut by a high, narrow bridge, and thence continues over the marsh to the "White Hart," at Temple Mills. The ford which was in use when this road was the ancient way into Essex has continued as a ford to this day, but a bridge is now (July, 1883) in course of erection on the spot, so that the ford will be no longer necessary. It is not quite clear whether Mr. J. T. Smith wrote only in fun or seriously, in his "Book for a Rainy Day," about crossing "the Lea" with "the lowing herd;" but, at all events, the fording of cattle at this point is a frequent occurrence, the meadows affording excellent pasturage.

Of Old Ford, Bow, and Stratford, and other places through which the Lea passes in its course to join the Thames, we have already spoken.

It is stated by Campbell, in his "Political Survey of Great Britain," that the Lea was the first river distinguished by the care of the Legislature in rendering it navigable.[†]

The first instance of a Parliamentary provision for the navigation of the Lea, however, was made as far back as the reign of Henry IV. (1424). The Act passed in the thirteenth year of Elizabeth (1570) was for making the navigation more perfect by the formation of a new cut from London to the town of Ware, and ten years later the river was cleansed and widened as far as that town, and made navigable by an Order in Council. It was ultimately determined by the Star Chamber that the river should be made free for barges and boats, and several Acts of Parliament dealing with the

---

* See *ante*, p. 508.
† See Statute 13 Eliz., cap. 18.

matter were subsequently passed. Towards the end of the last century, it having been shown after a careful survey that great improvements could be made in the navigation by the formation of new cuts or canals out of, or into, the channel of the river between Hertford and Bromley, a sum of money was granted by Parliament for that purpose, and the formation of what is now known as the "Navigation Cut" was carried out. In 1868 an Act of Parliament was passed constituting a Board of Conservancy for the management of the River Lea,

instead of trustees, as of old. Of this Board five members are appointed by the landowners on the banks of the river and its tributaries, one by the barge-owners, one by the heads of the local authorities of towns on the river, two by the New River Company, two by the East London Water-works Company, one represents the Lord Mayor, Aldermen, and Common Council of London, and one the Metropolitan Board of Works. The funds arising from tolls are laid out in the improvement and maintenance of the navigation.

CHAPTER LXI.

THE RIVER THAMES.

"Oh, could I flow like thee, and make thy stream
My great example, as it is my theme !
Though deep, yet clear ; th ugh gentle, yet not dull
Strong without rage ; without o'erflowing full."—Sir John Denham.

The Thames as a Political Boundary, and as a Boundary of Counties—Tributary Rivers—Breadth of the River—Its General Aspect and Character of Scenery—The Embankments—Shoals and Floods—Tides—The Thames as the Common Highway of London—Anecdote of Cardinal Wolsey—Sir Walter Raleigh and Queen Elizabeth—Abdication of James II.—Funeral of Lord Nelson—Water Traffic in the Time of Richard II.—The Conservancy of the Thames—Boating on the Thames.

In the pages of Old and New London mention has been made, at some length, of the river Thames as the "silent highway" of London * ; but as only the part "above bridge" was there dealt with, our discourse here will be of the Pool and the lower reaches in the course of the river to its confluence with the German Ocean.

"At a very early period of English history," writes the author of Bohn's "London and its Vicinity," "the Thames appears to have been considered as a political boundary of great importance. The division of the country into shires is supposed to have been established on its present basis by King Alfred ; and we therein find that the Thames was taken as the boundary of many of these districts. . . . . Long before the time of Alfred the river was adopted as the political limit of the Roman provinces of Britannia Prima on the south, and of Flavia Cæsariensis on the north. In the seventh century, also, it formed one of the boundaries of the Saxon kingdoms of Mercia and West Seaxe, in the middle of England ; and of those of East Seaxe, South Seaxe, and Cantium on the eastern coast."

The Thames, we may remark in passing, rises in the south-eastern slopes of the Cotswold Hills, near Tetbury, and near Cheltenham. For about twenty miles it belongs wholly to Gloucestershire,

when, for a short distance it divides that county from Wiltshire. It then separates Berkshire first from Oxfordshire, and then from Buckinghamshire. Next it serves as the boundary line between the counties of Surrey and Middlesex ; and afterwards, to its mouth, between those of Kent and Essex. It falls into the sea at the Nore, which is about 110 miles nearly due east from the source of the river, and about twice that distance measured along its windings. The Thames is navigable for sea-going vessels as far as London Bridge, forty-five miles from the Nore, or nearly a fourth of its entire length, and for large barges, for nearly 130 miles above London Bridge, whilst the area of the basin drained by the river is estimated at above 6,500 miles.

In that portion of its course with which we have now to deal the Thames is joined by some half-dozen rivers of minor importance. The Lea, as we have seen, unites with it a little below Blackwall, on the northern shore ; whilst a little higher up, on the opposite side, the Deptford Creek forms the mouth of the Ravensbourne, which rises among the Surrey hills, in the neighbourhood of Hayes Common and Addiscombe. This river winds its course through Lewisham, and is navigable for a very short distance inland, when it dwindles down to a very insignificant mill-stream.

The next affluent of importance, on the Essex shore, is the Roding, which flows into the Thames

---

* See Vol. III., pp. 287-322.

at Barking Creek,* and is navigable as far as that very ancient town. A rivulet, called the Beam, springing from the hills round Havering-atte-Bower, falls in at Dagenham Reach ; and at Rainham Creek the Ingerburn, or Bourne brook—a stream which has a rather long course, but is of little size or importance—discharges itself. Further down, at Purfleet, another small stream from Childerditch Common is swallowed up in our mighty river. Passing again to the south side, we find that the Darent and the Cray, from the Kentish hills, join in the marshes of Dartford, shortly before falling into the Thames. In the last twenty miles of its course the Thames does not receive any affluent worth notice ; for the Medway does not join it till the Nore is reached.

In its passage through the metropolis the Thames varies in breadth from 260 to 500 yards. At London Bridge, the river at high tide is 290 yards across ; at Blackwall Wharf it is 380 ; at Gravesend it is 800 ; at Coal-house Point, where the Lower Hope Reach commences, it is 1,290 yards—being an increase of some 1,000 yards in about 29 miles ; about ten miles lower down, at the London Stone, by Yanlet Creek, where the jurisdiction of the Corporation of London ends, the river is nearly four miles and a half across ; whilst, as it approaches the Nore, it expands to seven miles broad.

" Though there are none of the wilder features of nature observable at the estuary of the Thames," writes Mr. James Thorne, in his " Rambles by Rivers," " the prospect is at least one of mingled amenity and grandeur. The broad calm river passes imperceptibly into the majestic sea. Along the entrance of the united Thames and Medway ride some of those magnificent ships whose thunders have made the prowess of the British navy memorable in the annals of the world. In continual passage are vessels of every class and of every nation, bringing hither the fruits of every clime, or bearing to every shore the products of British skill. One who has followed the Thames from its parent rock, through so many beautiful and fertile districts ; past so many places dignified by the memory of great events and illustrious men, of British worth and British genius ; by so many trophies which mark the peaceful triumphs of British wealth and commerce, now that he contemplates this parting scene, may well regard with pride and admiration the noble river which so greatly contributes to the grandeur and the glory of his country and his countrymen. And as he looks

forth on the ocean sprinkled over with the shipping of the world, it will almost seem that the language is verified in which one of our older poets addressed his native land :

" ' Now all the riches of the globe beside,
    Flow into thee with every tide ;
And all that Nature doth thy soul deny
The growth is of thy fruitful industry ;
    And all the proud and dreadful sea,
And all his tributary streams,
    A constant tribute pays to thee,
And all the liquid world is one extended Thames.' "
                                        COWLEY.

" It will require no very great stretch of imagination," writes Mr. S. C. Hall in the " Book of the Thames," " to pass from the little streamlet in Trewsbury Mead to the ' Pool ' below the Tower. The river, born in a sequestered nook, grows and gathers strength until it bears on its bosom ' a forest of masts ;' enriches the greatest and most populous city of any age ; ministers to the wants and luxuries of nearly three millions of people— there alone ; becomes the mainstay of commerce, and the missionary of civilisation to mankind, carrying innumerable blessings throughout the Old World and the New ; yet ever the active auxiliary, and never the dangerous ally—keeping from its birth to its close the character so happily conveyed by the famous lines of the poet :

' Though deep, yet clear ; though gentle, yet not dull ;
  Strong without rage ; without o'erflowing, full.'

Few, therefore, are the poets of England who have no word for ' Old Father Thames !' Even its minor enjoyments have been fertile themes for the muse ; and numerous are they who laud the 'gentle craft' of the angler, whose ' idle time is never idly spent ' beside the river, which, above all others, invites to contemplation, and promotes familiar intercourse with Nature. Here, too, the botanist and the entomologist gather a rich harvest of instruction ; while to the landscape painter, wander where he will, it is ever an open volume of natural beauties, which are the only veritable teachers of art."

The general character of the scenery of the Thames is that of a calm and tranquil beauty, rather than of bold and romantic grandeur. The scenery on either side, and particularly on the Essex shore, is somewhat flat and dull, rising, however, into little hillocks away in the distance ; but this dulness is compensated for by the broad expansive reaches that occur all along its course. The banks, or river walls, along the Essex shore, as we have shown in a previous chapter, * are mostly artificial, the meadows being, in places, below the level of the river at high water. The general construction of these embankments is what is technically called the "earthen mound." It consists of a heap of earth, the section of which forms a scalene triangle, with the side towards the river inclined at an angle of about 20°, and that towards the land at one of about 45°. They are fortified chiefly by tiers of stakes, driven into the river face of the wall, and the intervals filled in with lumps of chalk or stone, rammed in to a level with the heads of the stakes or "stalks," as they are more generally called. Since the river steamer has added its "churning" power to the influence of tide and wind, however, the wall has been faced with a granite pavement.

"The banks of the lower part of the Thames," observes the author of Bohn's "Pictorial Handbook of London," "are marked by the same want of a definite plan which renders the upper part of the stream less useful than it might be made. The period at which they were first formed is very remote, being by some supposed to date as far back as the time of the Romans. This, indeed, seems very probable, for the manner in which the banks are executed, though eminently successful, is marked by all the clumsiness of a first essay. The marshes they protect from the river are sometimes (as at Woolwich) not less than four feet three inches below the level of the high water in spring tides. Those of the Isle of Dogs are now (1854) being enclosed by an embankment upon piles, with a superstructure of brickwork, executed in conformity with a plan prepared by Mr. Walker, under the direction of the Navigation Committee; thus indicating that the attention of that body has been fairly called to the necessity of co-ordinating all encroachments upon the channel of the river to one general system. The result of the several works upon the bed of the Thames, and the demolition of the old bridge, has been hitherto to lower the bed, and to compromise the safety of several of the bridges in the stream, and of some of the buildings on the shore. . . . . Moreover, in the lower Thames, that is to say, in those parts of its course below London Bridge, numerous shoals exist, which are highly prejudicial to the safety of the navigation, whilst at the same time, there is no reason why they might not be carried further out towards the embouchure if the course of the river were regularised, and the dredging operations made to conform to the necessities of the port. The shoals exist in the parts of the Thames in which the deep sea navigation terminates, where, in fact, from the more energetic action

THE THAMES—BARKING REACH.

of the tides, the floods from the upper country begin to deposit the matter they hold in solution."

The occasional floods which occur in the valleys of the Thames and the Lea arise entirely from the surface waters, hardly ever from the melting of snow in the higher lands near their sources. Indeed, the climate of this part of England, and the feeble elevation of its hills, does not admit of the fall of snow in quantities sufficient to affect the sources of the river supply. Under these circumstances the floods are found to occur in the rainy seasons—in November and December, in

of the London Dock on the north, and the St. Saviour's Dock on the south; a similar shoal was formed opposite to the Lime Kiln Dock; another in a wide reach a little above the Greenland Docks; a fourth near Deptford Creek. Opposite Saunders Ness, shoals have been formed on each side of the river, owing to the check given to its velocity by the abrupt bend which it here assumes; whilst a small shoal in the middle of the stream, a little lower down than these side ones, appears to have owed its origin to the interference which it produces in the direction of the currents. Another small

THE THAMES—WOOLWICH REACH.

April and May, without, however, being in any manner peculiarly confined to those months. The flood waters brought down to the rivers are highly charged with earthy matter, and the germs of organised life; they, in fact, materially influence the formation of the alluvial deposits of the rivers. The volume of water brought down by the Thames not being sufficient to form a delta, the particles which the stream holds in solution are gradually deposited on the mudbanks, and form shifting shoals, which extend from about Woolwich to the Nore, and even beyond.

Numerous shoals have existed in the bed of the river near the entrance to the Pool, but in most instances these have been reduced by dredging. For instance, a shoal existed on the north shore, opposite to the recesses formed by the east entrance

shoal has been produced in the still water opposite the entrance of the West India Docks.

Below the above-mentioned points of the river it is very difficult, from the nature of the currents, to define with certainty the exact position of the shoals; still less would it be possible to effectually remove them, or to stop their formation. A writer on the physical geography of the Thames, observes, "At Woolwich the water becomes brackish at spring tides, and the greater specific gravity it thence attains modifies the conditions of the deposition of the matter it holds in suspension. The difference between the lengths of time during which the flood and the ebb tides prevail also diminishes as the river approaches the sea. Moreover, the action of the current upon the shores of the embouchure at the same time that it removes the land on both sides, and thus changes the form of the outfall, so also does it carry into those portions of the estuary where still water is to be met with the materials resulting from the degradation of the shores. The variations of the tides from the neap to the spring, the changes in the force and direction of the deep-sea current—possibly from the effects of storms in very different and distant latitudes—the irregularities of the volume of fresh water brought down from the upper regions of the Thames, combine to render its *régime* in the lower and wider portions of its course very irregular and capricious. The sands of the Nore vary often in their outline, and their distance from the surface of the water ; the erosive force of the current upon the banks also varies in intensity, according to the action of the causes shortly enumerated above.

"The tide in the Thames ascends about fifteen miles above London Bridge to Teddington, below which place the river is exposed to the action of the tides from a peculiar combination of causes. The tide-wave from the Atlantic divides at Land's End into two streams, one of which runs up the British Channel, and enters the Thames round the North Foreland ; the other passes along the west coast of England and Scotland, and returns southward by the eastern shore and enters the Thames also, after passing the Yarmouth Roads. The tide in the river is then composed of two tidal waves, distant twelve hours from each other, so that the day and night tides are equal ; the tides meet between the Foreland and the Kentish Knock. The velocity of the wave from the North Foreland to London is very great, being about fifty miles per hour ; above the bridges, from the resistances it meets, the velocity is so much diminished that the wave is not propagated more rapidly than twelve miles an hour on the average. The difference of time of high water between London Bridge and Richmond is one hour eighteen minutes . . . Professor Airy observed that the rise of the water in the Thames, at a given interval from low water—in half an hour, for instance—is considerably more than its descent in the same interval before low water. There exists, in fact, the rudiment of a bore. The duration of slack water, or the interval between the change of direction of the stream, is forty minutes during the spring tides and thirty-seven minutes during the neaps, at Deptford. The vulgar establishment is the interval by which the time of high water follows the moon's transit on the day of new and full moon. What Sir John Lubbock calls the corrected establishment, or the lunar hour of high water, freed from the semi-menstrual irregularity, is found to

be, at the London Docks, one hour twenty-six minutes. The interval of the high tide and moon's transit is, however, affected by a considerable inequality, which goes through its period twice in a month, depending on the moon's distance from the sun in right ascension, or on the solar time of the moon's transit. Its value is two hours. The direction of the winds has a great influence on the tides of the Thames, not only as to the height they attain, but also as to their duration. Thus, with north-westerly gales, they do not rise so high, nor does the flood run so long as with the wind in any other quarter. With south-westerly gales, however, and with those from the east, the tides often rise as much as four feet above their usual levels."

In the old chronicles and memoirs that have been rescued from oblivion will be found many a graphic description of the use made of the river as the common highway of London. "These old writers," observes Charles Knight, in his "London," "were noble hands at scene-painting. What a picture Hall gives us of the populousness of the Thames !—a perfect contrast to Wordsworth's—

‘ The river glideth at his own sweet will '—

in the story which he tells us of the Archbishop of York, after leaving the widow of Edward IV. in the sanctuary of Westminster, sitting ' alone below on the rushes, all desolate and dismayed,' returning home to York Place in the dawning of the day ; ' and when he opened his windows and looked on the Thames, he might see the river full of boats of the Duke of Gloucester, his servants watching that no person should go to the sanctuary, nor none should pass unsearched.' " Cavendish, in his " Life of Wolsey," furnishes as graphic a description of the great cardinal hurrying to and fro on the highway of the Thames between his imperious master and the injured Katharine, when Henry had become impatient of the tedious conferences of the Court at Blackfriars, sitting on the question of his divorce, and desired to throw down with the strong hand the barriers that kept him from the Lady Anne :—" Thus the court passed from session to session, and day to day, in so much that a certain day the king sent for my lord at the breaking up one day of the court to come to him into Bridewell. And, to accomplish his commandment, he went unto him, and being there with him in communication in his grace's privy chamber from eleven till twelve of the clock and past at noon, my lord came out and departed from the king, and took his barge at the Black Friars, and so went to his house at Westminster. The Bishop of Carlisle, being with him in his barge, said unto him (wiping the sweat from his face), ' Sir,' quoth he, 'it is a very hot day.' 'Yea,' quoth my lord cardinal, 'if ye had been as well chafed as I have been within this hour, ye would say it were very hot.'"

But it is rather with "below bridge" than "above bridge" that we have to deal here. Not only between Westminster and Blackfriars, nor even the Tower, but also between the Tower and Greenwich, was the Thames especially the royal road. When Henry VII. willed the coronation of his queen, Elizabeth, she came from Greenwich, attended by "barges freshly furnished with banners and streamers of silk." When Henry VIII. avowed his marriage with Anne Boleyn, she was brought by "all the crafts of London" from Greenwich to the Tower, "trumpets, shawms, and other divers instruments all the way playing and making great melody." The river was not only the festival highway, but the more convenient one, for kings as well as subjects. Hall tells us in his "Chronicles": "This year (1536), in December, was the Thames of London all frozen over, *wherefore* the king's majesty, with his beautiful spouse, Queen Jane, rode throughout the City of London to Greenwich." The "Privy Purse Expenses of Henry VIII." contain several items of sums paid to watermen for waiting with barge and boat. The barge was evidently always in attendance upon the king, and the great boat was used for the conveyance of household stuffs and servants from Westminster to Greenwich or to Richmond. On one occasion, in 1531, we find a record of payment "to John, the king's bargeman, for coming twice from Greenwich to York Place with a great boat with books for the king." Later on we see the "great Eliza" on the Thames in all her pomp, as Raleigh saw her out of his prison window in the Tower, in 1592, as described in a letter from Arthur Gorges to Cecil :—"Upon a report of her majesty's being at Sir George Carew's, Sir W. Raleigh having gazed and sighed a long time at his study window, from whence he might discern the barges and boats about the Blackfriars stairs ; suddenly he brake out into a great distemper, and sware that his enemies had on purpose brought her majesty thither to break his gall in sunder with Tantalus' torment, that when she went away he might see death before his eyes; with many such-like conceits. And, as a man transported with passion, he swore to Sir George Carew that he would disguise himself, and get into a pair of oars to ease his mind with but a sight of the queen."

James II., on his abdication, availed himself of the river transit as far as Gravesend, in his journey to France. The provisional government and the Prince of Orange had come to the conclusion that James would turn his face towards France, his majesty having had the choice of either returning to London or retiring to the Continent, as he should think fit. James accordingly returned to London, and invited his son-in-law, the Prince of Orange, to meet him at Whitehall, that they might "amicably settle the distractions of the nation." What William and his party wanted, however, was the immediate expatriation of the king, which could be converted into a virtual abdication ; and to this end they drove, being assisted by some whom James still considered his personal friends. The king was waited upon at the palace by his ex-minister, Halifax, and told that he must go to Ham House, near Richmond, as the Prince of Orange intended entering London on the following morning. James, we are told, merely said that Ham was cold and damp, and that he should prefer going to Rochester. "As this was a step towards France," writes the author of the "Comprehensive History of England," "he was soon informed that his son-in-law agreed ; and about noon on the following day James embarked in the royal barge for Gravesend. He was attended by the Lords Arran, Dumbarton, Lichfield, Aylesford, and Dundee, and followed and watched by a number of Dutch troops in other boats. . . . That night he slept at Gravesend, and on the morrow he proceeded to Rochester." Thence, as readers of English history know, the king was rowed down the Medway in a small boat, and then, embarking on board a fishing-smack, which had been hired for the voyage, passed over in safety to the coast of France.

Among the "processions" on the Thames in more recent times, was that which conveyed the remains of Lord Nelson, after lying in state in the Painted Hall of Greenwich Hospital, to Whitehall, on the 8th of January, 1806, preparatory to their interment in St. Paul's Cathedral.

From the time of Fitz-Stephen, at the beginning of the thirteenth century, to that of "the moral Gower," as Chaucer calls him, it may be easily imagined that the water-communication between one part of London and another, and between London and Westminster, was constantly upon the increase. A portion of London Bridge was movable, and this enabled vessels of burden to pass up the river to unload at Queenhithe and other wharves. "Stairs (called bridges) and water-gates," writes Charles Knight, "studded the shores on both sides. Palaces arose, such as the Savoy, where the powerful nobles kept almost regal state. The courts of law were fixed at Westminster, and thither the citizens and strangers from the country daily resorted, preferring the easy highway of the Thames to the almost impassable road that led from Westminster to the village of Charing, and thence onward to London. John Lydgate, who wrote in the time of Henry V., has left us a very curious poem, entitled 'London Lyckpeny.' He gives us a picture of his coming to London to obtain legal redress of some grievance, but without money to pursue his suit. Upon quitting Westminster Hall, he says—

'Then to Westminster *Gate* I presently went.'

This is undoubtedly the Water-gate; and without describing anything beyond the cooks, whom he found busy with their bread and beef at the gate, 'when the sun was at high prime,' he adds,

'Then unto *London* I did me hie.'

By water he no doubt went, for through Charing he would have made almost a day's journey. Wanting money, he has no choice but to return to the country, and having to go 'into Kent,' he applies to the watermen at Billingsgate:

'Then hied I me to Billingsgate,
  And one cried *hoo!*—go we hence?
I pray'd a bargeman, for God's sake,
  That he would spare me my expense;
"Thou 'scap'st not here," quoth he, "under two pence." '

"We have a corroboration of the accuracy of this picture in Lambarde's 'Perambulation of Kent.' The old topographer informs us that in the time of Richard II. the inhabitants of Milton and Gravesend agreed to carry in their boats, from London to Gravesend, a passenger, with his truss and farthell, for twopence. The poor Kentish suitor, without twopence in his pocket to pay the Gravesend bargemen, takes his solitary way on foot homeward. The *gate* where he was welcomed with the cry of *hoo*—ho, ahoy!—was the great landing-place of the coasting vessels; and the king here anciently took his toll upon imports and exports."

"In the beginning of the seventeenth century," writes Charles Knight, "the river was at the height of its glory as the great thoroughfare of London. Howell maintains that 'the river of Thames hath not her fellow, if regard be had to those forests of masts which are perpetually upon her; the variety of smaller wooden bottoms plying up and down; the stately palaces that are built upon both sides of her banks so thick; which made divers foreign ambassadors affirm that the most glorious sight in the world, take water and land together, was to come upon a high tide from Gravesend and shoot the bridge at Westminster.' Of the 'smaller wooden bottoms,' Stow computes that there were

in his time as many as two thousand; and he makes the very extraordinary statement that there were forty thousand watermen upon the rolls of the company, and that they could furnish twenty thousand men for the fleet. The private watermen of the court and of the nobility were doubtless included in this large number."

The Conservancy of the Thames by the Corporation of London, as shown in a previous chapter,* extends from Staines in the west to Yantlet Creek in the east, a distance of about eighty miles, the Lord Mayor acting as bailiff over the waters, in preserving its fisheries and channels, and as meter of marketable commodities—fruit, vegetables, salt, oysters, corn, and coal. The rules and bye-laws for the regulation of the watermen and lightermen, and also for the regulation of the steamboat and other traffic on the river, are drawn up by the court of mayor and aldermen in their capacity as Conservators of the Thames. By the Thames Conservancy Acts and the Thames Navigation Acts, passed between the years 1857 and 1878, special bye-laws have been framed for regulating the traffic on the river during boat-races. One of these bye-laws is to the effect that "any vessel being on the river Thames between Cricklade, in the county of Wilts, and Yantlet Creek in the county of Kent, on the occasion of any boat-race, regatta, public procession, or launch of any vessel, or any other occasion when large crowds assemble thereon, shall not pass thereon so as to obstruct, impede, or interfere with the boat-race, regatta, procession, or launch, or endanger the safety of persons assembling on the river, or prevent the maintenance of order thereon; and the master of every such vessel, on any such occasion as aforesaid, shall observe the directions of the officer of the Conservators engaged in superintending the execution of this bye-law; and if any such master fails in any respect to comply with the requirements of this bye-law, or does anything in contravention thereof, he shall be deemed guilty of an offence against this bye-law, and shall for every such offence be liable to a penalty of not exceeding £5."

Boating has always been a favourite pastime with Londoners, who still largely indulge in it; and it is but right, therefore, that stringent rules should be laid down to guard against accidents.

The loss of life upon the Thames, by collision of vessels and other accidents, is of frightful amount; as many as 500 persons are, on an average, annually drowned in the river, and one-third of that number in the Pool. The most disastrous catastrophe that has taken place on the river of late years occurred at Gallion's Reach, near Blackwall, on the evening of the 3rd of September, 1878, when upwards of 500 persons lost their lives through a collision between an outward-bound vessel called the *Bywell Castle*, and a river steamboat named the *Princess Alice*, which was returning from a pleasure-trip heavily laden with passengers.

"From steeple-chasing," writes Lord William Lennox in " Drafts on my Memory," "I turn to boating, a delightful pastime before the introduction of river steamers played such havoc with it in the more frequented parts of the river.

' Some o'er the Thamis rowed the ribboned fair,

writes Byron in 'Childe Harold'; and unquestionably, however agreeable it might have been in the days of the noble poet to have found oneself like Dibdin's 'Jolly Young Watermen, never in want of a *fair*,' we should scarcely like in these days to trust any lovely daughter of Eve in a frail wherry subject to the tender mercies of the steamboat captains. The Thames, like the roads of England, have been completely sacrificed to steam ; and a morning sail or an evening pull on the water is now only to be ranked among the pleasures of memory. Some seventeen years ago boating was a great amusement, both to the higher and the humbler classes ; and in those days there were some splendid six, eight, and ten-oared boats, manned by the flower of the English nobility. Now the steamboats have entirely monopolised Father Thames; and since the time these fire-flies have taken possession of the no longer 'silent highway,' oars and sculls are at a sad discount. Who now would venture his life in a wherry, when, owing to the modern invention of 'steam for the million,' boats are whizzing up and down the river from sunrise to sunset, dodging in and out, dashing and slashing very much after the principle of the cutting-in, panel-breaking coachman of the Fourth George's time ? What would the water poet, that renowned king of scullers of 1630, John Taylor, have said, had he lived during the present period ; he that was wont to boast that he often ferried the immortal Shakespeare from Whitehall to Paris Garden, or his contemporary Ben Jonson from the Bankside to the Rose and Hope playhouses? With his tirade against coaches, then but lately introduced, what would he have said to the modern importation of cabs, 'buses, and other vehicles, from the well-appointed four-in-hand 'team,' to a Whitechapel cart ? The poor water poet must have drowned himself in his own element : for mark

what a picture he drew even then of the fearful calamity that assailed his vocation :—" I do not inveigh,' says honest John, 'against any conveyances that belong to persons of worth or quality, but only against the caterpillar swarm of hirelings. *They have undone my poor trade* whereof I am a member ; and though I look for no reformation, yet I expect the benefit of an old proverb, ' Give the losers leave to speak.' This infernal swarm of trade-spillers (coaches) have so overrun the land that we can get no living upon the water; for I dare truly affirm that every day in any term, especially if the court be at Whitehall, they do rob us of our living, and carry five hundred and sixty fares daily from us. I pray you look into the streets, and the chambers or lodgings in Fleet Street or the Strand, how they are pestered with them, especially after a masque or play at the Court, when even the very earth quakes and trembles, the casements chatter, patter, and clatter, and such a confused noise is made, so that a man can neither sleep, speak, hear, write, nor eat his dinner or supper quiet for them.'"

In 1815 a sporting event came off on the Thames, namely, a grand rowing match for two hundred sovereigns, between "Squire" Osbaldeston, with Mitchell, of Strand Lane, and Captain Bentinck, of the Guards, with Cobb, of Whitehall ; the terms being to row a pair of oars from Vauxhall to Kew Bridge. The details of this race, and of one or two others shortly after, are thus given in Lord W. Lennox's "Drafts on my Memory" :—" At the word 'off' Mr. Osbaldeston's boat shot half a length ahead, and the boats remained in this position until within a few yards of Battersea Bridge, when the Captain laid out, and the boats were about even. Soon after the church had been passed the opponents changed places, and from this point the gallant Guardsman continued to gain, winning the match at length by four minutes and a half. A wonderful feat took place in September of the same year, when Messrs. Bishop and Horneman accomplished the task of rowing with a pair of oars from London Bridge to Gravesend, up to Richmond Bridge, and back to Westminster (a distance of nearly a hundred miles) in the short space of thirteen hours and thirty-five minutes—an hour and twenty-five minutes within the time of the wager. What made this exploit so wonderful was, that from Gravesend to Erith Reach, they had a heavy sea and a dead 'noser,' as I can vouch for, for it nearly water-logged their boat, and capsized mine.

"In 1830 I was present at a most extraordinary match against time, made by a distinguished amateur, F. Cresswell, Esq., for fifty sovereigns, that he and William Lewis, a waterman of Old Swan Stairs, would row in a Thames wherry from Billingsgate down to Gravesend, up through Richmond Bridge, and back to the Old Swan, in thirteen hours and a half. At starting the odds were two to one in favour of time. The day was calm, although it rained heavily for some time, and the tide in their favour almost the whole of the way to Gravesend. They turned without landing, so as to avail themselves of the flowing tide, and on their return, the tide above Sion House being favourable, they reached the Swan Stairs at 5. 20, winning their match by an hour and forty minutes."

Having thus far laid before the reader a general view of the chief features of Old Father Thames, we will, in the opening chapter of our next volume deal with the Pool and its commercial activity, and then ask the reader to accompany us in an imaginary trip as far as the most easterly limits of the Thames Conservancy, and jurisdiction of the Lord Mayor.